American Ethnic Writers

American Ethnic Writers

Volume 1

Ai — Lionel G. García

Editors, Revised Edition
The Editors of Salem Press

Editor, First Edition
David Peck
California State University, Long Beach

SALEM PRESS, INC.
Pasadena, California   Hackensack, New Jersey

Library of Congress Cataloging-in-Publication Data
American ethnic writers / editors, the editors of Salem Press. — Rev. ed.
    p. cm. — (Magill's choice)
    Includes bibliographical references and index.
    ISBN 978-1-58765-462-6 (set : alk. paper) — ISBN 978-1-58765-463-3 (vol. 1 : alk. paper) — ISBN 978-1-58765-464-0 (vol. 2 : alk. paper) — ISBN 978-1-58765-465-7 (vol. 3 : alk. paper) 1. American literature—Minority authors—Bio-bibliography—Dictionaries. 2. Minority authors—United States—Biography—Dictionaries. 3. Ethnic groups in literature—Dictionaries. 4. Minorities in literature—Dictionaries. I. Salem Press.
    PS153.M56A414 2008
    810.9′920693—dc22

                                                                    2008018357

First Printing

Contents

Contents

Publisher's Note

Diverse ethnic literatures are more than ever a mainstay of the high school and undergraduate curriculum. This edition of *American Ethnic Writers* covers not only the core writers and the classics of African American, Asian American, Hispanic/Latino, Jewish American, and Native American novels, short stories, plays, and poetry—but many recent voices as well. These volumes offer authoritative coverage, essential for the school and college library shelf.

This significantly expanded edition more than doubles the length of the original two-volume set (published in 2000) by adding a third volume: 89 new authors have been added to the original 136, and 493 works have been added to the original 217, for a total coverage of more than 700 literary works. Material has been added from the best of Salem's previously published essays in *Critical Survey of Drama, Second Revised Edition* (2003), *Critical Survey of Long Fiction, Second Revised Edition* (2000), *Critical Survey of Poetry, Second Revised Edition* (2002), *Cyclopedia of World Authors, Fourth Revised Edition* (2003), *Magill Book Reviews* (online), *Magill's Survey of American Literature* (2006), *Masterplots II, African American Literature Series* (1994), *Masterplots II, Women's Literature Series* (1995), *Notable African American Writers* (2006), and *Notable Latino Writers* (2005). In addition, new material has been added: All listings of the authors' works and the "Suggested Readings" have been updated, and the biographies of many authors who have recently died as well as those still living have been updated as well.

The result is a fully current collection, in one compact set, of the best of our coverage of the most important ethnic literary voices—ranging from the Harlem Renaissance through the blossoming of Chicano literature to contemporary American ethnic and multiethnic voices in the twenty-first century. All major American minority cultures are covered: African American, Asian American, Jewish American, Hispanic/Latino, Native American; the set also includes 94 women. The authors represented here are identified with one or more of the following ethnicities: African American (103), Caribbean (5), Chilean American (1), Chinese American (14), Cuban American (7), Dominican American (1), Filipino American (4), Japanese American (7), Jewish American (31), Korean American (1), Mexican American (24), Native American (20), Peruvian American (2), Puerto Rican (12), South and Southeast Asian American (6), Spanish American (1), and Vietnamese American (1).

The works covered are equally diverse in genre, falling into one or more of the following categories: autobiographies and biographies (43), children's and young adult literature (7), drama (71), essays (35), ethnography (1), family histories (2), history (3), letters (2), memoirs (13), novellas (5), novels (259), philosophy (1), poetry (159), short fiction (99), social criticism (10), sociological study (1), and speeches (3).

Arranged alphabetically by author, each essay begins with the name of the writer as best known; any "also known as" name (such as a birth name or pseudonym); birth date and place; and death date and place (if applicable); an identification of the author's ethnicity or ethnicities (e.g., Japanese American); a summary description of the writer's significance. The text of each essay opens with a biographical sketch, which includes a guide to the pronunciation of the author's name, if difficult to pronounce. There follow one or more analytical sections focusing on

xi

up to ten of the author's best-known and most often studied works. For each of these core novels, plays, short stories, or poems, we list the work's title, genre, and year of publication, followed by at least a page of analysis. A fully updated "Suggested Readings" section, which closes every essay, lists up to a dozen print resources for further study. Altogether, more than 1,500 additional reading sources are listed. Finally, each essay is signed by the academicians and other experts who contributed it.

Volume 3 concludes with a General Bibliography and a list of Web Sites for further study, as well as five indexes: Author Index, Authors by Ethnic Identity, Titles by Ethnic Identity, Titles by Genre, and a straight alphabetical Title Index. These indexes are designed to give students and others the greatest variety of access to the essays' coverage. In addition, the front matter to each volume provides a Complete List of Contents.

We are indebted to the more than 280 scholars who contributed to the revised edition; their names and affiliations are found in the list of contributors that follows.

List of Contributors

McCrea Adams
Independent Scholar

Timothy Dow Adams
University of West Virginia

Patrick Adcock
Independent Scholar

Cami D. Agan
Oklahoma Christian University

Vivian R. Alexander
Independent Scholar

Amy Allison
Independent Scholar

Heather Russell Andrade
Barry University

Debra D. Andrist
University of St. Thomas

Karen Antell
University of Oklahoma

Gerald S. Argetsinger
Rochester Institute of Technology

Karen L. Arnold
Independent Scholar

Angela Athy
Bowling Green State University

Lisa R. Aunkst
Independent Scholar

Philip Bader
Independent Scholar

JoAnn Balingit
University of Delaware

Jane L. Ball
Independent Scholar

Janet M. Ball
The Mogollon Gazette

Carl L. Bankston III
Tulane University

Jack Vincent Barbera
University of Mississippi

James Barbour
Oregon State University

Paula C. Barnes
Hampton University

Dan Barnett
Butte College

Henry J. Baron
Calvin College

Kathleen M. Bartlett
Brevard Community College

Margaret Kent Bass
St. Lawrence University

Margaret W. Batschelet
University of Texas

Joseph F. Battaglia
Rutgers University

Cynthia S. Becerra
Humphreys College

Kate Begnal
Utah State University

Carol F. Bender
Alma College

Robert Bensen
Hartwick College

Alvin K. Benson
Brigham Young University

Jacquelyn Benton
Edgewood College

Milton Berman
University of Rochester

Cynthia A. Bily
Adrian College

Margaret Boe Birns
New York University and The New School for Social Research

Mary A. Blackmon
Hardin-Simmons University

Franz G. Blaha
University of Nebraska, Lincoln

Sandra F. Bone
Arkansas State University

Jo-Ellen Lipman Boon
Independent Scholar

J. H. Bowden
Indiana University Southeast

Jay Boyer
Arizona State University

Muriel W. Brailey
Wilberforce University

Harold Branam
Savannah State University

Marie J. K. Brenner
Bethel College

Wesley Britton
Grayson County College

Carl Brucker
Arkansas Tech University

Faith Hickman Brynie
Independent Scholar

Lori Hall Burghardt
University of Tennessee, Knoxville

Roland E. Bush
California State University, Long Beach

Rebecca R. Butler
Dalton College

Susan Butterworth
Independent Scholar

Gena Dagel Caponi
University of Texas, San Antonio

Emmett H. Carroll
Seattle University

Warren J. Carson
University of South Carolina, Spartanburg

Linda M. Carter
Morgan State University

Leonard Casper
Boston College

Mary LeDonne Cassidy
South Carolina State University

Thomas Cassidy
South Carolina State University

Russ Castronovo
University of Miami

Christine R. Catron
St. Mary's University

Susan Chainey
Sacramento City College

Cida S. Chase
Oklahoma State University

Nancy L. Chick
University of Georgia

Renny Christopher
California State University, Channel Islands

C. L. Chua
California State University, Fresno

J. Robin Coffelt
University of North Texas

David Conde
Metropolitan State College of Denver

Holly Dworken Cooley
Independent Scholar

Virginia M. Crane
California State University, Los Angeles

Shira Daemon
Independent Scholar

Dolores A. D'Angelo
Montgomery County (Maryland) Public Schools

Joyce Chandler Davis
Gadsden State Community College

Barbara Day
City University of New York

Frank Day
Clemson University

Jodi Dean
Hobart & William Smith Colleges

Mary Jo Deegan
University of Nebraska—Lincoln

Frenzella Elaine De Lancey
Drexel University

Bill Delaney
Independent Scholar

Francine Dempsey
The College of Saint Rose

List of Contributors

Joseph Dewey
University of Pittsburgh

Richard A. Eichwald
Independent Scholar

Thomas L. Erskine
Salisbury University

Don Evans
Trenton State College

Grace Farrell
Butler University

Nettie Farris
University of Louisville

Howard Faulkner
Washburn University

James Feast
Baruch College, City University of New York

John W. Fiero
University of Louisiana, Lafayette

Edward A. Fiorelli
St. John's University

David Marc Fischer
Independent Scholar

T. A. Fishman
Clemson University

Anne Fleischmann
University of California, Davis

Ben Forkner
Independent Scholar

Robert Frail
Centenary College

Dean Franco
Wake Forest University

Tom Frazier
Cumberland College

Chris Freeman
St. John's University

Janet Fujimoto
California State University, Fresno

Constance M. Fulmer
Pepperdine University

Ann Davison Garbett
Averett College

Tanya Gardiner-Scott
Mount Ida College

Scott Giantvalley
Independent Scholar

Jill B. Gidmark
University of Minnesota

Craig Gilbert
Portland State University

Joyce J. Glover
University of North Texas

Dennis Goldsberry
College of Charleston

Vincent F. A. Golphin
The Writing Company

Charles A. Gramlich
Xavier University of Louisiana

James Green
Arizona State University

Robert Haight
Kalamazoo Valley Community College

Elsie Galbreath Haley
Metropolitan State College of Denver

Joyce Ann Hancock
Jefferson Community College

Betty L. Hart
University of Southern Indiana

Nelson Hathcock
Saint Xavier University

David M. Heaton
Ohio University

Terry Heller
Coe College

Diane Andrews Henningfeld
Adrian College

Cheryl Herr
Independent Scholar

Sarah Hilbert
Independent Scholar

Cynthia Packard Hill
University of Massachusetts—Amherst

Kay Hively
Independent Scholar

Arthur D. Hlavaty
Independent Scholar

James L. Hodge
Bowdoin College

Nika Hoffman
Crossroads School for Arts & Sciences

Pierre L. Horn
Wright State University

Edward Huffstetler
Bridgewater College

Theodore C. Humphrey
California Polytechnic University, Pomona

E. D. Huntley
Appalachian State University

Andrea J. Ivanov
Azusa Pacific University

Maura Ives
Texas A&M University

Martin Japtok
University of California, Davis

Helen Jaskoski
Independent Scholar

Philip K. Jason
United States Naval Academy

Shakuntala Jayaswal
University of New Haven

Jeffry Jensen
Independent Scholar

Jeff Johnson
Brevard Community College

Sheila Golburgh Johnson
Independent Scholar

Judith L. Johnston
Independent Scholar

Andrew O. Jones
University of California, Davis

Jane Anderson Jones
Manatee Community College

Leslie Ellen Jones
Independent Scholar

David Jortner
University of Pittsburgh

Rhona Justice-Malloy
Central Michigan University

Theresa M. Kanoza
Eastern Illinois University

Leela Kapai
University of the District of Columbia

Deborah Kaplan
Independent Scholar

Ludmila Kapschutschenko-Schmitt
Rider University

Richard Keenan
University of Maryland, Eastern Shore

Steven G. Kellman
University of Texas at San Antonio

Jacquelyn Kilpatrick
Governors State University

Anne Mills King
Prince George's Community College

Christine H. King
University of California, Davis

Judith Kitchen
State University of New York, College at Brockport

Laura L. Klure
Independent Scholar

Lynne Klyse
Independent Scholar

Mildred C. Kuner
Hunter College, City University of New York

Vera M. Kutzinski
Yale University

Gregory W. Lanier
The University of West Florida

Douglas Edward LaPrade
University of Texas—Pan American

Donald F. Larsson
Mankato State University

Norman Lavers
Arkansas State University

Michele Leavitt
University of North Florida

Katherine Lederer
Southwest Missouri State University

Linda Ledford-Miller
University of Scranton

Richard M. Leeson
Fort Hays State University

Christine Levecq
University of Liege

Leon Lewis
Appalachian State University

Guoqing Li
The Ohio State University

Janet E. Lorenz
Independent Scholar

Michael Loudon
Eastern Illinois University

Bernadette Flynn Low
Dundale Community College

R. C. Lutz
University of the Pacific

Joanne McCarthy
Tacoma Community College

Barbara A. McCaskill
University of Georgia

Robert McClenaghan
Independent Scholar

Gina Macdonald
Nicholls State University

James C. MacDonald
Humber College

Grace McEntee
Appalachian State University

Margaret McFadden
Appalachian State University

Ron McFarland
University of Idaho

S. Thomas Mack
University of South Carolina—Aiken

Sheila McKenna
University of Pittsburgh

Joseph McLaren
Hofstra University

A. L. McLeod
Rider University

Daryl F. Mallett
Independent Scholar

Anne B. Mangum
Bennett College

Lois A. Marchino
University of Texas at El Paso

Peter Markus
Independent Scholar

Charles E. May
California State University, Long Beach

Julia M. Meyers
North Carolina State University

Michael R. Meyers
Shaw University

Paula M. Miller
Biola University

Kathleen Mills
Independent Scholar

Laura Mitchell
California State University, Fresno

Christian H. Moe
Southern Illinois University, Carbondale

Anna A. Moore
Independent Scholar

Robert A. Morace
Daemon College

Earl Paulus Murphy
Harris-Stowe State College

Jamie Myers
Penn State University

H. N. Nguyen
University of California, Riverside

Margarita Nieto
California State University, Northridge

John Nizalowski
Mesa State College

Emma Coburn Norris
Troy State University

Sally Osborne Norton
University of Redlands

Rafael Ocasio
Agnes Scott College

Patrick O'Donnell
West Virginia University

Peter D. Olson
Independent Scholar

Cynthia Packard
University of Massachusetts, Amherst

Leslie Pearl
San Diego, California

David Peck
University of California, Long Beach

Allene Phy-Olsen
Austin Peay State University

Adrienne Pilon
Independent Scholar

Marjorie Podolsky
Pennsylvania State University, Behrend College

Andrew B. Preslar
Lamar University at Orange

Josephine Raburn
Cameron University

Brian Abel Ragen
Southern Illinois University—Edwardsville

Honora Rankine-Galloway
University of Southern Denmark

Ralph Reckley, Sr.
Independent Scholar

Rosemary M. Canfield Reisman
Independent Scholar

Barbara Cecelia Rhodes
Central Missouri State University

Janine Rider
Mesa State College

David Rigsbee
Virginia Tech

Christy Rishoi
Michigan State University

Danny Robinson
Bloomsburg University

St. John Robinson
Montana State University at Billings

Larry Rochelle
Johnson County Community College

Louise Connal Rodriguez
Truman College

Mary Rohrberger
University of Northern Iowa

Robert L. Ross
University of Texas at Austin

John K. Roth
Claremont McKenna College

Mark Sanders
College of the Mainland

Alexa L. Sandmann
University of Toledo

Richard Sax
Madonna University

Daniel M. Scott III
Rhode Island College

Barbara Kitt Seidman
Linfield College

Frank W. Shelton
Limestone College

Chenliang Sheng
Northern Kentucky University

Nancy Sherrod
Georgia Southern University

John C. Shields
Illinois State University

Wilma Shires
Cisco Junior College

Amy Beth Shollenberger
Independent Scholar

Hugh Short
Independent Scholar

Debra Shostak
The College of Wooster

R. Baird Shuman
University of Illinois at Urbana-Champaign

Thomas J. Sienkewicz
Monmouth College, Illinois

Charles L. P. Silet
Iowa State University

Carl Singleton
Fort Hays State University

Joseleyne Ashford Slade
Michigan State University

Genevieve Slomski
Independent Scholar

Marjorie Smelstor
University of Wisconsin—Eau Claire

Pamela J. Olubunmi Smith
University of Nebraska—Omaha

Rebecca G. Smith
Barton College

Virginia Whatley Smith
University of Alabama—Birmingham

Traci S. Smrcka
Hardin-Simmons University

Katherine Snipes
Eastern Washington University

Sherry G. Southard
Oklahoma State University

P. Jane Splawn
Purdue University

Brian Stableford
University College (Winchester, U.K.)

Trey Strecker
Ball State University

Philip A. Tapley
Louisiana College

Australia Tarver
Texas Christian University

Judith K. Taylor
Northern Kentucky University

Thomas J. Taylor
University of Akron

Betty Taylor-Thompson
Texas Southern University

Julie Tharp
*University of Wisconsin Center—Marshfield
Wood College*

Terry Theodore
University of North Carolina, Wilmington

Lorenzo Thomas
University of Houston—Downtown

Tony Trigilio
Northeastern University

Richard Tuerk
East Texas State University

William Vaughn
Appalachian State University

Martha Modena Vertreace
Kennedy-King College

Emil Volek
Arizona State University

Edward E. Waldron
Yankton College

Kelly C. Walter
Southern California College

Qun Wang
California State University, Monterey Bay

Gladys J. Washington
Texas Southern University

Patricia L. Watson
University of Georgia

Ron Welburn
Western Connecticut State University

Craig Werner
University of Wisconsin

John T. West III
Grambling State University

Gary Westfahl
University of California, Irvine

Barbara Wiedemann
Auburn University, Montgomery

Kathryn Ervin Williams
Michigan State University

Patricia A. R. Williams
Amherst College

Judith Barton Williamson
Sauk Valley Community College

David Willinger
City College of New York

Cynthia Wong
Western Illinois University

Pat M. Wong
Binghamton University

Gay Annette Zieger
Santa Fe Community College

Pronunciation Guide

Many of the names of personages covered in *American Ethnic Writers* may be unfamiliar to students and general readers. For these unfamiliar names, guides to pronunciation have been provided upon first mention of the names in the text. These guidelines do not purport to achieve the subtleties of the languages in question but will offer readers a rough equivalent of how English speakers may approximate the proper pronunciation.

VOWEL SOUNDS

Symbol	Spelled (Pronounced)
a	answer (AN-suhr), laugh (laf), sample (SAM-puhl), that (that)
ah	father (FAH-thur), hospital (HAHS-pih-tuhl)
aw	awful (AW-fuhl), caught (kawt)
ay	blaze (blayz), fade (fayd), waiter (WAYT-ur), weigh (way)
eh	bed (behd), head (hehd), said (sehd)
ee	believe (bee-LEEV), cedar (SEE-dur), leader (LEED-ur), liter (LEE-tur)
ew	boot (bewt), lose (lewz)
i	buy (bi), height (hit), lie (li), surprise (sur-PRIZ)
ih	bitter (BIH-tur), pill (pihl)
o	cotton (KO-tuhn), hot (hot)
oh	below (bee-LOH), coat (koht), note (noht), wholesome (HOHL-suhm)
oo	good (good), look (look)
ow	couch (kowch), how (how)
oy	boy (boy), coin (koyn)
uh	about (uh-BOWT), butter (BUH-tuhr), enough (ee-NUHF), other (UH-thur)

CONSONANT SOUNDS

Symbol	Spelled (Pronounced)
ch	beach (beech), chimp (chihmp)
g	beg (behg), disguise (dihs-GIZ), get (geht)
j	digit (DIH-juht), edge (ehj), jet (jeht)
k	cat (kat), kitten (KIH-tuhn), hex (hehks)
s	cellar (SEHL-ur), save (sayv), scent (sehnt)
sh	champagne (sham-PAYN), issue (IH-shew), shop (shop)
ur	birth (burth), disturb (dihs-TURB), earth (urth), letter (LEH-tur)
y	useful (YEWS-fuhl), young (yuhng)
z	business (BIHZ-nehs), zest (zehst)
zh	vision (VIH-zhuhn)

Complete List of Contents

Volume 1

Volume 2

Volume 3

American Ethnic Writers

Ai

(Florence Anthony)

BORN: Albany, Texas; October 21, 1947

AFRICAN AMERICAN, NATIVE AMERICAN, JAPANESE AMERICAN

*Ai renewed the dramatic monologue in poems that
record moments of public and private history.*

PRINCIPAL WORKS

POETRY: *Cruelty*, 1973; *Killing Floor*, 1979; *Sin*, 1986; *Cruelty/Killing Floor*,
1987; *Fate: New Poems*, 1991; *Greed*, 1993; *Vice: New and Selected Poems*,
1999; *Dread*, 2003
NONFICTION: "On Being One-Half Japanese, One-Eighth Choctaw, One-Fourth
Black, and One-Sixteenth Irish," 1974 (in *Ms.* magazine 6, no. 11)

Ai (ah-EE) was born with a rich multicultural heritage. Her mother's immediate ancestors were African American, Native American (Choctaw), and European American (Irish and Dutch). Her father's ancestors were Japanese. Ai once said that the
history of her family is the history of America. Rather than defining her identity
through ethnicity, however, she would insist on the uniqueness of personal identity.
Accordingly, one of the aims of her work is to destroy stereotypes. She has said that
she is "irrevocably tied to the lives of all people, both in and out of time." Consequently, whoever "wants to speak" in her poems "is allowed to speak regardless of
sex, race, creed, or color."

Ai grew up in Tucson, Arizona. When she was seven, her family moved to Las
Vegas, Nevada, for a year, then spent two years in San Francisco, California, before
returning to Tucson. They moved again when Ai was twelve, this time to Los Angeles, California, returning again to Tucson three years later, when Ai was fifteen.
Ai attended Catholic schools until the seventh grade. Her first poem, written when
she was twelve, was a response to an assignment by the nuns to write a letter from
the point of view of a Christian martyr who was going to die the next day. When she
was fourteen, intending to enter a contest for poems about a historical figure, Ai began writing poems regularly.

History was Ai's best subject in high school, which she attended in Tucson. At
the University of Arizona, also in Tucson, Ai found her identity in the "aesthetic atmosphere" of intellectual life. She graduated from the university in 1969 with a degree in Oriental studies. She earned an M.F.A. degree in creative writing from
the University of California at Irvine in 1971. When Ai published her first book

1

of poetry, *Cruelty*, in 1973, she became a nationally known figure, so striking were her grimly realistic and violent poems. Ai married the poet Lawrence Kearney in 1976. In 1979, her second book, *Killing Floor*, won the Lamont Poetry Prize. She separated from Kearney in 1981, and the couple divorced in 1984. In 1986, her third book, *Sin*, won an American Book Award from the Before Columbus Foundation. Her 1999 collection of new and selected poems, *Vice*, won the National Book Award and established her as a major poet despite the controversy surrounding her work. Ai held the Mitte Chair in Creative Writing for 2002-2003 at Southwest Texas State University. She became a professor of English at Oklahoma State University and moved to Stillwater, Oklahoma, where she continued to write.

Cruelty

TYPE OF WORK: Poetry
FIRST PUBLISHED: 1973

Ai is more concerned with social class than with racial identity or gender in *Cruelty*. The book is a series of poetic dramatic monologues spoken by members of the underclass in America. It is a searing indictment of societies that permit the existence of poverty.

Life itself is cruel for the speakers in *Cruelty*. The speaker in "Tenant Farmer" has no crops. The couple in "Starvation" have no food. In "Abortion," a man finds the fetus of his son wrapped in wax paper and thinks: "the poor have no children, just small people/ and there is room for only one man in this house." Men and women become alienated from each other in these conditions. The speaker in "Young Farm Woman Alone" no longer wants a man. In "Recapture," a man finds and beats a woman who has run off from him. In "Prostitute," a woman kills her husband, then goes out to get revenge on the men who use her.

Out of the agony of their lives, some of Ai's characters achieve transcendence through love. The couple in "Anniversary" has managed to stay together, providing a home for their son for many years, in spite of never having "anything but hard times." In "The Country Midwife: A Day," the midwife delivers a woman's child for "the third time between abortions." Beneath the mother "a stain . . . spreads over the sheet." Crying out to the Lord, the midwife lets her bleed. Ending the cycles of pregnancy for the woman, in an act of mercy, the midwife takes upon herself the cross of guilt and suffering.

Ai extends her study of the causes and consequences of poverty to other times and places in the second half of *Cruelty*. The figure in "The Hangman" smells "the whole Lebanese coast/ in the upraised arms of Kansas." In "Cuba, 1962," a farmer cuts off his dead wife's feet, allowing her blood to mix with the sugarcane he will sell in the village, so everyone can taste his grief. Medieval peasants are evoked by "The Corpse Hauler's Elegy," although the plague victims he carries could also be contemporary.

Violence increases in the final poems of the book, a sign of the violence in societies that perpetuate social injustice. In "The Deserter," a soldier kills the woman who gave him shelter in order to leave everything of himself behind. In "The Hitch-hiker," a woman is raped and killed by a psychopath in Arizona. In "The Child Beater," a mother beats her seven-year-old daughter with a belt, then gets out her "dog's chain leash." Ai has compassion for all of these people—including the killers—and she demands compassion for them from her readers.

Greed

TYPE OF WORK: Poetry
FIRST PUBLISHED: 1993

Greed is a collection of poems about the identity of America in the late twentieth century. In dramatic monologues spoken by famous or obscure Americans, Ai exposes amorality in the institutions of society, business, and private life. For most of the speakers, America has not kept its promises. Truth and justice are illusions in a society made more vicious, because of greed, than the Darwinian struggle for survival among animals. Money, power, drugs, sex—these are the gods of late twentieth century America.

To the African American speakers, slavery is still alive in the "big house" of white America. Violence is the result. In "Riot Act, April 29, 1992," a black man, going to get something on the day the wealth "finally trickled down," threatens to "set your world on fire." In "Self Defense," Marion Barry, mayor of Washington, D.C., trapped using crack cocaine by the FBI, warns: "The good ole days of slaves out pickin' cotton/ ain't coming back no more." In "Endangered Species," a black university professor, perceived as "a race instead of a man," is stopped by police while driving through his own neighborhood.

In "Hoover, Edgar J.," Ai indicts the director of the FBI for abuse of power. Hoover admits he has "files on everybody who counts" and "the will to use them." Deceptions by government are implicated in poems concerning the assassination of President John F. Kennedy. In "Jack Ruby on Ice," Ruby is refused sanctuary, in exchange for his testimony, by the Chief Justice of the United States. In "Oswald Incognito and Astral Travels," Oswald finds himself "trapped/ in the palace of lies,/ where I'm clothed in illusion/ and fed confusion with a spoon."

Other poems explore domestic violence and sexual abuse of children. In "Finished," a woman kills her husband after repeated episodes of physical abuse. In "Respect, 1967," such a man expresses rage "against the paycheck that must be saved for diapers/ and milk." The speaker in "Life Story" is a priest who sexually abuses young boys. As a child, he was abused by his uncle, also a priest. In "The Ice Cream Man," the speaker lures a little girl inside his truck to sexually molest her. He tells of his own abuse by his stepfather and his mother.

Ai offers little hope for the promise of America in *Greed*. She closes the book with the title poem, about the savings and loan scandal of the 1980's. The responsible working man in "Family Portrait, 1960" has little chance to succeed. Even so, he takes care of his sick wife, cooks dinner, oversees the baths of his young daughters, then dozes—"chaos kept at bay" for one more day.

SUGGESTED READINGS

Ackerson, Duane. "Ai: Overview." In *Contemporary Poets*, edited by Thomas Riggs. 6th ed. New York: St. James Press, 1996.

Bellamy, Joe David, ed. *American Poetry Observed: Poets on Their Work*. Urbana: University of Illinois Press, 1984.

Cramer, Steven. Review of *Fate*, by Ai. *Poetry* 159 (November, 1991): 108-111.

Field, C. Renee. "Ai." In *American Poets Since World War II, Third Series*, edited by R. S. Gwynn. Vol. 20 in *Dictionary of Literary Biography*. Detroit: Gale Group, 1992.

Flamm, Matthew. "Ai Came, Ai Saw, Ai Conquered." *The Village Voice* 31 (July 22, 1986).

Kilcup, Karen. "Dialogues of the Self: Toward a Theory of (Re)reading Ai." *Journal of Gender Studies* 7, no. 1 (March, 1998): 5-20.

Monaghan, Pat. Review of *Fate*, by Ai. *Booklist* 87 (January 1, 1991): 902.

Ostriker, Alicia. Review of *Sin*, by Ai. *Poetry* 144 (January, 1987): 231-237.

Seidman, Hugh. Review of *Killing Floor*, by Ai. *The New York Times Book Review*, July 8, 1979, 14.

Seshadri, Vijay. Review of *Dread*, by Ai. *The New York Times Book Review*, May 4, 2003.

Contributor: James Green

Meena Alexander

BORN: Allahabad, India; February 17, 1951

SOUTH ASIAN AMERICAN

*Alexander's work examines women in society from the
perspective of an expatriate feminist.*

PRINCIPAL WORKS

POETRY: *The Bird's Bright Ring: A Long Poem*, 1976; *I Root My Name*, 1977; *Without Place*, 1978; *Stone Roots*, 1980; *The Storm: A Poem in Five Parts*, 1989; *Night-Scene, the Garden*, 1992; *River and Bridge*, 1995; *Illiterate Heart*, 2002; *Raw Silk*, 2004

LONG FICTION: *Nampally Road*, 1991; *Manhattan Music*, 1997

NONFICTION: *The Poetic Self: Towards a Phenomenology of Romanticism*, 1979; *Women in Romanticism: Mary Wollstonecraft, Dorothy Wordsworth, and Mary Shelley*, 1989; *Fault Lines: A Memoir*, 1993; *The Shock of Arrival: Reflections on Postcolonial Experience*, 1996

EDITED TEXT: *Indian Love Poems*, 2005

MISCELLANEOUS: *House of a Thousand Doors: Poems and Prose Pieces*, 1988

Meena Alexander (MEE-nah Al-ehks-ZAN-dur) spent her early life in Kerala, a state at the southwestern tip of India. She received her English education in the Sudan, traveling between her parents' home in Africa and her grandparents' home in India. She received her bachelor's degree in 1969 from the University of Khartoum and a Ph.D. from the University of Nottingham in 1973. After teaching at universities in Delhi and Hyderabad, she moved to New York City in 1979. By that time she had already published three volumes of poetry; many more, along with literary studies and works in other genres, would follow.

Alexander describes herself as a "woman cracked by multiple migrations," acted on by the disparate and powerful influences of the languages and customs of the four continents on which she has lived. Although her works are written in English, she grew up speaking Malayalam, a Dravidian language of southwest India, and Arabic, the language of her Syrian Christian heritage, spoken in North Africa. Her writing reflects the tension created by the interplay of these influences and serves as a way to derive meaning from her wide range of experience.

The most prominent theme of Alexander's work is the difficulty inherent in being a woman, of having a woman's body and coping with the societal, physiological, and personal pressures on and responses to that body as it develops through childhood into maturity and middle age. Her grandmothers serve as mythical fig-

ures with whom Alexander closely identifies. Her perspective is further complicated by her alienation from the language and culture of her childhood and by her
need to recover something of that past. The images of fecundity and beauty with
which Alexander's work is suffused derive from her youth in Kerala; these images
may be juxtaposed with images of infirmity, sterility, or brutality, underscoring the
writer's need to integrate the fragmented components of her life as an expatriate
woman. The imagination provides a synthesis of the elements of history and personality in Alexander's work. Her poems "begin as a disturbance, a jostling in the
soul" which prompts her to write, seeking "that fortuitous, fleeting meaning, so
precious, so scanty."

House of a Thousand Doors

TYPE OF WORK: Poetry
FIRST PUBLISHED: 1988

House of a Thousand Doors is a collection of fifty-nine poems and prose pieces that
reflect Alexander's multicultural heritage and the tension it creates. The book is organized into three sections, the first and third sections serving as a synthesis for the
wide variety of subjects and themes treated in the body of the work. Many of the poems reflect the writer's subjective response to her experience; many also project or
create new experiences that underscore the importance of imagination as a lens
through which to focus the inner life into poetry.

   The title poem of *House of a Thousand Doors* uses the title metaphor to describe
the variety of forces that operate on the persona: gender, heritage, language, experience, ideology, and the search for meaning. A complex array of images embodies
these forces in the book, reflecting the author's sensitivity to their influence. Alexander uses her writing to integrate the diversity of her experience.

   Dominating the persona's early life is the figure of her grandmother, a powerful
member of the family who learned to exercise some control over the many lines of
force that affected her life. The mature awareness of the persona is imposed on the
re-created memory of herself as a girl watching the figure of the grandmother kneel
in turn before each of the thousand doors on a never-ending pilgrimage, "a poor
forked thing" praying for the favor of her ancestors. The grandmother becomes a
figure of myth and a symbol of tradition serving as the focus of many of the poems
in the collection. Conciliation and unity with the culture and solidity of the past are
central to *House of a Thousand Doors.*

   The three major sources of imagery in the book are family, culture, and nature.
Family images, though literal, have a universal quality—she describes finding her
grandmother's letters "in an old biscuit box" and wonders if her grandmother was,
like herself, "inventing a great deal." Other images reflect the diminution of women
at the behest of a patriarchal society; a cell door closing on a woman raped by the
police clangs "like an old bell left over by the British," while a portrait of the pacifist leader Mohandas Gandhi looks down from the wall. A third class of imagery,

the imagery of nature, reflects the persona's romantic theory of art; she laments, "My body/ part water/ part rock/ is searching for heaven." This searching brings her back to her past, real and mythical, and ultimately back to herself and her need for meaning.

SUGGESTED READINGS

Dave, Shilpa. "The Doors to Home and History: Post-colonial Identities in Meena Alexander and Bharati Mukherjee." *Amerasia Journal* 19 (Fall, 1993): 103.

Perry, John Oliver. Review of *Nampally Road*, by Meena Alexander. *World Literature Today* 65 (Spring, 1991): 364.

Contributor: Andrew B. Preslar

Sherman Alexie

BORN: Spokane Indian Reservation, Wellpinit, Washington; October 7, 1966

NATIVE AMERICAN

Alexie, an accomplished writer of poetry and fiction, is a spokesperson for the realities of reservation life.

PRINCIPAL WORKS

CHILDREN'S LITERATURE: *The Absolutely True Diary of a Part-Time Indian*, 2007
SHORT FICTION: *The Lone Ranger and Tonto Fistfight in Heaven*, 1993; *The Toughest Indian in the World*, 2000; *Ten Little Indians*, 2003
LONG FICTION: *Reservation Blues*, 1995; *Indian Killer*, 1996; *Flight*, 2007
POETRY: *I Would Steal Horses*, 1992; *Old Shirts and New Skins*, 1993; *The Man Who Loves Salmon*, 1998; *One Stick Song*, 2000; *Dangerous Astronomy*, 2005
SCREENPLAYS: *Smoke Signals*, 1998; *The Business of Fancydancing*, 2002
MISCELLANEOUS: *The Business of Fancydancing: Stories and Poems*, 1992; *First Indian on the Moon*, 1993; *The Summer of Black Widows*, 1996 (poems and short prose)

Sherman Alexie (SHUR-mahn ah-LEHK-see) is a Spokane-Coeur d'Alene Indian who grew up in Wellpinit, Washington, on a reservation. Alexie's father worked for the Bureau of Indian Affairs and his mother worked as a youth drug and alcohol counselor. The first of their five children to leave the reservation, Alexie attended Gonzaga University in Spokane for two years before entering Washington State University, where he studied creative writing with Alex Kuo. He graduated in 1991.

The seventy-seven-line free-verse poem "Horses," from *Old Shirts and New Skins*, typifies the passion, anger, and pain in some of his most effective poems. Focused on the slaughter of a thousand Spokane horses by General George Wright in 1858, the long lines echo obsessively: "1,000 ponies, the United States Cavalry stole 1,000 ponies/ from the Spokane Indians, shot 1,000 ponies & only 1 survived." The poem is one of Alexie's favorites at readings, where it acquires the incantatory power of the best oral poetry.

Although Alexie's poems often have narrative and dramatic qualities, he is also adept at the short lyric, and his published work includes examples of the sestina and the villanelle. "Reservation Love Song," from *The Business of Fancydancing*, reflecting on the poverty of reservation life, with its government-built housing and low-quality food, begins:

I can meet you
in Springdale buy you beer
& take you home
in my one-eyed Ford.

First Indian on the Moon is largely composed of prose poems. "Collect Calls" opens with an allusion to Crazy Horse, who appears often as a mythic figure in Alexie's writing: "My name is *Crazy Horse*, maybe it's *Neil Armstrong* or *Lee Harvey Oswald*. I am guilty of every crime; I was the first man on the moon." As in his fiction, Alexie tempers the anger and pain of his poems with satiric wit, as in "The Marlon Brando Memorial Swimming Pool," from *Old Shirts and New Skins*, in which activist Dennis Banks is imagined as "the first/ Native American real estate agent, selling a 5,000 gallon capacity dream/ in the middle of a desert." Not surprisingly, there is no water in the pool.

Sherman Alexie (© Marion Ettlinger)

The Lone Ranger and Tonto Fistfight in Heaven

TYPE OF WORK: Short fiction
FIRST PUBLISHED: 1993

Alexie's initial foray into fiction (except for a few stories sprinkled among his poems), *The Lone Ranger and Tonto Fistfight in Heaven* appeared before his twenty-seventh birthday and was awarded a citation from the PEN/Hemingway Award committee for best first book of fiction in 1993. Praising his "live and unremitting lyric energy," one reviewer suggested that three of the twenty-two stories in the book "could stand in any collection of excellence."

Critics have noted that the pain and anger of the stories are balanced by his keen sense of humor and satiric wit. Alexie's readers will notice certain recurring characters, including Victor Joseph, who often appears as the narrator; Lester Falls-Apart, the pompous tribal police chief; David WalksAlong; Junior Polatkin; and Thomas Builds-the-Fire, the storyteller to whom no one listens. These characters also appear in Alexie's first novel, *Reservation Blues* (1995), so the effect is of a community; in this respect, Alexie's writings are similar to the fiction of William Faulkner. One reviewer has suggested that *The Lone Ranger and Tonto Fistfight in Heaven* is almost a novel, despite the fact that Alexie rarely relies on plot development in the stories and does not flesh out his characters. It might more aptly be said that the stories come close to poetry, just as Alexie's poems verge on fiction. The stories range in length from less than three to about twenty pages, and some of the best, like "The First Annual All-Indian Horseshoe Pitch and Barbecue," leap from moment to moment, from one-liner to quickly narrated episode, much like a poem.

That story begins, "Someone forgot the charcoal; blame the BIA." The next sentence concerns Victor playing the piano just before the barbecue: "After the beautiful dissonance and implied survival, the Spokane Indians wept, stunned by this strange and familiar music." Survival is a repeated theme in Alexie's work. The story then jumps to a series of four short paragraphs, each beginning "There is something beautiful about. . . ." Then we are told that Simon won at horseshoes, and he "won the coyote contest when he told us that basketball should be our new religion." A paragraph near the end is composed of a series of questions, each beginning "Can you hear the dreams?" The last paragraph features a child born of a white mother and an Indian father, with the mother proclaiming: "Both sides of this baby are beautiful."

Beneath the anger, pain, and satiric edge of his stories, often haunted by the mythic figure of Crazy Horse and tinged with fantasy, Alexie offers hope for survival and reconciliation.

Reservation Blues

TYPE OF WORK: Novel
FIRST PUBLISHED: 1995

Alexie's first novel, *Reservation Blues*, was published before his thirtieth birthday and after the striking success of *The Business of Fancydancing*, a collection of poems and stories published by a small press when he was twenty-six. By the time his novel was being reviewed, nearly eight thousand copies of *The Business of Fancydancing* were in print, along with two additional collections of poetry, *Old Shirts and New Skins* and *First Indian on the Moon*, and a heralded book of short stories, *The Lone Ranger and Tonto Fistfight in Heaven*, all published in 1993.

In his novel Alexie reasserts an equation that he formed in "Imagining the Reservation," from *The Lone Ranger and Tonto Fistfight in Heaven*: "Survival = Anger × Imagination. Imagination is the only weapon on the reservation." *Reservation Blues* is arguably the most imaginative of his works to date, blending, among other things, the Faust myth with life on the "rez" and the dream of making it big in the music world. Alexie has performed in his own blues band.

The novel is haunted by the bad memories (the essence of the blues) and by several characters' nightmares, including Junior Polatkin, Victor, and Thomas Builds-the-Fire, all of whom are familiar from other stories and poems by Alexie. The role of the deity in the novel is played by Big Mom, who lives atop a mountain on the reservation and has powerful magic. The story gets under way when a black blues guitarist from Mississippi, Robert Johnson (a historical personage) who has sold his soul to the devil (a white man known as "The Gentleman") for a magic guitar wanders onto the reservation and passes his literally hot guitar to Victor.

On their way to success and fame the group acquires a pair of vocalists in Chess and Checkers, two Flathead women, and two groupies, Indian "wanna-be's," Betty and Veronica, named after characters in the Archie comic series. When Betty observes that white people want to be like Indians so they can live at peace with the earth and be wise, Chess says, "You've never spent a few hours in the Powwow Tavern. I'll show you wise and peaceful."

The destruction of the dream comes when the group goes to New York, where they find that their exploitative agents are none other than Phil Sheridan (source of the words "The only good Indian is a dead Indian") and George Wright (who commanded the soldiers that slaughtered the Spokane ponies in 1858, a recurring motif in Alexie's work). They work for Calvary Records. This novel encompasses broad humor, but the laughter is almost always painful. The satiric thrust, the travel, and the ironies attendant on innocents abroad suggest that *Reservation Blues* belongs to the tradition of Voltaire's *Candide* (1759).

Indian Killer

TYPE OF WORK: Novel
FIRST PUBLISHED: 1996

Unlike Alexie's earlier works, *Indian Killer* is starkly tragic. It begins with injustice, the virtual kidnapping of a newborn Native American baby so that a white couple can have the child they desire. Although at first their love seems enough to guarantee his happiness, in time John Smith comes to feel that he does not belong with them. However, not knowing even his mother's tribe, John cannot rejoin his people. He moves to Seattle, and there he finds an answer. He will become an Indian warrior, killing whites as a form of initiation into Native American society.

Informed that a Native American is responsible for the murders, a seemingly enlightened city reveals its deep-seated prejudice. A talk show host inflames the public and prompts acts of violence. However, he is really no worse than the "wannabe" Indians who profit by attaching themselves to a culture about which they know nothing. Alexie does not waste much sympathy even on well-meaning whites, like John's adoptive parents, and he ends his novel by predicting that other Native Americans will arise to avenge their people. *Indian Killer* is perceptive, well-crafted, and suspenseful; unfortunately, it does not offer much hope for the establishment of a peaceful, multicultural society.

One Stick Song

TYPE OF WORK: Poetry
FIRST PUBLISHED: 2000

The dark humor, deep feeling, and supple style that distinguish Alexie's novels and short stories about Native American experience in the United States are present in an especially forceful manner in *One Stick Song*, a collection of poems that function as a personal memoir that recollects and comments on his life as a Spokane/Coeur d'Alene Indian in contemporary America. Capitalizing on the possibilities for a multiplicity of expressive modes that a collection of poems affords, Alexie offers both a singularly personal and dauntingly candid vision of Indian society while recalling close friends and members of his family whose lives augment and personify the patterns he identifies.

The poems in the book are bracketed by two extended autobiographical fragments, "The Unauthorized Biography of Me," which conveys the content of Alexie's mind and spirit through the tone of its idiosyncratic observations, and "Sugar Town," which is a lament for and tribute to his father, as well as a meditation on his own growth toward maturity. Within this flexible frame, Alexie effectively uses a wide range of poetic forms to establish a recognizable, singular voice: Essentially laconic but capable of considerable passion; generally poised but sometimes very vulnerable; wary in anticipation of insults and rebuffs without closing contact with the world. Alexie often speaks with his own version of a contemporary American vernacular, characteristically in an expressionistic narrative called "The Warriors" which begins, "I hate baseball," and combines incidents from his youth with pointed, cogent cultural analysis. This mode is enlivened by sometimes startling moments of lyric fire, an introduction of the singing language that is at the core of the Native American oral tradition, which Alexie uses to create the emotional responses that mark his vivid depictions of humans in contact with one another, with the natural and with the supernatural or spirit world.

The title poem is a particularly powerful evocation of this tradition, a recollective story/song that works to reclaim centuries of loss by placing people in living memory. Its repetitive choral figures move toward a mood of revelation in which Alexie guides the reader to a view of a culture that is aslant from most popular conceptions, a new perspective on ancient ways that combats stereotypes while assembling an alternative identity that is compelling and persuasive in its vivid gathering of a life's imagery.

Ten Little Indians

TYPE OF WORK: Short fiction
FIRST PUBLISHED: 2003

In *Ten Little Indians*, Sherman Alexie continues his writing's practice of undermining the white world's expectations of Native Americans. All the old stereotypes are held up for ridicule at one time or another in these stories in which the Indians (they frequently call themselves by that term) mostly do not live on reservations, are mostly not alcoholic, do not necessarily have a special sense of union with the earth, and may in fact hold important jobs in computer technology or major in English at a university. At the same time, these characters are highly aware of their unique position in American culture and of whites' biased ideas about them.

In "The Search Engine," for example, Corliss is a Washington State University English major. Good brains, helpful high school teachers, and intense ambition got her to the university, despite discouraging comments from her family. Now, by accident, she has found a volume of poetry by a Native American on the library shelves. Many of the poems are set on the Spokane reservation, Corliss's own home, and she wonders why she has never heard of Harlan Atwater, their writer. Although she knows that the volume is uneven, she feels a special kinship with its author and longs to meet and talk with him. After an exhausting search, she locates him and finds that instead of the reservation, he had been adopted and raised in the city by a loving white couple.

Her last gesture in the story is to place Atwater's book, face out, on a bookstore shelf, so that all the world will see his poems. Like almost all Alexie's characters, she will combine respect for her origins with an ironic smile and a willingness to make her way as a Native American in the urban world of whites.

SUGGESTED READINGS

Alexie, Sherman. "Sending Cinematic Smoke Signals: An Interview with Sherman Alexie." Interview by Dennis West. *CINEASTE* 23, no. 4 (1998): 28-32.

Caldwell, E. K. *Dreaming the Dawn: Conversations with Native Artists and Activists.* Lincoln: University of Nebraska Press, 1999.

Fast, Robin Riley. *The Heart as a Drum: Continuance and Resistance in American Indian Poetry.* Ann Arbor: University of Michigan Press, 2000.

Fleck, Richard F., ed. *Critical Perspectives of Native American Fiction.* 2d ed. Pueblo, Colo.: Passeggiata Press, 1997.

Grassian, Daniel. *Understanding Sherman Alexie.* Columbia: University of South Carolina Press, 2005.

Kilpatrick, Jacquelyn. *Celluloid Indians: Native Americans and Film.* Lincoln: University of Nebraska Press, 1999.

Lincoln, Kenneth. *Sing with the Heart of a Bear: Fusions of Native and American Poetry, 1890-1999.* Berkeley: University of California Press, 2000.

McFarland, Ron. "'Another Kind of Violence': Sherman Alexie's Poems." *American Indian Quarterly* 21, no. 2 (Spring, 1997): 251-264.

Vickers, Scott B. *Native American Identities: From Stereotype to Archetype in Art and Literature.* Albuquerque: University of New Mexico Press, 1998.

Vizenor, Gerald, ed. *Narrative Chance: Postmodern Discourse on Native American Indian Literatures.* Norman: University of Oklahoma Press, 1993.

Contributor: Ron McFarland

Paula Gunn Allen

BORN: Cubero, New Mexico; October 24, 1939
DIED: Fort Bragg, California; May 29, 2008

NATIVE AMERICAN

*As a novelist, poet, literary critic, and scholar, Allen preserves
and creates Native American literature.*

PRINCIPAL WORKS

LONG FICTION: *The Woman Who Owned the Shadows*, 1983
POETRY: *The Blind Lion*, 1974; *Coyote's Daylight Trip*, 1978; *A Cannon Between
My Knees*, 1981; *Star Child: Poems*, 1981; *Shadow Country*, 1982; *Wyrds*,
1987; *Skins and Bones*, 1988; *Life Is a Fatal Disease: Collected Poems, 1962-
1995*, 1997
NONFICTION: *The Sacred Hoop: Recovering the Feminine in American Indian Tra-
ditions*, 1986; *Grandmothers of the Light: A Medicine Woman's Source Book*,
1991; *As Long as the Rivers Flow: The Stories of Nine Native Americans*, 1996
(with Patricia Clark Smith); *Off the Reservation: Reflections on Boundary-
Busting, Border-Crossing Loose Canons*, 1998; *Pocahontas: Medicine Woman,
Spy, Entrepreneur, Diplomat*, 2003
EDITED TEXTS: *Spider Woman's Granddaughters: Traditional Tales and Contemporary Writing by Native American Women*, 1989; *Voice of the Turtle: American
Indian Literature, 1900-1970*, 1994; *Hozho: Walking in Beauty*, 2001 (with Car-
olyn Dunn Anderson)

Paula Gunn Allen (PAH-luh guhn AL-lehn), as an American Indian woman, saw
her identity in relation to a larger community. She was proud to be part of an old and
honored tradition that appreciates the beautiful, the harmonious, and the spiritual.
She also recognized that since in the United States there are more than a million
non-Indians to every Indian, she had to work to stay connected to her heritage.

Allen frequently referred to herself as "a multicultural event"; people of many
ethnicities related to her. Her mother was a Laguna Indian whose grandfather was
Scottish American. Allen said that she was raised Roman Catholic, but living next
door were her grandmother, who was Presbyterian and Indian, and her grandfather,
who was a German Jew. Her father's family came from Lebanon; he was born in a
Mexican land-grant village north of Laguna Pueblo. She grew up with relatives
who spoke Arabic, English, Laguna, German, and Spanish. Her relatives shared
legends from around the world.

Even with such cultural diversity in her family, as a teenager Allen could find

15

Paula Gunn Allen (Tama Rothschild)

no Native American models for her writing. Consequently, she read Charlotte Brontë's *Jane Eyre: An Autobiography* (1847) about twenty times; her other literary favorites were Louisa May Alcott, Gertrude Stein, and the Romantic poets John Keats and Percy Bysshe Shelley. When she went to the University of New Mexico and wanted to focus on Native American literature in her Ph.D. program in English, it was impossible. The scholarship was not there to study. She came to write the books that she wanted to read and teach the courses that she wanted to take. Allen taught at San Francisco State University, at the University of New Mexico, in the Native American Studies Program at the University of California at Berkeley, and at the University of California, Los Angeles.

In enumerating her influences, Allen first honored her mother, who taught her not only to think like a strong Indian woman but also to treat animals, insects, and plants with the deep respect one customarily reserves for high-status humans. She honored her father for teaching her how to weave magic, memory, and observation into the tales she tells. Finally, the Indian collective unconscious remained the source of her vision of spiritual reality throughout her life and career.

The Sacred Hoop

TYPE OF WORK: Essays
FIRST PUBLISHED: 1986

The collection of essays *The Sacred Hoop: Recovering the Feminine in American Indian Traditions* documents the continuing vitality of Native American traditions and the crucial role of women in those traditions. The title comes from a lesson Allen learned from her mother: that all of life is a circle—a sacred hoop—in which everything has its place. These essays, like tribal art of all kinds, support the principle of kinship and render the beautiful in terms of the harmony, relationship, balance, and dignity that are the informing principles of Indian aesthetics. Indians understand that woman is the sun and the earth: She is grandmother, mother, thought, wisdom, dream, reason, tradition, memory, deity, and life itself.

The essays are all characterized by seven major themes that pertain to Native American identity. The first is that Indians and spirits are always found together.

Second, Indians endure. Third, the traditional tribal lifestyles are never patriarchal and are more often woman-centered than not. Tribal social systems are nurturing, pacifist, and based on ritual and spirit-centered, woman-focused worldviews. The welfare of the young is paramount, the complementary nature of all life forms is stressed, and the centrality of powerful, self-defining, assertive, decisive women to social well-being is unquestioned. Fourth, the physical and cultural destruction of American Indian tribes is and was about patriarchal fear and the inability to tolerate women's having decision-making capacity at every level of society. Fifth, there is such a thing as American Indian literature, and it informs all American writing. Sixth, all Western studies of American Indian tribal systems are erroneous because they view tribalism from the cultural bias of patriarchy. Seventh, the sacred ways of the American Indian people are part of a worldwide culture that predates Western systems.

These powerful essays are divided into three sections: "The Ways of Our Grandmothers," "The Word Warriors," and "Pushing Up the Sky." All of them testify to the value of American Indian traditions and the strength of the voices of Indian women. Allen identifies the Indian roots of white feminism as well as the role of lesbians in American culture, and she projects future visions for American Indian women, tribes, and literature.

Spider Woman's Granddaughters

TYPE OF WORK: Biography and short fiction
FIRST PUBLISHED: 1989

Spider Woman's Granddaughters, edited by Allen, is a collection of two dozen traditional tales, biographical writings, and short stories by seventeen accomplished American Indian women writers. All the women follow the tradition of Grandmother Spider, who, according to the Cherokee, brought the light of thought to her people, who were living as hostages in their own land. These stories are war stories, since all American Indian women are at war and have been for five hundred years.

Some of the selections are old-style stories; others deal with contemporary issues. All are by women intimately acquainted with defeat, with being conquered, and with losing the right and the authority to control their personal and communal lives. They have experienced the devastating destruction of their national and personal identities. They powerfully demonstrate the Indian slogan: We shall endure.

The first selection, "The Warriors," contains eleven stories of strong women who are self-defining, fearless, respectful, prayerful, and self-assertive. Their warpath is an odyssey through a brutal and hostile world. Each recognizes that the Indian family must continue to cling to tradition. A warrior must remember where she comes from; beauty is what gives human beings dignity; and the young must be taught how to keep their sense of value intact. These women warriors do not give up hope, even when they are dying, their children are stolen, and they are undergoing emotional and physical battering. They continue to resist when all the forces of a wealthy, powerful, arrogant, ignorant, and uncaring nation are mustered against them in order to coerce their capitulation.

The second section, "The Casualties," contains five selections about Indian women who have been wounded in the continuing war that seeks to destroy rather than enhance their individual and collective spiritual power. For example, Linda Hogan's "Making Do" is about a mother's powerlessness in the face of loss and grief. She clings to her tribal traditions and carves wooden birds, hoping to regain the power, healing, and grace that were traditionally put into carvings.

The third section, "The Resistance," contains eight selections that are more hopeful. Since the 1960's, Native Americans have become more involved in the administration of the economic and legal affairs of their tribes. "Deep Purple," by Allen, a Native American urban lesbian who loves a white woman, addresses the issue of colonization in the women's movement and tries to reclaim her connection to the spiritual powers of the past. Like all the granddaughters of Spider Woman, she is aware of her responsibilities, gifts, and identity.

Grandmothers of the Light

TYPE OF WORK: Essays and Native American tales
FIRST PUBLISHED: 1991

Described as a sourcebook for medicine women of the twenty-first century, *Grandmothers of the Light* does not provide actual instruction on how to become a medicine woman. It does, however, provide delightful tales from Native American oral tradition.

Allen's book is divided into four sections, three of which contain the tales. Part 1 introduces the reader to the mindset and concepts that will be encountered throughout the book. Allen explains the ritual tradition and the "Seven Ways of the Medicine Woman." The Universe of Power and female supernaturals are also discussed.

Part 2 presents tales of creation and the establishment of order in the cosmos and among the people. Including tales from the Keres, Maya, Cherokee, and Navajo, Allen notes similarities among the beings depicted in these diverse sources. Especially interesting is an Aztec tale set prior to the Spanish Conquest, concerning the troubled visions of Aztec priest-leaders who foresee the end of their empire with a fatalistic acceptance.

The tales in Part 3 contain female characters who exemplify proper conduct in dealings with supernatural persons and magical circumstances. A Lakota tale explains how the tribe came by its gift of the sacred pipe and the religion that helped them to live in harmony.

Part 4 addresses more contemporary issues, such as how the medicine ways have changed with the coming of modern civilization. Allen does not view these changes as always detrimental to what are living beliefs. Some of the accompanying tales are set in modern times, emphasizing the continued presence of supernaturals.

The last section gives brief histories of the tribes whose tales have been adapted for the book, followed by a glossary and bibliography.

Life Is a Fatal Disease

Type of work: Poetry
First published: 1997

Life Is a Fatal Disease brings together poetry Allen published over thirty years. Grouped thematically, the poems first explore the deadly condition that is American life—in its cities, on Indian reservations, in a mother's grief at the loss of her son, in the violence committed in the name of love—between men and women, between political enemies. The second part of the collection testifies to the toxicity of human existence: "we live in a browning season/ the heavy air blocking our breath." She records the "despair rising/ brown and stinking" in her students' eyes as they sit in her high school classroom, daring not to dream because "there is no future they can bear." The third part takes the words of the *Bhagavadgita* quoted by Robert Oppenheimer, "I am become death, destroyer of worlds," as an ironic affirmation. Only in claiming the union of both life and death, spirit and flesh, present and past, and traditional Laguna and contemporary urban American life can meaning be achieved.

Allen states, "to me a poem is a recording of an event of the mind." Critic Kenneth Lincoln says of Allen's poetry, "impression leads toward thought." A child's death, the victims of the war in Vietnam and on the streets, a grandmother's photograph, a hoop dancer at a powwow, a trendy Los Angeles street, and strong Indian women of history are events of the mind leading to thoughts on the nature of evil, the wholeness of the universe, the strength of will that survival demands.

Despite its title, *Life Is a Fatal Disease* expresses the hope of those who live thoughtfully and spiritually. In the wonderful poem "The Text Is Flesh," Allen draws together aspects of her culture and identity as Lebanese, Laguna Pueblo/ Sioux, and poet when she remarks that in the coffeehouses of Beirut and on "the res," people know "What there is is text and earth./ What there is is flesh./ And chanting flesh into death and life." This collection is such a chanting, unifying the disparate elements of her life, all of our lives.

Off the Reservation

Type of work: Essays
First published: 1998

The twenty pieces collected in *Off the Reservation* chart Allen's intellectual evolution since the 1960's and offer a provocative introduction to what she calls "contemporary coyote Pueblo American thought." Like the coyote, she assumes a self-consciously renegade stance vis-à-vis the Establishment, asserting through the book's subtitle that creativity lies, not in the wall-building divisiveness of Western thought, but in "Boundary-Busting" and "Border-Crossing" (activities for which her upbringing on the culturally heterogeneous Laguna Pueblo has aptly prepared her). Allen thus delivers repeated challenges to the assumed primacy of "pure" forms, whether they involve internal debates within the Native American community about standards for measuring one's authentic "indianness" or the literary preoccupation demanding that writers obediently refrain from mixing genres. Autobiographical reflection and academic discourse merge throughout these essays just as the sacred and secular coalesce within Native thought.

Off the Reservation is a learned, humane, and thoughtful book albeit one occasionally marred by ungrounded generalizations and dogmatic pronouncements. Allen offers fresh perspectives on familiar themes and leaves one mulling over her ideas long after the book is closed. For some readers her blend of erudition and political critique will violate the traditions of academic decorum; for others it will provide an inspiring example of academic work urgently conceived as an extension of a potent moral vision.

SUGGESTED READINGS

Allen, Paula Gunn. Interview by Quannah Karvar. *Los Angeles Times Book Review*, January 25, 1987.

_____. Interview by Robin Pogrebin. *The New York Times Book Review*, June 3, 1984.

Cook, Barbara. "The Feminist Journey in Paula Gunn Allen's *The Woman Who Owned the Shadows*." *Southwestern American Literature* 22 (Spring, 1997): 69-74.

Ferrell, Tracy J. Prince. "Transformation, Myth, and Ritual in Paula Gunn Allen's *Grandmothers of the Light*." *North Dakota Quarterly* 63 (Winter, 1996): 77-88.

Fisher, Dexter, ed. *The Third Woman: Minority Women Writers of the United States*. Boston: Houghton Mifflin, 1980.

Hanson, Elizabeth I. *Paula Gunn Allen*. Edited by Wayne Chatterton and James H. Maguire. Boise, Idaho: Boise State University Press, 1990.

Keating, AnaLouise. *Women Reading Women Writing: Self-Invention in Paula Gunn Allen, Gloria Anzaldúa, and Audre Lorde*. Philadelphia: Temple University Press, 1996.

Perry, Donna. "Paula Gunn Allen." In *Backtalk: Women Writers Speak Out*, edited by Donna Perry. New Brunswick, N.J.: Rutgers University Press, 1993.

Purdy, John."'And Then, Twenty Years Later . . .': A Conversation with Paula Gunn Allen." *Studies in American Indian Literatures* 9 (Fall, 1997): 5-16.

Toohey, Michelle Campbell. "Paula Allen Gunn's *Grandmothers of the Light*: Falling Through the Void." *Studies in American Indian Literatures* 12 (Fall, 2000): 35-51.

Contributor: Constance M. Fulmer

Isabel Allende

BORN: Lima, Peru; August 2, 1942

CHILEAN AMERICAN

*Allende brings a feminist perspective to the traditions of
Latin American literature.*

PRINCIPAL WORKS
CHILDREN'S LITERATURE: *Ciudad de las bestias*, 2002 (*City of the Beasts*, 2002); *El
bosque de los Pigmeos*, 2004 (*Forest of the Pygmies*, 2005); *La gorda de
porcelana*, 1984; *El reino del dragón de oro*, 2003 (*Kingdom of the Golden
Dragon*, 2004)
LONG FICTION: *La casa de los espíritus*, 1982 (*The House of the Spirits*, 1985); *De
amor y de sombra*, 1984 (*Of Love and Shadows*, 1987); *Eva Luna*, 1987 (English
translation, 1988); *El plan infinito*, 1991 (*The Infinite Plan*, 1993); *Hija de la
fortuna*, 1999 (*Daughter of Fortune*, 1999); *Portrait sépia*, 2000 (*Portrait in Se-
pia*, 2001); *Zorro*, 2005 (English translation, 2005); *Inés del alma mía*, 2006
(*Inés of My Soul*, 2006)
SHORT FICTION: (*Cuentos de Eva Luna*, 1990 (*The Stories of Eva Luna*, 1991)
NONFICTION: *Civilice a su troglodita: Los impertientes de Isabel Allende*, 1974;
Paula, 1994 (English translation, 1995); *Conversations with Isabel Allende*,
1999; *Mi país inventado*, 2003 (*My Invented Country: A Nostalgic Journey
Through Chile*, 2003)
MISCELLANEOUS: *Afrodita: Cuentos, recetas, y otros afrodisiacos*, 1997 (*Afrodite:
A Memoir of the Senses*, 1998)

The daughter of a Chilean diplomat, Isabel Allende (IHZ-ah-behl ah-YEHN-dee)
was born in Lima, Peru. Following her parents' divorce, she lived first with her
grandparents in Santiago and later with her mother and stepfather in Europe and the
Middle East. She returned to Chile as a young woman and began her career as a television and newsreel journalist and as a writer for a feminist journal.

In 1973, Allende found herself at the center of Chile's turbulent political life
when her uncle and godfather, the country's Marxist president Salvador Allende,
was assassinated during a military coup. In the months that followed, Allende
worked to oppose the new dictatorship headed by General Pinochet until fears for
her safety led Allende to move to Venezuela with her husband and two children.

Allende's first novel, *The House of the Spirits*, was published to international acclaim. It is a family saga set against a backdrop of political upheaval in an unnamed
South American country. Her second book, *Of Love and Shadows*, followed two

years later and also drew on her country's troubled history. Both works placed Allende firmly within the Latin American tradition of novels that take a strong stand in their fictionalized portrayals of political events. Allende's third novel, *Eva Luna*, traces the extraordinary life of its title character and the Austrian journalist who becomes her lover. All three novels are examples of the literary style known as Magical Realism, in which strange, supernatural occurrences are intermingled with everyday events. Allende's work, however, brings a distinctly feminist perspective to a literary style that is predominantly male.

Following her divorce from her husband of twenty years, Allende moved to the United States in the 1980's, where she remarried and settled in California. Her next novel, *The Infinite Plan*, draws on her American experience in its story of a man's life from his childhood in the barrios of Los Angeles to his adult search for meaning and happiness. In 1994, Allende published one of her most personal works, *Paula*, a chronicle of her daughter's death following a long illness. Allende examines her experience as a woman and a mother in her portrayal of love, pain, and loss.

Allende's position as a woman working within the traditions of Latin American literature has led her to create strikingly original stories and characters, and she remains a consistently intriguing and rewarding writer.

The House of the Spirits

TYPE OF WORK: Novel
FIRST PUBLISHED: *La casa de los espíritus*, 1982 (English translation, 1985)

The House of the Spirits, Allende's first novel, established her international reputation and remains her best-known work. Drawing on the Latin American literary style known as Magical Realism, the book tells the story of the Trueba family over several generations. Set in an unidentified South American country that resembles Allende's homeland, the novel chronicles the social and political forces that affect the family's fate.

The story begins with Esteban Trueba and his marriage to Clara del Valle, a young woman who possesses clairvoyant gifts and communicates easily with the spirit world. Their marriage produces a daughter, Blanca, and twin sons. Esteban also fathers a son by one of the peasant women on his family estate; years later his illegitimate grandson, a member of the secret police, will torture his legitimate granddaughter, Alba, a political prisoner. Esteban's political ambitions take him to the country's senate, where he opposes left-wing reform efforts, while Blanca's affair with an idealistic peasant boy results in Alba's birth. The boy becomes a populist songwriter and a leading figure in the Socialist movement. A subsequent leftist victory is short-lived, however, and the elected government is deposed in a military coup. Alba, who has married one of the leftist leaders, is arrested and tortured before her grandfather can secure her release. In an effort to come to terms with all that has happened to her and to her family, she sets about writing the book that will become *The House of the Spirits*.

Allende's novel has been compared to Gabriel García Márquez's masterpiece *Cien años de soledad* (1967; *One Hundred Years of Solitude*, 1970) in style and structure and in the use of Magical Realism, a technique that combines ordinary events with the fantastic and miraculous, giving rise to startling and vivid imagery. Allende herself maintains that much that seems incredible in the book is drawn from memories of her childhood. The characters of Esteban and Clara Trueba are based on her own maternal grandparents, and she began the book not as a novel but as a letter to her aging grandfather meant to reassure him that the family stories would live on through her. The book's political themes are also taken in part from Allende's family history; her uncle was Salvador Allende, the Socialist president slain in Chile's 1973 military coup.

Isabel Allende (Reuters/Gustau Nacarino/Archive Photos)

The House of the Spirits brings a strong female voice to the forefront of Latin American literature and offers a collection of vital female characters who embody the book's spirit of endurance, resilience, and courage.

Of Love and Shadows

TYPE OF WORK: Novel
FIRST PUBLISHED: *De amor y de sombra*, 1984 (English translation, 1987)

The protagonist of *Of Love and Shadows*, Irene, the daughter of an impoverished upper-class mother and her wayward husband, enjoys her life as a reporter of minor news items for a local women's magazine. Her stories are often accompanied with the photographs of Francisco Leal, who, unable to support himself with his degree in psychology, has taken up photography in the hope of earning his living in journalism. Francisco and Irene are caught up in their country's political intrigue when they are accidentally involved in a minor military skirmish while covering a story on a rural faith healer. From that moment, their lives remain in danger.

Although Francisco's father is a refugee from Fascist Spain who issues anti-government broadsides from his kitchen, it is not until his own run-in with the military authorities that Francisco really comes to understand the power and malignancy of the military government that controls his destiny. After the couple discover the secret burial ground of the police assassins, Irene is shot and the pair are in constant danger of being killed by the authorities. By the end of the novel, they have fled their native country for a life of exile and resistance.

This is a chilling novel. The presence of the military junta takes on a Kafkaesque quality as the young lovers become more and more involved in uncovering the secrets of the death squads. Isabel Allende has sketched a vivid portrait of what it means to be caught up in a world beyond one's own control.

Eva Luna

TYPE OF WORK: Novel
FIRST PUBLISHED: 1987 (English translation, 1988)

Eva Luna begins with the protagonist's account of her origins:

> My name is Eva, which means 'life,' according to a book of names my mother consulted. I was born in the back room of a shadowy house, and grew up amidst ancient furniture, books in Latin, and human mummies, but none of these things made me melancholy, because I came into the world with a breath of the jungle in my memory.

Conceived illicitly in a South American jungle, Eva Luna guides the reader through the picaresque story of her life. Like her mother Consuelo, she was born poor and was orphaned young. Unlike her mother, however, Eva rises to a position of relative power by the novel's end. Besides its wealth of poetically rendered detail and thoroughly believable characters, this novel is astoundingly rich in tenderness and insight, drama and humor, satire and compassion, history and myth. Eva is, like Allende, a seemingly natural and naturally inventive storyteller. Indeed, outdoing her rum-addled godmother, who creates her own Catholic saints, Eva creates *Bolero*, a mirror image of *Eva Luna*, for "The National Television." What she offers her television-viewing audience toward the novel's end is what Allende has already given her readers: that is, among other things, "clashes of snakebitten Indians, embalmers in wheelchairs, teachers hanged by their students, Ministers of State defecating in the bishops' plush chairs, and other atrocities that . . . defied all laws of the commercial television romance." Thanks must go to Allende for writing an excellent work of literature and for thereby defying with *Eva Luna* all the prevailing laws of America's commercial publishing industry.

The Infinite Plan

TYPE OF WORK: Novel
FIRST PUBLISHED: *El plan infinito*, 1991 (English translation, 1993)

The Infinite Plan was Allende's first novel following her move to the United States. Although it was written in Spanish, the book is set in California and chronicles the life of a European American man. Allende uses her characters' experiences to examine the factors that shaped the United States' social history in the decades following World War II. Her focus is the Latino culture in California, in which the main character comes of age.

As the book opens, young Gregory Reeves and his family are living a nomadic life as his father preaches a spiritual doctrine he calls the Infinite Plan. When the elder Reeves falls ill in Los Angeles, the family settles in the barrio (although they are not Latino). Gregory grows up experiencing life as a member of a minority group within the community. His closest friend is Carmen Morales, whose family comes to regard him as an honorary son. Following high school, Gregory leaves home for Berkeley and college while Carmen remains in the barrio until an unwanted pregnancy and near-fatal abortion make her an outcast.

Gregory leaves an unhappy marriage to serve a harrowing tour of duty in Vietnam, while Carmen lives abroad and begins designing jewelry. Both meet again in Berkeley, where Gregory embarks on an ambitious quest for success that leads him away from his youthful idealism and into a second failed marriage and problems with alcoholism. Carmen adopts her dead brother's half-Vietnamese son and discovers a strong sense of herself, marrying an old friend and settling in Italy. Gregory begins at last to take stock of his life and to see the pattern—the infinite plan—that has shaped it.

Allende's first novel set in her adopted country reflects her perspective on the United States as an immigrant. Her delight in tolerance and openness—matters of great importance to a writer whose life was marred by the repressive military coup in Chile in 1973—is apparent in her affectionate portrait of the freewheeling Berkeley of the 1960's. Her cultural identity as a Latina also comes into play in her portrayal of life in the barrio and the effect that religion and a patriarchal society has on Carmen.

Allende makes use in the novel of some aspects of the Latin American literary style known as Magical Realism, bringing a kind of heightened realism to the story, which blends realistic events with exaggerated or improbable ones. The result is a book filled with memorable characters that brings a fresh perspective to the post-World War II history and culture of the United States.

SUGGESTED READINGS

Allende, Isabel. *Conversations with Isabel Allende*. Edited by John Rodden. Austin: University of Texas Press, 1999.
_____. *My Invented Country: A Nostalgic Journey Through Chile*. New York: HarperCollins, 2003.

Correas Zapata, Celia. *Isabel Allende: Life and Spirits.* Houston, Tex.: Arte Público Press, 2002.

De Carvalho, Susan. "The Male Narrative Perspective in the Fiction of Isabel Allende." *Journal of Hispanic Research* 2, no. 2 (Spring, 1994): 269-278.

Hart, Patricia. *Narrative Magic in the Fiction of Isabel Allende.* Toronto: Associated University Presses, 1989.

Levine, Linda Gould. *Isabel Allende.* New York: Twayne, 2002.

Marketta, Laurila. "Isabel Allende and the Discourse of Exile." In *International Women's Writing, New Landscapes of Identity*, edited by Anne E. Brown and Marjanne E. Gooze. Westport, Conn.: Greenwood Press, 1995.

Rojas, Sonia Riquelme, and Edna Aguirre Rehbein, eds. *Critical Approaches to Isabel Allende's Novels.* New York: P. Lang, 1991.

Roof, Maria. "Maryse Conde and Isabel Allende: Family Saga Novels." *World Literature Today* 70, no. 2 (Spring, 1996): 410-416.

_____. "W. E. B. Du Bois, Isabel Allende, and the Empowerment of Third World Women." *CLA Journal* 39, no. 4 (June, 1996): 401-416.

Contributor: Janet E. Lorenz

Julia Alvarez

BORN: New York, New York; March 27, 1950

DOMINICAN AMERICAN

Alvarez expresses the complexities of having a cross-cultural identity and being an immigrant to the United States.

PRINCIPAL WORKS

CHILDREN'S LITERATURE: *The Secret Footprints*, 2000; *How Tía Lola Came to Stay*, 2001; *Before We Were Free*, 2002; *Finding Miracles*, 2004; *A Gift of Gracias*, 2005

LONG FICTION: *How the García Girls Lost Their Accents*, 1991; *In the Time of the Butterflies*, 1994; *¡Yo!*, 1997 (sequel to *How the García Girls Lost Their Accents*); *In the Name of Salomé*, 2000; *The Cafecito Story*, 2001

POETRY: *Homecoming: Poems*, 1984 (revised and expanded, 1996, as *Homecoming: New and Collected Poems*, 1996); *The Other Side/El otro lado*, 1995; *Seven Trees*, 1998; *Cry Out: Poets Protest the War*, 2003 (multiple authors); *The Woman I Kept to Myself*, 2004

NONFICTION: *Something to Declare*, 1998

EDITED TEXT: *Old Age Ain't for Sissies*, 1979

Although she was born in New York City, Julia Alvarez (JEW-lee-ah AHL-vah-rehs) spent much of her childhood in the Dominican Republic. Her parents were from the island. Her mother came from a well-positioned and wealthy family, but her father was rather poor. The family's divided economic position was tied to political problems within the Dominican Republic. Her father's family, which once was wealthy, supported the losing side during the revolution, while her mother's family benefited from supporting those who gained power. Julia's family, although poorer than most of their relatives, enjoyed a privileged position in the Dominican Republic.

Although she was raised in the Dominican Republic, Alvarez describes her childhood as "an American childhood." Her extended family's power, influence, American connections, and wealth led to Alvarez's enjoying many of the luxuries of America, including American food, clothes, and friends. When Alvarez's father became involved with the forces attempting to oust the dictator of the Dominican Republic, Rafaél Leonidas Trujillo Molina, the secret police began monitoring his activity. Immediately before he was to be arrested in 1960, the family escaped to the United States with the help of an American agent. In an article appearing in *American Scholar* ("Growing Up American in the Dominican Republic") published in

27

Julia Alvarez (Algonquin Books)

1987, Alvarez notes that all her life she had wanted to be a true American girl. She thought, in 1960, that she was going to live in her homeland, America.

Living in America was not quite what Alvarez expected. As her fictional but partly autobiographical novel *How the García Girls Lost Their Accents* hints, Alvarez was faced with many adjustments in America. She experienced homesickness, alienation, and prejudice. Going from living on a large family compound to living in a small New York apartment was, in itself, quite an adjustment. Alvarez's feeling of loss when moving to America caused a change in her. She became introverted, began to read avidly, and eventually began writing.

Alvarez attended college, earning degrees in literature and writing. She took a position as an English professor at Middlebury College in Vermont. She has published several collections of poetry, but her best-known work is her semiautobiographical novel *How the García Girls Lost Their Accents*. Alvarez can be praised for her portrayal of bicultural experiences, particularly for her focusing on the women's issues that arise out of such an experience.

How the García Girls Lost Their Accents

TYPE OF WORK: Novel
FIRST PUBLISHED: 1991

Set in New York City and the Dominican Republic, Alvarez's novel traces the lives of the four García sisters—Carla, Sandra, Yolanda, and Sofia—as they struggle to understand themselves and their cross-cultural identities. The novel is structured in three parts, focusing on the time spans of 1989-1972, 1970-1960, and 1960-1956. Throughout these years the García girls mature and face various cultural, familial, and individual crises. The sisters' mother, Laura, comes from the well-known, wealthy de la Torre family, who live in the Dominican Republic. The third part of the novel narrates the Garcías' flight from their homeland due to political problems within the country.

The Garcías immigrate to the United States, planning to stay only until the situation in their homeland improves. Once arriving in America, the sisters struggle to acclimate themselves to their new environment. The second part of the novel traces the sisters' formative years in the United States. Included among the numerous stories told are Yolanda's struggle to write an acceptable speech for a school event, Carla's trial of attending a new public school where she is bombarded by racial slurs, and Sandra's hatred of an American woman who flirts with her father during a family night out. In addition, part 2 narrates the García girls' summer trips to the Dominican Republic—their parents' way to keep them from becoming too Americanized. During these trips the García sisters realize that although they face great struggles as immigrants in the United States; they have much more freedom as young women in the United States than they have in the Dominican Republic.

Part 1 of the novel begins with Yolanda, who is known as the family poet, returning to the Dominican Republic as an adult. She discovers that the situation in her country has not changed. When she wants to travel to the coast alone, her relatives warn her against it. This early chapter sets Yolanda up as the primary narrator and introduces the tension between the traditions of the island and the new and different culture of the United States. In this first part, readers learn about the girls' young adult lives, primarily about their sexual awareness, relationships, and marriages. Virginity is a primary issue, for the sisters' traditions and customs haunt them as they negotiate their sexual awakenings throughout their college years in the United States. In short, it is in this first part in which readers learn precisely how Americanized the García girls have become, and throughout the rest of the novel readers learn how the girls have lost their "accents" gradually, throughout the years.

In the Time of the Butterflies

TYPE OF WORK: Novel
FIRST PUBLISHED: 1994

Three of the four daughters of Enrique and Mercedes Mirabal were murdered by the secret service of Dominican dictator Rafael Trujillo on November 25, 1960, as they returned from Puerto Plata, after paying their weekly visit to the imprisoned husbands of two of the sisters. Julia Alvarez, whose own family fled the Trujillo regime in August of 1960, when she was ten years old, captures in spine-tingling detail more than two decades of events that preceded these murders.

The first three sisters, Patria, Dede, and Minerva, were born between 1924 and 1926. Teresa Marie, nicknamed Mate, followed in 1935. Of the four, only Dede survived assassination, because she was unable to travel to Puerto Plata with her sisters on the appointed day. Alvarez, using first-person narration and dividing her book into sections headed always by the name of the sister who is talking, achieves a uniquely well-rounded development of her characters, who reveal themselves in their own sections but who are further revealed by each of the other sisters in their sections.

In the Time of the Butterflies tells the story of how four conventional, Roman Catholic sisters evolved into revolutionaries code-named "Mariposa"—"butterfly" in Spanish—after being reared as typical, submissive Hispanic women. By defying Trujillo, Minerva, the most independent and iconoclastic sister, gains both his respect and rage. As his megalomania increases, however, the Mirabals become his obsession. He arrested three of their husbands as well as Minerva and Mate, ultimately releasing the women to house arrest in Ojo de Agua. As Trujillo's obsession grows, he orchestrates their murders, which transform the sisters into martyrs venerated throughout Latin America.

¡Yo!

TYPE OF WORK: Novel
FIRST PUBLISHED: 1997

What readers learn about Yolanda García, the protagonist of this novel, they glean through sixteen discrete sections, all of which directly concern Yolanda. Many of these sections are interconnected. People who have known Yolanda reveal facets of her personality as they relate their encounters with her. From their revelations emerges a well-developed and complex portrayal of a multifaceted creative artist. The arrangement of the separate portions, each about twenty pages long, is vital to the cohesiveness of the book. Although any of the sections might be read meaningfully as separate entities, it is their placement that justifies identifying the book as a novel rather than a collection of character sketches or short stories. Yolanda is permitted to tell her own story only in the dialogue she has with the characters of each section, identified by such designations as "The Sisters," "The Mother," "The Caretakers," "The Maid's Daughter," and "The Third Husband." The result is a carefully structured novel from which the protagonist emerges as one of the best developed protagonists in recent literature. Alvarez's structure, perfect for the telling of her highly autobiographical tale, allows for the presentation of a central character more complex and diverse than she would have seemed had any other method of presentation been used.

The clue to the novel's autobiographical nature lurks in the title itself. Yo is both a shortened form of Yolanda and the Spanish word for "I." Readers, however, must be cautioned to remember that *¡Yo!* is a work of fiction and cannot be read as an autobiography presumed to be accurate in all of its details. Each of the sketches in this novel, along with presenting one or more characters as they interact with Yo, deals with some global theme. A political current relating to the despotic dictatorship of strongman Rafael Trujillo in the Dominican Republic underlies many of the individual sketches, in which Alvarez also deals with such broad and compelling matters as political oppression, spousal abuse, homosexuality, acquired immunodeficiency syndrome (AIDS), poverty and exploitation in the Third World, the problems faced by immigrants trying to reestablish themselves in alien cultures, and the effects of the creative temperament on those whose lives intersect with the life of an artist.

The first section of *¡Yo!*, called "Prologue," consists of one sketch, "The Sisters." It, like each sketch in the book, is identified with a descriptor, in this case "fiction." Other sections have such descriptors as "nonfiction," "poetry," "revelation," "confrontation," "characterization," and "tone," suggesting that Alvarez, a professor who was teaching writing at Middlebury College in Vermont when she wrote this book, perhaps composed along with her students, producing a sketch for each week of a sixteen-week semester, each sketch reflecting some major aspect of composition and contributing to an overall piece of creative writing, in this case a compelling novel.

The prologue is central to the novel as a whole. Yolanda García's sisters are uneasy about the liberties their sister takes in her writing with bits of private information she possesses about members of the family. They are concerned, as is Yolanda's mother in the first sketch in part 1, with what they regard as a violation of their privacy by a sister and daughter who, as the novel continues, is shown to be a natural storyteller but whose stories have sometimes created threatening situations.

The very last sketch, "The Father," touches on this subject as Carlos García, a member of the Dominican underground during the early years of his marriage, recalls how Yolanda, as a small child in Trujillo's Dominican Republic, placed the family in grave danger. Watching a movie with the family's neighbor General Molino, she boasted that her father—living in a dictatorial society where the possession of firearms by civilians was strictly banned—had a bigger gun than the one carried by the cowboy in the film. This sketch is particularly telling because it contains the veiled suggestion that Molino took some sexual liberties with the small child. Bouncing Yolanda on his knee and tickling her from time to time, the general says, watching the television screen, "Ay, look at that big gun, Yoyo!" to which she replies, "My papi has a bigger gun!" The sexual implications here are inescapable.

Each section carries its own specific theme that relates to a prevailing social or political crosscurrent. "The Landlady," whose descriptor is "confrontation," makes a strong feminist statement about spousal abuse. Marie Beaudry, who becomes Yolanda's landlady, suffers frequent beatings from a brutish husband who drinks too much. Like many abused wives, she denies that she is being abused, while blaming herself for motivating her husband's beatings. Yolanda finally confronts Clair Beaudry, the abusive husband, then forces Marie to confront him and to turn her life around. This section reveals Yolanda striving for tenure at the college in which she teaches. She needs a quiet place in which to work, but having signed a lease on the apartment the Beaudrys own, located above their own home, she finds that she cannot work there because their noise as they fight intrudes on her space, upsetting her greatly. Also, when the first rains come, she realizes that Clair Beaudry has, quite without conscience, rented her an apartment that floods in wet weather. The first flood destroys much of the material she has been working on in preparation for writing the book that she hopes will assure her being granted tenure.

Clair's reluctance to release Yolanda from her lease precipitates the confrontation that results, at Yolanda's instigation, in Marie's liberating herself from her abusive marriage. Clair Beaudry has reached the conclusion that Yolanda is a lesbian, although she is not, and accuses his wife of being drawn into Yolanda's web. Yolanda does have a close lesbian friend, Tammy Rosen, but the two are no more than friends. Yolanda also has been close to a male homosexual, Jordan Garfield, her college English professor, with whom she has maintained contact through the years. Garfield, married for more than thirty years, finally leaves his wife, Helena. He soon enters into a homosexual relationship with a much younger colleague, Matthews, who eventually takes a teaching job in San Diego, putting the two a continent apart. Their relationship, nevertheless, continues on a long-distance basis, with Garfield counting the time until he can retire, which will enable him to live with Matthews. Before this dream can be realized, however, Matthews reveals that he is dying of AIDS. Garfield, ever the caregiver, takes him in and tends him throughout what remains of his life. Alvarez is particularly sensitive in presenting the details of relationships that skirt the fringe of what society regards as normal and usual. She also retains a great consistency in developing her characters. Garfield, for example, is ever the caring person, fully aware of his commitment and responsibility to others.

A major concern in this novel is the Dominican Republic. Carlos García has immigrated with his wife and four daughters to the United States, giving up his profession, medicine, to do so. Only after years of doing menial work is he finally able to be certified to practice medicine in his adopted country. The family brings Primitiva, who worked for Laura García's family in the Dominican Republic, to the United States to be their maid. She eventually is able, with their help, to bring her daughter, Sarita, to live with her. The entire Primitiva/Sarita episode is intriguing in that it deals with a problem common in societies where large numbers of people are oppressed and live in grinding poverty. Primitiva, apparently, was impregnated by the husband of the family for whom she worked in the Dominican Republic, the well-to-do de la Torre family, from which Laura García comes. Primitiva's illegitimate daughter is, in all probability, the cousin of the García girls, although her social position is quite different from that of their cousin Lucinda, who also appears in the novel. Sarita is bright and is not bound by the social constraints that keep Lucinda from obtaining a college education, so, ironically, Sarita becomes a physician while Lucinda, brought back to the Dominican Republic before she has finished her formal education, is never able to have a career. The message is clear: Immigration to the United States places enormous hurdles before Third World people, but, as both Carlos and Sarita demonstrate, the United States is also a land of great opportunity in which immigrants of any social class can ultimately succeed and become contributing members of society.

Alvarez's technical experiments in this novel are noteworthy. Whereas most of the sketches focus on a central character who has in one way or another been a part of Yolanda García's life, two of the sketches, "The Sisters" and "The Caretakers," present two central characters who have had some crucial contact with the protagonist. Alvarez's most daring section, however, is "The Wedding Guests," in which the author experiments with the presentation of her narrative through the eyes of several characters, presented in brief segments, to whom she has introduced her readers earlier in the novel. This section, for all of its technical complexity, succeeds admirably and helps achieve a unity that adds an overall coherence to the larger work.

In *¡Yo!*, Alvarez consistently addresses the question of what it is to be a sensitive creative artist in the modern context and to be dissociated from one's native society. In this regard, *¡Yo!* is similar in its nostalgic tone to Cristina García's *Dreaming in Cuban* (1992) and *The Agüero Sisters* (1997).

In the Name of Salomé

TYPE OF WORK: Novel
FIRST PUBLISHED: 2000

In the Name of Salomé is intricately structured. It interweaves two stories: one of revolutionary Dominican poet Salomé Urena and one of her daughter, referred to as Camila. Camila was three when Salomé died. The stories of these two women unfold in alternating chapters. Those numbered in Spanish recount Salomé's story, those in English Camila's.

Salomé's story develops from beginning to end, Camila's story from the end of her professional life and her retirement to Cuba. As the book progresses, Camila's story moves backward through her earlier years. Only in the final pages do the two story lines coalesce.

Julia Alvarez explores timely issues of lasting social concern: Latin American politics, being orphaned, blended families, family relationships, the status of women, martial infidelity, forgiveness, lesbianism, multiculturalism, duty to one's country, and adjustment problems facing immigrants. Salomé, a revolutionary poet born in 1850, is a truly gifted writer. She marries Francisco Henriquez, nine years her junior, who, after her death, serves a four-month term as president of the troubled Dominican Republic.

Salomé's children are forced by Dominican political instability to disperse. Pedro immigrates to Argentina, becoming an eminent scholar and eventually a Norton lecturer at Harvard. Camila, after teaching in Cuba, becomes a Vassar professor. Her distinguished career ends in 1960 with her retirement and her return to Cuba, once her childhood sanctuary but now politically turbulent.

Alvarez, herself a Dominican, often focuses on the political unrest in the Dominican Republic. This book makes political statements in beguilingly personal and historically accurate ways.

SUGGESTED READINGS

Alvarez, Julia. "A Citizen of the World: An Interview with Julia Alvarez." In *Latina Self-Portraits: Interviews with Contemporary Women Writers*, edited by Bridget Kevane and Juanita Heredia. Albuquerque: University of New Mexico Press, 2000.
_____. "On Finding a Latino Voice." In *The Writing Life: Writers on How They Think and How They Work*, edited by Maria Arana. New York: Public Affairs Press, 2003.

_____. "An Unlikely Beginning for a Writer." In *Máscaras*, edited by Lucha Corpi. Berkeley, Calif.: Third Woman Press, 1997.

Bing, Jonathan. "Julia Alvarez: Books That Cross Borders." *Publishers Weekly* 243 (December 16, 1996).

Echevarria, Roberto Gonzalez. "Sisters in Death." *The New York Times Book Review* (December 18, 1994): 28.

Garcia-Johnson, Ronie-Richele. "Julía Alvarez." In *Notable Hispanic American Women*, edited by Diane Telgen and Jim Kamp. Detroit: Gale Research, 1993.

Johnson, Kelli Lyon. *Julia Alvarez: Writing a New Place on the Map*. Albuquerque: University of New Mexico Press, 2005.

Lyons, Bonnie, and Bill Oliver. "A Clean Windshield: An Interview with Julia Alvarez." In *Passion and Craft: Conversations with Notable Writers*. Urbana: University of Illinois Press, 1998.

Ortiz-Marquez, Maribel. "From Third World Politics to First World Practices: Contemporary Latina Writers in the United States." In *Interventions: Feminist Dialogues on Third World Women's Literature and Film*, edited by Ghosh Bishmupriya and Bose Brinda. New York: Garland, 1997.

Rosario-Sievert, Heather. "Conversation with Julia Alvarez." *Review: Latin American Literature and Arts* 54 (Spring, 1997): 31-37.

Rosenberg, Robert, ed. and director. *Women of Hope/Latinas Abriendo Camino: Twelve Ground Breaking Latina Women*. Bread and Roses Cultural Project. Princeton, N.J.: Films for Humanities, 1996.

Sirias, Silvio. *Julia Alvarez: A Critical Companion*. Westport, Conn.: Greenwood Press, 2001.

Contributors: Angela Athy and R. Baird Shuman

Rudolfo A. Anaya

BORN: Pastura, New Mexico; October 30, 1937

MEXICAN AMERICAN

*Anaya became one of the foremost Chicano novelists
of the twentieth century.*

PRINCIPAL WORKS

CHILDREN'S LITERATURE: *The Farolitos of Christmas: A New Mexico Christmas
Story*, 1987 (1995; illustrated edition); *Maya's Children: The Story of La
Llorona*, 1997; *Farolitos for Abuelo*, 1998; *My Land Sings: Stories from the Rio
Grande*, 1999; *Roadrunner's Dance*, 2000; *The Santero's Miracle: A Bilingual
Story*, 2004 (illustrated by Amy Cordova, Spanish translation by Enrique
Lamadrid)

DRAMA: *The Season of La Llorona*, pr. 1979; *Who Killed Don José?*, pr. 1987; *Billy
the Kid*, pb. 1995

LONG FICTION: *Bless Me, Ultima*, 1972; *Heart of Aztlán*, 1976; *Tortuga*, 1979; *The
Legend of La Llorona*, 1984; *Lord of the Dawn: The Legend of Quetzalcóatl*,
1987; *Alburquerque*, 1992; *Zia Summer*, 1995; *Jalamanta: A Message from the
Desert*, 1996; *Rio Grande Fall*, 1996; *Shaman Winter*, 1999; *Jemez Spring*, 2005

POETRY: *The Adventures of Juan Chicaspatas*, 1985 (epic poem); *Elegy on the
Death of Cesar Chávez*, 2000 (juvenile)

SCREENPLAY: *Bilingualism: Promise for Tomorrow*, 1976

SHORT FICTION: *The Silence of the Llano*, 1982; *Serafina's Stories*, 2004; *The Man
Who Could Fly, and Other Stories*, 2006

NONFICTION: *A Chicano in China*, 1986; *Conversations with Rudolfo Anaya*, 1998

EDITED TEXTS: *Voices from the Rio Grande*, 1976; *Cuentos Chicanos: A Short Story
Anthology*, 1980 (with Antonio Márquez); *A Ceremony of Brotherhood, 1680-
1980*, 1981 (with Simon Ortiz); *Voces: An Anthology of Nuevo Mexicano
Writers*, 1987; *Aztlán: Essays on the Chicano Homeland*, 1989; *Tierra: Contemporary Short Fiction of New Mexico*, 1989

MISCELLANEOUS: *The Anaya Reader*, 1995

Rudolfo Anaya (rew-DOHL-foh ah-NI-yah) began writing during his days as a student at the University of New Mexico. His poetry and early novels dealt with major
questions about his existence, beliefs, and identity. Anaya ended that phase of his
life by burning all of the manuscripts of his work.

After college he took a teaching job and got married. He found his wife to be a
great source of encouragement and an excellent editor and companion. Anaya be-

35

gan writing *Bless Me, Ultima* in the 1960's. He struggled with the work until in one of his creative moments Ultima appeared to him. She became the strongest character of the novel as well as the spiritual mentor for the novelist and the protagonist. Ultima led the way to a successful work. Anaya's next task was to get his novel published. After dozens of rejection letters from major publishers, Anaya turned to Quinto Sol Publications, a Chicano small press in Berkeley, California. The publishers not only accepted the work for publication but also recognized Anaya with the Quinto Sol Award for writing the best Chicano novel of 1972.

Bless Me, Ultima represents the first novel of a trilogy. The other two are *Heart of Aztlán* and *Tortuga*. *Heart of Aztlán* came as a result of Anaya's travels in Mexico during the 1960's, which raised the question of the relationship between the pre-Columbian Aztec world, called Aztlán, and Chicano destiny. *Tortuga* was inspired by a diving accident at an irrigation ditch during Anaya's high school days. The accident left Anaya disabled; the protagonist in the novel also experiences such events. The quality of the first three works enshrined Anaya as the foremost Chicano novelist of his time. His numerous other excellent works have confirmed this high regard. The essence of his literary production reflects the search for the meaning of existence as it is expressed in Chicano community life.

Anaya's works blend realistic description of daily life with the hidden magic of humanity; his work may be categorized as having the qualities of Magical Realism, which mingles, in a straightforward narrative tone, the mystical and magical with the everyday. Most of his developed characters reflect this duality.

Bless Me, Ultima

TYPE OF WORK: Novel
FIRST PUBLISHED: 1972

Bless Me, Ultima is Anaya's first novel of a trilogy that also includes *Heart of Aztlán* (1976) and *Tortuga* (1979). It is a psychological and magical portrait of a quest for identity by a child. In this classic work, Antonio, the protagonist, is subjected to contradicting influences that he must master in order to mature. These influences include symbolic characters and places, the most powerful of which are Ultima, a *curandera* (healer) who evokes the timeless past of a pre-Columbian world, and a golden carp, which swims the river waters of the supernatural and offers a redeeming future.

Antonio is born in Pasturas, a very small village on the Eastern New Mexican plain. Later, the family moves across the river to the small town of Guadalupe, where Antonio spends his childhood. His father belongs to the Márez family and is a cattleman; Antonio's mother is of the Luna family, whose background is farming. They represent the initial manifestation of the divided world into which Antonio is born. Division is a challenge he must resolve in order to find himself. Antonio's father wants him to become a horseman of the plain. Antonio's mother wants him to become a priest to a farming community, which is in the highest tradition of the Luna family.

The parents' wishes are symptoms of a deeper spiritual challenge facing Antonio involving his Catholic beliefs and those associated with the magical world of a pre-Columbian past. Ultima, the *curandera* and a creature of both worlds, helps guide Antonio through the ordeal of understanding and dealing with these challenges.

Ultima is a magical character who touches the core of Antonio's being. She supervised his birth. Later she comes to stay with the family in Guadalupe when Antonio is seven. On several occasions, Antonio is a witness to her power.

Antonio's adventure takes him beyond the divided world of the farmer and the horseman and beyond the Catholic ritual and its depictions of good and evil. With Ultima's help,

Rudolfo A. Anaya (Michael Mouchette)

he is able to bridge these opposites and channel them into a new cosmic vision of nature, represented by the river, which stands in the middle of his two worlds, and by the golden carp, which points to a new spiritual covenant.

The novel ends with the killing of Ultima's owl by one of her enemies. He discovered that the owl carried her spiritual presence. This killing also causes Ultima's death, but her work is done. Antonio can choose his destiny.

Heart of Aztlán

TYPE OF WORK: Novel
FIRST PUBLISHED: 1976

Heart of Aztlán is Anaya's second novel of a trilogy that includes *Bless Me, Ultima* (1972) and *Tortuga* (1979). It is a psychological portrait of a quest for Chicano identity and empowerment. It is the story of the Chávez family, who leave the country to search for a better life in the city only to discover that their destiny lies in a past thought abandoned and lost.

The story is carried by two major characters, Clemente Chávez, the father, and Jason, one of the sons. Jason depicts the adjustments the family has to make to everyday life in the city. Clemente undergoes a magical rebirth that brings a new awareness of destiny to the community and a new will to fight for their birthright.

The novel begins with the Chávez family selling the last of their land and leaving the small town of Guadalupe for a new life in Albuquerque. They go to live in Barelas, a barrio on the west side of the city that is full of other immigrants from the country.

The Chávezes soon learn, as the other people of the barrio already know, that their lives do not belong to them. They are controlled by industrial interests represented by the railroad and a union that has sold out the workers. They are controlled by politicians through Mannie García, "el super," who delivers the community vote.

In Barelas, Clemente also begins to lose the battle of maintaining control of the family, especially his daughters, who no longer believe in his insistence on the tradition of respect and obedience to the head of the family. The situation gets worse when Clemente loses his job in the railroad yard during a futile strike.

Clemente becomes a drunk and in his despair attempts to commit suicide. Crespín, a magical character who represents eternal wisdom, comes to his assistance and points the way to a new life. With Crespín's help, Clemente solves the riddle of a magical power stone in the possession of "la India," a sorceress who symbolically guards the entryway to the heart of Aztlán, the source of empowerment for the Chicano.

Clemente's rebirth takes the form of a journey to the magical mountain lake that is at the center of Aztlán and Chicano being. Reborn, Clemente returns to his community to lead the movement for social and economic justice. It is a redeeming and unifying struggle for life and the destiny of a people.

The novel ends with Clemente physically taking a hammer to the Santa Fe water tower in the railroad yard, a symbol of industrial might, before coming home to lead a powerful march on his former employers.

Tortuga

TYPE OF WORK: Novel
FIRST PUBLISHED: 1979

Tortuga is Anaya's third novel of a trilogy that also includes *Bless Me, Ultima* (1972) and *Heart of Aztlán* (1976). It is a tale of a journey to self-realization and supernatural awareness. In the story, Benjie Chávez, the protagonist, undergoes the ordeal of symbolic rebirth in order to take the place of Crespín, the keeper of Chicano wisdom who, upon his death, leaves that task to the protagonist.

At the end of *Heart of Aztlán*, Benjie is wounded by his brother Jason's rival. Benjie falls from a rail yard water tower and is paralyzed. He is transported to a hospital in the South for rehabilitation. His entry into the hospital is also symbolically an entry into a world of supernatural transformation.

The hospital sits at the foot of Tortuga Mountain, from which flow mineral springs with healing waters. Benjie is also given the name Tortuga (which means "turtle") after he is fitted with a body cast that makes him look like a turtle. What follows is a painful ordeal. The protagonist is subjected to demanding therapy and is exposed to every kind of suffering and deformity that can possibly afflict children. Not even this, however, prepares him for the visit to the "vegetable" ward, where rotting children—who cannot move or even breathe without the help of an iron lung—are kept alive.

It is in the vegetable ward that Tortuga meets Salomón, a vegetable, but one with supernatural insight into the human condition. Salomón enters Tortuga's psyche and guides him on the path to spiritual renewal. Salomón compares Tortuga's challenge with the terrible ordeal newly born turtles undergo as they dash to the sea. Most of them do not make it, as other creatures lie in wait to devour them. Tortuga must survive the path of the turtles' dash in order to arrive at his destiny, which is called "the path of the sun."

Another part of Tortuga's ordeal includes a moment when Danny, another important character, pushes him into a swimming pool, where he nearly drowns, surviving only because other people rush to his aid. Tortuga symbolically survives the turtle dash to the sea. The vegetables are not so lucky. One night Danny succeeds in turning off the power to their ward. With the iron lungs turned off, they all die.

The end of the novel and Tortuga's rehabilitation also bring the news that Crespín, the magical helper of Tortuga's home neighborhood, has died. The news of Crespín's death arrives along with his blue guitar, a symbol of universal knowledge, which is now in Benjie's care.

SUGGESTED READINGS

Baeza, Abelardo. *Man of Aztlan: A Biography of Rudolfo Anaya.* Austin, Tex.: Eakin Press, 2001.

Dick, Bruce, and Silvio Sirias, eds. *Conversations with Rudolfo Anaya.* Jackson: University of Mississippi Press, 1998.

Fernández Olmos, Margarite. *Rudolfo A. Anaya: A Critical Companion.* Westport, Conn.: Greenwood Press, 1999.

González-Trujillo, César A., ed. *Rudolfo A. Anaya: Focus on Criticism.* La Jolla, Calif.: Lalo Press, 1990.

Klein, Dianne. "Coming of Age in Novels by Rudolfo Anaya and Sandra Cisneros." *The English Journal* 81 (September, 1992).

Taylor, Paul Beekman. "Chicano Secrecy in the Fiction of Rudolfo A. Anaya." *Journal of the Southwest* 39, no. 2 (1997): 239-265.

Vasallo, Paul, ed. *The Magic of Words: Rudolfo Anaya and His Writings.* Albuquerque: University of New Mexico Press, 1982.

Contributor: David Conde

Maya Angelou
(Marguerite Johnson)

BORN: St. Louis, Missouri; April 4, 1928

AFRICAN AMERICAN

Through poems and autobiographical narratives,
Angelou describes her life as an African American,
single mother, professional, and feminist.

PRINCIPAL WORKS

CHILDREN'S LITERATURE: *Mrs. Flowers: A Moment of Friendship*, 1986 (illustrated by Étienne Delessert); *Life Doesn't Frighten Me*, 1993 (poetry; illustrated by Jean-Michel Basquiat); *Soul Looks Back in Wonder*, 1993; *My Painted House, My Friendly Chicken, and Me*, 1994; *Kofi and His Magic*, 1996; *Angelina of Italy*, 2004; *Izak of Lapland*, 2004; *Mikale of Hawaii*, 2004; *Renie Marie of France*, 2004

DRAMA: *Cabaret for Freedom*, pr. 1960 (with Godfrey Cambridge; musical); *The Least of These*, pr. 1966; *Encounters*, pr. 1973; *Ajax*, pr. 1974 (adaptation of Sophocles' play); *And Still I Rise*, pr. 1976; *King*, pr. 1990 (musical; lyrics with Alistair Beaton, book by Lonne Elder III; music by Richard Blackford)

POETRY: *Just Give Me a Cool Drink of Water 'fore I Diiie*, 1971; *Oh Pray My Wings Are Gonna Fit Me Well*, 1975; *And Still I Rise*, 1978; *Shaker, Why Don't You Sing?*, 1983; *Poems: Maya Angelou*, 1986; *Now Sheba Sings the Song*, 1987 (Tom Feelings, illustrator); *I Shall Not Be Moved: Poems*, 1990; *On the Pulse of Morning*, 1993; *The Complete Collected Poems of Maya Angelou*, 1994; *Phenomenal Woman: Four Poems Celebrating Women*, 1994; *A Brave and Startling Truth*, 1995; *Amazing Peace: A Christmas Poem*, 2005; *Mother: A Cradle to Hold Me*, 2006

SCREENPLAYS: *Georgia, Georgia*, 1972; *All Day Long*, 1974

SHORT FICTION: "Steady Going Up," 1972; "The Reunion," 1983

TELEPLAYS: *Black, Blues, Black*, 1968 (10 episodes); *The Inheritors*, 1976; *The Legacy*, 1976; *I Know Why the Caged Bird Sings*, 1979 (with Leonora Thuna and Ralph B. Woolsey); *Sister, Sister*, 1982; *Brewster Place*, 1990

NONFICTION: *I Know Why the Caged Bird Sings*, 1970 (autobiography); *Gather Together in My Name*, 1974 (autobiography); *Singin' and Swingin' and Gettin' Merry Like Christmas*, 1976 (autobiography); *The Heart of a Woman*, 1981 (autobiography); *All God's Children Need Traveling Shoes*, 1986 (autobiography); *Wouldn't Take Nothing for My Journey Now*, 1993 (autobiographical essays);

Even the Stars Look Lonesome, 1997; *A Song Flung Up to Heaven*, 2002 (autobiographical essays); *Hallelujah! The Welcome Table: A Lifetime of Memories with Recipes*, 2004 (memoir and cookbook)

Born Marguerite Johnson, rechristened Maya, and taking the professional name Angelou (an adaptation of the name of her first husband, Tosh Angelos), Maya Angelou studied music and dance with Martha Graham, Pearl Primus, and Ann Halprin. Her early career was as an actress and singer, to which she quickly added the roles of civil rights worker (as the northern coordinator for the Southern Christian Leadership Conference [SCLC], 1959-1960), editor (as associate editor for the *Arab Observer*, 1961-1962), educator (beginning with the School of Music and Drama at the University of Ghana's Institute of African Studies, 1963-1966), and finally writer—first as a reporter for the *Ghanaian Times* (1963-1965). During the late 1960's and 1970's she taught at many colleges and universities in California and Kansas. Since joining the faculty at Wake Forest University in 1981, she has been a sought-after speaker and is in many respects regarded as America's unofficial poet laureate, although she has yet to receive that honor.

Undoubtedly, Angelou's legacy will be her writings: Although the best-selling *I Know Why the Caged Bird Sings* was censored, her excellent work as an author in all genres has kept her story before the world. Angelou's early years have been burned into the minds of numerous readers. An image from this work centers on three-year-old Marguerite and four-year-old Bailey Johnson aboard a train, alone, traveling from California to their grandmother's home in Stamps, Arkansas, after the breakup of their parents' marriage. The two children wore their names and their destination attached to their clothes. This locomotive quest for family is both a factual part of and an apt metaphor for the life of the world-famous poet. Her first feeling of being truly at home, she has said, came in Africa, after she accompanied her second husband to Egypt and then traveled to Ghana.

A second image from Angelou's childhood involves the seven-year-old's rape by her mother's boyfriend. When no legal punishment followed, the rapist was murdered, possibly by the victim's uncles. Guilt following this incident drove Angelou inward, and she began reading the great works

Maya Angelou (AP/Wide World Photos)

of literature. Reading her way through the Stamps library, she fell in love with William Shakespeare and Paul Laurence Dunbar, among others. The child of a fractured nuclear family came to see herself as a child of the fractured human family.

By age thirteen Angelou had grown closer to her mother; at sixteen she became a mother herself. To earn a living for herself and her son Guy, she became a waitress, a singer, and a dancer. These and other occupations were followed by acting, directing, producing, and the hosting of television specials. She loved to dance, but when her knees began to suffer in her early twenties, she devoted her attention to her other love: writing. She began supporting herself through her writing in 1968. Her family came to include "sister friends" and "brother friends," as her troubled brother Bailey became lost in the worlds of substance abuse and prison. She married, but she has refused to attach a number to her marriages, as that might, she says, suggest frivolity, and she insists that she was never frivolous about marriage. To "brother friend" James Baldwin she gives much credit for her becoming an autobiographer. She assisted "brother friends" Martin Luther King, Jr., and Malcolm X in their work and pursued her own work to better the entire human family.

The hope that she found so significant in the 1960's is reflected in the poem she composed for Bill Clinton's presidential inauguration. The dream of King is evident in the words written and delivered by Angelou "on the pulse of [that] morning."

I Know Why the Caged Bird Sings

TYPE OF WORK: Autobiography
FIRST PUBLISHED: 1970

Angelou begins her autobiographical *I Know Why the Caged Bird Sings* with reflections about growing up black and female during the Great Depression in the small, segregated town of Stamps, Arkansas. Following their parents' divorce, Angelou, then three years old, moved to Stamps with her brother Bailey to live with their paternal grandmother and their uncle Willie. Their home was the general store, which served as the secular center of the African American community in Stamps. Angelou's memories of this store include weary farmworkers, the euphoria of Joe Louis's successful prizefight, and a terrifying nocturnal Ku Klux Klan hunt.

Angelou also recollects lively African American church services, unpleasant interracial encounters, and childhood sexual experimentation. An avid love of reading led the young Angelou to African American writers, including the poet Paul Laurence Dunbar, from whose verse Angelou borrows the title for her narrative.

Singing is heard in Angelou's memories of her segregated Arkansas school. At their grade-school graduation ceremony, Angelou and her classmates counter the racism of a condescending white politician with a defiant singing of James Weldon Johnson's "Lift Every Voice and Sing." For Angelou this song becomes a celebration of the resistance of African Americans to the white establishment and a key to her identity as an African American poet.

Angelou spends portions of the narrative with her mother in St. Louis and in California. She has a wild visit to Mexico with her father and is even a homeless runaway for a time. As a girl in St. Louis, Angelou is sexually abused by her mother's boyfriend. Following his trial and mysterious death, Angelou suffers a period of trauma and muteness. Later, an adolescent Angelou struggles with her sexual identity, fears that she is a lesbian, and eventually initiates an unsatisfactory heterosexual encounter, from which she becomes pregnant.

Angelou matures into a self-assured and proud young woman. During World War II, she overcomes racial barriers to become one of the first African American female streetcar conductors in San Francisco. Surviving the uncertainties of an unwanted pregnancy, Angelou optimistically faces her future as an unwed mother and as an African American woman.

All God's Children Need Traveling Shoes
TYPE OF WORK: Autobiography
FIRST PUBLISHED: 1986

All God's Children Need Traveling Shoes belongs to a series of autobiographical narratives tracing Angelou's personal search for identity as an African American woman. In this powerful tale, Angelou describes her emotional journey to find identity and ancestral roots in West Africa. Angelou reveals her excitement as she immigrates to Ghana in 1962 and attempts to redefine herself as African, not American. Her loyalty to Ghana's founding president, Kwame Nkrumah, reflects hope in Africa's and her own independence. She learns the Fanti language, toys with thoughts of marrying a prosperous Malian Muslim, communes with Ghanaians in small towns and rural areas, and identifies with her enslaved forebears. Monuments such as Cape Coast Castle, where captured slaves were imprisoned before sailing to America, stand on African soil as vivid reminders of an African American slave past.

In Ghana Angelou hopes to escape the lingering pains of American slavery and racism. Gradually, however, she feels displaced and uncomfortable in her African environment. Cultural differences and competition for employment result in unpleasant encounters between Ghanaians and African Americans. Despite such frustrations, Angelou's network of fellow African American emigrants offers mutual support and continuing hope in the African experience. A visit by Malcolm X provides much-needed encouragement, but his presence is also a reminder of ties with the United States. Angelou and her African American friends express their solidarity with the American Civil Rights movement by demonstrating at the United States embassy in Ghana.

As she sorts through her ambivalent feelings about Africa, Angelou also rethinks her role as mother. At the beginning of *All God's Children Need Traveling Shoes*, Angelou's son Guy almost dies in an automobile accident. Later in the narrative he develops a relationship with an older woman and struggles to gain admittance to the University of Ghana. In dealing with all these events, Angelou learns to balance her maternal feelings with her son's need for independence and self-expression. Finally recognizing the powerful ties binding her to American soil, Angelou concludes her narrative with a joyful journey home from Ghana and a renewed sense of identity as an African American.

I Shall Not Be Moved

TYPE OF WORK: Poetry
FIRST PUBLISHED: 1990

Maya Angelou's poetry draws on the rhythms of jazz, blues, and spirituals; despite its tough look at the hard facts of black life, it is ultimately forgiving and celebratory. Angelou's long poem "Our Grandmothers," perhaps her best, is emblematic of the entire work. It features the refrain, "I shall not be moved," epitomizing the love and determination of black women. The first woman who appears in this poem is significantly nameless, a slave mother running away with her children because the master is going to sell her and divide the family. Other women also appear as Angelou moves from the days of the slave trade to the modern-day black woman standing in the welfare line. Each of these women, however, has enormous resistance and resilience.

Angelou sympathizes as well with other struggling members of society. Her poems about the working poor are especially poignant—the girl who asserts, "Even minimal people/ can't survive on minimum wage," and Coleridge Jackson, a warehouse worker who is berated and diminished daily by his "little/ white bag of bones" boss.

Yet Angelou has the largeness of spirit to forgive even the former slave state of Virginia. She uses its natural beauty to signify the change, writing that dogwood blossoms form "round my/ head ringlets/ of forgiveness." Indeed, although Angelou presents a harshly realistic picture of black life, she also sees the humor, joy, and triumph of it. The final poem is a dirge for dead friends. She first mourns their loss, then looks at the larger picture, finding that "after a period peace blooms." Finally, because they were, "We can be. Be and be/ better. . . ." The entire volume is a triumph of overcoming.

Wouldn't Take Nothing for My Journey Now

TYPE OF WORK: Essays
FIRST PUBLISHED: 1993

Wouldn't Take Nothing for My Journey Now is a collection of twenty-four meditations, many of special interest to women, expressing Maya Angelou's views on subjects ranging from fashion and entertainment to sensuality and pregnancy, racism, and death. Two of the essays contain new poems, one for Angelou's mother, "Mrs. V. B.," and the other, untitled, on the similarities among all people despite racial diversity. Among the best pieces here are those that begin with some autobiographical incident from which Angelou draws an insight or lesson. The most interesting include "Power of the Word," focusing on the power of faith, particularly as illustrated in Angelou's own experience and in her grandmother, "Mamma," in Stamps, Arkansas, during the Great Depression; "Getups," demonstrating not only Angelou's love of richly colorful clothing but also a painful event from her years as a single mother of a small boy; and "Extending Boundaries," recounting an embarrassing experience from Angelou's early days as a writer in New York City. Angelou uses each incident to draw some point, though generally she offers her moral or advice with a light hand, often with humor, despite the seriousness of some of her subject matter. Her recurrent themes include self-knowledge and the necessity of honesty, prudence, and respect in the treatment of oneself and others.

Written in the simple, direct style that also characterizes Maya Angelou's poetry, these essays are particularly suitable for morning or evening reflection. They range in length from several pages to one paragraph, and each is an independent piece. They offer insight into the experience and philosophy of one of America's most celebrated women writers and practical advice for responsible yet pleasurable living.

Suggested Readings

Bloom, Harold, ed. *Maya Angelou*. Philadelphia: Chelsea House, 2001.

Elliott, Jeffrey M., ed. *Conversations with Maya Angelou*. Jackson: University Press of Mississippi, 1989.

Hagen, Lynn B. *Heart of a Woman, Mind of a Writer, and Soul of a Poet: A Critical Analysis of the Writings of Maya Angelou*. Lanham, Md.: University Press of America, 1996.

King, Sarah E. *Maya Angelou: Greeting the Morning*. Brookfield, Conn.: Millbrook Press, 1994.

Lisandrelli, Elaine Slivinski. *Maya Angelou: More than a Poet*. Springfield, N.J.: Enslow, 1996.

Lupton, Mary Jane. *Maya Angelou: A Critical Companion*. Westport, Conn.: Greenwood Press, 1998.

McPherson, Dolly A. *Order out of Chaos: The Autobiographical Works of Maya Angelou*. New York: P. Lang, 1990.

Pettit, Jayne. *Maya Angelou: Journey of the Heart*. New York: Lodestar Books, 1996.

Shapiro, Miles. *Maya Angelou*. New York: Chelsea House, 1994.

Williams, Mary E., ed. *Readings on Maya Angelou*. San Diego, Calif.: Greenhaven Press, 1997.

Contributors: Thomas J. Sienkewicz, Judith K. Taylor, and David Peck

Mary Antin

BORN: Polotzk, Russia; June 13, 1881
DIED: Suffern, New York; May 17, 1949

JEWISH

Antin's The Promised Land *is the classic Jewish American immigrant autobiography.*

PRINCIPAL WORKS

NONFICTION: *From Plotzk to Boston*, 1899; *At School in the Promised Land: Or, The Story of a Little Immigrant*, 1912 (selections from *The Promised Land*); *The Promised Land*, 1912; *They Who Knock at Our Gates: A Complete Gospel of Immigration*, 1914 (illustrated by Joseph Stella)

Mary Antin (MEHR-ree AN-tihn) was born in Polotzk in what was then czarist Russia. Antin's place of birth and her Jewishness determined what her identity would have been had her family stayed in Polotzk. Had they stayed, she would have been an Orthodox Jewish wife of a Jewish man, the mother of Jewish children, and a woman with only enough education to enable her to read the Psalms in Hebrew. As a Jew, she could not live beyond the pale of settlement in Russia and could never become assimilated into Russian society. As a young child, she felt stifled by this identity.

In *The Promised Land* she compares her moving at age thirteen to America, where she felt she had freedom to choose her own identity, to the Hebrews' escape from bondage in Egypt. In America, she received a free education in Boston public schools. She had access to public libraries. She had access to settlement houses, like Hale House (in which she later worked), where she experienced American culture. She had a freedom of which she could hardly dream in Europe. The woman who in Polotzk would never have become more than barely literate chose for herself in the New World the identity of a writer and social worker. At fifteen, she published her first poem in the *Boston Herald*. At eighteen, she published her first autobiographical volume, *From Plotzk to Boston*, which resulted in her being hailed as a child prodigy. Eventually, she reworked the material from this book into her masterpiece, *The Promised Land*.

After graduating from Girl's Latin School in Boston, Antin went to the Teachers' College of Columbia University in New York City and then to Barnard College, where she met and married Amadeus W. Grabau, a geologist, Columbia professor, and Gentile. She felt that her marriage cemented her chosen identity as a fully assimilated American. Although her husband eventually left her and settled in China, she never lost her faith in the possibilities of total assimilation into American society. She felt that since she had become fully assimilated, so could all other Jewish immigrants to the country she spoke of without irony as the promised land.

The Promised Land

TYPE OF WORK: Autobiography
FIRST PUBLISHED: 1912

The Promised Land is Antin's mature autobiography. In it, she tells the story of what she considers her escape from bondage in Eastern Europe and her finding of freedom in America. Early in the book, she compares herself to a treadmill horse who can only go round and round in the same circle. She sees herself in Polotzk in what was then Russia as imprisoned by her religion (Jews were allowed to live only in certain places in czarist Russia and to work only at certain trades) and her sex (among Orthodox Jews in Eastern Europe, women were not permitted education beyond learning to read the Psalms in Hebrew).

After her father suffered a long illness and as a result failed in business, he went to America. His family followed him to Boston, where Mary grew up. In America, she felt that she had all the freedom she lacked in the Old World. She could get free secular education. The public schools of Boston, she felt, opened new intellectual vistas for her. She also had access to public libraries and settlement houses that provided her with cultural activities. Thus, she felt she had "a kingdom in the slums."

She responded to America's possibilities by doing extremely well in school and by publishing her first poem when she was fifteen. Her father proudly bought copies of the newspaper in which it appeared and distributed it to friends and neighbors, bragging about his daughter the writer.

She became a member of the Natural History Club of Boston and, through it, learned about the lives of its members who, she felt, represented what was best about America, a country in which she felt she was a welcomed participant. Visiting many of the members in their homes, she became convinced that she had true equality in America.

In her book, Antin says that if she was able to accomplish so much, so can all immigrants. She admits that her father, because of an inability to master the English language and because of bad luck, did not prosper in the New World, but she still remains optimistic about America and about the possibilities of total assimilation for America's immigrant population. Whereas the Old World represents, for her, lack of freedom and a predetermined identity, she sees the New World as representing freedom and the ability to choose her own identity.

SUGGESTED READINGS

Antin, Mary. *Selected Letters of Mary Antin*. Edited by Evelyn Satz. Syracuse, N.Y.: Syracuse University Press, 2000.

Guttmann, Allen. *The Jewish Writer in America: Assimilation and the Crisis of Identity*. New York: Oxford University Press, 1971.

Liptzin, Sol. *The Jew in American Literature*. New York: Bloch, 1966.

Mindra, Mihai. *Strategists of Assimilation: Abraham Cahan, Mary Antin, Anzia Yezierska*. Bucharest: Romanian Academy, 2003.

Tuerk, Richard. "Jewish-American Literature." In *Ethnic Perspectives in American Literature: Selected Essays on the European Contribution*, edited by Robert J. DiPietro and Edward Ifkovic. New York: Modern Language Association of America, 1983.

Contributor: Richard Tuerk

Reinaldo Arenas

BORN: Holguín, Oriente, Cuba; July 16, 1943
DIED: New York, New York; December 7, 1990

CUBAN AMERICAN

Arenas's novels reflect his rural upbringing and his fight against Cuban revolutionary institutions that condemned him because of his homosexuality.

PRINCIPAL WORKS

DRAMA: *Persecución: Cuatro piezas de teatro experimental*, pb. 1986
LONG FICTION: *Celestino antes del alba*, 1967 (revised as *Cantando en el pozo*, 1982; *Singing from the Well*, 1987; part 1 of *The Pentagonía*); *El mundo alucinante*, 1969 (*Hallucinations: Being an Account of the Life and Adventures of Friar Servando Teresa de Mier*, 1971; also as *The Ill-Fated Peregrinations of Fray Servando*, 1987); *El palacio de las blanquísimas mofetas*, 1975 (as *Le Palais des très blanches mouffettes*, 1980; *The Palace of the White Skunks*, 1990; part 2 of *The Pentagonía*); *La vieja Rosa*, 1980; *Otra vez el mar*, 1982 (*Farewell to the Sea*, 1986; part 3 of *The Pentagonía*); *Arturo, la estrella más brillante*, 1984 (*Arturo, the Most Brilliant Star*, 1989, in *Old Rosa*); *La loma del ángel*, 1987 (*Graveyard of the Angels*, 1987); *El portero*, 1989 (*The Doorman*, 1991); *Old Rosa: A Novel in Two Stories*, 1989 (a combination of *La vieja Rosa* and *Arturo, la estrella más brillante*); *Viaje a La Habana*, 1990; *El color del verano*, 1991 (*The Color of Summer: Or, The New Garden of Earthly Delights*, 2000; part 4 of *The Pentagonía*); *El asalto*, 1991 (*The Assault*, 1994; part 5 of *The Pentagonía*)
POETRY: *El central*, 1981 (*El Central: A Cuban Sugar Mill*, 1984); *Voluntad de vivir manifestándose*, 1989
SHORT FICTION: *Con los ojos cerrados*, 1972 (revised as *Termina el desfile*, 1981); *Adiós a mamá: De La Habana a Nueva York*, 1995; *Mona, and Other Tales*, 2001
NONFICTION: *Necesidad de libertad*, 1985; *Antes que anochezca*, 1992 (*Before Night Falls*, 1993)

Reinaldo Arenas (ray-NAHL-doh ah-RAY-nahs) overcame a poor rural upbringing to become a renowned novelist and short-story writer. He belongs to a generation of young writers who received literary training in official programs to promote literacy among the Cuban poor. Such training, however, also involved heavy indoctrination by political organizations that promoted only revolutionary readings.

49

Although his career depended upon his incorporation into such a political agenda, Arenas refused to take an ideological stand. His decision caused him prosecution by legal authorities, imprisonment, and exile.

A superb storyteller, Arenas, in his first novel, *Singing from the Well*, presents young peasant characters who find themselves in an existentialist quest. Surrounded by a bleak rural environment, these protagonists fight the absolute poverty that keeps them from achieving their dreams. They also must confront their homosexual feelings, which force them to become outcasts. Although the subject of homosexuality is not an essential theme of the novel—the subject is merely hinted—Arenas's novel received a cold reception from Cuban critics.

Hallucinations brought Arenas's first confrontations with revolutionary critics and political authorities. Dissatisfied with the Castro regime, Arenas in the novel equates the Cuban Revolution to the oppressive forces of the Spanish Inquisition by drawing parallels between the persecutory practices of the two institutions. He also published the novel abroad without government consent, a crime punishable by law. That violation caused him to lose job opportunities and made him the target of multiple attempts at indoctrination, which included his imprisonment in a forced labor camp in 1970.

In spite of constant threats, Arenas continued writing antirevolutionary works that were smuggled out of the country by friends and published abroad in French translations. The theme of these works is constant: denunciation of Castro's oppressive political practices, most significantly the forced labor camps. The novels also decry the systematic persecution of homosexuals by military police and the relocation of homosexuals in labor camps.

After an incarceration of almost three years (1973-1976), Arenas made several attempts to escape from Cuba illegally. He finally succeeded in 1980, when he entered the United States by means of the Mariel boat lift. In the United States he continued his strong opposition to the Castro regime and re-edited the literary work he had written in Cuba. In addition, he intensified his interest in homosexual characters who, like his early young characters, find themselves in confrontation with the oppressive societies that punish them because of their sexual orientation. His open treatment of homosexuality makes him a forerunner of writers on that subject in Latin American literature. In 1987, Arenas received a diagnosis of AIDS and three years later took his own life by deliberately overdosing on drugs and alcohol. He had remained a staunch opponent of the Cuban government; in a suicide note he encouraged his compatriots to "continue fighting for freedom. . . . Cuba will be free. I already am."

Arturo, the Most Brilliant Star

TYPE OF WORK: Novel
FIRST PUBLISHED: *Arturo, la estrella más brillante*, 1984 (English translation, 1989)

Arenas's commitment to resisting and denouncing Cuba's indoctrination practices is evident in his short novel *Arturo, the Most Brilliant Star*. This work is also significant in that Arenas links his political views on the Cuban Revolution with his increasing interest in gay characters. The plot was inspired by a series of police raids against homosexuals in Havana in the early 1960's. The process was simple: The police picked up thousands of men, usually young men, and denounced them as homosexuals on the grounds of their wearing certain pieces of clothing commonly considered to be the garb of gay men. Those arrested had to work and undergo ideological training in labor camps.

Arturo is one of the thousands of gay men forced into a work camp. He becomes a fictional eyewitness of the rampant use of violence as a form of punishment. The novel's descriptions of the violence coincide with eyewitness accounts by gay men who have made similar declarations after their exile from Cuba.

Arturo faces the fact that a labor camp foments homosexual activity between the prisoners and the guards. A dreary and claustrophobic existence prompts some men to do female impersonations. If caught, those impersonators become a target of police brutality. Arturo, a social outcast, suffers rejection by his fellow prisoners because initially he does not take part in the female impersonations. Partly as the result of verbal and physical abuse, he joins the group at last and becomes the camp's best female impersonator. His transformation, especially his fast control of the female impersonator's jargon, reminds the reader of the revolutionary jargon forced upon the prisoners, which at first they resist learning but later mimic to ironic perfection.

Arturo's imagination forces him to understand his loneliness in the camp. In order to escape from the camp, he strives to create his own world, one that is truly fantastic and one of which he is king. The mental process is draining, and he has to work under sordid conditions that threaten his concentration, but he is successful in his attempt, and his world grows and extends outside the camp. The final touch is the construction of his own castle, in which he discovers a handsome man waiting for him on the other side of the walls. In his pursuit of his admirer, Arturo does not recognize that his imaginary walls are the off-limits fences of the camp. When he is ordered to stop, he continues to walk out of the camp, and he is shot dead by a military officer.

Arenas's novel represents the beginning of a literary trend in Latin America that presents homosexuals as significant characters. It also focuses on the sexual practices of homosexual men, something that was a literary taboo.

The Pentagonía

TYPE OF WORK: Novels
FIRST PUBLISHED: *Celestino antes del alba*, 1967 (*Singing from the Well*, 1987); *El palacio de las blanquísimas mofetas*, 1975 (*The Palace of the White Skunks*, 1990); *Otra vez el mar*, 1982 (*Farewell to the Sea*, 1986); *El color del verano*, 1991 (*The Color of Summer*, 2000); *El asalto*, 1991 (*The Assault*, 1994)

The Pentagonía documents life in Cuba from the early 1950's onward. Although the novels deal with a variety of themes and with diverse characters, one subject stands out as a common denominator: homosexuality. Many characters face sexual oppression by Cuban society and must fight for their incorporation into productive social roles.

Arenas's novels document the lives of various male characters from their childhood to adulthood, including their handling of their homosexuality. *Singing from the Well* opens the set by presenting children oppressed by poverty; these children also face the sexual dynamics of a highly chauvinistic society. The nameless characters are representative of Cuban homosexual youth and return as more mature characters in subsequent novels, which can be read as sequels.

The Palace of the White Skunks takes Arenas's coming-of-age themes one step further by removing an unhappy young man from his restrictive society. Inspired by claims of social equality, Fortunato joins Castro's guerrilla forces in the fight against the Cuban dictator. His dreams are shattered, however, by the strong antihomosexual attitude of men in the military forces. As a result of his being homosexual, Fortunato is labeled weak and imperfect, certainly not the model of the revolutionary man.

Farewell to the Sea abandons young characters to explore the life of a married man, who appears to be living a full life. Héctor is married and a proud father. He expresses total commitment to revolutionary ideology, for which the state has awarded him a free trip to a beach resort. There he meets a young man, with whom he has romantic encounters. When his friend is found dead in a remote area of the beach, Héctor decides to abandon his vacation. The reader comes to understand that Héctor is a homosexual man who despises the revolution, who has experienced homosexual life, but who is forced to live as a prorevolutionary heterosexual in order to survive.

Arenas wrote the last two novels while fighting AIDS-related illnesses. With *The Color of Summer* he makes his most direct attacks against revolutionary persecution of homosexuals. Characters have to lead lives of pretense in order to avoid the economic disaster that follows revelation of homosexuality. *The Assault* focuses on revolutionary censorship, showing how homosexuals are forced to turn against their own relatives. Physical violence abounds in Arenas's novels, reflecting on a violent revolutionary society.

SUGGESTED READINGS

Arenas, Reinaldo. "Reinaldo Arenas's Last Interview." Interview by Perla Rozencvaig. *Review: Latin American Literature and Arts* 44 (January/June, 1991): 78-83.

Foster, David W. *Gay and Lesbian Themes in Latin American Writing.* Austin: University of Texas Press, 1991.

Ocasio, Rafael. *A Gay Cuban Activist in Exile: Reinaldo Arenas.* Gainesville: University Press of Florida, 2007.

Paulson, Michael G. *The Youth and the Beach: A Comparative Study of Thomas Mann's "Der Tod in Venedig" ("Death in Venice") and Reinaldo Arenas's "Otra vez el mar" ("Farewell to the Sea").* Miami: Ediciones Universal, 1993.

Santí, Enrico M. "The Life and Times of Reinaldo Arenas." *Michigan Quarterly Review* 23 (Spring, 1984).

Soto, Francisco. *Reinaldo Arenas: The Pentagonia.* Gainesville: University Press of Florida, 1994.

Zéndegui, Ileana C. *The Postmodern Poetic Narrative of Cuban Writer Reinaldo Arenas.* Lewiston, N.Y.: Edwin Mellen Press, 2004.

Contributor: Rafael Ocasio

Molefi K. Asante
(Arthur Lee Smith, Jr.)

BORN: Valdosta, Georgia; August 14, 1942

AFRICAN AMERICAN

An authority on race and racism in America and author of more than fifty books, Asante is best known as a prolific activist, scholar, and spokesperson for Afrocentricity.

PRINCIPAL WORKS

POETRY: *The Break of Dawn*, 1964

NONFICTION: *Rhetoric of Black Revolution*, 1969; *Transracial Communication*, 1973; *Epic in Search of African Kings*, 1978; *Mass Communication: Principles and Practices*, 1979 (with Mary Cassata); *Afrocentricity: The Theory of Social Change*, 1980 (revised 1988); *The Afrocentric Idea*, 1987 (revised and expanded 1998); *Kemet, Afrocentricity, and Knowledge*, 1990; *The Book of African Names*, 1991; *Historical and Cultural Atlas of African Americans*, 1991 (revised as *The African American Atlas: Black History and Culture*, 1998; with Mark T. Mattson); *Thunder and Silence: The Mass Media in Africa*, 1992 (with Dhyana Ziegler); *Malcolm X as Cultural Hero, and Other Afrocentric Essays*, 1993; *Classical Africa*, 1994; *African American History: A Journey of Liberation*, 1995; *The African American Book of Names and Their Meanings*, 1999 (with Renée Muntaquim); *The Painful Demise of Eurocentrism*, 1999; *The Egyptian Philosophers: Ancient African Voices from Imhotep to Akhenaten*, 2000; *Culture and Customs of Egypt*, 2002; *One Hundred Greatest African Americans: A Biographical Encyclopedia*, 2002; *Erasing Racism: The Survival of the American Nation*, 2003

EDITED TEXTS: *The Voice of Black Rhetoric*, 1971 (with Stephen Robb); *Language, Communication, and Rhetoric in Black America*, 1972; *The Social Uses of Mass Communication*, 1977 (with Mary Cassata); *Handbook of Intercultural Communication*, 1979; *Contemporary Black Thought*, 1980 (with Abdulai Vandi); *African Culture: The Rhythms of Unity*, 1985 (with Kariamu Welsh Asante); *Handbook of International and Intercultural Communication*, 1989 (with William Gudykunst); *African Intellectual Heritage: A Book of Sources*, 1996 (with Abu Abarry); *Socio-cultural Conflict Between African American and Korean American*, 2000 (with Eungjin Min); *Transcultural Realities: Interdisciplinary Perspectives on Cross-Cultural Relations*, 2001 (with Virginia H. Milhouse and Peter O. Nwosu); *Egypt vs. Greece and the American Academy*, 2002 (with Ama Mazama); *Encyclopedia of Black Studies*, 2005 (with Mazama)

Born Arthur Lee Smith, Jr., to Arthur L. Smith and Lillie B. Wilkson Smith, Molefi Kete Asante (moh-LAY-fee KEH-tay ah-SAHN-tay) was reared in Valdosta, Georgia, where he experienced racial prejudice but also the sustaining influence of the black church. He attended Southwestern Christian College, receiving his associate of arts degree in 1962. He earned a bachelor's degree (cum laude) from Oklahoma Christian College in 1964, the year he published a collection of poems, *The Break of Dawn*. In 1965, he received a master's degree from Pepperdine University and, in 1968, a doctorate from the University of California at Los Angeles (UCLA).

In 1966, Asante began his teaching career at State Polytechnic College in California. Two years later, he secured a position in communication at Purdue University and chaired the Indiana State Civil Rights Commission on Higher Education and the Afro-American. In 1969, the year he became the founding editor of the *Journal of Black Studies*, he began teaching speech at UCLA.

Under the name Arthur L. Smith, Jr., Asante published *Rhetoric of Black Revolution* in 1969, during the height of the Black Power movement. The book traces black rhetoric from the nineteenth century to the 1960's. In 1970, Asante was appointed director of the UCLA Center for Afro-American Studies, where he remained until 1973, after which he taught at the State University of New York at Buffalo. He chaired the school's Department of Communication and was curator of the Center for Positive Thought. Published during this period, *Transracial Communication* addresses black-white interaction and emphasizes cultural perspectives.

One of the major turning points in Asante's identification with Africa occurred in 1975, when he changed his name. (The southern African name Molefi means "he keeps traditions.") During this period, he was appointed external examiner for the universities of Ibadan (Nigeria) and Nairobi (Kenya). In 1979, after a yearlong visiting professorship at Howard University, he traveled to Africa as a Fulbright professor at the Zimbabwe Institute of Mass Communication.

In 1980, the year he received the Outstanding Communication Scholar Award from Jackson State University, Asante published his first major work defining Afrocentric theory, *Afrocentricity: The Theory of Social Change*, which includes a foreword by his wife, Kariamu Welsh. ("Afrocentricity" can be defined as an attempt to place Africa at the center of black reality.) *Afrocentricity*, which discusses the contributions of such figures as Marcus Garvey, W. E. B. Du Bois, Frantz Fanon, Malcolm X, and Maulana Karenga, examines the spiritual concept of Nija, "collective" presentation of an Afrocentric worldview. Afrology, a methodological approach to the study of black people, is also addressed, along with "breakthrough strategies" to counter negative attitudes resulting from the "breakdown" of the West.

In 1984, Asante was appointed chair of the Department of African American Studies at Temple University, where he created the first Ph.D. program in African American studies. In 1985, in collaboration with his wife, he edited *African Culture: The Rhythms of Unity*, an impressive collection of articles by such writers as Wole Soyinka and John Henrik Clarke.

The Afrocentric Idea continued the critique of Eurocentrism, arguing against the universality of Western conceptions and proposing explanations of such African

American characteristics as Ebonics, or black language expression. Following publication of the revised edition of *Afrocentricity* in 1988, Asante published another collaborative work, *Handbook of Intercultural Communication*. In the 1990's, he explored Afrocentricity with an emphasis on Egyptian civilization in *Kemet, Afrocentricity, and Knowledge*, which poses alternate conceptions for understanding Afrocentricity. He also published a collaborative reference work providing maps, statistical data, and cultural information, the *Historical and Cultural Atlas of African Americans*. Another reference work, *The Book of African Names*, organizes African names by region. *Thunder and Silence*, a joint project with Dhyana Ziegler, explores from a historical perspective both print and electronic media in Africa.

In 1993, Asante's *Malcolm X as Cultural Hero, and Other Afrocentric Essays* was published, containing one essay on Malcolm X and, among others, "Afrocentricity, Women, and Gender," in which Afrocentricity is viewed as a humanizing force that challenges gender oppression. Furthermore, Asante addressed the need for Afrocentric perspectives in the schools by publishing such textbooks as *Classical Africa* and *African American History*. *African Intellectual Heritage*, edited with Abu Abarry, brings together a wide range of writings covering Africa and the African diaspora from ancient times to the late twentieth century. He also published books about Egypt, *The Egyptian Philosophers* and *Culture and Customs of Egypt*, and edited *Egypt vs. Greece and the American Academy*. He took up the question of cultural relations by coediting the texts *Socio-cultural Conflict Between African American and Korean American* and *Transcultural Realities*.

In the mid-1990's, Asante was made a traditional king in Ghana: Nana Okru Kete Asante Krobea I, Kyidomhene of Tafo.

Erasing Racism

TYPE OF WORK: Social criticism
FIRST PUBLISHED: 2003

Asante's knowledge of race and racism in America is sweeping, and he brings much of this knowledge to *Erasing Racism*. There are really two powerful visions in America, Asante argues, the Promise and the Wilderness, and African Americans live for the most part in the Wilderness, without access to the Promise. In seven chapters, he details the systemic racism in America, the history of injustice toward African Americans from slavery through current cases of police brutality, and describes the "wall of ignorance" keeping this long history of racial injustice from the public consciousness.

Much of Asante's book is a history of the abuse, but he ends with a call for unity and a six-point program for national survival. The key steps are an apology to the descendants of enslaved Africans for slavery itself, the retelling of American history in order to see the Wilderness as part of the national story, and an effort to open discussion of reparations as a way to repair that history. "I offer the suggestion that reparations will free whites from some degree of guilt and liberate African Americans from most of the heavy burden of inferiority and self-hatred rooted in the fact that the nation has never apologized for the historical abuse measured out to their ancestors." Americans need to listen to Asante's arguments and confront the tough truths within them.

SUGGESTED READINGS

Asante, Molefi K. "Afrocentric Curriculum." *Educational Leadership* 219 (December, 1991-January, 1992): 28-31.

_____. "The Afrocentric Idea in Education." *The Journal of Negro Education* 62 (Spring, 1991): 170-180.

Chowdhury, Kanishka. "Afrocentric Voices: Constructing Identities, [Dis]placing Difference." *College Literature* 24, no. 2 (June, 1997): 35.

Esonwanne, Uzo. Review of *Kemet, Afrocentricity, and Knowledge*, by Molefi K. Asante. *Research in African Literatures* 23 (Spring, 1992).

Ziegler, Dhyana, ed. *Molefi Kete Asante and Afrocentricity: In Praise and in Criticism*. Nashville: James C. Winston, 1995.

Contributor: Joseph McLaren

Jimmy Santiago Baca

BORN: Sante Fe, New Mexico; January 2, 1952

NATIVE AMERICAN, MEXICAN AMERICAN

Baca's poetry expresses the experience of a "detribalized Apache," reared in a Chicano barrio, who finds his values in family, the land, and a complex cultural heritage.

PRINCIPAL WORKS

DRAMA: *Los tres hijos de Julia*, pr. 1991
POETRY: *Jimmy Santiago Baca*, 1978; *Immigrants in Our Own Land*, 1979; *Swords of Darkness*, 1981; *What's Happening*, 1982; *Poems Taken from My Yard*, 1986; *Martín; &, Meditations on the South Valley*, 1987; *Black Mesa Poems*, 1989 (includes *Poems Taken from My Yard*); *Immigrants in Our Own Land, and Selected Earlier Poems*, 1990; *In the Way of the Sun*, 1997; *Set This Book on Fire*, 1999; *Que linda la brisa*, 2000 (with Benjamin Alier Sáenz; photographs by James Drake); *Healing Earthquakes: A Love Story in Poems*, 2001; *C-Train (Dream Boy's Story) and Thirteen Mexicans*, 2002; *Winter Poems Along the Rio Grande*, 2004; *Spring Poems Along the Rio Grande*, 2007
SCREENPLAY: *Bound by Honor*, 1993 (with Floyd Mutrux and Ross Thomas)
SHORT FICTION: *The Importance of a Piece of Paper*, 2004
NONFICTION: *A Place to Stand: The Making of a Poet*, 2001
MISCELLANEOUS: *Working in the Dark: Reflections of a Poet of the Barrio*, 1992 (essays, journal entries, and poetry)

Jimmy Santiago Baca (JIH-mee sahn-tee-AH-goh BAH-kah) began to write poetry as an almost illiterate *vato loco* (crazy guy, gangster) serving a five-year term in a federal prison. He was twenty years old, the son of Damacio Baca, of Apache and Yaqui lineage, and Cecilia Padilla, a Latino woman, who left him with his grandparents when he was two. Baca stayed with them for three years, then went into a boys' home, then into detention centers and the streets of Albuquerque's barrio at thirteen. Although he "confirmed" his identity as a Chicano by leafing through a stolen picture book of Chicano history at seventeen, he felt himself "disintegrating" in prison. Speaking of his father but alluding to his own situation when he was incarcerated, Baca observed: "He was everything that was bad in America. He was brown, he spoke Spanish, was from a Native American background, had no education."

As a gesture of rebellion, Baca took a guard's textbook and found that "sounds created music in me and happiness" as he slowly enunciated the lines of a poem

by William Wordsworth. This led
to a zealous effort at self-education,
encouraged by the recollection of
older men in detention centers who
"made barrio life come alive . . .
with their own Chicano language."
Progressing to the point where he
was writing letters for fellow prisoners, he placed a few poems in a
local magazine, *New Kauri*, and
achieved his first major publication
with *Immigrants in Our Own Land*,
a book whose title refers to the condition of inmates in a dehumanizing system and to his own feelings
of estrangement in American society. This was a turning point for
Baca, who realized that he could reclaim the community he was separated from and sing "the freedom
song of our Chicano dream" now
that poetry "had lifted me to my
feet."

Jimmy Santiago Baca (Lawrence Benton)

With this foundation to build on,
Baca started a family in the early
1980's, restored an adobe dwelling
in Albuquerque's South Valley, and wrote *Martín; &, Meditations on the South
Valley* because "the entire Southwest needed a long poem that could describe what
has happened here in the last twenty years." Continuing to combine personal history and communal life, Baca followed this book with *Black Mesa Poems*, which
links the landscape of the South Valley to people he knows and admires. Writing
with confidence and an easy facility in Spanish and English, Baca uses vernacular
speech, poetic form, ancient Mexican lore, and contemporary popular culture.

Martín; &, Meditations on the South Valley

TYPE OF WORK: Poetry
FIRST PUBLISHED: 1987

Told in the semiautobiographical voice of Martín, the two long poems "Martín" and
"Meditations on the South Valley" offer the moving account of a young Chicano's
difficult quest for self-definition amid the realities of the barrio and his dysfunctional family. Abandoned by his parents at a young age, Martín spends time with his
Indio grandparents and in an orphanage before striking out on his own at the age of

six. His early knowledge of his grandparents' heritage gives him the first indication that his quest for identity will involve the recovery of a sense of family and a strong connection with the earth.

As Martín grows older and is shuttled from the orphanage to his bourgeois uncle's home, he realizes that his life is of the barrio and the land and not the sterile world of the rich suburbs. Martín's quest eventually leads him on a journey throughout the United States in which he searches for himself amid the horrors of addiction and the troubled memories of his childhood. Realizing that he must restore his connection with his family and home, he returns to the South Valley by way of Aztec ruins, where he ritualistically establishes his connection with his Mother Earth and his Native American ancestry. "Martín" ends with the birth of his son and Martín's promise to never leave him. The cycle of abandonment and abuse seems to have ended, and Martín is on his way to becoming the good man he so strongly desires to be.

"Meditations on the South Valley" continues the story of Martín, reinforcing his newfound sense of identity. The poem begins with the burning of his house and the loss of ten years of writing. In the process of rebuilding his life, Martín and his family must live in the Heights, an antiseptic tract housing development that serves to reinforce his identification with the land of the South Valley. Told in brief sketches, the insights in "Meditations on the South Valley" encourage Martín to nurture the growing connections with his new family and his promise to his young son. The poem ends with the construction of his new home from the ruins of an abandoned flophouse in the South Valley. Martín's friends come together to construct the house, and, metaphorically, Martín and his life as a good Chicano man are reborn from the garbage piles and ashes of the house they reconstruct.

Black Mesa Poems

TYPE OF WORK: Poetry
FIRST PUBLISHED: 1989

Set in the desert of New Mexico, Baca's *Black Mesa Poems* explores the poet's continuing search for connections with his family, home, and cultural heritage. In vivid detail and striking imagery, the loosely connected poems catalog the poet's complex relationships with his past and the home he makes of Black Mesa.

Baca's intricate relationship to the land includes his knowledge of its history. He is keenly aware of the changes the land has gone through and the changes the people of that land have experienced. He writes of his personal sense of connection with arroyos and cottonwoods and of the conflicts between the earlier inhabitants of Black Mesa and the changes brought by progress. Dispossessed migrant workers are portrayed as the price of Anglo progress, and the arid land that once nourished strong cattle now offers only "sluggish pampered globs" from feedlots. Even the once sacred places have been unceremoniously "crusted with housing tracts." His people have been separated from their ancestral land, yet Baca celebrates his identification with the old adobe buildings and Aztec warriors in the face of modern Anglo society.

Despite nostalgia, Baca eludes naïve sentimentality by attaching himself to the land. His sense of self and identity with his race is rooted in the physical landscape of Black Mesa. He evokes a strong connection with the history of his people through rituals, including drum ceremonies that "mate heart with earth." Sketches evoke a rich sense of community life in the barrio. The poet presents himself in terms of his own troubled history, but he knows that the conflict between the "peaceful" man and the "destructive" one of his past is linked to the modern smothering of noisy jet fighters and invading pampered artists looking to his land for a "primitive place."

Memories and images of snapshotlike detail combine in these poems to create a portrait of a man defining himself in relation to his personal and cultural history. The poet knows he is "the end result of Conquistadores, Black Moors, American Indians, and Europeans," and he also notes the continuing invasion of land developers. Poems about his children combine memories of his troubled past with Olmec kings and tribal ancestors. The history of his ancestors' relationship with the land informs his complex and evolving sense of identity. Throughout the *Black Mesa Poems*, Baca's personal history becomes rooted in Black Mesa.

Working in the Dark

TYPE OF WORK: Essays, journal entries, and poetry
FIRST PUBLISHED: 1992

Baca's collection *Working in the Dark: Reflections of a Poet of the Barrio* is a blunt and honest gathering of essays, journal entries, and poetry that describes some of the more poignant incidents in a long journey that Baca has made from a "troubled and impoverished Chicano family" to a position of prominence as a widely admired poet. Baca's subject as a writer is the life and history of Albuquerque's South Valley. Baca passionately explores the crucial episodes in a process of self-growth and self-discovery beginning with his most desperate moments as an empty, powerless, inarticulate young man, through an expanding series of revelations about life and language in prison, and ending with his eventual construction of a self based on his relationships to the land, his family, and his identity as a "detribalized Apache" and Chicano artist.

The heart of the book is the fourth section, "Chicanismo: Destiny and Destinations." After covering his discovery in prison of the redemptive powers of language and his sense of a loss of Chicano culture in an Anglo world, Baca recalls the one positive feature of his youth: the three years he spent in the home of his grandparents before he was five. This memory kept a dim vision alive through the years when Baca began to realize that "none of what I did was who I was." In the first part of the "Chicanismo" section, Baca delivers a systematic critique of the methods used by a dominant Anglo culture to stereotype, demean, and distort Chicano life.

Drawing on his prison experience and on his troubles in school and in various temporary jobs, Baca describes how he felt doubly imprisoned as an immigrant in his own land and as one under the control of unknowing authorities.

As part of a plan to reclaim his cultural heritage, Baca reaches back into history to show how valuable and vital Chicano culture has been. In a satirical commentary on the Columbus quincentennial, which Baca debunks with a punning title "De Quiencentennial?" (whose quincentennial is it, anyway?), Baca introduces some of the positive, admirable facets of the life of the South Valley near Albuquerque. One of the strongest features of the life of *la raza* (the race) has been an oral tradition that, as Baca points out, has defied attempts to suppress or extinguish its vitality: "Our language, which I have inherited, is a symphony of rebellion against invaders." In the last section of the book, "Gleanings from a Poet's Journal," Baca demonstrates this linguistic power as he explains how he wrote in the dark when Chicanos could not find access to print, how the barrio is like an "uncut diamond" for the artist to shape, and how Baca responds to queries about his "Indian-ness."

SUGGESTED READINGS

Coppola, Vincent. "The Moon in Jimmy Baca." *Esquire*, June, 1993, 48-56.

Gish, Robert Franklin. *Beyond Bounds: Cross-Cultural Essays on Anglo, American Indian, and Chicano Literature*. Albuquerque: University of New Mexico Press, 1996.

Levertov, Denise. Introduction to *Martín; &, Meditations on the South Valley*, by Jimmy Santiago Baca. New York: New Directions, 1987.

Rector, Liam. "The Documentary of What Is." *Hudson Review* 41 (Summer, 1989): 393-400.

Schubnell, Mathias. "The Inner Landscape of the Self in Jimmy Santiago Baca's *Martín; &, Meditations on the South Valley*." *Southwestern American Literature* 21 (1995): 167-173.

Contributors: Leon Lewis and William Vaughn

James Baldwin

BORN: New York, New York; August 2, 1924
DIED: St. Paul de Vence, France; November 30, 1987

AFRICAN AMERICAN

*Baldwin's experiences as an African American
gay man became the source for essays and fiction
that were often angry but always honest.*

PRINCIPAL WORKS

CHILDREN'S LITERATURE: *Little Man, Little Man*, 1975
DRAMA: *The Amen Corner*, pr. 1954, pb. 1968; *Blues for Mister Charlie*, pr., pb. 1964; *A Deed from the King of Spain*, pr. 1974
LONG FICTION: *Go Tell It on the Mountain*, 1953; *Giovanni's Room*, 1956; *Another Country*, 1962; *Tell Me How Long the Train's Been Gone*, 1968; *If Beale Street Could Talk*, 1974; *Just Above My Head*, 1979
POETRY: *Jimmy's Blues: Selected Poems*, 1983
SCREENPLAY: *One Day, When I Was Lost: A Scenario Based on "The Autobiography of Malcolm X,"* 1972
SHORT FICTION: *Going to Meet the Man*, 1965
NONFICTION: *Notes of a Native Son*, 1955; *Nobody Knows My Name: More Notes of a Native Son*, 1961; *The Fire Next Time*, 1963; *Nothing Personal*, 1964 (with Richard Avedon); *No Name in the Street*, 1971; *A Rap on Race*, 1971 (with Margaret Mead); *A Dialogue*, 1975 (with Nikki Giovanni); *The Devil Finds Work*, 1976; *The Evidence of Things Not Seen*, 1985; *The Price of the Ticket*, 1985; *Conversations with James Baldwin*, 1989; *Collected Essays*, 1998; *Native Sons: A Friendship That Created One of the Greatest Works of the Twentieth-Century, Notes of "A Native Son,"* 2004 (with Sol Stein)

James Baldwin once dismissed his childhood as "the usual bleak fantasy." Nevertheless, the major concerns of his fiction consistently reflect the social context of his family life in Harlem during the Depression. The dominant figure of Baldwin's childhood was clearly that of his stepfather, David Baldwin, who worked as a manual laborer and preached in a storefront church. Clearly the model for Gabriel Grimes in *Go Tell It on the Mountain*, David Baldwin had moved from New Orleans to New York City, where he married Baldwin's mother, Emma Berdis. The oldest of what was to be a group of nine children in the household, James assumed a great deal of the responsibility for the care of his half brothers and half sisters. Insulated somewhat from the brutality of Harlem street life by his domestic duties, Baldwin, as

James Baldwin (© John Hoppy Hopkins)

he describes in *The Fire Next Time*, sought refuge in the church. Undergoing a conversion experience—similar to that of John in *Go Tell It on the Mountain*—at age fourteen in 1938, Baldwin preached as a youth minister for the next several years. At the same time, he began to read, immersing himself in works such as *Uncle Tom's Cabin* (1852) and the novels of Charles Dickens. Both at his Harlem junior high school, where the African American poet Countée Cullen was one of his teachers, and at his predominantly white Bronx high school, Baldwin contributed to student literary publications. The combination of family tension, economic hardship, and religious vocation provides the focus of much of Baldwin's greatest writing, most notably *Go Tell It on the Mountain*, *The Fire Next Time*, and *Just Above My Head.*

If Baldwin's experience during the 1930's provided his material, his life from 1942 to 1948 shaped his characteristic approach to that material. After he graduated from high school in 1942, Baldwin worked for a year as a manual laborer in New Jersey, an experience that increased both his understanding of his stepfather and his insight into America's economic and racial systems. Moving to Greenwich Village in 1943, Baldwin worked during the day and wrote at night for the next five years; his first national reviews and essays appeared in 1946. The major event of the Village years, however, was Baldwin's meeting with Richard Wright in the winter of 1944-1945. Wright's interest helped Baldwin secure first a Eugene F. Saxton Memorial Award and then a Rosenwald Fellowship, enabling him to move to Paris in 1948.

After his arrival in France, Baldwin experienced more of the poverty that had shaped his childhood. Simultaneously, he developed a larger perspective on the psychocultural context conditioning his experience, feeling at once a greater sense of freedom and a larger sense of the global structure of racism, particularly as reflected in the French treatment of North Africans. In addition, he formed many of the personal and literary friendships that contributed to his later public prominence. Baldwin's well-publicized literary feud with Wright, who viewed the younger writer's criticism of *Native Son* (1940) as a form of personal betrayal, helped establish Baldwin as a major presence in African American letters. Although Baldwin's first novel, *Go Tell It on the Mountain*, was well-received critically, it was not so financially successful that he could devote his full time to creative writing. As a result, Baldwin continued to travel widely, frequently on journalistic assignments, while writing *Giovanni's Room*, which is set in France and involves no black characters.

Returning to the United States as a journalist covering the Civil Rights movement, Baldwin made his first trip to the American South in 1957. The essays and reports describing that physical and psychological journey propelled Baldwin to the position of public prominence that he maintained for more than a decade. During the height of the movement, Baldwin lectured widely and was present at major events such as the March on Washington and the voter registration drive in Selma, Alabama. In addition, he met with most of the major African American activists of the period, including Martin Luther King, Jr., Elijah Muhammad, James Meredith, and Medgar Evers. Attorney General Robert Kennedy requested that Baldwin bring together the most influential voices in the black community, and, even though the resulting meeting accomplished little, the request testifies to Baldwin's image as a focal point of African American opinion. In addition to his political activity, Baldwin formed personal and literary relationships—frequently tempestuous ones—with numerous white writers, including William Styron and Norman Mailer. A surge in literary popularity, reflected in the presence of *Another Country* and *The Fire Next Time* on the best-seller lists throughout most of 1962 and 1963, accompanied Baldwin's political success and freed him from financial insecurity for the first time. He traveled extensively throughout the decade, and his visits to Puerto Rico and Africa were to have a major influence on his subsequent political thought.

Partly because of Baldwin's involvement with prominent whites and partly because of the sympathy for homosexuals evinced in his writing, several black militants, most notably Eldridge Cleaver, attacked Baldwin's position as "black spokesman" beginning in the late 1960's. As a result, nationalist spokesmen such as Amiri Baraka and Bobby Seale gradually eclipsed Baldwin in the public literary and political spotlights. Nevertheless, Baldwin, himself sympathetic to many of the militant positions, continued his involvement with public issues, such as the fate of the Wilmington, North Carolina, prisoners, which he addressed in an open letter to Jimmy Carter shortly after Carter's election to the presidency. In his later years, though he returned periodically to the South, Baldwin lived for much of the time in France and Turkey. It was in St. Paul de Vence, France, that he died, in 1987.

Go Tell It on the Mountain

TYPE OF WORK: Novel
FIRST PUBLISHED: 1953

The protagonist of *Go Tell It on the Mountain*, John Grimes, wants to be a man standing on his own; at the same time, he wants his father, Gabriel, to love him. He feels oppressed by his father and by his circumstances as a black youth in New York during the Depression. To achieve manhood, he must either accept his

heritage or embrace a world he instinctively feels is evil: the materialistic and oppressive white world.

In order to accept his heritage in the religious terms he understands, he must
come to terms with his father, the prophet and preacher. To John, it appears that Gabriel loves neither John nor his mother. John both loves and hates Gabriel; he wants
to kneel before God but not before his father.

Gabriel is a hard and passionate man who sees himself as chosen by God to found
a long line of preachers of the true gospel. Gabriel has made himself hard in order to
control his strong desires for worldly pleasure. If Gabriel does love his wife and
stepson, it is with the stern love of a judging God rather than the forgiving love of
Jesus. Gabriel seems to reserve tenderness for his wayward, natural son, Roy. Gabriel prefers that Roy continue the line of preachers and resents the fact that John is
more likely to be a preacher.

In the third of the novel's three parts, John experiences a religious conversion.
Though this conversion does not make his father love him as John hopes it may, it
allows John to feel compassion for Gabriel and for all suffering people whose
hearts' desires conflict with their souls' aspirations.

Baldwin has drawn on his childhood in Harlem to give authenticity to his story.
Because John, Gabriel, and other family members are so fully and deeply portrayed, this is a powerful first novel. Though the religious experiences of these
characters may seem sectarian, they are really universal. All of the major characters
are trying to build and sustain community in the face of dehumanizing oppression.
Their particular version of Christianity is an effective response to being captives in
a racist culture.

The Amen Corner

TYPE OF WORK: Drama
FIRST PRODUCED: 1954, pb. 1968

Like *Go Tell It on the Mountain*, *The Amen Corner* challenges the dichotomy between the holy Temple and the sinful Street, a tension that shapes the play's entire
dramatic structure. Accepted unquestioningly by most members of Sister Margaret
Alexander's congregation, the dichotomy reflects a basic survival strategy of
blacks making the transition from their rural southern roots to the urban North during the Great Migration. By dividing the world into zones of safety and danger,
church members attempt to distance themselves and, perhaps more important, their
loved ones from the brutalities of the city. As Baldwin comments in his introduction to the play, Sister Margaret faces the dilemma of "how to treat her husband and
her son as men and at the same time to protect them from the bloody consequences
of trying to be a man in this society." In act 1, Margaret attempts to resolve the dilemma by forcing her son David, a musician in his late teens, into the role of servant
of the Lord while consigning her estranged husband Luke, a jazz musician, to the
role of worldly tempter. Having witnessed the brutal impact of Harlem on Luke, she

strives to protect her son by creating a world entirely separate from his father's. Ultimately, however, the attempt fails as David's emerging sense of self drives him to confront a wider range of experience; meanwhile, Luke's physical collapse, which takes place in the "safe zone," forces Margaret to acknowledge her own evasions. The most important of these, which reveals Margaret's claim to moral purity as self-constructed illusion, involves her claim that Luke abandoned his family; in fact, she fled from him to avoid the pain caused by the death of a newborn daughter, a pain associated with sexuality and the Street.

As he did in *Go Tell It on the Mountain*, Baldwin treats the collapse of the dichotomies as a potential source of artistic and spiritual liberation. David recognizes that his development as a musician demands immersion in both the sacred and the secular traditions of African American music. Margaret attempts to redefine herself in terms not of holiness but of an accepting love imaged in her clutching Luke's trombone mouthpiece after his death. Both resolutions intimate a synthesis of Temple and Street, suggesting the common impulse behind the gospel music and jazz that sound throughout the play. The emotional implications of the collapse of the dichotomies in *The Amen Corner* are directly articulated when, following her acknowledgment that the vision on which she bases her authority as preacher was her own creation, Margaret says: "It's a awful thing to think about, the way love never dies!" This second "vision" marks a victory much more profound than that of the church faction that casts Margaret out at the end of the play. Ironically, the new preacher, Sister Moore, seems destined to perpetuate Margaret's moral failings. Although Sister Moore's rise to power is grounded primarily in the congregation's dissatisfaction with Margaret's inability to connect her spiritual life with the realities of the Street (Margaret refuses to sympathize with a woman's marital difficulties or to allow a man to take a job driving a liquor truck), she fails to perceive the larger implications of the dissatisfaction. Sister Moore's inability to see the depth of Margaret's transformed sense of love suggests that the simplifying dichotomies will continue to shape the congregation's experience.

Thematically and psychologically, then, *The Amen Corner* possesses a great deal of potential power. Theatrically, however, it fails to exploit this potential. Despite Baldwin's awareness that "the ritual of the church, historically speaking, comes out of the theater, the communion which is the theater," the structure of *The Amen Corner* emphasizes individual alienation rather than ritual reconciliation. In part because the play's power in performance largely derives from the energy of the music played in the church, the street side of Baldwin's vision remains relatively abstract. Where the brilliant prose of *Go Tell It on the Mountain* suggests nuances of perception that remain only half-conscious to John Grimes during his transforming vision, David's conversations with Luke and Margaret focus almost exclusively on his rebellion against the Temple while leaving the terms of the dichotomy unchallenged. In act 3, similarly, Margaret's catharsis seems static. The fact that Margaret articulates her altered awareness in her preacher's voice suggests a lingering commitment to the Temple at odds with Baldwin's thematic design. Although the sacred music emanating from the church is theoretically balanced by the jazz trombone associated with Luke, most of the performance power adheres to the gospel songs that provide an embodied experience of call and response; taken out of its performance context, the jazz seems a relatively powerless expression. As a result, *The Amen Corner* never escapes from the sense of separation it conceptually attacks.

Notes of a Native Son

TYPE OF WORK: Essays
FIRST PUBLISHED: 1955

Many readers consider Baldwin's nonfiction to be even finer than his fiction. His essays, which may be found in collections such as *Notes of a Native Son* (1955) and *Nobody Knows My Name: More Notes of a Native Son* (1961), are passionate and often scathing.

His personal feelings and experiences are freely expressed in his essays. His anger at black-white relations in America, his ambivalence toward his father, and his thoughts on such writers as Truman Capote, Norman Mailer, and William Faulkner are displayed openly. He is honest, and made enemies for it. On the other hand, he has many readers' respect for saying what he thinks.

Notes of a Native Son was Baldwin's first nonfiction collection, and it contains his "Autobiographical Notes" and three sections totaling ten essays. In "Autobiographical Notes," Baldwin sketches his early career—his Harlem birth, his childhood interest in writing, his journey to France. "Autobiographical Notes" and various essays describe the difficult process of Baldwin's establishment of his identity. Part 1 of *Notes of a Native Son* includes three essays. "Everybody's Protest Novel" examines *Uncle Tom's Cabin: Or, Life Among the Lowly* (1852), which Baldwin considers self-righteous and so sentimental as to be dishonest. "Many Thousands Gone" examines Richard Wright's *Native Son* (1940), which Baldwin describes as badly flawed. "*Carmen Jones:* The Dark Is Light Enough" is another biting review, of the Hollywood motion picture musical *Carmen Jones* (1955). Baldwin says that the film lacks imagination and is condescending to blacks. Part 2 contains three essays. "The Harlem Ghetto" is one of the most powerful, digging into the physical and emotional turmoil of Harlem, including problems between blacks and Jews. "Journey to Atlanta" looks at an African American singing group's first trip to the South. It is a humorous, cynical look at the treatment that the group, which included two of Baldwin's brothers, received. "Notes of a Native Son" examines Baldwin's anger and despair after his father's death.

Part 3 contains four essays. "Encounter on the Seine: Black Meets Brown" and "A Question of Identity" are about the feelings and attitudes of Americans in Paris in the 1940's and 1950's. "Equal in Paris" is Baldwin's account of being arrested and jailed, temporarily, in a case involving some stolen sheets that he did not steal. Baldwin describes the insight he had while in the hands of the French police: that they, in dealing with him, were not engaging in the racist cat-and-mouse game used by police in the United States. Finally, "Stranger in the Village" discusses Baldwin's time in a Swiss village and the astonished curiosity of people who had never seen a black person before. In all these essays, Baldwin explores his world and himself.

Giovanni's Room

TYPE OF WORK: Novel
FIRST PUBLISHED: 1956

Giovanni's Room was Baldwin's second novel, after *Go Tell It on the Mountain* (1953). It was a risky book for Baldwin because it openly explored male homosexuality at a time when few writers discussed gay themes. It almost went unpublished. Knopf had taken Baldwin's first novel but rejected *Giovanni's Room* and may even have suggested that Baldwin burn the manuscript to protect his reputation. Other rejections followed before Dial Press accepted the book for publication.

Baldwin, who was gay, had touched on homosexual love in "The Outing" (1951) and toward the end of *Go Tell It on the Mountain*, but *Giovanni's Room* was a frank portrayal of a gay man's feelings and torments. The book involves white rather than black characters, which added to the book's commercial and critical risk. *Giovanni's Room* focuses on David, an American expatriate living in Paris, France. Other characters include Hella, an American woman and David's lover, and Giovanni, an Italian who becomes David's gay partner. The story is narrated in first person by David.

Part 1 begins with Hella having left for America and Giovanni about to be executed. The rest is told primarily in flashbacks. In the flashbacks, David comes to Paris after a homosexual affair and attaches himself to Hella. He asks her to marry him, and she goes to Spain to think about it. During Hella's absence, David meets Giovanni, who works in a bar owned by a gay man. David and Giovanni are immediately drawn together and become lovers. David moves into Giovanni's room and the two are happy for a time. David cannot fully accept his gay identity, however, and reminds himself that Hella will return. In part 2, Giovanni and David's relationship sours, mainly because David begins to despise his own feelings and to resent Giovanni's affection. The tension increases when Giovanni loses his job.

Hella comes back and David returns to her without even telling Giovanni. He pretends to be purely heterosexual and finally breaks off his relationship with Giovanni, who is devastated emotionally. David and Hella plan to get married but then hear that Giovanni has murdered the owner of the bar where he once worked. Giovanni is sentenced to death. David stays with Hella during Giovanni's trial but finally gives in to his feelings and goes to the gay quarter. Hella sees him with a man and realizes David will never love her fully. She leaves for America, and David is left to think of Giovanni and to feel empty. David can neither accept his nature nor escape it.

Another Country

TYPE OF WORK: Novel
FIRST PUBLISHED: 1962

Another Country, Baldwin's greatest popular success, analyzes the effects of de-forming pressure and experience on a wide range of characters, black and white, male and female, homosexual and heterosexual. To accommodate these diverse consciousnesses, Baldwin employs the sprawling form usually associated with po-litical rather than psychological fiction, emphasizing the diverse forms of inno-cence and experience in American society. The three major sections of *Another Country*, "Easy Rider," "Any Day Now," and "Toward Bethlehem," progress gen-erally from despair to renewed hope, but no single consciousness or plot line pro-vides a frame similar to that of *Go Tell It on the Mountain*. Rather, the novel's struc-tural coherence derives from the moral concerns present in each of the various plots.

Casting a Melvillean shadow over the novel is the black jazz musician Rufus Scott, who is destroyed by an agonizing affair with Leona, a white southerner re-cently arrived in New York at the time she meets him. Unable to forge the inno-cence necessary for love in a context that repudiates the relationship at every turn, Rufus destroys Leona psychologically. After a period of physical and psychologi-cal destitution, he kills himself by jumping off a bridge. His sister Ida, an aspiring singer, and his friend Vivaldo Moore, an aspiring white writer, meet during the last days of Rufus's life and fall in love as they console each other over his death. Strug-gling to overcome the racial and sexual definitions that destroyed Rufus, they seek a higher innocence capable of countering Ida's sense of the world as a "whore-house." In contrast to Ida and Vivaldo's struggle, the relationship of white actor Eric Jones and his French lover Yves seems edenic. Although Baldwin portrays Eric's internal struggle for a firm sense of his sexual identity, their shared inno-cence at times seems to exist almost entirely outside the context of the pressures that destroyed Rufus. The final major characters, Richard and Cass Silenski, repre-sent the cost of the American Dream. After Richard "makes it" as a popular novel-ist, their personal relationship decays, precipitating Cass's affair with Eric. Their tentative reunion after Richard discovers the affair makes it clear that material suc-cess provides no shortcut to moral responsibility.

The majority of the narrative lines imply the impossibility of simple dissociation from institutional pressure. Ultimately, the intensity of Rufus's pain and the intri-cacy of Ida and Vivaldo's struggle overshadow Eric and Yves's questionable inno-cence. As Ida tells Vivaldo, "Our being together doesn't change the world." The at-tempt to overcome the cynicism of this perception leads to a recognition that meaningful love demands total acceptance. Ida's later question, "How can you say you loved Rufus when there was so much about him you didn't want to know?" could easily provide the epitaph for the entire society in *Another Country*.

The Fire Next Time

TYPE OF WORK: Civil rights manifesto
FIRST PUBLISHED: 1963

Baldwin frames the substance of his sermon inside a dedicatory letter to his nephew, "On the One Hundredth Anniversary of the Emancipation." He advises the nephew to accept white Americans—and do so lovingly—even though they have established a society that considers most black men worthless. Why? Because, says Baldwin, son of a minister and himself a former boy evangelist, all men are brothers and America is the black as well as the white man's house.

He then testifies to this text with an account of his youth and young manhood, covering events he previously narrated in essays collected as *Notes of a Native Son* and *Nobody Knows My Name*, and in his autobiographical first novel, *Go Tell It on the Mountain*. As a teenage preacher he finds himself active in the "church racket," which is only marginally superior to gambling, pimping, or trafficking in drugs. He soon becomes disillusioned with what he discovers to be a white man's God, in whose name white "Christians" behave arrogantly, cruelly, and self-righteously.

The next and more powerful temptation is represented by the Nation of Islam movement, headed by Elijah Muhammad and dedicated to the premises that, while Christianity is the white man's wicked rationale for oppressing blacks, the true religion is that of Allah; all white people are cursed devils whose sway will end forever in ten to fifteen years, with God now black and all black people chosen by Him for domination under the theology of Islam.

Baldwin describes an audience with Elijah: Muhammad is lucid, passionate, cunning—but he preaches a dogma of racial hatred that is no better than the reverse of whites' hatred for blacks.

Baldwin rejects it, saying to himself: "Isn't love more important than color?" He recognizes that the American blacks' complex fate is to deliver white Americans from their imprisonment in myths of racial superiority and educate them into a new, integrated sensitivity and maturity. Should such an effort fail, then the words of a slave song may come true: "God gave Noah the rainbow sign, No more water, the fire next time!"

"The Man Child"

TYPE OF WORK: Short fiction
FIRST PUBLISHED: 1965, in *Going to Meet the Man*

In Baldwin's collection of short fiction, three short stories are repeatedly anthologized and studied: "The Man Child," "Going to Meet the Man," and "Sonny's Blues." "The Man Child," the only story in *Going to Meet the Man* that has no black characters, scathingly describes whites, especially their violent propensities. The central character is Eric, an eight-year-old. The story opens as he, his mother, and his father are giving a birthday party for Jamie, his father's best friend. In the next scene Eric and his father walk together and then return to the party. After a brief summary of intervening events, the story moves forward in time to a day when Jamie meets Eric, entices him into a barn, and breaks his neck. The story described thus, its ending seems to be a surprise, and it certainly is a surprise to Eric. In fact, his sudden realization that he is in grave danger is an epiphany. "The Man Child" is thus a coming-of-age story, an account of a young person's realization of the dark side of adult existence. Eric, however, has little time to think about his realization or even to generalize very much on the basis of his intimation of danger before he is badly, perhaps mortally, injured.

The story, however, contains many hints that violent action will be forthcoming. A reader can see them even though Eric cannot, because Eric is the center of consciousness, a device perfected, if not invented, by Henry James. That is, Eric does not narrate the story so the story does not present his viewpoint, but he is always the focus of the action, and the story is in essence an account of his responses to that action. The difference between his perception of the events he witnesses (which is sometimes described and sometimes can be inferred from his actions) and the perception that can be had by attending carefully to the story encourages a reader to make a moral analysis and finally to make a moral judgment, just as the difference between Huck Finn's perception and the perception that one can have while reading *Adventures of Huckleberry Finn* (1884) at first stimulates laughter and then moral evaluation. Eric's lack of perception is a function of his innocence, a quality that he has to an even larger extent than has Huck Finn, and thus he is less able to cope in a threatening world and his injury is even more execrable. If the measure of a society is its solicitude for the powerless, the miniature society formed by the three adults in this story, and perhaps by implication the larger society of which they are a part, is sorely wanting.

To be more specific about the flaws in this society and in these persons, they enslave themselves and others, as is suggested very early in the story: "Eric lived with his father . . . and his mother, who had been captured by his father on some far-off unblessed, unbelievable night, who had never since burst her chains." Her husband intimidates and frightens her, and his conversation about relations between men and women indicates that he believes she exists at his sufferance only for sex and procreation. Her role becomes questionable because in the summary of events that happen between the first and last parts of the story one learns that she has lost the child she had been carrying and can no longer conceive. The two men enslave themselves with their notions about women, their drunkenness (which they misinterpret as male companionship), their mutual hostility, their overbearing expansiveness, in short, with their machismo. Eric's father is convinced that he is more successful in these terms. He has fathered a son, an accomplishment the significance of which to him is indicated by his "some day all this will be yours" talk with Eric between the two party scenes. Jamie's wife, showing more sense than Eric's mother, left him before he could sire a son. Jamie's violent act with Eric is his psychotic imitation of the relation of Eric's father to Eric, just as his whistling at the very end of the story is his imitation of the music he hears coming from a tavern. Eric is thus considered by the two men to be alive merely for their self-expression. His father's kind of self-expression is potentially debilitating, although somewhat benign; Jamie's version is nearly fatal.

"Going to Meet the Man"

TYPE OF WORK: Short fiction
FIRST PUBLISHED: 1965, in *Going to Meet the Man*

The title work of the collection, "Going to Meet the Man," is a companion to "The Man Child." Whereas the latter story isolates whites from blacks in order to analyze their psychology, the former story is about whites in relation to blacks, even though blacks make only brief appearances in it. The whites in these stories have many of the same characteristics, but in "Going to Meet the Man" those characteristics are more obviously dangerous. These stories were written during the height of the Civil Rights movement, and Baldwin, by means of his rhetorical power and his exclusion of more human white types, helped polarize that movement.

The main characters in "Going to Meet the Man" are a family composed of a southern deputy sheriff, his wife, and his son, Jesse. At the beginning of the story they are skittish because of racial unrest. Demonstrations by blacks have alternated with police brutality by whites, each response escalating the conflict, which began when a black man knocked down an elderly white woman. The family is awakened late at night by a crowd of whites who have learned that the black perpetrator has been caught. They all set off in a festive, although somewhat tense, mood to the place where he is being held. After they arrive the black man is burned, castrated, and mutilated—atrocities that Baldwin describes very vividly. This story, however, is not merely sensationalism or social and political rhetoric. It rises above those kinds of writing because of its psychological insights into the causes of racism and particularly of racial violence.

Baldwin's focus at first is on the deputy sheriff. As the story opens he is trying and failing to have sexual relations with his wife. He thinks that he would have an easier time with a black woman, and "the image of a black girl caused a distant excitement in him." Thus, his conception of blacks is immediately mixed with sexuality, especially with his fear of impotence. In contrast, he thinks of his wife as a "frail sanctuary." At the approach of a car he reaches for the gun beside his bed, thereby adding a propensity for violence to his complex of psychological motives. Most of his behavior results from this amalgam of racial attitudes, sexual drives, fear of impotence, and attraction to violence. For example, he recalls torturing a black prisoner by applying a cattle prod to his testicles, and on the way to see the black captive he takes pride in his wife's attractiveness. He also frequently associates blacks with sexual vigor and fecundity. The castration scene is the most powerful rendition of this psychological syndrome.

The deputy sheriff, however, is more than a mere brute. For example, he tries to think of his relation to blacks in moral terms. Their singing of spirituals disconcerts him because he has difficulty understanding how they can be Christians like himself. He tries to reconcile this problem by believing that blacks have decided "to fight against God and go against the rules laid down in the Bible for everyone to read!" To allay the guilt that threatens to complicate his life he also believes that there are a lot of good blacks who need his protection from bad blacks. These strategies for achieving inner peace do not work, and Baldwin brilliantly describes the moral confusion of such whites:

> They had never dreamed that their privacy could contain any element of terror, could threaten, that is, to reveal itself, to the scrutiny of a judgment day, while remaining unreadable and inaccessible to themselves; nor had they dreamed that the past, while certainly refusing to be forgotten, could yet so stubbornly refuse to be remembered. They felt themselves mysteriously set at naught.

In the absence of a satisfying moral vision, violence seems the only way to achieve inner peace, and the sheriff's participation in violence allows him to have sex with his wife as the story ends. Even then, however, he has to think that he is having it as blacks would. He is their psychic prisoner, just as the black man who was murdered was the white mob's physical prisoner.

Late in this story one can see that Jesse, the sheriff's eight-year-old son, is also an important character. At first he is confused by the turmoil and thinks of blacks in human terms. For example, he wonders why he has not seen his black friend Otis for several days. The mob violence, however, changes him; he undergoes a coming-of-age, the perversity of which is disturbing. He is the center of consciousness in the mob scene. His first reaction is the normal one for a boy: "Jesse clung to his father's neck in terror as the cry rolled over the crowd." Then he loses his innocence and it becomes clear that he will be a victim of the same psychological syndrome that afflicts his father: "He watched his mother's face . . . she was more beautiful than he had ever seen her. . . . He began to feel a joy he had never felt before." He wishes that he were the man with the knife who is about to castrate the black captive, whom Jesse considers "the most beautiful and terrible object he had ever seen." Then he identifies totally with his father: "At that moment Jesse loved his father more than he had ever loved him. He felt that his father had carried him through a mighty test, had revealed to him a great secret which would be the key to his life forever." For Jesse this brutality is thus a kind of initiation into adulthood, and its effect is to ensure that there will be at least one more generation capable of the kind of violence that he has just seen.

"Sonny's Blues"

TYPE OF WORK: Short fiction
FIRST PUBLISHED: 1965, in *Going to Meet the Man*

Whereas "The Man Child" has only white characters and "Going to Meet the Man" is about a conflict between whites and blacks, "Sonny's Blues" has only black characters. Although the chronology of "Sonny's Blues" is scrambled, its plot is simple. It tells the story of two brothers, one, the narrator, a respectable teacher and the other, Sonny, a former user of heroin who is jailed for that reason and then becomes a jazz musician. The story ends in a jazz nightclub, where the older brother hears Sonny play and finally understands the meaning of jazz for him. The real heart of this story is the contrast between the values of the two brothers, a contrast that becomes much less dramatic at the end.

The two brothers have similar social backgrounds, especially their status as blacks and, more specifically, as Harlem blacks. Of Harlem as a place in which to mature the narrator says, "boys exactly like the boys we once had been found themselves encircled by disaster. Some escaped the trap, most didn't. Those who got out always left something of themselves behind, as some animals amputate a leg and leave it in a trap." Even when he was very young the narrator had a sense of the danger and despair surrounding him:

> When lights fill the room, the child is filled with darkness. He knows that every time this happens he's moved just a little closer to that darkness outside. The darkness outside is what the old folks have been talking about. It's what they've come from. It's what they endure.

For example, he learns after his father's death that his father, though seemingly a hardened and stoical man, had hidden the grief caused by the killing of his brother.

At first the narrator believes that Sonny's two means for coping with the darkness, heroin and music, are inextricably connected to that darkness and thus are not survival mechanisms at all. He believes that heroin "filled everything, the people, the houses, the music, the dark, quicksilver barmaid, with menace; and this menace was their reality." Later, however, he realizes that jazz is a way to escape: He senses that "Sonny was at that time piano playing for his life." The narrator also has a few premonitions of the epiphany he experiences in the jazz nightclub. One occurs when he observes a group of street singers and understands that their "music seemed to soothe a poison out of them." Even with these premonitions, he does not realize that he uses the same strategy. After an argument with Sonny, during which their differences seem to be irreconcilable, his first reaction is to begin "whistling to keep from crying," and the tune is a blues. Finally the epiphany occurs, tying together all the major strands of this story. As he listens to Sonny playing jazz, the narrator thinks that

> freedom lurked around us and I understood, at last, that he could help us be free if we would listen, that he would never be free until we did. Yet, there was no battle in his face now. I heard what he had gone through, and would continue to go through.

The idea in that passage is essentially what Baldwin is about. Like Sonny, he has forged an instrument of freedom by means of the fire of his troubles, and he has made that instrument available to all, white and black. His is the old story of suffering and art; his fiction is an account of trouble, but by producing it he has shown others the way to rise above suffering.

The Evidence of Things Not Seen

TYPE OF WORK: Essay
FIRST PUBLISHED: 1985

An extended development of an essay on the Atlanta child murder case originally published in *Playboy* magazine, this extended essay examines the relationship between that case and the larger context of racial tension in the United States. Concentrating on the trial of Wayne Williams, Baldwin reiterates numerous themes from his past works: the interrelationship of victim and victimizer and the absence of any real concern on the part of the government for the black underclass.

Taking into account the political pressures on the black administration of Atlanta to close the case, Baldwin argues convincingly that the trial failed to establish Williams' guilt beyond a shadow of a doubt. Some of the most fascinating material in the book concerns the pattern of murders that provided the center of the persecution case. Emphasizing the continuity between the events in Atlanta and the history of racism in the United States, Baldwin points out that any set of events can be interpreted as a pattern, and that the pattern perceived reveals more about the perceiver than the events themselves.

Much of the cultural analysis in this book will be familiar to readers of Baldwin's previous novels and essays. Alternating between journalistic observation and historical meditation, Baldwin combines the rhetorical flourishes and moral intensity of the Afro-American preacher with a finely polished literary irony. Nevertheless, the new book lacks the power of Baldwin's best work, in part because of the familiarity of his positions and in part because of what seems a lingering uncertainty—perhaps inherent in the events—concerning the actual significance of the Atlanta tragedies.

The Price of the Ticket

TYPE OF WORK: Essays
FIRST PUBLISHED: 1985

Bringing together all of the author's substantial (and much of his relatively ephemeral) nonfiction, this volume provides a welcome opportunity for reassessing the development of James Baldwin's encounter with the political, moral, and intellectual complexities of the modern world. This opportunity seems particularly important since so much of Baldwin's work—and the reaction to that work—was, and is, intertwined with volatile racial issues and events that frequently excite a greater degree of passion than useful insight. Happily, what emerges from these diverse pieces, ranging from the early aesthetic essays through the politically influential *The Fire Next Time* to the introductory essay written specifically for the collection, is a clear sense that a large percentage of Baldwin's insights remain as relevant in 1985 as they were at the height of the civil rights movement.

In addition to providing a montage-style autobiography, Baldwin's essays provide an excellent introduction or recapitulation of the development of American racial relations since the 1930's. Reflecting the transitions from the relative optimism of the integrationist era to the militance of the late 1960's and on to the wary (and, at times, weary) determination of the Ronald Reagan backlash, Baldwin insists on clear acknowledgment of the conditions of life in black America. Perhaps his most important contribution to American culture, however, rests on his ability to address the interrelationship between those conditions and the spiritual dilemmas confronted by white Americans.

SUGGESTED READINGS

Balfour, Lawrie Lawrence, and Katherine Lawrence Balfour. *The Evidence of Things Not Said: James Baldwin and the Promise of American Democracy.* Ithaca, N.Y.: Cornell University Press, 2001.

Campbell, James. *Talking at the Gates: A Life of James Baldwin.* New York: Viking, 1991.

Kinnamon, Keneth, comp. *James Baldwin: A Collection of Critical Essays.* Englewood Cliffs, N.J.: Prentice-Hall, 1974.

Leeming, David. *James Baldwin: A Biography.* New York: Alfred A. Knopf, 1994.

McBride, Dwight A. *James Baldwin Now.* New York: New York University Press, 1999.

Miller, D. Quentin, ed. *Re-Viewing James Baldwin: Things Not Seen.* Philadelphia: Temple University Press, 2000.

Porter, Horace A. *Stealing the Fire: The Art and Protest of James Baldwin.* Middletown, Conn.: Wesleyan University Press, 1989.

Scott, Lynn Orilla. *James Baldwin's Later Fiction: Witness to the Journey.* East Lansing: Michigan State University Press, 2002.

Troupe, Quincy, ed. *James Baldwin: The Legacy.* New York: Simon & Schuster, 1989.

Weatherby, W. J. *James Baldwin: Artist on Fire.* New York: Donald I. Fine, 1989.

Contributors: Charles A. Gramlich, Terry Heller, Robert McClenaghan, Thomas J. Taylor, Terry Theodore, and Craig Werner

Toni Cade Bambara
(Miltona Mirkin Cade)

BORN: New York, New York; March 25, 1939
DIED: Philadelphia, Pennsylvania; December 9, 1995

AFRICAN AMERICAN

*Bambara saw herself as a literary combatant who
wrote to affirm the selfhood of blacks.*

PRINCIPAL WORKS

LONG FICTION: *The Salt Eaters*, 1980; *Those Bones Are Not My Child*, 1999
SCREENPLAYS: *The Bombing of Osage Avenue*, 1986 (documentary); *W. E. B. Du
Bois—A Biography in Four Voices*, 1995 (with Amiri Baraka, Wesley Brown,
and Thulani Davis)
SHORT FICTION: *Gorilla, My Love*, 1972; *The Sea Birds Are Still Alive: Collected
Stories*, 1977; *Raymond's Run: Stories for Young Adults*, 1989
EDITED TEXTS: *The Black Woman: An Anthology*, 1970; *Tales and Stories for Black
Folks*, 1971; *Southern Exposure*, 1976 (periodical; Bambara edited volume 3)
MISCELLANEOUS: "What It Is I Think I'm Doing Anyhow," *The Writer on Her Work*,
1981 (Janet Sternburg, editor); *Deep Sightings and Rescue Missions: Fiction,
Essays, and Conversations*, 1996

Given the name Miltona Mirkin Cade at birth, Toni Cade acquired the name
Bambara (BAHM-bah-rah) in 1970 after she discovered it as part of a signature on a
sketchbook she found in her great-grandmother's trunk. Bambara spent her formative years in New York and Jersey City, New Jersey, attending public and private
schools in the areas. Although she maintained that her early short stories are not
autobiographical, the protagonists in many of these pieces are young women who
recall Bambara's inquisitiveness as a youngster.

Bambara attended Queens College, New York, and received a bachelor of arts
degree in 1959. Earlier that year she had published her first short story, and she also
received the John Golden Award for fiction from Queens College. Bambara then
entered the City College of New York, where she studied modern American fiction,
but before completing her studies for the master's degree she traveled to Italy and
studied in Milan, eventually returning to her studies and earning the master's in
1963.

From 1959 to 1973, Bambara saw herself as an activist. She held positions as
social worker, teacher, and counselor. In her various roles, Bambara saw herself as

working for the betterment of the community. During the 1960's, Rutgers State University developed a strong fine arts undergraduate program. Many talented black artists joined the faculty to practice their crafts and to teach. Bambara was one of those talented faculty members. She taught, wrote, and participated in a program for raising the consciousness of minority women.

Like many artists during the 1960's, Bambara became involved in the black liberation struggle. She realized that all African Americans needed to be liberated, but she felt that black women were forgotten in the struggle. She was of the opinion that neither the white nor the black male was capable of understanding what it means to be a black female. White and black males created images of women, she argued, that "are still derived from their needs."

Toni Cade Bambara (Joyce Middler)

Bambara saw a kinship with white women but admitted: "I don't know that our priorities are the same." Believing that only the black woman is capable of explaining herself, Bambara edited *The Black Woman: An Anthology* (1970).

In 1973, Bambara visited Cuba, and in 1975 she traveled to Vietnam. Her travels led her to believe that globally, women were oppressed. Her experiences found expression in *The Sea Birds Are Still Alive*. In the late 1970's, Bambara moved to the South to teach at Spellman College. During this period she wrote *The Salt Eaters*, which focuses on mental and physical well-being. With her daughter, Bambara moved to Pennsylvania in the 1980's, where she continued her activism and her writing until her death from complications of colon cancer, in 1995.

Gorilla, My Love

TYPE OF WORK: Short fiction
FIRST PUBLISHED: 1972

Published in 1972, *Gorilla, My Love* is a collection of short stories written between 1959 and 1971. The book is an upbeat, positive work that redefines the black experience in America. It affirms the fact that inner-city children can grow into strong, healthy adults. It indicates clearly that black men are not always the weak, predatory element in the family but can be a strong, protective force. It intimates that African Americans are not the socially alienated, dysfunctional people that the mainstream society sometimes suggests. Instead, the stories project an image of a people who love themselves, who understand themselves, and who need no validation.

The fifteen short stories that compose the text are set in urban areas, and the narrative voices are usually streetwise, preadolescent girls who are extremely aware of their environment. The titular story, "Gorilla, My Love" is centered in the misunderstanding between a child and an adult. Jefferson Vale announces that he is getting married, but he has promised his preadolescent niece, Hazel, to marry her. Hazel sees her "Hunca" Bubba as a "lyin dawg." Although her uncle and her grandfather attempt to console her, Hazel believes adults "mess over kids, just cause they little and can't take em to court."

All of the stories are informative and entertaining. A story that typifies the anthology is "Playin with Ponjob," which details how a white social worker, Miss Violet, underestimates the influence of a local thug and is forced to leave the community. "Talkin Bout Sunny" explores the effects of the mainstream on the black male by pointing out how pressures from the larger community cause Sunny to kill his wife. "The Lesson" points out the disparity between the rich and the poor by telling of children window-shopping on Fifth Avenue. "Blues Ain't No Mockin Bird" details how one man protects his family from prying photographers employed by the welfare system.

What is significant in "Playin with Ponjob" is that Bambara does not depict Ponjob as being predatory. He is male, "jammed-up by the white man's nightmare." To the community, he is "the only kind of leader we can think of." In "Talkin Bout Sunny" Bambara indicates that the larger community is partly responsible for Sunny's actions, but she also indicates that the community of Sunny's friends is also responsible because they know of his distemper but do nothing. "The Lesson" teaches children that what one wealthy person spends on one toy can feed eight of them for a year. "Blues Ain't No Mockin Bird" indicates that the patriarch of an extended family can protect his own. The collection depicts African Americans as a strong, progressive people.

"Medley"

TYPE OF WORK: Short fiction
FIRST PUBLISHED: 1977, in *The Sea Birds Are Still Alive*

The most popular story from *The Sea Birds Are Still Alive*, "Medley" is the tale of Sweet Pea and Larry, a romantic couple who go through a poignant breakup in the course of the story. Though neither of them is a musician, both are music fans, and their showers together are erotic encounters in which they improvise songs together, pretending to be playing musical instruments with each other's bodies. Sweet Pea is a manicurist with her own shop, and her best customer is a gambler named Moody, who likes to keep his nails impeccable. Because he goes on a winning streak after she starts doing his nails, he offers to take her on a gambling trip as his personal manicurist, for which he pays her two thousand dollars. Sweet Pea takes the offer, though Larry objects, and when she gets back, he seems to have disappeared from her life. Nonetheless, she remembers their last night in the shower together, as they sang different tunes, keeping each other off balance but harmonizing a medley together until the hot water ran out.

Though Sweet Pea is faced with the choice of losing two thousand dollars or her boyfriend and chooses the money, the story does not attempt to say that she made the wrong choice. Rather, it is a snapshot of the impermanence of shared lives in Sweet Pea's modern, urban environment. This transience is painful but is also the basis for the enjoyment of life's beauty.

The Salt Eaters

TYPE OF WORK: Novel
FIRST PUBLISHED: 1980

The Salt Eaters opens with Velma Henry sitting on a stool in the South West Community Infirmary of Claybourne, Georgia, being healed by Minnie Ransom. Claybourne is a beehive of progressive activity. The Academy of the Seven Arts, run by James "Obie" Henry, Velma's husband, is the center of intellectual and social activities. Velma, performing the duties of seven employees, keeps the institution running. Overwhelmed by the infighting at the academy, her domestic problems with Obie, and her refusal to accept her spiritual powers, Velma has attempted suicide, and Minnie is laboring to "center" Velma, to make Velma whole.

The novel includes a spiritual plane where mortals interact with other life forms. Minnie Ransom operates on both planes. She is sitting opposite Velma while surrounded by her twelve disciples, the Master's Mind. Sometimes she reaches out and touches Velma physically. Other times she does "not touch [Velma] flesh on flesh, but touch[es] mind on mind from across the room or from across town." While Minnie is having these telepathic tête-à-têtes with Velma, she also confers at times with a spirit guide who helps her with the healing. When "centering" Velma becomes difficult, Minnie makes telepathic trips to the Chapel of the Mind to recharge her psychic energies.

The healing, which should take minutes, takes two hours—the time span of the novel. Velma, like Minnie, takes telepathic trips, during which she bumps into other characters, human and spiritual. These characters, filtered through Velma's subconscious, are for the most part what people the novel.

Bambara skillfully combines the European American traditional mode of storytelling with African and African American concepts and traditions. The Academy of the Seven Arts is concerned with empirical knowledge, but the institution is also concerned with teaching folk art and folk traditions. The medical center accommodates physicians who practice modern medicine, but the center also makes use of the skills of Minnie Ransom. The spring celebration is a ritual performed by human beings, but in Claybourne the quick and the dead perform this rite.

Bambara's concepts of the new age, guiding spirits, out-of-body experiences, and telepathic visions were not, at first, taken seriously. Reality is not, however, measured only by empirical evidence. Near-death experiences, guardian angels, and intergalactic travel are part of popular understanding. As the concept of reality expands, the significance of *The Salt Eaters* deepens.

"Raymond's Run"

TYPE OF WORK: Short fiction
FIRST PUBLISHED: 1989, in *Raymond's Run: Stories for Young Adults*

"Raymond's Run," a short story that forms the title of Bambara's collection for young adults, is about the relationship between the narrator, Hazel (not the same girl from "Gorilla, My Love," but about the same age); her retarded brother, Raymond; and another girl on the block, Gretchen. Hazel's reputation is as the fastest thing on two feet in the neighborhood, but coming up to the annual May Day run, she knows that her new rival, Gretchen, will challenge her and could win. Mr. Pearson, a teacher at the school, suggests that it would be a nice gesture to the new girl, Gretchen, to let her win, which Hazel dismisses out of hand. Thinking about a Hansel and Gretel pageant in which she played a strawberry, Hazel thinks, "I am not a strawberry... I run. That is what I'm all about." As a runner, she has no intention of letting someone else win.

In fact, when the race is run, she does win, but it is very close, and for all her bravado, she is not sure who won until her name is announced. More important, she sees her brother Raymond running along with her on the other side of the fence, keeping his hands down in an awkward running posture that she accepts as all his own. In her excitement about her brother's accomplishment, she imagines that her rival Gretchen might want to help her train Raymond as a runner, and the two girls share a moment of genuine warmth.

The central point of the story is captured by Hazel when she says of the smile she shared with Gretchen that it was the type of smile girls can share only when they are not too busy being "flowers or fairies or strawberries instead of something honest and worthy of respect ... you know ... like being people." The honest competition that brought out their best efforts and enticed Raymond to join them in his way brought them all together as people, not as social competitors trying to outmaneuver one another but as allies.

Deep Sightings and Rescue Missions

TYPE OF WORK: Short fiction, essays, interview
FIRST PUBLISHED: 1996

After her death from cancer in December, 1995, Toni Cade Bambara's friend and editor, Toni Morrison, pledged to collect Bambara's previously unpublished work. The result of that pledge, *Deep Sightings and Rescue Missions*, edited and prefaced by Morrison, is Bambara's first book since the early 1980's.

The anthology includes many selections that have never before appeared in print. The compilation of six stories, five essays, and an interview with the author showcases Bambara's extraordinary range as a writer, film critic, activist, and cultural worker.

Bambara's fiction is incisive and satisfying. "Going Critical" examines the relationship between Clara, a woman dying from radiation poisoning, and Honey, her spiritually gifted daughter whom Clara hopes will carry on her mission as a community advocate. All of the stories in the collection are about relationships, responsibility, and community.

Bambara's expertise and passion for filmmaking is evident throughout the book but especially in two essays. In "Reading the Signs, Empowering the Eye," Bambara explores the black independent film movement with a meticulous analysis of Julie Dash's 1992 lyric masterpiece, *Daughters of the Dust*. "School Daze" is an insightful appraisal of the complex themes, meanings, and implications of Spike Lee's film about class, caste, culture, and intracommunity dynamics at a southern black college.

In the essay "Deep Sight and Rescue Missions," Bambara takes the reader on a journey through downtown Philadelphia. Along the way, she examines the independent media movement as well as issues vital to people of color, including assimilation, accommodation, opportunism, and resistance.

"How She Came by Her Name," an interview by Louis Massiah, offers insights into Bambara's battle with cancer and into her development as a writer and activist.

In *Deep Sightings and Rescue Missions*, Bambara's prose is poetic and often confrontational, reflecting her honesty, passion, and commitment to issues of race, gender, and community.

SUGGESTED READINGS

Alwes, Derek. "The Burden of Liberty: Choice in Toni Morrison's *Jazz* and Toni Cade Bambara's *The Salt Eaters*." *African American Review* 30, no. 3 (Fall, 1996): 353-365.

Butler-Evans, Elliott. *Race, Gender, and Desire: Narrative Strategies in the Fiction of Toni Cade Bambara, Toni Morrison, Alice Walker*. Philadelphia: Temple University Press, 1989.

Collins, Janelle. "Generating Power: Fission, Fusion, and Post-modern Politics in Bambara's *The Salt Eaters*." *MELUS* 21, no. 2 (Summer, 1996): 35-47.

Evans, Mari, ed. *Black Women Writers (1950-1980): A Critical Evaluation.* Garden City, N.Y.: Anchor Press/Doubleday, 1984.

Hargrove, Nancy. "Youth in Toni Cade Bambara's *Gorilla, My Love.*" In *Women Writers of the Contemporary South*, edited by Peggy Whitman Prenshaw. Jackson: University Press of Mississippi, 1984.

Holmes, Linda J., and Cheryl A. Wall, eds. *Savoring the Salt: The Legacy of Toni Cade Bambara.* Philadelphia: Temple University Press, 2007.

Vertreace, Martha M. *Toni Cade Bambara.* New York: Macmillan Library Reference, 1998.

Willis, Susan. "Problematizing the Individual: Toni Cade Bambara's Stories for the Revolution." In *Specifying: Black Women Writing the American Experience.* Madison: University of Wisconsin Press, 1987.

Contributors: Ralph Reckley, Sr., Thomas Cassidy, and Judith Barton Williamson

Amiri Baraka
(LeRoi Jones)

BORN: Newark, New Jersey; October 7, 1934

AFRICAN AMERICAN

*Baraka's poetry, drama, and music criticism
make him one of the most influential African American
writers of his generation.*

PRINCIPAL WORKS

DRAMA: *The Baptism*, pr. 1964, pb. 1966; *Dutchman*, pr., pb. 1964; *The Slave*, pr., pb. 1964; *The Toilet*, pr., pb. 1964; *Experimental Death Unit #1*, pr. 1965, pb. 1969; *Jello*, pr. 1965, pb. 1970; *A Black Mass*, pr. 1966, pb. 1969; *Arm Yourself, or Harm Yourself*, pr., pb. 1967; *Great Goodness of Life (A Coon Show)*, pr. 1967, pb. 1969; *Madheart*, pr. 1967, pb. 1969; *Slave Ship: A Historical Pageant*, pr., pb. 1967; *The Death of Malcolm X*, pb. 1969; *Bloodrites*, pr. 1970, pb. 1971; *Junkies Are Full of (SHHH . . .)*, pr. 1970, pb. 1971; *A Recent Killing*, pr. 1973, pb. 1978; *S-1*, pr. 1976, pb. 1978; *The Motion of History*, pr. 1977, pb. 1978; *The Sidney Poet Heroical*, pb. 1979 (originally as *Sidnee Poet Heroical*, pr. 1975); *What Was the Relationship of the Lone Ranger to the Means of Production?*, pr., pb. 1979; *At the Dim'cracker Convention*, pr. 1980; *Weimar*, pr. 1981; *Money: A Jazz Opera*, pr. 1982; *Primitive World: An Anti-Nuclear Jazz Musical*, pr. 1984, pb. 1997; *The Life and Life of Bumpy Johnson*, pr. 1991; *General Hag's Skeezag*, pb. 1992; *Meeting Lillie*, pr. 1993; *The Election Machine Warehouse*, pr. 1996, pb. 1997

LONG FICTION: *The System of Dante's Hell*, 1965

POETRY: *Spring and Soforth*, 1960; *Preface to a Twenty Volume Suicide Note*, 1961; *The Dead Lecturer*, 1964; *Black Art*, 1966; *A Poem for Black Hearts*, 1967; *Black Magic: Sabotage, Target Study, Black Art—Collected Poetry, 1961-1967*, 1969; *In Our Terribleness: Some Elements and Meaning in Black Style*, 1970 (with Fundi [Billy Abernathy]); *It's Nation Time*, 1970; *Spirit Reach*, 1972; *Afrikan Revolution*, 1973; *Hard Facts*, 1975; *Selected Poetry of Amiri Baraka/ LeRoi Jones*, 1979; *Reggae or Not!*, 1981; *Transbluesency: The Selected Poems of Amiri Baraka*, 1995; *Wise, Why's, Y's*, 1995; *Funk Lore: New Poems, 1984-1995*, 1996; *Somebody Blew Up America, and Other Poems*, 2003; *Poco Low Coup*, 2004; *Mixed Blood: Number One*, 2005

SHORT FICTION: *Tales*, 1967; *The Fiction of LeRoi Jones/Amiri Baraka*, 2000; *Tales of the Out and the Gone*, 2006

NONFICTION: *"Cuba Libre,"* 1961; *The New Nationalism*, 1962; *Blues People: Negro Music in White America*, 1963; *Home: Social Essays*, 1966; *Black Music*, 1968; *A Black Value System*, 1970; *Kawaida Studies: The New Nationalism*, 1971; *Raise Race Rays Raze: Essays Since 1965*, 1971; *Strategy and Tactics of a Pan-African Nationalist Party*, 1971; *Crisis in Boston!*, 1974; *The Creation of the New Ark*, 1975; *The Autobiography of LeRoi Jones/Amiri Baraka*, 1984; *Daggers and Javelins: Essays*, 1984; *The Artist and Social Responsibility*, 1986; *The Music: Reflections on Jazz and Blues*, 1987 (with Amina Baraka); *Conversations with Amiri Baraka*, 1994 (Charlie Reilly, editor); *Jesse Jackson and Black People*, 1994; *Eulogies*, 1996; *Digging: Afro American Be/At American Classical Music*, 1999; *Bushwacked! A Counterfeit President for a Fake Democracy: A Collection of Essays on the 2000 National Elections*, 2001; *National Elections*, 2001; *The Essence of Reparation*, 2003; *Jubilee: The Emergence of African-American Culture*, 2003 (with others)

EDITED TEXTS: *The Moderns: New Fiction in America*, 1963; *Black Fire: An Anthology of Afro-American Writing*, 1968 (with Larry Neal); *African Congress: A Documentary of the First Modern Pan-African Congress*, 1972; *Confirmation: An Anthology of African-American Women*, 1983 (with Amina Baraka)

MISCELLANEOUS: *Selected Plays and Prose*, 1979; *The LeRoi Jones/Amiri Baraka Reader*, 1991; *Insomniacathon: Voices Without Restraint*, 1999 (audiocassette)

Amiri Baraka, as he has been known since 1967, was born Everett LeRoi Jones into a middle-class family in Newark, New Jersey. An excellent student whose parents encouraged his intellectual interests, Jones graduated from Howard University in Washington, D.C., in 1954 at the age of nineteen. After spending two years in the United States Air Force, primarily in Puerto Rico, he moved to Greenwich Village, where he embarked on his literary career in 1957. During the early stage of his career, Jones associated closely with numerous white avant-garde poets, including Robert Creeley, Allen Ginsberg, Robert Duncan, and Dianne DiPrima, with whom he founded the American Theatre for Poets in 1961. Marrying Hettie Cohen, a white woman with whom he edited the magazine *Yugen* from 1958 to 1963, Jones established himself as an important young poet, critic, and editor. Among the many magazines to which he contributed was *Down Beat*, the jazz journal in which he first developed many of the musical interests that were to have such a large impact on his later poetry. The political interests that were to dominate Jones's later work were unmistakably present as early as 1960 when he toured Cuba with a group of black intellectuals. This event sparked his perception of the United States as a corrupt bourgeois society and seems particularly significant in relation to his later socialist emphasis. Jones's growing political interest conditioned his first produced plays, including the Obie Award-winning *Dutchman* (1964), which anticipated the first major transformation of Jones's life.

Separating from Hettie Cohen and severing ties with his white associates, Jones moved from the Village to Harlem in 1965. Turning his attention to direct action within the black community, he founded the Black Arts Repertory Theatre and School in Harlem and, following his return to his native city in 1966, the

Spirit House in Newark. After marrying a black woman, Sylvia Robinson (Amina Baraka), in 1966, Jones adopted his new name, which means "Prince" (Ameer) "the blessed one" (Baraka), along with the honorary title of "Imamu." Over the next half dozen years, Baraka helped found and develop the Black Community Development and Defense Organization, the Congress of African Peoples (convened in Atlanta in 1970), and the National Black Political Convention (convened in Gary, Indiana, in 1972). As a leading spokesman of the Black Arts movement, Baraka provided support for young black poets and playwrights, including Larry Neal, Ed Bullins, Marvin X, and Ron Milner. During the Newark uprising/riot of 1967, Baraka was arrested for unlawful possession of firearms. Although he was convicted and given the maximum sentence after the judge read his poem "Black People!" as an example of incitement to riot, Baraka was later cleared on appeal.

Baraka supported Kenneth A. Gibson's campaign to become the first black mayor of Newark in 1970, but he later broke with Gibson over what he perceived as the bourgeois values of the administration. This disillusionment with black politics within the American system, combined with Baraka's attendance at the Sixth Pan-African Conference at Dar es Salaam in 1974, precipitated the subsequent stage of his political evolution. While not abandoning his commitment to confronting the special problems of African Americans in the United States, Baraka came to interpret these problems within the framework of an overarching Marxist-Leninist-Maoist philosophy. In conjunction with this second transformation, Baraka dropped the title "Imamu" and changed the name of his Newark publishing firm from "Jihad" to "People's War."

Baraka would continue to teach, lecture, and conduct workshops, and he is noted not only for his writings but also for his influence on young writers and social critics. As the editor of *Black Nation*, the organ of the Marxist organization the League of Revolutionary Struggle, Baraka exerted an influence that extended far beyond African American culture and politics to embrace other people of color. Native American writer Maurice Kenney, for example, credited Baraka for teaching ethnic writers how to open doors to important venues for their writing, to "claim and take" their place at the cultural forefront.

Amiri Baraka (Library of Congress)

Blues People

TYPE OF WORK: Essay
FIRST PUBLISHED: 1963

The first full-length analytical and historical study of jazz and blues written by an African American, *Blues People: Negro Music in White America* presents a highly original thesis suggesting that music can be used as a gauge to measure the cultural assimilation of Africans in North America from the early eighteenth century to the twentieth century. Broad in scope and insightfully opinionated, *Blues People* caused controversy among musicologists and other critics. Intending his remarks as negative criticism, Ralph Ellison was accurate in noting that Baraka is "attracted to the blues for what he believes they tell us of the sociology of Negro American identity and attitude."

Baraka contends that although slavery destroyed many formal artistic traditions, African American music represents certain African survivals. Most important, African American music represents an African approach to culture. As such, the music sustains the African worldview and records the historical experience of an oppressed people.

Baraka also argues that while Africans adapted their culture to the English language and to European musical instruments and song forms, they also maintained an ethnic viewpoint that is preserved and transmitted by their music. Stylistic changes in the music mirror historical changes in the attitudes and social conditions of African Americans. The chapter "Swing—From Verb to Noun" compares the contributions of African American and white jazz musicians in the 1920's and 1930's, demonstrating how some artists developed and extended an ethnic folk music tradition while others added what they learned from that tradition to the vocabulary of a more commercialized American popular music. Baraka's view that music is capable of expressing and maintaining a group identity leads to his assertion that even in later decades, increasingly dominated by the recording and broadcasting industry, African American artists continued to be the primary contributors and innovators. A classic work of its kind, *Blues People* offers an interesting view of how cultural products reflect and perhaps determine other social developments.

The Baptism

TYPE OF WORK: Drama
FIRST PRODUCED: 1964, pb. 1966

Baraka's early plays clearly reflect both his developing concern with issues of survival and his fascination with European American avant-garde traditions. *The Baptism*, in particular, draws on the conventions of expressionist theater to comment on the absurdity of contemporary American ideas of salvation, which in fact simply mask a larger scheme of victimization. Identified only as symbolic types, Baraka's characters speak a surreal mixture of street language and theological argot. While the slang references link them to the social reality familiar to the audience, their actions are dictated by the sudden shifts and thematic ambiguities characteristic of works such as August Strindberg's *Ett drömspel* (pb. 1902; *A Dream Play*, 1912) and the "Circe" chapter of James Joyce's *Ulysses* (1922).

The play's central character, named simply "the Boy," resembles a traditional Christ figure struggling to come to terms with his vocation. Baraka treats his protagonist with a mixture of irony and empathy, focusing on the ambiguous roles of the spirit and the flesh in relation to salvation. Pressured by the Minister to deny his body and by the cynical Homosexual to immerse himself in the profane as a path to the truly sacred, the Boy vacillates. At times he claims divine status; at times he insists, "I am only flesh." The chorus of Women, at once holy virgins and temple prostitutes, reinforces his confusion. Shortly after identifying him as "the Son of God," they refer to him as the "Chief Religious jelly roll of the universe." Given these irreconcilable roles, which he is expected to fulfill, the Boy's destiny as scapegoat and martyr seems inevitable; the dramatic tension revolves around the question of who will victimize him and why. Baraka uses a sequence of conflicting views of the Boy's role, each of which momentarily dominates his self-image, to heighten this tension.

Responding to the Homosexual's insistence that "the devil is a part of creation like an ash tray or senator," the Boy first confesses his past sins and demands baptism. When the Women respond by elevating him to the status of "Son of God/Son of Man," he explicitly rejects all claim to spiritual purity. The ambiguous masquerade culminates in an attack on the Boy, who is accused of using his spiritual status to seduce women who "wanted to be virgins of the Lord." Supported only by the Homosexual, the Boy defends himself against the Women and the Minister, who clamor for his sacrifice, ostensibly as punishment for his sins. Insisting that "there will be no second crucifixion," the Boy slays his antagonists with a phallic sword, which he interprets as the embodiment of spiritual glory. For a brief moment, the figures of Christ as scapegoat and Christ as avenger seem reconciled in a baptism of fire.

Baraka undercuts this moment of equilibrium almost immediately. Having escaped martyrdom at the hands of the mob (ironically, itself victimized), the Boy confronts the Messenger, who wears a motorcycle jacket embellished with a gold crown and the words "The Man." In Baraka's dream allegory, the Man can represent the Roman/American legal system or be a symbol for God the Father, both powers that severely limit the Boy's control over events. The Boy's first reaction to the Messenger is to reclaim his superior spiritual status, insisting that he has "brought love to many people" and calling on his "Father" for compassion. Rejecting these pleas, the Messenger indicates that "the Man's destroying the whole works tonight." The Boy responds defiantly: "Neither God nor man shall force me to leave. I was sent here to save man and I'll not leave until I do." The allegory suggests several different levels of interpretation: social, psychological, and symbolic. The Boy rejects his responsibility to concrete individuals (the mob he kills, the Man) in order to save an abstract entity (the mob as an ideal man). Ultimately, he claims his right to the martyr's death, which he killed the mob in order to avoid, by repudiating the martyr's submission to a higher power. Losing patience with the Boy's rhetoric, the Messenger responds not by killing him but by knocking him out and dragging him offstage. His attitude of boredom effectively deflates the allegorical seriousness of the Boy's defiance, a deflation reinforced by the Homosexual's concluding comment that the scene resembles "some really uninteresting kind of orgy."

The Baptism's treatment of the interlocking themes of sacrifice, ritual, and victimization emphasizes their inherent ambiguity and suggests the impossibility of moral action in a culture that confuses God with the leader of a motorcycle gang. Baraka's baptism initiates the Boy into absurdity rather than responsibility. If any sins have been washed away, they are resurrected immediately in pointless ritual violence and immature rhetoric. Although he does not develop the theme explicitly in *The Baptism*, Baraka suggests that there is an underlying philosophical corruption in European American culture, in this case derived from Christianity's tendency to divorce flesh from spirit. Increasingly, this philosophical corruption takes the center of Baraka's dramatic presentation of Western civilization.

Dutchman

TYPE OF WORK: Drama
FIRST PRODUCED: 1964, pb. 1964

A powerful one-act drama, *Dutchman* brought immediate and lasting attention to Baraka. The play is a searing two-character confrontation that begins playfully but builds rapidly in suspense and symbolic resonance. Set on a New York subway train, *Dutchman* opens with a well-dressed, intellectual, young African American man named Clay absorbed in reading a magazine. He is interrupted by Lula—a flirtatious, beautiful white woman a bit older than he. As Lula suggestively slices and eats an apple, she and Clay tease each other with bantering talk that becomes more and more personal. She reveals little about herself, but Lula is clearly in control of the conversation and the situation as she perceptively and provokingly challenges Clay's middle-class self-image. Lula is, in fact, a bit cruel. "What right do you have to be wearing a three-button suit and striped tie?" she asks. "Your grandfather was a slave, he didn't go to Harvard." Aware of his insecurities, Lula dares Clay to pretend "that you are free of your own history."

Clay's insecurities about his race, social status, and masculine prowess—slowly revealed as his answers shift from machismo to defensiveness—become the targets for Lula's increasingly direct taunts. Eventually, Lula's attempt to force Clay to see in himself the negative stereotypes of the black male—as either oversexed stud or cringing Uncle Tom—goad him into an eloquently bitter tirade. Black music and African American culture, he tells her, are actually repressions of a justified rage that has kept African American people sane in the face of centuries of oppression. Clay seems as desperate to prove this to himself as he is to convince Lula. He does not seem to know whether the rage or the repression has taken the greater toll on African American sanity. The scene escalates in dramatic force until Lula unexpectedly stabs Clay to death.

Baraka has said that *Dutchman* "is about how difficult it is to become a man in the United States." Nevertheless, the ancient symbolism of apple and temptation, and the myth of the ghostly pirate ship, *The Flying Dutchman*, used in Richard Wagner's opera and other literary works, are carefully suggested in Baraka's play and amplify the dimensions of racial conflict.

"The Screamers"

TYPE OF WORK: Short fiction
FIRST PUBLISHED: 1967, in *Tales*

Reprinted at least a half dozen times since its appearance in *Tales*, generally in collections of African American fiction, "The Screamers" is by far Baraka's best-known short story. The narrative covers one night in a black jazz nightclub in Newark (probably in the early 1950's) from the perspective of a young man listening to "Harlem Nocturne" and other popular dance tunes. What makes this night unique is the performance by saxophonist Lynn Hope, who in an inspired moment leads the musicians through the crowd and out into the streets. "It would be the form of the sweetest revolution, to hucklebuck into the fallen capital, and let the oppressors lindy hop out." The police arrive and attack the crowd, a riot ensues, and the marchers "all broke our different ways, to save whatever it was each of us thought we loved." The story has a number of elements common to Baraka's fiction: the positive depiction of African American cultural forms (including a kind of "bop" jazz language), the conflict between this culture and white oppressors, and the metaphor of black art—here it is music, but it could as easily stand for writing—as an inspirational cultural form which, while it cannot finally overcome white oppression, at least achieves a moment of heightened consciousness for the people (here called "Biggers," in reference to the central character, Bigger Thomas, of Richard Wright's 1940 novel *Native Son*) listening to the music and moved by it.

Selected Poetry of Amiri Baraka/LeRoi Jones

TYPE OF WORK: Poetry
FIRST PUBLISHED: 1979

Baraka helped define the Beat generation and served as a guide for the Black Arts movement of the 1960's. Baraka's work is simultaneously introspective and public; his combination of unrhymed open forms, African American vernacular speech, and allusions to American popular culture produces poems that express

Baraka's personal background while addressing political issues. Baraka's poetry draws upon the poetic techniques of William Carlos Williams and Charles Olson, and upon traditional oratory, ranging from the African American church to street-corner rapping.

Baraka has divided his work into three periods: his association with the Beats (1957-1963), his militant Black Nationalist period (1965-1974), and, after 1975, an adherence to Marxism and Third World anticolonial politics. These periods are marked by changes in the poet's ideology but not in his poetic style. Early poems such as "Hymn to Lanie Poo"—focusing on tension between middle-class and poor black people—and "Notes for a Speech" consider whether or not African Americans have a genuine ethnic identity and culture of their own as opposed to a segregated existence that only mirrors white America. This theme receives more attention in poems of the 1960's such as "Poem for Willie Best" and "Poem for HalfWhite College Students" that indict Hollywood stereotypes. Another collection, *Transbluesency*, represents much of Baraka's work after 1979.

Poems of the Black Nationalist period address questions of the poet's personal and racial identity. The poems of this period suggest that poetry itself is a means of creating individual and communal identity. In "Numbers, Letters" Baraka writes: "I can't be anything I'm not/ Except these words pretend/ to life not yet explained." Explicitly political poems, such as "The Nation Is Like Ourselves," propose that each person's efforts or failings collectively amount to a community's character. After 1975, poems such as "In the Tradition" argue—with some consistency with Baraka's earlier views—that although Marxism is the means to political progress, only an art of the people that insists on showing that "the universal/ is the entire collection/ of particulars" will prepare people to work toward a better future. "In the Tradition" and a later series titled "Why's" present musicians and political leaders as equally powerful cultural activists, reinforcing Baraka's idea that poetry is a force for change.

Daggers and Javelins

Type of work: Essays and lectures
First published: 1984

The essays and lectures collected in *Daggers and Javelins: Essays, 1974-1979* represent Baraka's vigorous attempt to identify an African American revolutionary tradition that could parallel anticolonial struggles in Third World countries of Africa, Asia, and South America. Baraka applies a Marxist analysis to African American literature in these essays.

Having become disappointed with the progress of the Black Power movement and its emphasis on grassroots electoral politics, Baraka came to Marxism with the zeal of a new convert. "The essays of the earliest part of this period," he writes, "are overwhelmingly political in the most overt sense." While some of the essays in *Daggers and Javelins* address jazz, film, and writers of the Harlem Renaissance, all of them do so with the purpose of assessing what Baraka calls their potential to contribute to a revolutionary struggle.

In "The Revolutionary Tradition in Afro-American Literature," Baraka distinguishes between the authentic folk and vernacular expression of African American masses and the poetry and prose produced by middle-class writers in imitation of prevailing literary standards. Considering the slave narratives of Frederick Douglass and others as the beginnings of a genuine African American literature, he criticizes works that promote individualism or are merely "a distraction, an ornament." Similarly, "Afro-American Literature and Class Struggle" and other essays consider how the economic structure of society affects the production and the appreciation of art. "Notes on the History of African/Afro-American Culture" interprets the theoretical writings of Karl Marx and Friedrich Engels and draws parallels between colonized African societies and the suppression of African American artistic expression by the American cultural mainstream.

Broadening his scope in essays on African and Caribbean authors, Baraka suggests that figures such as the Kenyan novelist Ngugi wa Thiong'o and the poet Aimé Césaire from Martinique can provide models for how African American artists can escape being co-opted into an elite that supports the status quo and, instead, produce art that offers a "cathartic revelation of reality" useful in promoting social change.

Conversations with Amiri Baraka

TYPE OF WORK: Letters
FIRST PUBLISHED: 1994

Readers of Amiri Baraka's books know the intensity of his rage against racism and economic injustice. Readers of these interviews collected by critic Charlie Reilly will catch a glimpse of the author as his political views evolved through three decades. Those interested in a static or logically consistent portrait of the author will be dismayed. Those fascinated by how an author must explore numerous meandering detours before arriving at a clearly defined path will find much of fascination.

Interviewers range from the famous (author Maya Angelou, television personality David Frost) to the obscure. Attitudes among these interviewers range from the fawning to the acidly critical. Baraka emerges from these interviews as a disarming mix of the erudite and the glib. His gifts as a satirist come to the fore when he pokes fun at white political leaders. He is less inspired when he lectures to his interviewers about his favorite cause of the time—whether Black Nationalism, Islam, or Marxism.

As consistently lively as Baraka's views on race and literature are, this collection makes for occasionally tedious reading. Baraka's early ties to Beat Generation writers such as Allen Ginsberg are touched upon in identical fashion in several interviews. A more substantial introduction by the editor would have provided a comprehensive mapping of the key trends in Baraka's literary career. As it stands, interviewers make references to Baraka's books in ways that presuppose the reader's acquaintance with such works. Nevertheless, the reader will find much to ponder as he or she witnesses Baraka shedding one ideological "suit of clothing" for another while maintaining a poetically lyrical perception of the world.

SUGGESTED READINGS

Baraka, Amiri. *Conversations with Amiri Baraka*. Edited by Charlie Reilly. Jackson: University Press of Mississippi, 1994.

Benston, Kimberly W., ed. *Imamu Amiri Baraka (LeRoi Jones): A Collection of Critical Essays*. Englewood Cliffs, N.J.: Prentice-Hall, 1978.

Brown, Lloyd W. *Amiri Baraka*. Boston: Twayne, 1980.

Effiong, Philip Uko. *In Search of a Model for African-American Drama: A Study of Selected Plays by Lorraine Hansberry, Amiri Baraka, and Ntozake Shange*. Lanham, Md.: University Press of America, 2000.

Fox, Robert Eliot. *Conscientious Sorcerers: The Black Post-modernist Fiction of LeRoi Jones/Baraka, Ishmael Reed, and Samuel R. Delaney*. New York: Greenwood Press, 1987.

Gwynne, James B., ed. *Amiri Baraka: The Kaleidoscopic Torch*. Harlem, N.Y.: Steppingstones Press, 1985.

Lacey, Henry C. *To Raise, Destroy, and Create: The Poetry, Drama, and Fiction of Imamu Amiri Baraka (LeRoi Jones)*. Troy, N.Y.: Whitston, 1981.

Reilly, Charlie, ed. *Conversations with Amiri Baraka*. Jackson: University Press of Mississippi, 1994.

Sollors, Werner. *Amiri Baraka/LeRoi Jones: The Quest for a "Populist Modernism."* New York: Columbia University Press, 1978.

Watts, Jerry Gafio. *Amiri Baraka: The Politics and Art of a Black Intellectual*. New York: New York University Press, 2001.

Woodard, K. Komozi. *A Nation Within a Nation: Amiri Baraka (LeRoi Jones) and Black Power Politics*. Chapel Hill: University of North Carolina Press, 1999.

Contributors: Lorenzo Thomas, Robert McClenaghan, David Peck,
Judith K. Taylor, Thomas J. Taylor, and Craig Werner

Raymond Barrio

BORN: West Orange, New Jersey; August 27, 1921
DIED: Escondido, California; January 22, 1996

MEXICAN AMERICAN

Barrio's writing is concerned with gross inequalities
in a capitalist system, and he bases many of his characters
on the real lives of people he has known.

PRINCIPAL WORKS

CHILDREN'S LITERATURE: *The Fisherman's Dwarf*, 1968
DRAMA: *The Devil's Apple Corps: A Trauma in Four Acts*, pb. 1976
LONG FICTION: *The Plum Plum Pickers*, 1969; *Carib Blue*, 1990
NONFICTION: *The Big Picture: How to Experiment with Modern Techniques in Art*,
   1967 (revised as *Experiments in Modern Art*, 1968); *Art: Seen*, 1968; *The Prism*,
   1968; *Mexico's Art and Chicano Artists*, 1975

Raymond Barrio (RAY-mohnd BAHR-ree-oh) was born in West Orange, New Jersey, on August 27, 1921, to Spanish immigrants. His father, Saturnino, worked in a chemical factory in New Jersey and died as a result of his exposure to poisonous fumes there. Raymond's mother, Angelita (né Santos), was a Spanish dancer. Barrio once wrote in a letter that he and his brother lived with foster families while their mother pursued her career. He therefore grew up in a Protestant environment, despite his Catholic roots. In 1957, he married Yolanda Sánchez in Mazatlan, Mexico. They would have five children.

From 1936 until his death in 1996 (with the exception of his military service in Europe during World War II), Barrios lived in California. There he earned his bachelor of arts degree from the University of California at Berkeley in 1947 and a bachelor of fine arts degree from the Art Center College of Los Angeles in 1952. He taught courses in art, creative writing, Chicano culture and literature, and Mexican art in eight California institutions of higher education: San Jose State University, Ventura College, the University of California at Santa Barbara, West Valley College, De Anza College, Skyline College, Foothill College, and Sonoma State University. In 1964 he was awarded the Creative Arts Institute Faculty Grant by the University of California.

Barrio's major literary achievement was his novel *The Plum Plum Pickers*. Initially it was turned down by every publishing house to which Barrio offered it, so Barrios published it himself. It sold more than ten thousand copies in two years, becoming an underground classic. Barrio was as much a visual artist as he was a writer; he illustrated many of his own books. In fact, for most of his life he considered himself primarily an artist; teaching merely paid his family's bills.

The Plum Plum Pickers

TYPE OF WORK: Novel
FIRST PUBLISHED: 1969

Set in California's Santa Clara Valley during the summer and fall harvest season, *The Plum Plum Pickers* takes place in and around the fictional town of Drawbridge, and more specifically at the Western Grande Company's migrant housing project. The novel presents the dehumanized conditions of the mostly Mexican plum plum, or prune, pickers at the hands of the fruit company representatives: Mr. Quill, the grounds boss, and his superior and the company owner, Mr. Turner. The squalor of the migrant camps is a major element of the narrative and enhances the brutalized relations between not only Anglo bosses and Mexican laborers but also different groups within the farmworkers' Mexican community. The harsh reality of conditions is brought to the forefront in large part by the contrapuntal techniques employed in the narrative (which allow for contrasting views of the same topic) and the frequent attribution of animal qualities to individual characters.

Barrio published *The Plum Plum Pickers* privately in 1969. Its publication coincided with the unionizing activities of César Chávez, and the book appeared to illustrate the very conditions that Chávez sought to improve. The book was therefore an immediate popular success, although it received little critical attention, perhaps because of the poor quality of print and paper employed in its first printing. The novel has since maintained its position as one of the key novels of the Chicano movement of the late 1960's and early 1970's. A major reason for this is Barrio's use of an unusual narrative form, which incorporates such items as newspaper clippings, radio announcements, handwritten notes, and even a government agricultural manual. *The Plum Plum Pickers* set a new standard for Chicano fiction to follow.

SUGGESTED READINGS

Akers, John C. "Raymond Barrio." In *Chicano Writers, First Series*, edited by Francisco A. Lomelí. Vol. 82 in *Dictionary of Literary Biography*. Detroit: Gale, 1989.

Gray, Linda. "*The Plum Plum Pickers:* A Review." *Peninsula Bulletin* 11 (December, 1976).

Lomelí, Francisco A. "Depraved New World Revisited: Dreams and Dystopia in *The Plum Plum Pickers*." Introduction to *The Plum Plum Pickers*, by Raymond Barrio. Tempe, Ariz.: Bilingual Review Press, 1984.

Contributors: Kathleen M. Bartlett and St. John Robinson

Saul Bellow

Born: Lachine, Quebec, Canada; June 10, 1915
Died: Brookline, Massachusetts; April 5, 2005

Jewish

*Bellow was perhaps the first Jewish writer in America to reject
the categorization of his work as being Jewish American
literature; he became a major American novelist.*

Principal works

DRAMA: *The Wrecker*, pb. 1954; *The Last Analysis*, pr. 1964; *Under the Weather*, pr. 1966 (also known as *The Bellow Plays*; includes *Out from Under*, *A Wen*, and *Orange Soufflé*)

LONG FICTION: *Dangling Man*, 1944; *The Victim*, 1947; *The Adventures of Augie March*, 1953; *Seize the Day*, 1956; *Henderson the Rain King*, 1959; *Herzog*, 1964; *Mr. Sammler's Planet*, 1970; *Humboldt's Gift*, 1975; *The Dean's December*, 1982; *More Die of Heartbreak*, 1987; *The Bellarosa Connection*, 1989; *A Theft*, 1989; *The Actual*, 1997 (novella); *Ravelstein*, 2000; *Novels, 1944-1953*, 2003 (includes *Dangling Man*, *The Victim*, and *The Adventures of Augie March*)

SHORT FICTION: *Mosby's Memoirs, and Other Stories*, 1968; *Him with His Foot in His Mouth, and Other Stories*, 1984; *Something to Remember Me By: Three Tales*, 1991; *Collected Stories*, 2001

NONFICTION: *To Jerusalem and Back: A Personal Account*, 1976; *Conversations with Saul Bellow*, 1994 (Gloria L. Cronin and Ben Siegel, editors); *It All Adds Up: From the Dim Past to the Uncertain Future*, 1994

EDITED TEXT: *Great Jewish Short Stories*, 1963

Saul Bellow (sawl BEHL-loh) grew up in the polyglot slums of Montreal and Chicago. He was saved from a bleak existence by his love of learning. He acquired a knowledge of Yiddish, Hebrew, and French, in addition to Russian and English. His Russian immigrant parents were orthodox Jews; Bellow's exposure to other cultures led him to reject a purely Jewish identity. He discovered the work of Mark Twain, Edgar Allan Poe, Theodore Dreiser, and Sherwood Anderson, all leaders in shaping Americans' consciousness of their national identity.

After graduating from Northwestern University, Bellow obtained a scholarship to pursue graduate study in anthropology at the University of Wisconsin but found his real interest lay in creative writing. He considered his first two novels, *Dangling Man* and *The Victim*, "apprentice work." Not until the publication of *The Adventures of Augie March* did he achieve recognition as a major new voice in Amer-

Saul Bellow (© The Nobel Foundation)

ican fiction. He had forged a spontaneous, exuberant personal style that was
a poetic synthesis of lower-class vernacular, Yiddishisms, profuse neo-
logisms, the language of polite society, and the jargon of academia.

Bellow thought too much had been
made of persecution and exclusion. He
pointed to the exciting opportunities
for growth available to all Americans.
He insisted on being not a Jew addressing other Jews but an American
addressing other Americans. Creative
writing for him was an adventure in
self-discovery. He called his breakthrough novel *The Adventures of Augie
March* because he considered life an
adventure in spite of hardships, disap-
pointments, and failure. Bellow was
also inspirational as a teacher. He is
most closely identified with the University of Chicago. The fact that Bellow was married and divorced four
times reflects the quixotic spirit seen
in Augie March, Eugene Henderson,
and other autobiographical creations.

Among his numerous honors, Bellow received National Book Awards for *The
Adventures of Augie March* in 1954, *Herzog* in 1964, and *Mr. Sammler's Planet* in
1970. His crowning achievement was the Nobel Prize in Literature in 1976. Most of
his fiction concerns a search for self-realization in a confusing, often hostile world.
Bellow's heroes rarely know what they want but know what they do not want: They
are chronically dissatisfied with the complacency, inertia, and materialism around
them. Bellow will be best remembered for his example to writers attempting to discover and declare their identities, often as members of disadvantaged minorities.
Bellow expressed—and was shaped by—the adventurous, iconoclastic, and fiercely
democratic spirit of twentieth century America.

The Adventures of Augie March

TYPE OF WORK: Novel
FIRST PUBLISHED: 1953

The Adventures of Augie March is an autobiographical bildungsroman covering a
Jewish American's struggle to find himself, through trial and error, from the 1920's

through the 1940's. Bellow's hero-narrator Augie March is bewildered by the freedom and opportunities available to Jews in America after centuries of persecution and segregation in other lands.

Augie is a resilient but not a strongly motivated character. Not knowing what he wants, he allows himself to be misguided by a succession of domineering personalities, beginning with the family's tyrannical boarder, Mrs. Lausch, a refugee from czarist Russia, who tries to make him an Old World gentleman.

Augie and his older brother Simon have to go to work while still children to supplement the meager family income. Both quickly become hardened by the streets of Chicago. Criminal acquaintances involve Augie in felonies that nearly get him sent to prison. Augie, however, has a love for education and self-improvement because they offer hope of finding self-realization and escape from the ghetto. The combination of slang and erudite diction Augie uses in telling his story is an outstanding feature of the novel.

Simon is another domineering personality who tries to run Augie's life. Ruthless, money-hungry Simon cannot understand his younger brother's indifference to materialism and despises his bookworm mentality. They have a dynamic love-hate relationship throughout the novel.

Simon marries into a wealthy family and becomes a millionaire, but Augie sees that his unhappy brother is suicidal. Augie wants more from life than money and a loveless marriage. He tries shoplifting, union organizing, smuggling illegal immigrants, managing a punch-drunk boxer, and other fiascos. He experiences many changes of fortune. He plunges into love affairs with women who try to redirect his life. The most formidable is a huntress who collects poisonous snakes and trains an eagle to catch giant iguanas in Mexico.

When World War II comes, Augie joins the Merchant Marine and barely survives after his ship is torpedoed. After the war, he and his wife move to Europe, where he grows rich trading in black-market merchandise. At novel's end he still has not found himself. Augie finds that he has settled for a comfortable but shallow existence, but he realizes that other people have no better understanding of who they are or what they want than he does himself.

During the 1950's and 1960's *The Adventures of Augie March* was popular with young readers because they identified with a protagonist who rejected traditional values and sought self-realization in a world seemingly doomed to atomic annihilation.

Seize the Day

TYPE OF WORK: Novella
FIRST PUBLISHED: 1956

Tommy Wilhelm is a loser. He is divorced, unemployed, broke, undereducated, self-indulgent, and dependent (on pills and his father, among other things). He lives in a hotel in New York City and wants desperately to put his life in order. Tommy, like all Bellow protagonists, has trouble determining how to cope with the modern world.

One of the symbols of Tommy's problems, and those of modern society generally, is his relationship with his father. Tommy's father lives in the same hotel and is disgusted with his son's weakness. He refuses to give the one thing Tommy wants most—sympathy.

Tommy makes one last grasp for success by investing in the commodities market under the dubious influence of Dr. Tamkin. His money quickly evaporates and with it his hopes.

At this lowest point, however, Tommy has an epiphany. He accidentally happens into a church during a funeral and, after looking at the body of a man he does not know, breaks into uncontrollable weeping. Tommy weeps for the man, for himself, and for the human condition. He is transported beyond his own particular problems to a cathartic suffering for all humankind.

Bellow sees the problems of the modern world as essentially matters of the spirit. In a high-pressure, pluralistic, threatening, materialistic world, people must find a way to live and to remain human. Tommy does this by recognizing that human beings, for all their weaknesses—or perhaps because of them—must accept and share one another's burdens. Bellow offers this important response to the modern condition in a comic tale that is a contemporary classic, one which later helped win for him the Nobel Prize.

Humboldt's Gift

TYPE OF WORK: Novel
FIRST PUBLISHED: 1975

The narrator of *Humboldt's Gift*, Charlie Citrine, is a somewhat diminished version of Bellow, a writer of fiction and nonfiction whose career and reputation have flourished during the same years that Humboldt's have declined. Even after death, the outrageous, eccentric figure of Humboldt looms large in Charlie's life, never far out of sight as Charlie grapples with a late-midlife crisis populated by agents, lawyers, accountants, gangsters, lovely ladies, and former wives (his own and Humboldt's).

Set mainly in Chicago in the early 1970's, with frequent flashbacks to an earlier New York, the novel in fact begins when Charlie's Mercedes is vandalized by an ambitious young hoodlum to whom he owes a small gambling debt. The hoodlum, known variously as Ronald or Rinaldo Cantabile, soon intervenes in Charlie's life as a strange kind of "angel" bent on reacquainting him with the life of the common man. Here too the figure of Von Humboldt Fleischer looms, as Cantabile's wife is preparing a doctoral dissertation on Humboldt's life and work.

Haggling over children and finances with his former wife Denise, inevitably attracted to the treacherous young divorcée, Renata Koffritz, Charlie is again haunted by Humboldt's memory when he learns that Humboldt has bequeathed him some apparently worthless papers. Later, marooned in Madrid with Renata's young son after she has deserted them both to elope with a prosperous undertaker, Charlie will learn from the ubiquitous Cantabile that Humboldt's papers indisputably prove his and Charlie's authorship of a pirated script that has since been very profitably filmed. Although daunted by the prospect of further legal action, Charlie will in fact take steps to recover Humboldt's "gift," the tangible evidence of his warped but gifted personality.

James Atlas's life of Schwartz, published in 1977, revealed that many of Humboldt's more implausible actions were directly drawn from Schwartz's life, leaving the line between life and art even more blurred than before. The novel remains one writer's eulogy, testament, and testimony to a difficult but oddly rewarding friendship.

More Die of Heartbreak

TYPE OF WORK: Novel
FIRST PUBLISHED: 1987

For its first thirty pages or so, *More Die of Heartbreak* is exhilarating. Sentences that no one else could have written follow one another in rapid-fire bursts: "What you have to consider is a Jew who moves into the vegetable kingdom, studying leaves, bark, roots, heartwood, sapwood, flowers, for their own sake." They come to the reader via the narrator, thirty-five-year-old Kenneth Trachtenberg, a professor of Russian literature at a midwestern university. While it is abundantly clear that the self-deprecating Kenneth is not to be confused with his creator, he voices many of Bellow's concerns (and is given many good lines). Thus, the novel's opening pages report on America's (and the modern world's) spiritual malaise, updating the diagnosis offered in *Humboldt's Gift* and *The Dean's December*.

All this, the reader assumes, is a prologue to the unfolding of the action—which, as Kenneth outlines it, centers on his relationship with his widowed uncle, Benn Crader, an eminent botanist and a good man, and Benn's disastrous marriage to a much younger woman, Matilda Layamon, not long after having escaped at the last minute from what would have been an equally unsatisfactory union. As Kenneth's narrative proceeds, however, the reader gradually comes to realize that the "prologue" is of a piece with the rest: This is a story in which virtually all the action takes place offstage or in the past, to be recounted in Kenneth's summary or in his reconstruction of conversations with Benn.

Clearly Bellow was aware of the risks: that his readers, deprived of suspense, would quickly weary of Kenneth's digressive ways; that the novel's diagnosis and obliquely proposed cure would remain at the level of commentary. The result is a challenging and at times exasperating book—one that frustrates while it enlightens and delights.

SUGGESTED READINGS

American Studies International 35 (February, 1997).

Atlas, James. *Bellow.* New York: Random House, 2000.

Bellow, Saul. "Moving Quickly: An Interview with Saul Bellow." *Salmagundi* (Spring/Summer, 1995): 32-53.

Bigler, Walter. *Figures of Madness in Saul Bellow's Longer Fiction.* Bern, Switzerland: Peter Lang, 1998.

Bloom, Harold, ed. *Saul Bellow.* New York: Chelsea House, 1986.

Boyers, Robert. "Captains of Intellect." *Salmagundi* (Spring/Summer, 1995): 100-108.

Cronin, Gloria L., and L. H. Goldman, eds. *Saul Bellow in the 1980's: A Collection of Critical Essays.* East Lansing: Michigan State University Press, 1989.

Freedman, William. "Hanging for Pleasure and Profit: Truth as Necessary Illusion in Bellow's Fiction." *Papers on Language and Literature* 35 (Winter, 1999): 3-27.

The Georgia Review 49 (Spring, 1995).

Hollahan, Eugene, ed. *Saul Bellow and the Struggle at the Center.* New York: AMS Press, 1996.

Kiernan, Robert. *Saul Bellow.* New York: Continuum, 1989.

Miller, Ruth. *Saul Bellow: A Biography of the Imagination.* New York: St. Martin's Press, 1991.

Pifer, Ellen. *Saul Bellow Against the Grain.* Philadelphia: University of Pennsylvania Press, 1990.

Contributor: Bill Delaney

Arna Bontemps

BORN: Alexandria, Louisiana; October 13, 1902
DIED: Nashville, Tennessee; June 4, 1973

AFRICAN AMERICAN

Bontemps, recognized as a scholar and historian of the Harlem Renaissance, is considered one of the most significant African American writers.

PRINCIPAL WORKS

CHILDREN'S LITERATURE: *Popo and Fifina: Children of Haiti*, 1932 (with Langston Hughes); *You Can't Pet a Possum*, 1934; *Sad-Faced Boy*, 1937; *The Fast Sooner Hound*, 1942 (with Jack Conroy); *We Have Tomorrow*, 1945; *Slappy Hooper: The Wonderful Sign Painter*, 1946 (with Conroy); *The Story of the Negro*, 1948; *Chariot in the Sky: A Story of the Jubilee Singers*, 1951; *Sam Patch*, 1951 (with Conroy); *The Story of George Washington Carver*, 1954; *Lonesome Boy*, 1955; *Frederick Douglass: Slave, Fighter, Freeman*, 1959; *Famous Negro Athletes*, 1964; *Mr. Kelso's Lion*, 1970; *Young Booker: Booker T. Washington's Early Days*, 1972; *The Pasteboard Bandit*, 1997 (with Hughes); *Bubber Goes to Heaven*, 1998

DRAMA: *St. Louis Woman*, pr. 1946 (with Countée Cullen)

LONG FICTION: *God Sends Sunday*, 1931; *Black Thunder*, 1936; *Drums at Dusk*, 1939

POETRY: *Personals*, 1963

SHORT FICTION: *The Old South*, 1973

NONFICTION: *Father of the Blues*, 1941 (with W. C. Handy; biography); *They Seek a City*, 1945 (with Jack Conroy; revised as *Anyplace but Here*, 1966); *One Hundred Years of Negro Freedom*, 1961 (history); *Free at Last: The Life of Frederick Douglass*, 1971; *Arna Bontemps-Langston Hughes Letters, 1925-1967*, 1980

EDITED TEXTS: *The Poetry of the Negro*, 1949 (revised 1971; with Langston Hughes); *The Book of Negro Folklore*, 1958 (with Hughes); *American Negro Poetry*, 1963; *Great Slave Narratives*, 1969; *Hold Fast to Dreams*, 1969; *The Harlem Renaissance Remembered*, 1972

Arna Bontemps (AHR-nah bahn-tahm), at age twenty-one, accepted a teaching position in New York City at the beginning of the Harlem Renaissance. Through his poetry, novels, short stories, and essays, he became one of that movement's defining writers. Bontemps, whose father was a bricklayer and whose mother, a school-

Arna Bontemps (Library of Congress)

teacher, instilled in him a love of books, was born in Louisiana but, because of white threats against his family, was reared and educated in California, where he graduated from Pacific Union College in 1923.

The Bontemps family settled in the Watts section of Los Angeles in 1905. At the time, they were the only African American family in the neighborhood. When Bontemps was twelve years old, his mother died, and he was sent to live with relatives in the California countryside. There, by becoming his Uncle Buddy's "companion and confidant in the corn rows," Bontemps gained access to a living embodiment of southern black folk culture. According to Bontemps, Uncle Buddy was an "old derelict" who drank alcohol and loved "dialect stories, preacher stories, ghost stories, slave and master stories. He half-believed in signs and charms and mumbo-jumbo, and he believed wholeheartedly in ghosts." Concerned by Uncle Buddy's influence, Bontemps's father sent his son to a white boarding school, admonishing him, "Now don't go up there acting colored." Fifty years later, the rebuke still rankled: Recalling his father's advice in 1965, Bontemps exclaimed, "How dare anyone, parent, schoolteacher, or merely literary critic, tell me not to act colored?" Pride in color and heritage stamps all Bontemps's works.

The African American experience is at the heart of all Bontemps's work. His novel *God Sends Sunday*, which he and Countée Cullen adapted for Broadway in 1946, is based loosely on the life of Uncle Buddy. The work offers a glimpse of the southern racing circuit through the eyes of a black jockey in the late 1800's. Another novel, *Black Thunder*, is based on Gabriel Prosser's slave rebellion. Bontemps edited an anthology, *Great Slave Narratives*, and *The Book of Negro Folklore* in 1958. With Langston Hughes, Bontemps edited *The Poetry of the Negro 1746-1949* (1949). Bontemps was a central figure in the rediscovery and dissemination of African American literature.

Bontemps was a librarian at Fisk University from 1943 to 1965. Although he left to teach at the University of Illinois and then at Yale during the late 1960's, he returned to Fisk in 1971 and remained there until his death in 1973.

God Sends Sunday

TYPE OF WORK: Novel
FIRST PUBLISHED: 1931

In *God Sends Sunday*, set in the 1890's, Bontemps depicts a diminutive black jockey, Little Augie, who lives on a Red River plantation in Louisiana with his older sister. Because he was born with a caul over his face, he is thought to be lucky. He discovers a talent for riding horses, which serves him well when he escapes to New Orleans on a steamboat and becomes a jockey. Augie grows rich, arrogant, and ostentatious. He falls in love with a beautiful young mulatto, Florence Desseau, but learns, to his sorrow, that she is the mistress of his rich white patron. Going to St. Louis to find a woman like Florence, Augie falls in with a crowd of prostitutes, gamblers, and "sugar daddies," one of whom he murders when the man bothers Augie's woman. Returning to New Orleans, Augie at last has Florence as his lover. However, she deserts him, taking his money and possessions. Augie's luck fades, and he declines rapidly into penury and alcoholism. In California, Augie commits another "passion murder" and escapes to Mexico.

The novel exhibits a remarkable joie de vivre among its black characters, but they are primarily caricatures within a melodramatic plot. Bontemps uses black dialect and folklore effectively, making especially good use of the blues, for which Augie has a great affection.

"A Summer Tragedy"

TYPE OF WORK: Short fiction
FIRST PUBLISHED: 1935, in *Opportunity*

"A Summer Tragedy" is Bontemps's best-known, most frequently anthologized, and perhaps most successful short story because of its artistic interlacing of setting, symbolism, characterization, and folklore. As Bontemps's biographer, Kirkland C. Jones, has observed, this story is "to the Bontemps canon what 'Sonny's Blues' has become to Baldwin's short fiction efforts—outstanding."

An elderly black couple, Jennie and Jeff Patton, have for decades been tenant farmers on Greenbrier Plantation in an unnamed southern state. The Pattons are ill, frail, and barely ambulatory; Jennie is nearly blind. Their five adult children have all died in violent situations, none of which is specified, suggesting that life for blacks, particularly the young, was dangerous and uncertain in the South.

The opening scene reveals the old couple dressing in their clean but threadbare black "Sunday-best." Their actions are described slowly and painfully as they prepare for some great, momentous occasion. The story is set in the fullness of the green, fecund, early summer fields; all of nature—plants, animals, and birds—seems to be celebrating life, youth, warmth, and procreation, as contrasted with the aging, pinched, wintry, weary, and deathlike lives of Jennie and Jeff. Nevertheless, they affirm their love for each other and resolve to persevere in their plans, which are not clear to the reader until late in the story. At first, Bontemps's narrative seems almost naturalistic in the tradition of Theodore Dreiser as the Pattons reflect upon their lives of hard, monotonous, futile labor which has left them only more debt-ridden. Their existence seems to be a cruel trap, a vicious, meaningless struggle. They own an old, battered, hard-to-crank Model-T Ford that will later serve a vital but ominous purpose.

Yet the story is not merely documentary with dreary details. Jeff and Jennie are presented as three-dimensional characters through a psychological point of view that allows the reader to share their thoughts, feelings, and memories. Bontemps has also skillfully used folk motifs to provide both verisimilitude and foreshadowing. For example, the Pattons' sickly "frizzly" chickens, which are supposed to protect the farm from evil spirits by devouring them, seem to be as death-doomed as their owners.

Jeff reflects on the many mules he has worn out in his years of plantation toil. His stingy employer has allowed him to have only one mule at a time; thus a long succession of mules has been killed by excessive and unremitting toil. Jeff is not aware that he is symbolically a mule for whom the callous old Major Stevenson has also had no sympathy. Moreover, Jeff himself has never felt pity for a man who is too weak to work.

Passing a neighbor's house on the journey through the countryside, Jennie is silently amused to think that their neighbor, Delia, who sees the Pattons' car drive past, is consumed with curiosity to know their destination. Delia, it seems, had once made passes at Jeff when he was a young married man. By refusing to supply Delia with any information, Jennie feels she is punishing her neighbor for her long-ago indiscretion. Such details help to humanize and individualize Bontemps's characters, making them psychologically credible. The reader gradually becomes aware that because of the couple's love for each other and their fear that one may grow too weak to help the other, they are determined to perish together.

As the Pattons near the high banks of the river levee, they can hear the rushing water. They drive over the levee and into the dark, swirling water. (Some readers contend that the stream is Louisiana's Red River, which flows near Bontemps's birthplace.) In death, Jeff and Jennie have preserved their independence and dignity. As the car sinks, one wheel sticks up out of the mud in a shallow place—fate's ironical monument to the lives and courageous deaths of Jeff and Jennie Patton. Free of histrionics and sentimentality, this well-handled story is, as critic Robert Bone contends, truly "compelling."

Black Thunder

TYPE OF WORK: Novel
FIRST PUBLISHED: 1936

Black Thunder, Bontemps's defining novel, is a fictionalized account of the early nineteenth century Gabriel Insurrection, in Virginia. The novel, which chronicles the Gabriel Prosser-led rebellion against the slave owners of Henrico County, was generally lauded by critics as one of the most significant black American works of fiction. Richard Wright praised the work for dealing forthrightly with the historical and revolutionary traditions of African Americans.

Gabriel Prosser, a slave convinced that anything "equal to a grey squirrel wants to be free," urges the other slaves to revolt against their owners. The rebellion is hastened when a brutal slave owner whips a slave, Bundy, to death. Even though the rebellion ultimately fails, Gabriel Prosser nonetheless emerges as a potent hero. The "power of black folk" credo is central to *Black Thunder*. Bontemps's treatment of Bundy's funeral is faithful in detail to the customs of the time. Bontemps's use of signs and portents pushes the story to its heroic ending. Stunning characterizations of Pharaoh, Drucilla, Ben, and Gabriel become multileveled, believably universal personalities through Bontemps's skillful use of folk material. Elements of magic appear in *Black Thunder* just as they appear in folktales and beliefs as recorded by collectors.

Bundy's spirit returns to haunt Pharaoh, the slave who betrays the rebellion and whose death is foreshadowed. Use of charms and countercharms is rampant, conjure-poisoning looms at all times, and rebellious slaves debate omens in the stars. The tapestry that Bontemps weaves shows the intricate beliefs of slaves to be colorful and compelling. Bontemps's narrative techniques have origins in black folklore about death, ghosts, and spirits.

Black Thunder's strength, largely, is in its depiction of an alternate worldview, which, while retaining the power to sanctify or punish, is painfully adapting to a new land and people. Critics note that Bontemps situates his story in the politics of the times: Readers see blame for slave unrest placed at the feet of Thomas Jefferson during John Quincy Adams's bitter reelection campaign. Bontemps depicts the Virginia legislature debate considering sectional segregation of blacks, slaves and free, and chronicles the press. *Black Thunder* was written during the 1930's; some critics believe it reflects the mood of the Depression.

Drums at Dusk

TYPE OF WORK: Novel
FIRST PUBLISHED: 1939

Drums at Dusk, like *Black Thunder*, is a historical novel in which Bontemps makes use of slave narratives and legal records to establish background for the black rebellion leading to Haiti's independence and Toussaint-Louverture's ascendancy. Bontemps centers the story on a young girl of French ancestry, Celeste Juvet, and Diron de Sautels, an aristocratic young Frenchman who claims membership in Les Amis des Noirs, embraces enthusiastically the ideas of writers of the French Revolution, and works as an abolitionist. Celeste and her grandmother reside on a large plantation where the owner's cousin, Count Armand de Sacy, abuses ailing slaves and mistreats his mistresses, abandoning them at his uncle's. De Sacy is deeply disliked, and when several slaves foment an insurrection, the aristocrats are overturned and rebel leaders successfully seize power.

Diron de Sautels's radical opinions influence young blacks, and they fight with three other groups for political control of Santo Domingo: rich aristocrats, poor whites, and free mulattos. *Drums at Dusk* describes with melodramatic sensationalism the sybaritic lives of the wealthy and their sexual exploitation of light-skinned black women. Moreover, the novel describes graphically the heinous conditions on the slave ships and on many of the plantations. The patricians' cruelty and abuse lead to a rapid spread of liberal ideology and the rise of such leaders as Toussaint-Louverture.

In spite of its faults, Bontemps's last novel, like his second one, emphasizes the universal need and desire for freedom, which he intimates is as necessary for the survival of human beings as water, air, food, and shelter.

Great Slave Narratives

TYPE OF WORK: Edited text
FIRST PUBLISHED: 1969

Great Slave Narratives, Bontemps's 1960's revival of a once-popular American literary genre, is a compilation of three book-length narratives written by former slaves. During much of the nineteenth century, slave narratives were best sellers for American publishers. The reintroduction of this literary form was inspired by the Black Power movement of the 1960's and 1970's and the resurgent interest in black culture and the African American experience. Readers were again curious about how it felt to be black and a slave; they wanted to know how the world looked through the eyes of one who had achieved a measure of freedom by effort and suffering. Who, readers wanted to know, were the people who had passed through the ordeal, and how had they expressed their thoughts and feelings?

Bontemps chose for this book three outstanding examples of the genre. The first, *The Interesting Narrative of the Life of Olaudah Equiano, or Gustavus Vassa, the African* (1789), by Olaudah Equiano, who was given the name Gustavus Vassa, gained wide attention, and is particularly interesting for the author's vivid recall of his African background. In 1794, it went into its eighth edition, with many more to follow in America and Europe.

The second book, *The Fugitive Blacksmith; Or, Events in the History of James W. C. Pennington, Pastor of a Presbyterian Church, New York, Formerly a Slave in the State of Maryland, United States* (1850), is the tale of a full-blooded African who was honored with the degree of doctor of divinity by the University of Heidelberg, Germany. Yale University denied him admission as a regular student but did not interfere when he stood outside the doors of classrooms in order to hear professors lecture. Pennington also was the first black to write a history of his people in America: *A Text Book of the Origin and History of the Colored People* (1841).

The final narrative in the trilogy, *Running a Thousand Miles for Freedom: Or, The Escape of William and Ellen Craft from Slavery* (1860), an exciting story of a courageous slave couple's escape, is perhaps the high point in the development of the slave narrative genre. Apparently no two slaves in their flight from subjugation to freedom ever thrilled the world so much as did this handsome young couple. Not everyone was pleased, however. President James Polk was so infuriated by their success that he threatened to use the Fugitive Slave Law and the military in their re-capture. By then the Crafts were in England.

Bontemps, in his introduction to *Great Slave Narratives*, explained the importance of this "half-forgotten history," placing it in the context of American literature: "Hindsight," he wrote, "may yet disclose the extent to which this writing, this impulse, has been influential on subsequent American writing, if not indeed on America's view of itself. . . . The standard literary sources and the classics of modern fiction pale in comparison as a source of strength."

The Old South

TYPE OF WORK: Short fiction
FIRST PUBLISHED: 1973

The Old South, Arna Bontemps's collection of short stories, contains fourteen selections, the first of which is an important essay, "Why I Returned," an account of his early life in Louisiana and California and his later life in Alabama and Tennessee. All of the selections are set in the South of the 1930's (a time when this region was yet unchanged and thus "old") or concern characters from the South. Some of the stories are also autobiographical—"The Cure," "Three Pennies for Luck," "Saturday Night"—and some are sharply satirical portraits of influential white women: a wealthy patron of young black musicians in "A Woman with a Mission" and a principal of a black boarding school in "Heathens at Home." The titles of these latter stories are self-explanatory.

Bontemps was brought up in the Seventh-day Adventist Church, for which his father had abandoned the Creoles' traditional Catholicism. The boarding school and college Bontemps attended as well as the academy where he taught in Alabama were sponsored by the Adventists. Though Bontemps did not remain active in this church, he was deeply religious all his life. Several of his stories thus have religious settings and themes, including "Let the Church Roll On," a study of a black congregation's lively charismatic church service. Bontemps was early influenced by music, since his father and other relatives had been blues and jazz musicians in Louisiana. "Talk to the Music," "Lonesome Boy, Silver Trumpet," and "A Woman with a Mission" all concern young black musicians.

Several selections concern black folk culture and folklore: "The Cure," "Lonesome Boy, Silver Trumpet," and "The Devil Is a Conjurer." The latter story reflects the human desire to invest nature with a sense of the mysterious, which unimaginative men find foolish and unprofitable. In addition, at least seven of Bontemps's stories, including the three named above, involve a young boy or man seeking or discovering meaning and worth in family and community, which some Bontemps scholars believe was a principal desire in the author's own life. Bontemps's short stories treat sensitive political, economic, and social themes that are also employed in his two novels of slave revolts, *Black Thunder* and *Drums at Dusk*.

"Boy Blue" concerns an escaped black murderer who is hunted down and killed after he commits a second homicide. The action in this story is seen from two perspectives, that of a young child and of the criminal himself. Critic Robert Bone argues that the criminal named Blue is in fact "Bontemps's apotheosis of the blues hero." In his best stories Bontemps achieves an aesthetic distance, a mastery of literary form, and a belief in transcendence in spite of his characters' struggles in a world that often denies them human value. Though Bontemps's stories have been compared with those of Richard Wright, Bontemps's are less angry and acerbic.

SUGGESTED READINGS

Bone, Robert. "Arna Bontemps." *Down Home: A History of Afro-American Short Fiction from Its Beginnings to the End of the Harlem Renaissance.* New York: G. P. Putnam's Sons, 1975.

Canaday, Nicholas. "Arna Bontemps: The Louisiana Heritage." *Callaloo* 4 (October-February, 1981): 163-169.

Jones, Kirkland C. "Bontemps and the Old South." *African American Review* 27, no. 2 (1993): 179-185.

_____. *Renaissance Man from Louisiana: A Biography of Arna Wendell Bontemps.* Westport, Conn.: Greenwood Press, 1992.

Reagan, Daniel. "Voices of Silence: The Representation of Orality in Arna Bontemps' *Black Thunder.*" *Studies in American Fiction* 19 (Spring, 1991): 71-83.

Stone, Albert. "The Thirties and the Sixties: Arna Bontemps' *Black Thunder.*" In *The Return of Nat Turner: History, Literature, and Cultural Politics in Sixties America.* Athens: University of Georgia Press, 1992.

Yardley, Jonathan. Review of *The Old South. The New York Times Book Review*, December, 1973, 11.

Contributors: Barbara Day and Philip A. Tapley

Cecilia Manguerra Brainard

BORN: Cebu, Philippines; November 21, 1947

FILIPINO AMERICAN

Brainard has reminded American readers of how
Filipinos earned their independence.

PRINCIPAL WORKS

LONG FICTION: *Song of Yvonne*, 1991 (pb. in U.S. as *When the Rainbow Goddess Wept*, 1994); *Magdalena*, 2002
SHORT FICTION: *Woman with Horns, and Other Stories*, 1987; *Acapulco at Sunset, and Other Stories*, 1995
NONFICTION: *Philippine Woman in America: Essays*, 1991; *Cecilia's Diary, 1962-1969*, 2003
EDITED TEXTS: *Fiction by Filipinos in America*, 1993; *Contemporary Fiction by Filipinos in America*, 1997; *Growing Up Filipino: Stories for Young Adults*, 2003

Born one year after the Philippines gained its independence, Cecilia Manguerra Brainard (seh-SEE-lee-ah mahn-GEHR-rah BRAYN-urd) was surrounded from the start with a sense of her country's having been born at almost the same time as herself. After centuries of Spanish colonialism, more than four decades of American control, and four years of Japanese occupation, finally, in 1946, Filipinos were free to determine their own future. The Americans had helped prepare for this moment through elective models and had fought side by side with Filipinos during the war, and the Americans were vital to the difficult postwar reconstruction, but Brainard grew up well aware of her fellow Filipinos' own proud contributions toward establishment of an independent Philippines. The street on which she lived in Cebu was called Guerrillero Street in honor of her father, a guerrilla and then a civil engineer involved in rebuilding shattered Philippine cities. Many of the anecdotes in her first novel, *Song of Yvonne*, came from tales of war remembered by her family.

As a result, even when Brainard left home for graduate studies at the University of California at Los Angeles in the late 1960's, she brought with her an identity as a Filipina. She married a former member of the Peace Corps, Lauren Brainard, who had served on Leyte, an island close to Cebu. In California, she worked on documentary film scripts and public relations from 1969 to 1981. Then she began the newspaper columns later collected in *Philippine Woman in America*, which describe the enrichment and frustration felt by Philippine Americans who are straddling two cultures. Conscious of her own Americanization and anxious to provide her three sons with cultural choices, she formed Philippine American Women Writers and Artists, an organization intent on publishing remembered legends and scenes from the contributors' childhoods. Brainard's organization was intended to provide a continuum of presence from varied pasts to a shared future. Such dedication to the "memory of a people" is in the ancient Philippine tradition of the female *babaylan*, or priestess.

Woman with Horns, and Other Stories
TYPE OF WORK: Short fiction
FIRST PUBLISHED: 1987

The stories in this collection by Brainard derive from the author's attempt to compensate for the fact that Filipino culture, for hundreds of years, was considered too primitive to be significant in the eyes of nations such as Spain, the United States, and Japan. The author's nationalism (reinforced by nostalgia after her immigration to California) is reinforced by her placing many of the tales in Ubec—the reverse spelling of Cebu, the Philippine island of the author's birth. The fact that invading forces so often destroyed or neglected native records provided the final impulse for Brainard to depend on her imagination for invention of details wherever history has been forced to remain silent. Her stories also show her division of allegiance between her native land and her adopted country.

An example of Brainard's creative approach to history is found in the story "1521." The failure of Ferdinand Magellan to complete his circumnavigation of the world is usually explained by his coming between two hostile Filipino chiefs. Yet "1521" suggests that Lapu-Lapu may have killed Magellan in revenge for the death of Lapu-Lapu's infant son at Spanish hands. "Alba," however, shows more tolerance when, in 1763, during the English occupation of Manila, Doña Saturnina gives birth to a fair-skinned son. The son is accepted by her husband. Similarly, in "The Black Man in the Forest" old guerrilla general Gregorio kills an African American soldier but will not let his body be cannibalized despite near-starvation brought on by the Philippine-American War. The title story recounts how, in 1903, an American public health director finds renewed interest in life, after the death of his wife, with Agustina, a seductive Filipina widow. The effects of war are remarked in "Miracle at Santo Niño Church," in which Tecla suffers nightmares about the Japanese who bayoneted her family. "The Blue-Green Chiffon Dress" uses the period of the Vietnam War as occasion for a brief encounter between Gemma and a soldier heading back to combat. "The Discovery" describes a Filipina's torn loyalties between her American husband and a former Filipino lover who, like her homeland, seems ravaged by time and violent circumstance.

The collection does not observe the historical sequence. For the modern Filipino, perhaps, all past time is being experienced for the first time by a people whose history has been withheld from them. In any given period, however, Filipino resilience has proved to outweigh victimization. Melodrama in the stories' circumstances repeatedly gives way to quietude and certitude.

SUGGESTED READINGS

Casper, Leonard. *Sunsurfers Seen from Afar: Critical Essays, 1991-1996.* Metro
  Manila, Philippines: Anvil, 1996.
Zapanta Manlapaz, Edna. *Songs of Ourselves.* Metro Manila, Philippines: Anvil,
  1994.

Contributor: Leonard Casper

Edward Kamau Brathwaite

BORN: Bridgetown, Barbados, West Indies; May 11, 1930

AFRICAN AMERICAN CARIBBEAN

Brathwaite epitomizes the intensified ethnic and
national awareness of his generation of writers, whose
writing seeks to correct the destructive effects of
colonialism on West Indian sensibility.

PRINCIPAL WORKS

DRAMA: *Four Plays for Primary Schools*, pr. 1961; *Odale's Choice*, pr. 1962, pb. 1967

POETRY: *Rights of Passage*, 1967; *Masks*, 1968; *Islands*, 1969; *The Arrivants: A New World Trilogy*, 1973 (includes *Rights of Passage*, *Masks*, and *Islands*); *Days and Nights*, 1975; *Other Exiles*, 1975; *Black + Blues*, 1977; *Mother Poem*, 1977; *Word Making Man: A Poem for Nicólas Guillèn*, 1979; *Sun Poem*, 1982; *Third World Poems*, 1983; *Jah Music*, 1986; *X/Self*, 1987; *Sappho Sakyi's Meditations*, 1989; *Shar*, 1990; *Middle Passages*, 1992; *Words Need Love Too*, 2000; *Ancestors: A Reinvention of "Mother Poem," "Sun Poem," and "X/Self,"* 2001; *Born to Slow Horses*, 2005; *DS (2): dreamstories*, 2007

SHORT FICTION: *Dreamstories*, 1994

NONFICTION: *Folk Culture of the Slaves in Jamaica*, 1970; *The Development of Creole Society in Jamaica, 1770-1820*, 1971; *Caribbean Man in Space and Time*, 1974; *Contradictory Omens: Cultural Diversity and Integration in the Caribbean*, 1974; *Our Ancestral Heritage: A Bibliography of the Roots of Culture in the English-Speaking Caribbean*, 1976; *Wars of Respect: Nanny, Sam Sharpe, and the Struggle for People's Liberation*, 1977; *Barbados Poetry, 1661-1979: A Checklist*, 1979; *Jamaica Poetry: A Checklist*, 1979; *The Colonial Encounter: Language*, 1984; *History of the Voice: The Development of Nation Language in Anglophone Caribbean Poetry*, 1984; *Roots: Essays in Caribbean Literature*, 1993; *The Zea Mexican Diary*, 1993

EDITED TEXT: *New Poets from Jamaica: An Anthology*, 1979

Edward Kamau Brathwaite (kah-MAW BRATH-wayt) was born Lawson Edward Brathwaite in Bridgetown, Barbados, on May 11, 1930, the son of Hilton Brathwaite and Beryl Gill Brathwaite. He enrolled at Harrison College in Barbados but won the Barbados Scholarship in 1949, enabling him the next year to read history at Pembroke College, University of Cambridge, England. He received an honors degree in 1953 and the Certificate of Education in 1955.

His earliest published poems appeared in the literary journal *Bim*, beginning in 1950. The poems of that decade, some of which are collected in *Other Exiles* and, in revised form, in *The Arrivants*, portray an estranged world fallen from grace, a world that can be redeemed through poetic vision—a creative faith that sustains the more complex fashionings of his later work. Brathwaite shared with other West Indian writers of his generation a strong sense of the impossibility of a creative life in the Caribbean and the equal impossibility of maintaining identity in exile in England or North America. That crisis of the present he understood as a product of his island's cultural heritage fragmented among its several sources: European, African, Amerindian, and Asian.

His reading of history at Cambridge heightened both his sense of the European culture that had been the dominant official culture of the West Indies and his need to understand the African culture that had come with the slaves on the Middle Passage. His search led him to Africa, where from 1955 to 1962 he served as an education officer in Kwame Nkrumah's Ghana. His career in Ghana (and in Togoland in 1956-1957 as United Nations Plebiscite Officer) provided the historical and local images that became *Masks*, the pivotal book of *The Arrivants*. In Ghana, he established a children's theater and wrote several plays for children (*Four Plays for Primary Schools*, 1961, and *Odale's Choice*, 1962). He married Doris Welcome in 1960, and has a son, Michael Kwesi Brathwaite.

Brathwaite returned to the West Indies after an exile of twelve years to assume a post as Resident Tutor at the University of the West Indies in St. Lucia (1962-1963) and to produce programs for the Windward Islands Broadcasting Service. His return to the Caribbean supplied the focus that his poetry had lacked:

> I had, at that moment of return, completed the triangular trade of my historical origins. West Africa had given me a sense of place, of belonging; and that place . . . was the West Indies. My absence and travels, at the same time, had given me a sense of movement and restlessness—rootlessness. It was, I recognized, particularly the condition of the Negro of the West Indies and the New World.

The exploration of that sense of belonging and rootlessness in personal and historic terms is the motive for Brathwaite's subsequent work in poetry, history, and literary criticism. He began in 1963 as lecturer in history at the University of the West Indies at Kingston, Jamaica; he became a professor of social and cultural history there. He earned his Ph.D. at the University of Sussex in England (1965-1968). His dissertation became *The Development of Creole Society in Jamaica, 1770-1820*, a study of the assimilation of cultures by various groups within the colonial hierarchy.

During the 1980's, Brathwaite continued to produce important literary criticism and poetry collections. The 1986 death of his wife, Doris, marked a critical juncture in his career. The shock came in the midst of a series of publications that year: a retrospective collection of essays (*Roots: Essays in Caribbean Literature*); a retrospective collection of poems (*Jah Music*); and Doris's own labor of love, the bibliography *EKB: His Published Prose and Poetry, 1948-1986*. Another blow came in

1988, when Hurricane Gilbert virtually destroyed Brathwaite's house and buried most of his library in mud, entombing an unequaled collection of Caribbean writing as well as Brathwaite's own papers. Even more harrowing was a 1990 break-in and physical attack against Brathwaite in his Marley Manor apartment in Kingston, Jamaica. These events helped in his decision to leave Jamaica in 1991, when he began his tenure at New York University, teaching comparative literature. He would later remarry, to Beverley Reid, and spend the years 1997-2000 at his home CowPastor in Barbados. He was the winner of the 2006 Griffin Poetry Prize, the world's richest poetry prize. Other honors include the Neustadt International Prize for Literature, the Bussa Award, and the Casa de las Américas Prize.

The Arrivants

TYPE OF WORK: Poetry
FIRST PUBLISHED: 1973

That movement can be discerned in the three books of *The Arrivants* through the poet's reconstruction of racial history and his tracing of his personal history. *Rights of Passage*, the first book of the trilogy, contains the restless isolation of his early life in Barbados that sends him into exile in England and Africa, as well as a recollection of the first phase of the black diaspora, the advent of the slave trade and the Middle Passage. The original dispersal of tribes from Ethiopia to West Africa, as well as his own search for his African origins, is the subject of *Masks*. In *Islands*, racial and personal histories merge in the exile's return to the West Indies. The fruits of that return will become manifest in his planned second trilogy.

Readers of *The Arrivants* who focus on its historical dimension figure Brathwaite as the epic poet of the black diaspora, while those who focus on the autobiography make him the hero of the poem. Taking both approaches as valid, with the binocular vision that the poem requires, one can see that the central figure of the rootless, alienated West Indian in exile and in search of home is the only possible kind of hero for a West Indian epic. That questing poet's voice is, however, often transformed into the voice of a precolonial African being fired upon by a white slaver; the Rastafarian Brother Man; Uncle Tom; a *houngan* (male high priest) invoking Legba; or some other historic or mythic figure. Brathwaite's use of personas, or masks, derives equally from the traditions of Greek drama (dramatic monologue) and African religious practice (chant or invocation). One communal soul speaks in a multiplicity of guises, and the poet thereby re-creates not only his own quest as victim and hero but also the larger racial consciousness in which he participates. The poet's many masks enable him to reconstruct his own life and the brutal history that created "new soil, new souls, new ancestors" out of the ashes of the past.

Combining racial history and personal quest in *The Arrivants*, Brathwaite has fashioned a contemporary West Indian myth. It is not the myth of history petrified into "progress" but that of a people's endurance through cycles of brutal oppression. Across centuries, across the ocean, and across the three books of this poem, images, characters, and events overlie one another to defy the myth of progress, leading in the poem only to heaven swaying in the reinforced girders of New York and to the God of capitalism floating in a soundless, airtight glass bubble of an office, a prisoner of his own creation. For the "gods" who tread the earth below, myth is cyclical, and it attaches them to the earth through the "souls" of their feet in repetitions of exodus and arrival.

The trilogy begins with one tribe's ancient crossing of the Sahara Desert, their wagons and camels left where they had fallen, and their arrival at a place where "cool/ dew falls/ in the evening." They build villages, but the cattle towns breed flies and flies breed plague, and another journey begins, for across the "dried out gut" of the riverbed, a mirage shimmers where

> trees are
> cool, there
> leaves are
> green, there
> burns the dream
> of a fountain
> garden of odours
> soft alleyways.

This is the repeated pattern of their history: exodus across desert, savanna, ocean; in caravan, ship, or jet plane; visitations of plague, pestilence, famine, slavery, poverty, ignorance, volcanoes, flood. The promised land is always elsewhere, across the parched riverbed ("Prelude") or in the bountiful fields of England, not in Barbados ("The Cracked Mother").

The connections between history and biography and the difficult process of destroying the colonial heritage in favor of a more creative mode of life are evident in the six poems that constitute the "Limbo" section of *Islands*. In "The Cracked Mother," the first poem of "Limbo," the dissociation of the West Indian's sensibility—regarding attitudes toward self, race, and country—threatens to paralyze the poet's dialectical movement toward a sustaining vision. The poet's rejection of his native land in favor of England is an acceptance of the colonial's position of inferiority. That attitude is instilled in young West Indians, historians such as Walter Rodney, Frantz Fanon, and Brathwaite have argued, by the system of colonial education that taught an alien and alienating value system. The debilitating effects of such an education are the subject of "The Cracked Mother." The three nuns who take the child from his mother to school appear as "black specks . . . / Santa Marias with black silk sails." The metaphor equates the nuns' coming with that of Columbus and anticipates the violence that followed, especially in the image of the nuns' habits as the sails of death ships. With her child gone, the mother speaks in the second part of the poem as a broken ("cracked") woman reduced to muttering children's word games that serve as the vehicle for her pain:

> See?
> She saw
> the sea . . .
> I saw
> you take
> my children . . .
> You gave your
> beads, you
> took
> my children . . .
> Christ on the Cross
> your cruel laws teach
> only to divide us
> and we are lost.

History provides the useful equation of nuns' habits with sails and the nuns' rosary with the beads that Columbus gave to the inhabitants of his "discovered" lands, but it is Brathwaite's own biography that turns metaphor into revelation in the last two parts of the poem, showing how ruinous the colonial mentality is, even to the point of rejecting the earth under one's feet (another "cracked mother") because it is not England.

Brathwaite's corrective begins in "Shepherd," the second poem of the "Limbo" section. Having recalled the damage of his early education and having felt again some of the old abhorrence of the colonial for himself, the poet returns to the African drumbeats of *Masks* to chant a service of possession or reconnection with the gods of his ancestors. The poet then addresses his peers in proverbs, as would an elder to his tribe:

> But you do not understand.
> For there is an absence of truth
> like a good tooth drawn from the tight skull
> like the wave's tune gone from the ship's hull
> there is sand
> but no desert where water can learn of its loveliness.

The people have gifts for the gods but do not give them, yet the gods are everywhere and waiting. Moving in *Islands* toward the regeneration promised in *Masks*, Brathwaite continues with "Caliban" to explore the potential for liberty inherent in the Cuban Revolution, then moves at the moment of triumph back into the slave ship and the limbo that contained the seeds of African religion and identity.

The "Limbo" section ends with the beautiful poem "Islands," which proposes the alternatives that are always present in every moment of Caribbean history: "So looking through a map/ of the islands, you see/ . . . the sun's/ slums: if you hate/ us. Jewels,/ if there is delight/ in your eyes." The same dichotomy of vision has surrounded every event and personage in the poem, all infolded upon the crucial event of the Middle Passage: Did it destroy a people or create one? Brathwaite's account of the voyage in "New World A-Comin" promises "new worlds, new waters, new/

harbours" on one hand, and on the other, "the flesh and the flies, the whips and the fixed/ fear of pain in this chained and welcoming port."

The gods have crossed with the slaves to new soil, and the poet has returned to the origin of his race to discover his communal selfhood in African rite, which requires participation by all to welcome the god who will visit one of them. *The Arrivants* is a long historical and autobiographical poem, and it is also a rite of passage for the poet-priest who invites the god to ride him. Brathwaite's incantatory poems in *Masks* are his learning of the priest's ways, which restores his spirit in *Islands*. The refrain "*Attibon Legba/ Ouvri bayi pou'moi*" ("Negus") is the Voodoo *houngan*'s prayer to the gatekeeper god Legba to open the door to the other gods. The prayer is answered in the final poem "*Jou'vert*" ("I Open"), where Legba promises

> hearts
> no longer bound
> to black and bitter
> ashes in the ground
> now waking
> making
> making with their
> rhythms some-
> thing torn
> and new.

Mother Poem

TYPE OF WORK: Poetry
FIRST PUBLISHED: 1977

In *Mother Poem*, the first book of Brathwaite's planned second trilogy, the central figure is not the restless poet but the mother he has left and returned to, the source of his life. The types of motherhood established in "The Cracked Mother" (*The Arrivants*) are reiterated here as the poet's human mother and his motherland, Barbados. Both "mothers" are established in the first poem, "Alpha," the origin. Barbados is the mother-island of porous limestone (thus absorbing all influence of weather and history), cut by ancient watercourses that have dried up in sterility. Her dead streams can be revived only by the transfigured human mother who "rains upon the island with her loud voices/ with her grey hairs/ with her green love." The transfiguration that occurs in the last lines of the book must wait, however, for the woman to endure the dream-killing, soul-killing life of the island that is dominated by "the man who possesses us all," the merchant, the modern agent of bondage ("nametracks").

The mother is his victim, no matter whether she "sits and calls on jesus name" waiting for her husband to come home from work with lungs covered with jute from the sugar sacks or whether she goes out after his death to sell calico cloth, half-soled shoes, and biscuits, or persuades her daughter to sell herself to the man who is waiting: "It int hard, leh me tell you/ jess sad/ so come darlin chile/ leh me tell he you ready you steady you go" ("Woo/Dove").

She gets no help from her men, who are crippled, destroyed, frightened, or sick from their lives of bondage to the merchant. One man goes to Montreal to work for nine years and sends back nothing ("Woo/Dove"), and another goes to work for life in the local plantation, brings nothing home, and loses three fingers in the cane-grinder ("Milkweed"). Nor does she receive comfort from her children, "wearing dark glasses/ hearing aids/ leaning on wine" ("Tear or pear shape"), who were educated by Chalkstick the teacher, a satirical composite of the colonial educator whose job is to see that his pupils "don't clap their hands, shake their heads, tap their feet" or "push bones through each others' congolese nostrils" ("Lix"). Nor does her help come from her sisters ("Dais" and "Nights") or from her Christianity ("Sam Lord").

Rather, the restoration of her powers as life-giver begins in the guttural, elemental, incantatory uttering of "Nametracks," where, as a slave-mother beaten by her owner, she reminds herself and her huddled children in dark monosyllables like the word game of "The Cracked Mother" that they will endure while "e di go/ e go di/ e go dead," that despite all his power, he "nevver maim what me." Her eyes rise from the plot of land she has bought with her meager earnings, the land that has sustained her and her children, to the whole island and a vision of revolutionary solidarity with her people: "de merchants got de money/ but de people got de men" ("Peace Fire"). With full realization that her child will be born to the life of "broken islands/ broken homes" ("Mid/Life"), in "Driftwood," the human mother still chooses to suffer the "pour of her flesh into their mould of bone." The poem ends with the mother re-created in clay by the potter who can work again, in stone by the sculptor whose skill has returned, and in her words gathered by the poet as rain gathering in the dry pools flows once more past the ruins of the slave and colonial world, re-freshing and renewing the ancient life of the island.

Sun Poem

TYPE OF WORK: Poetry
FIRST PUBLISHED: 1982

Brathwaite's second volume on Bajun life moves from *Mother Poem*'s focus on the female characters (and character) of the island to the male principle of the tropical sun and of the various sons of Barbados. The pun of sun/son is derived from a number of historical and mythological associations, including that of Christianity (Brathwaite renames himself Adam as the boy-hero of the poem and spells the pronoun "his" as "ihs" or Iesu Hominum Salvator) and various African traditions. The sun, for instance, contains "megalleons of light," the invented word associating it with the Egyptian god Ra's sun-ship, the galleons of European explorers, and the enormous nuclear energy that eclipses or perhaps anticipates the holocaust that Western man has in his power. The complexity of the sun/son as controlling metaphor, as it evokes various ethnic and historical images, extends through time and geographic space the significance of the narrative, even as it complements and completes the female principle of *Mother Poem*.

The mythologies evoked in the poem contribute to the meaning of the life of the son Adam, as he begins to understand the West Indian male's sunlike course of ascent, dominance, and descent, played out through the rituals of boyhood games and identity seeking, adolescence, adult sexual experience, marriage and paternity, and finally death. In an early encounter, Adam wrestles the bully Batto underwater in a life-or-death rite of passage that initiates him into the comradeship of his peers, but which, Brathwaite suggests, fails (as the other games that "had little meaning" fail) to prepare him for the struggles of adult manhood ("Son"). The types of fathers portrayed ("Clips") fall into roles available from Christian, bourgeois, and Rastafarian cultures that are equally dead-ended. These fathers are unable to pass on to their sons any mode of fulfilling identity or action, even as in his soliloquy the father laments his own diminishment, his being displaced as the head of his family by his own son.

The central incidents of Adam's life introduce him to the cares and costs of adulthood. On his Sunday school trip to the Atlantic coast, he enters the adult world, in part by hearing the story of Bussa's slave rebellion, a story of the painful price one pays for asserting his personhood ("Noom"). He conducts his courtship of Esse ("Return of the Sun") with a blithe but growing awareness of the consequences of one's sexual life in determining social and political roles ("Fleches"). The death of Adam's grandfather ("Indigone"), the final event in the poem, reveals to him the cyclical nature of manhood in which he begins to locate himself: "and i looked up to see my father's eye: wheeling/ towards his father/ now as i his sun moved upward to his eye." The cultural determinants of dispossession and lack of identity that so condition the natural progress and decline of masculine life are transcended in the poem's ultimate vision of a world capable of beginning anew. The final section ("Son") returns to the cosmic, creative domain of the poem's invocation ("Red Rising") but with a clarified focus on creation and growth as the first principles of the natural and hence human world. The image of emerging coral returns the reader to the genesis of the island at the beginning of *Mother Poem* ("Rock Seed"), completing the cycle of the poems with the "coming up coming up coming up" of his "thrilldren" to people a world renewed.

Middle Passages

TYPE OF WORK: Poetry
FIRST PUBLISHED: 1992

A collection of fourteen poems, *Middle Passages* has a running theme regarding the effects of slavery on Caribbean culture and on the world. The title also seems to evoke the grief caused by his wife's death in 1986, an event he personally referred to as "middle passages" in his book with excerpts from his personal diary, *The Zea Mexican Diary*. Thus the title also suggests a spiritual passage that death entails for both the dead and the living. Journeys, especially those to African roots, is a recurring theme in this volume.

"Columbe" suggests the beauty that Christopher Columbus and his entourage must have discovered upon their arrival in the Caribbean: "Yello pouis/ blazed like pollen and thin waterfalls suspended in the green." Told from the perspective of an island inhabitant watching the arrival, it also asks whether Columbus understood the violence to which his discovery would lead: "But did his vision/ fashion as he watched the shore/ the slaughter that his soldiers/ furthered here?"

Music and musicians are a strong presence in the collection as well. "Duke Playing the Piano at 70" pictures Duke Ellington's wrinkled hands as alligator skins gliding along a keyboard. Brathwaite uses a number of devices to evoke a sense of music to the printed page. Several poems call on the rhythm and cadence of different instruments to heighten the theme at hand: "Flutes" lyrically describes the sounds of bamboo flutes, while "Soweto," written about the Soweto massacre, draws on the rhythm of drums.

The history of violence against Africa plays a dominant role here, as it does in so many of Brathwaite's literary works. "The Visibility Trigger" surveys European history of using guns to kill and subdue Third World peoples. Another, "Stone," is dedicated to Mickey Smith, a poet and political activist who was "stoned to death on Stony Hill, Kingston" in 1983.

SUGGESTED READINGS

Brown, Stuart. *The Art of Kamau Brathwaite*. Bridgend, Mid Glamorgan, Wales: Seren, 1995.

Gowda, H. H. Anniah. "Creation in the Poetic Development of Kamau Brathwaite." *World Literature Today* 68, no. 4 (Autumn, 1994): 691.

McWatt, Mark A. "Edward Kamau Brathwaite." In *Fifty Caribbean Writers*, edited by Daryl Cumber Dance. New York: Greenwood Press, 1986.

Povey, John. "The Search for Identity in Edward Brathwaite's *The Arrivants*." *World Literature Written in English* 27 (1987): 275-289.

Rohlehr, Gordon. *Pathfinder: Black Awakening in "The Arrivants" of Edward Kamau Brathwaite*. Tunapuna, Trinidad: Gordon Rohlehr, 1981.

Ten Kortenaar, Neil. "Where the Atlantic Meets the Caribbean: Kamau Brathwaite's *The Arrivants* and T. S. Eliot's *The Waste Land*." *Research in African Literatures* 27, no. 4 (Winter, 1996): 15-27.

Thomas, Sue. "Sexual Politics in Edward Brathwaite's *Mother Poem* and *Sun Poem*." *Kunapipi* 9 (1987): 33-43.

Torres-Saillant, Silvio. *Caribbean Poetic: Towards an Aesthetic of West Indian Literature*. New York: Cambridge University Press, 1997.

Williams, Emily Allen. "Whose Words Are These? Lost Heritage and Search for Self in Edward Brathwaite's Poetry." *CLA Journal* 40 (September, 1996): 104-108.

World Literature Today 68, no. 4 (Autumn, 1994).

Contributor: Robert Bensen

Aristeo Brito

BORN: Ojinaga, Chihuahua, Mexico; October 20, 1942

MEXICAN AMERICAN

Brito writes about the history of his Chicano community and the relationship between the ruling class and its subordinates.

PRINCIPAL WORKS

LONG FICTION: *El diablo en Texas: Literatura chicana*, 1976 (*The Devil in Texas*, 1990)
MISCELLANEOUS: *Cuentos y poemas de Aristeo Brito*, 1974 (stories and poems)

The Chicano writer, poet, and educator Aristeo Brito (ah-rihs-TAY-oh BREE-toh) grew up in Presidio, Texas, which is located across the Rio Grande from Ojinaga. The river, extending approximately two thousand miles from the West Coast to the Gulf Coast, forms a divisional line separating the United States from Mexico. More than just a border, the river is also an imaginary barrier between the ideas, hopes, and aspirations of the two cultures.

In the introduction to Brito's poignant novel *The Devil in Texas*, Charles Tatum discusses Brito's life and the conditions in Ojinaga-Presidio during his youth, which spurred the writing of the novel. Brito was emotionally impacted by the plight of the Mexicans and Chicanos in Ojinaga-Presidio. These were poor people whose lack of education, lack of exposure outside their community, and domination by the white populace made only menial, low-paying, and backbreaking employment available to them: They worked in the irrigated fields that produced fruits, vegetables, and cotton.

After the Treaty of Guadalupe Hidalgo in 1848—the treaty of peace, friendship, limits, and settlement between the United States of America and the Mexican Republic—the Anglo population appropriated much of Texas from the Mexicans. The enforcers of the class system separating the poor Mexicans and Mexican Americans from the Anglos were the Texas Rangers. The Rangers were organized to restrict undocumented Mexican workers from crossing the border and to monitor the behavior of the Mexican and Mexican American population. Ongoing hostility existed between the Rangers and the Chicanos. The Rangers were regarded as protectors of Anglo interests, and they were terrorists against Mexicans and Mexican Americans.

As described in *The Devil in Texas*, the U.S. Border Patrol was considered a counterpart to the Rangers and was equally repressive. When a bridge was built over the Rio Grande between Ojinaga and Presidio, it was the Border Patrol that prevented "illegal" crossings. This bridge, and the continual surveillance over it,

123

restricted passage between Mexico and Texas. In the book, it represents an impediment to the Spanish-speaking people.

His early experiences in Ojinaga-Presidio had a profound effect on Brito, which would haunt him throughout his adulthood. In 1961 he graduated from Presidio High School as class valedictorian. Despite his academic accomplishments, Brito was unable to qualify for induction into the U.S. military because of low intelligence aptitude test scores. Like many local Mexican American youth, his comprehension of English was low. He vowed to become literate in both English and Spanish. In 1965 he graduated with distinction from Sul Ross University in Alpine, Texas, with a major in English. He subsequently received a master's degree in Spanish from the University of Arizona in Tucson.

A turning point in Brito's life occurred with his indoctrination into the Chicano movement. Nationwide, the Chicano movement had awakened cultural pride among Mexican American youth, and the movement was influential in assimilating these youth into American culture and waging war against social ills. Embittered by his experiences in Ojinaga-Presidio, Brito did not intend to return home. He felt compelled to go there, however, so that he could witness the changes he supposed had occurred in his absence. He took a leave from the completion of his doctoral studies in order to return home. Upon his arrival, he found that little had changed. People were still apathetic.

Brito's response was to write about the history of his community and the relationship between the ruling class and its subordinates. The result of his research and lifelong experiences was *The Devil in Texas*, a fictionalized version of his community's history. The novel is divided into three sections that represent Presidio's history in the years 1883, 1942, and 1970. *The Devil in Texas* was originally self-published in 1976. The book was translated into English in 1990.

Aristeo Brito received his Ph.D. from the University of Arizona in 1978 and has taught at the University of Arizona, the University of California at Santa Barbara, and Pima Community College in Tucson. He has been editor of the latter's bilingual literary magazine, *Llueve Tlaloc*, and has taught creative writing.

The Devil in Texas

Type of work: Novel
First published: *El diablo en Texas: Literatura chicana*, 1976 (English translation, 1990)

The Devil in Texas takes place in the town of Presidio, which means prison in Spanish. For the Mexicans who lived there when the town became part of Texas and for subsequent generations of Mexican Americans and Mexicans on both sides of the Rio Grande border, Presidio lived up to its name. The dry and barren land combined with rivalries and prejudice to imprison the workers in poverty and hopelessness. Brito's fragmented vignettes evoke the brutality of life in three periods of the area's history: 1883, 1942, and 1970.

The first section focuses on Ben Lynch, an Anglo landowner who makes his fortune from land stolen from Mexicans. He massacres twenty-six of his own workers and exploits the rest. Francisco Uranga starts a newspaper of protest against such injustices, but he is scorned as a troublemaker even by his own people.

By 1942, the United States Border Patrol has replaced the Texas Rangers as enforcers of Anglo interests, and the Mexican American workers have been displaced by the even-more exploited illegal immigrants. Much of this section is narrated by the unborn son of Francisco Uranga, who speaks from his mother's womb. He has been waiting more than a century to be born, to be the poet and chronicler who leads his people out of sorrow.

In the short section set in 1970, the embryonic narrator of part 2 is now an adult and returns to Presidio for his father's funeral, musing on his father's stunted opportunities. He is surprised to see how many of his father's friends are still living despite the hardships and discrimination they have faced. Their presence raises the hope that his people will unite in a new and victorious struggle.

SUGGESTED READINGS

Martinez, Julio A., ed. and comp. *Chicano Scholars and Writers*. Metuchen, N.J.: Scarecrow Press, 1979.

Martinez, Julio A., and Francisco A. Lomeli, eds. *Chicano Literature: A Reference Guide*. Westport, Conn.: Greenwood Press, 1985.

Tatum, Charles. Review of *El diablo en Texas*, by Aristeo Brito. *World Literature Today* 51, no. 4 (Autumn, 1977).

Contributors: Vivian R. Alexander and Lois A. Marchino

Gwendolyn Brooks

BORN: Topeka, Kansas; June 7, 1917
DIED: Chicago, Illinois; December 3, 2000

AFRICAN AMERICAN

*The first African American author to win the Pulitzer Prize
in poetry, Brooks affirms the power of ordinary people.*

PRINCIPAL WORKS

CHILDREN'S LITERATURE: *Bronzeville Boys and Girls*, 1956; *The Tiger Who Wore White Gloves*, 1974; *Very Young Poets*, 1983
LONG FICTION: *Maud Martha*, 1953
POETRY: *A Street in Bronzeville*, 1945; *Annie Allen*, 1949; *The Bean Eaters*, 1960; *Selected Poems*, 1963; *We Real Cool*, 1966; *The Wall*, 1967; *In the Mecca*, 1968; *Riot*, 1969; *Family Pictures*, 1970; *Aloneness*, 1971; *Black Steel: Joe Frazier and Muhammad Ali*, 1971; *Aurora*, 1972; *Beckonings*, 1975; *Primer for Blacks*, 1980; *To Disembark*, 1981; *Black Love*, 1982; *The Near-Johannesburg Boy*, 1986; *Blacks*, 1987; *Gottschalk and the Grand Tarantelle*, 1988; *Winnie*, 1988; *Children Coming Home*, 1991; *In Montgomery*, 2003
NONFICTION: *The World of Gwendolyn Brooks*, 1971; *Report from Part One*, 1972; *Young Poet's Primer*, 1980
EDITED TEXT: *Jump Bad: A New Chicago Anthology*, 1971

Gwendolyn Brooks's poetry bears the strong impress of Chicago, particularly of the predominantly black South Side where she lived most of her life. Although she was born in Topeka, Kansas, Brooks was taken to Chicago before she was a year old. In many ways she devoted her career to the physical, spiritual, and political exploration of her native city.

Brooks's life and writings are frequently separated into two phases, with her experience at the 1967 Black Writers' Conference at Fisk University in Nashville serving as a symbolic transition. Prior to the conference, Brooks was known primarily as the first black Pulitzer Prize winner in poetry. Although not politically unaware, she held to a somewhat cautious attitude. The vitality she encountered at the conference crystallized her sense of the insufficiency of universalist attitudes and generated close personal and artistic friendships with younger black poets such as Madhubuti, Walter Bradford, and Knight. Severing her ties with the mainstream publishing firm Harper and Row, which had published her first five books, Brooks transferred her work and prestige to the black-owned and operated Broadside Press of Detroit, Third World Press of Chicago, and Black Position Press, also of

Chicago. Her commitment to black publishing houses remained unwavering despite distribution problems that rendered her later work largely invisible to the American reading public.

Educated in the Chicago school system and at Wilson Junior College, Brooks learned her craft under Inez Cunningham Stark (Boulton), a white woman who taught poetry at the South Side Community Art Center in the late 1930's and 1940's. Brooks's mother, who had been a teacher in Topeka, had encouraged her literary interests from an early age. Her father, a janitor, provided her with ineffaceable images of the spiritual strength and dignity of "common" people. Brooks married Henry Blakely in 1939, and her family concerns continued to play a central role in shaping her career. The eleven-year hiatus between the publication of *Annie Allen* and *The*

Gwendolyn Brooks (© Jill Krementz)

Bean Eaters resulted at least in part from her concentration on rearing her two children, born in 1940 and 1951. Her numerous poems on family relationships reflect both the rewards and the tensions of her own experiences. Her children grown, Brooks concentrated on teaching, supervising poetry workshops, and speaking publicly. These activities brought her into contact with a wide range of younger black poets, preparing her for her experience at Fisk. As poet laureate of Illinois, she encouraged the development of younger poets through personal contact and formal competitions.

The division between the two phases of Brooks's life should not be overstated. She evinced a strong interest in the Civil Rights movement during the 1950's and early 1960's; her concern with family continued in the 1980's. Above all, Brooks lived with and wrote of and for the Chicagoans whose failures and triumphs she saw as deeply personal, universally resonant, and specifically black. She died in Chicago on December 3, 2000, at the age of eighty-three.

A Street in Bronzeville

TYPE OF WORK: Poetry
FIRST PUBLISHED: 1945

A Street in Bronzeville, Brooks's first poetry collection, poignantly reflects the reality of oppression in the lives of urban blacks. The poems portraying ordinary yet unforgettable individuals—from the flamboyant Satin Legs Smith to the sad hunchback girl who yearns for a pain-free life—launched Brooks's successful career. The poetic walk through Bronzeville begins with "the old-marrieds," whose longtime exposure to crowded conditions has eliminated loving communication from their lives.

The long-married couple is followed closely by poems exploring how life in a "kitchenette building" thwarts aspirations. Brooks wonders how dreams can endure in a fight with fried potatoes and garbage ripening in the hall. With honesty and love she portrays resilient characters: Pearl May Lee, whose man has been falsely accused of raping a white woman; Mame, the queen of the blues, who has no family and endures the slaps and pinches of rude men in the club where she sings; Moe Belle Jackson, whose husband "whipped her good last night"; and poor baby Percy, who was burned to death by his brother Brucie. Alongside this unblinking look at life's pain, Brooks now and then gently conveys humorous moments, such as the woman at the hairdresser who wants an upsweep to "show them girls" and the domestic worker who thinks her employer is a fool.

Alienation in city life is a theme Brooks explores unflinchingly. Matthew Cole seems to be a pleasant man, but in the dirtiness of his room, with fat roaches strolling up the wall, he never smiles. Maud, in the poem "Sadie and Maud," tries to escape Bronzeville by going to college but finds herself living alone, a thin brown mouse in an old house.

Composed of twelve poems, the last section of the book, "Gay Chaps at the Bar," is dedicated to Brooks's brother, Staff Sergeant Raymond Brooks, and other soldiers who returned from the war trembling and crying. The second poem, "still do I keep my look, my identity," affirms a soldier's individuality even as he dons a government-issue uniform and goes off to meet death on some distant hill. Each body has its pose, "the old personal art, the look."

Ultimately, the critique of America plays itself out in a critique of traditional literary form. Brooks parodies the sonnet in content and form. She uses slant rhyme for the entire collection because she thinks life in Bronzeville is "an off-rhyme situation."

"The Mother"

TYPE OF WORK: Poetry
FIRST PUBLISHED: 1945, in *A Street in Bronzeville*

One of the most powerful poems from *A Street in Bronzeville* is "The Mother," an exploration of the impact of an abortion on the woman who has chosen to have it. Brooks states that the mother "decides that *she*, rather than her world, will kill her children." Within the poem itself, however, the motivations remain unclear. Although the poem's position in the collection suggests that the persona is black, the poem neither supports nor denies a racial identification. Along with the standard English syntax and diction, this suggests that "The Mother," like poems such as "The Egg Boiler," "Callie Ford," and "A Light and Diplomatic Bird," was designed to speak directly of an emotional, rather than a social, experience, and to be as accessible to whites as to blacks. Re-creating the anguished perspective of a persona unsure whether she is victim or victimizer, Brooks directs her readers' attention to the complex emotions of her potential Everywoman.

"The Mother" centers on the persona's alternating desire to take and to evade responsibility for the abortion. Resorting to ambiguous grammatical structures, the persona repeatedly qualifies her acceptance with "if" clauses ("If I sinned," "If I stole your births"). She refers to the lives of the children as matters of fate ("Your luck") and backs away from admitting that a death has taken place by claiming that the children "were never made." Her use of the second-person pronoun to refer to herself in the first stanza reveals her desire to distance herself from her present pain. This attempt, however, fails. The opening line undercuts the evasion with the reality of memory: "Abortions will not let you forget." At the start of the second stanza, the pressure of memory forces the persona to shift to the more honest first-person pronoun. A sequence of spondees referring to the children ("damp small pulps," "dim killed children," "dim dears") interrupts the lightly stressed anapestic-iambic meter that dominates the first stanza. The concrete images of "scurrying off ghosts" and "devouring" children with loving gazes gain power when contrasted with the dimness of the mother's life and perceptions. Similarly, the first stanza's end-stopped couplets, reflecting the persona's simplistic attempt to recapture an irrevocably lost mother-child relationship through an act of imagination, give way to the intricate enjambment and complex rhyme scheme of the second stanza, which highlight the mother's inability to find rest.

The rhyme scheme—and Brooks can rival both Robert Frost and William Butler Yeats in her ability to employ various types of rhyme for thematic impact—underscores her struggle to come to terms with her action. The rhymes in the first stanza insist on her self-doubt, contrasting images of tenderness and physical substance with those of brutality and insubstantiality (forget/get, hair/air, beat/sweet). The internal rhyme of "never," repeated four times, and "remember," "workers," and "singers," further stresses the element of loss. In the second stanza, Brooks provides no rhymes for the end words "children" in line 11 and "deliberate" in line 21. This device draws attention to the persona's failure to answer the crucial questions of whether her children did in fact exist and of whether her own actions were in fact deliberate (and perhaps criminal). The last seven lines of the stanza end with hard "d" sounds as the persona struggles to forge her conflicting thoughts into a unified perspective. If Brooks offers coherence, though, it is emotional rather than intellectual. Fittingly, the "d" rhymes and off-rhymes focus on physical and emotional pain (dead/instead/made/afraid/said/died/cried). Brooks provides no easy answer to the anguished question: "How is the truth to be told?" The persona's concluding cry of "I loved you/ All" rings with desperation. It is futile but it is not a lie. To call "The Mother" an anti-abortion poem distorts its impact. Clearly portraying the devastating effects of the persona's action, it by no means condemns her or lacks sympathy. Like many of Brooks's characters, the mother is a person whose desire to love far outstrips her ability to cope with her circumstances and serves primarily to heighten her sensitivity to pain.

Perhaps the most significant change in Brooks's poetry involves her analysis of the origins of this pervasive pain. Rather than attributing the suffering to some unavoidable psychological condition, Brooks's later poetry indicts social institutions for their role in its perpetuation. The poems in her first two volumes frequently portray characters incapable of articulating the origins of their pain. Although the absence of any father in "The Mother" suggests sociological forces leading to the abortion, such analysis amounts to little more than speculation. The only certainty is that the mother, the persona of the sonnet sequence "The Children of the Poor," and the speaker in the brilliant sonnet "My Dreams, My Works Must Wait Till After Hell" share the fear that their pain will render them insensitive to love. The final poem of *Annie Allen*, "Men of Careful Turns," intimates that the defenders of a society that refuses to admit its full humanity bear responsibility for reducing the powerless to "grotesque toys." Despite this implicit accusation, however, Brooks perceives no "magic" capable of remedying the situation. She concludes the volume on a note of irresolution typical of her early period: "We are lost, must/ Wizard a track through our own screaming weed." The track, at this stage, remains spiritual rather than political.

"We Real Cool"

TYPE OF WORK: Poetry
FIRST PUBLISHED: 1966, in *We Real Cool*

Perhaps Brooks's single best-known poem is the title poem from the collection of the same name. In this poem, Brooks subjects a representative experience to intricate technical and thematic scrutiny, at once loving and critical. The poem is only twenty-four words long, including eight repetitions of the word "we." It is suggestive that the subtitle of "We Real Cool" specifies the presence of only seven pool players at the "Golden Shovel." The eighth "we" suggests that poet and reader share, on some level, the desperation of the group-voice that Brooks transmits. The final sentence, "We/ die soon," restates the carpe diem motif in the vernacular of Chicago's South Side.

On one level, "We Real Cool" appears simply to catalog the experiences of a group of dropouts content to "sing sin" in all available forms. A surprising ambiguity enters into the poem, however, revolving around the question of how to accent the word "we" that ends every line except the last one, providing the beat for the poem's jazz rhythm. Brooks said that she intended that the "we" *not* be accented. Read in this way, the poem takes on a slightly distant and ironic tone, emphasizing the artificiality of the group identity that involves the characters in activities offering early death as the only release from pain. Conversely, the poem can be read with a strong accent on each "we," affirming the group identity. Although the experience still ends with early death, the pool players metamorphose into defiant heroes determined to resist the alienating environment. Their confrontation with experience is felt, if not articulated, as existentially pure. Pool players, poet, and reader cannot be sure which stress is valid.

Brooks crafts the poem, however, to hint at an underlying coherence in the defiance. The intricate internal rhyme scheme echoes the sound of nearly every word. Not only do the first seven lines end with "we," but the penultimate words of each line in each stanza also rhyme (cool/school, late/straight, sin/gin, June/soon). In addition, the alliterated consonant of the last line of each stanza is repeated in the first line of the next stanza (Left/lurk, Strike/sin, gin/June), and the first words of each line in the middle two stanzas are connected through consonance (Lurk/strike, Sing/thin). The one exception to this suggestive texture of sound is the word "Die" that introduces both a new vowel and a new consonant into the final line, breaking the rhythm and subjecting the performance to ironic revaluation. Ultimately, the power of the poem derives from the tension between the celebratory and the ironic perspectives on the lives of the plain black boys struggling for a sense of connection.

The Warpland Poems

TYPE OF WORK: Poetry
FIRST PUBLISHED: 1968-1969

The Warpland poems—"The Sermon on the Warpland," "The Second Sermon on the Warpland," and "The Third Sermon on the Warpland"—mark Brooks's departure from the traditions of Euro-American poetry and thought represented by T. S. Eliot's *The Waste Land* (1922). The first two appeared in *In the Mecca*, and the last appeared in *Riot*. The sequence typifies Brooks's post-1967 poetry, in which she abandons traditional stanzaic forms, applying her technical expertise to a relatively colloquial free verse. This technical shift parallels her rejection of the philosophical premises of Euro-American culture. Brooks refuses to accept the inevitability of cultural decay, arguing that the "waste" of Eliot's vision exists primarily because of our "warped" perceptions. Seeing white society as the embodiment of these distortions, Brooks embraces her blackness as a potential counterbalancing force. The first "Sermon on the Warpland" opens with Ron Karenga's black nationalist credo: "The fact that we are black is our ultimate reality." Clearly, in Brooks's view, blackness is not simply a physical fact; it is primarily a metaphor for the possibility of love. As her poem "Two Dedications" indicates, Brooks sees the Euro-American tradition represented by the Chicago Picasso as inhumanly cold, mingling guilt and innocence, meaningfulness and meaninglessness, almost randomly. This contrasts sharply with her inspirational image of the Wall of Heroes on the South Side. To Brooks, true art assumes meaning from the people who interact with it. The wall helps to redefine black reality, rendering the "dispossessions beakless." Rather than contemplating the site of destruction, the politically aware black art that Brooks embraces should inspire the black community to face its pain with renewed determination to remove its sources. The final "Sermon on the Warpland" concludes with the image of a black phoenix rising from the ashes of the Chicago riot. No longer content to accept the unresolved suffering of "The Mother," Brooks forges a black nationalist politics and poetics of love.

"The Blackstone Rangers"

TYPE OF WORK: Poetry
FIRST PUBLISHED: 1987, in *Blacks*

Although her political vision influences every aspect of her work, Brooks maintains a strong sense of enduring individual pain and is aware that nationalism offers no simple panacea. "The Blackstone Rangers," about one of the most powerful Chicago street gangs, rejects as simplistic the argument—occasionally advanced by writers associated with the Black Arts movement—that no important distinction exists between the personal and the political experience. Specifically, Brooks doubts the corollary that politically desirable activity will inevitably increase the person's ability to love. Dividing "The Blackstone Rangers" into three segments— "As Seen by Disciplines," "The Leaders," and "Gang Girls: A Rangerette"— Brooks stresses the tension between perspectives. After rejecting the sociological-penal perspective of part 1, she remains suspended between the uncomprehending affirmation of the Rangers as a kind of government-in-exile in part 2, and the recognition of the individual person's continuing pain in part 3.

Brooks undercuts the description of the Rangers as "sores in the city/ that do not want to heal" ("As Seen by Disciplines") through the use of off-rhyme and a jazz rhythm reminiscent of "We Real Cool." The disciplines, both academic and corrective, fail to perceive any coherence in the Rangers' experience. Correct in their assumption that the Rangers do not want to "heal" themselves, the disciplines fail to perceive the gang's strong desire to "heal" the sick society. Brooks suggests an essential coherence in the Rangers' experience through the sound texture of part 1. Several of the sound patterns echoing through the brief stanza point to a shared response to pain (there/thirty/ready, raw/sore/corner). Similarly, the accent cluster on "Black, raw, ready" draws attention to the pain and potential power of the Rangers. The descriptive voice of the disciplines, however, provides only relatively weak end-rhymes (are/corner, ready/city), testifying to the inability of the distanced, presumably white, observers to comprehend the experiences they describe. The shifting, distinctively black, jazz rhythm further emphasizes the distance between the voices of observers and participants. Significantly, the voice of the disciplines finds no rhyme at all for its denial of the Rangers' desire to "heal."

This denial contrasts sharply with the tempered affirmation of the voice in part 2 that emphasizes the leaders' desire to "cancel, cure and curry." Again, internal rhymes and sound echoes suffuse the section. In the first stanza, the voice generates thematically significant rhymes, connecting Ranger leader *"Bop"* (whose name draws attention to the jazz rhythm that is even more intricate, though less obvious, in this section than in part 1) and the militant black leader *"Rap"* Brown, both nationalists whose "country is a Nation on no *map*." "Bop" and "Rap," of course, do not rhyme perfectly, attesting to Brooks's awareness of the gang leader's limitations. Her image of the leaders as "Bungled trophies" further reinforces her ambivalence. The only full rhyme in the final two stanzas of the section is the repeated "night." The leaders, canceling the racist association of darkness with evil, "translate" the image of blackness into a "monstrous pearl or grace." The section affirms the Blackstone Rangers' struggle; it does not pretend to comprehend fully the emotional texture of their lives.

Certain that the leaders possess the power to cancel the disfiguring images of the disciplines, Brooks remains unsure of their ability to create an alternate environment where love can blossom. Mary Ann, the "Gang Girl" of part 3, shares much of the individual pain of the characters in Brooks's early poetry, despite her involvement with the Rangers. "A rose in a whiskey glass," she continues to live with the knowledge that her "laboring lover" risks the same sudden death as the pool players of "We Real Cool." Forced to suppress a part of her awareness—she knows not to ask where her lover got the diamond he gives her—she remains emotionally removed even while making love. In place of a fully realized love, she accepts "the props and niceties of non-loneliness." The final line of the poem emphasizes the ambiguity of both Mary Ann's situation and Brooks's perspective. Recommending acceptance of "the rhymes of Leaning," the line responds to the previous stanza's question concerning whether love will have a "gleaning." The full rhyme paradoxically suggests acceptance of off-rhyme, of love consummated leaning against an alley wall, without expectation of safety or resolution. Given the political tension created by the juxtaposition of the disciplines and the leaders, the "Gang Girl" can hope to find no sanctuary beyond the reach of the whirlwind. Her desperate love, the more moving for its precariousness, provides the only near-adequate response to the pain that Brooks saw as the primary fact of life.

SUGGESTED READINGS

Bloom, Harold, ed. *Gwendolyn Brooks*. Philadelphia: Chelsea House, 2005.
Bolden, B. J. *Urban Rage in Bronzeville: Social Commentary in the Poetry of Gwendolyn Brooks, 1945-1960*. Chicago: Third World Press, 1999.

Brooks, Gwendolyn. *Conversations with Gwendolyn Brooks.* Edited by Gloria Wade Gayles. Jackson: University Press of Mississippi, 2003.

Bryant, Jacqueline Imani, ed. *Gwendolyn Brooks and Working Writers.* Chicago: Third World Press, 2007.

"Gwendolyn's Words: A Gift to Us." *Essence* 31, no. 11 (March, 2001): A18.

Hill, Christine M. *Gwendolyn Brooks: "Poetry Is Life Distilled."* Berkeley Heights, N.J.: Enslow, 2005.

Kent, George E. *A Life of Gwendolyn Brooks.* Lexington: University Press of Kentucky, 1990.

Melhem, D. L. *Gwendolyn Brooks: Poetry and the Heroic Voice.* Lexington: University Press of Kentucky, 1987.

Mootry, Maria K., and Gary Smith, eds. *A Life Distilled: Gwendolyn Brooks, Her Poetry and Fiction.* Urbana: University of Illinois Press, 1987.

Rhynes, Martha E. *Gwendolyn Brooks: Poet from Chicago.* Greensboro, N.C.: Morgan Reynolds, 2003.

Wright, Stephen Caldwell, ed. *On Gwendolyn Brooks: Reliant Contemplation.* Ann Arbor: University of Michigan Press, 1996.

Contributors: Carol F. Bender and Craig Werner

Claude Brown

BORN: New York, New York; February 23, 1937
DIED: New York, New York; February 2, 2002

AFRICAN AMERICAN

Brown's autobiography, Manchild in the Promised Land, *is considered one of the best and most realistic descriptions of coming-of-age in a black urban ghetto.*

PRINCIPAL WORKS
LONG FICTION: *The Children of Ham*, 1976
NONFICTION: *Manchild in the Promised Land*, 1965

By the time he was thirteen years old, Claude Brown had been hit by a bus, whipped with chains, thrown into a river, and shot in the stomach. Spending more time on the streets of Harlem than in school, Brown was an accomplished thief by the age of ten, when he became a member of the Forty Thieves, a branch of the infamous Buccaneers gang. In a desperate attempt to save their son from his early downward spiral into the penal system, the Browns sent Claude to live with his grandparents for a year. The sojourn seemed to have had little effect on him, because soon after his return to Harlem he was sent to the Wiltwyck School for emotionally disturbed boys.

Brown's early life was a seemingly endless series of events leading to one form or another of incarceration. All told, Brown was sent to reform school three times, and in between those times he ran con games and sold hard drugs. He avoided heroin addiction only because the one time he tried the drug he nearly died. Avoiding drug dependency may have been the key factor in his ability to escape the fate of early death or lengthy incarceration that met so many of his peers. Sensing that he would perish if he remained in Harlem, Brown moved to Greenwich Village at seventeen and began to attend night school.

As he began to understand that living in the ghetto did not mean a certain destiny of crime, misery, and poverty, he no longer believed that living in Harlem would inevitably ruin his life. While selling cosmetics he devoted many hours daily to playing the piano and eventually enrolled in and graduated from Howard University. During Brown's first year at Howard, he was urged to write about Harlem for a magazine by Ernest Papanek, who had been the school psychologist at Wiltwyck School. As Brown reflected on his life he began to understand what a difficult feat it is to survive the ghetto, and his writing describes the reasons for the general despair found there. The magazine article led to an offer from a publisher for Brown to write what eventually became *Manchild in the Promised Land.*

Brown earned a law degree and spent his life working on behalf of rehabilitating African American youth caught in the criminal justice system. He died in 2002 of respiratory failure.

Manchild in the Promised Land

TYPE OF WORK: Autobiography
FIRST PUBLISHED: 1965

Brown's classic autobiography *Manchild in the Promised Land* is a quintessentially American story of hardship and disadvantage overcome through determination and hard work, but with a critical difference. It became a best seller when it was published in 1965 because of its startlingly realistic portrayal of growing up in Harlem. Without sermonizing or sentimentalizing, Brown manages to evoke a vivid sense of the day-to-day experience of the ghetto, which startled many readers and became required reading, along with *The Autobiography of Malcolm X* (1965), for many civil rights activists.

Manchild in the Promised Land describes Brown's resistance to a life path that seemed predetermined by the color of his skin and the place he was born. In the tradition of the slave narrative of the nineteenth century, Brown sets about to establish his personhood to a wide audience, many of whom would write him off as a hopeless case. The book opens with the scene of Brown being shot in the stomach at the age of thirteen after he and his gang are caught stealing bedsheets off a laundry line. What follows is the story line most would expect of a ghetto child—low achievement in school, little parental supervision, and a sense of hopelessness about the future. There are crime, violence, and drugs lurking in every corner of Harlem, and young Sonny (Claude) falls prey to many temptations.

In spite of spending most of his early years committing various petty crimes, playing hooky from school, living in reform schools, and being the victim of assorted beatings and shootings, Brown manages to elude the destiny of so many of his boyhood friends—early death or successively longer incarcerations. Sensing that he would perish, literally or figuratively, if he remained on the path that seemed destined for him, he leaves Harlem for a few years and begins to chart a different outcome for his life, which includes night school, playing the piano, graduating from Howard University, and beginning law school.

Although Brown offers no formula for escaping the devastation that so often plagues ghetto life, he shows by example that it is possible to succeed in constructing, even in the ghetto, a positive identity.

SUGGESTED READINGS

Baker, Houston A., Jr. "The Environment as Enemy in a Black Autobiography: *Manchild in the Promised Land.*" *Phylon* 32, no. 1 (Spring, 1971).
Davis, Charles T. *Black Is the Color of the Cosmos: Essays on Afro-American Liter-*

ature and Culture, 1942-1981. Edited by Henry L. Gates, Jr. New York: Garland, 1982.

Fremont-Smith, Eliot. "Coming of Age in Harlem: A Report from Hell." *The New York Times*, August 14, 1965, p. 21.

Goldman, Robert M., and William D. Crane. *"Black Boy* and *Manchild in the Promised Land." Journal of Black Studies* 7, no. 2 (December, 1976).

Petesch, Donald A. *A Spy in the Enemy's Country.* Iowa City: University of Iowa Press, 1989.

Rampersad, Arnold. Review of *The Children of Ham*, by Claude Brown. *The New Republic* 174, no. 19 (May 8, 1976): 25-26.

Contributor: Christy Rishoi

Rosellen Brown

BORN: Philadelphia, Pennsylvania; May 12, 1939

JEWISH

Brown is noted for her perceptive treatment of alienation, displacement, exile, and disaster in seemingly ordinary American families.

PRINCIPAL WORKS

LONG FICTION: *The Autobiography of My Mother*, 1976; *Tender Mercies*, 1978; *Civil Wars: A Novel*, 1984; *Before and After*, 1992; *Half a Heart*, 2000
POETRY: *Some Deaths in the Delta, and Other Poems*, 1970; *Cora Fry*, 1977; *Cora Fry's Pillow Book*, 1994
SHORT FICTION: *Street Games*, 1974
EDITED TEXT: *The Whole Word Catalogue*, 1972 (with Marvin Hoffman, Martin Kushner, Philip Lopate, and Sheila Murphy)
MISCELLANEOUS: *A Rosellen Brown Reader: Selected Poetry and Prose*, 1992

Born in Philadelphia to Jewish parents, who moved frequently and much of the time lived in non-Jewish neighborhoods, Rosellen Brown came to feel that she had no roots. She found, however, that she could escape her loneliness by writing, and by the time she was nine she had decided to become a writer.

After earning a B.A. from Barnard College in 1960 and an M.A. from Brandeis University in 1962, Brown began working at her craft. In 1963, she married Marvin Hoffman, an English teacher, and in 1965 the couple went to Mississippi to teach at Tougaloo College and to participate with their black students in the Civil Rights movement. After the birth of her first child, Adina, Brown wrote most of the poems in her first published volume, *Some Deaths in the Delta, and Other Poems*, which were inspired by her often frightening experiences in Mississippi.

After three years at Tougaloo, Brown and her husband moved to Brooklyn, New York, where their daughter Elena was born. In 1972, she collaborated on a lucrative nonfiction volume entitled *The Whole Word Catalogue*. Her real interest, however, was short fiction, and her stories were appearing in magazines and in anthologies, including in the annual publication *O. Henry Prize Stories*, 1972, 1973, and 1976. In 1974, her collection *Street Games* appeared, which contains stories drawn from her multiethnic Brooklyn neighborhood. Most of the stories involve problems with relationships, often within the family.

Grants and honors signaled Brown's increasing status as a writer. In 1973-1974, Brown won a National Endowment for the Humanities creative writing grant. From

1973 to 1975, she was a Radcliffe Institute fellow. During the summer of 1974, she served as a member of the fiction staff at the prestigious Bread Loaf Writers' Conference.

By that time, the family had moved to New Hampshire, where they lived for more than eleven years and where they continued to spend their summers, even after moving to Houston. One day, while weaving, Brown had the experience of seeming to hear a woman's voice that she later identified as resembling that of a Jewish refugee she had met in Mississippi. The experience inspired Brown to write her novel *The Autobiography of My Mother*.

Brown's husband had been supportive of her writing from the start, but it was not until the children were in school that she began to have extended periods of time at her disposal. Even before then, she had been gaining insights and developing the themes that later dominated her novels. By having children, she said, she came to learn a great deal, not only about family ties but also about the precariousness of life. She first develops this theme fully in *The Autobiography of My Mother*. Haunted by a real-life story about a child who had fallen off a precipice when someone let go of its hand, Brown based her plot on that tragedy. Later works, too, reflect her belief that catastrophe is never far away. In *Tender Mercies*, a husband's momentary foolishness results in his wife's becoming a quadriplegic; in *Civil Wars*, the parents of two children die in an automobile accident, leaving the children to live with relatives they do not know; and in *Before and After*, whose plot was suggested by a murder trial in Houston, the teenage son of a respectable family commits a murder.

In her essay "Displaced Persons," Brown describes her fascination with the two most traditional regions of the United States, the South and New England. She was delighted with the southern atmosphere of Houston after moving there in the 1980's. Like her early poems, the novel *Civil Wars* is set in Mississippi. The collections *Cora Fry* and *Cora Fry's Pillow Book* describe the life of a New England woman, and both *Tender Mercies* and *Before and After* use similar small-town settings. In fact, in the latter novel the fictional family lives in Brown's own house in Peterborough, New Hampshire. *Half a Heart*, a complex novel dealing with race, mothers and daughters, and the lack of social commitment in the late 1990's, is set in the South.

In 1982, Brown began teaching in the University of Houston's creative writing program. She continued to win honors for her achievements, including being named "Woman of the Year" by *Ms.* magazine in 1984 and winning the Janet Kafka Award for best novel by an American woman for *Civil Wars*. With *Before and After*, she also attained popular success. Even before publication, the novel was scheduled for production as a motion picture, and soon after it appeared Brown's earlier novels were reissued as paperbacks. In 2000, she became writer-in-residence at Northwestern University. Although Brown has published poetry and short fiction and even experimented with drama, it is her novels for which she is best known. Many consider her to be one of the most compelling contemporary writers.

Before and After

TYPE OF WORK: Novel
FIRST PUBLISHED: 1992

Until Jacob Reiser admits to his parents that he killed his girlfriend, readers of *Before and After* are not sure that he committed the crime. The novel opens in a hospital emergency room as Carolyn Reiser, Jacob's mother, administers to the girl. She soon finds out that her son is accused of bludgeoning her to death.

None of the family members can believe that Jacob is guilty. His failure to appear at home casts suspicion on him, but Carolyn, his father Ben, and his sister Judith try to protect Jacob's innocence, both in their own minds and in material ways. Ben goes the furthest in this. When he finds a bloody jack handle in his son's car trunk, he removes that evidence before police can search the car.

The police eventually capture Jacob. He refuses at first to speak to his parents; it is only after they hire a lawyer and get him released on bail that he confesses to them. The family then splits over the issue of whether Jacob should tell the truth to his lawyer or let the lawyer represent him without knowing the complete story.

Chapters tell the story from three different characters' points of view. Carolyn and Judith's chapters are in the third person, but Ben relates events in the first person. This makes his emotions and his vehement defense of his son even more engaging. The conflict between Carolyn, a logical pediatrician, and Ben, a somewhat flighty artist, over how their son's defense should be conducted forms one strand of the story. Judith's chapters reveal Jacob's character and destroy the innocent image of him created by his parents' recollections, making plausible the idea that he could have killed his girlfriend. Jacob's story comes only through the experiences of others.

SUGGESTED READINGS

Craig, Patricia. "Cripples." *New Statesman* 98 (July 13, 1979): 62-63.

D'Erasmo, Stacey. "Home Fires." *The Nation*, September 28, 1992.

Epstein, Joseph. "Is Fiction Necessary?" *The Hudson Review* 29 (1976-1977): 593-594.

Hulbert, Ann. "In Struggle." *The New Republic* 190 (May 7, 1984): 37-40.

Mehren, Elizabeth. "Making Mayhem in Ordinary Lives." *Los Angeles Times*, September 3, 1992.

Rosenbert, Judith. "Rosellen Brown." *Publishers Weekly* 239 (August 31, 1992): 54-55.

Thurman, Judith. "Rosellen Brown." *Ms.* 13 (January, 1985): 82.

Contributor: Rosemary M. Canfield Reisman

Sterling A. Brown

BORN: Washington, D.C.; May 1, 1901
DIED: Takoma Park, Maryland; January 13, 1989

AFRICAN AMERICAN

*Brown is considered an important transitional figure
between the Harlem Renaissance era and the period
immediately following the Depression.*

PRINCIPAL WORKS

POETRY: *Southern Road*, 1932; *The Last Ride of Wild Bill, and Eleven Narrative Poems*, 1975; *The Collected Poems of Sterling A. Brown*, 1980
NONFICTION: *Outline for the Study of the Poetry of American Negroes*, 1931; *The Negro in American Fiction*, 1937; *Negro Poetry and Drama*, 1937; *The Negro Caravan*, 1941 (Arthur P. Davis and Ulysses Lee, editors); *A Son's Return: Selected Essays of Sterling A. Brown*, 1996 (Mark A. Sanders, editor)

Born into an educated, middle-class African American family, Sterling Allen Brown was the last of six children and the only son of Adelaide Allen Brown and the Reverend Sterling Nelson Brown. His father had taught in the School of Religion at Howard University since 1892, and the year Brown was born, his father also became the pastor of Lincoln Temple Congregational Church. The person who encouraged Brown's literary career and admiration for the cultural heritage of African Americans, however, was his mother, who had been born and reared in Tennessee and graduated from Fisk University. Brown also grew up listening to tales of his father's childhood in Tennessee, as well as to accounts of his father's friendships with noted leaders such as Frederick Douglass, Blanche K. Bruce, and Booker T. Washington.

Brown attended public schools in Washington, D.C., and graduated from the well-known Dunbar High School, noted for its distinguished teachers and alumni; among the latter were many of the nation's outstanding black professionals. Brown's teachers at Dunbar included literary artists such as Angelina Weld Grimké and Jessie Redmon Fauset. Moreover, Brown grew up on the campus of Howard University, where there were many outstanding African American scholars, such as historian Kelly Miller and critic and philosopher Alain Locke.

Brown received his A.B. in 1922 from Williams College (Phi Beta Kappa) and his M.A. in 1923 from Harvard University. Although he pursued further graduate study in English at Harvard, he never worked toward a doctorate degree; however, Howard University, the University of Massachusetts, Northwestern University,

141

Williams College, Boston University, Brown University, Lewis and Clark College, Lincoln University (Pennsylvania), and the University of Pennsylvania eventually granted him honorary doctorates. In September, 1927, he was married to Daisy Turnbull, who shared with him an enthusiasm for people, a sense of humor, and a rejection of pretentious behavior; she was also one of her husband's sharpest critics. She inspired Brown's poems "Long Track Blues" and "Against That Day." Daisy Turnbull Brown died in 1979. The Browns had one adopted child, John L. Dennis.

In 1927, "When de Saints Go Ma'ching Home" won first prize in an *Opportunity* writing contest. From 1926 to 1929, several of the poems that Brown later published in *Southern Road* were printed in *Crisis, Opportunity, Contempo*, and *Ebony and Topaz*. His early work is often identified with the outpouring of black writers during the Harlem Renaissance, for he shared with those artists (Claude McKay, Countée Cullen, Jean Toomer, and Langston Hughes) a deep concern for a franker self-revelation and a respect for the folk traditions of his people; however, Brown's writings did not reflect the alien-and-exile theme so popular with the writers of the Renaissance.

Brown's teaching career took him to Virginia Seminary and College, Lincoln University (Missouri), and Fisk University. He began teaching at Howard University in 1929 and remained there until his retirement in 1969. He was also a visiting professor at Atlanta University, New York University, Vassar College, the University of Minnesota, the New School, and the University of Illinois (Chicago Circle). Several years after coming to Howard University, Brown became an editor with the Works Progress Administration's Federal Writers' Project. Along with a small editorial staff, he coordinated the Federal Writers' Project studies by and about blacks. Beginning in 1932, Brown supervised an extensive collection of narratives by former slaves and initiated special projects such as *The Negro in Virginia* (1940), which became the model for other studies. His most enduring contribution to the project was an essay, "The Negro in Washington," which was published in the guidebook *Washington: City and Capital* (1937).

Brown's first fifteen years at Howard were most productive. During this period (1929-1945), he contributed poetry as well as reviews and essays on the American theater, folk expressions, oral history, social customs, music, and athletics to *The New Republic, The Journal of Negro Education, Phylon, Crisis, Opportunity*, and other journals. His most outstanding essay, "Negro Characters as Seen by White Authors," which appeared in *The Journal of Negro Education* in 1933, brought attention to the widespread misrepresentation of black characters and life in American literature. Only after Brown's retirement from Howard in 1969 did he begin reading his poems regularly there. This long neglect has been attributed to certain conservative faculty members' reluctance to appreciate a fellow professor whose interests were in blues and jazz. Brown was widely known as a raconteur. Throughout his career as a writer, he challenged fellow African American writers to choose their subject matter without regard to external pressures and to avoid the error of "timidity." He was a mentor who influenced the black poetry movement of the 1960's and 1970's, and poets such as Margaret Walker, Gwendolyn Brooks,

Langston Hughes, and Arna Bontemps, along with critics such as Addison Gayle and Houston Baker, learned from him.

In the five years before his retirement, Brown began to exhibit stress caused by what he perceived to be years of critical and professional neglect as well as unfulfilled goals. Inclined toward periods of deep depression, he was occasionally hospitalized in his later years. He died in Takoma Park, Maryland, on January 13, 1989.

Slim Greer Poems
Type of work: Poetry
First published: 1930-1933

The African American's ability to survive in a hostile world by mustering humor, religious faith, and the expectation of a utopian afterlife is portrayed in poems depicting the comical adventures of Slim Greer. The Slim Greer poems—"Slim Greer," "Slim Hears 'the Call,'" "Slim in Atlanta," "Slim in Hell," and "Slim Lands a Job"—reveal Brown's knowledge of the life of the ordinary black person and his ability to laugh at the weaknesses and foolishness of blacks and whites alike.

With their rich exaggerations, these poems fall into the tall tale tradition of folk stories. They show Slim in Arkansas passing for white although he is quite dark, or Slim in Atlanta laughing in a "telefoam booth" because of a law that keeps blacks from laughing in the open. In "Slim Lands a Job," the poet mocks the ridiculous demands that southern employers make on their black employees. Slim applies for a job in a restaurant. The owner is complaining about the laziness of his black employees when a black waiter enters the room carrying a tray on his head, trays in each hand, silver in his mouth, and soup plates in his vest, while simultaneously pulling a red wagon filled with other paraphernalia. When the owner points to this waiter as one who is lazy, Slim makes a quick exit. In "Slim in Hell," Slim discovers that Hell and the South are very much alike; when he reports this discovery to Saint Peter, the saint reprimands him, asking where he thought Hell was if not the South.

Southern Road
Type of work: Poetry
First published: 1932

The poetry of Sterling Brown is imbued with the folk spirit of African American culture. For Brown there was no wide abyss between his poetry and the spirit inherent in slave poetry; indeed, his works evidence a continuity of racial spirit from the slave experience to the African American present and reflect his deep understanding of the multitudinous aspects of the African American personality and soul.

The setting for Brown's poetry is primarily the South, through which he traveled to listen to the folktales, songs, wisdom, sorrows, and frustrations of his people, and where the blues and ballads were nurtured. Brown respected traditional folk forms and employed them in the construction of his own poems; thus he may be called "the poet of the soul of his people."

Brown's first published collection of poems, *Southern Road*, was critically acclaimed by his peers and colleagues James Weldon Johnson and Alain Locke, because of its rendering of the living speech of the African American, its use of the raw material of folk poetry, and its poetic portrayal of African American folk life and thought. Later critics such as Arthur P. Davis, Jean Wagner, and Houston Baker have continued to praise his poetry for its creative and vital use of folk motifs. Some of the characters in Brown's poetry, such as Ma Rainey, Big Boy Davis, and Mrs. Bibby, are based on real people. Other characters, such as Maumee Ruth, Sporting Beasley, and Sam Smiley seem real because of Brown's dramatic and narrative talent. He is also highly skilled in the use of poetic techniques such as the refrain, alliteration, and onomatopoeia, and he employs several stanzaic forms with facility. Brown's extraordinary gift for re-creating the nuances of folk speech and idiom adds vitality and authenticity to his verse.

Brown is successful in drawing upon rich folk expressions to vitalize the speech of his characters through the cadences of southern speech. Though his poems cannot simply be called "dialect poetry," Brown does imitate southern African American speech, using variant spellings and apostrophes to mark dropped consonants. He uses grunts and onomatopoeic sounds to give a natural rhythm to the speech of his characters. These techniques are readily seen in a poem that dramatizes the poignant story of a "po los boy" on a chain gang. This poem follows the traditional folk form of the work song to convey the convict's personal tragedy.

Brown's work may be classed as protest poetry. Influenced by poets such as Carl Sandburg and Robert Frost, he is able to draw upon the entire canon of English and American poetry as well as African American folk material. Thus he is fluent in the use of the sonnet form, stanzaic forms, free-verse forms, and ballad and blues forms.

In *Southern Road*, several themes express the essence of the southern African American's folk spirit and culture. Recurring themes and subjects in Brown's poetry include endurance, tragedy, and survival. The theme of endurance is best illustrated in one of his most anthologized poems, "Strong Men," which tells the story of the unjust treatment of black men and women from the slave ship, to the tenant farm, and finally to the black ghetto. The refrain of "Strong Men" uses rhythmic beats, relentlessly repeating an affirmation of the black people's ability and determination to keep pressing onward, toward freedom and justice. The central image comes from a line of a Carl Sandburg poem: "The strong men keep comin on." In "Strong Men," Brown praises the indomitable spirit of African Americans in the face of racist exploitation. With its assertive tone, the rhythm of this poem suggests a martial song.

Some of the endurance poems express a stoic, fatalistic acceptance of the tragic fate of the African American, as can be seen in "Old Man Buzzard," "Memphis Blues," and "Riverbank Blues." Another important aspect of the endurance theme as portrayed by Brown is the poetic characters' courage when they are confronted with tragedy and injustice. In the poem "Strange Legacies," the speaker gives thanks to the legendary Jack Johnson and John Henry for their demonstration of courage.

"The Last Ride of Wild Bill"

TYPE OF WORK: Poetry
FIRST PUBLISHED: 1975, in *The Last Ride of Wild Bill*

Brown's poems reflect his understanding of the often tragic destinies of African Americans in the United States. No poet before Brown had created such a comprehensive poetic dramatization of the lives of black men and women in America. Brown depicts black men and women as alone and powerless, struggling nevertheless to confront an environment that is hostile and unjust. In this tragic environment, African American struggles against the schemes of racist whites are seen in "The Last Ride of Wild Bill," published in 1975 as the title poem of the collection of the same name. A black man falls victim to the hysteria of a lynch mob in "Frankie and Johnnie," a poem that takes up a familiar folktale and twists it to reflect a personal tragedy that occurs as a result of an interracial relationship. Brown emphasizes that in this story the only tragic victim is the black man. The retarded white girl, Frankie, reports her sexual experience with the black man, Johnnie, to her father and succeeds in getting her black lover killed; she laughs uproariously during the lynching. "Southern Cop" narrates the mindless killing of a black man who is the victim of the panic of a rookie police officer.

Yet Brown's poems show black people not only as victims of whites but also as victims of the whole environment that surrounds them, including natural forces of flood and fire as well as social evils such as poverty and ignorance. Rural blacks' vulnerability to natural disasters is revealed in "Old King Cotton," "New St. Louis Blues," and "Foreclosure." In these poems, if a tornado does not come, the Mississippi River rises and takes the peasant's arable land and his few animals and even traitorously kills his children by night. These poems portray despairing people who are capable only of futile questions in the face of an implacable and pitiless nature. The central character of "Low Down" is sunk in poverty and loneliness. His wife has left and his son is in prison; he is convinced that bad luck is his fate and that in the workings of life someone has loaded the dice against him. In "Johnny Thomas," the title character is the victim of poverty, abuse by his parents and society, and ignorance. (He attempts to enroll in a one-room school, but the teacher throws him out.) Johnny ends up on a chain gang, where he is killed. The poem that most strongly expresses African American despair of the entire race is "Southern Road," a convict song marked by a rhythmic, staccato beat and by a blues line punctuated by the convict's groaning over his accursed fate:

> My ole man died—hunh—
> Cussin' me;
> Old lady rocks, bebby
> huh misery.

"Remembering Nat Turner"

TYPE OF WORK: Poetry
FIRST PUBLISHED: 1980, in *The Collected Poems of Sterling A. Brown*

Brown's poems embrace themes of suffering, oppression, and tragedy yet always celebrate the vision and beauty of African American people and culture. One such deeply moving piece is "Remembering Nat Turner," a poem in which the speaker visits the scene of Turner's slave rebellion, only to hear an elderly white woman's garbled recollections of the event; moreover, the marker intended to call attention to Turner's heroic exploits, a rotting signpost, has been used by black tenants for kindling. A stoic fatalism can be seen in the poem "Memphis Blues," which nevertheless praises the ability of African Americans to survive in a hostile environment because of their courage and willingness to start over when all seems lost: "Guess we'll give it one more try." In the words of Sterling Brown, "The strong men keep a-comin' on/ Gittin' stronger. . . ."

SUGGESTED READINGS

Davis, Arthur P. "Sterling Brown." In *From the Dark Tower: Afro-American Writers, 1900-1960*. Washington, D.C.: Howard University Press, 1982.

Ekate, Genevieve. "Sterling Brown: A Living Legend." *New Directions: The Howard University Magazine* 1 (Winter, 1974): 5-11.

Sanders, Mark A. *Afro-Modernist Aesthetics and the Poetry of Sterling A. Brown*. Athens: University of Georgia Press, 1999.

Thelwell, Ekwueme Michael. "The Professor and the Activists: A Memoir of Sterling Brown." *The Massachusetts Review* 40, no. 4 (Winter, 1999/2000): 617-638.

Wagner, Jean. "Sterling Brown." In *Black Poets of the United States, from Paul Laurence Dunbar to Langston Hughes*. Urbana: University of Illinois Press, 1973.

Contributor: Betty Taylor-Thompson

William Wells Brown

Born: Lexington, Kentucky; c. 1814
Died: Chelsea, Massachusetts; November 6, 1884

African American

A former slave and an outspoken critic of slavery,
Brown wrote Clotel, *which is the first known novel*
written by an African American.

Principal works

DRAMA: *The Escape: Or, A Leap for Freedom: A Drama in Five Acts*, pb. 1858
LONG FICTION: *Clotel: Or, The President's Daughter*, 1853 (revised as *Miralda: Or, The Beautiful Quadroon*, 1860-1861; *Clotelle: A Tale of the Southern States*, 1864; and *Clotelle: Or, The Colored Heroine*, 1867)
POETRY: *The Anti-Slavery Harp*, 1848
NONFICTION: *Narrative of William W. Brown, a Fugitive Slave, Written by Himself*, 1847; *Three Years in Europe*, 1852; *The American Fugitive in Europe: Sketches of Places and People Abroad*, 1855; *St. Domingo: Its Revolution and Its Patriots*, 1855; *Memoir of William Wells Brown, an American Bondman*, 1859; *The Black Man, His Antecedents, His Genius, and His Achievements*, 1863; *The Negro in the American Rebellion: His Heroism and His Fidelity*, 1867; *The Rising Son: Or, The Antecedents and Advancement of the Colored Race*, 1873; *My Southern Home*, 1880; *The Travels of William Wells Brown*, 1991 (includes *Narrative of William Wells Brown, a Fugitive Slave*, 1847, and *The American Fugitive in Europe: Sketches of Places and People Abroad*, 1855; Paul Jefferson, editor)

The Southern laws that made slave literacy illegal were on the books for a reason. William Wells Brown, a former slave, employed his talents as a writer to argue for African American freedom. In the pre-Civil War years, his eloquence as an orator made him an important figure in the abolitionist crusade, and recognition of his literary activities led to appreciation of his pioneering uses of fiction to critique slavery.

Brown's speeches were often incisive and militant. He showed little admiration for those patriots (such as Thomas Jefferson) who, Brown pointed out, owned and fathered slaves even as they founded a new nation dedicated to liberty and equality. He questioned the respect that is generally accorded to the Declaration of Independence and to the Revolutionary War by revealing how these icons of American history failed to confront African enslavement. At an antislavery meeting in 1847 he

William Wells Brown (Associated Publishers, Inc.)

said that if the United States "is the 'cradle of liberty,' they have rocked the child to death."

Opponents of abolition often founded their arguments on racist assumptions. Brown's detractors made much of the fact that Brown's father was a white man (probably his master's brother) and implied that his achievements stemmed from the "white blood" of his father. For example, when Brown traveled to Europe to gain overseas support for abolitionism, an English journalist sneered that Brown was "far removed from the black race . . . his distinct enunciation evidently showed that a white man 'spoke' within."

Brown never sought to deny his racial heritage. In later versions of *Clotel* published in 1860 and 1864, Brown recast his mulatto hero as a black rebel. As he makes clear in *Narrative of William W. Brown, a Fugitive Slave, Written by Himself,* his works were motivated by a deep commitment to the plight of the three million American slaves, a number that included his own family. Brown's literary efforts undertaken in behalf of his enslaved brethren were no doubt supported by his earlier role in secreting fugitive slaves to Canada.

These fugitives often fled slavery, as Brown had himself, at the price of severing familial ties. He dramatized the strain that slavery places upon family connections in *Clotel,* the first known African American novel. Creating a historical fiction from the well-known fact that Jefferson had a slave mistress, Brown details the outrage of the auction block, the struggle for autonomy, and the tragic ends of slave women who could trace their bloodlines to the author of the Declaration of Independence. The mixed heritage of his heroines—white and black, free and enslaved—points to the contradictions of a nation that idealized liberty even as it practiced slavery.

The Narrative of William W. Brown, a Fugitive Slave

TYPE OF WORK: Autobiography
FIRST PUBLISHED: 1847

In his slave narrative, Brown assailed the prevailing notion of his time that slaves lacked legal or historical selfhood. His autobiography asserts that he has an autonomous identity. *The Narrative of William W. Brown, a Fugitive Slave, Written by Himself*, like many of the stories written by former slaves, does more than chronicle a journey from bondage to freedom. The work also reveals the ways in which the former slave author writes a sense of self, denied by the South's "peculiar institution," into existence.

So great was slavery's disregard of black personhood that William, as a boy on a Kentucky plantation, is forced to change his name when his master's nephew, also named William, comes to live as part of the white household. Brown never forgets this insult. He writes of his flight across the Mason-Dixon Line: "So I was not only hunting for my liberty, but also hunting for a name." He finds a name by accepting as his surname that of an Ohio Quaker, Wells Brown, who gives him food and shelter during his escape. He also insists on retaining his first name, showing that his conception of freedom includes the ability to define, shape, and control one's own identity.

Brown is careful to record that his achievement of an unfettered identity is not without its tragic consequences. His personal freedom is undercut by reminders that his mother and siblings remain enslaved. When an escape undertaken in 1833 with his mother fails, his mother is sent to the Deep South, and Brown temporarily gives up his plans of liberty. His repeated sorrowful musings about his mother and sister suggest that Brown's freedom and self-definition are processes infused not only with hope and triumph but also with alienation and loss. His statement that "the fact that I was a freeman . . . made me feel that I was not myself" registers his ambivalence at forever leaving his family in order to find liberty.

Although his purpose is at times weakened by a tragic family history that includes memories of his sister's sale and visions of his mother performing hard labor on a cotton plantation, his understanding of national history lends resolve and determination to his quest. His thoughts of "democratic whips" and "republican chains" work to expose the severe contradictions that haunt the United States and reinforce his decision to risk becoming a fugitive once again in an attempt to reach Canada. In this way, Brown's personal narrative functions as national criticism. His narrative is an American autobiography and an unflinching examination of America.

The American Fugitive in Europe

TYPE OF WORK: Autobiography
FIRST PUBLISHED: 1855

Brown's two travel narratives, *The Narrative of William Wells Brown, a Fugitive Slave* (1847) and *The American Fugitive in Europe: Sketches of Places and People Abroad* (1855), were ably edited by Paul Jefferson in 1991, which made the 1855 sketches available in a modern edition.

The narrative features Brown's travels to an International Peace Conference at Paris (1849) and his residence in England, prolonged by the passage of a new Fugitive Slave Law (1850). His encounters with the racial prejudice of Americans and his amazement at its European opposite form one fascinating dimension of the work. Also of interest are Brown's impressions of European literary figures, statesmen, and institutions and his vivid descriptions of the people he encountered, their dress, occupations, and living conditions in London of the Crystal Palace era, in England's Great Houses, and in laborers' cottages.

SUGGESTED READINGS

Andrews, William L. *To Tell a Free Story: The First Century of Afro-American Autobiography, 1760-1865.* Urbana: University of Illinois Press, 1986.

Ellison, Curtis W., and E. W. Metcalf, Jr. *William Wells Brown and Martin R. Delany: A Reference Guide.* Boston: G. K. Hall, 1978.

Ernest, John. *Resistance and Reformation in Nineteenth-Century African-American Literature: Brown, Wilson, Jacobs, Delany, Douglass, and Harper.* Jackson: University Press of Mississippi, 1995.

Farrison, William Edward. *William Wells Brown: Author and Reformer.* Chicago: University of Chicago Press, 1969.

Jackson, Blyden. *The Long Beginning, 1746-1895.* Vol. 1 in *A History of Afro-American Literature.* Baton Rouge: Louisiana State University Press, 1989.

Sekora, John, and Darwin T. Turner, eds. *The Art of Slave Narrative: Original Essays in Criticism and Theory.* Macomb: Western Illinois University Press, 1982.

Thorpe, Earl E. *Black Historians: A Critique.* New York: William Morrow, 1971.

Whelchel, L. H., Jr. *My Chains Fell Off: William Wells Brown, Fugitive Abolitionist.* Lanham, Md.: University Press of America, 1985.

Contributor: Russ Castronovo

Ed Bullins
(Kingsley B. Bass, Jr.)

BORN: Philadelphia, Pennsylvania; July 2, 1935

AFRICAN AMERICAN

Bullins's work challenges easy preconceptions concerning the relationship between politics and aesthetics. He sees no inherent contradiction between the use of experimental techniques and the drive to reach a mass audience alienated from the dominant social/economic/racial hierarchy.

PRINCIPAL WORKS

DRAMA: *Clara's Ole Man*, pr. 1965, pb. 1969 (one act); *Dialect Determinism: Or, The Rally*, pr. 1965, pb. 1973 (one act); *How Do You Do?*, pr. 1965, pb. 1968 (one act); *The Theme Is Blackness*, pr. 1966, pb. 1973 (one act); *The Electronic Nigger*, pr. 1968, pb. 1969 (one act); *Goin' a Buffalo*, pr. 1968, pb. 1969; *In the Wine Time*, pr. 1968, pb. 1969; *A Son, Come Home*, pr. 1968, pb. 1969 (one act); *Five Plays*, pb. 1969 (includes *Clara's Ole Man, A Son, Come Home, The Electronic Nigger, Goin' a Buffalo*, and *In the Wine Time*); *In New England Winter*, pb. 1969, pr. 1971; *The Gentleman Caller*, pr. 1969, pb. 1970; *We Righteous Bombers*, pr. 1969 (as Kingsley B. Bass, Jr.; adaptation of Albert Camus' play *Les Justes*); *The Duplex*, pr. 1970, pb. 1971; *The Pig Pen*, pr. 1970, pb. 1971; *A Ritual to Raise the Dead and Foretell the Future*, pr. 1970, pb. 1973; *Street Sounds*, pr. 1970, pb. 1973; *The Devil Catchers*, pr. 1971; *The Fabulous Miss Marie*, pr. 1971, pb. 1974; *House Party*, pr. 1973 (lyrics; music by Pat Patrick); *The Theme Is Blackness*, pb. 1973 (collection); *The Taking of Miss Janie*, pr. 1975, pb. 1981; *Home Boy*, pr. 1976 (lyrics; music by Aaron Bell); *Jo Anne!*, pr. 1976, pb. 1993; *Daddy*, pr. 1977; *Sepia Star: Or, Chocolate Comes to the Cotton Club*, pr. 1977 (lyrics; music by Mildred Kayden); *Storyville*, pr. 1977 (revised pr. 1979; music by Kayden); *Michael*, pr. 1978; *Leavings*, pr. 1980; *Steve and Velma*, pr. 1980; *A Sunday Afternoon*, pr. 1989 (with Marshall Borden); *A Teacup Full of Roses*, pr. 1989; *I Think It's Going to Turn Out Fine*, pr. 1990; *American Griot*, pr. 1991 (with Idris Ackamoor); *Salaam, Huey Newton, Salaam*, pr. 1991 (one act); *Boy x Man*, pr. 1995; *Mtumi X*, pr. 2000

LONG FICTION: *The Reluctant Rapist*, 1973

POETRY: *To Raise the Dead and Foretell the Future*, 1971

SCREENPLAYS: *Night of the Beast*, 1971; *The Ritual Masters*, 1972

EDITED TEXTS: *New Plays from the Black Theatre*, 1969 (with introduction); *The*

New Lafayette Theater Presents: Plays with Aesthetic Comments by Six Black Playwrights, 1974 (with introduction)
MISCELLANEOUS: *The Hungered Ones: Early Writings,* 1971 (stories and essays)

Intensely protective concerning the details of his private life, Ed Bullins (BUHL-lihnz) nevertheless became a highly visible force in the development of African American theater beginning in the mid-1960's. Reared primarily by his civil servant mother in North Philadelphia, Bullins attended a predominantly white grade school before transferring to an inner-city junior high, where he became involved with the street gang called the Jet Cobras. Like his semiautobiographical character Steve Benson (*The Reluctant Rapist, In New England Winter, The Duplex*), Bullins suffered a near-fatal knife wound, in the area of his heart, in a street fight. After dropping out of high school, he served in the United States Navy from 1952 to 1955. In 1958, he moved to California, where he passed his high school graduation equivalency examination and attended Los Angeles City College from 1961 to 1963.

Bullins's 1963 move to San Francisco signaled the start of his emergence as an influential figure in African American literary culture. The first national publication of his essays in 1963 initiated a period of tremendous creativity extending into the mid-1970's. Actively committed to Black Nationalist politics by 1965, he began working with community theater organizations such as Black Arts/West, the Black Student Union at San Francisco State College, and Black House of San Francisco, which he founded along with playwright Marvin X. The first major production of Bullins's drama, a program including *How Do You Do?, Dialect Determinism,* and *Clara's Ole Man,* premiered at the Firehouse Repertory Theater in San Francisco on August 5, 1965. At about the same time, Bullins assumed the position of minister of culture with the Black Panther Party, then emerging as a major force in national politics. Breaking with the Panthers in 1967, reportedly in disagreement with Eldridge Cleaver's decision to accept alliances with white radical groups, Bullins moved to Harlem at the urging of Robert MacBeth, director of the New Lafayette Theater.

Bullins's first New York production, *The Electronic Nigger,* ran for ninety-six performances following its February 21, 1968, debut at the American Place Theatre, where it was moved after the original New Lafayette burned down. Combined with his editorship of the controversial "Black Theatre" issue of *The Drama Review* (Summer, 1968), the success of *The Electronic Nigger* consolidated Bullins's position alongside Baraka as a major presence within and outside the African American theatrical community. Between 1968 and 1976, Bullins's plays received an average of three major New York productions per year at theaters, including the New Lafayette (where Bullins was playwright-in-residence up to its 1973 closing), the American Place Theatre, the Brooklyn Academy of Music, Woodie King's New Federal Theatre at the Henry Street Settlement House, Lincoln Center, and the La Mama Experimental Theater.

Bullins wrote *A Sunday Afternoon* with Marshall Borden and "a pseudo-satiric monster horror play, a take-off on B-movies," called *Dr. Geechie and the Blood Junkies,* which he read at the Henry Street Settlement House in New York in the

Ed Bullins (AP/Wide World Photos)

summer of 1989. The La Mama theater staged *I Think It's Going to Turn Out Fine*, based on the Tina Turner story, in 1990, and *American Griot* (coauthored with Idris Ackamoor, who also acted in the play) in 1991. *Salaam, Huey Newton, Salaam*, a one-act play on the aftermath of the black revolution, premiered at the Ensemble Studio Theater in 1991.

Bullins has also taught American humanities, black theater, and play making at Contra Costa College, in San Pablo, California. He settled in Emeryville, near Oakland, and started a theater there called the BMT Theatre (Bullins Memorial Theatre, named after his son, who died in an automobile accident).

He continued his formal education at Antioch University in San Francisco, where he received his bachelor's degree in liberal studies (English and playwriting) in 1989. After he completed his master's degree in playwriting at San Francisco State University in 1994, he was appointed professor of theater at Northeastern University in 1995. In 1996 he was made acting director of Northeastern University's Center for the Arts, and his *Boy x Man*, which premiered a year earlier in Greensboro, North Carolina, was staged at the Arts Black Box Theater in Boston. Three years later many of his plays were presented at a retrospective at the Schomberg Center for Research in Black Culture in New York. An avid supporter of local drama, he has written two ten-minute plays for the Boston Theater Marathon and works with the ACT Theater Group in Roxbury, where he mentors young playwrights and conducts workshops. In 2000 his play *Mtumi X* was produced, and his play *Goin' a Buffalo* was adapted to film and screened at the New York International Film and Video Festival in New York's Madison Square Garden.

A radical playwright in both the simple and the complex senses of the term, Bullins consistently challenges the members of his audience to test their political and aesthetic beliefs against the multifaceted reality of daily life in the United States. Committed to a revolutionary Black Nationalist consciousness, he attacks both liberal and conservative politics as aspects of an oppressive context dominated by a white elite. Equally committed to the development of a radical alternative to European American modernist aesthetics, he incorporates a wide range of cultural materials into specifically black performances. The clearest evidence of Bullins's radical sensibility, however, is his unwavering refusal to accept any dogma, white or black, traditional or revolutionary, without testing it against a multitude of perspectives and experiences. Throughout a career that has earned for him serious consideration alongside O'Neill and Tennessee Williams as the United States' greatest dramatist, Bullins has subjected the hypocrisies and corruptions of European and African American culture to rigorous examination and reevaluation. Refusing to accept any distinctions between aesthetics and politics or between the concerns of the artist and those of the mass community, Bullins demands that his audience synthesize abstract perception and concrete experience. Providing a set of terms useful to understanding the development of these concerns in his own work, Bullins defines a constituting dialectic in the black theatrical movement that emerged in the mid-1960's:

> This new thrust has two main branches—the *dialectic of change* and the *dialectic of experience*. The writers are attempting to answer questions concerning Black survival and future, one group through confronting the Black/white reality of America, the other, by heightening the dreadful white reality of being a modern Black captive and victim.

Essentially, the dialectic of change focuses attention on political problems demanding a specific form of action. The dialectic of experience focuses on a more "realistic" (though Bullins redefines the term to encompass aspects of reality frequently dismissed by programmatic realists) picture of black life in the context in which the problems continue to condition all experience. Reflecting his awareness that by definition each dialectic is in constant tension with the other, Bullins directs his work in the dialectic of change to altering the audience's actual experience. Similarly, his work in the dialectic of experience, while rarely explicitly didactic, leads inexorably to recognition of the need for change.

Bullins's work in both dialectics repudiates the tradition of the Western theater, which, he says, "shies away from social, political, psychological or any disturbing (revolutionary) reforms." Asserting the central importance of non-Western references, Bullins catalogs the "elements that make up the alphabet of the secret language used in Black theater," among them the blues, dance, African religion and mysticism, "familial nationalism," mythscience, ritual-ceremony, and "nigger street styles." Despite the commitment to an African American continuum evident in the construction and content of his plays, Bullins by no means repudiates all elements of the European American tradition. Even as he criticizes Brechtian epic theater, Bullins employs aspects of Brecht's dramatic rhetoric, designed to alienate the audience from received modes of perceiving theatrical and, by extension, political events. It is less important to catalog Bullins's allusions to William Shakespeare, O'Neill, Camus, or Genet than to recognize his use of their devices alongside those of Baraka, Soyinka, and Derek A. Walcott in the service of "Black artistic, political, and cultural consciousness."

Most of Bullins's work in the dialectic of change, which he calls "protest writing" when addressed to a European American audience and "Black revolutionary writing" when addressed to an African American audience, takes the form of short satiric or agitpropic plays. Frequently intended for street performance, these plays aim to attract a crowd and communicate an incisive message as rapidly as possible. Influential in the ritual theater of Baraka and in Bullins's own "Black Revolutionary Commercials," this strategy developed out of association with the Black Nationalist movement in cities such as New York, Detroit, Chicago, San Francisco, and Newark. Reflecting the need to avoid unplanned confrontations with police, the performances described in Bullins's influential "Short Statement on Street Theater" concentrate on establishing contact with groups unlikely to enter a theater, especially black working people and individuals living on the margins of society—gang members, junkies, prostitutes, and street people. Recognizing the impact of the media on American consciousness, Bullins frequently parodies media techniques, satirizing political advertising in "The American Flag Ritual" and "selling" positive black revolutionary images in "A Street Play." Somewhat longer though equally direct, "Death List," which can be performed by a troupe moving through the neighborhood streets, alerts the community to "enemies of the Black People," from Vernon Jordan to Whitney Young. Considered out of their performance context, many of these pieces seem simplistic or didactic, but their real intent is to realize Bullins's desire that "each individual in the crowd should have his sense of reality confronted, his consciousness assaulted." Because the "accidental" street audience comes into contact with the play while in its "normal" frame of mind, Bullins creates deliberately hyperbolic images to dislocate that mind-set in a very short period of time.

Dialect Determinism

TYPE OF WORK: Drama
FIRST PRODUCED: 1965, pb. 1973

When writing revolutionary plays for performance in traditional theaters, Bullins tempers his rhetoric considerably. To be sure, *Dialect Determinism*, a warning against trivializing the revolutionary impulse of Malcolm X, and *The Gentleman Caller*, a satiric attack on master-slave mentality of black-white economic interaction, both resemble the street plays in their insistence on revolutionary change. *Dialect Determinism* climaxes with the killing of a black "enemy," and *The Gentleman Caller* ends with a formulaic call for the rise of the foretold "Black nation that will survive, conquer and rule." The difference between these plays and the street theater lies not in message but in Bullins's way of involving the audience. Recognizing the different needs of an audience willing to seek out his work in the theater but frequently educated by the dominant culture, Bullins involves it in the analytic process leading to what seem, from a black nationalist perspective, relatively unambiguous political perceptions. Rather than asserting the messages at the start of the plays, therefore, he developed a satiric setting before stripping away the masks and distortions imposed by the audience's normal frame of reference on its recognition of his revolutionary message.

Along with Baraka, Marvin X, Adrienne Kennedy, and others, Bullins helped make the dialectic of change an important cultural force at the height of the Black Nationalist movement, but his most substantial achievements involve the dialectic of experience. Ranging from his impressionistic gallery plays and politically resonant problem plays to the intricately interconnected Twentieth Century Cycle, Bullins's work in this dialectic reveals a profound skepticism regarding revolutionary ideals that have not been tested against the actual contradictions of African American experience.

The Twentieth Century Cycle

TYPE OF WORK: Drama
FIRST PRODUCED: 1968-1991

The Twentieth Century Cycle, Bullins's most far-reaching confrontation with the American experience, brings together most of his theatrical and thematic concerns and seems destined to stand as his major work. Several of the projected twenty plays of the cycle have been performed, including *In the Wine Time, In New England Winter, The Duplex, The Fabulous Miss Marie, Home Boy, Daddy*, and *Salaam, Huey Newton, Salaam*. Although the underlying structure of the cycle remains a matter of speculation, it clearly focuses on the experience of a group of black people traversing various areas of America's cultural and physical geography during the 1950's, 1960's, and 1970's. Recurring characters, including Cliff Dawson, his nephew Ray Crawford, Michael Brown (who first appeared in a play not part of the cycle, *A Son, Come Home*), and Steve Benson, a black intellectual whose life story resembles Bullins's own, serve to unify the cycle's imaginative landscape. In addition, a core of thematic concerns, viewed from various perspectives, unites the plays.

In the Wine Time, the initial play of the cycle, establishes a basic set of thematic concerns, including the incompatibility of Ray's romantic idealism with the brutality and potential violence of his northern urban environment. Stylistically, the play typifies the cycle in its juxtaposition of introverted lyricism, naturalistic dialogue, technological staging, and African American music and dance. Individual plays combine these elements in different ways. *In New England Winter*, set in California, draws much of its power from a poetic image of the snow that takes on racial, geographical, and metaphysical meanings in Steve Benson's consciousness. Each act of *The Duplex* opens with a jazz, blues, or rhythm-and-blues song that sets a framework for the ensuing action. *The Fabulous Miss Marie* uses televised images of the Civil Rights movement both to highlight its characters' personal desperation and to emphasize the role of technology in creating and aggravating their problems of perception. Drawing directly on the reflexive rhetoric of European American modernism, *In New England Winter* revolves around Steve Benson's construction of a "play," involving a planned robbery, which he plans to enact in reality but which he also uses as a means of working out his psychological desires.

Ultimately, Bullins's *Salaam, Huey Newton, Salaam* extends Bullins's vision into an imaginary future to depict the former Black Panther leader down and out in the wake of a black revolution. Bullins suggests that each of these approaches reflects a perspective on experience actually present in contemporary American society and that any vision failing to take all of them into account will inevitably fall victim to the dissociation of ideals and experience that plunges many of Bullins's characters into despair or violence. While some of his characters, most notably Steve Benson, seem intermittently aware of the source of their alienation and are potentially capable of imaginative responses with political impact, Bullins leaves the resolution of the cycle plays to the members of the audience. Portraying the futility of socially prescribed roles and of any consciousness not directly engaged with its total context, Bullins continues to challenge his audience to attain a perspective from which the dialectic of experience and the dialectic of change can be realized as one and the same.

Street Sounds

TYPE OF WORK: Drama
FIRST PRODUCED: 1970, pb. 1973

Street Sounds, parts of which were later incorporated into *House Party*, represents Bullins's adaptation of the gallery approach pioneered by poets such as Robert Browning, Edgar Lee Masters (*Spoon River Anthology*, 1915), Melvin B. Tolson (*Harlem Gallery*, 1969), Gwendolyn Brooks (*A Street in Bronzeville*, 1945), and Langston Hughes (*Montage of a Dream Deferred*, 1951). By montaging a series of thirty- to ninety-second monologues, Bullins suggests the tensions common to the experience of seemingly disparate elements of the African American community. Superficially, the characters can be divided into categories such as politicians (Harlem Politician, Black Student), hustlers (Dope Seller, The Thief), artists (Black Revolutionary Artist, Black Writer), street people (Fried Brains, Corner Brother), working people (Errand Boy, Workin' Man), and women (The Loved One, The Virgin, Harlem Mother). None of the categories, however, survives careful examination; individual women could be placed in every other category; the Black Revolutionary Artist combines politics and art; the Harlem Politician, politics and crime. To a large extent, all types ultimately amount to variations on several social and psychological themes that render the surface distinctions far less important than they initially appear.

Although their particular responses vary considerably, each character in *Street Sounds* confronts the decaying community described by The Old-timer: "They changin' things, you know? Freeways comin' through tearin' up the old neighborhood. Buildings goin' down, and not bein' put up again. Abandoned houses that are boarded up, the homes of winos, junkies and rats, catchin' fire and never bein' fixed up." As a result, many share the Workin' Man's feeling of being "trapped inside of ourselves, inside our experience." Throughout the play, Bullins portrays a deep-seated feeling of racial inferiority that results in black men's obsession with white women (Slightly Confused Negro, The Explainer) and a casual willingness to exploit or attack other blacks (The Thief, The Doubter, Young West Indian Revolutionary Poet). Attempting to salvage some sense of freedom or self-worth, or simply to find momentary release from the struggle, individuals turn to art, sex, politics, or drugs, but the weight of their context pressures each toward the psychological collapse of Fried Brains, the hypocritical delusions of the Non-Ideological Nigger, or the unfounded self-glorification of The Genius. Even when individuals embrace political causes, Bullins remains skeptical. The Theorist, The Rapper, and The Liar, who ironically echoes Bullins's aesthetic when he declares, "Even when I lie, I lie truthfully.... I'm no stranger to experience," express ideological positions similar to those Bullins advocates in the dialectic of change. None, however, seems even marginally aware that his grand pronouncements have no impact on the experience of the black community. The Rapper's revolutionary call—"We are slaves now, this moment in time, brothers, but let this moment end with this breath and let us unite as fearless revolutionaries in the pursuit of world liberation!"—comes between the entirely apolitical monologues of Waiting and Bewildered. Similarly, the Black Revolutionary Artist's endorsement of "a cosmic revolution that will liberate the highest potential of nationhood in the universe" is followed by the Black Dee Jay's claim that "BLACK MEANS BUY!" The sales pitch seems to have a great deal more power than the nationalist vision in the lives of the Soul Sister and the Corner Brother, whose monologues frame the Black Revolutionary Artist-Black Dee Jay sequence.

One of Bullins's characteristic "signatures" is the attribution of his own ideas to characters unwilling or unable to act or inspire others to act on them. Reflecting his belief that, without action, ideals have little value, Bullins structures *Street Sounds* to insist on the need for connection. The opening monologue, delivered by a white "Pig," establishes a political context similar to the one that Bullins uses in the dialectic of change, within which the dialectic of experience proceeds. Reducing all blacks to a single type, the nigger, Pig wishes only to "beat his nigger ass good." Although Bullins clearly perceives the police as a basic oppressive force in the ghetto, he does not concentrate on highlighting the audience's awareness of that point. Rather, by the end of the play he has made it clear that the African American community in actuality beats its own ass. The absence of any other white character in the play reflects Bullins's focus on the nature of victimization as experienced within and perpetuated by the black community. The Harlem Mother monologue that closes the play concentrates almost entirely on details of experience. Although she presents no hyperbolic portraits of white oppressors, her memories of the impact on her family of economic exploitation, hunger, and government indifference carry more politically dramatic power than does any abstraction. This by no means indicates Bullins's distaste for political analysis or a repudiation of the opening monologues; rather, it reflects his awareness that abstract principles signify little unless they are embedded in the experience first of the audience and, ultimately, of the community as a whole.

The Taking of Miss Janie

TYPE OF WORK: Drama
FIRST PRODUCED: 1975, pb. 1981

Although Bullins consistently directs his work toward the African American community, his work in the dialectic of experience inevitably involves the interaction of blacks and whites. *The Taking of Miss Janie*, perhaps his single most powerful play, focuses on a group of California college students, several of whom first appeared in *The Pig Pen*. In part a meditation on the heritage of the 1960's Civil Rights movement, *The Taking of Miss Janie* revolves around the sexual and political tensions between and within racial groups. Although most of the characters are readily identifiable types—the stage directions identify Rick as a cultural nationalist, Janie as a California beach girl, Flossy as a "soul sister"—Bullins explores individual characters in depth, concentrating on their tendency to revert to behavior patterns, especially when they assume rigid ideological or social roles. The central incident of the play—the "rape" of the white Janie by Monty, a black friend of long standing—provides a severely alienating image of this tendency to both black and white audiences. After committing a murder, which may or may not be real, when the half-mythic Jewish beatnik Mort Silberstein taunts Monty for his inability to separate his consciousness from European American influences, Monty undresses Janie, who does not resist or cooperate, in a rape scene devoid of violence, love, anger, or physical desire. Unable to resist the pressures that make their traditional Western claim to individuality seem naïve, both Janie and Monty seem resigned to living out a "fate" that in fact depends on their acquiescence. Monty accepts the role of the "black beast" who rapes and murders white people, while Janie plays the role of plantation mistress. Although these intellectually articulate characters do not genuinely believe in the reality of their roles, their ironic attitude ultimately makes no difference, for the roles govern their actions.

Although the rape incident provides the frame for *The Taking of Miss Janie*, Monty and Janie exist in a gallery of characters whose collective inability to maintain individual integrity testifies to the larger dimensions of the problem. Rick and Len enact the classic argument between nationalism and eclecticism in the black political/intellectual world; Peggy tires of confronting the neuroses of black men and turns to lesbianism; "hip" white boy Lonnie moves from fad to fad, turning his contact with black culture to financial advantage in the music business; several couples drift aimlessly into interracial marriages. Alternating scenes in which char-

acters interact with monologues in which an individual reflects on his future development, Bullins reveals his characters' inability to create alternatives to the "fate"
within which they feel themselves trapped. Although none demonstrates a fully developed ability to integrate ideals and experiences, several seem substantially less
alienated than others. In many ways the least deluded, Peggy accepts both her lesbianism and her responsibility for her past actions. Her comment on the 1960's articulates a basic aspect of Bullins's vision: "We all failed. Failed ourselves in that serious time known as the sixties. And by failing ourselves we also failed in the test of
the times." Her honesty and insight also have a positive impact on the black nationalist Rick, who during a conversation with Peggy abandons his grandiose rhetoric
on the "devil's tricknology" (a phrase adopted from the Nation of Islam)—rhetoric
that masks a deep hostility toward other blacks. Although he has previously attacked her as a lesbian "freak," Rick's final lines to Peggy suggest another aspect of
Bullins's perspective: "Ya know, it be about what you make it anyway." Any ade-
quate response to *The Taking of Miss Janie* must take into account not only Peggy's
survival strategy and Rick's nationalistic idealism but also Janie's willed naïveté
and the accuracy of Mort's claim that, despite his invocation of Mao Zedong,
Malcolm X, and Frantz Fanon, Monty is still on some levels "FREAKY FOR
JESUS!" Bullins presents no simple answers nor does he simply contemplate the
wasteland. Rather, as in almost all of his work in both the dialectic of change and
the dialectic of experience, he challenges his audience to make something out of the
fragments and failures he portrays.

Boy x Man

TYPE OF WORK: Drama
FIRST PRODUCED: 1995

In *Boy x Man* (the *x* means "times," as in multiplication), Bullins constructs a memory play in which a young man's return to attend his mother's funeral prompts him
to remember his boyhood with his mother and her "friend," who raised him as a son.
The song "Blues in the Night," his first crib memory, provides the transition to
scenes from the 1930's and 1940's. Ernie's mother, Brenda, is a single mom and
dancer whose life improves dramatically when she meets Will, who lacks ambition
but who nevertheless provides his "family" with much-needed stability. The play
includes a series of highly emotional vignettes, including the following: Brenda's
reliving of her discovery of her dead mother; Will's reliving of his Nazi concentration camp experiences; and, to provide balance, Will's attending and listening to
Negro League baseball games. Bullins provides his audience with a glimpse of the
problems, prejudice, and tensions that black American families encounter; but because many of the problems are not confined to the black experience, the play reflects on American life in general.

SUGGESTED READINGS

DeGaetani, John L. *A Search for a Postmodern Theater: Interviews with Contemporary Playwrights*. New York: Greenwood Press, 1991.

Hay, Samuel A. *Ed Bullins: A Literary Biography*. Detroit: Wayne State University Press, 1997.

Herman, William. *Understanding Contemporary American Drama*. Columbia: University of South Carolina Press, 1987.

Contributors: Thomas L. Erskine, Thomas J. Taylor, and Craig Werner

Carlos Bulosan

BORN: Binalonan, Pangasinan, Luzon, Philippines; November 2, 1911
DIED: Seattle, Washington; September 11, 1956

FILIPINO AMERICAN

Bulosan provides the best introduction to the lives of
Filipino immigrant workers in America.

PRINCIPAL WORKS

LONG FICTION: *The Power of the People*, 1986; *All the Conspirators*, 1998
POETRY: *Letter from America*, 1942; *The Voice of Bataan*, 1943; *Now You Are Still, and Other Poems*, 1990
SHORT FICTION: *The Laughter of My Father*, 1944; *The Philippines Is in the Heart: A Collection of Stories*, 1978; *If You Want to Know What We Are: A Carlos Bulosan Reader*, 1983 (E. San Juan, Jr., editor); *The Power of Money, and Other Stories*, 1990; *On Becoming Filipino: Selected Writings of Carlos Bulosan*, 1995 (E. San Juan, Jr., editor); *The Cry and the Dedication*, 1995 (E. San Juan, Jr., editor)
NONFICTION: *America Is in the Heart*, 1946; *Sound of Falling Light: Letters in Exile*, 1960
EDITED TEXT: *Chorus for America: Six Philippine Poets*, 1942
MISCELLANEOUS: *Bulosan: An Introduction with Selections*, 1983 (compiled by E. San Juan, Jr.)

Carlos Bulosan (BOO-loh-sahn) never forgot his background as a Filipino farmer's son. He expressed the pride he had in this background as well as the severe social situations that small farmers as well as other hired workers faced in their day-to-day attempts to earn a livelihood. A turning point in Bulosan's life, which fixed in his memory and conscience the small farmers' and hired workers' need for a voice, came when Bulosan's father lost the family's small farm and entered the world of serfdom—slavery—in his native Philippines.

Bulosan learned one important lesson from his father: Bulosan saw his father retain his personal identity by confronting his daily tasks and hardships with laughter and cunning. His father showed how one is able to speak as loudly against injustices through satire and laughter as through political diatribe. Bulosan recounts many stories of his father in the numerous pieces that appeared in leading American publications.

In search of a better life, Bulosan worked his way to America, landing in Seattle on July 22, 1930, and found himself on the streets with others looking for work dur-

162

ing the Depression. The good life escaped Bulosan because jobs were few and because extreme jingoism was rampant in America at the time. Although Bulosan never intended to lose his identity as a Filipino, those with whom he came into contact constantly berated him for being an outsider and a Filipino.

Bulosan began to take whatever job he could find, always being relegated to secondary positions because of his ethnicity. As hard as he tried to fit into the American Dream of a better life, he was denied entrance. Bulosan chronicles his father's difficult life in America as an unwanted outsider in his autobiographical novel, *America Is in the Heart*. Bulosan's dream of a life better than that of his father was never realized. He soon learned that

Carlos Bulosan (Courtesy, APIHDC)

he, too, was a slave to those controlling the jobs. This no doubt contributed to Bulosan's strong support and activity in the many workers' movements that arose during his life. Bulosan's hard life also, no doubt, contributed to his early death.

America Is in the Heart

TYPE OF WORK: Autobiography and novel
FIRST PUBLISHED: 1946

In this poignant tale of immigrant dreams and racial discrimination, Bulosan depicts growing up in the Philippines, voyaging to the United States, and enduring years of hardship and despair as an itinerant laborer and union organizer on the West Coast.

Bulosan gives his readers the uncomfortable perspective of harsh discrimination because of racial and economic status. The actual form of the book, however, is difficult to characterize. Unlike a novel, it contains real-life situations, but neither is it autobiography, in the strictest sense. Though narrated in the first person by a character named Carlos Bulosan, the book is neither really nor exclusively an account of his life. For example, unlike the book's narrator, the real Bulosan was not as impoverished. Bulosan states that the events in the book are a composite: They happened either to him or to someone he knew or heard about. The book, then, is a conglomerate portrait of Filipino American life in the early twentieth century, but Bulosan presents the events as personal history so that the reader is more likely to take what he says to be truth. The use of the first-person narrative voice conveys immediacy and energy, arousing sympathy in a way that a third-person narrative would not.

This is an "everyperson" story, an immigrant myth. As such, it is very episodic in nature, depicting brief or extended encounters first with one character who was influential to Bulosan and then moving on to another character. The voice of Bulosan is constant throughout the novel, and two of his brothers emerge periodically throughout, although no other long-term relationships are described.

The book shows Bulosan growing up in a small barrio, or village, in the central Philippines, working in the fields with his father, selling salted fish with his mother, and attending school as he was able. At seventeen, he immigrates to the United States, landing in Seattle and being sold for five dollars to a labor contractor. He moves from one manual job to another up and down the Washington and California coasts, depending on which crops are ready to harvest. He becomes a union organizer and experiences abuse and cruelty at the hands of white leaders and townspeople. His hospitalization for two years because of tuberculosis enables him to read an average of a book a day and to write newsletters that promote the union cause.

America Is in the Heart is a coming-of-age story from an immigrant's point of view. The first third of the book shows Bulosan's youth within the circle of his impoverished but loving family. In the beginning of the second third of the book, Bulosan is optimistic and naïve as he lands on the shores of Seattle at seventeen. Although he is soon duped, sold for hire, and abused, his disillusion never breaks his spiritual faith in the United States or his desire to forge ahead in his own intellectual development and for the welfare of all Filipino workers. He is forced by "oldtimers," the more seasoned Filipino laborers, into losing his virginity with a Mexican prostitute; his maturity cannot be complete without this sexual awakening. The final third of the book depicts the fruits of his adult labor: the formation of fledgling labor unions and the beginnings of a grassroots network that will begin to hold white owners and managers accountable for humane working and living conditions for their immigrant itinerant laborers.

SUGGESTED READINGS

Evangelista, Susan, ed. *Carlos Bulosan and His Poetry: A Biography and Anthology*. Seattle: University of Washington Press, 1985.
Lee, Rachel C. *The Americas of Asian American Literature: Gendered Fictions of Nation and Transnation*. Princeton, N.J.: Princeton University Press, 1999.
San Juan, E., Jr. *Carlos Bulosan and the Imagination of the Class Struggle*. New York: Oriole Editions, 1976.
_____, ed. *Introduction to Modern Pilipino Literature*. New York: Twayne, 1974.

Contributors: Tom Frazier and Jill B. Gidmark

Julia de Burgos

BORN: Carolina, Puerto Rico; February 17, 1914
DIED: New York, New York; July 6, 1953

PUERTO RICAN

*Burgos stands out as a early feminist activist at a
time when Puerto Rican culture restricted women to
the traditional roles of spouse and mother.*

PRINCIPAL WORKS

POETRY: *Poema en veinte surcos*, 1938; *Canción de la verdad sencilla*, 1939 (*Song
of the Simple Truth: The Complete Poems*, 1997); *El mar y tú: Otros poemas*,
1954; *Obra poética*, 1961; *Antología poética*, 1975; *Roses in the Mirror*, 1992

Born into a poor peasant family in rural Puerto Rico, Julia de Burgos (JEW-lee-ah
duh BEHR-gohs), a remarkably intelligent girl, received schooling because of
money collected among her equally poor neighbors. Eventually she earned a teaching degree. Her experiences as a rural teacher and her agrarian background added
to her deep concern for the exploited workers and for the women subjected to male-
chauvinist cultural patterns. Her contact with common people also ignited her
interest in local politics, especially in independence-seeking revolutionary movements.

Burgos is best known for her strongly feminist poems. Her poetry is thematically
diverse; it includes an inclination to the erotic and to social activism. Burgos's feminist poems present a philosophical consideration of the role of women in Puerto
Rican society. By such questioning, Burgos explores womanhood issues in her efforts to break away from restrictive social patterns. Her definition of womanhood
encompasses multiple facets: the woman yearning for motherhood (which she herself never fulfilled), the social nonconformist who openly challenges sexist traditions, and the devoted citizen and political activist.

Her political involvement with the Puerto Rican Nationalist Party, which ag-
gressively promoted the independence of Puerto Rico by means of revolutionary
guerrilla warfare, added to her poetry a marked sense of patriotism. Her idea of a
pure, lush countryside clashed with the realities of an increasingly urbanized and,
therefore, Americanized Puerto Rico. Committed to international activism, Burgos
also wrote against fascism in Spain during that country's civil war.

Burgos's life can be examined as an example of a commitment to fight social injustice. At a time when racial discrimination was rampant, Burgos, a woman of
black descent, fought such restrictions. Racism was certainly her major problem

upon arriving in New York City in 1942, where she lived until her death. In New York, although she was a renowned poet and fully bilingual, Burgos was obliged to take menial jobs. She fought back, however, by writing against such oppression. Her alcoholism led to her early death.

Burgos stands out as a early feminist activist at a time when Puerto Rican culture restricted women to the traditional roles of spouse and mother. The inclusion of feminism in her poetic production, which she links to political activism, puts Burgos on the cutting edge of an incipient movement in Puerto Rico and in the United States. It may be more significant, however, that her life reflected her cherished beliefs.

"To Julia de Burgos"

TYPE OF WORK: Poetry
FIRST PUBLISHED: 1938, in *Poema en veinte surcos*

"To Julia de Burgos" is part of *Poema en veinte surcos* (poem in twenty furrows), whose poems focus mainly on social hierarchies and on the relationship between the individual and society. Both these elements are combined in "To Julia de Burgos," which is remarkable both for the clarity and conviction of its voice and for the conflict and tension inherent within that voice.

The poem is a critique of Julia de Burgos as the world knows her. The speaker, who is not—and perhaps cannot—be named (and is referred to only as "I") accuses this "false" Julia de Burgos of being the superficial, transparent embodiment of the "real" Julia de Burgos; that is, the independent, free-thinking, soulful creator (who is, presumably, the author of the poem). The difference between the two, the speaker says, is simple: The real Julia de Burgos is her own creation, while the Julia de Burgos to whom the poem is directed is merely a creation of the outside world, someone who succumbs to societal expectations:

> You curl your hair and paint your face. Not I:
> I am curled by the wind, painted by the sun.

Here, the hostility is directed from one female to another; the speaker criticizes Julia de Burgos's submission to social hierarchies and ideas of where a woman's "place" should be. The real Julia de Burgos is the only one aware of the other's inauthenticity; her accusations stem from a unique vantage point. She has deep insight into the mind-set and hierarchies to which her false self belongs, and by placing her voice in the third person she is able to launch a scathing social critique of the author's own weaknesses, of women's conformity to perceived perceptions, and of the oppressive nature of Puerto Rico's upper class.

SUGGESTED READINGS

Kattau, C. "The Plural and the Nuclear in 'A Julia de Burgos.'" *Symposium—A Quarterly Journal in Modern Foreign Literatures* 48, no. 4 (Winter, 1995): 285-293.

Vásquez, Carmen, et al. *La Poésie de Julia de Burgos, 1914-1953*. Paris: Indigo, 2005.

Vicioso, Sherezada. *Julia de Burgos: La Nuestra*. Santo Domingo, Dominican Republic: Dirección General Feria del Libro, 2004.

Contributors: Rafael Ocasio and Anna A. Moore

Octavia E. Butler

BORN: Pasadena, California; June 22, 1947
DIED: Seattle, Washington; February 24, 2006

AFRICAN AMERICAN

*Butler's portrayal of the "loner" of science and
adventure fiction is given depth and complexity by the
implied treatment of sexual and racial prejudices and the
direct treatment of social power structures. Examining love
and miscegenation, male-female roles, the responsibilities
of power, and the urge to survive, Butler invites readers
to reexamine long-standing attitudes.*

PRINCIPAL WORKS

LONG FICTION: *Patternmaster*, 1976; *Mind of My Mind*, 1977; *Survivor*, 1978; *Kindred*, 1979; *Wild Seed*, 1980; *Clay's Ark*, 1984; *Dawn*, 1987; *Adulthood Rites*, 1988; *Imago*, 1989; *Parable of the Sower*, 1993; *Parable of the Talents*, 1998; *Fledgling*, 2005

SHORT FICTION: "Crossover," 1971; "Near of Kin," 1979; "Speech Sounds," 1983; "Bloodchild," 1984; "The Evening and the Morning and the Night," 1987

NONFICTION: "Birth of a Writer," 1989 (later renamed "Positive Obsession"); "Furor Scribendi," 1993

MISCELLANEOUS: *Bloodchild, and Other Stories*, 1995 (collected short stories and essays)

Octavia E. Butler grew up in a family that reflected some of the hard realities for African Americans. Her father, who died when she was very young, shined shoes; her mother, who had been taken from school at the age of ten, supported herself by working as a maid.

Reared by her mother, grandmother, and other relatives, Butler felt most comfortable in the company of her adult relatives, even while she was uncomfortable with a social system that routinely denied their humanity. She was tall for her age, shy, bookish, and further set off from her peer group by strict Baptist prohibitions against dancing and the use of makeup. Her escape from a less-than-satisfactory everyday life was provided by her ability to write. She began writing when she was about ten years old and began to experiment with science fiction one day at age twelve, when she decided that she could write a better story than the one of the poor science-fiction film she was watching on television.

Her family did not support her decision to write, and her teachers did not support her choice of science fiction as a medium. She attended Pasadena City College and then California State College at Los Angeles, where she was unable to major in creative writing but took a potpourri of other subjects. After attending evening writing classes at the University of California at Los Angeles (UCLA), she met science-fiction writer Harlan Ellison through the Writers Guild of America, and he brought her to the Clarion Science Fiction Writers Workshop in 1970. Butler continued her study of science-fiction writing in classes taught by Ellison at UCLA. Although she had sold some of her science fiction as early as 1970, her breakthrough publication came in 1976 with *Patternmaster*, with which she began the Patternist series. She went on to fashion a successful career that was cut short by a fatal stroke in 2006.

Octavia E. Butler presented a version of humanity as a congenitally flawed species, possibly doomed to destroy itself because it is both intelligent and hierarchical. In this sense, her work does not follow the lead of Isaac Asimov's *Foundation* series (1951-1993), Arthur C. Clarke's *2001: A Space Odyssey* (1968), and similar science fiction in offering an optimistic, rational, and agreeable view of humanity. As Butler herself said, she did not believe that imperfect human beings can create a perfect world.

Butler's diverse societies are controlled by Darwinian realities: competition to survive, struggle for power, domination of the weak by the strong, parasitism, and the like. Within this framework, there is room for both pain and hope, for idealism, love, bravery and compassion, for an outsider to challenge the system, defeat the tyrant, and win power. There is, however, no happy ending but a conclusion in which the lead characters have done their best and the world (wherever it is) remains ethically and morally unchanged.

In contemplative but vividly descriptive prose, Butler tells her story from the first- or third-person perspective of someone who is passive or disfranchised and is forced by events or other characters to take significant action. In order to fulfill her destiny, often the protagonist— most often a black woman—must do or experience something not only unprecedented but also alien and even grotesque. What begins as an act of courage usually ends as an act of love, or at least understanding. Through an alien, alienated, or excluded person, a crucial compromise is struck, civilization is preserved in some form, and life goes on.

Octavia E. Butler (Beth Gwinn)

Butler's fiction reflects and refracts the attempts—and failures—of the twentieth century to deal with ethnic and sexual prejudice. She frequently used standard images of horror, such as snakelike or insectlike beings, to provoke an aversion that the reader is unable to sustain as the humanity of the alien becomes clear. Being human does not mean being faultless—merely familiar. Therefore, each of her human, nonhuman, and quasi-human societies displays its own form of selfishness and, usually, a very clear power structure. The maturity and independence achieved by the protagonists imply not the advent of universal equality and harmony but merely a pragmatic personal obligation to wield power responsibly. Characters unable to alter or escape the order of things are expected to show a sort of noblesse oblige.

Kindred

TYPE OF WORK: Novel
FIRST PUBLISHED: 1979

Butler's most atypical work in terms of genre is *Kindred*, published in 1979. While the protagonist is shuttled helplessly back and forth between 1824 and 1976 in a kind of time travel, this device is of no intrinsic importance to the message of the story. At one point, the heroine, Edana, asks herself how it can be that she—the as yet unborn black descendant of a nineteenth century slaveholder—can be the instrument of keeping that slaveholder alive until he fulfills his destiny and fathers her ancestor. By asking, she preempts the reader's own curiosity, and when there is no answer, the story simply moves forward.

Kindred uses a black woman of the 1970's and her white husband to probe beneath the surface stereotypes of "happy slave" on one hand and "Uncle Tom" on the other. When Edana and Kevin are separated by the South of 1824 into slave and master, they each begin unwillingly to imbibe the feelings and attitudes of the time from that perspective. The impact of the novel results from Butler's ability to evoke the antebellum South from two points of view: the stubborn, desperate attempts of blacks to lead meaningful lives in a society that disregards family ties and disposes of individuals as marketable animals; and the uncomprehending, sometimes oppressively benevolent ruthlessness of a ruling class that defines slaves in terms of what trouble or pleasure they can give.

The Patternist Series

TYPE OF WORK: Novels
FIRST PUBLISHED: 1976-1984

Butler began her science-fiction novels with the Patternist series, and in this series the reader can observe the beginning of her development from a writer of well-crafted science/adventure fiction to a writer who recalls in her own way the reflectiveness of Ray Bradbury.

First written but third published was *Survivor*, the tale of an orphaned Afro-Asian girl who becomes a "wild human" in order to survive in a harsh environment. She is found and adopted, in an atypical act of reaching out, by two members of the Missionaries—a nouveau-Fundamentalist Christian sect. The Missionaries' escape from a hostile Earth takes them to a planet inhabited by furred bipeds, whom they regard as less than human. These beings are, in fact, a science-fiction version of the noble savage, but the protagonist is alone in recognizing their nobility. Internally untouched by Missionary dogma, she is truly socialized as a captive of the Tehkohn and, in the end, chooses them as her own people. Her survival and success require an understanding of the color classes of fur among the Tehkohn, where blue is the highest color, suggesting a tongue-in-cheek reference to "blue blood." She makes her own way by dint of qualities often found in protagonists of adventure novels: physical agility, courage, and adaptability.

Patternmaster features an appealing duo, with the younger son of the Patternmaster—the psychic control-central of a society of advanced human beings—confronting and defeating his brutal older brother in an unwanted competition to succeed their father. His helper, mentor, and lover is a bisexual Healer; he trusts her enough to "link" with her in order to pool their psionic power. She teaches him that Healing is, paradoxically, also a deadly knowledge of the body with which he can defeat his brother. Thus, trust and cooperation overcome ambition and brutality. The "mutes" of this novel are nontelepathic human beings whose vulnerability to cruelty or kindness and inability to control their own destinies reflect the earlier status of slaves in America.

Mary, in *Mind of My Mind*, is a "latent" who must undergo a painful transition in order to become a full-fledged telepath. The pain and danger of this passage from adolescence to adulthood are emblematic of the turmoil of coming-of-age everywhere and of the physical or psychological pain that is required as the price of initiation in many, if not all, societies. The deadened, sometimes crazed, helplessness of latents who cannot become telepaths but must continue to live with the intrusive offal of other people's thoughts is a powerful metaphor for people trapped in poverty, and some of the horrors Butler paints are familiar.

Mary has no choice at first. The founder of her "people," a nontelepathic immortal named Doro, prescribes her actions until she acquires her power. He senses danger only when she reaches out reflexively to control other, powerful telepaths, thus forming the first Pattern. Mary's destruction of the pitiless Doro, like the death of the older brother in *Patternmaster* and of the rival alien chief in *Survivor*, is foreordained and accomplished with a ruthlessness appropriate to the society and to the character of the victim. The incipient change in Butler's style is evident here in the comparative lack of adventure-action sequences and in the greater concentration on psychological adaptation to and responsible use of social power.

The technique of historical reconstruction is seen again in *Wild Seed*, whose evocation of Ibo West Africa owes something to the work of writers such as Chinua Achebe. *Wild Seed* traces Doro and Anyanwu from their seventeenth century meeting in West Africa to the establishment of Doro's settlements in America. Doro is a centuries-old being who lives by "taking" another man's or woman's body and leaving his previous body behind. Anyanwu is a descendant of Doro. She is a "wild seed" because she has unexpectedly developed the power to shape-shift, becoming young or old, an animal, fish, or bird, at will. Their relationship is completely one-sided, since Doro could "take" her any time he chose, although he would not acquire her special abilities. His long life and unremitting efforts to create a special people of his own have left him completely insensitive to the needs and desires of others. Anyanwu finally achieves some balance of power simply by being willing to die and leave Doro without the only companion who could last beyond a mortal lifetime.

The last Patternist novel, *Clay's Ark*, introduces the reader to those brutish enemies of both Patternist and "mute" humanity, the Clayarks, so named because the disease that created them was brought back to Earth on a spaceship called "Clay's Ark." The disease culls its victims, killing some and imbuing others with a will to live that overcomes the horror of their new existence. They become faster and stronger, and their children evolve even further, taking on animal shapes and attributes of speed, power, and heightened senses but retaining human thought and use of their hands. In the guise of a horror story, *Clay's Ark* follows the first Clayarks' attempt to come to terms with their condition and live responsibly, shut off from civilization. Their failed attempt demonstrates that it is not possible to contain cataclysmic natural change, but the story enlists the reader's sympathy for human beings who suffer even as they afflict others.

The Xenogenesis Series

TYPE OF WORK: Novels
FIRST PUBLISHED: 1987-1989

With the exception of *Clay's Ark*, in which there is much action, the pace of Butler's novels slows progressively; action is increasingly internalized and psychological. Moral judgments and the contest of right versus wrong dwindle to insignificance. The next, and quite logical, development is the Xenogenesis series: *Dawn, Adulthood Rites*, and *Imago*. This series confirmed Butler as a science-fiction writer of sufficient depth to be of significance beyond the genre.

The change from her originally projected title for the series is informative. "Exogenesis" would have implied merely genesis effected from outside humanity. "Xenogenesis" has both text and subtext. Its meaning is the production of an organism altogether and permanently unlike the parent. The subtext is a function of the best-known English word built on the same root: xenophobia, fear and dislike of that which is foreign or alien. Butler makes the series title a statement of the thesis she will address.

Many of the techniques and themes of her earlier, developing style come to fruition here: The alternating use of first- and third-person narrative, the slow pace of a plot laden with psychological development and sensory perceptions, the meticulous foreclosure of value judgments, the concern with hierarchy and responsibility, the objective observation of feelings of revulsion for that which is alien, and those feelings' gradual dissipation as the alien becomes familiar and therefore less threatening. Action in the series is sparse, normally kept to the minimum necessary to maintain the pace of psychological and social observation. In some ways, it is a chilling series of seductions of human beings by an alien, benevolent oppressor. In some ways, it is a demonstration of the infinite capacity of humanity to seek satisfaction in the destruction of itself and others.

Words used to describe two of Butler's shorter works in the 1984 and 1987 issues of *The Year's Best Science Fiction* may serve here as a characterization of the Xenogenesis series: "strange, grotesque, disturbing . . . and ultimately moving," a "tale of despair, resignation, and, most painfully, hope." It is apparently to examine the capacity of human beings to adapt, to survive, and perhaps stubbornly to pursue a self-destructive course of action that Butler has created the nightmarish situation that the reader encounters in *Dawn*.

In a world devastated by nuclear exchange between East and West, the dying remnants of humanity survive largely in the Southern Hemisphere. The heroine of *Dawn* is an African, Lilith, whose name suggests the demonic goddess of Hebrew tradition, the famous medieval witch who appears in Johann Wolfgang von Goethe's *Faust* (1808, 1833), and the medieval, alternate "first mother" who was put aside in favor of Eve.

Enter the Oankali, a nonviolent race of benevolent parasites and genetic engineers, who exist for the opportunity of combining with other species to acquire new cellular "knowledge" and capabilities. They live for miscegenation. They are trisexual: male, female, and ooloi. The ooloi is the indispensable link between male and female—channeling, altering, or amplifying all genetic material and sexual contact, including transfer of sperm and pleasurable sensations. The ooloi is capable of internal healing; for example, one cures Lilith of a cancer and finds the cancer to be an exciting new biological material with which to work.

The Oankali blend with another species by linking a male and female of that species and a male and female Oankali through an ooloi. Thereafter, independent conception is not possible for those members of that species. The progeny are "constructs," who, at least at first, resemble their direct parents but carry genetic change within them. Lilith's first husband is killed in *Dawn*, but she bears his child posthumously because Nikanj, the ooloi that has chosen her, has preserved his seed. The resultant humanoid male child is the protagonist of *Adulthood Rites*, while a much later child of Lilith with another husband and the same Oankali parents is the protagonist of *Imago*.

Lilith is at first appalled by even the more humanoid Oankali, with their Medusan tentacles and sensory arms. She is gradually acclimated to them, cooperates with them to save humanity, bears children with them, is overwhelmed by the sensory pleasure they can give, and becomes sympathetic to their need to unite with other species, but she is never fully resigned. In *Imago*, Lilith compares the Oankali's description of the "flavors" of human beings to physical cannibalism and implies that the spiritual equivalent is no less predatory.

Lilith's conversion from complete repugnance in *Dawn*, a stylistic tour de force, shapes the following novels, as human beings are ultimately allowed a choice of living with the Oankali, staying behind on a doomed and barren Earth, or living in an experimental, all-human world on Mars. The Oankali, who seem to make decisions as a kind of committee-of-the-whole, foresee that the same old combination of intelligence and hierarchical tendencies (in a rather Darwinian sense) will lead this last outpost of humanity to destroy itself. No one convincingly denies it.

Butler's stylistic virtuosity also extended to narrative person. *Dawn* is a third-person account of Lilith's absorption into the Oankali social structure; *Adulthood Rites* is the third-person narrative of Akin, a male-human construct, who convinces the more rational human beings left on Earth to trust the Oankali and convinces the Oankali to offer the humans the choice of planetary residences.

Imago is a first-person account of Jodahs, a child whose transformation to adulthood reveals it to be an ooloi. Use of the first-person narrative to tell the story of an apparent human who becomes wholly alien in both psychology and physiology is risky but rewarding. Through the eyes of a being routinely referred to as "it" in its own society, the reader observes its benevolent stalking and drug-induced brainwashing of human mates and the final planting of a seed that will grow into an organic town and then an organic spaceship, which will carry Jodahs and his people to new worlds for new genetic blendings.

Imago's conclusion serves as a reminder that Butler's imaginary worlds are primarily arenas for hard, necessary decisions in the business of survival. There is compassion as well as bitterness, and love as well as prejudice, but there is no triumph or glory. There is only doing what must be done as responsibly as possible.

Parable of the Sower
TYPE OF WORK: Novel
FIRST PUBLISHED: 1993

Parable of the Sower was published in 1993. It is set in California in 2024. The narrator is a fifteen-year-old African American girl who lives with her family in the fictitious town of Robledo, some twenty miles from Los Angeles. At the time of the story, the social order has nearly disintegrated. Society consists of "haves" and "have-nots." The haves live in walled and fortified neighborhoods; the have-nots roam outside the walls along with packs of wild dogs and drug addicts called "Paints," whose addiction imbues them with an orgasmic desire to burn things. Apparently due to the follies of humankind, the climate has been altered, and the entire world is in a state of near-collapse. Disease is rampant, natural disasters are frequent, and though there are stores, some jobs, and even television programming, the social order, at least in California, is almost gone.

Against this backdrop, the heroine, Lauren Olamina, founds a new religion named Earthseed. The novel takes the form of a journal Lauren keeps. Entries are dated and each chapter is prefaced with a passage from the new religion, the essence of which is that everything changes, even God. In fact, God is change.

Butler said that humankind is not likely to change itself but that humans will go elsewhere and be forced to change. When the Paints destroy Lauren's neighborhood and most of her family, she treks north toward Canada, and new members join her group, one by one. Most survive and reach their destination, a burned farm in Oregon. The ending is a classic Butler resolution: There is no promised land; people who have not changed generally perish. Lauren has changed nothing in society; she has merely adapted and learned to survive. The structure, style, and plot of *Parable of the Sower* are all deceptively simple. Beneath the surface of the story, the novel deals directly with social power, its use and abuse, and its possible consequences.

SUGGESTED READINGS

Barr, Marleen S. *Lost in Space: Probing Feminist Science Fiction and Beyond.* Chapel Hill: University of North Carolina Press, 1993.

Dubey, Madhu. "Folk and Urban Communities in African American Women's Fiction: Octavia Butler's *Parable of the Sower.*" *Studies in American Fiction* 27, no. 1 (1999): 103-128.

Foster, Frances Smith. "Octavia Butler's Black Female Future Fiction." *Extrapolation* 23 (Spring, 1982): 37-49.

Govan, Sandra Y. "Connections, Links, and Extended Networks: Patterns in Octavia Butler's Science Fiction." *Black American Literature Forum* 18 (1984): 82-87.

Jesser, Nancy. "Blood, Genes, and Gender in Octavia Butler's *Kindred* and *Dawn.*" *Extrapolation* 43, no. 1 (2002): 36-61.

McCaffery, Larry. "Interview with Octavia E. Butler." In *Across the Wounded Galaxies.* Urbana: University of Illinois Press, 1990.

Mitchell, Angelyn. "Not Enough of the Past: Feminist Revisions of Slavery in Octavia Butler's *Kindred.*" *MELUS* 26, no. 3 (2001): 51-75.

Roberts, Robin. *A New Species: Gender and Science in Science Fiction.* Urbana: University of Illinois Press, 1993.

Shinn, Thelma. "The Wise Witches: Black Woman Mentors in the Fiction of Octavia E. Butler." In *Conjuring: Black Women, Fiction, and Literary Tradition,* edited by Marjorie Pryse and Hortense Spillers. Bloomington: Indiana University Press, 1985.

Contributors: James L. Hodge and John T. West III

Abraham Cahan

BORN: Podberezy, Lithuania; July 6, 1860
DIED: New York, New York; August 31, 1951

JEWISH

*As a novelist and a journalist, Cahan was a
voice for his fellow Jewish immigrants.*

PRINCIPAL WORKS

LONG FICTION: *Yekl: A Tale of the New York Ghetto*, 1896; *The White Terror and the
Red: A Novel of Revolutionary Russia*, 1905; *The Rise of David Levinsky*, 1917
SHORT FICTION: *The Imported Bridegroom, and Other Stories of the New York
Ghetto*, 1898
NONFICTION: *Historye fun di Fareynigte Shtaaten: Mit Eyntselhayten vegen der
Entdekung un Eroberung fun Amerika*, 1910; *Bleter fun mayn leben*, 1926-1931
(5 volumes; *The Education of Abraham Cahan*, 1969); *Grandma Never Lived in
America: The New Journalism of Abraham Cahan*, 1985
EDITED TEXT: *Hear the Other Side: A Symposium of Democratic Socialist Opinion*,
1934

As a young man in Russia, Abraham Cahan (KAY-hahn) experienced many different identities: pious Jew, Russian intellectual, nihilist. By his early twenties, in response to prevalent anti-Semitism and recent pogroms, Cahan had become a full-
fledged revolutionary socialist, dedicated to the overthrow of the czar and hunted
by the Russian government. Hoping to create in America a prototype communist
colony in which Jew and Gentile were equal, Cahan immigrated to New York in
1882.

Upon his arrival, Cahan modulated his outspoken socialism and embarked on a
distinguished career as a Yiddish-language journalist, English teacher, and novelist. As editor for the Yiddish-language *Jewish Daily Forward*, Cahan transformed
the paper from a dry mouthpiece for socialist propaganda into a vital community
voice, still socialist in its leanings but dedicated to improving the lives of its audience.

One of the early realists, Cahan is appreciated for his frank portrayals of immigrant life. *Yekl: A Tale of the New York Ghetto*, Cahan's first novel in English, follows the rocky road toward Americanization of Yekl Podkovnik, a Russian Jewish
immigrant desperately trying to assimilate. Faced with two choices for a wife, Yekl
chooses the more assimilated Mamie over his Old World spouse, Gitl, but for all his
efforts to become "a Yankee," Yekl's tale ends on a melancholy note, demonstrat-

ing that he is unable to break out of his immigrant identity simply by changing his clothes, his language, and his wife.

Cahan's sense of the loss and confusion faced by immigrants to America is also evident in *The Rise of David Levinsky*. This masterful novel tells the rags-to-riches story of a clothier who, despite his wealth and success, is lonely and forlorn, distant from his Russian Jewish beginnings, and alienated from American culture. Following the publication of *Yekl*, Cahan was ushered into the national spotlight by William Dean Howells, who had encouraged many other regional and ethnic writers. Cahan's career in mainstream English-language publishing, however, was short-lived. After *The Rise of David Levinsky*, Cahan wrote no more fiction in English, choosing instead to act as a mentor for other writers and to pour his energies into the *Jewish Daily Forward*.

The Rise of David Levinsky

TYPE OF WORK: Novel
FIRST PUBLISHED: 1917

In 1913, in response to a request from the popular *McClure's* magazine for articles describing the success of Eastern European immigrants in the U.S. garment trade, Cahan wrote several short stories instead. Subsequently published as a novel, these pieces of fiction permitted Cahan to explore problematic aspects of the process of Americanization, produce vignettes of immigrant Jewish life, and describe the development of a major American industry.

Cahan uses the life of David Levinsky to explore three interrelated themes. From the opening paragraph, in which Levinsky asserts that although he is a millionaire he is not a happy man, Cahan examines the ambiguous meaning of success and the personal and psychological cost of achieving material gains. Success distances Levinsky from his friends—the companions who came to America with him and those who helped him during his early and difficult years in the New World. His great wealth overawes them, making them uncomfortable in his presence. In turn, Levinsky can never be certain whether people associate with him out of friendship or because they hope to get some of his money. His business success is accomplished through methods that are unethical when they are not illegal, in violation of the values he learned as a child. Appealing to the Social Darwinist creed of "survival of the fittest" to justify his actions, Levinsky is too insecure psychologically to be certain he is, in fact, truly one of "the fittest."

A second major theme is the development of the American ready-to-wear clothing industry and the surprisingly rapid rise to prominence within that industry of recent Russian Jewish immigrants. Levinsky's success illustrates how this occurred, but the contradictions between his methods and his inherited values make the meaning of success ambiguous.

The third theme, the process of adaptation to American life by Russian Jewish immigrants of Levinsky's generation, takes up large segments of the novel. Levinsky experiences the teeming Lower East Side, with its peddlers and markets, its storefront synagogues of recent immigrants, their poverty-stricken homes, and their vigorous intellectual life. As he rises in wealth, Levinsky describes the over-furnished homes of the wealthy, their religious compromises, and the lavish resort hotels that also serve as marriage marts. The novel contains a social history of Jew-ish immigrants in the years before World War I, as they adapt to a new American reality.

In fulfilling the commission from *McClure's*, Cahan used his fictional manufac-turer to show how, in the late 1880's and early 1890's, Russian Jews replaced Ger-man Jews at the head of the cloak-and-suit trade. Levinsky, always short of cash during his early years, learned to use unethical subterfuges to postpone payment of his bills. He could undercut major firms on prices because the Orthodox East Euro-pean Jewish tailors he hired were willing to work longer hours for lower wages in return for not having to work on Saturday. Concentrating his clothing line on a few successful designs, frequently illegally copied from those of established manufac-turers, Levinsky achieved an economy of operation that permitted him to sell styl-ish goods at low prices, a process that made fashionable clothes readily available to the majority of American women.

When Cahan turned his *McClure's* short stories into a longer work, with far greater depth of characterization and scope of social observation, he created the first major novel portraying the Jewish experience in America. In effect, he also created a new literary genre within which there have been many followers. Such ac-claimed writers as Bernard Malamud, Philip Roth, and Saul Bellow have continued to explore themes first articulated by Cahan.

SUGGESTED READINGS

Chametzky, Jules. *From the Ghetto: The Fiction of Abraham Cahan.* Amherst: University of Massachusetts Press, 1977.
Marovitz, Sanford E. *Abraham Cahan.* New York: Twayne, 1996.
Mindra, Mihai. *Strategists of Assimilation: Abraham Cahan, Mary Antin, Anzia Yezierska.* Bucharest: Romanian Academy, 2003.
Sanders, Ronald. *The Downtown Jews: Portraits of an Immigrant Generation.* New York: Harper & Row, 1969.

Contributors: Anne Fleischmann and Milton Berman

Hortense Calisher

BORN: New York, New York; December 20, 1911

JEWISH

*Calisher uses sexuality as a metaphor to explore
the convolutions and unpredictable twists of the human
psyche. Beyond "feminist," her work compassionately
probes the psychology of human motivations.*

PRINCIPAL WORKS

LONG FICTION: *False Entry*, 1961; *Textures of Life*, 1963; *Journal from Ellipsia*,
1965; *The New Yorkers*, 1969; *Queenie*, 1971; *Standard Dreaming*, 1972; *Eagle
Eye*, 1973; *On Keeping Women*, 1977; *Mysteries of Motion*, 1983; *The Bobby-
Soxer*, 1986; *Age*, 1987; *The Small Bang*, 1992 (as Jack Fenno); *In the Palace of
the Movie King*, 1993; *In the Slammer with Carol Smith*, 1997; *Sunday Jews*,
2002

SHORT FICTION: *In the Absence of Angels: Stories*, 1951; *Tale for the Mirror: A Novella and Other Stories*, 1962; *Extreme Magic: A Novella and Other Stories*,
1964; *"The Railway Police" and "The Last Trolley Ride,"* 1966; *The Collected
Stories of Hortense Calisher*, 1975; *Saratoga, Hot*, 1985; *The Novellas of
Hortense Calisher*, 1997

NONFICTION: *Herself*, 1972; *Kissing Cousins: A Memory*, 1988; *Tattoo for a Slave*,
2004

Hortense Calisher's (KAL-ih-shur) background was secular-Jewish, with an often
emphasized splash of the southern—her father was from Richmond, Virginia.
(Both Calisher's father and paternal grandfather were married and started families
late, as do many of her fictional males.) Born and educated in New York City (her
B.A. is from Barnard College, where she studied literature and philosophy), she
lived there or nearby for most of her life. After graduation from college, she worked
as a salesclerk, as a model, and for some years as a social worker. In 1935 she married Heaton Bennett Heffelfinger, an engineer by whom she had a son and a daughter and from whom she was divorced in 1958. In 1959 she married Curtis Harnack,
also a writer, who, like her first husband, was a Gentile. In her autobiographical collection *Herself*, which includes thoughts on writing, on values, and on her contemporaries, she expresses a preference for Christian men. Also in *Herself*, Calisher
obliquely mentions her children, referring once or twice to emotional problems her
daughter had when reaching maturity but otherwise saying little about domestic
matters. She does indicate that she spent much time traveling for the United States

Information Agency in the 1950's; on a trip to the Far East she noted that Japanese writers had maintained that their own literature differed from Western literature in that they had no sense of original sin. If that is so, there is a definite Eastern quality to Calisher's fiction.

Calisher was awarded a Guggenheim Fellowship in 1952 and 1953 and received many other awards, both literary and academic. She wrote that she does not care for academic life, nor does she believe much in creative writing classes. Nonetheless, she served on the faculties of Barnard College, Sarah Lawrence College, Brandeis University, Columbia University, Bennington College, Washington University, and Brown University.

Although she wrote poetry in the 1930's, Calisher published none of it. She saw her first story, "A Box of Ginger," in print in *The New Yorker* in 1948. Her best-known and most often anthologized story, "In Greenwich There Are Many Gravelled Walks," is another early effort, and in it much is encapsulated that appears with variations in her other work. In this story Peter, a young heterosexual man who has driven his hysterical and sometimes nymphomaniacal mother to a sanatorium, decides to visit the apartment of an older friend, a homosexual. The middle-aged man is another recurring type, a remittance man whose family pays him to keep his distance; he is in the process of leaving his lover for another, who is in the room when Peter visits. The daughter of the fickle remittance man arrives, and while conversation continues in the front room, the rejected lover jumps to his death, the replacement makes himself scarce, and Peter and the young woman get acquainted. All of this occurs in a very few pages. As Calisher has said, "a story is an apocalypse, served in a very small cup."

Calisher's characters are sophisticated, and they often seem to resemble the characters in Henry James's works. They are intellectuals, certainly, but people whose approach to life is primarily aesthetic. Indeed, she often has been compared to James and to Marcel Proust, though in *Herself* she notes that she read these authors only after she was established. In short, her stories are ones similar to many that appear in *The New Yorker*, whose editors for a long time enjoyed first-refusal rights on what she wrote. Critics have commented that Calisher's novels are essentially the same type of fiction as her short stories, only longer.

Most often, sexuality is the metaphor Calisher uses to explore the convolutions and unpredictable twists of the human psyche. Her characters have hidden curiosities that are revealed at least in part; these revelations hint at more mysteries yet unexplored, and not necessarily sexual ones. While her characters generally experience some defeat and feelings of hopelessness, Calisher's work champions self-awareness and the principles of love. She has, especially, been praised for her insight into women's lives, but her work could not be labeled "feminist." Indeed, it is much broader, compassionately probing the psychology of human motivations.

In the Palace of the Movie King

TYPE OF WORK: Novel
FIRST PUBLISHED: 1993

In the Palace of the Movie King is a variation on the theme of the transportational journey, which is a common thread among a number of Calisher's novels and short stories, including *Journal from Ellipsia*, *On Keeping Women*, and *Age*. In this narrative, her protagonist, film director Paul Gonchev, a perpetual "outsider," is removed from the world he knows and, after a series of dramatic and traumatic dislocations, comes to realize the emptiness of his life, the meaninglessness of political boundaries, and the significance of his relationships to his wife and children. This is a novel of picaresque adventures with a postmodern European twist, as Gonchev deals with shifting political realities as well as fundamental existential questions.

Gonchev's adventures in the "West" include his kidnapping; a period of being unable to speak any language but the Japanese of his boyhood; an affair with his interpreter, which ends unhappily because of the differences in their ethnicities; encounters with professional dissidents and their dissatisfied wives; interactions with faceless government departments; and ultimately, reunion with his beloved wife, who has had her own series of adventures.

In this novel, Calisher is at the peak of her powers of observation and description. Readers should not be put off by her prose, which has a tendency to be subtle, elliptical, and complex. This novel is an ambitious, elegant examination of the meanings of place, politics, art, and love in a world defined by isolation and separation.

SUGGESTED READINGS

Aarons, Victoria. "The Outsider Within: Women in Contemporary Jewish American Fiction." *Contemporary Literature* 28, no. 3 (1987): 378-393.

Calisher, Hortense. "The Art of Fiction: Hortense Calisher." Interview by Allen Gurganus, Pamela McCordick, and Mona Simpson. *The Paris Review* 29 (Winter, 1987): 157-187.

_____. Introduction to *The Novellas of Hortense Calisher*. New York: The Modern Library, 1997.

_____. "*Saturday Review* Talks to Hortense Calisher." *Saturday Review* 11 (July/August, 1985): 77.

Hahn, Emily. "In Appreciation of Hortense Calisher." *Wisconsin Studies in Contemporary Literature* 6 (Summer, 1965): 243-249.

Shinn, Thelma J. *Radiant Daughters: Fictional American Women*. Westport, Conn.: Greenwood Press, 1986.

Snodgrass, Kathleen. *The Fiction of Hortense Calisher*. Newark: University of Delaware Press, 1993.

Contributor: J. H. Bowden

Bebe Moore Campbell

BORN: Philadelphia, Pennsylvania; 1950
DIED: Los Angeles, California; November 27, 2006

AFRICAN AMERICAN

*Campbell offers telling portraits of
people of many backgrounds.*

PRINCIPAL WORKS

CHILDREN'S LITERATURE: *Sometimes My Mommy Gets Angry*, 2003 (Earl B. Lewis, illustrator); *Stompin' at the Savoy*, 2006
LONG FICTION: *Your Blues Ain't Like Mine*, 1992; *Brothers and Sisters*, 1994; *Singing in the Comeback Choir*, 1998; *What You Owe Me*, 2001; *Seventy-two Hour Hold*, 2005
NONFICTION: *Successful Women, Angry Men: Backlash in the Two-Career Marriage*, 1986 (revised 2000); *Sweet Summer: Growing Up with and Without My Dad*, 1989

As a child, Bebe Moore Campbell spent her school years in Philadelphia with her mother and her summers in North Carolina with her father. She writes of this divided life in *Sweet Summer: Growing Up with and Without My Dad*, drawing sharp contrasts between the two worlds. She credits both parents with shaping her into a writer.

Her mother, an avid storyteller, designated Sundays as church day and library day. Having learned the value of stories and writing, Campbell composed stories for her father, cliff-hangers designed to elicit his immediate response. By the third grade, she knew that she wanted to be a writer; however, not until her mother gave her a book written by an African American did she feel affirmed in that ambition. The knowledge that African Americans wrote books gave her the permission she needed to pursue her dream.

Campbell earned a B.S. degree in elementary education at the University of Pittsburgh, later teaching elementary school for ten years in Pittsburgh, Atlanta, and Washington, D.C. An early marriage ended in divorce. Campbell, as her mother had, assumed the responsibilities of a single parent. Her writing career began when the editor of *Essence* gave a lecture at Howard University. Campbell hurriedly handed her young daughter, Maia, to a friend for care so that she could chase the woman to the ladies room and tell her of her writing aspirations. The woman, impressed, helped Campbell enter the publishing world. Campbell moved to Los Angeles in the early 1980's. There she married a banker, Ellis Gordon, Jr., who also had a child, a son named Ellis Gordon III.

In the early 2000's, Campbell turned her efforts to writing for younger readers. Her book *Sometimes My Mommy Gets Angry* addresses a parent's bipolar disorder from a young daughter's point of view, and *Stompin' at the Savoy*, for elementary schoolchildren, expressed the joy of jazz and dance through a child's eyes. Diagnosed with brain cancer in her mid-fifties, Campbell died in Los Angeles in 2006.

Your Blues Ain't Like Mine

TYPE OF WORK: Novel
FIRST PUBLISHED: 1992

Your Blues Ain't Like Mine was inspired by the 1955 murder of Emmett Till, an African American teenager from Chicago who was killed in Mississippi after speaking to a white woman. Till's death was widely discussed in the African American community, and Campbell grew up feeling that she had known him. Since his murderers were never brought to justice, she sought in *Your Blues Ain't Like Mine* to create a fictional world in which the justice that society withheld exists. The novel showcases her ability to portray many diverse characters.

The plot chronicles the aftermath of the murder of Armstrong Todd, an event that reverberates in the lives of two families, one black and one white. The novel opens in 1955 in Hopewell, Mississippi, where Armstrong, a fifteen-year-old African American, has come from Chicago to spend the summer with his grandmother. Unused to the ways of the South, he is not aware of the consequences that await him for speaking to Lily Cox, a white woman. When Armstrong is killed by Lily's husband Floyd, family members of the murderer and the victim are forced to examine their lives in relation to this act.

Over time Lily comes to realize that Armstrong's death was prompted more by Floyd's desire to please his father than to protect her. This growing awareness causes her to question her passive allegiance to her husband, a role which she had been taught that women should assume. This shift is furthered by her daughter Doreen, who is not afraid to stand up to her father, a man from whom she feels her mother needed more protection than from Armstrong.

In Chicago, Todd's parents, Delotha and Wydell, must deal with their feelings of guilt and failure that their son's death produces. Delotha's identity is bound up in her obsession to produce another male child to take Armstrong's place, a son whom she must protect from white people. Yet her resolve is pitted against Wydell's reluctance to be a father again, born of his fear of failing yet another child. Eventually, another son, W. T., is born to them, a boy threatening to be lost not to whites but to the streets of Chicago. When Wydell takes his son to Hopewell, another aspect of the interwoven identities of the two families surfaces.

When the novel opens, Lily Cox is listening to the singing of African Americans as they work the cotton fields. She says that the music makes her feel "strong and hopeful," as if she were being healed. When the novel closes, Wydell shows his son where he and others worked the fields, explaining to him that the workers battled the harshness of their lives with song. The songs recalled by Wydell form the back-drop of Lily's life. Both acknowledge song as a source of healing for broken souls. Campbell has said that the title of her novel reflects some irony. In some ways all blues are the same, since human pain is human pain.

Brothers and Sisters

TYPE OF WORK: Novel
FIRST PUBLISHED: 1994

Her second novel, *Brothers and Sisters*, is set around another event affecting the African American community. Rodney King, an African American motorist, was beaten by police officers in Los Angeles in 1992. The beating was captured on videotape, but the policemen were found not guilty in their first trial, resulting in riots. Delving into the aftermath of this event, *Brothers and Sisters* explores the way in which race affects the relationship between an African American woman, bank manager Esther Jackson, and a white woman, loan officer Mallory Post. Mallory holds a position coveted by Esther but denied her because of racism. These two women are cautious friends, neither completely comfortable with the other race—one filled with underlying anger, the other always fearful of appearing ra-cially insensitive. Esther is the sort of woman who will not date "down": She is in-sistent on running a kind of financial background check on her suitors. Mallory

Bebe Moore Campbell (Courtesy, Gordon/Barash Associates, Inc.)

urges Esther to relax her demand for upward mobility and to date the mail-truck driver because he is nice and will treat her well. Campbell notes that Mallory, as a middle-class white woman, has "the freedom to exercise these choices because she's not so clutched about trying to get to the next rung on the ladder and thinking she's got to be with the proper partner to get there."

Campbell hoped that the novel would "serve as a kind of blueprint, to help people foster racial understanding." She says that "our strengths lie in saluting our differences and getting along." While she is aware that many of the problems in the black community have to do with institutionalized racism, she also feels that "African-Americans need to begin to look really closely and make some movement toward changing the problems" and to recognize that some of them are the result of choices they have made. The response to *Brothers and Sisters* was uncommon, in that hundreds of discussion groups formed to come to terms with its issues. In Prince George's County, Maryland, an area with a large black population as well as a relatively stable white one, the book became the basis of a community project: People studied the impact of bias and sought ways to deal effectively with communication breakdowns between races.

Campbell laments the abandonment of the old neighborhoods, feeling that integration should not entail embracing white communities at the expense of black ones. She urges middle-class blacks to stay in touch with those less fortunate, to mentor the young. She feels that men, in particular, must take steps toward regaining control of their children and of the streets. In an interview with Martha Satz published in the *Southwest Review* (Spring, 1996), she observed that the Million Man March, with its resultant reawakening of moral, ethical, familial, and racial responsibilities, may have been responsible for the dramatically lower number of arson incidents in Detroit on Halloween of that year.

Singing in the Comeback Choir

Type of work: Novel
First published: 1998

Singing in the Comeback Choir is the story of Malindy Walker, a once-famous entertainer who has fallen ungracefully into old age, with its sometimes attendant sense of the pointlessness of the battle. Her life consists mainly of stealthily smoking and drinking, despite admonitions from her doctor. Based loosely on Alberta Hunter, jazz legend of the 1940's and 1950's, Malindy is a fiercely independent soul who has no intention of bowing to her granddaughter's wish to have her cared for (and closely supervised) in a senior citizen compound. The old neighborhood in which she lives has fallen into ruin, but Malindy's friends are there; memories of her great triumphs, of her sequined gowns and the applause, seem to sustain her. Her underlying sadness is over her diminished singing ability. She sees herself as finished, so she partakes of the fleeting pleasures of alcohol and nicotine.

Her granddaughter, Maxine Lott McCoy, a highly successful television producer with a relatively good marriage and a child on the way, is a professional who bears some resemblance to Campbell herself. She comes to the rescue of her grandmother, only to find that she herself is the one who needs to be rescued—from the high-powered yet insular and protected world in which she has lost touch with her origins. Therein lies the point of the novel. The old neighborhoods are dying because they have been abandoned by those who could give them life, the ones who are capable of regeneration. Maxine is saddened by what is left of her grandmother's street and by the dead eyes of the neighborhood boy she once knew; now grown and playing at being a man, he curses her and makes sexually threatening gestures. She confronts him but sees that he is the wave of the future unless others can intervene and help.

Part of Campbell's intent in the novel was "to talk about the work that needs to be done" in order to salvage and rebuild the decaying neighborhoods and despairing lives. She has noted that she wants "black folks to do the hard work that we've done in the past that we haven't been doing as much in the years following the Civil Rights movement."

Bebe Campbell's early works were primarily nonfiction. Her first book, *Successful Women, Angry Men: Backlash in the Two-Career Marriage*, delves into the effect of the feminist movement on family structure, most notably the shifting gender roles that result when women, either of necessity or in quest of self-actualization, seek work outside the home, sometimes upsetting the balance within. Her second work, *Sweet Summer: Growing Up with and Without My Dad*, is her memoir as a child of divorce having to spend the school year with her mother in Philadelphia and the summer with her father in North Carolina. The book was hailed for showing loving relationships in the black community and for stressing the importance of men or male figures in young girls' lives. Poet Nikki Giovanni praised it for providing "a corrective to some of the destructive images of black men that are prevalent in our society" and doing so with great vitality and clarity. Campbell has produced nonfiction articles for a wide range of publications, including *Essence*, *The New York Times*, *The Washington Post*, the *Los Angeles Times*, *Black Enterprise*, *Working Mother*, *Adweek*, *Ms.*, and *Glamour*; she was a contributing editor for *Essence*, *Black Enterprise*, and *Savvy*. In the 1990's, she became a regular commentator on National Public Radio's Morning Edition.

SUGGESTED READINGS

Campbell, Bebe Moore. "Bebe Moore Campbell: Her Memoir of 'A Special Childhood' Celebrates the Different Styles of Her Upbringing in a Divided Black Family." Interview by Lisa See. *Publishers Weekly*, June 30, 1989, 82-84.

_____. "Interview with Bebe Moore Campbell." Interview by Jane Campbell. *Callaloo* 22, no. 4 (1999): 954-973.

Chambers, Veronica. "Which Counts More, Gender or Race?" *The New York Times Magazine*, December 25, 1994, 16-19.

Edgerton, Clyde. "Medicine for Broken Souls." *The New York Times Book Review*, September 20, 1992, 13.

Ladson-Billings, Gloria. *"Your Blues Ain't Like Mine:* Keeping Issues of Race and Racism on the Multicultural Agenda." *Theory into Practice* 35, no. 4 (1996): 248-256.

Olendorf, Donna, ed. *Contemporary Authors.* Vol. 139. Detroit, Mich.: Gale Research, 1993.

Powers, Retha. "A Tale of Two Women." *Ms.*, September/October, 1994, 78.

Satz, Martha. "I Hope I Can Teach a Little Bit: An Interview with Bebe Moore Campbell." *Southwest Review* 81 (Spring, 1996): 195-213.

See, Lisa. "Bebe Moore Campbell." *Publishers Weekly*, June 30, 1989, 82-83.

Winter, Kari J. *"Brothers and Sisters*, by B. M. Campbell." *African American Review* 31, no. 2 (Summer, 1997): 369-372.

Contributors: Jacquelyn Benton and Gay Annette Zieger

Lorene Cary

BORN: Philadelphia, Pennsylvania; November 29, 1956

AFRICAN AMERICAN

Whether writing about her own life or writing about
women from history or contemporary women, Cary
offers varied insights into African American life.

PRINCIPAL WORKS
LONG FICTION: *The Price of a Child*, 1995; *Pride*, 1998
NONFICTION: *Black Ice*, 1991 (autobiography)

Lorene Cary (lohr-REEN KAR-ree), who became a freelance writer in the 1980's, gained prominence in the 1990's for her autobiography and novels. Education had always been a dominant factor in her life. The daughter of teachers John and Carole (née Hamilton) Cary, Lorene was raised in Philadelphia and one of its suburbs, Yeadon, where she attended public schools.

In the early 1960's, Cary's parents decided that their daughter, who was about to enter first grade, should attend the Lea School, where musical instrument lessons, French classes, an individualized reading series, and advanced Saturday morning classes were offered. Although the Carys lived outside the Lea School district, Carole Cary convinced the principal to consider her daughter for admission. After Cary passed an I.Q. test, she was placed in Lea's top first-grade class. By the time Cary was a teenager, her family had moved to Yeadon.

She transferred from the public high school and spent her junior and senior years at the elite Saint Paul's School in Concord, New Hampshire, after a friend of the family told her that the formerly all-male, segregated boarding school was offering scholarships to African American girls. She was one of only three or four girls in her classes, and during her first year, all the teachers were men. Her years at Saint Paul's were successful; she wrote articles for a school publication, was elected senior class vice president, and was the recipient of the Rector's Award. Cary graduated from Saint Paul's in 1974. Fourteen years later, she wrote about her days as a Saint Paul's coed in an article for *American Visions*.

Cary then expanded the article into her autobiography, *Black Ice*, her most critically acclaimed and well-known book. In *Black Ice*, Cary documents her experiences as a member of the generation of African American students who were the first of their race to attend elite prep schools during the stage of school integration that occurred after the public school desegregation efforts of the 1950's and 1960's. The American Library Association selected *Black Ice* as one of its Notable Books

188

in 1992. Cary's autobiography has been compared with Maya Angelou's *I Know Why the Caged Bird Sings* (1970). *Black Ice* is a valuable addition to the tradition of African American first-person narrative that extends back to the 1700's.

Cary continued her education at the University of Pennsylvania, where she earned a B.A. and an M.A. in English in 1978. Cary, as a recipient of a Thouron Fellowship, then studied Victorian literature and religion at England's Sussex University, where she completed her second M.A. in 1979. One year later, Cary was an apprentice at *Time* magazine, and in 1981 she became an associate editor of *TV Guide*. She became a freelance writer in 1983, and her articles appeared in such periodicals as *Essence*, *The Philadelphia Inquirer Sunday Magazine*, *Obsidian*, *Mirabella*, and *American Visions*. In 1993 she was a contributing editor for *Newsweek*.

Cary began her career as an educator at Saint Paul's in 1982, where she taught for one year and was a trustee from 1985 to 1989. She also taught at Antioch University, Philadelphia campus; Philadelphia University of the Arts; and the University of Pennsylvania, where she became a faculty member in the Department of English in 1995. Her novel, *The Price of a Child*, based on a nineteenth century African American woman who was a fugitive slave as well as an abolitionist, and *Pride*, her interpretation of the lives of four contemporary black women, were published during her tenure at the University of Pennsylvania.

Cary combined her dual careers as an author and educator in 1998 in the form of Art Sanctuary. She founded this nonprofit program, located in North Philadelphia at the Church of the Advocate, a National Historic Landmark Building, as a lecture and performance series presenting African American writers and artists to the community. Cary continued to reside in Philadelphia with her husband, writer and editor Robert C. Smith, with whom she had two daughters.

Black Ice

TYPE OF WORK: Autobiography
FIRST PUBLISHED: 1991

Black Ice provides glimpses into the mind and life of a young girl attending a prestigious prep school in New England. In 1971, Lorene Cary, an academically gifted African American teenager from Philadelphia, is invited to attend St. Paul's School in New Hampshire. Cary looks forward to the educational challenge and is excited to learn about upper-class and New England living, money, power, and the handsome Mike Russell, a St. Paul's senior who helps recruit new African American students.

Cary unravels and compares her childhood experiences to her adolescent ones at St. Paul's. She enters the school as an ambitious student with a mission to "turn it out," both academically and socially. Amid both successes and failures, her first year's experiences range from romance and sex to the mischief of petty stealing, lying, and smoking marijuana. The older Cary feels a different pressure in her second year, serving as the first female vice president, making decisions that, at times, alienate her from some of her closest friends. She experiences a frustrating self-awakening as she realizes that she lacks skills that her upper-class schoolmates take for granted. After graduation, she goes on to earn degrees from the University of Pennsylvania. Returning to teach at St. Paul's, where she later becomes a trustee, she feels that her bittersweet experience changed her into a "crossover artist."

Black Ice, a moderately toned autobiography, captures the contradictions of youth. Cary's memoir is grounded in vivid particulars: childhood songs and stories, the acute embarrassments and delights of adolescence. She divulges personal secrets while subtly revealing the silent isolation she felt as a student at St. Paul's.

The Price of a Child

TYPE OF WORK: Novel
FIRST PUBLISHED: 1995

Based on an actual story, *The Price of a Child* is a moving and suspenseful account of a courageous woman's attempts to obtain freedom for herself and for others. After dreaming of freedom all her life, Virginia (Ginnie) Pryor finally has a chance to escape from the Virginian Jackson Pryor, father of two of her three children. With the help of the Philadelphia Underground Railroad, Ginnie, her daughter, and her older son walk away from Pryor and take refuge with the Quicks, a large, prosperous black family, active in the abolitionist cause.

However, even in the North there are problems. Ginnie, now Mercer Gray, cannot forget the baby she left behind. She also worries about Pryor's efforts to get her back or to avenge himself on her rescuers. Within the Quick family there are the usual conflicts, often between amorous men and their wives, who are too tired from hard work and childbearing to be interested. Ironically, the two characters who seem made for each other, Mercer and the personable Tyree Quick, cannot marry because, to his regret, Tyree already has a wife.

In the end, the lovers part, Tyree to take care of his extended family, Mercer to continue speaking out against slavery and for women's rights, exposing herself to the salacious curiosity of her audience, as well as to threats from mobs of Northern anti-abolitionists. However, at the end of this memorable novel, the heroine's virtue is rewarded, for as a gift from Tyree, Mercer receives "the price of a child," that is, enough money to recover the little boy she lost.

SUGGESTED READINGS

Bigelow, Barbara Carlisle, ed. "Lorene Cary." In *Contemporary Black Biography: Profiles from the International Black Community*, vol. 3, edited by Michael L. LeBlanc. Detroit: Gale, 1993.
Woodson, Rose. "Lorene Cary." In *Facts On File Encyclopedia of Black Women in America*, vol. 2, edited by Darlene Clark Hine. New York: Facts On File, 1997.

Contributor: Linda M. Carter

Carlos Castaneda

BORN: Cajamarca, Peru(?); December 25, 1925(?)
DIED: Los Angeles, California; April 27, 1998

PERUVIAN AMERICAN

*A controversial anthropologist whose novelistic writings
attracted a large following beginning in the 1970's, Castaneda
is best known for his novel-like study of Yaqui culture and
ritual peyote use,* The Teachings of Don Juan.

PRINCIPAL WORKS

NONFICTION: *The Teachings of Don Juan: A Yaqui Way of Knowledge,* 1968 (fictionalized ethnographic study); *A Separate Reality: Further Conversations with Don Juan,* 1971; *Journey to Ixtlán: The Lessons of Don Juan,* 1972; *Tales of Power,* 1974; *The Second Ring of Power,* 1977; *The Eagle's Gift,* 1981; *The Fire from Within,* 1984; *The Power of Silence: Further Lessons of Don Juan,* 1987; *The Art of Dreaming,* 1993; *The Active Side of Infinity,* 1998; *Magical Passes: The Practical Wisdom of the Shamans of Ancient Mexico,* 1998; *The Wheel of Time: The Shamans of Ancient Mexico, Their Thoughts About Life, Death, and the Universe,* 1998

Carlos Castaneda (KAR-lohs kahs-tahn-NAY-dah) is a controversial anthropologist whose novelistic writings have attracted a large following. He claims to have been born in São Paulo, Brazil, on December 25, 1935. Some reference works concur with this place of birth but list December 25, 1931, as the date. Castaneda claims that he was born into a prominent Italian family of another name, that his mother died when he was a child, and that his father was a professor of literature. According to his story, he legally took the name Castaneda in 1959. Yet United States immigration records indicate that he was born in Cajamarca, Peru, on December 25, 1925, the son of César Arana Burungaray, a goldsmith, and Susan Castaneda Nova. According to these records, he was using the name Castaneda as early as 1951. When confronted with these discrepancies, Castaneda dismissed them as inconsequential.

Castaneda graduated from the Colegio Nacional de Nuestra Señora de Guadalupe and later studied painting and sculpture at the National School of Fine Arts in Lima. In 1951, he immigrated to Los Angeles, California. He initially studied psychology at Los Angeles City College between 1955 and 1959. In the latter year, he became a student at the University of California at Los Angeles (UCLA), where he received a B.A. in anthropology in 1962. He studied intermittently at UCLA over the next nine years, earning an M.A. in 1964 and a Ph.D. in 1970. While a student, Castaneda spent five years in Mexico, apprenticed to a Yaqui sorcerer. It was his account of this apprenticeship that would bring him literary celebrity.

Castaneda's field of graduate study was ethnomethodology, and as early as 1960 he had set out to study the ritual use of medicinal and psychotropic plants by American Indians in the southwestern United States. In the summer of that year, he met Don Juan Matus, an aged member of the Yaqui tribe, who was reputed to have extraordinary powers. First in Arizona and later in Sonora, Mexico, Don Juan initiated Castaneda into the ritual use of peyote and other hallucinogens. By the autumn of 1965, Castaneda had almost come to regard the visionary states shared with the old Indian as an alternate reality, one totally at odds with the rationalistic Western tradition. Castaneda turned the notes he had taken during his apprenticeship into a master's thesis. In 1968, the University of California Press published the work under the title *The Teachings of Don Juan: A Yaqui Way of Knowledge*. The modest run of two thousand copies excited great interest. The book was reissued as a paperback and immediately became a best seller. It was taken up by the antiestablishment counterculture, which viewed Don Juan as a folk hero and Castaneda as his amanuensis.

Also in 1968, Castaneda returned to Mexico to show Don Juan the book in which he was the central character. There, Castaneda had more experiences that defied his scientific rationalism. The result was *A Separate Reality: Further Conversations with Don Juan*. Other books followed in rapid succession: *Journey to Ixtlán*, an account of nonpsychedelic-related exercises practiced during the author's apprenticeship, and *Tales of Power*, which recounts further and even more extravagant experiences with Don Juan, now joined by another sorcerer, Don Genaro. Castaneda's doctoral dissertation was essentially the text of *Journey to Ixtlán*. *The Second Ring of Power*, which tells of Castaneda's encounter with Don Juan's female disciples, was received with mixed reviews.

Castaneda's earlier writings are linear in their narrative and temporal structure. In later books, such as *The Eagle's Gift, The Fire from Within, The Power of Silence*, and *The Art of Dreaming*, he presents the reader with the process of remembering the events that occurred in the multilayered and multidimensional time he spent with Don Juan. He also confronts the memory of Don Juan and his party moving beyond death and journeying into infinity with their awareness intact.

The system of knowledge that Castaneda learned from Don Juan proposes that, by making a minute account of their lives through a practice called recapitulation, people can acquire the necessary energy to challenge the objective existence of this world. An essential step in the process of gaining energy involves eradicating the ego and self-importance. As a practitioner of this system of knowledge, Castaneda did not defend himself or his works from criticism.

Castaneda's subject matter and personality made him a controversial figure. Despite his defenders within the academic community, when Castaneda received his Ph.D. in anthropology, the more staid members of the profession reacted as if the University of California had granted a doctorate in magic. After becoming famous, Castaneda gave interviews in which his date and place of birth, his parents' names,

Carlos Castaneda (AP/Wide World Photos)

and the entire history of his childhood conflicted with the official record. Even the date of his Ph.D. ranges from 1970 to 1973 in contemporary reference works. Castaneda maintained that Don Juan had marked him with the responsibility to succeed him as a guide for others in their quest for knowledge. Some critics implied that, because no one except Castaneda had actually seen Don Juan, the books might be largely works of imagination. (Two of Castaneda's colleagues and fellow apprentices of Don Juan, Florinda Donner-Grau and Taisha Abelar, later published narratives recounting their apprenticeships with Don Juan from a female viewpoint.) Nevertheless, some critics were of the opinion that Castaneda was essentially a gifted novelist and that the literal truth of his accounts was not a crucial factor.

Castaneda attempted to teach at the University of California at Irvine but discovered that he was too much of a celebrity to lecture effectively there. He subsequently led a rather reclusive life, working with a few of his students to present and elucidate the principles of "Tensegrity." The discipline of Tensegrity, based on specialized physical movements that were discovered by the shamans who founded Don Juan's system of knowledge, purportedly enable the practitioner to gather sufficient energy or impetus to navigate into other worlds. Castaneda died near UCLA in Westwood (a part of Los Angeles), on April 27, 1998.

Castaneda's books have sold in the millions and have been translated into several languages. Their gripping narrative and descriptive power and the beguiling and awesome alternatives that they present to ordinary existence have contributed to their popularity. As F. Scott Fitzgerald became the spokesperson for the Jazz Age, Castaneda caught the spirit (or one major part of the spirit) of the turbulent 1960's and 1970's and of the New Age movement that emerged from these years: a radical questioning of the values of American life, even of the American perception of reality.

The Teachings of Don Juan

TYPE OF WORK: Ethnography
FIRST PUBLISHED: 1968

The Teachings of Don Juan: A Yaqui Way of Knowledge introduces the mystical character of Juan Matu, a Yaqui Indian from Sonora, Mexico. Born in the Southwest in 1891, Don Juan lived in Mexico until 1940. He then immigrated to Arizona, where he met Castaneda and, in 1961, accepted him as an apprentice in Yaqui sorcery. Until 1965, he instructed Castaneda in becoming a "man of knowledge" through experience with "nonordinary reality."

The teaching required the use of hallucinogenic drugs, and much of the book chronicles Castaneda's visions while under their influence. The sorcerer teaches Castaneda the procedures for growing, collecting, and preparing drug-yielding plants. Castaneda's altered states of consciousness frighten and bewilder him, and he repeatedly calls on Don Juan for rational explanations. The Indian counters with metaphysics and insists that his pupil form his own understandings. Don Juan defines a man of knowledge as one "who has, without rushing or faltering, gone as far as he can in unraveling the secrets of power." Only he who challenges and defeats the four "natural enemies"—fear, clarity, power, and old age—can become such a man. He recommends "a path with heart." All paths lead nowhere, he says, but those with heart make for a joyful journey.

Becoming a man of knowledge requires in-depth learning, unbending intent, strenuous labor, and the possession of an ally. An ally is either "the smoke" (psilocybin from mushrooms) or jimson weed. "The smoke will set you free to see anything you want to see," Don Juan claims. A third drug, mescaline (peyote), is not an ally but a protector and teacher. Don Juan claims that mescaline has an identity of its own outside the user. In contrast, an ally resides within, bestowing the ability to perform fantastic feats, such as assuming animal form.

Although presented as a work of ethnographic research and published as a master's thesis in anthropology, the book is widely agreed to be fiction. The work is condemned by some as a hoax. Whether truth or fabrication, it has been widely read and served to consolidate the role of hallucinogens in Native American religious rituals with the psychedelic movement of the 1960's and 1970's.

SUGGESTED READINGS

De Mille, Richard. *Castaneda's Journey: The Power and the Allegory*. Rev. ed. Santa Barbara, Calif.: Capra Press, 1978.
Keen, Sam. *Voices and Visions*. New York: Harper & Row, 1974.
Sánchez, Víctor. *The Teachings of Don Carlos: Practical Applications of the Works of Carlos Castaneda*. Translated by Robert Nelson. Santa Fe, N.Mex.: Bear, 1995.
Williams, Donald Lee. *Border Crossings: A Psychological Perspective on Carlos Castaneda's Path of Knowledge*. Toronto: Inner City Books, 1981.

Contributors: Patrick Adcock, Margarita Nieto, and Faith Hickman Brynie

Ana Castillo

BORN: Chicago, Illinois; June 15, 1953

MEXICAN AMERICAN

Castillo's writing reflects her involvement in Chicano and Latino political and cultural movements, as well as her strong commitment to feminist and environmental concerns.

PRINCIPAL WORKS

CHILDREN'S LITERATURE: *My Daughter, My Son, the Eagle, the Dove: An Aztec Chant*, 2000
LONG FICTION: *The Mixquiahuala Letters*, 1986; *Sapogonia*, 1990 (revised 1994); *So Far from God*, 1993; *Peel My Love Like an Onion*, 1999; *The Guardians*, 2007
POETRY: *Otro Canto*, 1977; *The Invitation*, 1979 (second edition 1986); *Women Are Not Roses*, 1984; *My Father Was a Toltec*, 1988; *My Father Was a Toltec and Selected Poems, 1973-1988*, 1995; *I Ask the Impossible*, 2001; *Watercolor Women/Opaque Men*, 2005
SHORT FICTION: *Ghost Talk*, 1984; *The Antihero*, 1986; *Subtitles*, 1992; *Loverboys: Stories*, 1996
TRANSLATION: *Esta Puente, Mi Espalda*, 1988 (*This Bridge Called My Back: Writings by Radical Women of Color*; Cherríe Moraga and Gloria Anzaldua, editors)
NONFICTION: *Massacre of the Dreamers: Essays on Xicanisma*, 1994
EDITED TEXTS: *The Sexuality of Latinas*, 1993; *Recent Chicano Poetry/Neueste Chicano-Lyrik*, 1994; *Goddess of the Americas/La Diosa de las Américas*, 1996

One of the most prominent and versatile Chicana writers in the United States, Ana Castillo (AH-nah kahs-TEE-yoh) is the author of poetry, novels, critical essays, translations, and edited texts. The Chicago-born Castillo first became known as a poet. Her writing reflects her involvement in Chicano and Latino political and cultural movements, as well as her strong commitment to feminist and environmental concerns. Among the many grants and awards she has received are the Carl Sandburg Literary Award in Fiction in 1993 for *So Far from God*, a Before Columbus Foundation American Book Award in 1987 for *The Mixquiahuala Letters*, and National Endowment for the Arts Poetry Fellowships in 1990 and 1995. She has taught and lectured at several American and European universities.

Castillo began publishing poetry while she was still a student at Northeastern Illinois University, from which she graduated with a degree in liberal arts in 1975. She first published in journals such as *Revista Chicano-Riqueño*, and her first collection, *Otro Canto*, appeared in 1977. This was followed by *The Invitation* in 1979, the same year that she received an M.A. in Latin American and Caribbean studies from the University of Chicago.

Castillo's early poems reveal her involvement in *El Movimiento* (the Chicano/ Latino civil rights movement), as well as her developing feminism and her poetic use of eroticism. The theme of social protest in *Otro Canto* appears in poems such as "A Christmas Carol: c. 1976," spoken in the voice of a Chicana facing divorce and poverty amid memories of her childhood dreams. Other frequently noted poems from the volume include "Napa, California" and "1975." *The Invitation* displays Castillo's disillusionment with the persistent sexism of the male-dominated Civil Rights movement. Castillo's response in *The Invitation* is to appropriate the erotic, rejecting taboos and clichés through a female speaker who explores and defines her sexuality in her own terms.

In 1984, a year after the birth of her son, Marcel Ramón Herrera, selections from *Otro Canto* and *The Invitation* were reprinted, along with new pieces, in *Women Are Not Roses*. Castillo's rejection of antifeminist stereotypes appears in the volume's title poem, as well as in "The Antihero," in which Castillo explores the male need to construct and objectify the feminine. *My Father Was a Toltec and Selected Poems, 1973-1988* is noted for its treatment of Chicana identity in poems such as "Ixtacihuatl Died in Vain" and the political resonance of the utopian "In My Country."

Castillo began writing her first novel, *The Mixquiahuala Letters*, at the age of twenty-three. Published ten years later, in 1986, *The Mixquiahuala Letters* is an epistolary novel that records the shifting relationship of two Latinas: Teresa, the author of the letters, and the artist Alicia. Their friendship becomes a record of betrayals through which Castillo explores internalized sexism and the negation of lesbian desire. Castillo's main characters meet in Mexico; through their experiences in Mexico and the United States, Castillo probes race, class, and gender issues from a variety of perspectives. This strategy is enhanced by Castillo's experimental provision of multiple sequences in which the letters can be read. Although the novel is dedicated to Julio Cortázar, Castillo's strongest literary influence was the controversial *Novas Cartas Portuguesas* (1972) by the "three Marias" (Maria Barreno, Maria Horta, and Maria Costa), a work that inspired Castillo's presentation of sexuality and her challenge of Catholicism.

In 1990, Castillo moved from California to Albuquerque, New Mexico. In that same year, she published *Sapogonia*, a novel set in the mythical country of Sapogonia, the home of all mestizos. The novel depicts the obsession of Máximo Madrigal with singer and activist Pastora Aké. Máximo's need to dominate Pastora is presented both as the legacy of the conquest, with the European-identified Máximo playing out the role of conquistador, and as a function of the cultural position of women who, like Pastora, participate in their own objectification.

The 1993 publication of Castillo's novel *So Far from God*, along with the republication of *Sapogonia*, marked her crossover from small presses into the mainstream publishing market. Set in New Mexico, *So Far from God* illustrates the expansion of Castillo's political vision to issues such as environmentalism and presents a new focus on Latino spirituality and popular culture. Castillo's main characters, Sofia and her daughters Esperanza, Fe, Caridad, and La Loca, enact a late twentieth century version of the martyrdom of Saint Sophia. However, while Sofia's daughters fall victim to war, toxic chemicals, and violence, Sofia becomes a paragon of strength and survival. Although tragic at times, *So Far from God*, like many of Castillo's works, also reveals her ironic sense of humor.

Many of Castillo's political concerns are presented in her book of essays, *Massacre of the Dreamers: Essays on Xicanisma*. Castillo develops a Chicana feminism that addresses the history of the colonized woman, taking into account her sexuality and her spirituality, both of which must be freed from institutional oppression. In 1996, Castillo published the short-story collection *Loverboys*, which was centered on the theme of desire, both homosexual and heterosexual. The novel *Peel My Love Like an Onion* returned to the subject of flamenco dancing and music explored in *Sapogonia* and delved into the erotic lives of its main characters. Her varied works have firmly established Castillo as an influential Latina feminist writer and theorist.

So Far from God

TYPE OF WORK: Novel
FIRST PUBLISHED: 1993

So Far from God is a tragicomic exploration of the cultural and temporal collisions in the Chicana world. The novel tells the story of two decades in the life of Sofia and her four daughters in a small New Mexico town, blending melodrama, visions, recipes, Catholicism, folklore, and miracles through an intimate, conversational tone that incorporates Latino slang and regional dialect. Parodying the Latin American *telenovela*, or soap opera, the protagonists are soap opera stereotypes. The plot is filled with ironies, and it contrasts the fantasy of the *telenovela* genre with the realities of Chicana lives. The novel's admiration and empathy are for the Chicana—the men in the book are damaged or weak.

Fe, ambitious, assimilated into the white culture, and perfectly groomed, is ashamed of her family. To reach her dream of middle-class respectability, she works overtime at a factory, where she contracts cancer and dies. The beautiful Caridad, sexually promiscuous after her annulled marriage, is attacked and mutilated. She uses spirituality to reconnect with the mysticism of her heritage, and she becomes a hermit, healer, and channeler. She falls in love with Esmeralda, a lesbian whose Mexican roots mystically connect them. The two die holding hands, leaping from a mesa, called by a Mexican deity. Unlike Fe, who was "plain dead," they achieve a mythic status. Esperanza, a television journalist and the only college-educated sister, is kidnapped and killed in Saudi Arabia. Emotionally connected to the Native American church, her visionary form converses with Caridad. La Loca, the youngest and most visionary, dies of AIDS even though she has had no physical contact with people other than her mother and sister since the age of three.

Sofia endures. Abandoned by her gambling husband (who returns twenty years later), she raises her daughters alone, establishes herself as mayor, and organizes cooperatives to improve the economic stability of the impoverished town. The novel ends with her founding of the Society of Mothers of Martyrs and Saints as a tribute to La Loca. This act takes a sardonic twist as the society develops into a purveyor of kitsch. Consistent with the oral tradition, the novel relates cherished Latino traditions. As a scathing commentary of the complexities of the Chicana existence, it also portends cultural decline.

Watercolor Women/Opaque Men

TYPE OF WORK: Novel and poetry
FIRST PUBLISHED: 2005

That *Watercolor Women/Opaque Men* is an epic novel in verse detracts neither from its narrative power nor from the troubling story Ana Castillo tells of what the woman protagonist—referred to only as "Ella" (the Spanish for "she")—endures as an "American." Particularizing racism, sexism, and homophobia to the story of this one "nameless" Chicana enables Castillo to make her point more harshly: Life for any outsider but particularly for a lesbian Chicana is not easy, even after She has fully embraced her lesbian self as well as her Mexican heritage.

Told in a sequence of vignettes about Ella and her relatives, the novel follows She from her early days as the child of hard-working illegal field hands in California, through the turbulent 1960's in hippy San Francisco, into and out of a marriage, finally arriving at the point where Ella finally is fully "her self": a single mother of a son and a lover of women. The aunts, uncles, and Ella's immediate family serve to reflect Ella's own circumstances as someone who has been disenfranchised from her own Mexican heritage by her family's attempt at a better life in the United States as well as to illustrate how difficult it is to achieve that "better" life once in America.

The powerful influences in her life are her female relatives, especially an aunt who teaches her self-reliance while on a trip to Chicago. From there, Ella journeys more or less alone, even when married, through the American caste system and endures. That she is essentially always alone is perhaps the main point of this book: Strong women, especially women on the outside, have no other choice. "She" succeeds, but no one except her one aunt offered any help.

Although *Watercolor Women/Opaque Men* is angry, it is, more important, instructive and enlightening: Anyone wishing to gain insight into what it means to be a minority in America will learn much from reading this novel.

SUGGESTED READINGS

Alarcón, Norma. "The Sardonic Powers of the Erotic in the Work of Ana Castillo."
In *Breaking Boundaries: Latina Writing and Critical Readings*, edited by

Asuncion Horno-Delgado et al. Amherst: University of Massachusetts Press, 1989.

Aldama, Fredereick Luis. *Brown on Brown: Chicano/a Representations of Gender and Ethnicity*. Austin: University of Texas Press, 2005.

Curiel, Barbara Brinson. "Heteroglossia in Ana Castillo's *The Mixquiahuala Letters*." *Discurso Literario* 7, no. 1 (1990).

Delgadillo, Theresa. "Forms of Chicana Feminist Resistance: Hybrid Spirituality in Ana Castillo's *So Far from God*." *Modern Fiction Studies* 44 (Winter, 1998): 888-889.

Lanza, Carmela D. "Hearing the Voices: Women and Home and Ana Castillo's *So Far from God*." *MELUS* 23 (Spring, 1998): 65-79.

Pérez-Torres, Rafael. *Movements in Chicano Poetry: Against Myths, Against Margins*. New York: Cambridge University Press, 1995.

Quintana, Alvina. "Ana Castillo's *The Mixquiahuala Letters:* The Novelist as Ethnographer." In *Criticism in the Borderlands: Studies in Chicano Literature, Culture, and Ideology*, edited by Héctor Calderón and José David Saldívar. Durham, N.C.: Duke University Press, 1991.

Walter, Roland. "The Cultural Politics of Dislocation and Relocation in the Novels of Ana Castillo." *MELUS* 23 (Spring, 1998): 81-97.

Yarbro-Bejarano, Yvonne. "The Multiple Subject in the Writing of Ana Castillo." *American Review* 20, no. 1 (Spring, 1992).

Contributors: Maura Ives and Susan Chainey

Lorna Dee Cervantes

BORN: San Francisco, California; August 6, 1954

MEXICAN AMERICAN

*Acting as a mediator between the Chicano community and a
mainstream English-speaking audience, Cervantes uses
autobiography to translate the experiences of her ethnic and
gender communities to a broader audience.*

PRINCIPAL WORKS

POETRY: *Emplumada*, 1981; *From the Cables of Genocide: Poems on Love and
Hunger*, 1991; *Drive: The First Quartet*, 2006

Although Lorna Dee Cervantes (LOHR-nah dee sur-VAHN-tehs) grew up in an urban, working-class barrio, she was raised to speak English because of her family's
fear of racism. As a result, gender issues and ethnicity and language issues play major roles in her poetry. In keeping with such themes, Cervantes describes herself as
a Chicana poet, with all the ethnic, gender, and language markers expressed or implied. Furthermore, she means that description to be subversive. When a group or
individual self-defines, it is an exercise of power, which leads to self-determina-
tion, an act historically denied to women and members of minority ethnic groups.

Cervantes notes that women and Chicanos' common experiences and challenges
are in the first case due to machismo and patriarchy and in the second due to racial
prejudice and economic exploitation. This unites either group but alienates it from
other groups. While the visionary power of poetry can invoke an idealized, utopian
world, the real world is beset by social problems, making social revolution necessary. Poetry serves Cervantes as a form of resistance, another means of subversion.
She employs narrative poems to represent the real world of conflicts and lyrical poetry for contemplation and meditation. The former deal most specifically with ethnicity and gender, particularly male-female sexual relationships. The lyrical poems
frequently bemoan the necessity of social commitment and responsibility.

Language serves Cervantes as a power strategy. For example, she juxtaposes
versions of her poems in English and Spanish. She does not translate poems, as one
poem is not the same as the other: Each develops independently in its own language. She also employs interlingualism—that is, Spanish within English plus barrio dialect—in order to establish her version of literary style rather than follow canonical traditions and customs.

Cervantes's use of autobiography as a poetic strategy has offended some members of her family, who feel that she discloses too many personal details. Her inten-

tion, however, is to record and translate the experiences of the historical and collective ethnic and gender communities to larger audiences rather than to emphasize her family's experiences. Furthermore, she sees herself as a mediator between the Chicano community (a largely oral culture) and the English-speaking audience (a largely print culture). In fact, she portrays herself as a scribe in her poem "Beneath the Shadow of the Freeway." Her grandmother is represented as Queen and her mother as Knight.

Cervantes earned an undergraduate degree from San Jose State University in 1984 and a doctorate from University of California, Santa Cruz, in the history of consciousness in 1990. She has taught creative writing at the Universities of Colorado at Denver and at Boulder. Cervantes received two grants from the National Endowment for the Arts and one from the Fine Arts Works Center. She also won a Pushcart Prize, a Provincetown Fellowship, a London Meadow Fellowship, and a Lila Wallace/Readers Digest Foundation Writers Award (1995). She was named Outstanding Chicana Scholar by the National Association of Chicano Scholars. She has served as a judge for the Poetry Society of America's William Carlos Williams Award and as a panelist for Arizona State Arts Commission.

"Beneath the Shadow of the Freeway"

TYPE OF WORK: Poetry
FIRST PUBLISHED: 1981, in *Emplumada*

"Beneath the Shadow of the Freeway" is probably Cervantes's best-known poem. In spite of its title and all its natural imagery, however, "Beneath the Shadow of the Freeway" is really a celebration of the power of women. In language that lifts her thoughts to a mythic level, Cervantes creates a powerful statement of Latina strength and a reminder about those—particularly men—who so often take it away.

The poem is broken into six numbered parts; all except the first contain verse stanzas themselves. In the first section, the narrator describes the house she lives in with her mother and her grandmother, who "watered geraniums/ [as] the shadow of the freeway lengthened." "We were a woman family," the narrator declares in the next stanza and introduces her main theme. Her mother warns her about men, but the narrator models herself more on her grandmother, who "believes in myths and birds" and "trusts only what she builds/ with her own hands." A drunken intruder (perhaps the mother's ex-husband) tries to break into the house in section 5 but is scared away. In the final stanza the mother warns the narrator, "'Baby, don't count on nobody,'" but the narrator confesses to the reader that "every night I sleep with a gentle man/ to the hymn of the mockingbirds," plants geraniums, ties her hair up like her grandmother, "and trust[s] only what I have built with my own hands." The poem is thus a celebration of three generations of women and contains the promise that women can be independent and still find love.

SUGGESTED READINGS

Crawford, John F. "Notes Toward a New Multicultural Criticism: Three Works by Women of Color." In *A Gift of Tongues: Critical Challenges in Contemporary American Poetry*, edited by Marie Harris and Kathleen Aguero. Athens: University of Georgia Press, 1987.

"Lorna Dee Cervantes." In *After Aztlán: Latino Poets of the Nineties*, edited by Ray González. Boston: David R. Godine, 1993.

"Lorna Dee Cervantes." In *The Bloomsbury Guide to Women's Literature*, edited by Claire Buck. New York: Prentice Hall, 1992.

McKenna, Teresa. "'An Utterance More Pure than Word': Gender and the Corrido Tradition in Two Contemporary Chicano Poems." In *Feminist Measures: Soundings in Poetry and Theory*, edited by Lynn Keller and Cristianne Miller. Ann Arbor: University of Michigan Press, 1994.

Madsen, Deborah L. *Understanding Contemporary Chicana Poetry*. Columbia: University of South Carolina Press, 2000.

Sánchez, Marta Ester. "The Chicana as Scribe: Harmonizing Gender and Culture in Lorna Dee Cervantes' 'Beneath the Shadow of the Freeway.'" In *Contemporary Chicana Poetry: A Critical Approach to an Emerging Literature*. Berkeley: University of California Press, 1985.

Savin, Ada. "Bilingualism and Dialogism: Another Reading of Lorna Dee Cervantes' Poetry." In *An Other Tongue: Nation and Ethnicity in the Linguistic Borderlands*, edited by Alfred Arteaga. Durham, N.C.: Duke University Press, 1994.

Seator, Lynette. "*Emplumada:* Chicana Rites-of-Passage." *MELUS* 11 (Summer, 1984): 23-38.

Wallace, Patricia. "Divided Loyalties: Literal and Literary in the Poetry of Lorna Dee Cervantes, Cathy Song, and Rita Dove." *MELUS* 18 (Fall, 1993): 3-19.

Contributors: Debra D. Andrist and David Peck

Barbara Chase-Riboud

BORN: Philadelphia, Pennsylvania; June 26, 1939

AFRICAN AMERICAN

Chase-Riboud's writing explores power relationships as they are shaped by race, gender, and social and political needs.

PRINCIPAL WORKS

LONG FICTION: *Sally Hemings*, 1979; *Valide: A Novel of the Harem*, 1986 (revised 1988); *Echo of Lions*, 1989; *The President's Daughter*, 1994; *Hottentot Venus*, 2003

POETRY: *From Memphis and Peking*, 1974; *Portrait of a Nude Woman as Cleopatra*, 1987

Barbara DeWayne Chase-Riboud (chays-rih-BOOD) was born and raised in Philadelphia, the only child of a building contractor and a medical assistant. She won her first art prize at age eight. She received a bachelor's of fine arts from Temple University in 1957 and a master's of fine arts from Yale University in 1960. In 1961 she married the French photojournalist Marc Eugène Riboud, with whom she had two sons, David and Alexis. She made her home in Europe, mostly in Paris and Rome. After her divorce in 1981, she married Sergio Tosi, an Italian art historian and expert. She traveled widely in Africa and the Near and Far East and was the first American woman to be admitted to the People's Republic of China after the revolution in 1949. Asked if she felt like an expatriate, she answered: "It takes me three hours to get from Paris to New York, so I don't really believe in expatriatism anymore."

Chase-Riboud became a popular writer almost overnight with the publication of *Sally Hemings*, which sold more than one million copies and won the Janet Heidinger Kafka Prize for best novel by an American woman in 1979. Ten years later, *Echo of Lions* sold 500,000 copies and confirmed Chase-Riboud's reputation as a solid historical novelist who likes to bring historical figures out of an undeserved obscurity.

Her original literary vocation, though, was in poetry. *From Memphis and Peking* combines a strong sensual appeal with the expression of a desire to travel through time, in the form of a quest for her ancestry, and space, in an exploration of the cultures of Africa, America, and China. In 1988, she won the Carl Sandburg Poetry Prize for *Portrait of a Nude Woman as Cleopatra*, a tortured unveiling of the Egyptian queen's public and private lives. Even before becoming a poet, Chase-Riboud was a sculptor with an international reputation. She received many fellowships and awards for her work, including a John Hay Whitney Foundation Fellowship in 1957-1958 for study at the American Academy in Rome, a National Endowment for the Arts Fellowship in 1973, and a Van der Zee Award in 1995. Her several honorary doctorates include one from Temple University in 1981. In 1996 she received a Knighthood for Contributions to Arts and Letters from the French government.

Chase-Riboud's historical novels offer a strongly diversified exploration of power relationships as they are shaped by race, gender, and social and political needs. Slavery figures prominently in each novel, not only in its aberrations and its violence but also in the complex configurations of relationships it produces.

Barbara Chase-Riboud (Courtesy, Author)

The hairsplitting legal separation of the races is rendered incongruous by the intertwined blood ties exemplified in the extended interracial Jefferson family. More controversially, the notions of slave and master lose their sharp distinction in front of multiple forms of attraction and manipulation. It is the theme of profoundly mixed heritage and history, embodied in miscegenation, that ultimately dominates. The "outing" of hidden or mysterious women, such as Sally Hemings or Valide, bespeaks a desire to shake taboos and renew our understanding of world history.

Chase-Riboud's intellectual inquisitiveness, her multilingual and multicultural experience, and her artistic sensibility successfully collaborate in these re-creations of large portions of world history, whose visual power is attained through precise and often poetic descriptions of places, events, clothes, and physiognomies. Especially engaging are the nuanced renderings of the characters' psychological and emotional turmoil, whether Catherine the Great or the African Joseph Cinque. These are historical novels in the pure Scottian tradition, which depict a welter of official historical events while bringing them to life with invented but eminently plausible depictions of the private lives that lie in the gaps. The sense of wide-ranging tableau is enhanced by a narrative technique that often jumps between numerous characters' perspectives in successions of relatively short chapters. One can even hear echoes from one novel to another, as Sally Hemings is discussed by John Quincy Adams in *Echo of Lions* or Thomas Jefferson figures in *Valide*'s Tripoli episode, and *The President's Daughter* even reproduces scenes from *Sally Hemings*.

In October, 1997, Chase-Riboud filed a plagiarism suit against film director Steven Spielberg, accusing him of stealing "themes, dialogue, characters, relationships, plots, scenes, and fictional inventions" from *Echo of Lions* for his 1997 film *Amistad*. The suit ended with an out-of-court settlement, but during the controversy plagiarism charges were turned against Chase-Riboud, for both *Echo of Lions* and *Valide*. Although she admitted that not mentioning her sources was an inexperienced writer's oversight, she pointed out that she often weaves "real documents and real reference materials" into her novels; *The President's Daughter* contains nine pages of author's notes on historical sources.

Sally Hemings

TYPE OF WORK: Novel
FIRST PUBLISHED: 1979

This novel is a fictional biography of Sally Hemings, President Thomas Jefferson's slave mistress (in November, 1998, a *Nature* magazine article revealed, thanks to deoxyribonucleic acid [DNA] evidence, that Jefferson had at least fathered Hemings's last child). Primarily inspired by Fawn M. Brodie's 1974 biography *Thomas Jefferson: An Intimate History* and by the Hemings family's oral testimony, Chase-Riboud re-creates known historical events and characters, filling them out with nuanced and convincing psychological and emotional texture. The official facts are: Sally Hemings accompanied Jefferson's daughter Maria to Paris in June of 1787 to join him there, and they all came back to America in October of 1789. A scandal broke out during Jefferson's first term as president, when he was accused of having a son with his slave Sally, an allegation Jefferson never publicly denied; all seven of Sally's children were conceived when Jefferson was present at Monticello, his estate in Virginia, and all her children were either allowed to run away or freed by Jefferson's will. According to Sally's son Madison Hemings, whose memoirs appeared in the Pike County (Ohio) *Republican* in 1873, his mother was pregnant with Jefferson's child when they came back from Paris, and Jefferson had promised her that he would free their children when they turned twenty-one.

The novel, which is told mostly from Sally's point of view, explores with great subtlety the emotional torture involved in a love story between a slave mistress and her master. Her alternate references to him as "my master" or "my lover" reflect her changing evaluation of herself as someone who gave up her freedom for love. A reminder of her surrender is provided by her brother James, who exhorts her to stay in France, where they are legally free, who keeps reproaching her for choosing a golden prison, and who ultimately dies in mysterious circumstances. The relationship with Jefferson is presented realistically, as Sally occupies the underside of his public life, which echoes back into her life though remains frustratingly out of reach. Her rare excursions into public spaces lead to unpleasant confrontations with future vice president Aaron Burr and future First Lady Dolley Madison, reminding her of the limits imposed on her identity by the outside world. The recurring silences between her and her lover, which become a motif in the book, symbolize the extent of her invisibility and powerlessness. As a consequence she starts wielding power indirectly and subversively, as she takes over the keys of the house from her mother and decides to methodically attain freedom for each of her children. Ultimately, though, it is the love that defines her more than her slavehood.

Sally's story is told as a flashback, after the census taker Nathan Langdon visits her in her cabin in 1830 and decides to mark her and her two sons down as white, thereby replaying the white world's many attempts to erase her identity. The novel thus explicitly defines itself as a response to the silences and taboos of American history, as signified by the burning of letters and the ripping up of portraits. Langdon's interviews with sixth president John Quincy Adams, Burr, and painter John Trumbull, inserted in the middle of the novel, ensure a definite link between Sally Hemings's private life and the representatives of public history and lend her story long-overdue weight and legitimacy.

Although Jefferson remains an elusive figure throughout the book, some personality traits come out forcefully, such as the strength of his desires and passions under a facade of equanimity and his streak of despotism despite his egalitarian principles. The Jefferson family, and Virginia society more generally, are shown to be shot through with violence and decay, as evidenced by Jefferson's granddaughter's death at the hands of an abusive husband and George Wythe's and his mulatto son's murders by his nephew. The theme of lying to oneself and to others in order to preserve a semblance of social order would remain a dominant one in Chase-Riboud's oeuvre.

Valide

TYPE OF WORK: Novel
FIRST PUBLISHED: 1986

In *Valide*, Chase-Riboud transports her exploration of power relationships under slavery to the Ottoman Empire at the turn of the nineteenth century. The novel starts with the death of the sultana Valide in 1817, then retraces her rise from American slave of sultan Abdülhamid I after her capture by Barbary pirates to Ikbal (favorite) to Kadine (official wife) to Valide, queen mother. The subtle political and psychological analysis uncovers the complex usages of power and powerlessness in a profoundly hierarchical and ritualistic social structure. Under her new name, Naksh-i-dil ("embroidered tongue"), she becomes slowly acquainted with the intrigues, alliances, and corruption that condition survival in the harem and that constitute the only possible form of resistance against engulfment by boredom and lassitude. She learns to use her body to wield power over the sultan and her female companions, and love is shown to be merely "a mixture of need and power, lust and loneliness."

The microcosmos of the harem reflects the wider geopolitical struggles of the empire with France, England, and Russia. As a young woman, Naksh-i-dil realizes that the sultan himself is a slave, whose power oscillates between treasons, alliances, and demonstrations of military prowess. Later, as Valide, she displays more political insight than her son and becomes his mastermind; for example, she forces a peace treaty with the Russians as an alliance against French emporer Napoleon I. The parallels and contrasts with Russian empress Catherine the Great, whose triumphant trip through the newly acquired Crimea turns out to be an illusion of grandeur, intensify the theme that "there was no absolute tyranny, just as there was no absolute slavery." By zeroing in on numerous historical figures, such as Russian statesman Grigory Aleksandrovich Potemkin, the sultan Selim III, and American admirals, the novel skillfully captures the intermingling of public and private lives. Detailed descriptions of settings (including a map of the harem), as well as information on social mores, help place this book in the best tradition of the historical novel.

Echo of Lions

TYPE OF WORK: Novel
FIRST PUBLISHED: 1989

Echo of Lions recounts the true ordeal of fifty-three kidnapped Mende Africans taken to Havana and sold to two Cuban planters, José Ruiz and Pedro Montez. On their way to the plantation aboard the *Amistad*, the Africans rebelled and killed the captain and the cook, while two sailors escaped. The Spaniards, kept alive to help steer the ship back to Africa, tricked the mutineers by navigating east by day and northwest by night. After their capture off Long Island, the Africans underwent three trials for murder and piracy, the last one in the Supreme Court in March, 1841, which declared them free. The *Amistad* story, which fascinated the American public at the time, put forth the view of slaves as mere property to be returned to their owners, according to a treaty with Spain, against their constitutional rights as persons illegally captured from their home country. The novel presents a skillful mixture of public and private history, providing minute descriptions of the slaves' tribulations, their court trials, their incarceration conditions, the New England abolitionist scene, and political debates, all the while infusing them with the historical characters' intimate thoughts and perspectives. Joseph Cinque, the Africans' charismatic leader, who, even though the case did little for the abolition of slavery in America, became a symbol of black pride and the right to freedom, as well as John Quincy Adams, who defended the case before the Supreme Court, receive a splendidly nuanced psychological treatment. In occasionally poetic passages Cinque tries to make sense of his new surroundings, recalls the beauty of his native land, and dreams of his wife; excerpts from Adams's diary bring to light his anxious but intense commitment. Several fictional characters, such as a wealthy black abolitionist and his beautiful daughter, help provide social and emotional texture to the wide-ranging historical material.

The President's Daughter

TYPE OF WORK: Novel
FIRST PUBLISHED: 1994

A follow-up to *Sally Hemings*, *The President's Daughter* chronicles the life of Harriet Hemings, Thomas Jefferson's white-skinned, red-haired slave daughter, as she leaves Monticello, travels through Europe, and marries a pharmacist in Philadelphia. After his death and burial in Africa, she marries his twin brother and raises seven children, passing as a white woman until her death. This novel of epic proportions gives Harriet's life a wide public resonance by associating it closely with a stream of historical events, such as Jefferson's death, the legal twists and turns of the institution of slavery, the Civil War (the Gettysburg battle, in particular), even the European presence in South Africa. Its descriptions of various social circles, such as Philadelphian high society and abolitionist groups, its renderings of long conversations on issues of the day, and its lengthy time span, give it a nineteenth century novel's consistency. Its themes, though, are painfully contemporary. Besides the continued exploration of filial love and power relationships, the novel concentrates on the psychological tortures of Harriet as an impostor and betrayer of her two families, the white and the black. The motif of fingerprints as an unmistakable bearer of identity is complicated when Harriet loses hers after burning her hand and sees the signs of her identity thus irrecoverably lost. The local theme of slavery as an institution based on fake premises and dependent on duplicity and lies reaches a philosophical dimension when Jefferson's Paris lover, Maria Cosway, whom Harriet visits in her Italian convent, teaches her that "nothing is real" and "everything is illusion." The theme of race relations receives a more bitter treatment in this sequel, as even love cannot seem to rise above gulfs of incomprehension.

SUGGESTED READINGS

Rushdy, Ashraf H. A. "'I Write in Tongues': The Supplement of Voice in Barbara Chase-Riboud's *Sally Hemings.*" *Contemporary Literature* 35, no. 1 (1994): 100-135.

_____. "Representing the Constitution: Embodiments of America in Barbara Chase-Riboud's *Echo of Lions.*" *Critique: Studies in Contemporary Fiction* 36, no. 4 (Summer, 1995): 258-280.

Stout, Candace Jesse. "In the Spirit of Art Criticism: Reading the Writings of Women Artists." *Studies in Art Education* 41, no. 4 (2000): 346-361.

Contributor: Christine Levecq

Denise Chávez

BORN: Las Cruces, New Mexico; August 15, 1948

MEXICAN AMERICAN

*Chávez's poetry, fiction, and numerous plays show
Mexican American women searching for personal identity
and space in a complex cultural environment.*

PRINCIPAL WORKS
LONG FICTION: *Face of an Angel*, 1994; *Loving Pedro Infante*, 2001
SHORT FICTION: *The Last of the Menu Girls*, 1986
NONFICTION: *A Taco Testimony: Meditations on Family, Food, and Culture*, 2006

Denise Chávez (CHAH-vehs) was born in the desert Southwest, and she writes about the Native Americans, Mexican Americans, Anglo-Americans, and others who provide the region's rich cultural tapestry. Her works consistently focus on the strength and endurance of ordinary working-class Latino women.

Chávez had twelve years of Catholic schooling and started writing diaries and skits while still in elementary school. She received her bachelor of arts degree in theater from New Mexico State University in 1971, her master of fine arts in theater from Trinity University in San Antonio, Texas, in 1974, and her master of arts in creative writing from the University of New Mexico in 1984. During her school years she worked in a variety of jobs—in a hospital, in an art gallery, and in public relations. She also wrote poetry, fiction, and drama, always with emphasis on the lives of women. She taught at Northern New Mexico Community College, the University of Houston, Artist-in-the-Schools programs, and writers' workshops.

Chávez has written numerous plays and literary pieces, which she often performed or directed, including a national tour with her one-woman performance piece. Her plays have been produced throughout the United States and Europe. Her plays (mostly unpublished), written in English and Spanish, include *Novitiates* (1971), *The Flying Tortilla Man* (1975), *Rainy Day Waterloo* (1976), *The Third Door* (1978), *Sí, hay posada* (1980), *The Green Madonna* (1982), *La morenita* (1983), *El más pequeño de mis hijos* (1983), *Plague-Time* (1984), *Novena Narrativas* (1986), and *Language of Vision* (1987).

The Last of the Menu Girls, interrelated stories about a young Chicana, and the novel *Face of an Angel* have established Chávez's high reputation as a fiction writer. Both works address critical questions of personal and cultural identity with extraordinary wit and compassion. Chávez has a striking ability to create a sense of individual voice for her characters, and she makes that voice resonate for readers who may or may not be familiar with the places and people about whom she writes.

The Last of the Menu Girls

TYPE OF WORK: Short fiction
FIRST PUBLISHED: 1986

Chávez's *The Last of the Menu Girls* is a collection of seven interrelated stories about Rocío Esquibel, a young Mexican American woman in southern New Mexico who seeks to understand herself, her family, and her community. Rocío's development from girl to woman gives unity to the collage of stories. As Rocío observes those around her, she provides a portrait of a culturally diverse community and a clear insight into the human condition.

The title story introduces Rocío at age seventeen beginning her first job as an aide in a hospital in her hometown. It is the summer of 1966. One of her tasks is to take menus to patients and get their requests for meals. Rocío studies the patients with great attention. She sees them as individuals with differing needs, and her heart reaches out to them so fully that she suspects she is too emotional for the job. Her emotional investment, however, helps Rocío understand others and makes her better able to understand herself. By the end of the summer Rocío has been promoted to other duties in the hospital, and the system has changed; she is literally the last of the menu girls. Her compassion for others continues to serve her well as a way of understanding herself and her relationship to the world.

In the other stories Rocío increasingly looks to the past, to her personal history, and to that of her Mexican American culture. She also tries to envision the future, to create the woman she hopes to be. By the end of the stories, Rocío has found her mission. As her mother says, it would take a lifetime to write even the story of their home; there are stories all around. Rocío dedicates herself to writing the lives of the ordinary people she knows, people who often cannot speak for themselves. In the process of telling their stories, Rocío will speak for herself and for her culture.

Face of an Angel

TYPE OF WORK: Novel
FIRST PUBLISHED: 1994

Face of an Angel specifically addresses the quest for identity of Soveida Dosamantes, a hardworking waitress at El Farol Mexican Restaurant in southern New Mexico. The rich cast of characters around Soveida provides detailed portraits of the lives of Mexican, American, and Mexican American working-class men and women in the Southwest. The work describes these characters' various struggles to know themselves and to be accepted in a multicultural setting. The novel speaks compellingly of the importance of the individual self and the social attitudes that allow the individual freedom to function.

Soveida, who narrates most of the novel, has grown up in Agua Oscura, a fictional small town in the desert Southwest. Soveida explores the boundaries of her life through her interactions with her mother Dolores, her grandmother Mama Lupita, her cousin Mara, and a wide cast of other townspeople. As Chávez brings this population of memorable characters to life, their actions and motivations are shown to be reflections of social attitudes about race, ethnicity, gender, and class. It is difficult for them to break through these received attitudes to wholeness and acceptance of others. Soveida, for example, seems destined to repeat the same mistakes other women in her family made in their choice of partners, and she becomes involved with a number of lazy and hurtful men, including her two husbands.

Soveida eventually writes a handbook for waitresses, called "The Book of Service," based on her thirty years of work at El Farol. The advice she gives about service reflects her ideas about her life and her connections with other people, and it shows her growing sense of pride in herself as a Chicana. She has learned to question and reject the limited roles assigned to Mexican American women in a male-dominated society, and instead she develops a philosophy that encompasses individual strength and endurance combined with a genuine respect for others, as shown through service.

Soveida's philosophy is reinforced by the novel's unrestrained, irreverent, and hilarious scenes, by the effective use of colloquial bilingual speech, and by the in-depth exploration of such universal issues as poverty, personal relationships, illness, and death. Chávez's characters are all individuals with distinctive voices, and she draws them together in ways that show the possibilities of changing social prejudices. Her major themes focus on the rights and responsibilities of the individual and on the need for an evolving social consciousness.

SUGGESTED READINGS

Balassi, William, John F. Crawford, and Annie O. Eysturoy, eds. *This Is About Vision: Interviews with Southwestern Writers.* Albuquerque: University of New Mexico Press, 1990.

Farah, Cynthia. *Literature and Landscape: Writers of the Southwest.* El Paso: Texas Western Press, 1988.

Lannan Foundation. *Readings and Conversations: Readings by Lucille Clifton; Conversation with Denise Chávez.* Santa Fe, N.Mex.: Author, 2000.

Reed, Ishmael. *Hispanic American Literature.* New York: HarperCollins, 1995.

Contributor: Lois A. Marchino

Charles Waddell Chesnutt

BORN: Cleveland, Ohio; June 20, 1858
DIED: Cleveland, Ohio; November 15, 1932

AFRICAN AMERICAN

*Chesnutt was one of the first African American writers
to examine honestly and in detail the racial problems of
black people in America after the Civil War.*

PRINCIPAL WORKS

LONG FICTION: *Mandy Oxendine*, wr. 1897, pb. 1997; *A Business Career*, wr. 1898, pb. 2005 (Matthew Wilson and Marjan van Schaik, editors); *The House Behind the Cedars*, 1900; *The Marrow of Tradition*, 1901; *Evelyn's Husband*, wr. 1903, pb. 2005 (Matthew Wilson and Marjan van Schaik, editors); *The Colonel's Dream*, 1905; *Paul Marchand, F.M.C.*, wr. 1921, pb. 1998; *The Quarry*, wr. 1928, pb. 1999

SHORT FICTION: *The Conjure Woman*, 1899; *The Wife of His Youth, and Other Stories of the Color Line*, 1899

NONFICTION: *The Life of Frederick Douglass*, 1899; *The Journals of Charles W. Chesnutt*, 1993; *"To Be an Author": The Letters of Charles W. Chesnutt, 1889-1905*, 1997; *Charles W. Chesnutt: Essays and Speeches*, 1999; *Selected Writings*, 2001 (SallyAnn H. Ferguson, editor); *An Exemplary Citizen: Letters of Charles W. Chesnutt, 1906-1932*, 2002

When Charles Waddell Chesnutt (CHEHZ-nuht) was nine years old, his family moved to Fayetteville, North Carolina, where he spent his youth. Although he was of African American descent, his features barely distinguished him from Caucasians. He learned, however, that family blood was very important in determining a person's social and economic prospects.

Chesnutt's mother died in 1871, when he was thirteen years old. Two years later, he left school to teach in order to supplement the family income. In 1878, he married Susan Perry, a fellow teacher and daughter of a well-to-do black barber in Fayetteville. He had begun teaching in 1877 at the new State Colored Normal School in Fayetteville, and in 1880 he became principal of the school.

On a job-hunting trip to Washington, D.C., in 1879, Chesnutt was unable to find work. He had been studying stenography and hoped to obtain a job on a newspaper. In 1883, he was able to begin a new career as a stenographer and reporter in New York City, and shortly afterward he moved to Cleveland, where he was first a clerk and then a legal stenographer. Two years later, he began studying law, and in 1887,

Charles Waddell Chesnutt (Cleveland Public Library)

he passed the Ohio bar examination with the highest grade in his group. He opened his own office as a court reporter in 1888.

Between 1887 and 1899, beginning with the publication of "The Goophered Grapevine" by *The Atlantic Monthly*, he achieved some success as a short-story writer. In 1899, when Houghton Mifflin published two collections of his short stories, he gave up his profitable business and began writing novels full time—something he had dreamed of doing for many years.

His first published novel, *The House Behind the Cedars*, had some commercial success, but the next, *The Marrow of Tradition*, did not. In 1901, two years after he had closed his stenographic firm, he reopened it. Deciding to write short stories once more in 1903 and 1904, he sent them to *The Atlantic Monthly*, where he had found success earlier, but only one, "Baxter's Procrustes," was accepted. His novel *The Colonel's Dream*, published in 1905, failed to attract the attention of the public. The public of the early 1900's was not ready for the controversial subject matter of his novels and later short stories or for the sympathetic treatment of the black characters in them. It did not want to read literature that had African Americans as the main characters, that presented their problems in a predominantly white world, and that were written with a sympathy for blacks rather than whites. Chesnutt retired from creative writing as a profession in 1905, and thereafter he published only nonfiction.

During the rest of his life, Chesnutt concentrated on managing his business affairs, on participating in civic affairs, and on working on behalf of black people. He was an active member of the Rowland Club, an exclusive male literary group in Cleveland, although at first he was denied membership in this club because of his race. During the last twenty-seven years of his life, he managed to find time to travel in Europe and to help educate his three children. He was a member of the Cleveland Chamber of Commerce and the National Arts Club; he also helped establish Playhouse Settlement (now Karamu House).

Before 1905, he had been politically and socially active in helping to advance the cause of black people, and he continued to be active throughout his life. In 1901, he worked to have W. H. Thomas's *The American Negro* withdrawn from circulation. The same year, he chaired the Committee on Colored Troops for the 35th National Encampment of the Grand Army of the Republic in Cleveland. In 1904, he became a member of the Committee of Twelve, organized by Booker T. Washington, and in 1905 he was a member of the Cleveland Council of Sociology. He addressed the National Negro Committee, which later became the NAACP, and served as a member of its General Committee. He protested the showing of the film *The Birth of a Nation* (1915), which glorified the Ku Klux Klan, and, more important, he protested the treatment of black soldiers. He participated in the First Amenia Conference, called by Joel Spingarn in 1916. He was awarded the Spingarn Medal by the NAACP in 1928.

Chesnutt dreamed of being a novelist, and he believed that racial issues such as the problems of passing, miscegenation, and racial assimilation had to be the subject of serious fiction. He found, though, that if he tried to write novels that would be commercially successful, publishers would not accept them, and if he tried to write works that examined racial issues honestly and with sympathy for blacks, the public would not accept these topical but controversial novels. Nonetheless, Chesnutt was the first African American fiction writer to present an honest portrayal of the racial problems of black people in America after the Civil War, at a time when many Americans preferred to ignore those problems. Chesnutt may have been a victim, just as his characters sometimes are. The themes that he could present most effectively and that he felt compelled to present were ones that the public would not accept; thus, he did not continue to write novels and may have been prevented from developing as a literary artist.

In addition, Chesnutt may have had to compromise to get his views before readers in America. He believed that Americans had an unnatural fear of miscegenation. Because of this fear, the person of mixed blood was an outcast in society and was almost forced by society to pass for white to try to obtain the American Dream. Ironically, those forced into passing and marrying whites began again the miscegenation cycle that was so feared by whites. Anglo-Saxon racial purity was something that should not be preserved, Chesnutt believed. Intermingling and integration would improve humanity biologically, but, more important, blacks would then be able to have the rights they should have as human beings. Only by eliminating laws against intermarriage and social interaction between the races would blacks gain true social, economic, and political equality.

"The Goophered Grapevine"

TYPE OF WORK: Short fiction
FIRST PUBLISHED: 1899, in *The Conjure Woman*

The Conjure Woman contains narratives revealed through the accounts of a Northern white person's rendition of the tales of Uncle Julius, a former slave. This storytelling device lays the foundation for Chesnutt's sociological commentary. The real and perceived voices represent the perspectives he wishes to expose, those of the white capitalist and the impoverished, disadvantaged African American. The primary persona is the capitalist, while the perceived voice is that of the struggling poor. Chesnutt skillfully melds the two perspectives.

The preeminent story of the collection is "The Goophered Grapevine." This story embodies the overriding thematic intent of the narratives in this collection. Chesnutt points out the foibles of the capitalistic quest in the post-Civil War South, a venture pursued at the expense of the newly freed African American slave. He illustrates this point in "The Goophered Grapevine" by skillfully intertwining Aunt Peggy's gains as a result of her conjurations and Henry's destruction as a result of man's inhumanity to man. Chesnutt discloses his ultimate point when the plantation owner, McAdoo, is deceived by a Yankee horticulturist and his grape vineyard becomes totally unproductive.

Running episodes, such as Aunt Peggy's conjurations to keep the field hands from consuming the grape crop and the seasonal benefit McAdoo gains from selling Henry, serve to illustrate the interplay between a monied white capitalist and his less-privileged black human resources. McAdoo used Aunt Peggy to deny his field laborers any benefit from the land they worked, and he sold Henry every spring to increase his cash flow and prepare for the next gardening season.

The central metaphor in "The Goophered Grapevine" is the bewitched vineyard. To illustrate and condemn man's inhumanity to man, Chesnutt contrasts the black conjure woman's protection of the grape vineyard with the white Yankee's destruction of it. McAdoo's exploitation of Henry serves to justify McAdoo's ultimate ruin. Through allegory, Chesnutt is able to draw attention to the immorality of capitalistic gain through a sacrifice of basic humanity to other people.

"Po' Sandy"

TYPE OF WORK: Short fiction
FIRST PUBLISHED: 1899, in *The Conjure Woman*

Following the theme of inhumanity established in "The Goophered Grapevine," "Po' Sandy" highlights the abuse of a former slave laborer. Accordingly, a situation with a folkloric variation is used to convey this message. Sandy, Master Marabo's field hand, is shifted from relative to relative at various points during the year to perform various duties. During the course of these transactions, he is separated from his second common-law wife, Tenie. (His first wife has been sent to work at a distant plantation.) Tenie is a conjurer. She transforms Sandy into a tree, and she changes him back to his original state periodically so that they can be together. With Sandy's apparent disappearance, Master Marabo decides to send Tenie away to nurse his ailing daughter-in-law. There is therefore no one left to watch Sandy, the tree. The dehumanizing effects of industrialization creep into the story line at this point. The "tree" is to be used as lumber for a kitchen at the Marabo home. Tenie returns just in time to try to stop this transformation at the lumber mill, but she is deemed "mad."

Sandy's spirit thereafter haunts the Marabo kitchen, and no one wants to work there. The complaints are so extensive that the kitchen is dismantled and the lumber donated toward the building of a school. This structure is then haunted, too. The point is that industrialization and economic gain diminish essential human concerns and can lead to destruction. The destruction of Sandy's marital relationships in order to increase his usefulness as a field worker justifies this defiant spirit. In his depiction of Sandy as a tree, Chesnutt illustrates an enslaved spirit desperately seeking freedom.

"The Conjurer's Revenge"

TYPE OF WORK: Short fiction
FIRST PUBLISHED: 1899, in *The Conjure Woman*

"The Conjurer's Revenge," also contained in *The Conjure Woman*, illustrates Chesnutt's mastery of the exemplum. The allegory in this work conveys a strong message, and Chesnutt's evolving skill in characterization becomes apparent. The characters' actions, rather than the situation, contain the didactic message of the story. Some qualities of the fable unfold as the various dimensions of characters are portrayed. Consequently, "The Conjurer's Revenge" is a good example of Chesnutt's short imaginative sketch. These qualities are also most characteristic of Chesnutt's early short fiction.

"The Conjurer's Revenge" begins when Primus, a field hand, discovers the conjure man's hog alone in a bush one evening. Concerned for the hog and not knowing to whom the animal belongs, Primus carries it to the plantation where he works. Unfortunately, the conjurer identifies Primus as a thief and transforms Primus into a mule. Chesnutt uses this transformation to reveal Primus's personality. As a mule, Primus displays jealousy when other men show an attraction to his woman, Sally. The mule's reaction is one of shocking violence in instances when Sally is approached by other men. The mule has a tremendous appetite for food and drink, an apparent compensation for his unhappiness. Laying the foundation for his exemplum, Chesnutt brings these human foibles to the forefront and illustrates the consequences of even the mildest appearance of dishonesty.

The conjurer's character is also developed more fully as the story progresses. After attending a religious revival, he becomes ill, confesses his act of vengeance, and repents. During the conjurer's metamorphosis, Chesnutt captures the remorse, grief, and forgiveness in this character. He also reveals the benefits of human compassion and concern for other human beings. A hardened heart undergoes reform and develops an ability to demonstrate sensitivity. Nevertheless, the conjurer suffers the consequences of his evil deed: He is mistakenly given poison by a companion and dies before he completely restores Primus's human features, a deed he undertakes after repenting. The conjurer dies prematurely, and Primus lives with a clubfoot for the rest of his life.

"The Wife of His Youth"

TYPE OF WORK: Short fiction
FIRST PUBLISHED: 1899, in *The Wife of His Youth*

Features of Chesnutt's more mature writing emerge in the series of narratives which make up *The Wife of His Youth, and Other Stories of the Color Line*. The stories in this collection center on the identity crisis experienced by African Americans, portraying their true human qualities in the face of the grotesque distortions wrought by racism. In order to achieve his goal, Chesnutt abandons his earlier imaginative posture and embraces realism as a means to unfold his message. The dimensions of his characters are therefore appropriately self-revealing. The characters respond to the stresses and pressures in their external environment with genuine emotion; Mr. Ryder in "The Wife of His Youth" is no exception.

"The Wife of His Youth" follows the structural pattern that appears to typify the narratives in the collection. This pattern evolves in three phases: crisis, character response, and resolution. The crisis in "The Wife of His Youth" is Mr. Ryder's attempt to reconcile his new and old ways of life. He has moved North from a southern plantation and entered black middle-class society. Adapting to the customs, traditions, and mores of this stratum of society is a stressful challenge for Mr. Ryder. Tensions exist between his old life and his new life. He fears being unable to appear as if he belongs to this "blue vein" society and exposing his lowly background. This probable eventuality is his constant preoccupation.

The "blue veins" were primarily lighter-skinned blacks who were better educated and more advantaged than their darker counterparts. Relishing their perceived superiority, they segregated themselves from their brothers and sisters. It is within this web of social clamoring and essential self-denial that Mr. Ryder finds himself. The inherent contradictions of this lifestyle present a crisis for him, although a resolution is attained during the course of the narrative.

Mr. Ryder's efforts to fit into this society are thwarted when his slave wife appears at his doorstep on the day before a major social event that he has planned. He is about to introduce the Blue Vein Society to a widow, Mrs. Dixon, upon whom he has set his affections. The appearance of Liza Jane, his slave wife, forces Mr. Ryder to confront his new life. This situation also allows Chesnutt to assume his typically moralizing tone. Mr. Ryder moves from self-denial to self-pride as he decides to present Liza Jane to his society friends instead of Mrs. Dixon. The narrative ends on a note of personal triumph for Mr. Ryder as he proudly introduces the wife of his youth to society.

"The Passing of Grandison"

TYPE OF WORK: Short fiction
FIRST PUBLISHED: 1899, in *The Wife of His Youth*

Chesnutt does not totally relinquish his allegiance to the use of myth in *The Wife of His Youth, and Other Stories of the Color Line*. The myth of the ascent journey, or the quest for freedom, is evident in several stories in the collection, among them "The Passing of Grandison" and "Uncle Wellington's Wives." Following the structured pattern of crisis, character response, and resolution, "The Passing of Grandison" is a commentary on the newly emerging moral values of the postbellum South. Colonel Owens, a plantation owner, has a son, Dick, who is in love with a belle named Charity Lomax. Charity's human values reflect the principles of human equality and freedom, and the challenge that she presents to Dick Owens becomes the crisis of the narrative.

Dick is scheduled to take a trip North, and his father insists on his being escorted by one of the servants. Grandison is selected to accompany his young master. Charity Lomax challenges Dick to find a way to entice Grandison to remain in the North and receive his well-deserved liberation. Charity's request conflicts with the values held by Dick and Grandison. Dick believes that slave/master relationships are essential to the survival of the South. Grandison holds that servants should be unequivocally loyal to their masters.

In spite of Dick's attempts to connect Grandison unobtrusively with the abolitionist movement in the North, the former slave remains loyal to Dick. Grandison's steadfastness perplexes Dick because his proposed marriage to Charity is at risk if he does not succeed in freeing Grandison. After a series of faulty attempts, Dick succeeds in losing Grandison. Dick then returns home alone and triumphant. Grandison ultimately returns to the plantation. He had previously proven himself so trustworthy that goodwill toward him is restored. To make the characterization of Grandison realistic, however, Chesnutt must have him pursue his freedom.

In a surprise ending typical of Chesnutt, Grandison plans the escape of all of his relatives who remain on the plantation. They succeed, and in the last scene of the narrative, Colonel Owens spots them from a distance on a boat journeying to a new destination. "The Passing of Grandison" successfully achieves the social and artistic goals of *The Wife of His Youth, and Other Stories of the Color Line*. Chesnutt creates characters with convincing human qualities and captures their responses to the stresses and pressures of their environment. While so doing, he advocates the quest for human freedom.

"Uncle Wellington's Wives"

TYPE OF WORK: Short fiction
FIRST PUBLISHED: 1899, in *The Wife of His Youth*

"Uncle Wellington's Wives" contains several of the thematic dimensions mentioned above. The story concerns the self-identity of the African American and the freedom quest. Wellington Braboy, a light-skinned mulatto, is determined to move North and seek his freedom. His crisis is the result of a lack of resources, primarily financial, to achieve his goal.

Braboy is portrayed as having a distorted view of loyalty and commitment. He justifies stealing money from his slave wife's life savings by saying that, as her husband, he is entitled to the money. On the other hand, he denies his responsibility to his slave wife once he reaches the North. In order to marry a white woman he denies the legality of a slave marriage.

Chesnutt takes Braboy on a journey of purgation and catharsis as he moves toward resolution. After being subjected to much ridicule and humiliation as a result of his mixed marriage, Braboy must honestly confront himself and come to terms with his true identity. Abandoned by his wife for her former white husband, Braboy returns to the South. This journey is also a symbolic return to himself; his temporary escape from himself has failed.

Milly, Braboy's first wife, does not deny her love for him, in spite of his previous actions. Milly receives and accepts him with a forgiving spirit. Chesnutt capitalizes on the contrast between Braboy's African and Anglo wives. The African wife loves him unconditionally because she has the capacity to know and understand him, regardless of his foibles. Braboy's Anglo wife was frustrated by what she considered to be irreparable inadequacies in his character and abandoned him.

"Cicely's Dream"

TYPE OF WORK: Short fiction
FIRST PUBLISHED: 1899, in *The Wife of His Youth*

In his character development, Chesnutt repeatedly sought to dispel some of the stereotypical thinking about African Americans. An example of his success in this effort is found in "Cicely's Dream," set in the period of Reconstruction. Cicely Green is depicted as a young woman of considerable ambition. Like most African Americans, she has had very little education and is apparently limited in her capacity to achieve. She does have, however, many dreams.

Cicely's crisis begins when she discovers a wounded man on her way home one day. The man is delirious and has no recollection of who he is. Cicely and her grandmother care for the man until his physical health is restored, but he is still mentally distraught. The tenderness and sensitivity displayed by Cicely keep the stranger reasonably content. Over a period of time, they become close and eventually pledge their love to each other. Chesnutt portrays a caring, giving relationship between the two lovers, one that is not complicated by any caste system that would destroy love through separation of the lovers. This relationship, therefore, provides a poignant contrast to the relationships among blacks during the days of slavery, and Chesnutt thereby exposes an unexplored dimension of the African American.

Typically, however, there is a surprise ending: Martha Chandler, an African American teacher, enters the picture. She teaches Cicely and other black youths for one school term. During the final program of the term, the teacher reveals her story of lost love. Her lover had been killed in the Civil War. Cicely's lover's memory is jolted by the teacher's story, and he proves to be the teacher's long-lost love. The happy reunion is a celebration of purely committed love. Again, Chesnutt examines qualities in African Americans that had largely been ignored. He emphasizes the innate humanity of the African American in a natural and realistic way, combining great artistic skill with a forceful moral vision.

The House Behind the Cedars

TYPE OF WORK: Novel
FIRST PUBLISHED: 1900

Between 1890 and 1899, Chesnutt greatly expanded and revised "Rena Walden," a short story, until it became *The House Behind the Cedars*. At first, he focused on how color consciousness can destroy an interracial marriage and then on the predominant issue of whether a mulatto should cross the "color line." In March, 1899, he wrote journalist and diplomat Walter Hines Page that the Rena Walden story was the strong expression of a writer whose themes dealt primarily with the American color line. When he wrote to his daughters in the fall of 1900, he indicated that he hoped for "a howling success" from *The House Behind the Cedars*, "a strong race problem novel." The story of Rena Walden and her brother was the first in which the problems of Americans concealing their African heritage were studied with a detached and compassionate presentation of individuals on the various sides of the issue.

The novel can be divided into two parts: Rena in white society, in which her brother is the major focus, and Rena in black society, in which she becomes the focus. The novel is set in Patesville, North Carolina, a few years after the Civil War. John Warwick, who has changed his name from Walden, has left Patesville and gone to South Carolina, where he has become a lawyer and plantation owner, acquiring wealth and position. He and his sister Rena are the children of a quadroon mother Molly and a white man who has died. John has returned to Patesville to help his beautiful sister escape the restrictions of color by teaching her how to pass for white. She is a success at the boarding school in South Carolina to which he takes her. As proof of her success in passing, George Tryon, a good friend of John and a white, wants to marry Rena, but she is not sure she should marry him without telling him of her mixed blood. John and Rena indirectly discuss the pros and cons of passing and intermarriage. A series of coincidences leads to an unexpected meeting between George and Rena; he learns of her heritage, and the engagement is broken. Rena returns home to her mother and the house behind the cedars.

A chapter interlude that gives the Walden family history separates the first part of the novel from the second. John tries to persuade his sister to return to South Carolina with him or to take money and go North or West, where she can pass for white and marry someone even better than George, but she refuses to leave Patesville. She has decided to accept her destiny and be of service to her people, whom she has rediscovered. After this point, the reader is told little more about John.

Rena meets Jeff Wain, an influential and prosperous mulatto from a rural county, who is seeking a schoolteacher. Rena accepts the position, not realizing Jeff has a personal as well as a professional interest in her. Jeff is not as admirable a character as he first appears. As he pays her more and more attention, she is upset and repulsed. Once again, coincidence plays a part in the plot. George Tryon happens to learn of her presence near a place he is visiting. When he sees her, he realizes that he loves her and that his love is stronger than his racial prejudice. The same day that George decides to declare his love, Jeff decides to do so too. Rena fears both of the men and leaves hastily for her mother's house behind the cedars. After exposure and fatigue have overcome her, Frank Fowler, a childhood friend and a conscientious black workman, finds her and carries her to her home, where she dies. Rena realizes before she dies that Frank loved her the best.

Chesnutt seeks to lead his readers to share his perspective rather than lecturing them. He delays revealing that John and Rena are mulattoes. To create sympathy for them first, he presents them simply as persons of humble origins who are attempting to achieve prosperity and happiness. Chesnutt passes John and Rena for white with the reader before he lets the reader know that they are mulattoes who have chosen or will deliberately choose to pass for white.

John Walden is the first black character in American fiction to decide to pass for white and, at the same time, to feel that his decision is legally and morally justified. Believing that the color of his skin tells him that he is white, he has no psychological problems concerning his choice to pass. He is not a stereotype. Intelligent and industrious, he patiently trains himself so that he can achieve the American Dream. At the beginning of the novel, the reader learns that he has become a prosperous lawyer and plantation owner after leaving Patesville; in the second part of the novel, after he has not been successful in helping Rena pass for white, he returns to South Carolina to regain his position.

The characters are not fully developed and remain stick figures, although Chesnutt is partially successful in creating human interest for them. While Chesnutt attempts to create pity for her, Rena is simply a victim who accepts her fate, like other antiassimilationist mulattoes of the time. Another character, Dr. Green, is no more than a vehicle to present the traditional southern viewpoint. Two figures, Molly Walden and George Tyron, retain some individuality. Molly, as an unprotected free black woman in the slave South, is a product of her environment. With the circumstances that she faces, she can do little other than be the kept mistress for the white plantation owner, who has died but left her the house behind the cedars.

Chesnutt does not want the reader to feel contempt for her or to be repulsed by her actions; her position is rendered dispassionately. George Tyron, on the other hand, undergoes great emotional upheaval and has a change of view that is probably meant to be instructive. He is tied to the traditional code of the southern gentleman but is not deluded about his prerogatives as a southern aristocrat. Rather, he is meant to be the best of the new South. His realization that he loves Rena and that her racial heritage is not important comes too late; she dies before he is able to do anything about it. He does not blame her for passing, and Chesnutt expects the reader not to blame her.

The Marrow of Tradition
TYPE OF WORK: Novel
FIRST PUBLISHED: 1901

The Marrow of Tradition is the story of two families: The Carterets stand for the New South aristocracy with its pride and prejudice, and the Millers, who are of mixed blood, represent the qualities of the new black. The lives of the families are intertwined because the wives are half sisters. Janet Miller, however, has been cheated of her inheritance by Olivia Carteret, and Olivia constantly struggles with the problem of accepting Janet as her rightful sister.

The novel's message—a study of white supremacist politics in a small southern town after the Civil War—is more relevant to the problems encountered by the husbands than those facing the wives. Dr. Adam Miller is a brilliant young surgeon denied opportunity in his hometown of Wellington (Wilmington, North Carolina). Major Philip Carteret, editor of the town's newspaper, seeks to seat a white supremacist regime in the local government. If he is successful, Adam Miller's position will be even more intolerable than it has been.

At the end of the novel, Major Carteret stirs up a riot during which Dr. Miller's son is killed. Immediately after the death of the Millers' child, the son of the Carterets becomes ill, and Adam Miller is the only person who can perform the surgery necessary to save the child's life. At first, Miller refuses, but after Olivia Carteret humbles herself before her half sister and pleads with her to help save the Carterets' son, Janet Miller convinces her husband to change his mind and operate. The child is saved.

The Marrow of Tradition was too controversial a novel for the public. Americans were not ready for the subject of white supremacist politics and the political injustice existing in the South. Chesnutt himself was concerned that the novel approached fanaticism. He believed that he should not speak so plainly concerning these matters if he hoped to succeed as a fiction writer.

SUGGESTED READINGS

Andrews, William L. *The Literary Career of Charles W. Chesnutt*. Baton Rouge: Louisiana State University Press, 1980.

Chesnutt, Charles Waddell. *"To Be an Author": Letters of Charles W. Chesnutt, 1889-1905*. Edited by Joseph R. McElrath, Jr., and Robert C. Leitz III. Princeton, N.J.: Princeton University Press, 1997.

Duncan, Charles. *The Absent Man: The Narrative Craft of Charles W. Chesnutt*. Athens: Ohio University Press, 1998.

Gleason, William. "Chesnutt's Piazza Tales: Architecture, Race, and Memory in the Conjure Stories." *American Quarterly* 51 (March, 1999): 33-77.

Heermance, Noel. *Charles Chesnutt: America's First Great Black Novelist*. Hamden, Conn.: Archon Books, 1974.

Keller, Frances Richardson. *An American Crusade: The Life of Charles Waddell Chesnutt*. Provo, Utah: Brigham Young University Press, 1978.

Lehman, Cynthia L. "The Social and Political View of Charles Chesnutt: Reflections on His Major Writings." *Journal of Black Studies* 26 (January, 1996).

McElrath, Joseph R., Jr., ed. *Critical Essays on Charles W. Chesnutt*. New York: G. K. Hall, 1999.

McFatter, Susan. "From Revenge to Resolution: The (R)evolution of Female Characters in Chesnutt's Fiction." *CLA Journal* 42 (December, 1998): 194-211.

Pickens, Ernestine Williams. *Charles W. Chesnutt and the Progressive Movement*. New York: Pace University Press, 1994.

Render, Sylvia. *Charles W. Chesnutt*. Boston: Twayne, 1980.

Wonham, Henry B. *Charles W. Chesnutt: A Study of the Short Fiction*. New York: Twayne, 1998.

Contributors: Earl Paulus Murphy, Sherry G. Southard, and Patricia A. R. Williams

Alice Childress

BORN: Charleston, South Carolina; October 12, 1916
DIED: New York, New York; August 14, 1994

AFRICAN AMERICAN

*Breaking with the tradition of African American drama to
her time, Childress wrote plays about the concerns of black
women, including the female psychological journey.*

PRINCIPAL WORKS

CHILDREN'S LITERATURE: *A Hero Ain't Nothin' but a Sandwich*, 1973; *Rainbow
Jordan*, 1981; *Those Other People*, 1989
DRAMA: *Florence*, pr. 1949, pb. 1950; *Just a Little Simple*, pr. 1950; *Gold Through
the Trees*, pr. 1952; *Trouble in Mind*, pr. 1955, pb. 1971; *Wedding Band: A Love/
Hate Story in Black and White*, staged 1966, televised 1973, pb. 1973; *The World
on a Hill*, pb. 1968; *The Freedom Drum*, pr. 1969 (music by Nathan Woodard;
retitled *Young Martin Luther King*); *String*, pr. 1969 (staged; pb. 1971, pr. 1979;
televised; adaptation of a Guy de Maupassant story); *Wine in the Wilderness*, pr.
1969 (televised, pb. 1969, pr. 1976 [televised]); *Mojo: A Black Love Story*, pr.
1970, pb. 1971; *The African Garden*, pb. 1971 (with Woodard); *When the Rattlesnake Sounds*, pb. 1975 (for children); *Let's Hear It for the Queen*, pb. 1976 (for
children); *Sea Island Song*, pr. 1979 (with Woodard; pr. 1984 as *Gullah*); *Moms:
A Praise Play for a Black Comedienne*, pr. 1987 (with Woodard)
LONG FICTION: *A Short Walk*, 1979
SCREENPLAY: *A Hero Ain't Nothin' but a Sandwich*, 1978
SHORT FICTION: *Like One of the Family: Conversations from a Domestic's Life*, 1956
EDITED TEXT: *Black Scenes: Collection of Scenes from Plays Written by Black Peo-
ple About Black Experience*, 1971

Alice Childress (CHIHL-drehs) was five years old when Her parents separated and
she was sent to live with her maternal grandmother, who had seven children of her
own. Although Grandmother Eliza was a poverty-stricken former slave with only a
fifth-grade education, she was intellectually curious and self-educated. Childress
credited her grandmother with teaching her how to observe and encouraging her to
write. Her grandmother also took her to Salem Church in Harlem, where Alice
learned storytelling from the Wednesday night testimonials. Childress was educated in New York public schools, leaving before she graduated from high school.
She encountered racial prejudice at school but recalled several teachers who made a
difference, encouraging her to read and introducing her to the library.

Childress revealed little about her private life, but it is known that she married and divorced Alvin Childress, who played Amos on television's *Amos 'n' Andy Show*. The couple had a daughter, Jean, born on November 1, 1935, who was raised by her mother. To support herself and her child while she tried to establish her writing and acting career, Childress held a variety of jobs, including domestic servant, salesperson, and insurance agent. Through these jobs, she became acquainted with numerous working-class people, whose lives became the basis of characters in her later plays and novels.

In 1941 Childress joined the American Negro Theatre (ANT), which met in the Schomburg Library in Harlem. Like all ANT members, Childress participated in all aspects of theater, though her main interest was acting. She stayed with ANT for eleven years but was frustrated by the emphasis on issues important to black men and the consequent neglect of black women's issues and roles. When she tried to act in the theater at large, she ran into problems because she was considered too light-skinned to play black roles but not fair enough to play whites. Although she starred in the Broadway production of *Anna Lucasta* (1944-1946) and did some work in radio and television, Childress finally concluded that she would be better able to express herself as a writer.

Interested in creating complex and realistic black female characters, Childress wrote *Florence*, a one-act play that she hoped would show that African American drama did not have to be sensational to be significant. This drama, about a working-class black woman on her way to New York to rescue her daughter from a failed career in the theater, opened new areas to African American theater, eventually influencing Amiri Baraka's Black Revolutionary Theater and woman-centered African American dramatists such as Ntozake Shange. Childress's next plays did not focus on women, however. One was a reworking of Langston Hughes's serialized articles, *Simple Speaks His Mind*, published in the *Chicago Defender*, as a musical review titled *Just a Little Simple*.

In 1955, Childress returned to her controversial subjects and assertive black women characters with *Trouble in Mind*, a play about a black actress trying to maintain her dignity while playing menial roles. The play was well received Off-Broadway, but Broadway options were abandoned because producers considered it too risky for the commercial theater. It was presented twice by the British Broadcasting Corporation (BBC), however. Childress received the Obie Award for *Trouble in Mind* in 1956, becoming the first woman to receive the award.

Also in 1956, Childress published *Like One of the Family: Conversations from a Domestic's Life*, a series of vignettes or monologues that incorporated sketches from her *Baltimore Afro-American* column "Here's Mildred," which she would write through 1958. The column and book centered on Mildred, a domestic servant modeled on Childress's aunt. On July 17, 1957, she married a musician named Nathan Woodward. She and Woodward collaborated on a number of projects; he wrote music for her play *Sea Island Song*, later produced as *Gullah*.

During the 1960's, Childress focused on writing plays. She chose to ignore white audiences and focused on controversial topics, which made production difficult. During this period, she wrote *Wedding Band: A Love/Hate Story in Black and*

Alice Childress (Ray Grist)

White, which focused on interracial lovers; *The Freedom Drum* (later retitled *Young Martin Luther King*); *String*, an adaptation of Guy de Maupassant's story "A Piece of String"; and *Wine in the Wilderness*, on revolution and black males' problematic attitudes toward black women.

Also during this period, Childress participated in a variety of communities of writers and scholars. In 1965 she was part of a BBC panel discussion, "The Negro in American Theater," which also included James Baldwin, LeRoi Jones (Amiri Baraka), and Langston Hughes. The writer Tillie Olsen recommended Childress for an appointment at the Radcliffe Institute for Independent Study, where she worked on her writing from 1966 to 1968.

During the 1970's Childress traveled extensively to study drama and other arts: to the Soviet Union in 1971; to Beijing and Shanghai, China, in 1973; and to Ghana, West Africa, in 1974. She also shifted the focus of her own writing at this time, producing a young adult novel, *A Hero Ain't Nothin' but a Sandwich* and its screenplay; two plays for children, *When the Rattlesnake Sounds*, about a summer in the life of escaped slave Harriet Tubman, and *Let's Hear It for the Queen*; and *A Short Walk*, a novel. Also in 1979, Childress's play *Sea Island Song*, which had been commissioned by the South Carolina Arts Commission, was presented in Columbia and Charleston, South Carolina, during the observance of Alice Childress Week.

In the 1980's, Childress continued to write and speak out. She wrote her second young adult novel, *Rainbow Jordan*, in 1981. She was artist-in-residence at the University of Massachusetts, Amherst, in 1984. Her final works were *Moms: A Praise Play for a Black Comedienne*, based on the life of comedienne "Moms" Mabley, and a novel, *Those Other People*. Her daughter Jean died of cancer in May, 1990. Four years later, Childress died of cancer, in Queens.

Childress addressed issues of gender and race through her black female characters. She worked against stereotypes prevalent in both black and white American literature to present ordinary women—strong, searching for their identities, and standing up to prejudices based on class, gender, and race. Even when she wrote about controversial topics such as miscegenation, her characters and the situations were realistic and believable. Her explorations laid the groundwork for later African American women playwrights such as Ntozake Shange and Sonia Sanchez.

Childress's unwillingness to compromise her principles or play to white audiences cost her in terms of production and visibility. However, she attracted the attention of feminist scholars in the 1980's and 1990's, and she has always had the attention of African American theater people. Elizabeth Brown-Guillory calls her the mother of African American professional theater, and the debt that those who followed her owe to her pioneering work in presenting realistic and complex black women characters supports that title.

Trouble in Mind

TYPE OF WORK: Drama
FIRST PRODUCED: 1955, pb. 1971

Childress uses two tried-and-true theatrical devices in *Trouble in Mind*: a play-within-a-play and metadrama, focusing on an examination of theater itself. Placed in the larger context of the Civil Rights movement, with allusions to Rosa Parks and Martin Luther King, Jr., the play features Wiletta Mayer, a veteran actress who has been cast in an antilynching drama written by a white playwright. Although Wiletta and the other veteran black actors have been conditioned to accept the denigrating conditions of working in white-controlled theater, she cannot justify her character's advising her son to give himself up to a lynch mob. When she argues against the play and its portrayal of blacks, the cast is dismissed with the clear implication that Wiletta will not be called for the next rehearsal. The play-within-the-play, however, has made clear the problems of stereotypes of African Americans.

Wedding Band

TYPE OF WORK: Drama
FIRST PRODUCED: 1966, pb. 1973

This play about the ten-year romantic relationship of a black seamstress, Julia, and a white baker, Herman, was not well received either by blacks, who saw it as integrationist, or whites, who were offended by the topic of miscegenation. In the world of the play, Julia receives little support from her black neighbors, who do not see her relationship with Herman as positive in any way, or from Herman's mother and sister, who make racist comments and try to sabotage the relationship. When Herman develops influenza, collapsing in Julia's home, the situation is serious because the same laws that have prevented Julia and Herman's marriage will result in their prosecution if the relationship is discovered. Julia calls in Herman's mother, but instead of help, she gets abuse. She does stand up to her, though, claiming her place as her daughter-in-law. The play examines problematic relationships between black and white women and between black women themselves, as well as the interracial love relationship.

Wine in the Wilderness

TYPE OF WORK: Drama
FIRST PRODUCED: 1969, pb. 1969

Wine in the Wilderness is set in the apartment of a middle-class black artist during a 1960's Harlem riot. Childress depicts the arrogance and ignorance of the black middle class in the artist's treatment of a young lower-class black woman, Tommy (Tomorrow Marie). The artist, Bill, has been working on a triptych dedicated to black womanhood—as Bill understands it. He has completed two of the panels, one depicting "innocent" black girlhood, the second a beautiful, regal woman representing an idealized Mother Africa. He has been looking for a model for the third panel—the "lost" black woman of his imagination, rude and vulgar, the antithesis of the African queen. His neighbors find Tommy during the riot, and she, believing that she is to be the model for an ideal woman in the artist's work, goes with them to his apartment. When she realizes the truth, she confronts the group. Finally Bill understands his shortsightedness and persuades "his" Tomorrow to pose for the new center panel as woman of the future. The middle-class assimilationists learn to value an assertive black woman.

SUGGESTED READINGS

Austin, Gayle. "Alice Childress: Black Woman Playwright as Feminist Critic." *Southern Quarterly* 25 (Spring, 1987): 53-62.

Brown-Guillory, Elizabeth. "Black Women Playwrights Exorcizing Myths." *Phylon* 48 (Fall, 1997): 229-239.

_____. *Their Place on the Stage: Black Women Playwrights in America*. Westport, Conn.: Greenwood Press, 1988.

Childress, Alice. Interview by Kathleen Betsko and Rachel Koenig. In *Interviews with Contemporary Women Playwrights*. New York: Beech Tree Books, 1987.

Dugan, Olga. "Telling the Truth: Alice Childress as Theorist and Playwright." *The Journal of Negro History* 81 (1996): 123-137.

Jennings, LaVinia Delois. *Alice Childress*. New York: Twayne, 1995.

Maguire, Roberta S. "Alice Childress." In *Twentieth-Century American Dramatists, Third Series*, edited by Christopher Wheatley. Vol. 249 in *Dictionary of Literary Biography*. Detroit: Gale Group, 2001.

Contributor: Elsie Galbreath Haley

Frank Chin

BORN: Berkeley, California; February 25, 1940

CHINESE AMERICAN

*Author of the first Asian American play produced on the
New York stage, Chin is among the first few writers to
present the experiences of Chinese Americans.*

PRINCIPAL WORKS

DRAMA: *The Chickencoop Chinaman*, pr. 1972, pb. 1981; *The Year of the Dragon*,
pr. 1974, pb. 1981
LONG FICTION: *Donald Duk*, 1991; *Gunga Din Highway*, 1994
SHORT FICTION: *The Chinaman Pacific and Frisco R.R. Co.*, 1988
TELEPLAYS: *The Bel Canto Carols*, 1966; *S.R.T., Act Two*, 1966; *And Still Cham-
pion . . .* , 1967; *Ed Sierer's New Zealand*, 1967; *A Man and His Music*, 1967; *The
Report*, 1967; *Searfair Preview*, 1967; *The Year of the Ram*, 1967; *Mary*, 1969;
Rainlight Rainvision, 1969; *Chinaman's Chance*, 1971
NONFICTION: *Bulletproof Buddhists, and Other Essays*, 1998
EDITED TEXTS: *Aiiieeeee! An Anthology of Asian-American Writers*, 1974 (with
others; Asian American writing); *The Big Aiiieeeee!*, 1991; *Born in the USA: A
Story of Japanese America, 1889-1947*, 2002

A fifth-generation Chinese American, Frank Chin has been witness to a most dramatic chapter in the history of his people. The chapter started with the 1943 repeal
of the racially discriminatory Chinese Exclusion Act of 1882. Chin has lived in a
social and cultural environment that tends to distort the image of his people and to
ignore their history. Chin sees it as his mission to restore their image and remember
the heroism, the pioneering spirit, and the sufferings of his people by writing about
them from a Chinese American perspective. His plays and novels are informed by
his knowledge of the history of Chinese Americans, his understanding of their cultural heritage, and his vision of their future.

Chin believes that the history of Chinese Americans constitutes a heroic and vital part of the history of the American West. In the 1970's, his sense of history was
accompanied by a pessimistic prediction. Chin was aware that legislative racism
had turned the Chinese American community into a bachelor society in the past and
that euphemized discrimination was luring many young Chinese Americans toward assimilation. Hence, he declared in an essay, "Yellow Seattle," that Chinese
America was doomed to extinction. This kind of pessimism permeates the two
plays that he wrote in the 1970's: *The Chickencoop Chinaman* and *The Year of the*

Dragon. Pervading these works is an atmosphere of gloom, decay, and death, with bitter young people full of self-contempt renouncing their racial identity and with their families and communities falling apart. The apparent revival of Chinatown and the growth of the Chinese community in the 1980's seem to have helped change Chin's view. Such a change is discerned in *Donald Duk,* in which an atmosphere of renewal and jubilant celebration prevails. In the play, a family and a community conscientiously and successfully pass on their heritage from one generation to another in San Francisco's Chinatown.

The Chickencoop Chinaman

TYPE OF WORK: Drama
FIRST PRODUCED: 1972, pb. 1981

The Chickencoop Chinaman is a subtle depiction of the experiences of a Chinese American writer who loses and then regains his racial identity and cultural heritage. Laced with historical allusions to legislative and euphemized discrimination against Chinese Americans, the play centers on a visit the writer, Tam Lum, makes to Pittsburgh to collect materials for a documentary film about a famous black boxer. The events that take place during his visit make him realize that what he

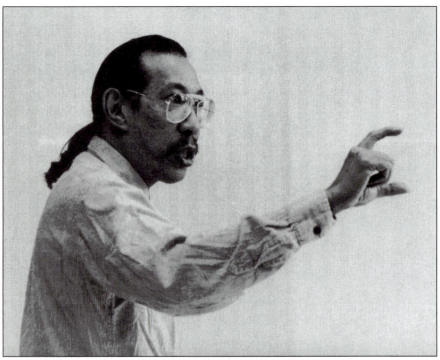

Frank Chin (Corky Lee)

should do is pursue the lonely mission of telling stories to the unassimilated children of the Chinese railroad builders and gold miners.

The play begins with Tam telling an airline hostess that he was born to be a writer for "the Chinamans sons of Chinamans." As the ensuing scenes show, he has never had a chance to write about the heroism of his people. When a boy, he used to sit in the kitchen, listening to his grandmother's stories of the Chinese railroaders, but he heard no such stories on the radio. In his desperate search for a hero of his own race, he imagined that the Lone Ranger with his mask was a Chinese American in disguise. To his dismay, the Ranger turned out to be a decrepit white racist who ordered Tam to go back to Chinatown to preserve his culture.

Ironically, there was no Chinatown to which Tam could return to preserve his culture, for the old people there were trying to forget their history in order to survive. They urged him to destroy the past and get assimilated. Thus, he turned his back on his father, eradicated his memory of the railroaders, and married a white woman. A few years later, he found himself incompetent as a writer, deserted by his wife, and forgotten by his children. In order to keep himself busy and give his children a gift, he decided to make a film about a black former boxer and his father, Mr. Popcorn, who lived in Pittsburgh.

In Pittsburgh, Tam discovers that the boxer has invented a father. Mr. Popcorn adamantly refuses to play a fake father in a documentary film and chastises Tam for betraying his real father. Tam's plan for the film collapses; however, he learns that he must be true to his own identity and fulfill his destiny. The play ends with Tam standing in a kitchen, asking a group of children to turn off the radio and listen to the stories that his grandmother used to tell him about the Chinese railroaders in the Old West.

The Year of the Dragon

TYPE OF WORK: Drama
FIRST PRODUCED: 1974, pb. 1981

The Year of the Dragon is an anguished depiction of a Chinese American man and his family, in conflict between the younger generation's urge toward assimilation and the older generation's obsession with tradition. Set in the late 1960's in San Francisco's Chinatown, the play represents Frank Chin's artistic expression of his view that historically Chinese America is doomed. The play begins with Fred Eng, a tour guide in Chinatown, welcoming a group of tourists and wishing them happiness in the Year of the Dragon. He speaks like Charlie Chan, but he wants to drop his phony accent and just be himself. Fred cannot be just himself; he knows that tourists expect a Chinese American to speak like Charlie Chan.

Fred wanted to be a writer and went to college, but his ailing father, Wing Eng, called him back to Chinatown to take over the father's travel agency and care for Fred's mother, Hyacinth, and two younger siblings, Mattie and Johnny. The ensuing scenes show that Wing has gathered his family, including his first wife from China, so that he can die as a Chinese would like to, surrounded by a happy family and assured that Fred will stay in Chinatown to care for his two mothers. Wing's family is by no means happy. His first wife, who has just arrived from China and whose expected presence causes resentment from others, seems to feel out of place in her husband's home. Hyacinth frequently escapes to the bathroom to sing her lullaby. Mattie, who has "married out white" like many other Chinese Americans, cannot stand her father's home. She urges the family to "forget Chinatown and be just people." Johnny is a juvenile delinquent still on probation, and Fred is torn between his obligation to his father as a son and his sense of himself as an individual. He plans to stay in Chinatown for a while but have everyone else leave for Boston after his father dies. He urges Johnny to marry a white girl.

Wing vehemently rejects Fred's plan, insisting that Fred and his two mothers should stay in Chinatown. He dies amid a violent argument with his son while the festive sounds are floating into the house. At the end of the play, Fred appears like "a shrunken Charlie Chan," welcoming tourists to Chinatown.

Donald Duk

TYPE OF WORK: Novel
FIRST PUBLISHED: 1991

Donald Duk is a psychologically realistic depiction of a fifth-generation Chinese American boy who, by learning his family history and his cultural heritage, frees himself from the trauma caused by the racial stereotyping of his people. Set in San Francisco's Chinatown during a New Year's celebration, the novel delineates the initiation of its protagonist, Donald Duk, in a manner that interweaves history, legend, surrealistic dreams, and psychological realism.

Donald is troubled more by his racial identity than by his funny name. Repeatedly he has heard people at school and in the media say that his people are traditionally timid and passive, introverted and nonassertive; therefore, they are alien to American heroism and pioneering spirit. He is thus filled with self-contempt and tormented by everything Chinese. With the Chinese New Year approaching, he becomes more and more depressed and withdrawn, for the New Year will provide another opportunity for his schoolteachers to repeat in class the same thing that everybody else says about his people.

The New Year during which Donald completes the first twelve-year cycle of his life (there are twelve years in the Chinese zodiac) is the right time for the elders in his family and in the community to tell him what everybody has chosen not to say about his people. From these elders he learns that his people came from a land that had produced its own Robin Hoods, and that Chinese railroaders, his great-great grandfather among them, blasted their way through Nevada, lived in tunnels carved in deep frozen snow for two winters, set a world record in track-laying, and went on strike for back pay and Chinese foremen for Chinese gangs. He is so fascinated with these railroaders' heroism and pioneering spirit that scenes of their toil and struggle appear one after another in his dreams.

Through careful library research, Donald determines that his dreams are actually flashbacks to the real events that have been excluded in history books by the majority culture. With his newly gained understanding of the cultural heritage of his people, he is eager to go back to school to challenge the stereotype of his people with his story about their courage and assertiveness.

SUGGESTED READINGS

Chua, C. L. "*The Year of the Dragon*, by Frank Chin." In *A Resource Guide to Asian American Literature*, edited by Sau-ling Wong and Stephen Sumida. New York: Modern Language Association, 2001.

Goshert, John Charles. *Frank Chin*. Boise, Idaho: Boise State University, 2002.

Kim, Daniel Y. *Writing Manhood in Black and Yellow: Ralph Ellison, Frank Chin, and the Literary Politics of Identity*. Stanford, Calif.: Stanford University Press, 2005.

Kim, Elaine H. *Asian American Literature: An Introduction to the Writings and Their Social Context*. Philadelphia: Temple University Press, 1982.

_____. "Frank Chin: The Chinatown Cowboy and His Backtalk." *Midwest Quarterly* 20 (Autumn, 1978): 78-91.

Ling, Jinqi. *Narrating Nationalisms: Ideology and Form in Asian American Literature*. New York: Oxford University Press, 1998.

McDonald, Dorothy Ritsuko. Introduction to *"The Chickencoop Chinaman" and "The Year of the Dragon": Two Plays by Frank Chin*. Seattle: University of Washington Press, 1981.

Wong, Sau-ling. *Reading Asian American Literature: From Necessity to Extravagance*. Princeton, N.J.: Princeton University Press, 1993.

Yin, Xiao-huang. *Chinese American Literature Since the 1850's*. Urbana: University of Illinois Press, 2000.

Contributor: Chenliang Sheng

Louis H. Chu

BORN: Toishan, Kwangtung Province, China; October 1, 1915
DIED: New York, New York; 1970

CHINESE AMERICAN

*Chu is acknowledged as the first Chinese American
novelist to depict Chinatown life realistically.*

PRINCIPAL WORK
LONG FICTION: *Eat a Bowl of Tea*, 1961

Born in China, Louis Chu immigrated to America when he was nine years old. Thus Asia and America played significant roles in his formative experience. In *Eat a Bowl of Tea*, Chu's only published novel, he writes knowledgeably and feelingly about life in a rural community of South China as well as about life in New York's urban Chinatown. Chu's life and career in the United States followed a pattern of education and employment that many immigrants would envy. After completing high school in New Jersey, Chu attended Upsala College, earning his degree in 1937. He then attended New York University, obtaining an M.A. in 1940. Two years of graduate study at the New School for Social Research in New York rounded off his formal education. During World War II, Chu served in the Signal Corps of the U.S. Army. In 1940, he married Pong Fay, who had been born and raised in China; they brought up four children in Hollis, New York, a Queens suburb, where they made a Chinese-speaking home.

Things Chinese American were very much a part of Chu's career. From 1951 to 1961, he was a disc jockey for radio station WHOM in New York City (he was the only Chinese American disc jockey in the city). His radio show, called *Chinese Festival*, could be heard four evenings a week. In 1961, Chu went to work for the city's Department of Welfare and became the director of a center in New York's Chinatown. He was also an entrepreneur, being the owner of the Acme Company, and played an active role in the Chinatown community, holding the post of executive secretary of the Soo Yuen Benevolent Association for more than a decade.

Chu's experience and observation provided ample grist for the mill of his novel, *Eat a Bowl of Tea*, whose protagonist wrestles with issues of traditional Confucian filial duty, marital infidelity, and his identity as a Chinese in America during the 1940's.

Eat a Bowl of Tea

TYPE OF WORK: Novel
FIRST PUBLISHED: 1961

Widely acclaimed by Asian American writers and critics, Chu's *Eat a Bowl of Tea* is the first Chinese American novel that realistically depicts New York's Chinatown bachelor society in the United States shortly after World War II. The novel focuses on the struggles of a young Chinese American who attempts to define his identity.

As the novel opens, it is revealed that the protagonist, Wang Ben Loy, a bridegroom of two months, has become impotent. Ben Loy is a Chinese American in his twenties, a filial son, obedient to his Confucian father, Wah Gay, who left him in China for twenty-five years while establishing himself in America.

Wah Gay, owner of a gambling establishment in Chinatown, sends for Ben Loy, who works as a waiter, joins the U.S. Army, then returns to waiting tables at a Chinese restaurant. Ben Loy alleviates his frustrations by regularly patronizing prostitutes; unfortunately, he contracts several venereal diseases. In 1948, Ben Loy fulfills his filial duty by marrying Mei Oi, a China-born daughter of Wah Gay's longtime friend.

Neglected by her husband, Mei Oi becomes pregnant by Ah Song, a notorious Chinatown philanderer. Chu appears sympathetic with women by implying that husbands must share blame for the infidelity of their wives when sexual and emotional needs are unsatisfied.

Mei Oi passes off the expected child as Ben Loy's, but when Ah Song is sighted sneaking from her apartment, Chinatown buzzes with gossip. Feeling disgraced, Wah Gay ambushes Ah Song after a tryst at Mei Oi's apartment and slices off his left ear. Justice is served when the unofficial Chinatown judicial system condemns Ah Song to five years' ostracism. Having lost face, Wah Gay exiles himself.

Ben Loy and Mei Oi go west to San Francisco, where Mei Oi has a baby whom Ben Loy accepts. They look forward to having others after Ben Loy's impotence is cured by a Chinese herbalist, who makes him "eat a bowl of tea" of medicinal herbs. Most important, Ben Loy breaks from the patriarchal control of his traditionalist Confucian father and becomes the arbiter of his Asian American identity.

SUGGESTED READINGS

Cheng Lok Chua. "Golden Mountain: Chinese Versions of the American Dream in Lin Yutang, Louis Chu, and Maxine Hong Kingston." *Ethnic Groups* 4 (1982).

Cheung, King-Kok, and Stan Yogi. *Asian American Literature. An Annotated Bibliography.* New York: Modern Language Association of America, 1988.

Gong, Ted. "Approaching Cultural Change Through Literature." *Amerasia Journal* 7 (1980).

Hsiao, Ruth Y. "Facing the Incurable: Patriarchy in *Eat a Bowl of Tea.*" In *Reading the Literatures of Asian America*, edited by Shirley Geok-lin Lim and Amy Ling. Philadelphia: Temple University Press, 1992.

Li-Shu-yan. "Otherness and Transformation in *Eat a Bowl of Tea* and *Crossings.*" *MELUS* 18 (1993).

Contributors: C. L. Chua and Janet Fujimoto

Sandra Cisneros

BORN: Chicago, Illinois; December 20, 1954

MEXICAN AMERICAN

*Cisneros's work introduced a powerful and zestful
Latina voice to American literature.*

PRINCIPAL WORKS

CHILDREN'S LITERATURE: *Hairs = Pelitos*, 1984
LONG FICTION: *The House on Mango Street*, 1984; *Caramelo*, 2002
POETRY: *Bad Boys*, 1980; *The Rodrigo Poems*, 1985; *My Wicked, Wicked Ways*,
1987; *Loose Woman*, 1994
SHORT FICTION: *Woman Hollering Creek, and Other Stories*, 1991
MISCELLANEOUS: *Vintage Cisneros*, 2004

Sandra Cisneros (SAHN-drah sihz-NAY-rohs) was born in Chicago in 1954 to a
Mexican father and a Mexican American mother. She grew up in a working-class
family with six brothers; her family expected her to follow the traditional female
role. Her lonely childhood growing up with six males and the family's constant
moving contributed to her becoming a writer. The family moved frequently—from
house to house and from Chicago to Mexico City—which caused constant upheav-
als. She felt trapped between the American and the Mexican cultures, not belonging
in either one. Understandably, Cisneros withdrew into a world of books. The family
finally settled down in a Puerto Rican neighborhood on the north side of Chicago.
This setting provided Cisneros with the inspiration for her first novel, *The House on
Mango Street* and the characters who appear in it.

   Cisneros attended Loyola University in Chicago and graduated in 1976 with a
B.A. in English. She was the only Hispanic majoring in English at the time, a unique
situation that isolated her from her peers. During her junior year at Loyola, she
came in contact with her cultural roots and the Chicago poetry scene, influences to
which she would later return in her writings.

   Cisneros moved to Iowa, where she earned a master's degree in creative writing
at the University of Iowa Writers' Workshop in 1978. During her two years there,
she felt lonely and displaced. A particularly unsettling experience occurred, one
that ultimately helped her find her narrative voice and her writing subjects. During
a seminar discussion of Gaston Bachelard's *The Poetics of Space* (1957), Cisneros
discovered that his use of "house" as a metaphor differed radically from her understanding. She realized that Bachelard and her classmates shared a communal understanding of "house," one that she did not possess. Recognizing her otherness, she

decided to write about subjects and memories close to her life but foreign to her classmates: third-floor flats, fear of rats, drunk and abusive husbands, all unpoetic subjects. At the same time, she found her literary voice, one which had been there but she had suppressed.

Before developing her career as a writer, Cisneros worked as a teacher, counselor, and arts administrator. She also began writing autobiographical sketches about her life experiences and continues to write about "those ghosts that haunt [her], that will not [let] her sleep." She is internationally recognized for her poetry and fiction in which she intermingles English and Spanish. Her poetry and short stories, though not copious, have earned for her recognition as an outstanding Latina writer.

Although Cisneros has written four volumes of poetry, it is her fiction for which she is best known. *The House on Mango Street* received the 1985 Before Columbus American Book Award. This work, which took her five years to complete, provides a feminine perspective on growing up. The collection of forty-four narratives relates the experiences of Esperanza Cordero, the Hispanic adolescent narrator. The sketches describe her experiences as she matures and discovers life in a poor Hispanic urban ghetto. The house on Mango Street symbolizes her search for self-identity as she yearns for "a house all [her] own."

The House on Mango Street

TYPE OF WORK: Novella
FIRST PUBLISHED: 1984

The House on Mango Street speaks in an adolescent Chicana's voice of coming-of-age in a poor Chicago neighborhood in the mid-twentieth century. Cisneros's first book of fiction received immediate acclaim, becoming a widely studied text in schools and universities.

The novella consists of sketches, each exploring some aspect of the experiences of the narrator, Esperanza Cordero, after her family moves into a house of their own. These sketches are drawn from Cisneros's own life; her family moved into a Puerto Rican neighborhood on Chicago's North Side during her twelfth year. Cisneros discovered this voice and subject in resistance against the pressure to conform to what she felt was, at the University of Iowa Writers' Workshop, a "terrible East-coast pretentiousness." She realized that growing up Chicana in Chicago set her apart from most other writers. Esperanza's story also is one of resistance, especially against the expectations for women in her culture. She and her family have dreamed of having an even grander home, but she discovers strongly ambivalent feelings about home once they have one. On one hand, it is a place to be and to become. On the other, it is a sort of prison, especially for women.

In "The Family of Little Feet," Esperanza and two girlfriends get high-heeled shoes and wander playfully into the neighborhood, imagining themselves adults. At first, when men notice them and women seem jealous, they enjoy the attention, but when a drunk demands a kiss from Esperanza in exchange for a dollar, she and her friends flee and get rid of the shoes. Every other specifically feminine artifact and feature becomes a potential trap: hips, cooking, dresses, physical beauty, and most of all houses. Repeatedly, wives and daughters are locked in houses, where they serve men.

Finally, Esperanza dreams of a house of her own, one that is not her husband's or her father's but hers. At the end of the novella, Esperanza begins the story again, revealing that her book has become her house on Mango Street, the home in her heart that her best female mentors have told her to find. By writing, she gets hold of it, and in this way she can have a home and still resist becoming a man's property.

Sandra Cisneros (Rubén Guzmán)

My Wicked, Wicked Ways

TYPE OF WORK: Poetry
FIRST PUBLISHED: 1987

There is little of Cisneros's signature blend of English and Spanish in this collection, though several pieces tell of growing up Chicana, one rebellious girl among six brothers. The book's first section captures the guileless sing-song of a schoolgirl. There's a cold baby in a satin box, "like a valentine,"in the corner of Lucy's pink living room, and there's sick, sad Abuelito, "who used to laugh like the letter k."

By the second section, the girl has become a lover, "thenotorious/ one/ leg wrapped/ around/ the door." Her girlfriend chugs Pabst in redneck bars, and her father warns her that a Sandra Cisneros in Mexico "was arrested for audacious crimes/ that began by disobeying fathers."

The third section is a handful of postcards from exotic places. She walks alone under stars through a field of poppies in the south of France. She muses to lovers, and to lovers who might have been. She drags furniture out of a burning house on the island of Hydra and praises that "paradise of symmetry," the derriere of Michelangelo's "David."

The collection closes with a series of love poems that are richly sensual and often furious. The affair, with its many good-byes, is angular and adulterous: "you who never admitted a public grace./ We of the half-dark who were unbrave."

Cisneros has written a prefatory poem that is worth the price of the book, a terrific psychic summary of the years that created these poems. "I chucked the life/ my father'd plucked for me," she explains, ". . . winched the door with poetry and fled."

Woman Hollering Creek

TYPE OF WORK: Short fiction
FIRST PUBLISHED: 1991

Woman Hollering Creek, and Other Stories is a widely admired collection of short stories. Most of the stories are set in Texas, some in Mexico. Most deal with the pressures upon Chicanas to conform to traditional ideas of femininity.

The title story is about Cleo, a naïve Mexican girl who marries a Mexican American. She soon finds herself pregnant with her second child, isolated in a foreign land where she cannot even speak with most people. Her frustrated husband beats her, destroying the dreams of happiness in marriage she learned from Mexican soap operas. When she flees, she gets help from a woman who hollers joyfully as they cross the Woman Hollering Creek bridge, teaching Cleo a new meaning for the creek's name and another way to be a woman.

Two stories explore the problem of being "the other woman": "Never Marry a Mexican" and "Eyes of Zapata." This role may seem to be a form of rebellion against conventional women's roles, but a mistress's role can be as restrictive as a wife's, and the price of what freedom it offers proves high. The narrator of "Bien Pretty" more successfully breaks free of traditional forms, living an artist's life, taking lovers as she is inclined, learning that she can be in control, even after losing lovers. She becomes determined to change the image of women in love she sees in soap operas; she wants to re-create them as people who make things happen.

Cisneros described writing this collection as a community project. She met friends at a San Antonio diner on weekends, drew on the unbelievable things they discussed, and then shared her drafts while revising them. This approach accounts in part for the variety of voices and forms. Two especially witty pieces are "Little Miracles, Kept Promises" and "Los Boxers." The first consists of notes left at saints' shrines, many requests for divine intervention in amusing problems. The final long note recounts the writer's discovery that the Virgin Mary is a multifaceted goddess who has helped her begin to escape the restrictive traditional woman's role. "Los Boxers" is the monologue of a widower who has learned to do his own laundry; he explains to a young mother the economies he has discovered by applying masculine intelligence to "woman's work." Using many voices, this collection explores themes of gender and identity in twentieth century Latino and general American culture.

Loose Woman

TYPE OF WORK: Poetry
FIRST PUBLISHED: 1994

In "Night Madness Poem," Sandra Cisneros identifies her main speaking voice in *Loose Woman:* "I'm the crazy lady they warned you about./ The she of rumor talked about—/ and worse, who talks." These are mostly love poems, spoken by a mature woman who loves hard, who takes risks and accepts the consequences. She takes and abandons lovers and is abandoned in turn. She experiences the ecstasy and pain traditionally identified with women in love but embraces these experiences with abandon, swagger, and joy. Sometimes victimized, she refuses to let the victim's role define her. This attitude is evident in a long title: "I Am So Depressed I Feel Like Jumping in the River Behind My House but Won't Because I'm Thirty-Eight and Not Eighteen."

In these often witty poems, one especially humorous strategy is role reversal. In "Full Moon and You're Not Here," the speaker opens in the traditional male voice, calling the lover who has had to leave to pick up a son at scouts, "Cinderella." Only in the last few lines does it become clear that the voice complaining of the lover's inconvenient family ties is female. In "Los Desnudos," she imagines her lover in the position of Goya's *The Naked Maja*. In "Down There," she opens with a portrait of a male proud of his rebellious enjoyment of filth, then takes her turn to glory in the beauty of her menstrual blood.

Although it is sometimes helpful to know Spanish, nearly all of these poems communicate upon first reading. With more familiarity, one sees ever more clearly how they are funny, rich in allusion, and thought-provoking, and how they revel in the power of language to make love and to break things.

SUGGESTED READINGS

Brady, Mary Pat. "The Contrapuntal Geographies of *Woman Hollering Creek, and Other Stories.*" *American Literature* 71 (March, 1999): 117-150.

Cisneros, Sandra. "On the Solitary Fate of Being Mexican, Female, Wicked, and Thirty-three: An Interview with Writer Sandra Cisneros." Interview by Pilar E. Rodríguez Aranda. *The Americas Review* 18, no. 1 (1990): 64-80.

Cruz, Felicia J. "On the 'Simplicity' of Sandra Cisneros' *The House on Mango Street.*" *Modern Fiction Studies* 47, no. 4 (2001): 910-946.

Doyle, Jacqueline. "More Room of Her Own: Sandra Cisneros' *The House on Mango Street.*" *MELUS* 19 (Winter, 1994): 5-35.

Griffin, Susan E. "Resistance and Reinvention in Sandra Cisneros' *Woman Hollering Creek.*" In *Ethnicity and the American Short Story*, edited by Julie Brown. New York: Garland, 1997.

Matchie, Thomas. "Literary Continuity in Sandra Cisneros's *The House on Mango Street.*" *The Midwest Quarterly* 37 (Autumn, 1995): 67-79.

Miriam-Goldberg, Caryn. *Sandra Cisneros: Latina Writer and Activist.* Berkeley Heights, N.J.: Enslow, 1998.

Mullen, Harryette. "'A Silence Between Us Like a Language': The Untranslatability of Experience in Sandra Cisneros's *Woman Hollering Creek.*" *MELUS* 21 (Summer, 1996): 3-20.

Olivares, Julian. "Sandra Cisneros' *The House on Mango Street,* and the Poetics of Space." *The Americas Review* 15, nos. 3/4 (1987): 160-170.

Thompson, Jeff. "'What Is Called Heaven?' Identity in Sandra Cisneros's *Woman Hollering Creek.*" *Studies in Short Fiction* 31 (Summer, 1994): 415-424.

Wyatt, Jean. "On Not Being *La Malinche:* Border Negotiations of Gender in Sandra Cisneros's 'Never Marry a Mexican' and 'Woman Hollering Creek.'" *Tulsa Studies in Women's Literature* 14 (Fall, 1995): 243-271.

Contributor: Terry Heller

Eldridge Cleaver

BORN: Wabbaseka, Arkansas; August 31, 1935
DIED: Pomona, California; May 1, 1998

AFRICAN AMERICAN

Cleaver's Soul on Ice, *an electrifying mixture of confessional writing and social commentary, is one of the major documents of the 1960's.*

PRINCIPAL WORKS

NONFICTION: *Soul on Ice*, 1968; *Eldridge Cleaver's Black Papers*, 1969; *Post Prison Writings and Speeches*, 1969; *Soul on Fire*, 1978; *Target Zero: A Life in Writing*, 2006 (Kathleen Cleaver, editor)

Eldridge Cleaver (EHL-dridj KLEE-vur) was born in the small village of Wabbaseka, Arkansas, near Little Rock. In 1946, he moved with his family to Rose Hill, a mainly Chicano neighborhood in the Los Angeles area. Cleaver was first arrested, for stealing bicycles, in 1947, and in 1949 he was sent to reform school, where he became a Roman Catholic. He explains in *Soul on Ice* that he chose the Catholic Church because "all the Negroes and Mexicans went there."

In 1954, Cleaver was sent to prison for selling marijuana. Four years later he was charged with attempted rape and assault with intent to kill and was sent to Folsom Prison, from which he was paroled in November, 1966. Shortly thereafter, he joined the militant Black Panther Party and married Kathleen Neal. The publication of *Soul on Ice* in February, 1968, marked Cleaver's appearance as a self-educated intellectual to be reckoned with. In the work he speaks fluently on issues that were sensitive among blacks and whites. He attacks writer James Baldwin for his alleged bowing to whites, condemns homosexuality as a "sickness," and reviles black women. *Soul on Ice* began a crucial year for Cleaver. On April 6, Cleaver was wounded in a shoot-out with the Oakland police that resulted in Bobby Hutton's death. As a result of this incident, Cleaver's parole was revoked. Faced with return to prison, Cleaver fled to Montreal and on to Havana.

Cleaver was kept under guard for seven months in Cuba before being sent in 1969 to Algiers, where his hatred for capitalism intensified. In 1970, he led a group of eleven on a trip to Pyongyang, North Korea, and on to Hanoi and Peking. In 1971, Cleaver was expelled from the Black Panthers by party leader Huey Newton. When two groups of black Americans hijacked planes to Algiers, Algeria forced the Cleavers to move to Paris, where they obtained legal residence in 1974.

The two years he spent in Paris proved crucial to Cleaver; his thinking turned

conservative. In late 1975, he returned to the United States as an evangelical Christian. He was arrested but released in 1976 on $100,000 bail. In the 1980's, he sup-
ported Ronald Reagan's presidency, but his active career as an evangelist began to
falter. He and Kathleen were divorced in 1985, and he struggled with drug problems and had to be hospitalized when, in 1994, he was injured during a drug deal
gone bad. Upon his release, he worked for San Francisco's Black Chamber of Commerce and taught at a Miami Bible college, but convictions for burglary and cocaine possession ensued, and he died in Southern California on May 1, 1998, at
Pomona Valley Medical Center for reasons his family asked to remain undisclosed.

Soul on Ice

TYPE OF WORK: Essays
FIRST PUBLISHED: 1968

The seventeen essays collected in *Soul on Ice* contribute to the long tradition of
prison writing. In the first essay, "On Becoming," Cleaver recalls his earlier association in Soledad prison with angry young blacks who "cursed everything American." His reading of Thomas Paine, Voltaire, and the writings of Vladimir Ilich
Lenin convinced Cleaver of the nearly universal confusion that ruled in the realm of
political and social affairs. Cleaver became an iconoclast who took the writings

Eldridge Cleaver (Library of Congress)

of Russian anarchist Mikhail Bakunin and Russian revolutionary Sergey Nechayev (1847-1882) as his guide to political life.

Following his release from Soledad, Cleaver became obsessed with "The Ogre," or the white woman, cultivated an image of himself as an outlaw, and committed rape as an "insurrectionary act." Imprisonment at Folsom forced him to look at himself and to write to save himself. "I had to find out who I am and what I want to be, what type of man I should be, and what I could do to become the best of which I was capable." *Soul on Ice*, then, among other things, is a discovery of identity.

Almost half a century after their writing, most of the essays retain considerable power. "The White Race and Its Heroes," for example, offers penetrating insights into race relations in "schizophrenic" America, although its vision of a world revolution led by people of color turns out to have lacked prescience. "Lazarus, Come Forth" analyzes the significance of the black celebrity in a clear-eyed account of the Muhammad Ali boxing match with Floyd Patterson. "Notes on a Native Son" attacks James Baldwin for what Cleaver perceives as "the hatred for blacks permeating his writings" and for Baldwin's "flippant, schoolmarmish dismissal" of Norman Mailer's *The White Negro* (1957), which Cleaver found "prophetic and penetrating." Cleaver's contempt for Baldwin is complicated by Cleaver's judgment of homosexuality as a sickness and by Cleaver's charge that the homosexual Baldwin criticized Richard Wright because Baldwin despised Wright's masculinity.

Two of the more important themes in *Soul on Ice* are the identification of white oppression of blacks in the United States with white colonial capitalist exploitation of minorities everywhere, especially in Vietnam, and a rather mystical ethic of love and sexuality preached in "The Primeval Mitosis." "The Primeval Mitosis" analyzes the power relations between the sexes and the black and white races. *Soul on Ice* resists dismissal as a period piece. The book continues to impress with its energy and powers of intelligent observation.

SUGGESTED READINGS

Oliver, John. *Eldridge Cleaver: Ice and Fire!* Plainfield, N.J.: Logos International, 1977.

Rajiv, Sudhi. *Forms of Black Consciousness*. New York: Advent Books, 1992.

Rout, Kathleen. *Eldridge Cleaver*. Boston: Twayne, 1995.

Waldrep, Sheldon. "'Being Bridges': Cleaver/Baldwin/Lorde and African American Sexism and Sexuality." *Journal of Homosexuality* 26, no. 2/3 (1994): 167-181.

Contributor: Frank Day

Lucille Clifton

BORN: Depew, New York; June 27, 1936

AFRICAN AMERICAN

*Clifton's unique strength in poetry is her
understated complexity in celebrating all life
as an African American woman.*

PRINCIPAL WORKS

CHILDREN'S LITERATURE: *The Black BC's*, 1970; *Some of the Days of Everett Anderson*, 1970; *Everett Anderson's Christmas Coming*, 1971; *All Us Come Cross the Water*, 1973; *The Boy Who Didn't Believe in Spring*, 1973; *Everett Anderson's Year*, 1974; *The Times They Used to Be*, 1974; *My Brother Fine with Me*, 1975; *Everett Anderson's Friend*, 1976; *Three Wishes*, 1976; *Amifika*, 1977; *Everett Anderson's 1-2-3*, 1977; *Everett Anderson's Nine Month Long*, 1978; *The Lucky Stone*, 1979; *Sonora Beautiful*, 1981; *Everett Anderson's Goodbye*, 1983; *One of the Problems of Everett Anderson*, 2001

POETRY: *Good Times*, 1969; *Good News About the Earth*, 1972; *An Ordinary Woman*, 1974; *Two-Headed Woman*, 1980; *Good Woman: Poems and a Memoir, 1969-1980*, 1987; *Next: New Poems*, 1987; *Quilting: Poems, 1987-1990*, 1991; *The Book of Light*, 1993; *The Terrible Stories*, 1996; *Blessing the Boats: New and Selected Poems, 1988-2000*, 2000; *Mercy*, 2004

NONFICTION: *Generations: A Memoir*, 1976

Lucille Clifton's parents had little education but were avid readers, and she grew to love books. Her father's stories steeped her in ancestral heritage, going back to Mammy Caroline, who was born in 1822 in Dahomey, Africa, seized as a child, and enslaved in the United States for much of her life. Caroline and other family members appear in *Generations: A Memoir* and in many of Clifton's poems.

Clifton's mother wrote and recited poetry. At age ten, Clifton became interested in writing, having learned from her mother that it is a means of self-expression. Being a writer never occurred to Clifton; she simply wrote. The first in her family to attend college, she had intellectual black friends, studied drama, and performed in plays—developing her voice and lyricism, and, in her writing, experimenting with sparse punctuation. In 1958, she married Fred Clifton, a philosophy professor. Continuing to write, Clifton did not attempt to have any poems published until her work was solicited. This happened when she was thirty-three, happily married, and with six children under the age of ten.

By then, Clifton had a wealth of education, experiences, and a growing family

Lucille Clifton (AP/Wide World Photos)

from which to draw for her writing. Her first published book of poetry, *Good Times*, focuses on difficulties in urban life. The book also honors strength and celebration in the face of adversity. In Clifton's second volume, she turns away from "white ways" to affirm "the Black." She celebrates her religious heritage and joins many contemporaries in celebrating racial heritage. With succeeding years and poetry volumes, Clifton's themes, subjects, and style have changed little.

Clifton has also achieved acclaim, and has been more prolific, in writing children's books. Some themes, ideas, and points of view found in her poetry are also found in her children's literature. In her children's books, too, Clifton cultivates identity, values, and pride.

Good Times

TYPE OF WORK: Poetry
FIRST PUBLISHED: 1969

Hesitant to call herself a poet in spite of wide literary acclaim, Clifton has noted that poetry is her heart. She has unassumingly identified herself as a black woman, a wife, and mother who "makes poems." Her poems celebrate all of life—its daily realities, its mysteries, and, most significantly, its continuity. She has claimed that celebrating life is what she is about; her poems validate the claim.

Beginning with *Good Times*, Clifton has capitalized on what she knows best. Virtually all her poems fall into one or more of three broad areas of focus: family, African American experience, and female sensibility.

Clifton is a lyric poet whose work is unpretentious and has little rhyme. She continually achieves her goal of rendering big ideas in simple ways. Through short poems of simple language she relates brief portraits, encounters, or disturbances that are neatly presented in a few lines. Clifton seems more guided by consciousness or heart than form or structure. Her use of precise, evocative images is masterful, as evidenced in "miss rosie," which describes the title character as "a wet brown bag of a woman." In that poem, and many others, what Clifton does not say is part of the poem's power. Always significant are her use of spaces, few capital letters, and vernacular. In "homage to my hair," the poet changes from standard English to a black dialect with great effect; in "holy night," Mary speaks in a Caribbean dialect. Clifton's use of metaphor is frequent, compelling, and nowhere better than in "lucy and her girls," relating the power of family ties to natural phenomena. The contrast and tension Clifton achieves through frequent juxtaposition of concepts, as in "inner city," are laudatory. Many of her lines are memorable, as "my mouth is a cave of cries" in "chemotherapy." Only occasionally didactic, sometimes humorous, typically subtle or understated, Clifton's poetry has emotion, conviction, moral stance, Christian tenets, and hope. It has changed little through the years, except to sometimes reflect aging and all that that implies. Always, Clifton defines and affirms the African American experience, politically and aesthetically, with originality, voice, dignity, and pride. She has twice been nominated for the Pulitzer Prize in poetry.

Clifton's early work was frequently inspired by her family, especially her children, and was often a celebration of African American ancestry, heritage, and culture. In the title poem of this collection, Clifton reminds all children, "oh children think about the/ good times." She juxtaposes society's perceptions and her own in the opening poem of the collection—"in the inner city/ or/ like we call it/ home"— in order to honor the place she lives. Believing in the humanity of all people, she calls on each person, regardless of ancestry, to take control of his or her life. Of Robert, in the poem by the same name, she states he "married a master/ who whipped his mind/ until he died," suggesting through the image that the union was one of mutual consent. Her impatience with humans of all kinds who do not strive to improve their lot is a theme begun with this collection and continued throughout her more than three decades of publishing. Another theme that arises here is optimism, as in "Flowers": "Oh/ here we are/ flourishing for the field/ and the name of the place/ is Love."

An Ordinary Woman

TYPE OF WORK: Poetry
FIRST PUBLISHED: 1974

An Ordinary Woman includes poems divided into two sections, beginning with "Sisters," a celebration of family and relationships. "The Lesson of the Falling Leaves" includes the following line:

> the leaves believe
> such letting go is love
> such love is faith
> such faith is grace
> such grace is god
> i agree with the leaves.

It is a testimony to hope, a theme that runs throughout her work. Consistently juxtaposing past with present, Clifton provides wisdom to guide the future, as in the example of "Jackie Robinson":

> ran against walls
> without breaking.
> in night games
> was not foul
> but, brave as a hit
> over whitestone fences
> entered the conquering dark.

Two-Headed Woman

TYPE OF WORK: Poetry
FIRST PUBLISHED: 1980

Two-Headed Woman, which invokes the African American folk belief in a "Two-Headed Woman," with its overtones of a voodoo conjurer, begins with a section titled "Homage to Mine," moves on to "Two-Headed Woman," and concludes with "The Light That Came to Lucille Clifton." While Clifton's works often have allusions to Christianity, as in the "Some Jesus" series in *Good News About the Earth*, she refers to other faiths as well, including the Hindu goddess Kali, from "An Ordinary Woman," providing evidence of her openness to multiple ways of knowing. As a "Two-Headed Woman," in the opening poem of that section, Clifton says she has "one face turned outward/ one face/ swiveling slowly in." Spirituality and mysticism pervade this collection, as the final poem attests, with its reference to the "shimmering voices" of her ancestors, whom the poet has heard singing in the "populated air."

Good Woman

TYPE OF WORK: Poetry
FIRST PUBLISHED: 1987

One theme of the poems in this collection involves Clifton's ethnic pride, as is reflected in "After Kent State": "white ways are/ the way of death/ come into the/ black/ and live." This volume also contains a section called "Heroes," which directly extends this first theme, and ends the book with a section called "Some Jesus":

> I have learned
> some few things
> like when a man
> walk manly
> he don't stumble
> even in the lion's den.

While the gender is male, Clifton would not limit the message to men. Overall, her early work heralds African Americans for their resistance to oppression and their survival of racism.

Quilting

TYPE OF WORK: Poetry
FIRST PUBLISHED: 1991

In five parts, each of the first four named for traditional quilt patterns, "Log Cabin," "Catalpa Flower," "Eight-Pointed Star," and "Tree of Life," *Quilting* seems pieced together, as a quilt. It ends with a single poem, "Blessing the Boats," in "prayer," as if the spiritual life serves as the connecting threads. Clifton honors those whose roles in history have brought about change, like "February 11, 1990" dedicated to "Nelson Mandela and Winnie," and "Memo" which is dedicated "to Fannie Lou Hamer." The poem's "questions and answers" ends with "the surest failure/ is the unattempted walk."

The Terrible Stories

TYPE OF WORK: Poetry
FIRST PUBLISHED: 1996

In *The Terrible Stories*, Clifton chronicles the terrible stories of her own life, which include her struggle with breast cancer, and the terrible stories of her people, which include slavery and the prejudice that has survived time. The book ends with a question: Referring to the biblical David, the poet asks how this David will be remembered "if he stands in the tents of history/ bloody skull in one hand, harp in the other?" Clifton's ability to look at history—ancient, contemporary, or personal—and find redemption in it gives humanity a way to face and survive its failures; this perspective shows her consistent faith in grace.

SUGGESTED READINGS

Anaporte-Easton, Jean. "Healing Our Wounds: The Direction of Difference in the Poetry of Lucille Clifton and Judith Johnson." *Mid-American Review* 14, no. 2 (1994).

Clifton, Lucille. "I'd Like Not to Be a Stranger in the World: A Conversation/ Interview with Lucille Clifton." Interview by Michael Glaser. *The Antioch Review* 58, no. 3 (2000): 310-328.

Holladay, Hilary. *Wild Blessings: The Poetry of Lucille Clifton.* Baton Rouge: Louisiana State University Press, 2004.

Jordan, Shirley, ed. *Broken Silences: Interviews with Black and White Women Writers.* New Brunswick, N.J.: Rutgers University Press. 1993.

Lannan Foundation. *Readings and Conversations: Readings by Lucille Clifton; Conversation with Denise Chávez.* [United States]: Author, 2000.

Lupton, Mary Jane. *Lucille Clifton: Her Life and Letters.* Westport, Conn.: Praeger, 2006.

Madhubuti, Haki. "Lucille Clifton: Warm Water, Greased Legs, and Dangerous Poetry." In *Black Women Writers, 1950-1980: A Critical Evaluation*, edited by Mari Evans. New York: Doubleday, 1984.

Mullaney, Janet Palmer, ed. *Truthtellers of the Times: Interviews with Contemporary Woman Poets.* Ann Arbor: University of Michigan Press, 1998.

White, Mark Bernard. "Sharing the Living Light: Rhetorical, Poetic, and Social Identity in Lucille Clifton." *CLA Journal* 40, no. 3 (1997): 288-305.

Whitley, Edward. "'A Long Missing Part of Itself': Bringing Lucille Clifton's *Generations* into American Literature." *MELUS* 26, no. 2 (2001): 47-64.

Contributors: Sandra F. Bone and Alexa L. Sandmann

Jesús Colón

BORN: Cayey, Puerto Rico; January 20, 1901

PUERTO RICAN

*Colón's sketches document the Puerto Rican
immigrant experience, validating the role of average
Puerto Rican immigrants and "the deep traditions of striving
for freedom and progress that pervade our daily life."*

PRINCIPAL WORKS
NONFICTION: *A Puerto Rican in New York, and Other Sketches*, 1961; *The Way It
Was, and Other Writings*, 1993

Jesús Colón (heh-ZEWS koh-LOHN) was involved as an activist with the Puerto
Rican and Latino communities in New York City. He understood the plight of the
poor, working-class immigrant, since he had held a variety of odd jobs, from dish-
washer to dockworker. A committed socialist, Colón wrote from New York for a
socialist newspaper, *Justicia*, published in Spanish in Puerto Rico. He also contributed articles in English to the New York-based socialist newspapers *The Daily
Worker* and *The Worker*. His publications denounced violations against the working class, and they opposed biased attitudes against the Puerto Rican, the Latino,
and the African American populations. His 1961 anthology gathers together some
of those articles, some of them published for the first time in English.

Colón's background as a newspaper reporter directly influenced his sketches.
Born to a humble peasant family, Colón aims to offer a kinder view of the Puerto Rican experience by recapturing key moments of his own life and stressing particular
folk traditions as representative of Puerto Rican culture. His struggle to succeed in
New York City, where he arrived at sixteen, illustrates the saga of the Puerto Ricans
generally, who since the 1920's have come to that city by the thousands. Colón protests the generally negative attitude toward Puerto Ricans and instead offers his
own life as example of the Puerto Rican experience in New York, a life that is a
combination of strong, fulfilling, and discouraging emotions.

Colón's sketches place the writer as protagonist in stories that attempt to illustrate specific traits of the Puerto Rican personality. His narrative is highly dependent upon his memories, which go back to his childhood in rural Puerto Rico during
the first decade of the twentieth century. Displaying his ability to remember incidents from several decades before, Colón recalls the readers who entertained tobacco wrappers, some of whom were so well read that they could recite long literary
passages from memory. Listening to men reading and commenting on literature

made the boy Colón aware of social injustice toward the working class.

Colón's stories bring together a number of colorful characters who inhabit the Puerto Rican barrios of New York. His book, with its commitment to document the Puerto Rican immigrant experience, stands out as a rich sociological treatise. Colón's major contribution may be his ability to validate the role of average Puerto Rican immigrants as protagonists of their own stories. For Colón, the history of the Puerto Rican community is not to be found in the "sentimental, transient and ephemeral, or bizarre and grotesque in Puerto Rican life" but in "the deep traditions of striving for freedom and progress that pervade our daily life."

A Puerto Rican in New York

TYPE OF WORK: Autobiography
FIRST PUBLISHED: 1961

The sketches in *A Puerto Rican in New York* place the writer as protagonist in stories that attempt to illustrate specific traits of the Puerto Rican personality. His narrative is highly dependent upon his memories, which go back to his childhood in rural Puerto Rico during the first decade of the twentieth century. Displaying his ability to remember incidents from several decades before, Colón recalls the readers who entertained tobacco wrappers, some of whom were so well read that they could recite long literary passages from memory. Listening to men reading and commenting on literature made the boy Colón aware of social injustice toward the working class.

Colón's stories bring together a number of colorful characters who inhabit the Puerto Rican barrios of New York. His book, with its commitment to document the Puerto Rican immigrant experience, stands out as a rich sociological treatise. Colón's major contribution may be his ability to validate the role of average Puerto Rican immigrants as protagonists of their own stories. For Colón, the history of the Puerto Rican community is not to be found in the "sentimental, transient and ephemeral, or bizarre and grotesque in Puerto Rican life" but in "the deep traditions of striving for freedom and progress that pervade our daily life."

SUGGESTED READINGS

Colón, Jesús. *The Jesús Colón Papers*. New York: Evelina López Antonetty Puerto Rican Research Collection, Centro de Estudios Puertorriqeños, Hunter College, 1991.
_____. *The Way It Was, and Other Writings*. Edited with an introduction by Edna Acosta-Belen and Virginia Sanchez Korrol. Houston, Tex.: Arte Público, 1993.

Contributor: Rafael Ocasio

Lucha Corpi

BORN: Jáltipan, Veracruz, Mexico; April 13, 1945

MEXICAN AMERICAN

Corpi addresses border issues and three cultures—indigenous Mexican, mixed modern Mexican, and Anglo—and works to sensitize the male literary tradition to women's issues.

PRINCIPAL WORKS

CHILDREN'S/YOUNG ADULT LITERATURE: *Where Fireflies Dance*, 1997
LONG FICTION: *Delia's Song*, 1989; *Eulogy for a Brown Angel*, 1992; *Cactus Blood*, 1995; *Black Widow's Wardrobe*, 1999
POETRY: *Palabras de mediodía/Noon Words*, 1980; *Variaciones sobre una tempestad/ Variations on a Storm*, 1990
EDITED TEXT: *Máscaras*, 1997

Lucha Corpi (LEW-chah KOR-pee), called Luz, was born and socialized in Mexico. At an early age, she began to give recitals and read poems in public, encouraged by her teachers. Her youthful adventures with her brother included visiting the ruined house of the revolutionary fighter Juan Sebastián. Afterward, the siblings listened to music from the jukebox at the neighborhood cantina but were caught by their mother. Later, as an adult, Corpi sang and told stories to her own son.

Corpi immigrated at nineteen, in 1965, to San Francisco with her husband. Their son was born there. Five years later they divorced. It is notable that Corpi did not write until living in the Chicano community after the divorce. Mexican literary traditions are stronger than Anglo ones in her work, which employs the codes and conventions of the Hispanic lyrical and romantic tradition, echoing the works of Pablo Neruda, Gabriel García Márquez, and Federico García Lorca. Corpi's work presupposes knowledge of Mexican popular expressions and legends such as that of *La Llorona*, the ghost woman who seeks her children.

Because of the author's emigration and divorce, Corpi's work explores the boundaries between Anglo and Mexican cultures and life in a society that permits women to express themselves in writing. She writes her fiction in English and her poetry in Spanish (and collaborates with her longtime translator, Catherine Nieto-Rodríguez, on the bilingual versions). Corpi addresses border issues and three cultures (the indigenous Mexican, the mixed modern Mexican, and the Anglo) as she writes about four areas of human experience: the natural world, the cultural overlay, the pagan aspect, and artistic expression. Among her most potent symbols are the bridge (emigration) and the Virgin of Guadalupe (the long-suffering woman).

256

Critics note that while Corpi's works presuppose an audience of women, she avoids overt textual markers of sex, keeps her literary voice impersonal, and concerns herself with the representation of female consciousness. Corpi examines her own emotions and those of her characters by using images rather than expository prose. In Corpi's mind, women's tragedies are caused by men's insensitivity to women, and she means to sensitize male literary tradition to women's issues.

Corpi holds a B.A. from the University of California at Berkeley and an M.A. in comparative literature from San Francisco State University. She began to teach English as a second language in Oakland, California, in 1973. She has served as coordinator of the Chicano Studies Library at the University of California at Berkeley, as president of the Centro Chicano de Escritores, and as a member of the feminist mystery novel circle Sisters in Crime.

Her *Eulogy for a Brown Angel* won a PEN/Josephine Miles Award and a Multicultural Exchange Award for best book of fiction. The bilingual children's book *Where Fireflies Dance* was named to the 2000-2001 Texas Bluebonnet Award master list of the Texas Library Association. In addition, she received the Lila Wallace-Reader's Digest Foundation Writers Award in 1995 for outstanding Chicana literature, a National Endowment for the Arts Fellowship, and the Latino Hallmark Book Award.

Delia's Song
TYPE OF WORK: Novel
FIRST PUBLISHED: 1989

Delia's Song recounts a young woman's maturation amid the student riots and civil rights movements of the late 1960's. The novel begins with a flashback that suggests the intensity of Delia's emotional state before switching to the central event, which took place earlier in the novel's chronology. The novel's three sections outline the pain and excitement of this turbulent period through Delia's emergence from naïveté into a new social and sexual maturity.

The novel's events are strongly autobiographical, echoing a Mexican American woman's quest for literary respect, sexual identity and equality, an academic degree, and a fulfilling love during the political transformations of late-1960's California. One of the most effective social themes of *Delia's Song* is the disturbing reality of sexism as it is experienced in Chicano culture. Delia must struggle against her own family's limiting attitudes as well as those of her colleagues. Her two brothers, both dead (one shot as a soldier in Vietnam, the other killed by a drug overdose), receive the affections of their mother that Delia desires and deserves. The deepest expression of her struggle for sexual and intellectual identity takes place within, as she moves from an idealistic girl to a fully developed artist, academic, and partner in love.

The disjointed plot requires the reader to remain attentive to narrative cues in order to make sense of the events, but the unconventional structure is one of the novel's best features. Dreams, sprinkles of family history, and memories all interrupt the plot. Stream-of-consciousness flashbacks, vignettes of dream imagery, bits of journal entries, family oral histories, and even newspaper clippings are used as narrative elements. The story is presented from the limited-omniscient point of view, filtered principally through the emotions and mind of Delia, but taking liberties by revealing the thoughts of other characters as well. This structure reflects one of the main themes: that life happens all at once, at the level of consciousness, and has meaning to the degree that people have awareness of it. Delia's life makes sense only when looked at as an entire fabric, not as a series of logically related events.

SUGGESTED READINGS

Armstrong, Jeanne. *Demythologizing the Romance of Conquest*. Westport, Conn.: Greenwood Press, 2000.

Brinson-Piñeda, Barbara. "Poets on Poetry: Dialogue with Lucha Corpi." *Prisma* 1, no. 1 (1979).

Sánchez, Marta Ester. "Prohibition and Sexuality in Lucha Corpi's *Palabras de mediodía/Noon Words*." In *Contemporary Chicana Poetry: A Critical Approach to an Emerging Literature*. Berkeley: University of California Press, 1985.

Contributors: Debra D. Andrist and Joyce Ann Hancock

Victor Hernández Cruz

BORN: Aguas Buenas, Puerto Rico; February 6, 1949

PUERTO RICAN AFRICAN AMERICAN

Cruz incorporates traditional Spanish, New York-Puerto Rican slang, and black English in his writing to explore his multiethnic heritage.

PRINCIPAL WORKS

POETRY: *Papo Got His Gun! and Other Poems*, 1966; *Snaps*, 1969; *Mainland*, 1973; *Tropicalization*, 1976; *By Lingual Wholes*, 1982; *Rhythm, Content & Flavor*, 1989; *Red Beans*, 1991; *Panoramas*, 1997; *Maraca: New and Selected Poems, 1965-2000*, 2001; *The Mountain in the Sea: Poems*, 2006
NONFICTION: *Doing Poetry*, 1970
EDITED TEXTS: *Stuff: A Collection of Poems, Visions and Imaginative Happenings from Young Writers in Schools—Opened and Closed*, 1970 (with Herbert Kohl); *Paper Dance: Fifty-five Latino Poets*, 1995 (with Virgil Suarez and Leroy V. Quintana)

Victor Hernández Cruz (VEE-tohr hehr-NAN-dehz crewz) was born in Aguas Buenas, Puerto Rico, a small town about twenty miles from San Juan. The streets were unpaved, but he absorbed the native song and poetry as well as the poetic declamations of his grandfather and uncle. His family migrated to New York in 1954 and settled in the tenements of the Lower East Side of Manhattan. He attended Benjamin Franklin High School and began to write verse. At sixteen, he composed his first collection of poetry, *Papo Got His Gun! and Other Poems*. Cruz and his friends duplicated and distributed five hundred copies to local bookstores.

In 1967, the *Evergreen Review* helped launch his career when it featured several of these poems. Thus, while still in high school, he became a published poet. In New York, he edited *Umbra* magazine from 1967 to 1969 and was cofounder of the East Harlem Gut Theater. In 1969, he released his second collection of poems, *Snaps*, and gained national attention. In the 1960's, his neighborhood had become a center of intellectual and social ferment as part of the Civil Rights movement. Beat poetry, protest poetry, and feminist poetry mixed with political activism and music to form the social milieu. Ishmael Reed, Allen Ginsberg, and LeRoi Jones (Amiri Baraka) were major influences, and Cruz was intrigued by the developing Nuyorican (New York/Puerto Rican) poetry movement, which often claims him.

In 1969, he moved to Berkeley, California, to become poet in residence at the

University of California. He then served in the ethnic studies department of San Francisco State College from 1971 to 1972. In 1973, he published a third collection of poems, *Mainland*, which chronicles his migrations from New York to California and back again. In 1974, he received the Creative Arts Public Service Award. He worked with the San Francisco Art Commission (1976) and the Mission Neighborhood Center (1981). In April, 1981, *Life* magazine featured Cruz in its celebration of twelve North American poets. With novelist Ishmael Reed, he formed the Before Columbus Foundation.

In 1989, Cruz earned a National Endowment for the Arts creative writing award. After the publication of *Rhythm, Content & Flavor*, he moved back to Aguas Buenas, where he was born. He came into close contact with the local oral traditions and was deeply affected by them. In 1991, the year in which he won a John Simon Guggenheim Memorial Foundation Fellowship, he recorded these sensations in *Red Beans*, and next he began working on a book of poems in Spanish. He served as a visiting professor at the University of California at San Diego (1993) and at the University of Michigan, Ann Arbor (1994). Cultural critic Bill Moyers interviewed Cruz for an eight-part Public Broadcasting Service series, *The Language of Life*, which aired June 23 to July 28, 1995. This program was subsequently released in book and audiocassette formats.

Cruz's legendary ability to give dynamic poetry readings has twice made him World Heavyweight Poetry Champion in Taos, New Mexico. He has also participated in discussions and readings sponsored by La Fundación Federico García Lorca and at the Universidad de Alcalá. He has been short-listed for the prestigious Lenore Marshall Poetry Prize and the Griffen Poetry Prize.

Snaps
TYPE OF WORK: Poetry
FIRST PUBLISHED: 1969

After the early success of *Papo Got His Gun! and Other Poems*, a chapbook that had gained notice in *Evergreen Review*, Random House published *Snaps*. This collection's hip, barrio voice, its jazzy rhythms, and its snapshot technique of realistically portraying street life bought Cruz immediate recognition. Random House honored his irreverence for grammar and formalities of style and thus helped launch the young poet's ongoing fascination with the relationship of sound and sense, of language and life.

The poems capture the true essence of urban ghetto life. Clacking subways, dance clubs, smoking, girl-watching, and knife fights form the gritty realities of life on the street, and the rapid staccato of half-learned English enriches the poems. Cruz's language here is the sublanguage used to present Spanish Harlem's subculture. His speaker in these primarily narrative poems uses street slang as well as surrealistic humor to create a vivid picture of the danger and energy of the culturally diverse Lower East Side. There is constant movement: on subways, uptown, downtown, inside, outside, walking, driving. In "Megalopolis," the speaker presents snapshots from the window of a car moving through the urban sprawl of the East Coast:

> let those lights & trees & rocks
> talk/ going by/ go by   just sit
> back/ we/ we go into towns/   sailing the
> east coast/ westside drive   far-off
> buildings look like castles/ the kind
> dracula flies out of/ new england of houses

The poem goes on to end with quick vignettes of a poet inciting riot, urban bombs, "laurence welk-reader's digest ladies" with bouffant hairdos secured with hair spray, billboards "singing lies," and "the night of the buildings/ . . . singing magic words/ of our ancestors." This ending points to another aspect of Cruz's poetry: traveling through time as well as space.

Mainland
Type of work: Poetry
First published: 1973

Mainland records Cruz's poetic migration across the United States. The motion/ mobility theme of *Snaps* here moves from intracity travel to interstate and, finally, to international migrations. The collection begins in New York, traverses the Midwest to California and the Southwest, and ends with a visit to Puerto Rico, followed by the return to New York.

These poems show the power of the memory of the Caribbean—its music and dance, its food, language, people, and culture—all working to recenter the poet once he returns to the realities of New York urban life. "The Man Who Came to the Last Floor," which ends the collection, employs surrealistic humor. A Puerto Rican immigrant with a bag of tropical seeds arrives in New York and rents a sixth-floor apartment. Singing and dancing in his apartment, he accidentally flings the seeds of tropical fruits from his window.

> A policeman was walking down the avenue
> and all of a sudden took off his hat
> A mango seed landed nicely into his
> curly hair

The policeman does not notice the seed, which then grows into a flourishing five-foot tree that bears a mango. With this surreal image, Cruz presents the subtle, almost subversive, "tropicalization" accomplished by immigrants as they plant seeds to revitalize the northern urban landscape.

Tropicalization

TYPE OF WORK: Poetry
FIRST PUBLISHED: 1976

In an increasingly lyrical vein, Cruz collects in *Tropicalization* the images and rhythms of the Caribbean in poetry and prose poems. This collection presents a renewed vision of the United States, tropicalized, surrealistically transformed by the beat of its Hispanic population. Here Cruz uses more experimental structures to capture the spiritual side of barrio life, and he also enlarges upon the blending of Spanish and English ("Spanglish," or code-switching), always a characteristic of his work. He handles English as an amalgam capable of easily incorporating new words and innovative syntaxes.

In "Side 24," he cheerfully juxtaposes English and Spanish, cement and tropical oranges (*chinas*):

> Walk el cement
> Where las chinas roll
> Illuminating my path
> Through old streets

As part of the "ethnic" avant-garde, Cruz does not regard his Puerto Rican home with anger or despair, as Abraham Rodriguez does, nor does he look back with sadness, as does Judith Ortiz Cofer. He cheerfully delights in his ethnic identity, which he sees as tropicalizing the North, as bringing oranges and salsa to the cement and the chill of the United States.

By Lingual Wholes

TYPE OF WORK: Poetry
FIRST PUBLISHED: 1982

Continuing his themes of contrasting and merging the sounds of two cultures and languages, Cruz again includes both poetry and prose in his 1982 *By Lingual Wholes*. This collection is slower paced and more pensive than the earlier works; again, music, dance, and Spanglish coalesce in a dynamic and positive expression of multiculturalism. Cruz removes barriers of culture and language, illustrating the wholeness possible in living in and creating from two cultures and languages.

The title suggests the wordplay that will follow as Cruz proves himself a master of pun, whimsy, paradox, and concrete poetry. In addition, these poems explore a deeper heritage of Puerto Rican folklore and myth, as well as a whole range of historical events and characters. Never didactic, Cruz invites the reader to participate in genial handshakes across cultures.

In the sixth poem of the collection, "Listening to the Music of Arsenio Rodriguez Is Moving Closer to Knowledge," Cruz pays tribute to the blind African Cuban musician and composer. In New York, the Caribbean community enjoyed this music under the label "salsa." The speaker raves about salsa's power and gaily ridicules researchers who attempt to study it and "understand" it. They totally miss the dance music's intrinsic warmth and tropical passion, which is to be experienced and absorbed, not analyzed and understood.

"Listening to the Music of Arsenio Rodriguez Is Moving Closer to Knowledge"

TYPE OF WORK: Poetry
FIRST PUBLISHED: 1982, in *By Lingual Wholes*

The central feature of "Listening to the Music of Arsenio Rodriguez Is Moving Closer to Knowledge," from the title to the final line ("Has it rained?"), is its lightheartedness and sense of whimsy. Rodriguez was a blind percussionist, player of the *tres* (a small nine-stringed guitar), composer, and bandleader. His impact on the mambo style in Cuba in the 1930's was immeasurable, and he was responsible for the mambo craze that took the northeastern United States by storm in the early 1950's.

The poem salutes Afro-Cuban music and the great musician in its title. At the same time, it ridicules those "researchers" who would attempt to study the results of its impact. The stuff of knowledge is in the music; to study its aftereffects—the "puddles of water" that the listeners have become—is inane. Some things, such as sensuous music, cannot be analyzed; they should simply be experienced. The poem's vivid irony lies in the comparison of the researchers' scrutiny of the pools of water with the knowledge the speaker and his friends gain from directly experiencing the music. The poem satirizes the academicians' preoccupation with the puddles; they are unaware of the water's essence and intangible qualities. Theirs is the kind of intellect that cannot rise to "dance *el son*."

The neighbors, represented by Doña Flores, love the music and willingly liquefy under its spell. "Flores" means flowers, and, as Mrs. Flores is affected, so are the flowers in stanza 4 that "dance/—in the wind." The poem's organic spontaneity creates a bridge in stanza 3 between Flores and flowers: the people, who are lively and beautiful, and the metaphorical essence and spirit of the people. The water is warm because it is metaphorically equated with those who are alive and, in their exultation, transformed. The poem ends with the researchers seeking answers to their absurd questions. They have missed the beauty and truth of the music of Arsenio Rodriguez: They will never be wise.

Rhythm, Content & Flavor

TYPE OF WORK: Poetry
FIRST PUBLISHED: 1989

In his collection, *Rhythm, Content & Flavor*, Cruz selects poems from his earlier works and adds a new work, "Islandis: The Age of Seashells." Here he continues to interweave images of the urban and natural worlds. Also the poet reaffirms his Puerto Rican culture as the source of music and knowledge. Like lost Atlantis, with its tropical breezes and its kinship with the ocean, Puerto Rico creates a music reminiscent of the medieval "music of the spheres." As he also notes elsewhere, poetry for Cruz is "la salsa de Dios"; God is the origin of all poetry and music, and poetry is the music of God.

Red Beans

TYPE OF WORK: Poetry
FIRST PUBLISHED: 1991

Red Beans contains poems, prose essays, and a manifesto on poetry. The "red" of the title is the color of beans, shirts, earth, the Red Sea, "Red pepper/ In a stew," all representing the vitality and urgency Cruz finds in the "red beings," his Puerto Rican ancestors. He also draws on his earliest memories of hearing English in "Snaps of Immigration": "At first English was nothing/ but sound/ Like trumpets doing yakity yak." Later, the sound of poetic language is celebrated in "An Essay on Williams Carlos Williams":

> I love the quality of the
> spoken thought
> As it happens immediately
> uttered into the air
> Not held inside and rolled
> around for some properly
> schemed moment

Cruz continues to emphasize the naturalness, the oral spontaneity of true poetry. "Corsica" adds a focus on the joyful interplay of cultures and languages that had always been a theme in Cruz's poetry. He announces that Puerto Rico and Corsica are "holding hands" underneath the "geologic plates," that both islands see the same moon. Never narrowly ethnic, Cruz celebrates the creative merger of culture and language. He ends this volume showing his receptivity to other cultures:

> I wait with a gourd full
> of inspiration
> For a chip to fall from

The festival fireworks
To favor me
And set me on fire.

Panoramas

TYPE OF WORK: Poetry
FIRST PUBLISHED: 1997

The poems and essays of *Panoramas* present a civilized and gracious tone as they transport the reader to the magic world of the Caribbean, which celebrates its blend of Taino, African, and Spanish legacies. They also illuminate Latin American/Caribbean culture in the United States and beyond. Rather than conflict, Cruz suggests a harmonious merger and a creative synthesis of disparate ideas and people.

The Mountain in the Sea

TYPE OF WORK: Poetry
FIRST PUBLISHED: 2006

Victor Hernández Cruz was one of the earliest and most influential voices of the Nuyorican writers, and his poetry has always been marked by a rich blending of English and Spanish and of imagery that calls up both the vibrant and musical life on the streets of New York's Lower East Side and the tender details of Puerto Rican food, home, agriculture, and climate. With this new volume, Cruz's poetry is further enriched with language and imagery from a new source: the North African Arabic culture of Morocco, where Cruz and his wife Amina live for part of each year. Now the poetry integrates vocabulary in English, Spanish, and Arabic, and alludes to Christianity and Islam, in an exciting bridge of cultures that is as natural as the ocean connecting Cruz's three homelands.

The poems in *The Mountain in the Sea* are in three sections. The first, "Other Shores," explores Cruz's first sensory impressions of the markets, homes, foods, and music of Morocco. "Portraits," the second section, contains nineteen of what Cruz calls "tribute poems," biographical portraits of people who have inspired him. The first two poems, "Rafael Hernández" and "Felipe Rodriguez," honor Puerto Rican immigrants to New York. Memories preserved in this section include the early television appearance of President Dwight Eisenhower, the music of The Harptones, the mystical apparitions of the Virgin of Monserrate and the Virgin of Guadalupe, and the poetry of Jorge Luis Borges.

In the third section, "Island Waves," Cruz returns to Puerto Rico, which he has written about throughout his career. With these poems, however, he sees his native land with new eyes, finding echoes of North Africa in the daily rhythms of Puerto Rican life. Cruz's poetry shows how the same moon, the same rain, and the waves on the Mediterranean and the Caribbean wash over the lands and the people of these distant lands.

SUGGESTED READINGS

Aparicio, Frances R. "'Salsa,' 'Maracas,' and 'Baile': Latin Popular Music in the Poetry of Victor Hernández Cruz." *MELUS* 16 (Spring, 1989/1990): 43-58.

Cruz, Victor Hernández. "Victor Hernández Cruz." Interview by Bill Moyers. In *The Language of Life: A Festival of Poets.* New York: Doubleday, 1995.

Kanellos, Nicolás. *Victor Hernández Cruz and La Salsa de Dios.* Milwaukee: University of Wisconsin Press, 1979.

Torrens, James. "U.S. Latino Writers: The Searchers." *America* 167 (July 18-25, 1992).

Waisman, Sergio Gabriel. "The Body as Migration." *Bilingual Review* 19 (May 1, 1944): 188-192.

Contributors: Marie J. K. Brenner and Ron Welburn

Countée Cullen

Born: New York, New York; May 30, 1903
Died: New York, New York; January 9, 1946

African American

*Cullen, one of the most prolific poets of
the Harlem Renaissance, combined English poetic
styles with racial themes and identities.*

Principal works

CHILDREN'S LITERATURE: *The Lost Zoo (A Rhyme for the Young, but Not Too
Young)*, 1940; *My Lives and How I Lost Them*, 1942
DRAMA: *Medea*, pr., pb. 1935 (translation of Euripides); *One Way to Heaven*, pb.
1936 (adaptation of his novel); *St. Louis Woman*, pr. 1946 (adaptation of Arna
Bontemps's novel *God Sends Sunday*); *The Third Fourth of July*, pr., pb. 1946
(with Owen Dodson; one-act)
LONG FICTION: *One Way to Heaven*, 1932
POETRY: *Color*, 1925; *The Ballad of the Brown Girl: An Old Ballad Retold*, 1927;
Copper Sun, 1927; *The Black Christ, and Other Poems*, 1929; *The Medea, and
Some Poems*, 1935; *On These I Stand: An Anthology of the Best Poems of
Countée Cullen*, 1947
EDITED TEXT: *Caroling Dusk*, 1927

Countée Cullen (KOWN-tee KUHL-lehn) recognized early in his life that he
wanted to use poetry to express his belief that a poet's skin color should not dictate
style and subject matter in a poem. He began writing poetry while in high school.
Cullen, a Phi Beta Kappa honoree from New York University, had already published *Color* by the time he entered graduate school at Harvard University. With a
master's in English and three additional books of poetry, Cullen was widely known
as the unofficial poet laureate of the Harlem Renaissance.

In his introduction to *Caroling Dusk: An Anthology of Verse by Negro Poets*,
Cullen set forth many of the ideas that shaped his identity as a poet and an African
American. He believed that poetry elevated any race and that African American poets could benefit from using the rich traditions of English and American verse. Cullen also chose not to include dialect poetry in his anthology, viewing this style as
out of date, restrictive, and best left to the white poets who were still using it.

Cullen was not ashamed of his race, nor did he deliberately seek white approval. He did feel that he should be receptive to many ideas to enhance his poetry.
Many of his poems, such as "Incident," "From the Dark Tower," and "Colors," pro-

Countée Cullen (Library of Congress)

test racism and bigotry. However, in his collection *The Black Christ, and Other Poems*, themes of love and death prevail. Such themes show the influence of the British Romantic poets John Keats and Percy Bysshe Shelley. Keats especially was Cullen's artistic mentor. Cullen records his response to having visited Keats's grave in "Endymion," a poem celebrating the power of Keats's lyricism.

Cullen's use of genteel traditions and the black experience caused dilemmas and conflicts throughout his writing career. Critics praised Cullen for his skillful use of the sonnet form, but they castigated him when he did not use racial experiences as the primary source of his themes. However, even as he cautioned Harlem Renaissance poets about excessive use of racial themes, he published a novel about Harlem characters, *One Way to Heaven*.

Cullen wrote nearly as much prose as he did poetry. While serving from 1926 through most of 1928 as literary editor of *Opportunity*, a magazine vehicle for the National Urban League, Cullen wrote several articles, including book reviews, and a series of topical essays for a column called "The Dark Tower" about figures and events involved in the Harlem Renaissance. He also wrote many stories for children, most of which are collected in *My Lives and How I Lost Them*, the "autobiography" of Cullen's own pet, Christopher Cat, who had allegedly reached his ninth life. Earlier, in 1932, the poet had tried his hand at a novel, publishing it as *One Way to Heaven*.

In addition to articles, reviews, stories, and a novel, the poet translated or collaborated in the writing of three plays, one of them a musical. From 1934 until his death, Cullen taught French and English at Frederick Douglass Junior High School, guiding students in the traditions that made him a celebrated poet.

In 1935, Cullen translated Euripides' *Medea* for the volume by the same name; in 1942, Virgil Thomson set to music the seven-verse choruses from Cullen's translation. With Owen Dodson, Cullen wrote the one-act play *The Third Fourth of July*, which appeared posthumously in 1946. The musical was produced at the Martin Beck Theater on Broadway, where it ran for 113 performances; this production also introduced Pearl Bailey as the character Butterfly.

The Black Christt

TYPE OF WORK: Poetry
FIRST PUBLISHED: 1929

The intense need expressed here, to see God as literally black, predicts the long narrative poem of 1929, *The Black Christ*. This poem, perhaps more than any other of Cullen's poems, represents his attempt to portray black heroism, the second tenet of the Black Aesthetic. Briefly the poem tells the tale of Jim, a young black man who comes to believe it is inevitable that he will suffer death at the hands of an angry lynch mob. Miraculously, after the inevitable lynching has indeed occurred, the young man appears to his younger brother and mother, much as Jesus of Nazareth, according to the Gospels, appeared before his disciples. Christ has essentially transformed himself into black Jim. Although the poem contains such faults as a main character who speaks in dialect at one point and waxes eloquent at another and one speech by Jim who, pursued by the mob, speaks so long that he cannot possibly escape (one may argue that he was doomed from the start), it has moments of artistic brilliance.

Jim "was handsome in a way/ Night is after a long, hot day." He could never bend his spirit to the white man's demands: "my blood's too hot to knuckle." Like Richard Wright's Bigger Thomas, Jim was a man of action whose deeds "let loose/ The pent-up torrent of abuse," which clamored in his younger brother "for release." Toward the middle of the poem, Jim's brother, the narrator, describes Jim, after the older brother has become tipsy with drink, as "Spring's gayest cavalier"; this occurs "in the dim/ Half-light" of the evening. At the end, "Spring's gayest cavalier" has become the black Christ, Spring's radiant sacrifice, suggesting that "Half-light" reveals only selective truths, those one may be inclined to believe are true because of one's human limitations, whereas God's total light reveals absolute truth unfettered. Following this suggestion, the image "Spring's gayest cavalier" becomes even more fecund. The word "cavalier" calls up another poem by Hopkins, "The Windhover," which is dedicated to Christ. In this poem, the speaker addresses Christ with the exclamation, "O my chevalier!" Both "cavalier" and "chevalier" have their origins in the same Latin word, *caballarius*. Since Cullen knew both French and Latin and since Hopkins's poems had been published in 1918, it is reasonable to suggest a more than coincidental connection. At any rate, "Spring's gayest cavalier" embodies an example of effective foreshadowing.

Just before the mob seizes Jim, the narrator maintains that "the air about him shaped a crown/ Of light, or so it seemed to me," similar to the nimbus so often appearing in medieval paintings of Christ, the holy family, the disciples, and the saints. The narrator describes the seizure itself in an epic simile of nine lines. When Jim has been lynched, the younger brother exclaims, "My Lycidas was dead. There swung/ In all his glory, lusty, young,/ My Jonathan, my Patrocles." Here Cullen brings together the works of John Milton, the Bible, and Homer into one image that appears to syncretize them all. Clearly, the poet is attempting to construct in Jim a hero of cosmic proportions while at the same time managing to unify, if only for a moment, four grand traditions: the English, the biblical, the classical, and the African American.

The octave of "From the Dark Tower" states the poem's problem in an unconventional, perhaps surprising manner by means of a series of threats. The first threat introduces the conceit of planting, to which the poem returns in its last pair of couplets. The poet begins, "We shall not always plant while others reap/ The golden increment of bursting fruit." The planting conceit suggests almost immediately the image of slaves working the fields of a Southern plantation. Conjuring up this memory of the antebellum South but then asserting by use of the future tense ("We *shall* not") that nothing has changed—that is, that the white world has relegated today's African Americans to their former status as slaves, not even as good as second-class citizens—Cullen strikes a minor chord of deep, poignant bitterness felt by many contemporary blacks. Yet, what these blacks produce with their planting is richly fertile, a "bursting fruit"; the problem is that "others reap" this "golden increment." The poet's threat promises that this tide of gross, unjust rapine will soon turn against its perpetrators.

The next few lines compound this initial threat with others. These same oppressed people will not forever bow "abject and mute" to such treatment by a people who have shown by their oppression that they are the inferiors of their victims. "Not everlastingly" will these victims "beguile" this evil race "with mellow flute"; the reader can readily picture scenes of supposedly contented, dancing "darkies" and ostensibly happy minstrel men. "We were not made eternally to weep" declares the poet in the last line of the octave. This line constitutes the *volta*, or turning point, in the poem. All the bitterness and resentment implied in the preceding lines is exposed here. An oppressed people simply will not shed tears forever; sorrow and self-pity inevitably turn to anger and rebellion.

The first four lines of the sestet state cases in defense of the octave's propositions that these oppressed people, now identified by the comparisons made in these lines as the black race, are "no less lovely being dark." The poet returns subtly to his planting conceit by citing the case of flowers that "cannot bloom at all/ In light, but crumple, piteous, and fall." Cullen takes his reader from the infinite heavens to finite flowers of earth, grasping universal and particular significance for his people and thereby restoring and bolstering their pride and sense of worth.

Then follow the piercing, deep-felt last lines: "So, in the dark we hide the heart that bleeds,/ And wait, and tend our agonizing seeds." As with "Yet Do I Marvel," Cullen has effectively combined the structures of the Petrarchan and Shakespearean sonnets by concluding his poem with this trenchant, succinct couplet. The planting conceit, however, has altered dramatically. What has been "golden increment" for white oppressors will yet surely prove the "bursting fruit" of "agonizing seeds." The poem represents, then, a sort of revolutionary predeclaration of independence. This "document" first states the offenses sustained by the downtrodden, next asserts their worth and significance as human beings, and finally argues that the black people will "wait" until an appropriate time to reveal their agony through rebellion. Cullen has here predicted the anger of James Baldwin's *The Fire Next Time* (1963) and the rhetoric of the Black Armageddon, a later literary movement led by such poets as Amiri Baraka, Sonia Sanchez, and Nikki Giovanni.

Whereas these figures of the Black Armageddon movement almost invariably selected unconventional forms in which to express their rebellion, Cullen demonstrated his respect for tradition in voicing his parallel feelings. Although Cullen's work ably displays his knowledge of the traditions of the Western world, from Homer to Keats (and even Edna St. Vincent Millay), it equally enunciates his empathy with black Americans in its celebration of the Black Aesthetic. At the same time that his poetry incorporates classicism and English Romanticism, it affirms his black heritage and the black American experience.

On These I Stand

Type of work: Poetry
First published: 1947

On These I Stand: An Anthology of the Best Poems of Countée Cullen is a collection of the formerly published poems for which Cullen wanted to be remembered. Written during the 1920's and 1930's, these poems are from such works as *Color* (1925), *Copper Sun* (1927), *The Ballad of the Brown Girl* (1927), *The Black Christ, and Other Poems* (1929), and *The Medea, and Some Poems* (1935). Cullen also includes six new poems on subjects ranging from a tribute to John Brown ("A Negro Mother's Lullaby") to the evolution from birth to death ("Dear Friends and Gentle Hearts"). Cullen maintains the style of classical lyricists such as British poet John Keats in this collection, using rhymed couplets, ballads, or sonnet forms.

Color emphasizes racial themes and shows the influence of ideas associated with the Harlem Renaissance. There are religious overtones in some of the poems about the burden of racial oppression. The speaker recognizes a loss of faith but laments the racial prejudice against more religious blacks in "Pagan Prayer." Cullen's Simon the Cyrenian transcends his race by helping Christ bear the cross in "Simon the Cyrenian Speaks." The poem for which Cullen is widely known, "Yet Do I Marvel," questions the value of God's decision to give creative talent to a black person, whose talents are ignored.

Cullen joined other Harlem Renaissance writers in using African motifs. In "Heritage," one of the longer poems in *Color*, the speaker asks the question, What is Africa to me? An exotic and stereotyped image of Africa emerges, and the question is unanswered.

The selections from *Copper Sun* and *The Black Christ, and Other Poems* show that gradually Cullen moved away from ideas about racial identity to those that preoccupy a Romantic mind influenced by Keats, Percy Bysshe Shelley, or Edna St. Vincent Millay. There are numerous poems on love, death, and the difficulties of the creative spirit in overcoming the burdens of the physical self.

To complete *On These I Stand*, Cullen chose examples from *The Lost Zoo* (1940), his book of poems for children. "The Wakeupworld" and "The-Snake-That-Walked-Upon-His-Tail" instruct and delight. The collection *On These I Stand* attests Cullen's Romantic vision, his attraction to Harlem Renaissance themes, and his depiction of the African American experience.

"Yet Do I Marvel"

TYPE OF WORK: Poetry
FIRST PUBLISHED: 1947, in *On These I Stand*

"Yet Do I Marvel," perhaps Cullen's most famous single poem, displays the poet during one of his most intensely lyrical, personal moments; yet this poem also illustrates his reverence for tradition. The sonnet, essentially Shakespearean in rhyme scheme, is actually Petrarchan in its internal form. The Petrarchan form is even suggested in the rhyme scheme; the first two quatrains rhyme *abab, cdcd* in perfect accord with the Shakespearean scheme. The next six lines, however, break the expected pattern of yet another quatrain in the same scheme; instead of *efef* followed by a couplet *gg*, the poem adopts the scheme *ee ff gg*. While retaining the concluding couplet (*gg*), the other two (*eeff*) combine with the final couplet, suggesting the Petrarchan structure of the sestet. The poem is essentially divided, then, into the octave, wherein the problem is stated, and the sestet, in which some sort of resolution is attempted.

Analysis of the poem's content shows that Cullen chooses the internal form of the Petrarchan sonnet but retains a measure of the Shakespearean form for dramatic effect. The first eight lines of the poem express by means of antiphrastic statements or ironic declaratives that the poem's speaker doubts God's goodness and benevolent intent, especially in his creation of certain limited beings. The poem begins with the assertion that "I doubt not God is good, well-meaning, kind" and then proceeds to reveal that the speaker actually believes just the opposite to be true; that is, he actually says, "I do doubt God is good." For God has created the "little buried mole" to continue blind and "flesh that mirrors Him" to "some day die." Then the persona cites two illustrations of cruel, irremediable predicaments from classical mythology, those of Tantalus and Sisyphus. These mythological figures are traditional examples: Tantalus, the man who suffers eternal denial of that which he seeks, and Sisyphus, the man who suffers the eternal drudgery of being forced to toil endlessly again and again only to lose his objective each time he thinks he has won it.

The illustration of the mole and the man who must die rehearses the existential pathos of modern human beings estranged from God and thrust into a hostile universe. What appeared to be naïve affirmations of God's goodness become penetrating questions that reveal Cullen himself in a moment of intense doubt. This attitude of contention with God closely resembles that expressed by Gerard Manley Hopkins in his sonnet "Thou Art Indeed Just, Lord." The probing questions, combined with the apparent resolve to believe, are indeed close; one might suggest that Cullen has adapted Hopkins's struggle for certainty to the black predicament, the real subject of Cullen's poem. The predicaments of Tantalus and Sisyphus (anticipating Albert Camus's later essay) comment on a personal problem, one close to home for Cullen himself. The notion of men struggling eternally toward a goal, thinking they have achieved it but having it torn from them, articulates the plight of black artists in America. In keeping with the form of the Petrarchan sonnet, the ninth line constitutes the *volta*, referring to a "turn" toward some sort of resolution. From ironic questioning, the persona moves to direct statement, even to a degree of affirmation. "Inscrutable His ways are," the speaker declares, to a mere human being who is too preoccupied with the vicissitudes of his mundane existence to grasp "What awful brain compels His awful hand," this last line echoing William Blake's "The Tyger." The apparent resolution becomes clouded by the poem's striking final couplet: "Yet do I marvel at this curious thing:/ To make a poet black, and bid him sing!"

The doubt remains; nothing is finally resolved. The plight of the black poet becomes identical with that of Tantalus and Sisyphus. Like these figures from classical mythology, the black poet is, in the contemporary, nonmythological world, forced to struggle endlessly toward a goal he will never, as the poem suggests, be allowed to reach. Cullen has effectively combined the Petrarchan and the Shakespearean sonnet forms; the sestet's first four lines function as an apparent resolution of the problem advanced by the octave. The concluding couplet, however, recalling the Shakespearean device of concentrating the entire poem's comment within the final two lines, restates the problem of the octave by maintaining that, in the case of a black poet, God has created the supreme irony. In "Yet Do I Marvel," Cullen has succeeded in making an intensely personal statement; as James Johnson suggested, this poem "is motivated by race." Nevertheless, not only race is at work here. Rather than selecting a more modern form, perhaps free verse, the poet employs the sonnet tradition in a surprising and effective way, and he also shows his regard for tradition by citing mythological figures and by summoning up Blake.

"Heritage"

TYPE OF WORK: Poetry
FIRST PUBLISHED: 1947, in *On These I Stand*

Beauty and classical mythology were not the only elements of tradition that Cullen revered. Indeed, he forcefully celebrated his own African heritage, exemplifying the first of the tenets of the Black Aesthetic. "Heritage" represents his most concentrated effort to reclaim his African roots. This 128-line lyric opens as the persona longs for the song of "wild barbaric birds/ Goading massive jungle herds" from which through no fault of his own he has been removed for three centuries. He then articulates Johnson's observation that this poet is ever "seeking to free himself and his art" from the bonds of this heritage. The poem's speaker remarks that, although he crams his thumbs against his ears and keeps them there, "great drums" always throb "through the air." This duplicity of mind and action forces upon him a sense of "distress, and joy allied." Despite this distress, he continues to conjure up in his mind's eye "cats/ Crouching in the river reeds," "silver snakes," and "the savage measures of/ Jungle boys and girls in love." The rain has a particularly dramatic effect on him: "While its primal measures drip," a distant, resonant voice beckons him to "'strip!/ Off this new exuberance./ Come and dance the Lover's Dance!'" Out of this experience of recollection and reclaiming his past comes the urge to "fashion dark gods" and, finally, even to dare "to give You [one God, the]/ Dark despairing features."

SUGGESTED READINGS

Baker, Houston A., Jr. *A Many-Colored Coat of Dreams: The Poetry of Countée Cullen.* Detroit: Broadside Press, 1974.

Bronz, Stephen H. "Countée Cullen." In *Roots of Negro Racial Consciousness: The 1920's, Three Harlem Renaissance Writers.* New York: Libra, 1964.

Ferguson, Blanche E. *Countée Cullen and the Negro Renaissance.* New York: Dodd, Mead, 1966.

Onyeberechi, Sydney. *Critical Essays: Achebe, Baldwin, Cullen, Ngugi, and Tutuola.* Hyattsville, Md.: Rising Star, 1999.

Perry, Margaret. *A Bio-bibliography of Countée Cullen.* Westport, Conn.: Greenwood Press, 1971.

Schwarz, A. B. Christa. *Gay Voices of the Harlem Renaissance.* Bloomington: Indiana University Press, 2003.

Tuttleton, James W. "Countée Cullen at 'The Heights.'" In *The Harlem Renaissance: Revaluations*, edited by Amritjit Singh, William S. Shiver, and Stanley Brodwin. New York: Garland, 1989.

Contributors: Australia Tarver and John C. Shields

Nicholas Dante

(Conrad Morales)

BORN: New York, New York; November 22, 1941
DIED: New York, New York; May 21, 1991

PUERTO RICAN

Dante was coauthor of A Chorus Line, *the longest-running show in Broadway history, which documented the personal and professional struggles of Broadway dancers.*

PRINCIPAL WORK

DRAMA: *A Chorus Line*, pr. 1975 (libretto, with James Kirkwood; conceived, choreographed, and directed by Michael Bennett; music by Marvin Hamlisch; lyrics by Edward Kleban)

Nicholas Dante (NIH-koh-las DAHN-tay), born Conrado Morales, was coauthor of *A Chorus Line*, the longest-running show in Broadway history. *A Chorus Line*, which documented the personal and professional struggles of Broadway dancers, was performed at the Shubert Theater 6,137 times between 1975 and 1990. Dante began his career as a dancer and hoped that his work on *A Chorus Line* would serve as a catalyst to a new career as a writer: "It's the first thing I ever wrote. . . . I've been dancing all my life. Now I hope I can be a writer."

Although Dante planned to major in journalism, he dropped out of Cardinal Hayes High School at the age of fourteen because of negative reactions to his homosexuality. When he was a boy, writing in the genre of fantasy served as an outlet for his emotions, but after dropping out of school he stopped writing because he believed that a writer had to have an education. He supported himself by working as a drag queen and began studying dance. In 1965, he worked summer stock in St. Louis. The experience in summer stock encouraged him to write again; he believed he could write better material. Dante wrote two unproduced musicals: "The Orphanage" and "Dr. Jekyll and Mr. Hyde." In 1968, he performed in his first Broadway show, *I'm Soloman*, and continued working as a dancer in the choruses of several Broadway musicals.

Dante's work on *A Chorus Line* began in 1974 during two twelve-hour taping sessions of dancers recounting their life stories. During these sessions, Dante told his life story, which would become the monologue of Paul, the longest monologue in the show. Dante told how he had hidden both his homosexuality and his profession from his parents; they only knew that he worked in theater. When his parents

275

arrived backstage at the Jewel Box Revue for a surprise visit, they found him dressed as a showgirl. Dante felt relieved when his father told the producer, "Take care of my son."

Although Dante had begun work on *A Chorus Line* using material from the taped sessions, the script was not completed until after the show was cast and in rehearsal. After the second rehearsal, James Kirkwood, a seasoned writer, was brought in to work with Dante, and the show began taking shape. Kirkwood had written Dante's favorite book, *Good Times/Bad Times* (1968), and the two had an amiable working relationship. However, because the writing of the show was a collaboration, Dante felt that he did not get the credit he deserved for his writing, especially from the dancers whose stories were woven into the script. Although he worked on the show for eight months before Kirkwood joined the collaborative team, Kirkwood's name appeared first in the credits. Furthermore, Dante argues that the idea that the show be in the form of a montage was his own, rather than that of Michael Bennett (the show's producer), who received credit. Nevertheless, Dante received the Pulitzer Prize for *A Chorus Line*, as well as the Tony Award, the Drama Desk Award, and the New York Drama Critics Circle Award.

Dante was unable to repeat the success of *A Chorus Line*. He wrote the book to an unsuccessful musical, *Jolson Tonight*, which toured the United States in the early 1980's. He also wrote an unproduced screenplay, "Fake Lady," which explores the character Paul San Marco from *A Chorus Line*. Dante had trouble dealing with the pressure of repeating such a phenomenal early success, and he received no help from Bennett on further writing projects. Kirkwood and others on the creative team had made more money than he had, and Dante's financial advisers had managed his money poorly.

Before Dante died of acquired immunodeficiency syndrome (AIDS) in 1991, he had found peace with himself. He attributed his newfound sense of wholeness to participation in an unorthodox therapy using mind-expanding drugs and caring for his senile mother, Maria Guadalupe Morales, who had moved in with him following the death of his father, Conrado Morales. He thought that the therapy allowed him to come to terms with his childhood problems, and taking care of his mother, who did not even know what day it was, allowed him to understand the insignificance of whether or not he was famous. After years of drifting, he became motivated to write again and believed he could find success again. When he died, he was working on a new play titled *A Suite Letting Go*, about a man caring for his elderly senile mother.

A Chorus Line

TYPE OF WORK: Drama
FIRST PRODUCED: 1975

Nicholas Dante, Michael Bennett, and James Kirkwood wrote *A Chorus Line* in 1975. The play is largely based on thirty hours of tape from a meeting of twenty-two dancers in New York City in January, 1974, in which the group shared their stories and their reasons for dancing. The result is a musical based heavily on real-life experiences in the cutthroat world of dance; in fact, the character Paul is closely based on Dante's experiences as a struggling actor and homosexual in New York City. The production was met with immediate critical acclaim and quickly moved to Broadway, where it played for many years and won a Pulitzer Prize.

The plot is relatively simple. A director, Zach (based on Bennett), auditions a series of dancers, narrowing the field based on ability to sing, dance, and explain the importance of their art. As the pool gets smaller, the audience becomes more intimately acquainted with each individual and with the themes that carry through many of the dancers' lives: broken families, ambition, and the sacrifice of personal relationships in pursuit of a career on stage. Perhaps as a result, those few dancers chosen form their own sort of family. They have no guarantee that the show will last longer than its opening night, but the group finds hope under the stage's lights and joy in the audience's applause.

SUGGESTED READINGS

Mandelbaum, Ken. *"A Chorus Line" and the Musicals of Michael Bennett.* New York: St. Martin's Press, 1989.

"Nicholas Dante." *Variety*, May 27, 1991, p. 57.

Sanchez, Alberto Sandoval. *"A Chorus Line:* Not Such a 'One Singular Sensation' for Puerto Rican Crossovers." *Ollantay* 1, no. 1 (January, 1993): 46-60.

Viagas, Robert, Baayork Lee, and Thommie Walsh. *On the Line: The Creation of "A Chorus Line."* New York: William Morrow, 1990.

Contributors: Nettie Farris and Anna A. Moore

Angela Davis

BORN: Birmingham, Alabama; January 26, 1944

AFRICAN AMERICAN

Davis's autobiographical work explores the development
of the African American political consciousness in
the late twentieth century.

PRINCIPAL WORKS

NONFICTION: *If They Come in the Morning: Voices of Resistance*, 1971 (with others); *Angela Davis: An Autobiography*, 1974; *Women, Race, and Class*, 1981; *Women, Culture, and Politics*, 1989; *The Angela Y. Davis Reader*, 1998; *Blues Legacies and Black Feminism: Gertrude "Ma" Rainey, Bessie Smith, and Billie Holiday*, 1998; *Are Prisons Obsolete?*, 2003

Primarily known as a political activist, Angela Davis began writing as a result of her activities within the Black Liberation movement of the late 1960's and early 1970's. Her work consistently explores the destructive influences of racism, sexism, and economic inequality on the development of African Americans, women, and the poor. Davis felt the full impact of racism beginning with her childhood, having been born and raised in segregated Birmingham. The racial inequality that prevailed particularly in the American South did much to shape her consciousness as an African American. In her autobiography, for example, she expresses her determination as a child to "never harbor or express the desire to be white" in spite of the fact that most whites lived what in comparison to hers was a privileged life.

Davis attended Elizabeth Irwin High School in New York. She studied philosophy at Brandeis University, the Sorbonne in Paris, the University of Frankfurt, and the University of California at San Diego. In 1968, she officially joined the Communist Party, having concluded that "the emancipation of all oppressed groups" could be achieved through the emancipation of the proletariat.

As a result of her membership in the Communist Party, the Board of Regents of the University of California fired Davis from her teaching position at UCLA in 1969; she was reinstated after a trial. Charged with murder and kidnapping in connection with an escape attempt from a California courthouse, Davis was arrested and imprisoned in 1970 after spending several months on the run. She was tried and acquitted in 1972.

Davis's early writings center on the difficulties African Americans face in trying to establish a positive African American identity and political consciousness within a system that is racially oppressive. In *If They Come in the Morning:*

Voices of Resistance and *Angela Davis: An Autobiography*, Davis presents a personal account of the ways the legal and penal systems stifle the African American community and political expression. In her autobiography, she touches on what it means to be an African American woman in a racially and sexually divided society. She explores this issue in greater detail in her works on the problems of racial division within the women's movement, *Women, Race, and Class* and *Women, Culture, and Politics*. Many critics claim that in presenting her ideas from a decidedly Marxist perspective, Davis deprives her writing of personal insight. Most contend, however, that in spite of her ideological viewpoint, she gives a unique and passionate voice to the experience of African American women.

Angela Davis (Library of Congress)

Angela Davis

TYPE OF WORK: Autobiography
FIRST PUBLISHED: 1974

Angela Davis: An Autobiography, Davis's most notable literary work, is the personal narrative of her development as an African American and feminist political activist. The autobiography explores how the forces of institutionalized racism shaped her consciousness as an African American and compelled her to seek political solutions. Her personal account also explores how her experiences as a woman in a movement dominated by males affected her awareness of the special challenges African American women face in overcoming sexism and racism.

The autobiography opens not with Davis's birth but with her flight from California legal authorities. She was charged with murder and kidnapping in relation to a failed escape attempt at a California courthouse. Her constant self-awareness as an African American woman attempting to evade discovery within an overwhelmingly white society underscores the problems African Americans have in establishing their identity. From the writer's perspective, the charges against her stemmed not from a legal system that seeks justice but from a legal system that works to destroy those who fight to change the system.

As a child in racially segregated Birmingham, Alabama, Davis's fight to establish such an identity began at an early age. Growing up on "Dynamite Hill," a racially mixed neighborhood that acquired its name from the frequent bombings of African American residences, she was, as a child, aware of the danger of simply being black and of fighting for the right to have an equal voice in society. In detailing her experiences within the Black Liberation movement, Davis expresses her growing awareness of attempts to stifle the voices of African American women in particular within the movement. Communism, she contends, would eradicate all such oppression.

Davis is further convinced of the oppressive nature of the American legal system after she is captured and incarcerated to await trial. She describes continual attempts by the prison authorities to control the minds of her fellow prisoners through humiliating and nonsensical rules. She also gives an account of attempts to deprive her of her basic rights as a prisoner. When she is finally acquitted, Davis sees the verdict not as a vindication of the legal system but as a vindication of the political efforts to fight racial oppression. Many critics contend that Davis's constant focus on political ideology prevents her from giving an honest and insightful account of her experiences in her autobiography. Most agree, however, that, in spite of such perceived flaws, the autobiography presents a powerful portrait of an African American woman passionately devoted to her battle against oppression.

SUGGESTED READINGS

Aptheker, Bettina. *The Morning Breaks: The Trial of Angela Davis*. 2d ed. Ithaca, N.Y.: Cornell University Press, 1999.

Davis, Angela. "Globalism and the Prison Industrial Complex: An Interview with Angela Davis." Interview by Avery F. Gordon. *Race and Class* 40, nos. 2/3 (1998/1999): 145-157.

Nadelson, Regina. *Who Is Angela Davis? The Biography of a Revolutionary*. New York: P. H. Wyden, 1972.

Perkins, Margo V. *Autobiography as Activism: Three Black Women of the Sixties*. Jackson: University Press of Mississippi, 2000.

Contributor: Lisa R. Aunkst

Samuel R. Delany

BORN: New York, New York; April 1, 1942

AFRICAN AMERICAN

*Delany is an intensely self-analytical explorer of the
linguistic and imaginative possibilities of science fiction.*

PRINCIPAL WORKS

LONG FICTION: *The Jewels of Aptor*, 1962; *Captives of the Flame*, 1963 (revised
1968, as *Out of the Dead City*); *The Towers of Toron*, 1964; *The Ballad of Beta-2*,
1965; *City of a Thousand Suns*, 1965; *Babel-17*, 1966; *Empire Star*, 1966; *The
Einstein Intersection*, 1967; *Nova*, 1968; *The Fall of the Towers*, 1970 (includes
revised versions of *Out of the Dead City*, *The Towers of Toron*, and *City of a
Thousand Suns*); *The Tides of Lust*, 1973 (also known as *Equinox*); *Dhalgren*,
1975; *Triton*, 1976 (also known as *Trouble on Triton*); *Empire*, 1978; *Tales of
Nevèrÿon*, 1979; *Nevèrÿona: Or, The Tale of Signs and Cities*, 1983; *Stars in My
Pocket Like Grains of Sand*, 1984; *Flight from Nevèrÿon*, 1985; *The Bridge of
Lost Desire*, 1987 (also known as *Return to Nevèrÿon*); *Hogg*, 1993; *They Fly at
Çiron*, 1993; *The Mad Man*, 1994

SHORT FICTION: *Driftglass: Ten Tales of Speculative Fiction*, 1971 (revised and expanded, 2003, as *Aye and Gomorrah*); *Distant Stars*, 1981; *Atlantis: Three
Tales*, 1995

NONFICTION: *The Jewel-Hinged Jaw: Notes on the Language of Science Fiction*,
1977; *The American Shore: Meditations on a Tale of Science Fiction by Thomas
M. Disch*, 1978; *Heavenly Breakfast: An Essay on the Winter of Love*, 1979;
Starboard Wine: More Notes on the Language of Science Fiction, 1984; *The
Straits of Messina*, 1987; *The Motion of Light in Water: Sex and Science-Fiction
Writing in the East Village, 1957-1965*, 1988 (memoir); *Silent Interviews*, 1994;
Longer Views, 1996; *Bread and Wine: An Erotic Tale of New York City, an Auto-
biographical Account*, 1998; *Shorter Views: Queer Thoughts and the Politics of
the Paraliterary*, 1999; *Times Square Red, Times Square Blue*, 1999; *Nineteen
Eighty-Four: Selected Letters*, 2000; *About Writing: Seven Essays, Four Let-
ters, and Five Interviews*, 2005

EDITED TEXT: *Quark: A Quarterly of Speculative Fiction*, 1970-1971 (with Marilyn
Hacker)

Samuel Ray Delany, Jr., was born April 1, 1942, to Samuel Ray Delany, Sr., a funeral director, and Margaret Carey (née Boyd) Delany, a clerk in a local library.
Delany's early education took place at Dalton, an exclusive, primarily white school

on the East Side. He then attended the Bronx High School of Science, where the average intelligence quotient of the students was 140. Although his scores in most subjects were excellent (particularly in math), Delany's school career was often made more difficult by what would much later be diagnosed as dyslexia. His parents had forced him to become right-handed, and, partially as a result, Delany had immense difficulty with spelling, with a particular propensity for writing words backward. A broken and jumbled mishmash of misspellings, his writing was opaque even to him once he had forgotten the intended meaning of the words. His parents always encouraged him to write, however, because they had been told by a tutor that if Delany wrote as much as possible his spelling would have to improve. His mother read to him constantly, and his father even read aloud Mark Twain's *Adventures of Huckleberry Finn* (1884), chapter by chapter.

Toward the end of his Dalton years, Delany began to write short stories. He also began reading science fiction, including the works of such writers as Theodore Sturgeon, Alfred Bester, and Robert Heinlein. After being graduated from Dalton in 1956, Delany attended the Bronx High School of Science, where he was encouraged in his writing by some of his teachers and by a fellow student and aspiring poet, Marilyn Hacker. After high school graduation in 1960, Delany received a fellowship to the Breadloaf Writers' Conference in Vermont, where he met Robert Frost and other professional writers.

He continued to write, supporting himself as a folksinger in Greenwich Village clubs and cafés. On August 24, 1961, he and Marilyn Hacker were married. Although their marriage of more than thirteen years was open and loosely structured (the couple often lived apart), Hacker and Delany were highly influential on each other as he developed his fiction and she her poetry (Hacker's influence is especially strong in *Babel-17*). Delany submitted his first published book, *The Jewels of Aptor*, to Ace Books, where Hacker worked, at her suggestion. Hacker herself is the model for Rydra Wong, the heroine of *Babel-17*. Delany attended City College in New York City (now City University of New York) in 1960 and again from 1962 to 1963, but dropped out to finish *Babel-17* (1966).

Delany's life in New York over the next several years, including his personal relationships and a near nervous breakdown in 1964, figures in a number of his works from *Empire Star* to *Dhalgren*. After *The Jewels of Aptor*, he completed a trilogy, *The Fall of the Towers*, and in 1964 reenrolled at City College of New York, where he edited the campus poetry magazine, *The Promethean*. He soon dropped out again and in 1965, after completing *The Ballad of Beta-2*, went with a friend to work on shrimp boats in the Gulf of Mexico.

At this point, Delany's writing was beginning to return enough to help support him, and, after completing *Babel-17* and *Empire Star*, he used the advance money to tour Europe and Turkey during 1965 and 1966, an experience that influenced both *The Einstein Intersection* and *Nova*.

When he returned to the United States, Delany became more involved in the science-fiction community, which was beginning to take notice of his work. He attended conferences and workshops and met both established science-fiction writers and younger authors, including Joanna Russ and Thomas Disch, who would both become good friends. In 1967, The Science Fiction Writers of America awarded *Babel-17* the Nebula Award for best novel (shared with *Flowers for Algernon* by Daniel Keyes), and in 1968 the award again went to Delany, this time for both *The Einstein Intersection* and the short story "Aye and Gomorrah."

During the winter of 1967, while Hacker was living in San Francisco, Delany moved in with a New York rock group called The Heavenly Breakfast, who lived communally. This experiment in living, recorded in *Heavenly Breakfast*, is reflected in *Dhalgren*. By 1968, Delany was becoming firmly established as an important science-fiction writer. He had won three Nebulas; had a new book, *Nova*, published; had begun to receive critical acclaim from outside science-fiction circles; and had spoken at the Modern Language Association's annual meeting in New York. During the next few years, while working on *Dhalgren*, he devoted himself to a number of other projects, including reviewing and filmmaking. He received the Hugo Award in 1970 for his short story "Time Considered as a Helix of SemiPrecious Stones," and in the same year began coediting, with Marilyn Hacker, *Quark: A Quarterly of Speculative Fiction*. The journal—which published writers such as Russ, Disch, R. A. Lafferty, and others who experimented with both form and content in the genre—ceased publication in 1971 after four issues.

In 1972, Delany worked for D. C. Comics, writing the stories for two issues of *Wonder Woman* and the introduction of an anthology of *Green Lantern/ Green Arrow* comics. In 1973, he joined Hacker in London, where he continued to work on *Dhalgren* and sat in at the University of London on classes in language and philosophy, which profoundly influenced his later writing. Completing *Dhalgren*, Delany began work on his next novel, *Triton*, which was published in 1976.

On January 14, 1974, Hacker gave birth to a daughter, Iva Hacker-Delany, in London. Delany, with his family, returned to the United States late in 1974 to take the position of Visiting Butler Chair Professor of English, SUNY-Buffalo, a post offered him by Leslie Fiedler. At this time, Hacker and Delany agreed to a separation and Hacker returned to London (they were divorced in 1980). Delany completed *Triton* and in September, 1976, accepted a fellowship at the University of Wisconsin—Milwaukee's Center for Twentieth Century Studies. In 1977, he collected some of his critical essays in *The Jewel-Hinged Jaw* and in 1978 published *The American Shore*, a book-length study of a Disch short story.

During the 1980's, Delany spent much of his time in New York, writing, looking after Iva, and attending conferences and conventions. His major project in that decade was the creation of the "sword-and-sorcery" fantasy Nevèrÿon series. The impact of the acquired immunodeficiency syndrome (AIDS) crisis is seen in the latter two books, especially *Flight from Nevèrÿon*. In 1984, Delany collected more of his criticism in *Starboard Wine* and also received the Pilgrim Award for achievement in science-fiction criticism from the Science Fiction Research Association. Delany's only science-fiction work in that decade was *Stars in My Pocket Like Grains of Sand*, the first part of a planned "dyptich." In 1988, he published his autobiographical recollections about his earlier years in *The Motion of Light in Water*, and he became a professor of comparative literature at the University of Massachusetts at Amherst.

During the 1990's Delany produced a great deal of writing and gained the recognition of being, in the words of critic and author James Sallis, "among our finest and most important writers." The most controversial of Delany's 1990's publications are his erotic novels—*Equinox, Hogg,* and *The Mad Man*—and his 1998 comic-book-format erotic autobiography, *Bread and Wine. Equinox* appeared briefly in 1973, and *Hogg*'s scheduled publication that same year was canceled. Both went back into print in the mid-1990's, along with the release of *The Mad Man,* the only one of the three erotic novels composed in the 1990's. While these books have disturbed and challenged many readers and scholars of Delany's work, a number of critics, most notably Norman Mailer, have defended them as examples of Delany's belief in pushing the boundaries of literature and of dealing with sexual subjects with absolute openness.

Delany also published two important nonfiction works in the 1990's: *Silent Interviews,* a collection of Delany's written interviews with subjects ranging from racism to aesthetic theory; and *Longer Views,* a collection of Delany's major essays on art, literature, and culture. Finally, there were two new works of fiction: *Atlantis,* a collection of three mainstream stories set in the 1920's, and *They Fly at Çiron,* a fantasy novel which appeared in 1993 but became widely available two years later. Delany also won the William Whitehead Award for Lifetime Achievement in Gay Literature in 1993 and was the guest of honor at the World Science-Fiction Convention at London, England in 1995. That year he was also a visiting writer at the universities of Minnesota and Idaho, and in 1997 he was a visiting professor at Michigan State University. In January of 2000, he joined the faculty in the English department at the State University of New York at Buffalo.

Dhalgren

TYPE OF WORK: Novel
FIRST PUBLISHED: 1975

Dhalgren begins with an archetypal scenario: A young man, wearing only one sandal and unable to remember his name, wanders into Bellona, a midwestern city which has suffered some nameless catastrophe. In the course of the novel's 880 pages, he encounters the city's remaining residents; goes through mental, physical, and sexual adventures; becomes a local legend; and leaves. In its complexity and its ambitious scope, *Dhalgren* invites comparison with a handful of contemporary novels, including Vladimir Nabokov's *Ada or Ardor* (1969) and Thomas Pynchon's *Gravity's Rainbow* (1973), which make Joycean demands of the reader. Unlike many other science-fiction novels set in a post-holocaust society, *Dhalgren* is not concerned with the causes of the breakdown, nor does it tell of an attempt to create a new society out of the ashes of the old. There is no need for such a reconstruction. Bellona's catastrophe was unique; the rest of the country and the world are unaffected. Separated from outside electronic communication and simply abandoned by the larger society, Bellona has become a center of attraction for outcasts and drifters of all descriptions as well as remaining a home to its own disenfranchised, notably the city's black population. The city has become a place of absolute freedom, where all can do and be whatever they choose, yet it is not in a state of anarchy. There are rules and laws that govern the city, but they are not recorded or codified.

To the newcomer (and to a first reader of the book), these "rules" seem random and unpredictable. Clouds obscure the sky, so that time of day has little meaning, and the days themselves are named arbitrarily. Direction in this city seems constantly to shift, in part because people change the street signs at whim. Fires burn throughout the city, but listlessly and without pattern. When the clouds do part, they might reveal two moons in the night sky or a sun that covers half the sky. The protagonist (who comes to be known simply as The Kid) must define his identity in terms of these shifting relationships, coping with the ever-fluid patterns Bellona offers.

The price of failing to work within the web and to accommodate reality—even an unreal reality—is exemplified by the Richards family, white middle-class citizens who try to maintain a semblance of the life they had known and are going mad as a result. The Kid begins his stay in Bellona by working for the Richardses, helping them to move upstairs in their apartment complex, away from a "nest" of "Scorpions," the mostly black street gangs who wander through the city. (The Scorpions themselves are almost as annoyed and bothered by the Richardses.) The move is futile—the Richardses are no happier or saner in their new apartment, and their son accidentally dies during the move; The Kid is not paid his promised wages (in any case, money is useless in Bellona). Still, the job has helped The Kid to adjust to Bellona's society, and he has begun to write poetry in a notebook he has found. As he nears the end of his job, he finds himself becoming, almost by accident, a Scorpion and eventually the leader of a "nest." His poetry is published, and he becomes, within the city, famous.

The characters and events of *Dhalgren* are rich and detailed enough in themselves to make the book notable. It is Delany's attention to form, though, that makes the book so complex and the act of reading it so disruptive. Not only are the city and its events seemingly random, but the plot and characterization are likewise unpredictable. Questions remain unanswered, few elements are fully resolved, and the answers and resolutions that are given are tentative and possibly misleading. Near the end of the novel, The Kid believes that he has discovered his name, but this is never confirmed. He leaves Bellona at the end of the book, but his fate is left obscure. The Kid is, moreover, an unreliable center of consciousness. He was once in a mental institution, so the reader must doubt his perceptions (he unaccountably loses stretches of time; after his first sexual encounter early in the book, he sees the woman he was with turn into a tree). He is also ambidextrous and possibly dyslexic, so that the random ways in which Bellona seems to rearrange itself may be the result of The Kid's own confusion. At the same time, though, Delany gives the reader reason to believe The Kid's perception; others, for example, also witness the impossible double moons and giant sun.

Dhalgren is not a book that will explain itself. A palimpsest, it offers new explanations on each reading. The Kid's notebook contains observations by an unknown author which tempt the reader to think that they are notes for the novel *Dhalgren*; there are minor but significant differences, however, between notes and text. The last phrase of the novel, ". . . I have come to," runs into the first, "to wound the autumnal city," recalling the circular construction of *Finnegans Wake* (1939). Unlike the river of James Joyce's dream book, though, *Dhalgren* does not offer the solace of such a unitary construction. The two phrases do not, after all, cohere, but overlap on the word "to." If anything, the construction of the book echoes the "optical chain" made of mirrors, prisms, and lenses that The Kid and other characters wear. Events and phrases within the book do not exactly repeat, but imprecisely mirror, one another. Certain events and phenomena, such as the giant sun, are magnified as if by a lens; others are fragmented and dispersed, as a prism fragments light into the visible spectrum.

Ultimately, Delany's Bellona is a paradigm of contemporary society. Within this seeming wasteland, though, the author finds not solace and refuge in art and love, as so many modern authors have, but the very source and taproot of art and love. Delany's epigraph reads, "You have confused the true and the real." Whatever the "reality" of the city, the book's events, or The Kid's ultimate fate, "truth" has been discovered. The Kid no longer needs the city, and his place is taken by a young woman entering Bellona in a scene that mirrors The Kid's own entrance. Even the "reality" of this scene is not assured, as The Kid's speech fragments into the unfinished sentences of the notebook. "Truth," finally, is provisional, whatever is sufficient for one's needs, and requires to be actively sought and separated from the "real."

Triton

TYPE OF WORK: Novel
FIRST PUBLISHED: 1976

Triton has two sections: The first is "Some Informal Remarks Toward the Modular Calculus, Part One," and the second is "An Ambiguous Heterotopia." The first section's title links *Triton* to a series of Delany's quasi-allegorical fictions, including the appendix to *Tales of Nevèrÿon* (1979), "Some Informal Remarks Toward the Modular Calculus, Part Three," and his remarkable memoir and analysis of the advent of acquired immunodeficiency syndrome (AIDS) in New York, "The Tale of Plagues and Carnivals: Or, Some Informal Remarks Toward the Modular Calculus, Part Five" (in *Flight from Nevèrÿon*, 1985). A calculatedly convoluted essay on the language of science fiction appears at the end of *Triton* as "Appendix B."

Triton's second section's title refers to the subtitle of Ursula K. Le Guin's *The Dispossessed: An Ambiguous Utopia* (1974) and stresses the fact that, unlike most Utopian novels, *Triton* describes a society in which the differences among individuals—especially differences in sexuality—are not merely tolerated but encouraged to flourish, thus lending the anarchy of difference a constructive and creative thrust. The addition of this element of calculated flamboyance to the traditional story of the ideal society does not rob Delany's Utopia of its ambiguity. An ambiguity arising from Utopian fiction is the truth that one person's Utopia is another person's hell. The hero of *Triton*, Bron Helstrom, retains the only sexual trait that can still be called a perversity in the book's utopia: an inability to exploit in a fully satisfying manner the Utopia's rich potential for pleasure. This personal perversity is reflected in the plot on a larger scale when the scrupulously nonaggressive society of Triton is horribly maimed by the war fought between the Outer Satellites and the conservative Worlds of the inner solar system.

Unlike many of Delany's protagonists, Helstrom is not a version of the author. Delany's memoir *The Motion of Light in Water* (1988) includes an account of the young author's meeting with a prawn fisherman named Ron Helstrom, who seems to have provided a model for the character's stubborn masculinity. The fictional Helstrom is a kind of negative image of Delany's own sexuality and values. The author's identity is not only mirrored in The Spike—the novel's writer character—but also is transfigured and magnified into the Tritonian society to which Helstrom cannot adapt.

Although it did not have the commercial success of *Dhalgren*, *Triton* is tremendously impressive as an exploration of the personal and social possibilities inherent in freedom from traditional gender roles. The book is even more spectacular in its deployment of the narrative strategies of science fiction; it is a landmark work within the genre.

Tales of Nevèrÿon
TYPE OF WORK: Novel
FIRST PUBLISHED: 1979

Not all Delany's stories are science-fiction tales set in the future. For example, the loosely related stories found in the *Tales of Nevèrÿon* collection are set in a mythical past. These stories owe much to the genre of swashbuckling fantasy fiction called sword-and-sorcery, though they depart as radically from the conventions of that genre as *Dhalgren* does from science fiction.

Sword-and-sorcery is, itself, a marginalized literature. It has received little respect from mainstream critics, even those willing to admit, grudgingly, that science fiction has something to offer. However, in the hands of some writers (Robert E. Howard, Fritz Leiber, Karl Edward Wagner) sword-and-sorcery has achieved notable commercial success and generated enough small press scholarship to deserve broader critical consideration.

Delany is, according to James Sallis in *Ash of Stars: On the Writing of Samuel R. Delany* (1996), "the man who would intellectualize" sword-and-sorcery. Certainly, Delany's *Nevèrÿon* stories have contributed two things to the genre. First, while sword-and-sorcery must develop a historical "feel," most writers achieve this with descriptions of walled cities, ruins, and swordfights. The focus is on large-scale, dramatic events—war being a favorite. A common criticism here is that readers seldom see how armies are fed or how cities survive in the absence of an economy other than trade.

Delany's *Nevèrÿon* stories, in contrast, develop a sense of history by focusing on exactly those details that other writers neglect. In "The Tale of Gorgik," the first *Nevèrÿon* story, the reader learns of docks and warehouses, of sailors and slaves. The main trade item described is not jewels or exotic furs but little rubber balls.

"The Tale of Old Venn" shows readers the ship builders and fishing boats. The astrolabe's invention is part of the story's background, and the development of an early writing system leads one character, Norema, to thoughts on origins and philosophy.

Although sword-and-sorcery is generally set at a time when cultures are moving from barter to monetary economies and from rural to urban societies, most writers use these facts only to force characters into motion. Delany makes the change to a monetary economy a major focus of such stories as "The Tale of Potters and Dragons," where attempts to control the rubber-ball trade and the change from three-legged to four-legged pots are important plot developments. Is it coincidence that one character is named Madam Keyne (reminiscent of John Maynard Keynes, the economist)?

Delany's second contribution to sword-and-sorcery is his far greater emphasis on character than on the plot and action that drive most work in the genre. In fact, there is little plot at all in the *Nevèrÿon* stories. There are certainly no larger-than-life characters. Gorgik, who appears in most of the tales and is the closest Delany comes to a barbarian warrior, is, in fact, a "civilized" man and has the psychological scars to prove it. Only "The Tale of Dragons and Dreamers" has much fighting, and it is not an imprisoned Gorgik who does it. It is Small Sarg, a youth, who handles the killing.

Many characters in the *Nevèrÿon* stories are women, but not in the usual roles of princess, harlot, or woman warrior (the only woman warrior is named Raven). Instead, women are merchants, inventors, and fishers. There is a part-time prostitute whose story is told in "The Tale of Rumor and Desire"; this is Clodon, a man.

Stars in My Pocket Like Grains of Sand

TYPE OF WORK: Novel
FIRST PUBLISHED: 1984

To open this brilliant and intricate work is to enter a fully realized alternate universe where everything, even language, is disquietingly familiar yet also alien—everything, that is, except the workings of the human heart.

On the surface, Delany begins with a story of lost and found love. Korga, a mind-altered laborer called a "rat," is the only survivor of a planetwide catastrophe; his rescuers not only repair his body but also inbue him with the ancient knowledge of a long-dead master. Marq Dyeth is a galactic diplomat from a planet where humans and the native species, evelmi, live in amicable closeness. To gain access to Rat's newfound knowledge, the galactic rulers determine that he and Marq are each other's "perfect erotic object" and place him under Marq's tutelage. The resulting relationship is a brief and intense one, quickly terminated when it is realized that Rat's knowledge and presence could bring down the entire society.

Delany demolishes readers' most cherished prejudices, including the concept of gender, sexual taboos, the family unit, and the structure of entire societies. Even the formalities of a diplomatic dinner party are exploded in a fantastic scene at once hilarious and subtly disturbing. Over all flow Delany's lyrical words, rising finally to a moving epilogue on the intensity of human experience. Readers will return to their mundane world forever changed by Delany's vision of a brave, new universe.

The Motion of Light in Water
TYPE OF WORK: Memoir
FIRST PUBLISHED: 1988

The Motion of Light in Water: Sex and Science-Fiction Writing in the East Village, 1957-1965 is Delaney's account of his late adolescence and early adulthood. The memoir stops short of the period when he became a literary pioneer, but it examines in great detail the personal experiences that were later to feed that work. Its primary concern is the awakening of the author's homosexual identity, augmented—and slightly confused—by his early marriage to Marilyn Hacker, a white poet, and their setting up home on the Lower East Side of Manhattan.

The memoir describes—but not in strictly chronological order—Delany's unsteady emergence from the educational hothouse of the Bronx High School of Science into the "real world" of work and marriage. It contemplates, with slightly self-demeaning but sympathetic fascination, his early and precocious adventures in science-fiction writing and the gradual forging of his highly distinctive literary voice. It ends, after an astonishing profusion of erotic encounters, with his setting forth from the city of his birth to cross the Atlantic and explore the Old World, modestly recapitulating the kind of experiential quest pursued by all the heroes of his early novels.

The text of *The Motion of Light in Water* is broken into brief numbered subchapters, some of which have further subchapters presumably introduced as elaborations and afterthoughts, emphasizing that it grew in a mosaic fashion rather than being written in a straightforward, linear manner. The second edition of the book is further augmented, offering additional testimony to the relentless curiosity with which the author has repeatedly worked through the catalog of his experiences.

The Motion of Light in Water is remarkable for its frankness and for its scrupulousness. It attains a paradoxical combination of warm intimacy and clinical objectivity that is unique. The analysis of actual experiences is combined with and subtly tempered by an extended reflection on the vagaries of memory. The metaphorical title refers to the essential elusiveness of the process by which the filtration of memory converts the raw material of incident and confrontation into the wealth of self-knowledge. There are very few works that capture the elusiveness of memory and celebrate its mercurial quality as well as Delany's.

Times Square Red, Times Square Blue

TYPE OF WORK: Social criticism
FIRST PUBLISHED: 1999

What are the civic and humane values and benefits of a seedy strip of city street best known for its porn moviehouses, midnight hustlers, and dubious retail stores? If the street in question is New York's Forty-second, and the strip Times Square, then city authorities and real estate developers have been unanimous in answering: no values or benefits at all. Therefore, theaters must be closed, buildings razed, customers and residents relocated, and a "new" Forty-second Street built which will be a theme-park version of a better, cleaner and above all "safer" New York. Manhattan as a mall.

Delany offers a different and more interesting answer in *Times Square Red, Times Square Blue*. The importance of this seemingly tawdry piece of real estate, Delany claims, is that the unreclaimed Times Square offered a precious place where people could cross all manner of boundary lines: racial, economic, emotional, and sexual. It was an area that not only permitted but encouraged complex relationships that de-emphasized the artificial barriers and underscored that common humanity which linked those who came there. It was, Delany argues, a place where people could be human beings, in all the messy, sometimes inconvenient but often rewarding ways that they express that humanity.

Now, Delany notes, Forty-second Street and the old Times Square are but a memory. They have been made safe for "family values" but at the cost of truly human values. Where once people could come, perhaps in darkness and anonymity to bridge the gaps between them, now there is only the sterile brightness that forbids even fumbling attempts at communication. Times Square may be safer today, Delany concludes, but it is much less human.

SUGGESTED READINGS

Barbour, Douglas. *Worlds Out of Words: The SF Novels of Samuel R. Delany*. London: Bran's Head Books, 1979.
Dery, Mark. "Black to the Future: Interviews with Samuel R. Delany, Greg Tate, and Tricia Rose." *The South Atlantic Quarterly* 92 (Fall, 1993): 735-778.
Fox, Robert Elliot. *Conscientious Sorcerers: The Black Postmodernist Fiction of LeRoi Jones/Amiri Baraka, Ishmael Reed, and Samuel R. Delany*. New York: Greenwood Press, 1987.
Freedman, Carl. *Critical Theory and Science Fiction*. Hanover, N.H.: Wesleyan University Press, 2000.

Kelso, Sylvia. "'Across Never': Postmodern Theory and Narrative Praxis in Samuel R. Delany's Nevèrÿon Cycle." *Science-Fiction Studies* 24 (July, 1997): 289-301.

McEvoy, Seth. *Samuel R. Delany.* New York: Frederick Ungar, 1984.

Reid-Pharr, Robert F. "Disseminating Heterotopia." *African American Review* 28 (Fall, 1994): 347-357.

Review of Contemporary Fiction 16 (Fall, 1996).

Sallis, James, ed. *Ash of Stars: On the Writing of Samuel R. Delany.* Jackson: University Press of Mississippi, 1996.

Slusser, George Edgar. *The Delany Intersection: Samuel R. Delany Considered as a Writer of Semi-Precious Words.* San Bernardino, Calif.: Borgo Press, 1977.

Tucker, Jeffrey Allen. *A Sense of Wonder: Samuel R. Delany, Race, Identity, and Difference.* Middletown, Conn.: Wesleyan University Press, 2004.

Weedman, Jane. *Samuel R. Delany.* Mercer Island, Wash.: Starmont House, 1982.

Contributors: Brian Stableford, Donald F. Larsson, Jo-Ellen Lipman Boon, and John Nizalowski

Toi Derricotte

BORN: Detroit, Michigan; April 12, 1941

AFRICAN AMERICAN

*Coming of age as a writer during the Black Arts
movement of the 1970's, Derricotte forced the American
poetry establishment to rethink its assumptions about
African Americans and women.*

PRINCIPAL WORKS

POETRY: *The Empress of the Death House*, 1978; *Natural Birth*, 1983; *Captivity*,
1989; *Tender*, 1997
NONFICTION: *Creative Writing: A Manual for Teachers*, 1985 (with Madeline
Bass); *The Black Notebooks: An Interior Journey*, 1997

Born April 12, 1941, into a Detroit family separated from most of the city's African
American community by class and lighter skin, Toinette Derricotte (toy-NEHT
DEHR-ree-kawt) wrote as a way to find solace in an existence filled with alienation. "Tender," the title poem of her fourth major collection, opens: "The tenderest
meat comes from the houses where you hear the least squealing." This insight says
much about what it was like to be the daughter of Benjamin Sweeney Webster, a
mortician, and Antonia Banquet Webster Cyrus, a systems analyst. The young girl
quickly learned to hide her thoughts on the page.

Writing is a first passion, but after high school, the shy teen studied psychology
at Wayne State University with visions of a doctorate. Plans changed in December,
1961, when she gave birth to son Anthony, and in July, 1962, Derricotte married
artist Clarence Reese. The union lasted two years. In 1967, she married banker
Bruce Derricotte. They separated in 1991.

Parenthood's realities led Derricotte to major in special education. She started
teaching in 1964 with the Manpower Program. She finished a bachelor's degree in
1965. In 1966, Derricotte became a teacher for mentally and emotionally challenged
students at Detroit's Farand School. In 1969, Derricotte left her hometown to teach
remedial reading at Jefferson School in Teaneck, New Jersey. The job lasted a year.

She taught for money, but always wrote. In 1973, Derricotte began a four-year
stint on the *New York Quarterly* staff. The following year she started a fifteen-year
residency with the New Jersey State Council on the Arts Poet-in-the-Schools program. Those years set the direction of her life as author, mentor, and teacher.

The Empress of the Death House, her first collection, was published in 1978. The
next year she founded a retreat to foster the development of African American poets

in a culturally sensitive atmosphere. That involvement ended in 1982 but was re-born in 1996, when she collaborated with Cornelius Eady to create Cave Canem, a summer workshop in upstate New York.

In 1983, *Natural Birth* was published. Derricotte graduated from New York University with a master's degree in creative writing the next year. The 1985 publication of *Creative Writing: A Manual for Teachers*, coauthored with Madeline Bass, followed.

In 1988, twenty-one years after she left home for New Jersey, Derricotte moved to Norfolk, Virginia, to teach at Old Dominion. The next year, *Captivity* was published. In 1990, she spent a year as Commonwealth Professor in the English Department of George Mason University in Fairfax, Virginia. In 1991, she moved to the University of Pittsburgh.

Throughout her writing career, Derricotte has immersed herself in readings, contributions to various magazines and journals, and teaching at institutions such as the University of South Florida and the College of Charleston. She has won recognition and fellowships from the Academy of American Poets and the National Endowment for the Arts. She won the nomination for the 1998 Pushcart Prize, a Folger Shakespeare Library Poetry Book Award, a Lucille Medwick Memorial Award from the Poetry Society of America, and a United Black Artists' Distinguished Pioneering of the Arts Award.

The Empress of the Death House
TYPE OF WORK: Poetry
FIRST PUBLISHED: 1978

Derricotte is unique in her confessional treatment of racial identity. "My skin causes certain problems continuously, problems that open the issue of racism over and over like a wound," she once wrote. That statement hangs over her photograph on the African American Literature Book Club Web site as tribute to the talent she displays in the ability to turn poignant racial episodes into instruments that sometimes strike readers' consciences with jackhammer force and, at other times, soothe their souls.

Derricotte's early works focused on death and birth. The theme is heavy in her first book, *The Empress of the Death House*, where "The Grandmother Poems" discuss her childhood experiences in her grandparents' Detroit funeral home. Her mother's stepfather owned the business. Although she was sickly, the woman used two thousand dollars of her own money to send Derricotte's father to mortuary school, so that he might join a more stable line of work.

The Empress of the Death House grapples with the plight of women who survive abuse in an effort to sort out her feelings about her grandmother and mother. The understanding was a step on the path to self-awareness and helped her to understand her personal reactions to motherhood. In *The American Book Review*, reviewer Joe Weixlmann, who wrote about *Natural Birth*, said *The Empress of the Death House* opens readers' eyes to the "indifference or contempt" with which the world treats African American women.

Natural Birth

TYPE OF WORK: Poetry
FIRST PUBLISHED: 1983

Natural Birth is an extension of Derricotte's investigation into African American women. The collection candidly probes the birth process as an experience that hurts too much and humiliates. This poem is a "tour de force, at once a book-length experimental poem, an exploration of the extremes of human experience, and an examination of the social construction of identity," Woodson wrote of the 1983 Crossing Press version. Of the 2000 edition, Eileen Robinson wrote in *Black Issues Book Review*:

> *Natural Birth* is a triumph of one woman's spirit that will appeal to readers who are looking for depth, emotion, originality and truth. . . . Derricotte has completed a moving testament to teenage mothers, and mothers everywhere, who survive the miracle of birth. It is also a special gift to their children who grow stronger for understanding the very human fears and pains of the women who brought them here.

Natural Birth takes writings about death, birth, and transcendence to another level. Derricotte reaches for the truth that most unwed mothers might like to tell. She reaches inside the experience of childbirth for the thoughts that most mothers might want to share.

In *Contemporary Authors*, Derricotte is quoted as saying that her Catholic school education taught that confession made a person "whole" or "back into a state of grace." She concludes:

> As a black woman, I have been consistently confused about my "sins," unsure of which faults were in me and which faults were the results of others' projections. . . . [T]ruth-telling in my art is also a way to separate my "self" from what I have been taught to believe about my "self," the degrading stereotypes about black women.

Captivity

TYPE OF WORK: Poetry
FIRST PUBLISHED: 1989

Captivity shifted the focus from gender to race, sliding from portraits of general poverty to intricate sketches of urban students. The book places the U.S. slave experience at the root of many issues in today's black experience. The dehumanization and commercialization of African Americans' slave ancestors have been cited as root causes of black poverty, fractured family structures, violence, and continued oppression. *Village Voice* reviewer Robyn Selman called the book "a personal exploration yielding truths that apply to all of us."

Tender

TYPE OF WORK: Poetry
FIRST PUBLISHED: 1997

Derricotte's fourth book of poetry, *Tender*, does a similar favor. The uncharacteristically short title poem appears to talk about meat and begins:

> The tenderest meat
> comes from the houses
> where you hear the least
>
> squealing.

It does not take much reflection to see the metaphor about pain-filled lives. In the collection's preface, Derricotte urges readers to use the poem as a hub in exploring, as she describes the book's structure, "a seven-spoked wheel." The poet continues to wrestle with the meanings of death, birth, and transcendence. She writes, "Violence is central to our lives, a constant and unavoidable reality."

Derricotte's enduring legacy might be that, as she herself observed of Emily Dickinson, she does not flinch, whether the subject is political or sexual, and that courage is especially well demonstrated in *Tender*. For example, in "Clitoris," she discusses oral sex and her emotional response to it graphically and with lush imagery.

Like many in her generation, Derricotte never let go of the optimism of the 1960's about a positive evolution in U.S. attitudes toward and treatment of women and blacks. At the same time, she does not hesitate to display bitter disappointment at where we are along the road. For example, in "After a Reading at a Black College," also from *Tender*, she looks forward with both hope and skepticism:

> Maybe one day we will have
> written about this color thing
> until we've solved it. Tonight
> when I read my poems about
> looking white, the audience strains
> forward with their whole colored
> bodies . . .
> . . . .
> . . . though frightened
> I don't stop the spirit.
> *Hold steady*, Harriet Tubman whispers
> *Don't flop around.*

Once again, the best part of Derricotte's work is that, no matter how scathing, it is unapologetic. "People would like inspiring books that tell them what to do, something like *Five Steps Not to Be a Racist*," she told Don Lee in a 1996 interview in *Ploughshares*, the Emerson College literary journal. "That's just not the truth. The easy solutions don't really prepare one for the hard work that needs to be done." She goes on:

> I feel the need to represent what's not spoken. . . . I discover a pocket in myself that hasn't been articulated, then I have to find a form to carry that. Speaking the unspeakable is not that hard. The difficulty is in finding a way to make it perfect, to make it have light and beauty and truth inside it.

The Black Notebooks

TYPE OF WORK: Autobiography
FIRST PUBLISHED: 1997

Toi Derricotte's *The Black Notebooks: An Interior Journey* is an intimate portrait of a black woman who has "passed invisibly into the white world." Along the way, through these passages, Derricotte has experienced racism from the outside, through the slanted cast of the public eye, as well as from the inside, through her own sense of insecurity and fear. Derricotte documents these encounters with her own blackness through a series of journal entries. These entries offer the reader the rare opportunity to listen into this private dialogue on race relations, as witnessed and recorded by Derricotte the professor, the artist, the woman, the wife, and resident in an all-white neighborhood outside of New York City, where Derricotte lived when she first began writing this book, twenty years before publication, while "in the middle of a severe depression." She articulates what it is like to be perceived as something and someone she is not. On the surface, Derricotte might "pass" as being white, but on the inside, underneath her skin, she is all black. The most powerful moments in this book, on this interior journey, re-create those instances when Derricotte's skin color has not been seen as it is: those times when, in other words, others—that is, whites—have seen her to be one of them. Do I tell them the truth? Derricotte asks. Do I tell them who I am: that I am black? These questions form the heart of Derricotte's story. At an artist's colony where she is the lone black artist in residence, she confides to the page: "I am afraid to come out as a black person, to bear that solitude, that hatred, that invisibility." When Derricotte finally does come out and expose who and what she is, the response is, "You're not really black." How the world perceives her is a constant and deep-cored source of inner and outer struggle for Derricotte—a struggle not to give in to the illusion of who she is not. Derricotte's struggle for self-acceptance, for her salvation, proves to be beatable, and the result of that victory is a book that rises up out of that battle, that tightening silence, that journey to an inner place of awakening where Derricotte brings forth and sings beautifully about what it means to be black.

Suggested Readings

Andrews, William, et al., eds. *The Oxford Companion to African American Literature*. New York: Oxford University Press, 1996.

Powers, William F. "The Furious Muse: Black Poets Assess the State of Their Art." *The Washington Post*, October 1, 1994, p. H1.

Robinson, Caudell, M. "Where Poets Explore Their Pain While Others Beware the Dog." *American Visions* 14, no. 5 (October, 1999): 30.

Contributor: Vincent F. A. Golphin

Owen Dodson

BORN: Brooklyn, New York; November 28, 1914
DIED: New York, New York; June 21, 1983

AFRICAN AMERICAN

*Hailed as the dean of African American drama, Dodson
is a literary forefather of black playwrights such as
Lorraine Hansberry and August Wilson as well
as black directors, including Lloyd Richards.*

PRINCIPAL WORKS

DRAMA: *Deep in Your Heart*, pr. 1935; *Including Laughter*, pr. 1936; *The Shining Town*, wr. 1937, pb. 1991; *Divine Comedy*, pr. 1938, pb. 1974 (music by Morris Mamorsky); *The Garden of Time*, pr. 1939 (music by Shirley Graham); *Everybody Join Hands*, pb. 1943; *New World A-Coming*, pr. 1943, pb. 1944; *The Third Fourth of July*, pb. 1946 (with Countée Cullen); *Bayou Legend*, pr. 1948, pb. 1971; *Till Victory Is Won*, pr. 1965 (with Mark Fax; opera); *Freedom, the Banner*, pb. 1984

LONG FICTION: *Boy at the Window*, 1951 (also known as *When Trees Were Green*, 1967); *Come Home Early Child*, 1977

POETRY: *Powerful Long Ladder*, 1946; *Cages*, 1953; *The Confession Stone*, 1968 (revised and enlarged as *The Confession Stone: Song Cycles*, 1970); *The Harlem Book of the Dead*, 1978 (with James Van De Zee and Camille Billops)

RADIO PLAYS: *Old Ironsides*, 1942; *Robert Smalls*, 1942; *The Midwest Mobilizes*, 1943; *Dorrie Miller*, 1944; *New World A-Coming*, 1945; *St. Louis Woman*, c. 1945 (adaptation of Countée Cullen and Arna Bontemps's play); *The Dream Awake*, 1969

SCREENPLAY: *They Seek a City*, 1945

SHORT FICTION: "The Summer Fire," 1956

NONFICTION: "Twice a Year," 1946-1947; "College Troopers Abroad," 1950; "Playwrights in Dark Glasses," 1968; "Who Has Seen the Wind? Playwrights and the Black Experience," 1977; "Who Has Seen the Wind? Part II," 1980

Owen Vincent Dodson, the grandson of former slaves and the ninth child of Nathaniel and Sarah Dodson, was born on November 28, 1914, in Brooklyn, New York. His father was a syndicated columnist and director of the National Negro Press. Before Owen's thirteenth birthday, death claimed four siblings and both parents; as a result, Owen and the other Dodson children lived with their older sister Lillian, an elementary schoolteacher. Dodson graduated from Thomas Jefferson

High School in 1932, earned a B.A. from Bates College in 1936 and an M.F.A. degree from the Yale School of Fine Arts's School of Drama in 1939.

At Bates, Dodson's passion for poetry and drama was evident. In response to his criticism of a sonnet by John Keats, his professor directed him to write sonnets himself, which Dodson did at the rate of four sonnets a week during his undergraduate years. This output enabled him to become a published poet while still an undergraduate. Also at Bates, he wrote and directed plays, and during his senior year he staged *The Trojan Women.*

At Yale, two of Dodson's best known plays, *Divine Comedy* and *The Garden of Time*, were first produced. Dodson, recognized as a promising poet, soon gained attention as an up-and-coming dramatist. Talladega College commissioned him to write a play, *Amistad*, commemorating the hundredth anniversary of the slave-ship mutiny led by Joseph Cinque.

After Dodson received his graduate degree from Yale, he began his career as an educator. He was employed by Spelman College and later at Hampton University. Dodson was one of the founders of the Negro Playwright Company in 1940. In 1942, during World War II, he enlisted in the Navy. While stationed at the Great Lakes Naval Training Center in Illinois, Dodson wrote and directed *Heroes on Parade*, a series of plays, including *Robert Smalls, John P. Jones, Booker T. Washington, Lord Nelson, Dorrie Miller, Everybody Join Hands, Old Ironsides, Don't Give Up the Ship, Freedom, the Banner*, and *Tropical Fable*. Some of these plays were performed by other military drama groups in the United States and abroad. Dodson received a medical discharge in 1943.

On June 26, 1944, twenty-five thousand people saw *New World A-Coming* at Madison Square Garden. Based on the production's success, Dodson was appointed executive secretary of the American Film Center's Committee for Mass Education in Race Relations. Other prominent committee members were Arna Bontemps, Langston Hughes, and Richard Wright. Dodson was a prolific dramatist. He collaborated with the well-known Harlem Renaissance poet Countée Cullen and wrote *The Third Fourth of July* and *Medea in Africa*, an adaptation of Euripides' *Mēdeia* (431 B.C.E.; *Medea*, 1781) that was based on Cullen's play *Medea* (pr., pb. 1935) and Dodson's *The Garden of Time.* Dodson also collaborated with composer Mark Fax and wrote two operas: *A Christmas Miracle* and *Till Victory Is Won.*

In 1947 Dodson joined the faculty of Howard University, and a decade later he was appointed chair of the drama department. He taught during the day and directed during the night. Indeed, during his long career he directed more than one hundred plays. In the fall of 1949, Dodson, Anne Cooke, and James Butcher led the Howard Players on a three-month tour of northwestern Europe. After the group's return to Washington, D.C., the United States government presented Howard University with the American Public Relations Award. During the 1954-1955 season, Dodson directed the premier performance of James Baldwin's *The Amen Corner* nine years before its Broadway debut. He also staged productions of plays by former Howard students, including Amiri Baraka (then known as LeRoi Jones).

In 1970, Dodson retired from Howard. However, his passion for the theater and poetry remained steadfast. He continued to direct plays and write poetry, in-

Owen Dodson (Courtesy of the New York Public Library)

cluding *The Confession Stone* and *The Harlem Book of the Dead.* Dodson taught at City College of New York and at York College in Queens. He died on June 21, 1983, in New York. Memorial services were held in Washington, D.C., and New York.

Although Dodson wrote poetry and two autobiographical novels, his plays remain his most significant theatrical accomplishment. In Dodson's plays, themes, plot, and characters are upstaged by language. His most widely known theatrical works are verse plays. He was one of the first playwrights, white or black, to effectively use verse drama. The epigraph ("It takes a powerful long ladder to climb to the sky/ An catch the bird of freedom for the dark") for Dodson's first volume of verse, *Powerful Long Ladder*, has relevance for his plays. The ladder is a metaphor for whatever individuals need, and the bird of freedom represents goals and desires. In *The Shining Town*, black women need to endure in order to reach financial stability. In *Divine Comedy*, the churchgoers need to turn away from a con man and empower themselves to obtain life's basic necessities. In *The Garden of Time*, the characters must realize that racism affects love. In *Bayou Legend*, Dodson's second full-length play, which critics have described as a fantasy and an allegorical poetic legend, Reve Grant fails to learn until it is too late that to compromise one's life is to compromise one's soul. He "chose the kingdom of compromise, of nothing, of mediocrity" as he longed for wealth and power.

The Shining Town

TYPE OF WORK: Drama
FIRST PUBLISHED: 1991 (wr. 1937)

The setting of this one-act play is a subway station in the Bronx during the Depression. New York is no "shining town" for the women who participate in a twentieth century version of a slave auction. African American domestic workers compete with one another for daily jobs offered by white women who pay extremely low wages. As the black women wait for their potential employers to arrive at the station, the atmosphere of gloom increases. The dark station corresponds with the women's despair. Dodson suggests that Abby, a little girl who accompanies her mother on her quest for employment, is doomed to the same fate. Dodson completed this play at Yale, but it was not produced there. One scholar, James V. Hatch, speculates that Dodson's less than flattering images of white women may be the reason *The Shining Town* was not produced at Yale.

Divine Comedy

TYPE OF WORK: Drama
FIRST PRODUCED: 1938, pb. 1974

Divine Comedy is another drama that Dodson completed at Yale. It premiered at Yale, was reviewed favorably in *Variety*, and remains one of his best-known plays. This verse play in two acts portrays a character based on Father Divine, the self-proclaimed religious leader. Dodson boldly focuses on an infamous black character at a time when a number of African American writers and scholars advocated positive images only. *The Shining Town*'s Depression-era time period is repeated here, and despair is also prevalent in this play. For example, a mother realizes she is rocking a dead baby. However, unlike *The Shining Town*, *Divine Comedy* does not have a pessimistic ending. The characters eventually realize they have to make their own lives better instead of depending on a religious charlatan. At the end, the characters proclaim: "We need no prophets./ This Winter is Autumn./ We need no miracles./ We *are* the miracle." Love is also an important factor in this play, as Cyril Jackson demonstrates the extremes to which a son will go to protect his mother.

The Garden of Time

TYPE OF WORK: Drama
FIRST PRODUCED: 1939

This three-act verse play, completed and produced at Yale, is Dodson's interpretation of Euripides' *Medea*. *The Garden of Time*, a drama of interracial relationships, begins in ancient Greece, and midway through the play the characters are in Georgia and Haiti. Concurrent with the shift in settings is the transformation of characters. Medea becomes Miranda, a Haitian, and Jason becomes John, a plantation owner's son. When *The Garden of Time* was staged at Yale, Shirley Graham was the play's only black actor. Graham, who was also enrolled in Yale's School of Drama, wrote the music for the play. *The Garden of Time* is one of Dodson's best-known plays and the winner of the Maxwell Anderson Verse Drama Award (second place) at Stanford University in 1942, yet ironically, it remains unpublished.

Dodson's plays provide insight into African American life, yet they are not limited to the black experience. Achieving universality in his writing was of primary importance to Dodson. His plays transcend cultures and time. *The Garden of Time*'s choral refrain, which was later titled "Circle One" and published in Dodson's *Powerful Long Ladder*, applies to the universality life experiences depicted in his plays: "Nothing happens only once,/ Nothing happens only here,/ . . . All the lands repeat themselves,/ Shore for shore and men for men."

SUGGESTED READINGS

Carbado, Devon W., Dwight A. McBride, and Donald Weise, eds. *Black Like Us: A Century of Lesbian, Gay, and Bisexual African American Fiction*. San Francisco: Cleis Press, 2002.

Dodson, Owen. Interview. In *Interviews with Black Writers*, edited by John O'Brien. New York: Liveright, 1973.

Hatch, James V. *Sorrow Is the Only Faithful One: The Life of Owen Dodson*. Urbana: University of Illinois Press, 1994.

Peterson, Bernard L., Jr. "Owen Dodson." In *Early Black American Playwrights and Dramatic Writers: A Biographical Directory and Catalog of Plays, Films, and Broadcasting Scripts*. New York: Greenwood Press, 1990.

Contributor: Linda M. Carter

Michael Dorris

BORN: Louisville, Kentucky; January 30, 1945
DIED: Concord, New Hampshire; April 11, 1997

NATIVE AMERICAN

*Dorris's works are among the best examples of fiction
and nonfiction featuring Native Americans.*

PRINCIPAL WORKS
CHILDREN'S LITERATURE: *Morning Girl*, 1992; *Guests*, 1994; *Sees Behind Trees*,
1996; *The Window*, 1997
LONG FICTION: *A Yellow Raft in Blue Water*, 1987; *Route Two*, 1990 (with Louise
Erdrich); *The Crown of Columbus*, 1991 (with Erdrich); *Cloud Chamber*, 1997
SHORT FICTION: *Working Men*, 1993
NONFICTION: *Native Americans: Five Hundred Years After*, 1977; *A Guide to Re-
search on North American Indians*, 1983 (with Arlene B. Hirschfelder and Mary
Gloyne Byler); *The Broken Cord: A Family's Ongoing Struggle with Fetal Alco-
hol Syndrome*, 1989; *Rooms in the House of Stone*, 1993; *Paper Trail: Essays*,
1994

Michael Dorris's involvement with Native American affairs came quite naturally.
The only child of a non-Native American mother and a Modoc father, Dorris spent
childhood vacations with relatives who lived on reservations in Montana and
Washington. His disdain for being called a Native American writer stemmed from
these early experiences; he learned to think of people as human beings rather than
as members of particular ethnic groups.

After his father's death, Dorris was raised by his mother, aunts, and grandmothers. The result of this feminine influence is apparent in his novel *A Yellow Raft in
Blue Water*, a story about three generations of women, narrated in their own voices.

In 1981, Dorris married Louise Erdrich, another author of mixed ancestry.
Dorris attributed his literary success to Erdrich, making her another of his women-
as-mentors. Dorris and Erdrich collaborated as they wrote, producing works that
authentically showcase Native Americans.

After his adopted son, Reynold Abel, was diagnosed with fetal alcohol syndrome, a preventable but debilitating condition caused by alcohol consumption
during pregnancy, Dorris began writing *The Broken Cord: A Family's Ongoing
Struggle with Fetal Alcohol Syndrome*. The book includes a touching autobiographical account provided by Reynold Abel. Its focus on alcohol abuse reflects
Dorris's concern that government policies are plunging Native Americans into a

health and education crisis, and continues his work as a Native American activist. The book won the 1989 National Book Critics Circle Award for General Nonfiction.

While a professor at Dartmouth, Dorris founded the Native American Studies Program and received the Indian Achievement Award. In 1991, his son was hit by a car and died. Dorris's son with Louise Erdrich, Jeffrey Sava, subsequently accused the couple of child abuse, leading to a prolonged court battle and later to the couple's divorce. Dorris later faced allegations of having abused a daughter. On April 10, 1997, Dorris took his own life at a motel in Concord, New Hampshire.

Dorris's empathy for Native Americans is apparent in his literary characters, who dramatize the often difficult living conditions of contemporary tribal members. It was the common experiences of humanity, however, that fueled Dorris's passion for writing. As an anthropologist who valued differences, Dorris used his literary voice to promote acceptance of diversity, touching on the basic elements of life that connect all people.

A Yellow Raft in Blue Water

TYPE OF WORK: Novel
FIRST PUBLISHED: 1987

A Yellow Raft in Blue Water, Dorris's first novel, chronicles incidents in the lives of his three women narrators. Readers have embraced the book, finding the story to be a compelling look at mothers and daughters. The novel opens with Rayona, a fifteen-year-old girl who is part Native American and part black. When her mother moves her to Montana to stay with her grandmother on a reservation, Rayona's mixed heritage makes her the target of prejudiced teens, damaging her already fragile self-esteem.

Eventually Rayona leaves the reservation and meets an understanding couple, who invite her to live with them. In Sky and Evelyn's modest home, Rayona feels accepted and begins to value commitment, self-sacrifice, and honesty as prime ways to define oneself. By the novel's end, Rayona develops the confidence and self-respect she needs to function in the tribal community and to be accepting of its diverse members.

Rayona learns to accept Christine and Ida, the other two main characters. Early in Christine's story, her sense of identity is complicated by an emotionally distant mother, who insists on being called "Aunt Ida." Christine's belief that she started life "in the hole" sends her on a quest for acceptance that leads to promiscuity, alcohol abuse, the fathers of her two children, and, finally, a fatal illness. As her life is ending, she moves toward harmony with herself, finally content simply to be Christine, a woman defined by the love of a good friend and forgiving family members.

Ida's story weaves together the autobiographies of all three women. During her teen years, her identity is negated by a family secret: She is not Christine's mother but her half sister. Ida's father and aunt, Christine's biological parents, persuade

Ida to pretend the baby is hers, saving the family from embarrassment. Ida's true sense of self is obscured by the roles she plays and the tales she has been spinning for forty years. As her story closes, she is tentatively considering an honest relationship with Rayona.

That Rayona, Christine, and Ida are Native American women struggling with poverty and abandoned by most of the men in their lives motivates their strength and independence. Diverse readers have identified with the three characters' emotions and experiences.

The Broken Cord

TYPE OF WORK: Autobiography
FIRST PUBLISHED: 1989

At first glance, *The Broken Cord* might appear to be a specialized study with limited appeal to the general reader, but that impression is quickly refuted: Any mother who ingests even moderate amounts of alcohol during pregnancy can produce fetal alcohol syndrome (FAS) in her child, and Dorris's treatise is both a practical primer and an eloquent prose poem detailing a poignant and growing problem the ramifications of which are social and legal as well as medical. The solutions to halting the birth of FAS children and to providing for FAS victims' lifelong care ultimately concern every reader.

"My son will forever travel through a moonless night with only the roar of wind for company," writes Dorris. "A drowning man is not separated from the lust for air by a bridge of thought, he is one with it, and my son, conceived and grown in an ethanol bath, lives each day in the act of drowning. For him there is no shore." Indeed, Dorris's son, Adam, exhibits all the characteristics of the classic FAS child, including "significant growth retardation both before and after birth; measurable mental deficit; altered facial characteristics; other physical abnormalities; and documentation of maternal alcoholism." Yet because FAS and its companion FAE (fetal alcohol effect) were not recognized conditions until the late twentieth century, the cause of Adam's learning difficulties remained misdiagnosed for years.

Eventually Dorris's role as an anthropologist and as the head of the Department of Native American Studies at Dartmouth University led him to work with specialists familiar with FAS and its devastating effect on Native American populations. Dorris learned that Adam is not unique; he discovered that Adam is one of thousands of such children born annually to women of every race and nationality who are themselves victims of poverty, ignorance, or low self-esteem. Dorris emphasizes that FAS may develop from an expectant mother's drinking as little as one cocktail or glass of wine or one can of beer a day, even on an irregular basis; the only insurance against FAS is total abstinence from alcohol consumption during pregnancy.

The Broken Cord helped draw national attention to this devastating syndrome and its long-term consequences. The book includes a foreword by Louise Erdrich and a final chapter by Adam, a touchingly unedited autobiography offered as a counterpoint and written at the suggestion of Adam's dad.

Working Men

TYPE OF WORK: Short fiction
FIRST PUBLISHED: 1993

The title of this collection suggests something of its thematic concerns. Many of these stories are about men who are more or less defined by the work they do. Yet the work they do is varied. Characters include an anthropologist, a traveling salesman, a designer of artificial lakes, and two railroad workers. The relation of the characters to their work varies as well. For the protagonist of "The Benchmark," his work is a vocation if not an obsession; characters in "Oui" and "Earnest Money" drift into whatever is available.

The men and their work exist within complex emotional relationships, treated by Dorris with a remarkable tonal variety. The almost total absence of humor in "The Benchmark" is unusual in Dorris's work, yet humor is seldom Dorris's only aim. The protagonist of "Qiana," who goes from buying a shirt on impulse, to an impulsive turnaround in his life, and finally to second thoughts about his impulses, makes readers smile; but the pain of his confusion and the pain he inflicts on others are honestly registered. At one level "Jeopardy" may be regarded as an ironic variation on the lore and legend of the traveling salesman, yet it is also a story of compelling emotional power.

The stories do not focus exclusively on men. As he established in *A Yellow Raft in Blue Water*, Dorris can create memorable female characters and, what is for a male writer even more remarkable, convincing and expressive female narrators, as in "Anything," "The Dark Snake," and "Decoration Day." The authenticity of the narrative voice in these stories suggests Dorris's mastery of language; he frequently achieves the intensity of poetry without abandoning the rhythms of American vernacular speech. *Working Men* reaffirms Dorris's importance as artist and working man.

Cloud Chamber

TYPE OF WORK: Novel
FIRST PUBLISHED: 1997

Rayona and her mother are carryovers from *A Yellow Raft in Blue Water*, which dealt with the Native American side of Rayona's heritage. The brilliantly written *Cloud Chamber* rounds out and completes the story with finely drawn portrayals of a fascinating line of resilient women.

In *Cloud Chamber*, Rose Mannion McGarry flees from Ireland ahead of British authorities who would prosecute her for her role in the uncovering of a British spy among Irish patriots. She takes with her the mild Martin McGarry, whom she married even though she is carrying the unborn child of the spy. The couple settles in a town near Lexington, Kentucky, where she gives birth to two sons.

Thereafter, the story of the family covers five generations in which the women show far more strength than the men. Rose, her daughter-in-law Bridie O'Gara McGarry, and Bridie's daughters Edna and Marcella, survive the weaknesses and early deaths of Rose's sons Andrew, a priest, and Robert, a consumptive. The women fight among themselves, but both Edna and Marcella conquer the disease that killed their father. Edna, finally the strongest of them all, rejects a belief that she has a vocation to be a nun to stay with the family. Marcella, with the connivance of her sister, defies segregation laws and convention and elopes with a young African American man and has a son, Elgin. He marries a Native American woman and becomes the father of Rayona, whose ceremonial adoption of the name of Rose as her Indian name signals a reconciliation among the women in her ancestry.

SUGGESTED READINGS

Chavkin, Allan, and Nancy Feyl Chavkin, eds. *Conversations with Louise Erdrich and Michael Dorris*. Jackson: University Press of Mississippi, 1994.

Couser, G. Thomas. "Raising Adam: Ethnicity, Disability, and the Ethics of Life Writing in Michael Dorris's *The Broken Cord*." *Biography* 21 (Fall, 1998): 421-444.

Farrell, Susan. "Colonizing Columbus: Dorris and Erdrich's Postmodern Novel." *Critique* 40 (Winter, 1999): 121-135.

Khader, Jamil. "Postcolonial Nativeness: Nomadism, Cultural Memory, and the Politics of Identity in Louise Erdrich's and Michael Dorris's *The Crown of Columbus*." *Ariel* 28 (1997): 81-101.

Owens, Louis. "Erdrich and Dorris's Mixedbloods and Multiple Narratives." In *Other Destinies: Understanding the American Indian Novel*. Norman: University of Oklahoma Press, 1992.

Rayson, Ann. "Shifting Identity in the Work of Louise Erdrich and Michael Dorris." *Studies in American Indian Literatures* 3 (Winter, 1991): 27-36.

Zabrowsky, Magdalena J., ed. *Other Americans, Other Americas*. Aarhus, Denmark: Aarhus University Press, 1998.

Contributor: Lynne Klyse

Frederick Douglass

(Frederick Augustus Washington Bailey)

BORN: Tuckahoe, Talbot County, Maryland; February, 1817?
DIED: Washington, D.C.; February 20, 1895

AFRICAN AMERICAN

Douglass wrote one of the most artistic, articulate,
and insightful slave narratives and lived a life dedicated
to championing black civil rights.

PRINCIPAL WORKS

LONG FICTION: *The Heroic Slave*, 1853

NONFICTION: *Narrative of the Life of Frederick Douglass, an American Slave,
Written by Himself*, 1845; *What to a Slave Is the Fourth of July?*, 1852; *The
Claims of the Negro Ethnologically Considered*, 1854; *The Anti-Slavery Move-
ment: A Lecture*, 1855; *My Bondage and My Freedom*, 1855; *Two Speeches by
Frederick Douglass*, 1857; *The Constitution of the United States: Is It Pro-
Slavery or Anti-Slavery? A Speech*, 1860; *Life and Times of Frederick Douglass,
Written by Himself*, 1881 (revised 1892); *The Lessons of the Hour*, 1894; *Fred-
erick Douglass: Selected Speeches and Writings*, 1999 (Philip S. Foner, editor)

EDITED TEXTS: *North Star*, 1847-1851; *Frederick Douglass' Paper*, 1851-1860;
Douglass' Monthly, 1859-1863; *New National Era*, 1870-1874

MISCELLANEOUS: *The Frederick Douglass Papers*, 1979-1992 (5 volumes); *The
Oxford Frederick Douglass Reader*, 1996 (William L. Andrews, editor)

Frederick Augustus Washington Bailey, who changed his name to Frederick
Douglass after escaping slavery, was the son of a slave mother and a white man,
probably his mother's master, Captain Aaron Anthony. He grew up in a variety of
slavery conditions, some very harsh. He nevertheless taught himself to read and
write and became a skilled caulker at the Baltimore shipyards.

In 1838, he escaped to New York disguised as a free sailor. After marrying Anna
Murray, a freewoman who had helped him escape, he moved with her to Massachusetts. He took the name Douglass and began working for the abolitionist cause. For
four years he was a popular and eloquent speaker for antislavery societies and in
1845 published his *Narrative of the Life of Frederick Douglass: An American
Slave*, one of the finest slave narratives.

As a precaution against recapture following the publication of his autobiography, Douglass went to England to lecture on racial conditions in the United

States. In late 1846, British friends purchased and manumitted Douglass, and the following year he returned to New York a free man.

Moving to Rochester, Douglass began an abolitionist newspaper, *The North Star* (later renamed *Frederick Douglass' Paper*), became an Underground Railroad agent, wrote in support of women's rights and temperance, and revised and expanded his autobiography. In 1859, he narrowly escaped arrest following John Brown's raid at Harpers Ferry. Although Douglass had not supported the raid, he was a friend of Brown. He fled to Canada, then England, returning months later when he learned of his daughter Annie's death.

Frederick Douglass (Library of Congress)

During the Civil War, Douglass urged the recruitment and equal treatment of blacks in the military (his two sons were early volunteers) and became an unofficial adviser to Abraham Lincoln on matters of race. After Lincoln's death, he opposed Andrew Johnson's pro-colonization stance and worked for black civil rights, especially suffrage.

A loyal supporter of the Republican Party, he was appointed to various posts by five presidents. In 1881, Douglass again updated his autobiography. The following year Anna Murray Douglass died. Two years later, Douglass married Helen Pitts, his white secretary, a marriage that shocked many. In 1889, President Benjamin Harrison appointed Douglass minister to Haiti. Douglass retired in 1891 but remained a powerful voice speaking out for racial equality until his death in 1895. He is remembered as not only the most prominent black American of his era but also a man whose life of commitment to the concept of equality made him an outstanding American for all times.

Narrative of the Life of Frederick Douglass

TYPE OF WORK: Autobiography
FIRST PUBLISHED: 1845

Frederick Douglass's *Narrative of the Life of Frederick Douglass, an American Slave, Written by Himself*, one of the finest nineteenth century slave narratives, is the autobiography of the most well-known African American of his time. The narrative chronicles Douglass's early life, ending soon after his escape from slavery when he was approximately twenty. It focuses on formative experiences that stand out in his life for their demonstration of the cruelty of slavery and of his ability to endure and transcend such conditions with his humanity intact.

Douglass's work follows the formula of many slave narratives of his day. He structures his story in a linear fashion, beginning with what little information he knew about his origins and progressing episodically through to his escape north. His recurring theme is the brutal nature of slavery, with an emphasis on the persevering humanity of the slaves despite unspeakable trials and the inhumanity of slave owners. Other themes common to Douglass's and other slave narratives are the hypocrisy of white Christianity, the linkage of literacy to the desire for and attainment of freedom, and the assurance that with liberty the former slave achieved not only a new sense of self-worth but also an economic self-sufficiency. Douglass's work is characteristic of the nineteenth century in that it is melodramatic and at times didactic.

Despite its conventional traits, however, Douglass's work transcends formulaic writing. The author's astute analyses of the psychology of slavery, his eloquent assertions of self, and his striking command of rhetoric lift this work above others in its genre. Particularly memorable scenes include young Frederick's teaching himself to read, the fight with the slave breaker Covey, the author's apostrophe to freedom as he watches sailboats on Chesapeake Bay, and his interpretation of slave songs as songs of sorrow.

When Douglass wrote this work in 1845, he had already earned a reputation as one of the most eloquent speakers for the Massachusetts Anti-Slavery Society. The *Narrative of the Life of Frederick Douglass* was published with a preface written by William Lloyd Garrison, which was followed by a letter by Wendell Phillips. An immediate success, the *Narrative of the Life of Frederick Douglass* soon went through five American and three European editions.

Douglass revised and enlarged the autobiography with later expansions, *My Bondage and My Freedom* (1855) and *Life and Times of Frederick Douglass* (1881, 1892). Although these later versions are of historical value for their extension of Douglass's life story and for their expansion on matters—such as his method of escape—that Douglass purposefully avoided in his first publication, critics generally agree that the spareness and immediacy of the original *Narrative of the Life of Frederick Douglass* renders it the most artistically appealing of the autobiographies.

Today Douglass's book has become canonical as one of the best of the slave narratives, as an eloquent rendering of the American self-made success story, as a finely crafted example of protest literature, and for its influence on two important genres of African American literature—the autobiography and the literary treatment of slavery.

My Bondage and My Freedom
TYPE OF WORK: Autobiography
FIRST PUBLISHED: 1855

Douglass's second autobiography was published eight years after his British friends purchased his freedom. Of the twenty-five chapters in *My Bondage and My Freedom*, the first twenty-two include events from *Narrative of the Life of Frederick Douglass*, such as his escape and early days as an abolitionist. *My Bondage and My Freedom* also includes chapters on Douglass's introduction to other abolitionists and his twenty-one-month stay in Great Britain, and the final chapter, "Various Incidents," includes his founding of *The North Star* and his family's move to Rochester. The appendix includes excerpts from Douglass's orations in England and the United States; his speech *What to a Slave Is the Fourth of July?* is also included. The appendix also contains Douglass's letter to his former master Thomas Auld; Douglass ends the letter by writing that he is a man and not Auld's slave.

Life and Times of Frederick Douglass
TYPE OF WORK: Autobiography
FIRST PUBLISHED: 1881

Douglass's third autobiography extends coverage of his life to 1891, four years prior to his death. Thus *Life and Times of Frederick Douglass* describes a century in which Douglass is born into slavery during the second decade and attains the status of statesman during the seventh and eighth. Part 1 ends with Douglass fleeing slavery in 1838. He provides more details about his escape in *Life and Times of Frederick Douglass* than in *Narrative of the Life of Frederick Douglass* and *My Bondage and My Freedom*. In part 2, Douglass offers more insight into his career as an abolitionist than he revealed in his previous autobiographies. His activities prior to the Civil War, during the war, and after the war are included; two instances are Douglass's recruitment of African American troops for the Fifty-fourth and Fifty-fifth Colored Regiments for the Civil War and his White House meeting with President Abraham Lincoln on behalf of the African American troops. Highlighted in parts 2 and 3 are Douglass's presidential appointments and his trip to Europe. As in *My Bondage and My Freedom, Life and Times of Frederick Douglass* provides glimpses into African American middle-class life as the Douglasses reside in New Bedford, Rochester, and Washington, D.C. Critics have stated that Douglass wrote *Life and Times of Frederick Douglass*, published decades after slavery's end, in order to remind people of slavery's injustices.

As founder and editor of *The North Star*, Douglass wrote most of the newspaper's articles and editorials. Among his writings in *The North Star/Frederick Douglass' Paper* are "Our Mind Is Made Up" (1847), a request for African American authors, editors, and orators to spearhead the quest for liberty and equality;

"Colorphobia—A Law of Nature?" (1848), an attack on America's preoccupation with skin color; "The Rights of Women" (1848), a report on the first United States women's rights convention; and "Here We Are, and Here We Stay" (1849), an assertion against the deportment of African Americans. Douglass was arguably the most eloquent nineteenth century orator, and during his lifetime his speeches were printed in his publications as well as in other sources such as the *National Anti-Slavery Standard* and *Pennsylvania Freeman*. Douglass's best-known speech is *What to a Slave Is the Fourth of July?* delivered in 1852. The next year, Douglass created *The Heroic Slave*, a historical novella based on a slave ship mutiny that is recognized as one of the first works of long fiction in African American literature.

SUGGESTED READINGS

Andrews, William L. *The Oxford Frederick Douglass Reader*. New York: Oxford University Press, 1997.

McFeely, William S. *Frederick Douglass*. New York: Norton, 1991.

Martin, Waldo E., Jr. *The Mind of Frederick Douglass*. Chapel Hill: University of North Carolina Press, 1984.

Preston, Dickson J. *Young Frederick Douglass: The Maryland Years*. Baltimore: The Johns Hopkins University Press, 1980.

Starling, Marion Wilson. *The Slave Narrative: Its Place in American History*. 2d ed. Washington, D.C.: Howard University Press, 1988.

Stone, Albert E. "Identity and Art in Frederick Douglass's *Narrative*." *CLA Journal* 17 (1973).

Sundquist, Eric J., ed. *Frederick Douglass: New Literary and Historical Essays*. New York: Cambridge University Press, 1990.

Contributors: Grace McEntee and Linda M. Carter

Rita Dove

BORN: Akron, Ohio; August 28, 1952

AFRICAN AMERICAN

Dove's poems give voice to the African American woman whose concerns are wider than region or race.

PRINCIPAL WORKS

DRAMA: *The Darker Face of the Earth*, pb. 1994, revised pb. 2000
LONG FICTION: *Through the Ivory Gate*, 1992
POETRY: *The Yellow House on the Corner*, 1980; *Museum*, 1983; *Thomas and Beulah*, 1986; *Grace Notes*, 1989; *Selected Poems*, 1993; *Mother Love*, 1995; *On the Bus with Rosa Parks*, 1999; *American Smooth*, 2004
SHORT FICTION: *Fifth Sunday*, 1985
NONFICTION: *The Poet's World*, 1995
EDITED TEXTS: *The Best American Poetry, 2000*, 2000; *Conversations with Rita Dove*, 2003 (Earl G. Ingersoll, editor)

Rita Dove acknowledges that her writing is influenced by a range of experiences. Consequently, Dove consistently avoids being pigeonholed. As an undergraduate at Miami University in Oxford, Ohio, she spent a year on a Fulbright Scholarship at the University of Tübingen, in West Germany, where she realized that a writer cannot have a limited view of the world. Although her earlier work was influenced by African American writers of the 1960's, she stands apart from African American writers who write primarily of the politics of ethnicity. Well educated, Dove allows her poetry to reflect her wide interests. Many poems allude to the visual arts and music. Poems in *Museum* discuss Catherine of Alexandria, Catherine of Siena, William Shakespeare, Friedrich Hölderlin, and Giovanni Boccaccio. The cross-cultural thrust of her writing is indicative of the influence that Dove's European experience had on her.

Dove's poetry uses family history as raw material. In *Thomas and Beulah*, Dove mixes fact and imagination to describe the lives of her maternal grandparents. A book-length narrative, the story of her family employs two separate points of view, that of her grandfather and that of her grandmother. Race is central to the story, but Dove focuses on the relationship that they had, in spite of the difference between their families. Winner of the 1987 Pulitzer Prize in poetry, the volume shows her concern with the voices of ordinary people. Through these lives she addresses more communal concerns. Dove's work acknowledges the existence of race problems but allows the human spirit to triumph.

Marriage to Fred Viebahn in 1979 produced one daughter, Aviva Chantal Tamu Dove-Viebahn. Dove's poetry of the time explores mother-daughter relationships, especially when the child is biracial. Such poems are evident in *Grace Notes*. Dove experiments with other literary forms. She has produced a verse play, short stories, and a novel. *Through the Ivory Gate*, her first novel, explores the interplay between autobiography and artifice. Virginia King, a character reflecting Dove's experiences, returns to Akron to work with young students. Learning the stories of her family confirms Virginia in her desire for a career in the theater.

In 1993, Dove became poet laureate of the United States. In that role, she worked with emerging writers, encouraging them to gain the breadth and depth of experience that would fuel their writing.

Grace Notes

TYPE OF WORK: Poetry
FIRST PUBLISHED: 1989

In *Grace Notes*, Dove explores the implications of being an African American who is prepared to step forward into a world broader than any limiting labels would suggest. Many poems focus on the relationship between her biracial child and herself, revealing how the child discovers and accepts these differences. Others show the daughter learning what it means to become a woman. Still other poems question the effect that the development of identity can have on the artist.

Dove sets the stage with the first poem, "Summit Beach, 1921," which examines the risk of being at the edge of development. A girl watches her friends dance as she rests her broken leg. She had climbed to the top of her father's shed, then stepped off. Dove shows that the girl wants to date but that her father had discouraged her. This poem suggests that the search for identity does not occur without risks because the search involves making choices.

Married to a German man, Dove's daughter learns to belong in both worlds. "Genetic Expedition" contains images that delve into the physical differences between the black mother and her biracial child. Beginning with images of her own body,

Rita Dove (Fred Viebahn)

Dove mentions that she resembles pictures of natives in the *National Geographic* more than she does her own daughter. Because of the *National Geographic*'s sensual, naked women, her father had not allowed the children to read the magazine. While Dove identifies physically with the bodies of these women, she acknowledges that her daughter's features and hair reflect her biracial heritage. Thus the poem exemplifies Dove's rootedness in her own culture while being open to other cultures.

Other poems that feature Dove's daughter show the child as she discovers her mother's body, the source of her life and future. "After Reading *Mickey in the Night Kitchen* for the Third Time Before Bed" describes a tender moment between mother and daughter as the daughter compares her budding body with her mother's mature body. Dove emphasizes the daughter's innocent curiosity and her delight at realizing what her future holds.

Several poems discuss artists searching for ways to express who they have come to be through their art. "Canary" looks at the difficulty of such inquiry. Focusing on Billie Holiday, the poem describes the downward spiral of her life. Whether it was more difficult for her to be black or to be female is the question of identity that Dove explores, suggesting that circumstances conspired to take away Holiday's power to carve out her own identity. Dove's poems allow the questions and implications of a search for identity to take shape as an ongoing process.

Through the Ivory Gate

TYPE OF WORK: Novel
FIRST PUBLISHED: 1992

Through the Ivory Gate is Dove's first novel. She brings her poetic skills to bear on this subtle and complex story of a bittersweet homecoming. Entertainer and aspiring actress Virginia King has never understood why her childhood was interrupted by a sudden move from Akron, Ohio, to Arizona and an apparently simultaneous change in her parents' characters. Coming back to Akron to teach puppetry in the public school, she is able to fill in pieces of her family's past that will help her in her search for self-definition. The family secrets she uncovers do not make her happy, but they do help her toward freedom.

The deft use of flashbacks allows Dove to weave into the present action scenes from King's childhood in Akron, her years in Arizona, her college experience, and her first attempts to use her education as a member of the traveling troupe "Puppets and People." Through King's perspective the reader sees the obvious and hidden prejudices of the time and place and the various ways King deals with these barriers to her career as an actress and her basic sense of self.

The most compelling presence in this novel, however, may be the puppets. Puppet lore and puppet activities dominate the present action, entrancing even readers who have been indifferent to this subject. The puppets become living beings as well as the various images we create for one another and ourselves. This is a book for rereading.

Mother Love

TYPE OF WORK: Poetry
FIRST PUBLISHED: 1995

Dove surmounts the inherent pitfalls of her overused source material, the myth of Demeter, by transforming it into something deeply personal. Most poets working this myth mistakenly try to enter a nonexistent past. Dove allows herself to be inhabited, and her Demeter emerges in contemporary idiom. The poet's assured manner allows control: She is both possessed and possessor.

Dove's Demeter consciousness reveals that every time a daughter walks out the door, the abduction by Hades begins again. Time insists on the loss of the daughter. This archetypal mother knows that her daughter must make her way in the world—with all its attendant risks. The Persephone aspect of Dove recalls, at twenty, enjoying the risks of visiting Paris (in "Persephone in Hell"). Although she felt the power of her mother's worry, she writes, "I was doing what she didn't need to know." She was, in fact, tempting fate, testing her ripeness against the world's (man's) treachery. She needed to know it and survive it.

In her foreword, Dove offers that her irregular sonnets lend themselves to the story of "a world gone awry." She enjoys "how the sonnet comforts even while its prim borders . . . are stultifying." Perhaps it is the very process of playing with the sonnet's strictures and gauging the appropriate license that has helped Dove find the voice (or voices) and shapes she needs to infuse life into materials that have so often generated hackneyed performances.

In *Mother Love*, narrative and dramatic elements are strong, yet there is no sacrifice of lyricism or any other poetic element. Constantly setting new challenges for herself and constantly growing, Rita Dove has again more than fulfilled the expectations of those who anointed her at the outset of her career.

The Yellow House on the Corner

TYPE OF WORK: Poetry
FIRST PUBLISHED: 1980

Poems in *The Yellow House on the Corner* often depict the collision of wish with reality, of heart's desire with the dictates of the world. This collision is made tolerable by the working of the imagination, and the result is, for Dove, "magic," or the existence of an unexplainable occurrence. It is imagination and the art it produces that allow the speaker in "This Life" to see that "the possibilities/ are golden dresses in a nutshell." "Possibilities" have the power to transform this life into something distinct and charmed. Even the woman driven mad with grief over the loss of her son (or husband?) in "The Bird Frau" becomes a testament to possibility in her desire to "let everything go wild!" She becomes a bird-woman as a way of reuniting with her lost airman, who died in the war over France. While her condition may be perceived as pathetic, Dove refuses to indulge sentimentality, instead seeing her madness as a form of undying hope.

The refusal to indulge sentimentality is a mark of Dove's critical intelligence. It allows her to interpose an objectifying distance between herself and the subject. She knows the absolute value of perspective, so that while she can exult in the freedom that imagination makes possible, she recognizes that such liberty has its costs and dangers too. Two poems in particular reveal this desire and her wariness: "Geometry" and "Sightseeing." In the former, Dove parallels the study of points, lines, and planes in space with the work of the poet: "I prove a theorem and the house expands:/ the windows jerk free to hover near the ceiling,/ the ceiling floats away with a sigh." Barriers and boundaries disappear in the imagination's manipulation of them, but that manipulation has its methodology or aesthetic: "I *prove* a theorem. . . ."

In "Sightseeing" the speaker, a traveler in Europe after World War II, comes upon what would seem to be a poem waiting to happen. The inner courtyard of a village church has been left just as it was found by the villagers after an Allied bombing raid. It is filled with the shattered cherubim and seraphim that had previously decorated the inner terrace of the building: "What a consort of broken dolls!" Yet the speaker repudiates any temptation to view the sight as the villagers must—"A terrible sign. . . ." Instead she coolly ponders the rubble with the detached air of a detective: "Let's look/ at the facts." She "reads" the scene and the observers' attention to it as a cautionary lesson. The "children of angels" become "childish monsters." Since she distinguishes herself from the devout villagers, she can also see herself and her companion in the least flattering light: "two drunks" coming all the way across the town "to look at a bunch of smashed statues."

This ability to debunk and subvert expectations is a matter of artistic survival for Dove and a function of her calm intelligence. As an African American poet she is aware of the tradition of letters she steps into. Two other poems imply that this tradition can be problematic. In "Upon Meeting Don L. Lee, in a Dream" Dove encounters Lee (now known as Haki R. Madhubuti), a leading figure in the Black Arts movement, which attempted to generate a populist, specifically black aesthetic. The figure that emerges from Dove's poem, however, is unable to change except to self-destruct: "I can see caviar/ Imbedded like buckshot between his teeth." Her dream-portrait of Lee deflates not only his masculinity but his status as cultural icon as well. In "Nigger Song: An Odyssey" Dove seems to hark back further for a literary forebear and finds one in Gwendolyn Brooks, the first black woman to win the Pulitzer Prize. Although by 1967 Brooks would have come to embrace the black nationalism that Lee embodied, Dove's poem echoes the Brooks of an earlier time, the composer of "We Real Cool." In her evocation of "the nigger night" Dove captures the same vibrant energy that Brooks both celebrates and laments with the realization that the energy of urban African American youth is allowed no purposeful outlet and will turn upon itself. She writes: "Nothing can catch us./ Laughter spills like gin from glasses."

Some of the most compelling poems in Dove's first book are in a group of vignettes and portraits from the era of American slavery. These poems not only reveal her historical awareness but also allow her to engage the issue of race from a distance. Dove wants her poetry to produce anger, perhaps, but not to be produced only by anger. One example of this aesthetic distance from emotion might be "The Abduction," a brief foray in the voice of Solomon Northrup. Northrup is a free black lured to Washington, D.C., by "new friends" with the promise of good work and then kidnapped and sold into bondage. Dove dwells on the duplicity of these men and Northrup's susceptibility to them. Yet no pronouncements are made. The poem ends with the end of freedom, but that ending has been foreshadowed by the tightly controlled structure of the poem itself, with each stanza shortening as the scope of the victim's world constricts to this one-line conclusion: "I woke and found myself alone, in darkness and in chains." The indignation and disgust that such an episode could call forth are left entirely to the reader.

Museum

TYPE OF WORK: Poetry
FIRST PUBLISHED: 1983

Museum is, as the title suggests, a collection of historical and aesthetic artifacts. The shaping impulse of the book seems to be retrospective, a looking back to people and things that have been somehow suspended in time by legend, by historical circumstance, by all-too-human emotional wish. Dove intends to delve beneath the publicly known side of these stories—to excavate, in a sense, and uncover something forgotten but vital. The book is filled with both historical and mythical figures, all sharing the single trait of muted voice. Thus, "Nestor's Bathtub" begins: "As usual, legend got it all/ wrong." The private torment of a would-be martyr is made public in "Catherine of Alexandria." In "The Hill Has Something to Say" the poet speculates on the buried history of Europe, the cryptic messages that a culture sends across time. In one sense, the hill is a metaphor for this book, a repository of signs and images that speak only to that special archaeologist, the reader.

In the section titled "In the Bulrush" Dove finds worthy subjects in unlikely places and draws them from hiding. "Banneker" is another example of her flair for evoking the antebellum world of slavery, where even the free man is wrongly regarded because of his race. In the scientist Benjamin Banneker she finds sensitivity, eloquence, and intelligence, all transformed by prejudice into mere eccentricity. Banneker was the first black man to devise an almanac and served on Thomas Jefferson's commission to lay out the city of Washington, D.C., but the same qualities that lifted him to prominence made him suspect in the eyes of white society. Dove redeems this crabbed conception of the man in an alliterative final passage that focuses attention on his vision:

> Lowering his eyes to fields
> sweet with the rot of spring, he could see

a government's domed city
rising from the morass and spreading
in a spiral of lights. . . .

A third section of the book is devoted entirely to poems about the poet's father, and they represent her efforts to understand him. It is a very personal grouping, made to seem all the more so by the preceding sections in which there is little or nothing directly personal at all.

In the final section, "Primer for the Nuclear Age," Dove includes what is one of her most impressive performances. Although she has not shown herself to be a poet of rage, she is certainly not inured to the social and political injustice she observes. Her work is a way of channeling and controlling such anger; as she says in "Primer for the Nuclear Age": "if you've/ got a heart at all, someday/ it will kill you." "Parsley," the final poem of *Museum*, summons up the rank insanity of Rafael Trujillo, dictator of the Dominican Republic, who, on October 2, 1957, ordered twenty thousand black Haitians killed because they could not pronounce the letter *r* in *perejil*, Spanish for parsley. The poem is divided into two sections; the first is a villanelle spoken by the Haitians; the second describes General Trujillo on the day of his decision. The second section echoes many of the lines from the Haitians' speech, drawing murderer and victim together, suggesting a disturbing complicity among all parties in this episode of unfettered power. Even though Dove certainly wants to draw attention to this event, the real subject here is the lyric poet's realm—that point at which language intersects with history and actually determines its course.

Thomas and Beulah

TYPE OF WORK: Poetry
FIRST PUBLISHED: 1986

Thomas and Beulah garnered the Pulitzer Prize, but it is more important for the stage it represents in Dove's poetic development. Her first two books reveal a lyric poet generally working within the bounds of her medium. The lyric poem denies time, process, change. It becomes a frozen moment, an emotion reenacted in the reading. In *Thomas and Beulah* she pushes at the limitations of the form by stringing together, "as beads on a necklace," a whole series of these lyric moments. As the poems begin to reflect upon one another, the effect is a dramatic unfolding in which the passing of time is represented, even though the sequence never establishes a conventional plot. To accomplish this end Dove creates a two-sided book: Thomas's side ("Mandolin," twenty-one poems) followed by Beulah's ("Canary in Bloom," twenty-one poems).

The narrative moves from Thomas's riverboat life and the crucial death of his friend Lem to his arrival in Akron and marriage, through the birth of children, jobs, illness, and death. Beulah's part of the book then begins, moving through her parents' stormy relationship, her courtship with Thomas, marriage, pregnancy, work, and death. These two lives transpire against the historical backdrop of the great migration, the Depression, World War II, and the March on Washington; however, these events are practically the only common elements in the two sides of the story. Thomas and Beulah seem to live separate lives. Their communication with each other is implicit in the survival of the marriage itself. Throughout, Dove handles the story through exacting use of imagery and character.

Thomas emerges as a haunted man, dogged by the death of his friend Lem, which occurs in the opening poem, "The Event." Thomas drunkenly challenges Lem to swim from the deck of the riverboat to an island in the Mississippi. Lem drowns in the attempt to reach what is probably a mirage, and Thomas is left with "a stinking circle of rags/ the half-shell mandolin." In "Courtship" he begins to woo Beulah, but the poem implies that the basis of their relationship will be the misinterpreted gesture and that Thomas's guilt has left him with a void. He casually takes a yellow silk scarf from around his neck and wraps it around her shoulders; "a gnat flies/ in his eye and she thinks/ he's crying." Thomas's gift, rather than a spontaneous transfer of warmth, is a sign of his security in his relative affluence. The show of vulnerability and emotional warmth is accidental. The lyric poet in Dove allows her to compress this range of possibility in the isolated gesture or image. Beulah's life is conveyed as a more interior affair, a process of attaining the wisdom to understand her world rather than to resist it openly. In "The Great Palace of Versailles" Beulah's reading becomes her secret escape from the nastiness of the whites for whom she works in Charlotte's Dress Shoppe. As she lies dying in the final poem, "The Oriental Ballerina," the contemplation of the tiny figurine seems a similar invitation to fantasy, but her sensibilities have always been attuned to seeing the world as it is, as it has to be, and the poem ends in a brief flurry of realistic details and an air of acceptance; there is "no cross, just the paper kiss/ of a kleenex above the stink of camphor,/ the walls exploding with shabby tutus. . . ."

SUGGESTED READINGS

Dove, Rita. "Coming Home." Interview by Steven Schneider. *The Iowa Review* 19 (Fall, 1989): 112-123.

_____. Interview by Judith Kitchen and others. *Black American Literature Forum* 20 (Fall, 1986): 227-240.

_____. "An Interview with Rita Dove." Interview by Malin Pereira. *Contemporary Literature* 40, no. 2 (Summer, 1999): 182-213.

Harrington, Walt. "A Narrow World Made Wide." *The Washington Post Magazine*, May 7, 1995, 13-19, 28-29.

McDowell, Robert. "The Assembling Vision of Rita Dove." *Callaloo* 9 (Winter, 1986): 61-70.

Pereira, Malin. *Rita Dove's Cosmopolitanism.* Urbana: University of Illinois Press, 2003.

Rampersad, Arnold. "The Poems of Rita Dove." *Callaloo: A Black South Journal of Arts and Letters* 9 (Winter, 1986): 52-60.

Steffen, Theresa. *Crossing Color: Transcultural Space and Place in Rita Dove's Poetry, Fiction, and Drama.* New York: Oxford University Press, 2001.

Walters, Jennifer. "Nikki Giovanni and Rita Dove: Poets Redefining." *Journal of Negro History* 85 (Summer, 2000): 210-217.

Contributors: Martha Modena Vertreace, Nelson Hathcock, and Philip K. Jason

W. E. B. Du Bois

BORN: Great Barrington, Massachusetts; February 23, 1868
DIED: Accra, Ghana; August 27, 1963

AFRICAN AMERICAN

Du Bois was the foremost African American intellectual of the twentieth century and a leader in civil rights and pan-Africanism.

PRINCIPAL WORKS

LONG FICTION: *The Quest of the Silver Fleece*, 1911; *Dark Princess*, 1928; *The Ordeal of Mansart*, 1957; *Mansart Builds a School*, 1959; *Worlds of Color*, 1961
NONFICTION: *The Suppression of the African Slave-Trade to the United States of America, 1638-1870*, 1896; *The Conservation of Races*, 1897; *The Philadelphia Negro*, 1899; *The Souls of Black Folk: Essays and Sketches*, 1903; *John Brown*, 1909; *Darkwater: Voices from Within the Veil*, 1920; *The Gift of Black Folk: The Negroes in the Making of America*, 1924; *Black Reconstruction: An Essay toward a History of the Part Which Black Folk Played in the Attempt to Reconstruct Democracy in America, 1860-1880*, 1935; *Black Folk Then and Now: An Essay in the History and Sociology of the Negro Race*, 1939; *Dusk of Dawn: An Essay Toward an Autobiography of a Race Concept*, 1940; *Color and Democracy: Colonies and Peace*, 1945; *The World and Africa: An Inquiry into the Part Which Africa Has Played in World History*, 1947; *In Battle for Peace: The Story of My Eighty-third Birthday*, 1952 (with Shirley Graham); *The Autobiography of W. E. B. Du Bois: A Soliloquy on Viewing My Life from the Last Decade of Its First Century*, 1968 (first pb. in Russian as *Vospominaniia*, 1962); *W. E. B. Du Bois Speaks: Speeches and Addresses, 1920-1963*, 1970 (Philip S. Foner, editor); *The Education of Black People: Ten Critiques, 1906-1960*, 1973 (Herbert Aptheker, editor); *Du Bois on Religion*, 2000 (Phil Zuckerman, editor); *Du Bois on Education*, 2002 (Eugene F. Provenzo, Jr., editor)

William Edward Burghardt Du Bois (dew-BOYS) was a towering intellectual who created a new language of protest and ideas to understand and guide the African American experience. He wrote fiction and nonfiction, infusing his writings with eloquence and anger. He envisioned a world with equality for all people, emphasizing social justice for Africans and their descendants throughout the New World.

Du Bois's chronicle of his childhood begins with a tale of small-town conventionality in rural Massachusetts, where he experienced a loving home. In 1888, he entered Fisk University and saw firsthand the "color line" dividing the South. After graduating from Fisk, he returned to Massachusetts, where he earned a doctorate in history at Harvard.

His first important academic position was a marginal one at the University of Pennsylvania, but it resulted in his brilliant exposition, *The Philadelphia Negro*. In that work he outlines the historical background of the black community in Philadelphia and documents its patterns of daily life.

In 1897, he accepted a position at the University of Atlanta, where he worked until 1910. He held a yearly conference, resulting in a series of edited books on such topics as African Americans and business, religion, and social life. In 1903, Du Bois published the literary masterpiece *The Souls of Black Folk*, the first of four autobiographies that connect his personal experience with that of his community.

W. E. B. Du Bois (Library of Congress)

In 1909, Du Bois helped organize the National Association for the Advancement of Colored People (NAACP). He became the first editor of their journal *Crisis* in 1910. For the next quarter century, Du Bois was a center of debate on pressing social issues, and he was personally responsible for many columns, opinions, and reviews in the journal.

By 1935, Du Bois was increasingly at odds with the leadership at the NAACP. He resigned his position there and returned to the University of Atlanta. He helped found the journal *Phylon*, which continues to provide an important voice for African American scholarship. Beginning in the 1920's, Du Bois turned his attention to international affairs, organizing pan-African conferences and observing the racist and classist practices of the Western nations. He became a Marxist and was attacked by other intellectuals. Du Bois was indicted by the United States for being an agent of a foreign power; the indictment was the result of his peace activism and leftist politics during the Cold War. Although he was acquitted, the accusation that his government made against him remained a source of bitterness.

Du Bois traveled widely around the world—after at first being denied a passport—and eventually settled in Ghana, whose leader, Kwame Nkrumah, was his friend. In Ghana, in his nineties, he began work on an encyclopedia of African culture. Much of Du Bois's vision of racial equality and African American achievement remained unfulfilled at his death in 1963.

The Philadelphia Negro

TYPE OF WORK: Sociological study
FIRST PUBLISHED: 1899

The Philadelphia Negro, Du Bois's second book, is an impressive sociological study of blacks in Philadelphia resulting from fifteen months of fieldwork the author did in Philadelphia's seventh ward in 1896 and 1897. Although this book has received less recognition than *The Souls of Black Folk* and *The Autobiography of W. E. B. Du Bois*, it deserves consideration.

This study was proposed by Susan B. Wharton, a member of the Executive Committee of the Philadelphia Settlement, who approached the provost of the University of Pennsylvania suggesting a scholarly investigation of the status of Philadelphia's black population. Du Bois, already well reputed as a black scholar, was an obvious choice to undertake this project. He agreed to leave his chairmanship of the classics department at Wilberforce University to undertake this investigation under the auspices of the University of Pennsylvania.

In August, 1896, Du Bois and his bride, Nina Gomer, moved into a small apartment in one of Philadelphia's worst neighborhoods and remained there for a year conducting door-to-door interviews with area residents (Du Bois estimated that he met with over five thousand people). He distributed and collected hundreds of questionnaires while simultaneously undertaking an in-depth study of the social history of Philadelphia so that his findings would reflect the broader environment in which his subjects lived and worked.

Du Bois ran statistical analyses of situations affecting black people. He studied the proportion of black to white inmates in Philadelphia's Eastern Penitentiary and found that 62 percent of the inmates were black, a shocking disparity given the city's proportion of blacks to whites. The reasons for this disparity, he concluded, were a lack of education and of vocational opportunities for blacks in Philadelphia. By extension, it could be assumed that similar disparities existed elsewhere in the North.

This book was the first thorough, scholarly study of the problems blacks faced at the turn of the century. It made considerable social and political impact and became a model for many future sociological studies based on fieldwork.

The Souls of Black Folk

TYPE OF WORK: Essays
FIRST PUBLISHED: 1903

The Souls of Black Folk is the passionate and eloquent story of an individual, W. E. B. Du Bois, and a group, African Americans. Du Bois could not forget that his world was divided by a color line. Du Bois calls the experience generated by the color line the veil and allows his readers to walk with him within the veil. He does this with songs of sorrow that introduce each chapter.

The second chapter begins with the famous lines: "The problem of the twentieth century is the problem of the color line." These prophetic words tell the story of American slaves and their descendants. One way to address these issues is to work for gradual change, as advocated by Booker T. Washington. Du Bois's criticism of Washington created a public debate about how to fight discrimination.

Du Bois then tells of entering Fisk University in Nashville, Tennessee. He experiences the Jim Crow world of the South and teaches children who must endure its cruelty. Du Bois soon moves from the elementary school to higher education, but before leaving the South, he travels through it. Jim Crow railway cars physically and socially segregate black and white passengers. Plantations dot the landscape, recalling the slavery that maintained them and continuing their legacy through tenant farming.

Du Bois reveals how the "faith of our fathers" is a communal heritage. Music and lyrics create a heritage from the past that lives in the present. Du Bois's faith is tested by the death of his first and only son, Burghardt, who was refused medical care because of the color line. Du Bois's keening cry against the evil that murdered his baby is heart-wrenching.

People are able to survive and triumph behind the veil, nevertheless, and the African American leader is the key to ending the color line. Alexander Crummell, a friend of Du Bois, was such a hero. Ordinary people can be revealed to be extraordinary too. Their paths may be hard, but their triumphs cause joy and celebration.

This book is a literary masterpiece that articulates the cost of hatred and the power to resist it. Although it has never been out of print, it was especially important in the 1960's, when it helped inspire the American civil rights struggle. Du Bois continued to tell his life story and the story of a people during the rest of his long, productive life. *The Souls of Black Folk*, however, is unique in its passion and eloquence. His inspirational language reaches all people who resist hatred.

Black Reconstruction
Type of work: History
First published: 1935

The historical study *Black Reconstruction* is a product of Du Bois's later years. Published in 1935, it is sometimes referred to as the author's most important work. In it, as in his doctoral dissertation and its subsequent publication in 1896 as *The Suppression of the African Slave-Trade to the United States of America, 1638-1870*, his chief objective is to correct much that has been written by white scholars about black history.

The post-Civil War era was generally depicted as a period during which freed slaves gained power and misused it. Most previous scholars depicted this as a period marked by scandal and corruption. Du Bois, however, writing his revisionist history in the depths of the Great Depression, believed that Reconstruction epitomized what democracy is really about. He chronicles how blacks who gained power imposed necessary reforms and worked toward the redistribution of wealth, thereby reflecting Du Bois's move toward communism in response to the economic crises African Americans faced during the Depression.

Du Bois followed this study in 1947 with *The World and Africa*, which was a further attempt to correct historical inaccuracies that portrayed his race in a less than favorable light. In both of these works, he emphasizes the exploitation of blacks by members of the dominant white society.

The Autobiography of W. E. B. Du Bois

TYPE OF WORK: Autobiography
FIRST PUBLISHED: *Vospominaniia*, 1962 (English edition, 1968)

The Autobiography of W. E. B. Du Bois: A Soliloquy on Viewing My Life from the Last Decade of Its First Century is the inspiring story of a foremost African American intellectual and civil rights leader of the twentieth century. Du Bois discusses his individual struggles and accomplishments, as well as his major ideas dedicated to promoting racial equality for Africans and African Americans. Moving from the reconstruction era after the U.S. Civil War, through World Wars I and II, to the height of the Cold War and the atomic age, Du Bois's personal reflections provide a critical, panoramic sweep of American social history. Du Bois did not simply observe the American scene; he altered it as a leader of African Americans in the American Civil Rights movement.

The chronological structure of the autobiography begins with five chapters on his travels to Europe, the Soviet Union, and China. After these travels, Du Bois announces the crowning ideological decision of his life: his conversion to communism. The remainder of the book answers the question: How did Du Bois arrive at this crucial decision in the last years of his life? Du Bois chronicles his life patterns of childhood, education, work for civil rights, travel, friendships, and writings. This information is written in such a way that it explains his decision to adopt communism as his political worldview.

Perhaps the most fascinating section of the book is Du Bois's account of his trial and subsequent acquittal in 1950 and 1951 for alleged failure to register as an agent of a foreign government, a sobering story of public corruption. His fundamental faith in American institutions, already strained by racism, was destroyed. He moved to Ghana and threw his tremendous energies into that nation as it shed its colonial experience.

The autobiography is subtitled as a soliloquy, but this categorization reflects the political realities of 1960 more than the specific literary form of speaking to oneself. At the time, the Cold War between the United States and the Soviet Union made communism an abhorrent choice to many Americans. The autobiography finally appeared in English in 1968, at a publishing house known for its communist writings. The autobiography is the least read of Du Bois's autobiographies, although it is an engaging exposition in which Du Bois shows his continuing growth and faith in human nature during his tenth decade.

SUGGESTED READINGS

Broderick, Francis L. *W. E. B. Du Bois: Negro Leader in a Time of Crisis.* Stanford, Calif.: Stanford University Press, 1959.

Byerman, Keith E. *Seizing the Word: History, Art, and Self in the Work of W. E. B. Du Bois.* Athens: University of Georgia Press, 1994.

Horne, Gerald, and Mary Young, eds. *W. E. B. Du Bois: An Encyclopedia.* New York: Greenwood Press, 2001.

Lewis, David Levering. *W. E. B. Du Bois: Biography of a Race, 1868-1919.* New York: H. Holt, 1993.

_____. *W. E. B. Du Bois: The Fight for Equality and the American Century, 1919-1963.* New York: Henry Holt, 2000.

Rampersad, Arnold. *The Art and Imagination of W. E. B. Du Bois.* Cambridge, Mass.: Harvard University Press, 1976.

Rudwick, Elliott M. *W. E. B. Du Bois: Voice of the Black Protest Movement.* Champaign: University of Illinois Press, 1982.

Contributors: Mary Jo Deegan and R. Baird Shuman

Paul Laurence Dunbar

BORN: Dayton, Ohio; June 27, 1872
DIED: Dayton, Ohio; February 9, 1906

AFRICAN AMERICAN

*Dunbar was one of the most popular American poets of
his time and America's first professional black writer.*

PRINCIPAL WORKS

LONG FICTION: *The Uncalled*, 1898; *The Love of Landry*, 1900; *The Fanatics*, 1901;
The Sport of the Gods, 1902
POETRY: *Oak and Ivy*, 1893; *Majors and Minors*, 1895; *Lyrics of Lowly Life*, 1896;
Lyrics of the Hearthside, 1899; *Lyrics of Love and Laughter*, 1903; *Lyrics of
Sunshine and Shadow*, 1905; *Complete Poems*, 1913
SHORT FICTION: *Folks from Dixie*, 1898; *The Strength of Gideon, and Other Stories*,
1900; *In Old Plantation Days*, 1903; *The Heart of Happy Hollow*, 1904; *The
Best Stories of Paul Laurence Dunbar*, 1938; *The Complete Stories of Paul
Laurence Dunbar*, 2006 (Gene Andrew Jarrett and Thomas Lewis Morgan,
editors)
MISCELLANEOUS: *In His Own Voice: The Dramatic and Other Uncollected Works of
Paul Laurence Dunbar*, 2002 (Herbert Woodward Martin and Ronald Primeau,
editors)

The creative genius and personal and professional tragedies of Paul Laurence
Dunbar (DUHN-bahr) have often been misunderstood by readers who neglect to
consider the poet in the context of his time, which was not just marked, but defined,
by all-encompassing racial politics. At the end of the nineteenth and beginning of
the twentieth century, commonly referred to by scholars of African American history as the nadir, Dunbar was a singular phenomenon, trapped between his audience's demands that he be the voice of his race and his own creative mandate that he
not be restricted to any given subject matter. Dunbar wrote not merely evocative
but enduring work, particularly as a poet. In addition to six volumes of verse, he
also wrote four collections of short stories and four novels in the twelve prolific
years before his untimely death at the age of thirty-three. Best known for his poems
and stories about the Southern rural black world from which he came, Dunbar also
wrote verse in standard English, often on black themes. His "We Wear the Mask" is
a classic revelation of what it means to be black and American, and his "Sympathy"
("I know why the caged bird sings!") is an ode to freedom with universal appeal.
    Dunbar was the only surviving child of Joshua and Matilda Glass Burton Mur-

phy Dunbar, former slaves who had taught themselves to read and write. They nurtured their son with stories of their Kentucky plantation years, the Underground Railroad, the Civil War, and emancipation. These accounts became an important part of Dunbar's consciousness of himself as an inheritor of a particular history and a voice for that identity. Ironically, however, white audiences exploited this work, even as they championed it, seeing it as a black confirmation of their stereotypical plantation tradition. Despite Dunbar's apparent compromise in this regard, black audiences reveled in and memorized his verses, representing as they did the first national exposure of the black experience rendered in high art.

Paul Laurence Dunbar (Library of Congress)

In 1898, Dunbar married Alice Ruth Moore, a Creole from New Orleans and a writer. The couple separated, however, in 1902, the result of tensions from within the marriage, including her family's disdain for the dark-skinned Dunbar and the demands of his professional life. These pressures contributed to Dunbar's failing health from tuberculosis and his general melancholy, from which his late work suffered. He died childless and broken in spirit in the house he shared with his mother in Dayton.

Lyrics of Lowly Life

TYPE OF WORK: Poetry
FIRST PUBLISHED: 1896

Reflective lyrics form a large segment of Dunbar's poetry. Some of his best poems of this type are found in *Lyrics of Lowly Life*, including the long stanzaic poem "Ere Sleep Comes Down to Soothe the Weary Eyes." This poem utilizes one sensory impression as a focal point for the lyrical evolution in the style of Keats. The sleep motif provides an avenue through which the persona's imagination enters the realm of reflection.

Through sleep's dream the persona is able to "make the waking world a world of lies—/ of lies palpable, uncouth, forlorn." In this state of subconscious reflection, past pains are revisited as they "come thronging through the chambers of the brain."

As the poem progresses, it becomes apparent that the repetitive echo of "ere sleep comes down to soothe the weary eyes" has some significance. This refrain begins and ends each stanza of the poem except the last. In addition to serving as a mood-setting device, this expression provides the channel of thought for the literary journey, which is compared with the "spirit's journeying." Dunbar's audience is thus constantly reminded of the source of his revelations.

Dunbar reveals his poetic thesis in the last stanza. He uses images from the subconscious state of life, sleep, to make a point about death. Prior to making this point, Dunbar takes the reader to the realm of reflective introspection: "So, trembling with the shock of sad surprise,/ The soul doth view its awful self alone." There is an introspective confrontation of the soul with itself, and it resolves

> When sleep comes down to seal the weary eyes
>
> . . . .
>
> Ah, then, no more we heed
> the sad world's cries
> Or seek to probe th' eternal mystery
> Or fret our souls at long-withheld replies.

The escape from pain and misery is death; there is no intermediary state which will eradicate that fact of life. Dunbar presents this notion with sympathy and sincerity. His metaphorical extensions, particularly those relative to the soul, are filled with compassion. The soul is torn with the world's deceit; it cries with "pangs of vague inexplicable pain." The spirit, an embodiment of the soul, forges ahead to seek truth as far as fancy will lead. Questioning begins then, and the inner sense confronts the inner being until truth emerges. Dunbar's presentation of the resolution is tender and gentle.

Dunbar wrote reflective lyrics in the vernacular as well. Espousing the philosophy of divine intention, Dunbar wrote "Accountability," a poem also found in *Lyrics of Lowly Life*. In this poem, the beliefs and attitudes of the persona are revealed in familiar language.

> Folks ain't got no right to
> censuah othah
> folks about dey habits;
>
> . . . .
>
> We is all constructed diff'ent
> d'ain't no two of
> us de same;
>
> . . . . . .
>
> But we all fits into places dat
> no othah ones
> could fill.

Each stanza in this poem presents a thesis and develops that point. The illustrations from the natural world support a creationist viewpoint. The persona obviously accepts the notion that everything has a purpose. The Creator gave the animals their members shaped as they are for a reason and so, "Him dat giv' de squr'ls de bushtails made de bobtails fu' de rabbits." The variations in nature are by design: "Him dat built de gread big mountains hollered out de little valleys"; "Him dat made de streets an' driveways wasn't shamed to make de alley." The poet establishes these notions in three quatrains, concluding in the fourth quatrain: "When you come to think about it, how it's all planned out it's splendid./ Nuthin's done er evah happens, dout hit's somefin' dat's intended." The persona's position that divine intention rules the world is thereby sealed.

Introspection is a feature of Dunbar's reflective lyrics. In "The Lesson," the persona engages in character revelation, interacts with the audience toward establishment of appropriate resolution, and participates in the action of the poem. These qualities are reminiscent of Browning's dramatic monologues. As the principal speaker sits by a window in his cottage, reflecting, he reports:

> And I thought of myself so sad and lone
> And my life's cold winter that knew no spring;
> Of my mind so weary and sick and wild
>   Of my heart too sad to sing.

The inner conflict facing the persona is revealed in these lines, and the perspective of self-examination is established. The persona must confront his sadness and move toward resolution. The movement toward resolution presents the dramatic occasion in the poem: "A thought stole into my saddened heart,/ And I said, 'I can cheer some other soul/ By a carol's simple art.'" Reflective introspection typically leads to improved character, a fundamental tenet in the Victorian viewpoint. Sustained by his new conviction and outlook, the persona "sang a lay for a brother's ear/ In a strain to soothe his bleeding heart."

The lyrical quality of "The Lesson" is strengthened by the movement in the poet's syntactic patterns. Feelings of initial despair and resulting joy and hope are conveyed through the poet's syntax. The sequential conjoining of ideas as if in a rushing stream of thought is particularly effective. The latter sections of the poem are noteworthy in this regard. This pattern gives the action more force, thereby intensifying the feeling. Dunbar presents an emphatic idea ("and he smiled . . .") and juxtaposes it to an exception ("Though mine was a feeble art"). He presents a responsive result ("But at his smile I smiled in turn") connected to a culminating effect ("And into my soul there came a ray"). With this pronouncement, the drama comes full circle from inner conflict through conversion to changed philosophical outlook. Dunbar captures each moment with appropriate vigor.

Dunbar's poetry of the rustic life and nature is pervasive in another poem from this collection, "The Old Apple-Tree." The primary lyrical quality of the poem is that the poetic message evolves from the poet's memory and imagination. Image creation is the medium through which Dunbar works here: His predominant image, dancing in flames of ruddy light, is an orchard "wrapped in autumn's purple haze."

Dunbar proceeds to create a nature scene that provides a setting for the immortalization of the apple tree. Memory takes the persona to the scene, but imagination re-creates events and feelings. The speaker in the poem admits that it probably appears ugly "When you look the tree all over/ Unadorned by memory's glow." The tree has become old and crooked, and it bears inferior fruit. Thus, without the nostalgic recall, the tree does not appear special at all.

Utilizing the imaginative frame, the speaker designs features of the simple rustic life, features that are typically British Romantic and peculiarly Wordsworthian. The "quiet, sweet seclusion" realized as one hides under the shelter of the tree and the idle dreaming in which one engages dangling in a swing from the tree are primary among these thoughts. Most memorable to the speaker is the solitary contentment he and his sweetheart found as they courted beneath the old apple tree.

> Now my gray old wife is Hallie
> An I'm grayer still than she
> But I'll not forget our courtin'
> 'Neath the old apple-tree.

The poet's ultimate purpose, to immortalize the apple tree, is fulfilled in the last stanza. The old apple tree will never lose its place in nature or its significance, for the speaker asks:

> But when death does come a-callin,'
> This my last request shall be,—
> That they'll bury me an' Hallie
> 'Neath the old apple-tree.

The union of man and nature at the culmination of physical life approaches a notion expressed in Wordsworth's poetry. This tree has symbolized the ultimate in goodness and universal harmony; it symbolizes the peace, contentment, and joy in the speaker's life. Here Dunbar's indebtedness to the Romantic traditions that inform his entire oeuvre is most profoundly felt.

Folks from Dixie

TYPE OF WORK: Short fiction
FIRST PUBLISHED: 1898

Dunbar's short fiction is often compared with that of his contemporary, Charles Waddell Chesnutt, who was also black and who wrote some accomplished plantation-based tales of black life. Chesnutt's stories are often peopled with characters who resist, undermine, and outsmart the white people who think they know them. The majority of Dunbar's black characters tend instead to manipulate and subvert white opposition and gain white approval by a show of sterling character: honesty, integrity, faithfulness, loyalty, love, redemptive suffering, forgiveness. Worse, some Dunbar stories cast uneducated black people as the ignorant, minstrel buffoons his white readers preferred. Yet nestled among this packing were also great stories for which he is well remembered, stories that reveal righteous anger over ignorance and racial injustice and contempt for those who perpetuate them.

There is plenty of "packing" in Dunbar's first story collection, *Folks from Dixie*. Several stories, such as "Mount Pisgah's Christmas 'Possum," represent uneducated black people as ludicrous bumpkins or grateful, indebted servants. "The Colonel's Awakening" is an extremely sentimental tale, dripping with the sort of pathos Thomas Nelson Page whipped into his plantation tales. In "Anner 'Lizer," Dunbar pokes fun at religious hypocrisy, while affirming the fact that people's emotional and spiritual needs are often deeply linked. "Jimsella," "Aunt Mandy's Investment," and "Nelse Hatton's Revenge" were written primarily for his post-Reconstruction black readers, who were still figuring out how to live now that the structure and restrictions of slavery no longer dictated their circumstances. Timely issues, which these stories address, were family responsibility, honesty, and integrity in businesses, which should serve the black community, and remembering and living the results of slavery and emancipation in ways that are not self-destructive.

"The Ordeal at Mt. Hope" and "At Shaft 11" are satisfying, well-constructed stories. The former is interesting for its autobiographical elements, its social commentary, and its "bootstrap economic" and educational philosophies as advocated by Booker T. Washington. The Reverend Howard Dokesbury steps off the train at Mt. Hope to take up his new post as Methodist preacher. The station house is run-down and filthy, like the rest of the town, and the indolent blacks, whites, and dogs view him with suspicion and malice. Dokesbury, understanding that any reconstruction of this community must happen one individual at a time, befriends 'Lias, one of the defeated young men. They collaborate on a small agricultural venture, and 'Lias gains confidence, feelings of self-reliance and self-esteem, and the financial base to go to the new industrial school to expand his skills. One by one, the townspeople are anxious to follow his example. Possibly Dunbar considered this story to be a blueprint for the betterment of the black masses, though he became increasingly critical of Washington's ideas, and by 1903 he warned of "educating the hand to the exclusion of the head." Dunbar gives Dokesbury his own physical characteristics, an occupation that Dunbar himself seriously considered and, even more important, some of his doubts and feelings of estrangement.

> He had always been such a loyal Negro, so proud of his honest brown . . . but . . . was he, after all, different from the majority of the people with whom he was supposed to have all thoughts, feelings, and emotions in common?

Increasingly, Dunbar discovered that education and class standing were great dividers among his people, and color-consciousness made it all much worse.

"At Shaft 11" takes place in a mining community in West Virginia where a strike is being broken with a crew of black miners. Violence erupts, and two heroes emerge: the Scottish foreman, Jason Andrews, and the black foreman, Sam Bowles, who unite for common cause and mutual benefit. Less believable than the previous story, it is a blueprint for how things might have been in a more perfect world but rarely were. Still, it is revealing as a Dunbar story: The black men fight back here, meeting violence with necessary violence, and winning their share of the American pie.

Lyrics of the Hearthside

TYPE OF WORK: Poetry
FIRST PUBLISHED: 1899

Dunbar's lyricism is substantially displayed in his love poetry, some of the best of which is found in this collection. In "A Bridal Measure," from *Lyrics of the Hearthside*, the poet's persona beckons maidens to the bridal throne. His invitation is spirited and triumphant yet controlled, reminiscent of the tradition in love poetry established by Ben Jonson. The tone, however, more closely approximates the carpe diem attitude of Robert Herrick.

> Come, essay a sprightly measure
> Tuned to some light song of pleasure.
> Maidens, let your brows be crowned
> As we foot this merry round.

The rhyming couplets carry the mood and punctuate the invitation. The urgency of the moment is extended further in the direct address: "Phyllis, Phyllis, why be waiting?/ In the woods the birds are mating." The poem continues in this tone, while adopting a pastoral simplicity.

> When the year, itself renewing
> All the world with flowers is strewing
> Then through Youth's Arcadian land
> Love and song go hand in hand.

The accentuation in the syntactic flow of these lines underlines the poet's intentions. Though the meter is irregular, with some iambs and some anapests, the force of the poet's exhortation remains apparent.

Dunbar frequently personifies abstractions. In "Love and Grief," also from *Lyrics of the Hearthside*, Dunbar espouses a morbid yet redemptive view of love. While the reflective scenario presented in this poem recalls Tennyson's meditations on death and loss, the poetic event echoes Wordsworth's faith in the indestructibility of joy. Utilizing the heroic couplet, Dunbar makes an opening pronouncement:

Out of my heart, one treach'rous winter's day
I locked young Love and threw the key away.
Grief, wandering widely, found the key
And hastened with it, straightway, back to me.

The drama of grief-stricken love is thus established. The poet carefully clarifies his position through an emphatic personification of Grief's behavior: "He unlocked the door/ and bade Love enter with him there and stay." Being a lyric poet of redemptive sensibility, Dunbar cannot conclude the poem on this note. The "table must turn," as it does for Wordsworth in such situations. Love then becomes bold and asks of Grief: "What right hast thou/ To part or parcel of this heart?" In order to justify the redemptive quality he presents, Dunbar attributes the human frailty of pride to Love, a failing which invites Grief. In so doing, the poet's philosophical intuitiveness emerges with a measure of moral decorum. Through the movement in the syntactic patterns, the intensity of the drama is heightened as the poem moves to resolution. Dunbar utilizes a variety of metrical patterns, the most significant of which is the spondee. This poetic foot of two accented syllables allows the poet to proclaim emphatically: "And Love, pride purged, was chastened all his life." Thus, the principal emotion in the poem is redeemed.

The brief, compact lyrical verse, as found in Browning, is among Dunbar's typical forms. "Love's Humility," in *Lyrics of the Hearthside*, is an example:

As some rapt gazer on the lowly earth
Looks up to radiant planets, ranging far
So I, whose soul doth know thy wondrous worth
Look longing up to thee as to a star.

This skillfully concentrated simile elevates love to celestial heights. The descriptive detail enhances the power of the feeling the poet captures and empowers the lyrical qualities of the poem with greater pathos.

Lyrics of the Hearthside also contains some of Dunbar's best nature poetry. "In Summer" captures a mood of merriment stimulated by nature. The common man is used as a model of one who possesses the capacity to experience this natural joy. Summer is a bright, sunny time; it is also a time for ease, as presented in the second stanza. Introducing the character of the farmer boy in stanza 3, Dunbar presents a model embodiment of the ease and merriment of summer. Amid the blades of green grass and as the breezes cool his brow, the farmer boy sings as he plows. He sings "to the dewy morn" and "to the joys of life." This behavior leads to some moralizing, to which the last three stanzas of the poem are devoted. The poet's point is made through a contrast:

O ye who toil in the town.
And ye who moil in the mart
Hear the artless song, and your faith made strong
Shall renew your joy of heart.

Dunbar admonishes the reader to examine the behavior of the farm boy. Elevation of the simple, rustic life is prevalent in the writings of early British Romantic poets and postbellum African American writers alike. The admonition to reflect on the rustic life, for example, is the same advice Wordsworth gives in "The Old Cumberland Beggar." Both groups of writers agree that there are lessons to be learned through an examination of the virtues of the rustic life. In this vein, Dunbar advises: "Oh, poor were the worth of the world/ If never a song were heard." He goes further by advising all to "taunt old Care with a merry air."

The Strength of Gideon

TYPE OF WORK: Short fiction
FIRST PUBLISHED: 1900

Dunbar's second collection of short stories, *The Strength of Gideon, and Other Stories*, reveals a wide spectrum of his thought and style. The title work and "Mammy Peggy's Pride" typify the plantation stories that champion the virtues of the race, such as honor, loyalty, dignity, faithfulness, selflessness, and a sense of duty and responsibility. Mammy Peggy, still the faithful, postemancipation house servant, so identifies with her owners' former aristocratic place in southern society that she almost cannot adapt to the alliances and reconciliation necessary for a new day. Gideon's strength is his sense of duty and responsibility in keeping his word to his old master, even though he loses the woman he loves and who loves him. Dunbar's intent is to glorify race relations of an earlier day in the interest of race relations of his own day, which were marked by increasing enmity and violence. It is as if he hopes to calm would-be lynchers and segregationists and reassure potential friends of the race, with the admonition to "remember who these people are."

"The Ingrate" is based on Dunbar's father's experiences as a slave, a fugitive on the Underground Railroad to Canada, and a Union soldier. The former slaveholder sees his former slave's name on a Union roster and feels grievously abused that he taught "the ingrate" to read and cipher because he used these accomplishments against him. "The Case of 'Ca'line,'" subtitled "A Kitchen Monologue," is a sassy piece, which anticipates Langston Hughes's Simple and Alberta K. Johnson stories.

Though there is enough melodramatic action in "The Tragedy at Three Forks" for a novel, this antilynching story is not entirely unsuccessful. Reflecting the usual circumstances of lynchings, the two victims are innocent, and the reader understands that this evil bloodthirst will continue as long as white people are motivated by guilt, ignorance, immorality, cruelty, base instincts, and mob violence. Other stories point out other kinds of white injustice. In "One Man's Fortunes," a worthy black college graduate goes out to get a job and, like Dunbar himself, meets defeat and deception in the white world. Others warn of the folly of migrating to the urban North, where hardship and evil await. The last story in the collection, "Silas Jackson," could have been a prototype for the beginnings of James Weldon Johnson's

Autobiography of an Ex-Coloured Man (1912) and Ralph Ellison's *Invisible Man* (1952). Here, too, the young, country innocent has a vision of a better life, and, through a series of ever more blinding incidents involving white "benefactors" and black charlatans, he finds himself in New York City, where he thinks he has "made something of himself." Here Silas's fortunes take a characteristic Dunbarian turn, and he returns home "spent, broken, hopeless, all contentment and simplicity gone." Portending death more than reunion with "the old folks at home," it is an ambiguous, unsettling end to the collection.

The Heart of Happy Hollow

TYPE OF WORK: Short fiction
FIRST PUBLISHED: 1904

The stories of this collection take place during and after Reconstruction and are concerned with the strengths and weaknesses of the southern black community in the aftermath of slavery and the strained, even violent circumstances it was forced to endure as it claimed the benefits of freedom. "The Scapegoat" is Dunbar's most successful story about how African Americans were, and are, used as America's political pawns. It is also one of the first stories by a black writer to locate an alternate, undermining seat of power in the barbershop/newsstand. "The Lynching of Jube Benson" is Dunbar's other antilynching story, this one narrated by one of the lynchers, as in James Baldwin's work. Though its impact is fueled by sentiment, it is unrelenting and unforgiving in its indictment. Other stories, primarily for a black audience, warn of the dangers of boastfulness, vanity, cowardice, self-pity, class and color consciousness, and the reactionary fear of change and difference. Stories such as "The Promoter" and "The Boy and the Bayonet" reveal that Dunbar had discovered how to use humor and pathos without sacrificing his characters' humanity. At the time of his death, his strongest work was no longer in poetry but in short fiction, a genre that allowed him to be more realistic, relevant, and true to himself and his people.

Lyrics of Sunshine and Shadow

TYPE OF WORK: Poetry
FIRST PUBLISHED: 1905

The subjects of love and death are treated in Dunbar's lyrics of melancholy, one of the major moods found in the poet's lyrical verse. "Yesterday and To-morrow," in *Lyrics of Sunshine and Shadow*, is an example of Dunbar's lyric of melancholy. The mood of this poem is in the tradition of the British Romantic poets, particularly that of Wordsworth. Dunbar treats the melancholy feelings in this poem with tenderness and simplicity. The persona expresses disappointment with the untimeliness of life's events and the uncertainties of love. This scenario intimates a bleak future.

"Yesterday and To-morrow" is developed in three compact quatrains. Each quatrain envelops a primary emotion. The first stanza unfolds yesterday's contentment in love. The lover remembers the tender and blessed emotion of closeness with his lover: "And its gentle yieldingness/ From my soul I blessed it." The second stanza is reminiscent of the metaphysical questionings and imagery of Donne: "Must our gold forever know/ Flames for the refining?" The lovers' emotions are compared with precious metal undergoing the fire of refinement: Their feelings of sadness are released in this cynical question.

In the third quatrain, Dunbar feeds the sad heart with more cynicism. Returning to the feelings of disappointment and uncertainty, the persona concludes: "Life was all a lyric song/ Set to tricksy meter." The persona escapes in cynicism, but the poem still ends on a hopeless note.

SUGGESTED READINGS

Alexander, Eleanor. *Lyrics of Sunshine and Shadow: The Tragic Courtship and Marriage of Paul Laurence Dunbar and Alice Ruth Moore.* Albany: New York University Press, 2001.

Best, Felton O. *Crossing the Color Line: A Biography of Paul Laurence Dunbar.* Dubuque, Iowa: Kendall/Hunt, 1996.

Gentry, Tony. *Paul Laurence Dunbar: Poet.* Los Angeles: Melrose Square, 1993.

Hudson, Gossie Harold. *A Biography of Paul Laurence Dunbar.* Baltimore: Gateway Press, 1999.

McKissack, Patricia C. *Paul Laurence Dunbar: A Poet to Remember.* Chicago: Children's Press, 1984.

Martin, Jay, ed. *A Singer in the Dawn: Reinterpretations of Paul Laurence Dunbar.* New York: Dodd, Mead, 1975.

Turner, Darwin T. "Paul Laurence Dunbar: The Rejected Symbol." *Journal of Negro History* (January, 1967): 1-13.

Wiggins, Lida Keck. *The Life and Works of Paul Laurence Dunbar.* Nashville, Tenn.: Winston-Derek, 1992.

Contributors: Cynthia Packard Hill and Patricia A. R. Williams

Andrea Dworkin

BORN: Camden, New Jersey; September 26, 1946
DIED: Washington, D.C.; April 9, 2005

JEWISH

Dworkin, a radical feminist, presents alternative
views of sexuality and gender roles in society.

PRINCIPAL WORKS

LONG FICTION: *Ice and Fire*, 1986; *Mercy*, 1990
SHORT FICTION: *The New Woman's Broken Heart*, 1980
NONFICTION: *Woman Hating: A Radical Look at Sexuality*, 1974; *Our Blood: Prophecies and Discourses on Sexual Politics*, 1976; *Pornography: Men Possessing Women*, 1981; *Right-Wing Women*, 1983; *Intercourse*, 1987; *Pornography and Civil Rights: A New Day for Women's Equality*, 1988 (with Catharine A. MacKinnon); *Letters from a War Zone: Writings, 1976-1989*, 1989; *Life and Death: Unapologetic Writings on the Continuing War Against Women*, 1997; *Scapegoat: The Jews, Israel, and Women's Liberation*, 2000; *Heartbreak: The Political Memoir of a Feminist Militant*, 2002
EDITED TEXT: *In Harm's Way: The Pornography Civil Rights Hearings*, 1997 (with Catharine A. MacKinnon)

Andrea Dworkin (DWOHR-kihn) was born to left-wing Jewish parents. Inspired by the peace movement of the 1960's, she participated in a number of antiwar demonstrations. It was at one of these demonstrations that she had the experience that changed her life. At eighteen she was arrested and taken to the Women's House of Detention. Her treatment there was brutal: Bullying, harsh internal examinations, and authoritarian contempt left her emotionally and physically scarred. Released after four days, Dworkin hemorrhaged vaginally for two weeks.

Dworkin spoke out publicly about her trauma in an attempt to learn why any woman should be humiliated in so sexual a way. Her marriage to a Dutch anarchist awakened her to the reality of sexual violence in relationships; he beat her severely until she escaped from him with the help of feminist friends. She was an intelligent, educated woman who had been graduated from Bennington College, but she could not prevent herself from being hurt.

Dworkin describes her childhood as one that taught her to defy convention. As a Jewish child, she refused to sing Christmas carols such as "Silent Night" at school. When her brush with the law and her nightmarish marriage left her horrified by the status of women, she took action.

Woman Hating: A Radical Look at Sexuality, Dworkin's first major work, echoes the pain of her personal experiences of misogyny. Later books, such as *Our Blood: Prophecies and Discourses on Sexual Politics* and *Intercourse*, go further into the implications of the sexual act itself. Dworkin analyzed the historical perceptions of rape and possession and of the biology of sexual contact. She also studied pornographic magazines in an attempt to understand how women are demeaned by pornography; this work led to her involvement in the feminist antipornography movement and to her testimony before the Attorney General's Commission on Pornography (the Meese Commission) in January of 1986. Many critics found Dworkin's lack of makeup, her unflattering clothes, and her heaviness to be unattractive, and Dworkin consequently had to relate to a double standard of beauty that did not apply to male writers, no matter how equally polemical they were. Dworkin's focus was to enlighten women about gender roles in society. When, in 2000, she published articles in the *New Statesman* and in *The Guardian* charging that she had been raped in a Paris hotel room, many did not believe her and dismissed the accusations. She overcame an ensuing bout with depression to write again and left a final book, *Writing America: How Novelists Invented and Gendered a Nation*, unfinished upon her death of complications from acute myocarditis in 2005.

Intercourse

TYPE OF WORK: Essay
FIRST PUBLISHED: 1987

Intercourse, one of Andrea Dworkin's most powerful books on sexuality in a repressive culture, is about self-disgust and self-hatred. Dworkin's "Amerika" is the modern world or, rather, the world that lives within the modern American. In "Amerika," sex is good, and liking it is morally right. In "Amerika," sex is defined solely as vaginal penetration. In "Amerika," women are happy to be passive and accepting while their men are aggressive and demanding. *Intercourse* attempts to question the rigid sexual roles that define the male as literally and figuratively on top of the woman and the symbolic implications of sexual contact—entry, penetration, and occupation.

Intercourse, documenting a series of literary excerpts and comments by and for women, develops Dworkin's theory that sexual congress is an act in which, typically, men rape women. The book's theory is that because the penis of a man goes inside a woman during the sexual act, intercourse is a hostile act of occupation, ready to degenerate into gynocide and cannibalism. Dworkin describes a woman's individuality as being surrounded by her body and bordered by her skin. The privacy of the inner self is essential to understanding exactly who one is. Thus, having no boundaries between one's own body and the body of another makes one feel invaded and skinless. The experience of being skinless is the primary force behind "Amerika's" sexuality, since "Amerikan" sexuality relies so heavily on the man being superior or on top of the woman.

Strictly speaking, however, it is not only the act of heterosexual penetration that causes one to lose one's sense of individuality. In *Intercourse*, even lesbianism seems to be no answer to the repressive society that Dworkin describes. The "real privacy" of the body can be as violated by another woman's objectification of her lover as it can be by a heterosexual rape. So long as women can stay outside each other's skins, metaphorically speaking, then and only then will they escape sexual domination of one another. One of Dworkin's earlier books, *Woman Hating: A Radical Look at Sexuality*, described heterosexual contact as acceptable so long as men do not insist on the superiority of an erect penis. In *Intercourse*, even a flaccid member does not negate female suppression in the sexual act. Dworkin's preoccupation was the obscenity of the ordinary; she encouraged women to scrutinize what they may have originally thought to be harmless, even trivial.

SUGGESTED READINGS

Allen, Amy. "Pornography and Power." *Journal of Social Philosophy* 32 (Winter, 2001): 512-531.

Blakely, Mary Kay. "Is One Woman's Sexuality Another Woman's Pornography?" *Ms.* 13 (April, 1985): 37-38.

Dworkin, Andrea. Letter to *The New York Times Book Review*, May 3, 1992, 15-16.

Eberly, Rosa A. *Citizen Critics: Literary Public Spheres*. Urbana: University of Illinois Press, 2000.

Green, Karen. "De Sade, de Beauvoir, and Dworkin." *Australian Feminist Studies* 15 (March, 2000): 69-81.

Jenefsky, Cindy. *Without Apology: Andrea Dworkin's Art and Politics*. Boulder, Colo.: Westview Press, 1998.

O'Driscoll, Sally. "Andrea Dworkin: Guilt Without Sex." *The Village Voice*, July 15-21, 1981.

Pagnaterro, Marisa Anne. "The Importance of Andrea Dworkin's *Mercy:* Mitigating Circumstances and Narrative Jurisprudence." *Frontiers* 19, no. 1 (1998): 147-166.

Palczewski, Catherine Helen. "Contesting Pornography: Terministic Catharsis and Definitional Argument." *Argumentation and Advocacy* 38 (Summer, 2001): 1-16.

Contributor: Julia M. Meyers

Cornelius Eady

BORN: Rochester, New York; January 7, 1954

AFRICAN AMERICAN

Emerging from the generation of African American
poets after the Black Arts movement, Eady explored his
working-class upbringing and his position as a black
poet in late twentieth century America.

PRINCIPAL WORKS

DRAMA: *Running Man*, pr. 1999 (libretto)

POETRY: *Kartunes*, 1980; *Victims of the Latest Dance Craze*, 1985; *BOOM BOOM BOOM*, 1988 (limited edition chapbook); *The Gathering of My Name*, 1991; *You Don't Miss Your Water*, 1995; *The Autobiography of a Jukebox*, 1996; *Brutal Imagination*, 2001

EDITED TEXTS: *Words for Breakfast*, 1998 (with Meg Kearney, Norma Fox Mazer, and Jacqueline Woodson); *Vinyl Donuts*, 2000 (with Kearney, Mazer, and Woodson)

Born in Rochester, New York, Cornelius Eady (EE-dee) began writing poems when he was only twelve. As chronicled in *You Don't Miss Your Water*, Eady's father posed a formidable emotional problem. High-school educated, the father, employed by the city water department, had difficulty accepting literature as a valid vocation. Consequently, Eady would struggle with feelings of estrangement until his father's death in 1993.

After graduating from Empire State College and then earning his M.F.A. from Warren Wilson College, Eady held teaching appointments at Sweet Briar College, the College of William and Mary, Sarah Lawrence College, Tougaloo College, and City College of New York. He was in the first generation of African American poets to succeed the formidable work of the Black Arts movement of the mid-twentieth century. That literary movement, an extension of the era's Civil Rights movement, created new interest in black identity. Eady continued that exploration, using his own working-class upbringing and his position as a black poet in late twentieth century America. That compelling honesty, coupled with his experiments in the sheer music of language, garnered Eady nominations for the Pulitzer Prize; he won the Lamont Prize from the Academy of American Poets in 1985.

While at the State University of New York at Stony Brook in the 1990's, he served as director of its famous poetry center. In 1999, Eady became distinguished writer-in-residence in the M.F.A. program at New York City's innovative New

School. In 1996, along with poet Toi Derricotte, Eady founded the Cave Canem (literally, "Beware of the Dog"), a popular program of summer workshops for African American poets.

Eady's poetry concerns the construction of identity, the dynamics of memory and reflection as part of the interrogation of the self, and the importance of recording that complex process. Like the blues, Eady's poetry centers on the struggle to define the isolated self within a chaotic world that harbors little possibility for redemption. Yet, like jazz, Eady's poetry also responds to a world that, given its essential unpredictability, can sustain authentic ecstasy. That texture, the self sustained between sadness and exuberance, is central to Eady's work. His poetry explores the roles he himself has played in the construction of his own identity. Not surprisingly, over the time Eady has been writing, this interrogation of the self has become more complex. Initially, Eady explored his role as urban poet; later, he examined more complex relational roles, that of husband, lover, teacher, and, supremely, son; he later began to confront his role as an African American, specifically the struggle to construct a viable black self amid the historical and social pressures of late twentieth century America.

The poetic line for such an investigation into the self is appropriately individual and resists conventional expectations of structure and sound. Rhythmic but not metric, Eady's lines can appear deceptively simple, direct, even conversational. However, it is freedom within a tightly manipulated form. Like improvisational jazz, which can, at first hearing, seem easy and effortless, Eady's poetry is a complex aural event. His poems consciously manipulate sounds, unexpected syncopations and cadences, enjambment, irregular spacings and emphasis, line length, and sound repetition to create an air of improvisation that is nevertheless a carefully textured sonic weave.

Given his willingness to experiment with bringing to the written word the rhythms of both jazz and blues and his belief in poetry as performed (that is, heard) art, it is not surprising that Eady would produced experimental theater pieces as part of a projected trilogy for the New York City-based Music-Theater Group; these involved original scores written by jazz cellist and longtime friend Diedre L. Murray. The first production, in 1997, was a staged recitation based on *You Don't Miss Your Water*, Eady's cycle of prose poems that recounts his father's death. In 1999 Eady provided the libretto for an experimental jazz opera based on the story of Murray's brother, a gifted man lost to a life of crime and heroin addiction. That production, *Running Man*, won two Obie Awards and was short-listed for both the New York Drama Critics Circle Award and the Pulitzer Prize. In 2001, *Brutal Imagination* was a finalist for the National Book Award in Poetry. Having taught at a number of prestigious universities, Eady was teaching at the University of Notre Dame in 2007.

Kartunes

TYPE OF WORK: Poetry
FIRST PUBLISHED: 1980

Kartunes is a portrait of the self as young poet, an exercise in testing the reach of the imagination and celebrating the role of a cocksure poet responding originally to the world. "I want to be fresh," he proclaims, "I want words/ to tumble off my lips/ rich enough/ to fertilize/ the ground." Giddy with imaginative possibilities, Eady improvises his narrative "I" into outlandish personas (the "cartoons" suggested by the title), many culled from pop culture: He is at turns an inept terrorist, a nerdy librarian, an unhappy woman forced into a witness protection program, a dying philanthropist anxious about the approaching afterlife, a man contemplating torching his own house, the legendary Headless Horseman selecting the appropriate pumpkin to hurtle, Popeye's nemesis Bluto groomed for a date, even Adolf Hitler posing before a mirror and dreaming of greatness.

Given such wild fluctuations in the narrative center, the poetry is given over to irreverent exuberance. Despite often centering on alienated characters existing within a contemporary environment of absurdity and brutality, the poems resist surrendering to emotional heaviness. The poems, themselves innovative in structure and sound (witness the wordplay of the collection's title), offer as resolutions the sheer animation of the engaged imagination, the possibility of love, and the ability of the world to stun with its unchoreographed wonder. With the confident insouciance of a young man, Eady argues that nothing is nobler than "laughing/ when nothing/ is funny anymore."

Victims of the Latest Dance Craze

TYPE OF WORK: Poetry
FIRST PUBLISHED: 1985

The interest in defining the poet and that confident sense of play animate Eady's follow-up collection, thematically centered on the metaphor of the dance. Here the world is in constant motion—the title poem, for example, details a pulsating urban neighborhood. Like William Carlos Williams (whose influence Eady has acknowledged), the poet responds to the seductive suasion of the world that too often goes unnoticed—to a cloud passing overhead, crows battling a strong wind, a waitress's purple nail polish, the leaden feel of November, the faint stirrings of April: "an entire world," he trumpets, "on the tip of my tongue." To respond to that world is to dance, a suggestive metaphor for the body's irresistible, spontaneous response to being alive, the electric moment of the "hands . . ./ Accidentally brush[ing] against the skirts of the world." Such animation makes problematic the life of the poet so vital in *Kartunes*.

In the closing poem, "Dance at the Amherst County Public Library," the poet describes himself as a "dancing fool who couldn't stay away from words." He concedes his jealousy over those who live so effortlessly and of his own poor efforts to capture secondhand that rich experience within his poetry, his "small graffiti dance." Yet the poetic lines here boldly strive to match the urgent call to respond originally to the world, capturing the improvisational feel of jazz: irregular patterning of lines, multiple stops and starts, a delightful matching of sounds, and wildly unanticipated rhythms.

The Gathering of My Name
TYPE OF WORK: Poetry
FIRST PUBLISHED: 1991

In Eady's ambitious third major collection, the tone considerably darkens as jazz gives way to the slower pull of the blues. In the opening poem, "Gratitude," Eady audaciously proffers love to those who have not welcomed him nor his poetry and confesses his greatest weakness is his "inability/ to sustain rage." It is a familiar brashness, and, indeed, the second poem ("Grace") offers one of those unexpected moments when the world sparkles: the sight of the neighborhood reflected in the waxed hood of a black sedan.

Yet quickly the poems concede to a more disturbing world that crushes dreams and sours love. For the first time, Eady addresses race. Poems introduce figures such as the tormented blues singer Leadbelly or jazz great John Coltrane in the aftermath of the 1963 bombing of a Baptist church in Birmingham, Alabama. In others, a waitress in Virginia refuses to serve a black man, a passing motorist hurls racial epithets at a black man's white wife, a car breaks down in the "wrong" neighborhood. Like the blues, these are poems of pain and bad luck, the curse of awareness, the dilemma of disappointment, and the need to define the self in a harsh world. What is the poet to do? "Get it all out," Eady demands in "The Sheets of Sounds," the remarkable closing piece that is a tour de force of metrical audacity. Here, Eady captures in language the technical virtuosity and improvisational sound of Coltrane himself: "What do I have to lose,/ Actually,/ By coming right out/ And saying/ What I mean/ To say?" Honesty then compels the poet/jazz artist to let loose the spirit in all its outrage, to push art if only for a moment into uncompromising expression, the "loud humility" of a man giving himself the right to claim, as a refrain insists with typographical variations: "This is who I am."

You Don't Miss Your Water
TYPE OF WORK: Poetry
FIRST PUBLISHED: 1995

Appropriately, then, in Eady's fourth collection readers feel (for the first time in his work) the nearness of the poet himself. Dropping his elaborate personas,

Cornelius Eady (© Miriam Berkley)

Eady speaks forthrightly of his own life. The twenty-one prose poems are stark narratives without poetic frills and without clean chronological sequencing. The reader is given an unblinking record of a son's estrangement from a father in the face of mortality, the honest struggle to come to terms with the difficult wisdom of the blues lines, "You don't miss your water/ 'til your well runs dry." Eady refuses to sentimentalize the father (he is at turns miserly, stubborn, distant, even unfaithful) or himself (he cremates the body to save money), or even death (he records the indignities of hospital treatment and the impersonal efficiency of agencies that manage the paperwork). Titles recall traditional blues songs, and the mood is elegiac, sobering, eloquent: "This is how life, sharpened to a fine point, plunges into what we call hope."

If Eady's first three volumes speak of how the imagination takes hold of the world and shapes individual identity, here he acknowledges the depth of the inevitable experience of loss and how that experience is as well part of any construction of identity. In the volume's rich closing poem, "Paradiso," Eady decides that language itself, disparaged in his earlier work as secondhand graffiti, is the sole conjurer of the afterlife, that the "key to any heaven is language."

The Autobiography of a Jukebox

TYPE OF WORK: Poetry
FIRST PUBLISHED: 1996

The Autobiography of a Jukebox is a kind of summary text. It is divided into four sections, each of which centers on themes drawn from earlier works: the heavy intrusion of loss; the ugly realities of racism; the glorious transcendence of art, specifically jazz, within this environment of oppression; and those small unexpected moments that trigger deep emotional responses and make such a world endurable. The volume begins where *You Don't Miss Your Water* ends: dealing with harsh loss—indeed, opening poems linger within recollections of Eady's father. With bluesy feel, other poems follow characters who discover the wounding of love, the certainty of bad luck, and the humiliations of poverty.

In the second section, Eady confronts the angry indignation over the 1991 beating of citizen Rodney King by Los Angeles police officers, the federal trial in which the white officers were acquitted, and the riots that followed. It is Eady's first lengthy examination of the social dimension of the self and specifically how black identity must be defined within an oppressive white culture. To maintain dignity and to touch grace within such an environment, Eady offers in the third section portraits of jazz artists (and pioneer rocker Chuck Berry), black musicians who forged from such oppression the stuff of their art: "What/ Hurts is beautiful, the bruise/ Of the lyric." However, it is not sufficient simply to relish such aesthetic artifacts.

In the closing section Eady quietly affirms what his first two volumes trumpeted: the imagination's ability to be stunned by the accidental encounter with something that triggers a minor epiphany in a flawed world that still permits awe—a woman with dreadlocks crossing a street, a tray of cornbread at a posh reception, the electric flow of an urban mall, the tangy smells of a bakery. Yet, hard on the death of Eady's father and the anger over the King beating, these slender moments of grace are suddenly significant in ways the earlier volumes could not suggest.

Brutal Imagination

TYPE OF WORK: Poetry
FIRST PUBLISHED: 2001

In *Brutal Imagination* Eady's career-long interest in defining the self takes on new maturity as he projects himself, within two unrelated poem cycles, out of the matrix of his own experience. In the first section Eady conjures the spirit, and voice, of the black kidnapper that mother Susan Smith invented as an alibi to cover the 1994 murder of her two infant sons. Eady uses that lie to investigate the white culture of anger, bigotry, and anxiety within which all black identity must be fashioned. In a biting middle section, Eady suggests the dimensions of this dilemma by giving voice to the sorry racist stereotypes fashioned by a white imagination unwilling to grant blacks the dignity and complexity of legitimate selfhood: Uncle Tom, Uncle Ben, Aunt Jemina, Buckwheat, Stepin Fetchit. The faux-kidnapper—witty, articulate, probing, caring—dominates the cycle and, specifically, the symbiotic relationship between Smith and her invention, Eady suggesting how necessary the black stereotype is for whites. In the closing poem, "Birthing," which draws excerpts from Smith's actual confession, the conjured kidnapper extends compassion to the mother, imagining the actual killing and the desperate loneliness of Smith herself driven to do the unimaginable.

The second section contains pieces from the libretto of *Running Man*. Although offered without the haunting jazz score of the original production and without the dramatic interplay of performance, the pieces nevertheless succeed in a conjuring of a sort far different from Susan Smith's. A southern black family, devastated by the death of its only son, struggles to explain why such a promising young man succumbed to the very life of crime that made credible the vicious lie of Susan Smith.

Within the interplay of their elegiac recollections, the poetic line tightly clipped for maximum effect, the young man himself is conjured and speaks of his own promise lost to the anger of limited social expectations within the white system and to the easy out of drug addiction and crime. He is the "running man" never sure where he was running from or to: "Where I come from/ A smart black boy/ Is like being a cat/ With a duck's bill." Chained to history—the cycle begins in an old slave cemetery—blacks, whatever their talent or aspirations, must withstand the larger predatory white culture that can leave them helpless, like "fish, scooped from a pond." It is a powerful assessment of black identity at the twentieth century's close.

SUGGESTED READINGS

Carroll, Rebecca. *Swing Low: Black Men Writing*. New York: Carol Southern Books, 1995.

Harper, Michael S., and Anthony Walton, eds. *Every Shut Eye Ain't Asleep: An Anthology of Poetry by African Americans Since 1945*. Boston: Little, Brown, 1994.

Hawkins, Shayla. "Cave Canem: A Haven for Black Poets." *Poets & Writers* 29, no. 2 (March/April, 2001): 48-53.

Quashie, Kevin Everod. "Cornelius Eady." In *New Bones: Contemporary Black Writers in America*, edited by Joyce Lausch, Keith Miller, and Quashie. Saddle River, N.J.: Prentice-Hall, 2001.

Young, Kevin, ed. *Giant Steps: The New Generation of African-American Writers*. New York: Perennial, 2000.

Contributor: Joseph Dewey

Lonne Elder III

BORN: Americus, Georgia; December 26, 1931
DIED: Woodland Hills, California; June 11, 1996

AFRICAN AMERICAN

Elder's Ceremonies in Dark Old Men *dissects the love and power relations within a family, revealing the adverse situation of African Americans living in a racially torn nation.*

PRINCIPAL WORKS

DRAMA: *Ceremonies in Dark Old Men*, pr. 1965 (revised pr., pb. 1969); *Charades on East Fourth Street*, pr. 1967, pb. 1971 (one act); *Splendid Mummer*, pr. 1988
SCREENPLAYS: *Melinda*, 1972; *Sounder*, 1972 (adaptation of William H. Armstrong's novel); *Sounder, Part Two*, 1976; *Bustin' Loose*, 1981 (with Richard Pryor and Roger L. Simon; adaptation of a story by Pryor)
TELEPLAYS: *Camera Three*, 1963 season; *The Terrible Veil*, 1963; *N.Y.P.D.*, 1967-1968 season; *McCloud*, 1970-1971; *Ceremonies in Dark Old Men*, 1975 (adaptation of his play); *A Woman Called Moses*, 1978 (miniseries based on Marcy Heidish's book); *The Negro Ensemble Company*, 1987
NONFICTION: "Comment: Rambled Thoughts," in *Black Creation*, 1973; "Lorraine Hansberry: Social Consciousness and the Will," in *Freedomways*, 1979

Lonne Elder III (LAH-nee EHL-dur) was born in Americus, Georgia, on December 26, 1931, to Lonne Elder II and Quincy Elder. While he was still an infant, his family moved to New York and New Jersey. He was orphaned at the age of ten and ended up living with relatives on a New Jersey farm. Rural life, however, was not for him, and, after he ran away a few times, he was sent to live with his uncle, a numbers runner, in Jersey City.

In 1949, Elder entered New Jersey State Teachers College, where he stayed less than a year. He then moved to New York City and took courses at the Jefferson School and the New School for Social Research, while becoming involved in the movement for social equality for black people. In 1952, he was drafted into the United States Army. While stationed near Fisk University, in Nashville, Tennessee, he met the poet and playwright Robert Hayden, who encouraged Elder with his writing.

Back in New York City in 1953, Elder shared an apartment with the aspiring playwright Douglas Turner Ward and began studying acting. Supporting himself through jobs as a dockworker, waiter, and poker dealer, among other things, he pursued his acting career, appearing on Broadway in 1959 in *A Raisin in the Sun* and with the Negro Ensemble Company (cofounded by Ward) in Ward's play *Day of Absence* (pr. 1965). During this time, he met such prominent black writers as Lorraine Hansberry and John Oliver Killens, married Betty Gross (in 1963), and wrote his first play. This work, "A Hysterical Turtle in a Rabbit Race," written in 1961 but never performed or published, broached Elder's favored topic of how a black family can be pulled apart by prejudice and false standards.

In 1965, his masterpiece, *Ceremonies in Dark Old Men*, was performed, earning for him fame and critical success. Along with his other ventures, such as writing television scripts for such shows as *N.Y.P.D.* and *McCloud*, it netted for him a number of awards and honors, including a fellowship to the Yale School of Drama in 1966-1967. His next play to be produced was the one-act *Charades on East Fourth Street*, which did not have the impact of his previous drama. It was performed in 1967.

In 1970, sick of New York City, Elder moved with his second wife, Judith Ann Johnson, whom he had married in 1969, to California. He was hoping to improve the depiction of African Americans in Hollywood productions, and he did just that in his screenplay *Sounder* in 1972. After the critical success of this film, he continued working in the industry, producing more serious work about black life and tradition, such as his follow-up television script *Sounder, Part Two* (1976) and his television presentation about Harriet Ross Tubman, *A Woman Called Moses* (1978), as well as writing an occasional comedy, such as the 1981 Richard Pryor film *Bustin' Loose*.

In 1988, Elder returned briefly to the theater with *Splendid Mummer*, a historical play about a black expatriate actor who left the United States in the 1820's to practice his art in Europe. The play was liked by critics but was not a popular success and was not published. Elder continued to be primarily devoted to his goal of working in television and film to provide a positive and realistic view of African American life until his death in 1996.

Ceremonies in Dark Old Men
TYPE OF WORK: Drama
FIRST PRODUCED: 1965, pb. 1969

Elder's *Ceremonies in Dark Old Men* deals with the survival of the black family under duress. For Elder, the family is not a collection of autonomous individuals but a dynamic set of relationships. In *Ceremonies in Dark Old Men*, Elder focuses on how each family member's decisions crucially hinge on the words and actions of each other member. The playwright indicates, moreover, that under stressful conditions the equilibrium of such a black family is a fragile thing, because the family is a working unit in a larger society that is controlled by white people to the disadvantage of black persons. The drama records how, under increasing pressure, the family disintegrates in some ways while it grows in others. Thus, Elder combines social criticism with a subtle look at the inner workings of families.

In much of post-World War II American theater, including such works as Arthur Miller's *Death of a Salesman* (pr., pb. 1949) and Tennessee Williams's *The Glass Menagerie* (pr. 1944, pb. 1945), the family is portrayed as entrapping and destructive of individualism. The family may stifle a son by forcing him to support it, as in Williams's play, or it may ruin his life by giving him false views, as happens to Biff in Miller's work; in either case, however, the family is inimical to self-reliance. By contrast, in *Ceremonies in Dark Old Men*, each family member has a role that is both constricting and sustaining, while each member either grows or diminishes as a result of the family's overall adaptation to the outside world.

At first sight, the family in Elder's play is organized in stereotypical "culture of poverty" fashion, with a female, the daughter Adele, being the de facto head of the house, since she supports the other, male family members. The two sons with the father, the nominal ruler of the house, are shiftless characters; the father, Russell, presides over a defunct barbershop, while his elder son, Theo, is a hapless loser, and the younger one, Bobby, a sneak thief. As the story develops, however, the audience learns that the three are not as parasitical as they first appeared. The father, for example, had been the mainstay of the family, earning a living as a professional dancer until his legs failed and he was unceremoniously dropped from his place. When viewers see the father returning from a day of job-hunting humiliation, they also learn that, as an over-the-hill black man, he has little hope of finding work.

The thrust of the play, however, is not to exonerate any individual but to show that the current operation of the family is, given the way the odds are stacked against prosperity for minority group members, probably the best possible. This view is shown by the simple, but fundamental, device of ending the first act with the beginning of a basic change in the household arrangements (as Theo sets up a viable, if illegal, business) and then jumping ahead a few months for the second act. In this way, in the second act, the audience can see how Theo's changed status, as he takes on a more manly role in the family and supports the others by working long hours, affects the personalities and actions of each of the others, often adversely. Adele, for example, no longer having to bear tremendous responsibility, lets herself go, running around with a notorious skirt chaser. Bobby, who never felt threatened by his brother, since Theo was as ambitionless as he was, now begins sullenly competing with him, becoming a big-time hoodlum.

This is not to say that, because there is more tension in the family after Theo begins working than previously, the old organization was better. Rather, Elder indicates—especially toward the end of the second act, when the family begins to calm down and Adele gives up her playboy boyfriend—that each set of family relationships is highly interdependent and serves as an essential means to help the members orient themselves to the outside world. Elder also indicates that each transition between different familial "steady states" will involve special periods of stress.

In his plays, it is clear that Elder is critical of the position that black persons are forced to occupy in the American economy, and it also may be evident that his anger is more latent than expressed. Rather than have his characters complain about the system, he makes the audience experience the constant feeling of failure that hovers over a family whose members are not fully employed, especially when, to a large degree, their unemployment is not their fault. In relation to one character, however, Elder's social criticism is less oblique. This character, Blue Haven, is a self-styled black activist, who, curiously, is not interested in fighting injustice and oppression through protests and political action; rather, he prefers to steal the clients of white people's liquor and gambling establishments by setting up bootleg and numbers operations of his own. In this portrayal, Elder reveals a satirical side to his talent and shows that he is as critical of black persons as he is of white ones, insofar as he shows that black residents of Harlem are more interested in supporting Blue Haven's "enterprises" than the businesses run by more bona fide progressives.

Elder's treatment of this character also reveals another point about his methods. Throughout most of the play, Blue Haven obtains little sympathy from the audience, being not only a sharper but also a hypocrite. Yet in a powerful monologue that he delivers in a confrontation with Theo, who accuses Blue Haven of exploiting him, Blue Haven presents his own tortured dreams, showing that he is capable of much deeper feeling than it would have been thought possible. This emotional monologue lifts him in the audience's estimation and establishes Elder's goal of giving every character his or her due.

The generosity in Elder's treatment of his characters, seen not only in the way he allows each to develop a voice but also in his mutualistic conception of the family, does have certain drawbacks. As none of the characters is larger than the others, none, in this tale of wrecked hopes, gains the type of tragic stature obtained by the leading characters in the Williams and Miller plays mentioned above. That is to say, none has the broken splendor of a Willy Loman, because, as each family member's choices are heavily dependent on others' situations, no character ever has to face the anxiety of bearing total responsibility for his or her actions. Thus, a character can never rise to the grandeur associated with an acceptance of such responsibility. Furthermore, as a number of critics have noted, Elder's evenhandedness sometimes hints at a distance between him and his creations, since his equal treatment of each problem reveals that he was not aroused by any of his characters' tribulations. Such an attitude can lead to the pathos and power of a given dramatic situation not being fully asserted.

One compensation for these drawbacks is compassion. Elder refuses to make any of his characterizations, even of such comic figures as Blue Haven, into caricatures. He extends to each a measure of respect and understanding. Further, Elder's undistorted, accepting view of his characters and their world matches their general realism. His characters are aware of their own and others' limitations and are largely accustomed to, though hurt by, their social inferiority. The family members tend to treat each new vicissitude with relatively good humor. Thus, near the end of the first act, when everyone is momentarily glum about future prospects, the father, having leeringly accepted Theo's proposal that he work with Blue Haven but being none too happy about it, engages in a little tap dancing. Although his steps are clumsy, the boys cheer him on, caught up in their infectious attempt to celebrate a dubious alliance. The frequent joking of the father and sons works to this same end, lightening the burdens they must bear.

Charades on East Fourth Street

TYPE OF WORK: Drama
FIRST PRODUCED: 1967, pb. 1971

Elder's ability to create a multisided situation is found in his other published drama, *Charades on East Fourth Street*. This play belongs to a genre, delved into by black playwrights of the 1960's, that might be called "ritual drama." Ritual dramas were a component of the rebellious Black Arts movement that emphasized theater as a social ritual, such as the Catholic Mass, that worked to renew symbolically a society's cohesion. These works provided a way of going back to the sources of theater, as is evident in such dramas as the medieval mystery plays. Ritual dramas retold the story of Christ's passion, and, as the centerpiece of a worldview, its reenactment served to rededicate viewers to a common purpose as they reempathized with their binding social myth. Numerous modern authors, such as T. S. Eliot, have turned back to the roots of drama, but African American writers often gave this turn a perverse twist.

One of the most brilliant of the black writers' ritual dramas was *Dutchman* (pr., pb. 1964) by LeRoi Jones (who later changed his name to Amiri Baraka). In this play, a black college student flirts with an initially willing white woman on a subway, but the game turns ugly, and she stabs him. All the other white passengers join her in disposing of the corpse. The ritual, then, is the sacrifice of a young African American male, portrayed as the glue holding together white society. Thus, *Dutchman*, pretending to reveal white America's ideological foundations, actually serves up an indictment of how, it claims, the United States can unite only by scapegoating its minorities.

It may be surmised from this plot recapitulation that such plays could easily become shrill. Although this is not the case with *Dutchman*, because of the author's use of three-dimensional characters, with the woman becoming a fury only in the last minutes, the same cannot be said for Elder's *Charades on East Fourth Street*. At points, his characters grow strident when they lecture one another about police brutality. This short play revolves around the actions of a band of black youths who have kidnapped a white policeman who they believe is guilty of raping a teenage girl. Then, in keeping with the title, *Charades on East Fourth Street*, the youths force the officer to act out a series of degrading scenes. For example, they strip him and put him in bed with a teenage girl, saying that they will send photographs to his wife. It can be seen that, in this sexual charade, he is acting out the same part that he supposedly plays in his oppression of the African American community.

As the play progresses, it grows more complex. It turns out, for example, that the gang has grabbed the wrong police officer. Furthermore, the audience learns that the majority of these black teenagers are not convinced of the utility of this kidnapping and are involved in it only because they have been pressured into acting by their leader. In a short (one-act) play such as this one, however, there is no room for excessive ambiguity. The fact that Elder does not give his black revolutionaries much conviction—the kind of fanaticism that Baraka's characters often display—

takes the wind out of the story's sails. Without the time to develop the gang's interplay or the anger to make the play an indictment, Elder heroically fails at a genre for which he has no aptitude.

It could be said that Elder's lack of success at agitational drama indicates that, for him, to write well he must follow his bent, which comes from depicting the complexity of characters and the networks they form. His defense of the African American family in his most important play, *Ceremonies in Dark Old Men*, does not rest on any encomiums of individual family members' virtues but on an insistence on the value of the family as a mechanism offering support and solidarity in the face of a hostile society. The worth of Elder's works lies in the evocative power of his affirmation, which itself rests on a sophisticated analysis of how a family functions as one, composed of the relationships of people rather than of people standing alone.

SUGGESTED READINGS

Eckstein, George. "Softened Voices in the Black Theater." *Dissent* 23 (Summer, 1976): 306-308.

Elder, Judyann. "*Ceremonies* Marks Tribute to Black History Month: Judyann Elder Directs Husband's Classic Play That Offers Sad but Hopeful Statement." Interview by Janice Arkatov. *Los Angeles Times*, February 5, 1988, p. 12.

Hay, Samuel A. *Ed Bullins: A Literary Biography*. Detroit, Mich.: Wayne State University Press, 1997.

Jeffers, Lance. "Bullins, Baraka, and Elder: The Dawn of Grandeur in Black Drama." *CLA Journal* 16 (September, 1972): 32-48.

Oliver, Myrna. "Lonne Elder III: Award-Winning Writer." *Los Angeles Times*, June 14, 1996, p. 28.

Contributor: James Feast

Stanley Elkin

BORN: Brooklyn, New York; May 11, 1930
DIED: St. Louis, Missouri; May 31, 1995

JEWISH

Through dark humor and inventive use of language,
Elkin captures a unique Jewish American identity.

PRINCIPAL WORKS

LONG FICTION: *Boswell: A Modern Comedy*, 1964; *A Bad Man*, 1967; *The Dick Gibson Show*, 1971; *The Franchiser*, 1976; *George Mills*, 1982; *Stanley Elkin's the Magic Kingdom*, 1985 (also known as *The Magic Kingdom*); *The Rabbi of Lud*, 1987; *The MacGuffin*, 1991; *Mrs. Ted Bliss*, 1995

SCREENPLAY: *The Six-Year-Old Man*, 1968

SHORT FICTION: *Criers and Kibitzers, Kibitzers and Criers*, 1965; *The Making of Ashenden*, 1972; *Searches and Seizures*, 1973; *The Living End*, 1979; *Stanley Elkin's Greatest Hits*, 1980; *Early Elkin*, 1985; *Van Gogh's Room at Arles: Three Novellas*, 1993

NONFICTION: *Why I Live Where I Live*, 1983; *Pieces of Soap: Essays*, 1992

Stanley Elkin (EHL-kihn) wrote darkly humorous works. About half of his characters are Jewish, mostly secular Jews. Many of them, however, resist assimilation into mainstream American life. In his short stories and novels, Elkin establishes Jewish identity in two major ways: He captures Jewish humor through the unique intonations of Jewish American speech, and he casts his characters in professions often entered by Jewish men.

A consummate stylist, Elkin often presents his characters as caught between their religious heritage, which they consider anachronistic and from which they have distanced themselves, and late twentieth century American society, into which they refuse to integrate. To repair a tattered self-image, the gentile protagonist in *Boswell: A Modern Comedy* forms a club for famous and successful people; he then cannot sacrifice his individuality by joining.

Although Elkin considered himself a novelist, *Criers and Kibitzers, Kibitzers and Criers*, which clearly established his identity as a Jewish writer, caused many readers and some critics to consider Elkin essentially as a short-story writer. Elkin clearly established his identity as a novelist, however, by producing more than ten novels.

Aside from *Criers and Kibitzers, Kibitzers and Criers*, about half of whose stories treat Jewish subjects, Elkin deals with Jews and Jewish themes in a number of his other books. *A Bad Man* focuses on Leo Feldman, a department store owner hemmed in by a crazy father and a tedious son. In "The Condominium," a novella in *Searches and Seizures*, Elkin focuses on shiva, the Jewish funeral rite.

In *The Franchiser*, Elkin puts Ben Flesh, adopted by Julius Finsberg during the Depression, into an unbelievable family of eighteen twins and triplets, all afflicted with degenerative diseases. In *George Mills*, however, in which the protagonists are gentile, Elkin sacrifices ethnic identity for universality.

The Franchiser

TYPE OF WORK: Novel
FIRST PUBLISHED: 1976

The protagonist of *The Franchiser* suffers from multiple sclerosis, a disease that deteriorates the nervous system. Between attacks of the disease, Ben Flesh roams the American landscape, "the packed masonry of states," looking after the massive network of franchises he has built upon an inheritance from his godfather, Julius Finsberg, an industrial kingpin. What Ben inherits from Finsberg, who has cheated Ben's father out of his share of a successful business, is not a substantial sum of money but the prime interest rate—"Not money but the use of money." With the low interest rates of the preinflationary 1960's, Ben is able to build up a financial empire consisting entirely of franchises—Fred Astaire Dance Studios, Kentucky Fried Chicken restaurants, Baskin-Robbins Ice Cream parlors. In fact, Ben has his hand in literally every franchise in the United States. Along with the interest rate, Ben has inherited a responsibility for Finsberg's children, eighteen in all. Like Ben, each of the Finsbergs suffers from an incurable disease, which is their physical inheritance from old Julius, bearer of bad genes. As he invests their money in his franchises, Ben becomes a lover to each of the Finsberg daughters and a confidant to each son, so that, between Ben and the children, business and familial relationships are interchangeable.

In his ramblings, Flesh might be seen as a reader and interpreter of cultural signs. He observes the minute phenomena of the human world and attempts to make connections between the scattered manifestations of life and death. Ben spends a lot of time with Patty Finsberg, who refers to herself as "The Insight Lady" because she is obsessed with the parallels to be drawn among disparate cultural events. While some of her insights are breathtaking, it is clear that Patty is paranoically concerned with "connections." From her, Ben learns that there is order in disorder, contradiction in synthesis. Flesh as a character is, then, like a reader of his own novel, who interprets his life and observations as a commentator might discuss the patterns and repetitions of a fiction. Then, too, Flesh is like a writer: As a franchiser, he both organizes and disseminates the separated units of his financial network. Almost continually in physical discomfort and confronting the visible evidence of his own death, Flesh looks outward, on life, for the external order that will confer meaning upon his existence.

Elkin has always been interested in the exaggerated peculiarities of the individual vision and voice; he is a master of intonation and nuance. Perhaps no other contemporary writer has so successfully captured the varied lifestyles and patois of contemporary Americans as they have been affected by the avid consumerism of their culture.

The MacGuffin

TYPE OF WORK: Novel
FIRST PUBLISHED: 1991

Set in a large unnamed American city in the Midwest that seems much like St. Louis, *The MacGuffin* is the story of some two days in the life of Bobbo Druff, commissioner of streets. The novel successfully functions on many levels; it exhibits a multifaceted complexity in that it is the story of a family, a love intrigue of the husband with mistress, a murder mystery, a tale of smuggling, and a political statement. While being all of these, it is mostly about Bobbo Druff and "The MacGuffin," his psychological other and controlling self.

Bobbo Druff, the narrator and main character of the story, is truly the only subject of this complex novel that has so many other threads and aspects. He represents the modern American, and his life embodies, for Elkin at least, life in America in the 1990's. He is materialistic and corrupt; he is neurotic, psychotic, and schizophrenic (and, importantly, justly so); he is intellectual, witty, and smart; he is hopelessly middle-class; he finds relief in life by incessantly getting high on coca leaves and taking at least four different prescription medicines; he is both humor and pathos—a strangely correct mixture.

Elkin's main purpose is to reveal the hopeless and meaningless entanglements of life in the United States in the 1990's—for the thinking and thoughtless alike. There is no escape from problems, no solution to them, only an awareness of facts that add up to craziness (a matter blended with humor and bitterness) in a world in which borderline insanity is necessary for survival. Bobbo Druff is not, however, insane; he is victimized by society

Stanley Elkin (© Miriam Berkley)

and politics and legalities—but yet entirely by self. Survival requires some control of the system in which one lives. For Druff and other characters, that system is corrupt, somehow defunct yet going on anyway.

The MacGuffin succeeds in making significant and correct statements about modern politics. The global situation is so involved that even such traditional enemies as the Arabs and Jews cannot disentangle themselves from the complexity of the various problems. They depend upon one another to have someone to hate, to have an enemy; just as certainly and more important, however, they depend upon one another to fund and sustain their own problems and hatreds.

Local politics, as exemplified by Druff, the mayor, other commissioners, and even the two chauffeurs, parallels the mess and havoc of larger problems. No one can be trusted in a world where friends serve the causes of enemies and, conversely, enemies serve the causes of friends—all knowingly, but never openly.

It is internal politics with which Elkin is doubtless most concerned. This is represented in Druff's family life with both his wife and son, and with his relationship with himself and The MacGuffin. The context of family politics finally makes it impossible for Druff to make sense out of the entanglements around him, even when he has full knowledge of all the facts. In *The MacGuffin*, Elkin's goal is to make a statement not merely about problems in the Middle East (he is actually little concerned about relations between Jews and Arabs) but rather about problems in self-definition facing all readers.

SUGGESTED READINGS

Bailey, Peter J. *Reading Stanley Elkin*. Urbana: University of Illinois Press, 1985.

Bargen, Doris G. *The Fiction of Stanley Elkin*. Frankfurt, Germany: Peter Lang, 1980.

Cohen, Sarah Blacher, ed. *Comic Relief: Humor in Contemporary American Literature*. Urbana: University of Illinois Press, 1978.

Dougherty, David C. *Stanley Elkin*. Boston: Twayne, 1990.

Gelfant, Blanche H. *The Columbia Companion to the Twentieth-Century American Short Story*. New York: Columbia University Press, 2000.

Olderman, Raymond M. *Beyond the Waste Land: The American Novel in the Nineteen Sixties*. New Haven, Conn.: Yale University Press, 1972.

Pinsker, Sanford. "Sickness unto Style." *Gettysburg Review* 7 (1994): 437-445.

Pughe, Thomas. *Comic Sense: Reading Robert Coover, Stanley Elkin, Philip Roth*. Boston: Birkhäuser, 1994.

Review of Contemporary Fiction 15 (Summer, 1995).

Contributors: R. Baird Shuman, Patrick O'Donnell, and Carl Singleton

Ralph Ellison

BORN: Oklahoma City, Oklahoma; March 1, 1914
DIED: New York, New York; April 16, 1994

AFRICAN AMERICAN

*In his writings, Ellison emphasizes his belief in integration
and pluralism in American society.*

PRINCIPAL WORKS

LONG FICTION: *Invisible Man*, 1952; *Juneteenth*, 1999 (John F. Callahan, editor)
SHORT FICTION: *Flying Home, and Other Stories*, 1996
NONFICTION: *Shadow and Act*, 1964; *The Writer's Experience*, 1964 (with Karl
Shapiro); *Going to the Territory*, 1986; *The Collected Essays of Ralph Ellison*,
1995 (John F. Callahan, editor); *Conversations with Ralph Ellison*, 1995 (Mary-
emma Graham and Amritjit Singh, editors); *Trading Twelves: The Selected Let-
ters of Ralph Ellison and Albert Murray*, 2000; *Living with Music: Ralph
Ellison's Jazz Writings*, 2001 (Robert O'Meally, editor)

A native of rural Oklahoma, Ralph Ellison (EHL-lih-suhn) moved to New York
City in 1936, where he met fellow black writer Richard Wright. Wright helped
Ellison begin his writing career. In 1938, Ellison joined the Federal Writers' Proj-
ect, which launched his educational and literary life.

In 1945, Ellison, who was then exploring and espousing leftist views, began
work on *Invisible Man*, a novel based on his post-World War II interest in racial
identity, ethnic unity, and social justice. *Invisible Man* won the National Book
Award and the Russwarm Award in 1953, catapulting Ellison into national prominence as an important black author. *Invisible Man* traces the life of a young African
American male who is attempting to define his identity in the context of his race and
of society as a whole. Ellison received numerous honors, including the 1969 Medal
of Freedom Award for his leadership in the black literary community.

Starting in 1952, Ellison taught at Bard College, Rutgers University, New York
University, and other institutions. In addition, he delivered public lectures, wrote
essays, and worked on a second novel. Less inclined to direct political involvement
than contemporaries such as Amiri Baraka and James Baldwin, Ellison participated
in the Civil Rights movement in a relatively quiet manner. He nevertheless
attracted political controversy during the rise of the African American nationalist movements in the mid-1960's. Refusing to endorse any form of cultural or political separatism, Ellison was attacked as an aesthetic European and a political
reactionary, especially after accepting appointments to the American Institute of

Ralph Ellison (National Archives)

Arts and Letters (1964) and to the National Council on the Arts and Humanities, acts that were interpreted as support for the Johnson administration's Vietnam policy. During the mid-1970's, however, these attacks abated as nationalist critics such as Larry Neal rose to Ellison's defense and a new generation of African American writers turned to him for aesthetic inspiration.

Though Ellison would publish two well-received collections of essays, *Shadow and Act* and *Going to the Territory*, he would never follow up his first novel with a second in his lifetime. He began writing his next novel around 1958, and over the years he was to publish numerous excerpts from it as a work-in-progress. A fire at his Plainsfield, Massachusetts, summer home destroyed much of the manuscript in 1967, causing him to have to painstakingly reconstruct it. Though he was to work on this project for the rest of his life, he never found a final form for the novel with which he felt comfortable, and it remained unfinished when he died of a heart attack in 1994.

Invisible Man

TYPE OF WORK: Novel
FIRST PUBLISHED: 1952

Frequently discussed as a novel addressing racial identity in modern, urban America, Ellison's masterpiece, *Invisible Man*, is also discussed regarding the larger issue of personal identity, especially self-assertion and personal expression in a metaphorically blind world. In the novel, the unnamed young black narrator is invisible within the larger culture because of his race. Race itself, in turn, is a metaphor for the individual's anonymity in modern life. The novel is scathing, angry, and humorous, incorporating a wide range of African American experiences and using a variety of styles, settings, characters, and images. Ellison uses jazz as a metaphor, especially that of the role of a soloist who is bound within the traditions and forms of a group performance.

The novel describes a series of incidents that show how racism has warped the American psyche. As a boy, the nameless narrator hears his grandfather say: "Undermine 'em with grins, agree 'em to death and destruction." Later, the youth sees a social function degenerate into a surrealistic and barbarous paroxysm of racism. Next, the narrator is expelled from a black college and heads north. After a job in a paint factory ends in shock treatment, the narrator heads to the big city and falls in with the Brotherhood, a group of political radicals. After realizing that the Brotherhood is just as power-hungry and manipulative as the other organizations and institutions that have victimized him, the narrator leaves the Brotherhood. He comes to understand that racism denies personal identity: As long as he is seen by others as a sample of a group rather than as an individual, he is invisible. The narrator finally becomes an urban hermit, living anonymously in a cellar and using pirated electricity.

The novel's narrator is typically viewed as representing a generation of intelligent African Americans born and raised in the rural South before World War II who moved to large cities such as New York to widen their opportunities. Such historical context aside, readers also see him as a black Everyman, whose story symbolically recapitulates black history. Attending a Southern black college, the narrator's idealism is built on black educator Booker T. Washington's teaching that racial uplift will occur by way of humility, accommodation, and hard work. The narrator's ideals erode, however, in a series of encounters with white and black leaders. The narrator learns of hypocrisy, blindness, and the need to play roles even when each pose leads to violence. The larger, white culture does not accept the narrator's independent nature. Accidents, and betrayals by educators, communists, and fellow African Americans, among others, show him that life is largely chaotic, with no clear pattern of order to follow. The narrator's complexity shatters white culture's predetermined, stereotyped notions of what role he should play. He finds himself obliged as a result to move from role to role, providing the reader a wide spectrum of personalities that reflect the range of the black community.

In the end the narrator rejects cynicism and hatred and advocates a philosophy of hope, a rejection mirroring Ellison's desire to write a novel that transcended protest novels, emphasizing rage and hopelessness, of the period. The narrator decides to look within himself for self-definition, and the act of telling his story provides meaning to his existence, an affirmation and celebration preceding his return to the world. He has learned first of his invisibility, second of his manhood.

In his later years, Ellison realized that his novel expands the meaning of the word "invisible." He observed that invisibility "touches anyone who lives in a big metropolis." A winner of numerous awards, including the National Book Award in 1953, *Invisible Man* has continually been regarded as one of the most important novels in twentieth century American literature.

Going to the Territory

TYPE OF WORK: Essays
FIRST PUBLISHED: 1986

Reasserting the democratic vision of Ellison's earlier writing, this eloquent collection of sixteen pieces (composed between 1957 and the early 1980's) incorporates many of Ellison's public speeches. Pieces written for specific occasions celebrate the achievements of composer Duke Ellington, novelist Richard Wright, artist Romare Bearden, and educator Inman Page. Each testifies to the diversity and style—the words are crucial to Ellison's sensibility—of Afro-American culture. Similarly, his responses to both white liberalism and black separatism insist that while Afro-American culture is unique, it is not separate from the pluralistic mainstream of the American experience.

The core of the book, however, lies in the more fully developed essays on the complexly intertwined aesthetic and moral responsibilities of the novelist in a democratic society. Although he remains curiously insensitive to the voices of women, Ellison is particularly perceptive concerning the ways in which mutually antagonistic cultures incorporate one another's influence through parody and unconscious imitation. "Society, Morality, and the Novel," "The Little Man at the Cheehaw Station," "An Extravagance of Laughter," and the title essay all rank with the finest prose of Walt Whitman, Ralph Waldo Emerson, William Carlos Williams, James Baldwin, and Adrienne Rich as classic statements of the constantly undervalued pluralistic ideal.

"Flying Home"

TYPE OF WORK: Short fiction
FIRST PUBLISHED: 1996, in *Flying Home*

Ralph Ellison's longest short story, "Flying Home," from the collection of the same name, is also his most richly satisfying accomplishment in the form. At the center of the story is Todd, a young black man whose lifelong dream of becoming a pilot crashes along with his plane when he flies into a buzzard on a training flight. Jefferson, an old black man who comes to Todd's rescue after the crash, tells him the buzzards are called "Jim Crows" locally, setting up an important level of symbolism about what has really caused Todd's crash. In fact, Todd has been training with the Tuskegee Airmen, a group of black World War II pilots who trained at the famed Tuskegee Institute but were only reluctantly deployed for combat missions. For Todd, this crash landing on a routine flight almost certainly means he will never get another chance to fly and, in his mind, will become the common black man he considers Jefferson to be, the worst fate he can imagine for himself.

Despite the younger man's hostility, Jefferson distracts the injured Todd by telling him a story about dying, going to heaven, and flying around so fast as to cause "a storm and a couple of lynchings down here in Macon County." In his story-within-a-story, Jefferson is stripped of his wings for flying too fast and is sent down to earth with a parachute and a map of Alabama. Todd, seeing only that this story has been twisted to mirror his own situation, snaps, "Why are you making fun of me?"—which, in fact, the old man is not doing. A feverish dream into which Todd drifts reveals not only the depth of his lifelong desire to fly but also the power of his grandmother's admonition:

> Young man, young man
> Yo arm's too short
> To box with God.

To Todd, becoming a pilot means taking a position higher than the majority white culture wants to allow black men of his time to occupy; it is the equivalent of boxing with God in his mind. To have failed as a pilot means not only to have made a mistake but also to have let down his entire race, something he cannot allow to happen. When Dabney Graves, the racist landowner on whose property Todd has crashed, arrives at the site, Todd snaps at the man and places his own life in danger. Jefferson, though, saves him by intervening and telling Graves that the army told Todd never to abandon his ship. Graves's temper is assuaged, and Jefferson and a young boy are allowed to take Todd to safety on a stretcher. The final image is of Todd watching a buzzard flying against the sun, glowing like a bird of flaming gold. This image suggests that though Todd will never fly again, his spirit will rise up like a phoenix from the ashes of his defeat, a victory made possible by the current of goodwill he can now allow himself to feel for Jefferson. Todd will begin to learn to love himself for who he is by loving others for who they are.

Juneteenth

TYPE OF WORK: Novel
FIRST PUBLISHED: 1999

Forty-seven years after the release of *Invisible Man*, Ellison's second novel was published. Ellison began working on *Juneteenth* in 1954, but his constant revisions delayed its publication. Although it was unfinished at the time of his death, only minor edits and revisions were necessary to publish the book.

Juneteenth is about a black minister, Hickman, who takes in and raises a little boy as black, even though the child looks white. The boy soon runs away to New England and later becomes a race-baiting senator. After he is shot on the Senate floor, he sends for Hickman. Their past is revealed through their ensuing conversation.

The title of the novel, appropriately, refers to a day of liberation for African Americans. Juneteenth historically represents June 19, 1865, the day Union forces announced emancipation of slaves in Texas; that state considers Juneteenth an official holiday. The title applies to the novel's themes of evasion and discovery of identity, which Ellison explored so masterfully in *Invisible Man.*

SUGGESTED READINGS

Benston, Kimberly, ed. *Speaking for You: The Vision of Ralph Ellison.* Washington, D.C.: Howard University Press, 1987.

Bloom, Harold, ed. *Ralph Ellison.* New York: Chelsea House, 1986.

Busby, Mark. *Ralph Ellison.* Boston: Twayne, 1991.

Callahan, John F. Introduction to *Flying Home, and Other Stories,* by Ralph Ellison. Edited by John F. Callahan. New York: Random House, 1996.

Jackson, Lawrence. *Ralph Ellison: Emergence of Genius.* New York: Wiley, 2001.

Nadel, Alan. *Invisible Criticism: Ralph Ellison and the American Canon.* Iowa City: University of Iowa Press, 1988.

O'Meally, Robert G. *New Essays on "Invisible Man."* New York: Cambridge University Press, 1988.

_____. *Ralph Ellison: A Biography.* New York: Alfred A. Knopf, 2007.

Schor, Edith. *Visible Ellison: A Study of Ralph Ellison's Fiction.* Westport, Conn.: Greenwood Press, 1993.

Watts, Jerry Gafio. *Heroism and the Black Intellectual: Ralph Ellison, Politics, and Afro-American Intellectual Life.* Chapel Hill: University of North Carolina Press, 1994.

Contributors: Wesley Britton, Thomas Cassidy, and Craig Werner

Louise Erdrich

BORN: Little Falls, Minnesota; June 7, 1954

NATIVE AMERICAN

Erdrich's poetry and novels represent some of the most creative and accessible writing by a Native American.

PRINCIPAL WORKS

CHILDREN'S LITERATURE: *Grandmother's Pigeon*, 1996 (illustrated by Jim La-Marche); *The Birchbark House*, 1999; *The Range Eternal*, 2002; *The Game of Silence*, 2004

LONG FICTION: *Love Medicine*, 1984 (revised and expanded, 1993); *The Beet Queen*, 1986; *Tracks*, 1988; *The Crown of Columbus*, 1991 (with Michael Dorris); *The Bingo Palace*, 1994; *Tales of Burning Love*, 1996; *The Antelope Wife*, 1998; *The Last Report on the Miracles at Little No Horse*, 2001; *The Master Butchers Singing Club*, 2003; *Four Souls*, 2004; *The Painted Drum*, 2005

POETRY: *Jacklight*, 1984; *Baptism of Desire*, 1989; *Original Fire: Selected and New Poems*, 2003

SHORT FICTION: "The Red Convertible," 1981; "Scales," 1982; "The World's Greatest Fisherman," 1982; "American Horse," 1983; "Destiny," 1985; "Saint Marie," 1985; "Fleur," 1987; "Snares," 1987; "Matchimanito," 1988; *The Best American Short Stories 1993*, 1993

NONFICTION: *The Blue Jay's Dance: A Birth Year*, 1995; *Books and Islands in Ojibwe Country*, 2003

Louise Erdrich (UR-drihch) was born to a Chippewa mother and a German American father, and her "mixed-blood" heritage is at the heart of her writing. The oldest of seven children and the granddaughter of the tribal chair of the Turtle Mountain Reservation, she has stated that her family was typical of Native American families in its telling of stories, and that those stories became a part of her and are reflected in her own work. In her poetry and novels, she explores Native American ideas, ordeals, and delights, with characters representing the European American and Native American sides of her heritage. Erdrich entered Dartmouth College in 1972, the year the Native American Studies Department was formed. The chair of that department was Michael Dorris, who later became her trusted literary collaborator and eventually her husband. Her work at Dartmouth was the beginning of a continuing exploration of her ancestry, the animating influence in her novels.

Erdrich frequently weaves stories in nonchronological patterns with multiple narrators. Her characters are multidimensional and entertaining while communicating the positives and negatives of Native American life in the twentieth century. Family relationships, community relationships, issues of assimilation, and the roles of tradition and religion are primary motifs in her novels. *Tracks, The Beet Queen, Love Medicine,* and *The Bingo Palace* form a quartet that follows four families living in North Dakota between the early 1930's and the late 1980's, exploring the relationships among themselves and within the larger cultures. The novel *The Crown of Columbus,* written with coauthor Michael Dorris, explores many of the same ideas and is a literary adventure story. In these novels about the search for identity, some of her characters are hopelessly caught between worlds, but most of her characters battle the hurt caused by mixed identities with humor, tenacity, and a will to construct their own sense of identity.

The result is some of the most accomplished and popular ethnic fiction available. The excellence of her work has earned for her numerous awards, including the National Book Critics Circle Award in 1984, and each of her five novels has achieved *The New York Times* best-seller list.

Love Medicine

TYPE OF WORK: Novel
FIRST PUBLISHED: 1984

A dazzling meld of Native American storytelling and postmodern literary craft, Erdrich's first novel, *Love Medicine,* was an immediate success. It quickly made the best-seller lists and gathered an impressive group of awards, including the National Book Critics Circle Award for fiction, the American Academy and Institute of Arts and Letters Award for best first novel, the Virginia McCormack Scully Prize for best book of 1984 dealing with Indians or Chicanos, the American Book Award, and the *Los Angeles Times* award for best novel of the year.

Sad and funny, realistic and lyrical, mystical and down-to-earth, the novel tells the story of three generations of four Chippewa and mixed-blood families—the Kashpaws, Morriseys, Lamartines, and Lazarres—from the 1930's to the 1980's. Seven separate narrators tell their own stories in a discontinuous time line, each a puzzle piece of its own, but by the novel's end there is one story, one jigsaw puzzle picture of lost identities and the often humorous but always meaningful efforts of a fragmented people to hold on to what is left to them.

The characters in *Love Medicine* experience individual forms of alienation caused by physical and emotional separation from the communal root of their existence. They contend with the United States government and its policies of allotment and commodities; the Catholic Church, which makes no allowances for the Chippewas' traditional religion; and with the seductive pull of life off the reservation, a life that cuts them off from the community whose traditions keep them centered and give them a sense of their identities. These three factors place the characters under the constant threat of loss of their culture. Erdrich makes this clear, but she presents the lives of her Native American characters as human experiences that readers who have no background in Native American cultures can readily understand. The three generations of characters in *Love Medicine* surface as human beings who deal with an unfair world with strength, frailty, love, anger, and most of all, a sense of humor.

The Beet Queen

TYPE OF WORK: Novel
FIRST PUBLISHED: 1986

Erdrich's second novel, *The Beet Queen*, is centered in the fictional little town of Argus, somewhere in North Dakota. Unlike her other novels of people living on reservations, the characters in this story are mostly European Americans, and those Native Americans who exist have very tenuous ties to their roots and to the reservation that lies just outside the town. Racism, poverty, and cultural conflict are not in the foreground in this novel, which makes it different from most novels by Native American authors. Instead, European Americans, Native Americans, and mixed-bloods are all in the same economic and cultural situation, and each of them is involved in a search for identity.

The prose in *The Beet Queen* is lyrical and finely crafted, as is evident in the description of Mary Adare, the novel's central character. Abandoned by a mother who literally vanishes in the air, she builds her identity by developing a solid grounding. She is described as heavy and immovable, and she makes a home for herself in a butcher shop that is described as having thick walls and green, watery light coming through glass block windows. She has found an earthy den, which attaches her to the one thing that will never abandon her—the earth. Her brother, Karl, is her opposite. Thin, flighty, always moving, he is a European American who fits perfectly the archetype of the Native American trickster figure. He is the destroyer, lover of men and women, game-player, and cocreator of the character who ties the main characters of the novel together, his daughter, Dot.

Dot is a strong, willful girl who is adored by her mother, a strong, mixed-blood Chippewa woman named Celestine, her Aunt Mary, and Walter Pfef, a town leader and her father's former lover. It is Dot, the Beet Queen in a contest fixed by Pfef, who brings together the web of characters who are otherwise loosely joined in fragile relationships. During the Beet Celebration in which she is to be crowned, her father returns. Pfef, Celestine, and Mary are also there, and Russell, Celestine's paralyzed war-hero brother, is the centerpiece of a float honoring veterans. Mary's vain cousin, Sita, is also there, although she is dead. When the day is over, the circle of family is complete. Poetic and graceful, *The Beet Queen* is widely recognized as one of Erdrich's finest accomplishments.

Tracks

TYPE OF WORK: Novel
FIRST PUBLISHED: 1988

Tracks is the third in the cycle of novels that began with *Love Medicine* and continued with *The Beet Queen*. *Tracks* is set farther back in time than the first two novels—during the period 1912 to 1924—and a number of characters from the earlier novels reappear.

The leading characters are Chippewa Indians, and the story is told through two narrators. First is the shrewd Nanapush, a tribal elder with a biting sense of humor, who survives epidemics of disease and despair and emerges as chief negotiator for the Chippewas in their dealings with the government over land. The second narrator is Pauline, a neurotic woman of mixed blood. She becomes a zealous convert to Catholicism, joins a convent, and shows herself eager for mortification. She still believes, however, in the traditional Indian myths. The third character of importance is the young Fleur Pillager, an alluring, mysterious, and dangerous woman who is thought to have a witch's power to be revenged on those who wrong her.

Erdrich writes with poetic vigor and a deep understanding of human passions. She empathizes with the old Indian ways and folk beliefs, in which dreams and visions are pregnant with meaning, the Earth is a living organism, and there is a spontaneous interflow between the human and the natural world. The austere, intense, magical world that she has created is a fine achievement; its strange force makes a lasting impression.

"Where I Ought to Be"

TYPE OF WORK: Essay
FIRST PUBLISHED: 1985, in *The New York Times Book Review*

In the essay "Where I Ought to Be: A Writer's Sense of Place," Erdrich explores the ways in which a sense of place changes the ways in which people think of themselves. Using examples from American authors of the last hundred and fifty years, she carefully compares and contrasts the approaches of European Americans and of Native Americans to a sense of place.

She begins the essay with a description of the Tewa Pueblo people's creation story. In that narrative, Grandmother Spider shows the people the Sandia Mountains and tells them the mountains are their home. Erdrich explains that the Tewa listening to that story would be living in the place where their ancestors lived, and the story would be a personal story and a collective story, told among lifelong friends and relatives.

In contrast with this view of a timeless, stable world, that of pre-invasion Native American cultures, Erdrich suggests that European American writers are invested in establishing a historical narrative for their landscapes. European American writers are interested in recording place, even predicting destruction, before their world changes again.

Erdrich proposes that the threat of destruction of place, such as in the extreme case of nuclear obliteration, may be one reason that writers catalog and describe landscapes so thoroughly. She takes the reader into a world of complete destruction, where nothing is left, and then she asks the reader to consider that this unthinkable thing has actually happened to the Native American population. "Many Native American cultures were annihilated more thoroughly than even a nuclear disaster might destroy ours, and others live on with the fallout of that destruction, effects as persistent as radiation—poverty, fetal alcohol syndrome, chronic despair." She points out that because of this, Native American writers have a different task. They "must tell the stories of contemporary survivors while protecting and celebrating the cores of cultures left in the wake of catastrophe."

Louise Erdrich (Michael Dorris)

She ends her essay with a description of her own sense of place, the area of North Dakota where she lived as a child. She points out that it is truly knowing a place that provides the link between details and meaning. A sense of place is, then, at the foundation of a sense of identity.

Baptism of Desire

TYPE OF WORK: Poetry
FIRST PUBLISHED: 1989

Erdrich peoples the fluid, shifting landscape of her poetry in this collection with Catholic saints and figures from classical myth and Native American legend: Saint Clare, the nine-headed Hydra, and the Chippewa trickster Potchikoo appear in these pages. Boundaries dissolve; the dead and the living share the same space, ghosts holy and otherwise.

In her notes to the book, Erdrich comments that most of the poems in the collection were written between the hours of two and four o'clock in the morning, during insomnia brought on by pregnancy. A number of voices in the poems painfully draw breath as if for the first time. The perspective may alternate between that of mother ("The Fence," "Birth") and child ("The Return," "The Flood"). Such fluidity of identity can be both terrifying and exhilarating, can provoke experiences of doubt and illumination. In "Hydra," Erdrich draws on the ambivalent imagery of the serpent as seducer and as initiator into the sacred mysteries; in the poem, the creature acts as muse: "you are my poetry . . . Your place/ is at my ear." As created by the poet's imagination, the world is a seductive place; one is "lured" into birth.

Erdrich notes that the German biochemist August Kekule von Stradonitz derived the ring structure of benzene with the help of a dream in which a snake was swallowing its tail. It is in a dreamlike, suggestible state that the metamorphosis of shapes and identities and the confounding of time and space occur, approximating the ritual of baptism. In the surreal landscape of dreams, the mundane and fantastical coexist: There are "mosquitoes/ dancing on the head of a pin." This interpenetration of the material and spiritual worlds characterizes both the sacramental and the poetic imagination.

Erdrich's use of religious imagery and the meditative quality of her rhythms contribute to the spiritual force of her poems. The reader struggles with them as if with Proteus, until true shapes are revealed and questions answered.

The Bingo Palace

TYPE OF WORK: Novel
FIRST PUBLISHED: 1994

The Bingo Palace adds to the cycle that began with *Love Medicine*. Unified mainly by the quest of its protagonist, Lipsha, to win Shawnee, *The Bingo Palace* is a rope drawing together many strands, just as, in Erdrich's central metaphor, the Kashpaw family is a rope of many strands complexly twisted together. Lipsha has been living away from the tribe in Fargo but is called home mysteriously by his grandmother, Lulu. He feels called to change his life. Is his mission to marry Shawnee, the beautiful and ambitious unwed mother? Or to prevent his half-uncle Lyman, the reputed father of Shawnee's child, from converting sacred tribal land into a casino and resort? Or to aid his father's escape from prison? Or to take his destined place as tribal medicine man after the death of his great grandmother, Fleur Pillager? Although Lipsha moves toward all of these goals, he achieves none of them, except perhaps for aiding his father in his escape. In the ten chapters he narrates, Lipsha focuses upon persuading Shawnee to marry him. The other chapters—narrated mainly by a communal voice of the reservation—call attention to the context of history and relationships within which Lipsha acts without full awareness.

Though early reviewers expressed skepticism about the novel's form, *The Bingo Palace* is Erdrich at her best; the book will reward rereading. Chronologically, this novel follows *Love Medicine*, which introduced most of the main characters. Like *Love Medicine*, *The Bingo Palace* abounds in anecdotes and legends that are at once funny and profound, revealing the rich and magical depth of the tribal life of Erdrich's Chippewas.

Tales of Burning Love
TYPE OF WORK: Novel
FIRST PUBLISHED: 1996

Tales of Burning Love, like *Love Medicine*, begins with June Kashpah's death during a 1981 North Dakota blizzard. The man who married her in a questionable ceremony and then drunkenly let her walk into the blizzard was Jack Mauser. For fourteen years, this incident haunts Jack. He becomes a leading contractor in Fargo, but this success is built upon concealment of growing debt and his Chippewa heritage. When his fifth marriage and his business collapse, Jack and his four living wives are pushed to reorder their lives.

The story takes place mainly off the Chippewa reservation in the materialistic white world of Fargo, but this world proves to be much like the Chippewa world of the other novels. It is filled with miracles that point to trickster powers who teach through absurdity and suffering. Most characters seem blind to such forces until pushed to extremes of suffering. Then they experience humorous visions that are healing and painful. Jack's second wife, Eleanor, visits with the recently dead Sister Leopolda while rolling across drifts in a blizzard wind. Jack finds forgiveness when a statue of Our Lady of the Wheat falls upon him.

Tales of Burning Love shares with the other North Dakota novels the conviction that the universe does not reveal how to love but still requires truthful and faithful love; the only alternative to burning love is freezing death. The stories are new, however, rich in character and situation. This novel is a worthy continuation of the series.

The Antelope Wife
TYPE OF WORK: Novel
FIRST PUBLISHED: 1998

In *The Antelope Wife*, Louise Erdrich's seventh novel, a U.S. Cavalry private, Scranton Roy, sent to quell a Native American uprising in Minnesota, mistakenly attacks a neutral village instead. He captures an Indian dog with an infant strapped to its back and rears the baby as his own. In this way the white Roy family begins its intricate relationship with the two Ojibwa families of Showano and Whiteheart Beads.

Typically, the book is peopled by many complex characters. The baby's grieving mother marries a man named Showano and bears twins. Her granddaughters Zosie and Mary Showano figure prominently as the twin mothers of Rozina Whiteheart Beads and grandmothers of Rozina's twin daughters. Meanwhile, Rozina, married to tribal businessman Richard Whiteheart Beads, falls in love with baker Frank Showano. That love triangle echoes the one formed years before by Zosie and Mary Showano and the grandson of Scranton Roy. Finally, Klaus Showano,

Frank's brother, is nearly destroyed by his infatuation with a seductive antelope woman, a creature of legend whom he meets at a powwow.

Welcome flashes of humor appear in the wisecracking monologues of the Indian dog Almost Soup, a four-legged standup comic who tells dirty dog stories. Black comedy also occurs at the disastrous wedding of Rozina and Frank Showano, where the bride's first husband menaces the wedding party and is felled by a blow to the head with a frozen turkey.

Erdrich is at her finest when she writes through Native American culture and consciousness. Here she returns to the lyricism of her earlier work, introducing a vital new group of characters. Her poetic skill and perceptive insights remain undimmed.

Four Souls

TYPE OF WORK: Novel
FIRST PUBLISHED: 2004

In *Four Souls*, the eighth installment in the series that began with *Love Medicine*, Fleur Pillager seeks redress from John James Mauser, the tycoon who left a trail of ruined Native American lives in his lust for wealth. Readers familiar with Fleur from the preceding novels in the cycle will delight in the story of this ferocious, taciturn woman. Erdrich's decision to allow Fleur's father and the aristocratic Polly Elizabeth Gheen to describe events rather than Fleur herself only serves to enhance the enigmatic nature of her personality.

Erdrich enriches Fleur's quest for revenge by contrasting it with Nanapush's desire to punish Shesheeb, a neighbor who flirts with Nanapush's wife, Margaret. While Nanapush's hilarious failures ultimately bring him closer to his wife, Fleur almost succeeds too well. She marries the man she originally intended to kill and bears him a son. The climax of the novel—a high-stakes poker game in which Fleur tries to win back her land—is one of the best scenes in Erdrich's oeuvre. While it would be easy to find fault with the shallowness of Mauser's character, one is more than compensated by the rich inner lives of Erdrich's Native Americans. *Four Souls* is a fitting addition to Erdrich's continuing saga.

SUGGESTED READINGS

Beidler, Peter G., and Gay Barton. *A Reader's Guide to the Novels of Louise Erdrich*. Columbia: University of Missouri Press, 1999.

Chavkin, Allan, ed. *The Chippewa Landscape of Louise Erdrich*. Tuscaloosa: University of Alabama Press, 1998.

Chavkin, Allan, and Nancy Feyl, eds. *Conversations with Louise Erdrich and Michael Dorris*. Jackson: University Press of Mississippi, 1994.

Erdrich, Louise. *Conversations with Louise Erdrich and Michael Dorris*. Edited by Allan Chavkin and Nancy Feyl Chavkin. Jackson: University Press of Mississippi, 1994.

Ferguson, Suzanne. "The Short Stories of Louise Erdrich's Novels." *Studies in Short Fiction* 33 (1996): 541-555.

Hafen, Jane P. "Sacramental Language: Ritual in the Poetry of Louise Erdrich." *Great Plains Quarterly* 16 (1996): 147-155.

Ludlow, Jeannie. "Working (in) the In-Between: Poetry, Criticism, Interrogation, and Interruption." *Studies in American Indian Literature* 6 (Spring, 1994): 24-42.

Stone, Brad. "Scenes from a Marriage: Louise Erdrich's New Novel—and Her Life." *Newsweek* 131, no. 12 (March 23, 1998): 69.

Stookey, Lorena Laura. *Louise Erdrich: A Critical Companion.* Westport, Conn.: Greenwood Press, 1999.

Wong, Hertha Dawn. *Louise Erdrich's "Love Medicine": A Casebook.* London: Oxford University Press, 1999.

Contributor: Jacquelyn Kilpatrick

Martín Espada

BORN: Brooklyn, New York; 1957

PUERTO RICAN

*Espada's poetic treatment of his immigrant roots
led Sandra Cisneros to dub him "the Pablo Neruda
of North American authors."*

PRINCIPAL WORKS

POETRY: *The Immigrant Iceboy's Bolero*, 1982; *Trumpets from the Islands of Their Eviction*, 1987 (expanded 1994); *Rebellion Is the Circle of a Lover's Hands = Rebelión es el giro de manos del amante*, 1990; *City of Coughing and Dead Radiators: Poems*, 1993; *Imagine the Angels of Bread: Poems*, 1996; *A Mayan Astronomer in Hell's Kitchen: Poems*, 2000; *Alabanza: New and Selected Poems, 1982-2002*, 2003; *The Republic of Poetry*, 2006

TRANSLATION: *The Blood That Keeps Singing: Selected Poems of Clemente Soto Vélez*, 1991 (with Camilo Pérez-Bustillo)

NONFICTION: *Zapata's Disciple: Essays*, 1998

EDITED TEXTS: *Poetry like Bread: Poets of the Political Imagination from Curbstone Press*, 1994 (expanded 2000); *El Coro: A Chorus of Latino and Latina Poetry*, 1997

Martín Espada (mahr-TEEN ehs-PAH-dah) was born and raised in Brooklyn, New York, by a Jewish mother and a Puerto Rican father. During the 1950's his father, Frank Espada, became active in the Civil Rights movement. Born in Puerto Rico, Espada's father also became one of the leaders of New York City's Puerto Rican community. Frank Espada taught his son to recognize how difficult it has been for minorities to make a living in the United States. Martín Espada came to appreciate the need for people of color to fight against injustice and poverty. His father took his young son to political rallies. At fifteen, Espada began to write poetry. In interviews, he has stated that he became obsessed with writing and that he would rather work on a poem than even sleep.

As a young adult, he held many odd jobs to help make a living, working as groundskeeper for a minor-league baseball park, bouncer in a bar, and bindery worker. Through his own hard work, he witnessed firsthand the many obstacles which people of color must try to overcome. Espada learned to be a "keen observer." He received a B.A. in history from the University of Wisconsin at Madison in 1981 and earned a law degree from Northeastern University School of Law in 1985. He went to work at a legal-aid office, Su Clínica Legal, located in the Boston area. His wife, Katherine, gave birth to a son in 1991. In 1993, Espada joined the English department at the University of Massachusetts, Amherst.

His first collection of poetry, *The Immigrant Iceboy's Bolero*, was published in 1982. For his first collection, Espada included some of his father's photographs. The title poem tells the story of his father coming to the United States. When Frank Espada was merely nine years old, he had to carry blocks of ice up flights of stairs in tenement buildings in his adopted country. Like other Latino immigrants who came to the United States in search of a better life, Espada's father had to endure injustices in order to make his way. Espada was influenced by the Chilean poet Pablo Neruda. Neruda wrote political poetry that spoke for the downtrodden. Espada wanted to write poems that challenged the reader as well as himself. For him, though, poetry was not to serve as propaganda; poetry should illuminate, engage, and educate.

Espada's second collection, *Trumpets from the Islands of Their Eviction*, speaks to the relationship that exists between Puerto Rico and the United States, wherein the United States is viewed as a shark and Puerto Rico as its prey. In 1990, he published *Rebellion Is the Circle of a Lover's Hands*. Not wishing to limit his audience to merely readers of English, Espada included a Spanish translation for each poem. The short lyric poem "Latin Night at the Pawnshop" details the fate of various musical instruments. These instruments have been abandoned and must face a tragic fate. Espada uses the "golden trumpet," the "silver trombone," and the "maracas" as stand-ins for Latin culture. *Rebellion Is the Circle of a Lover's Hands* was awarded the Paterson Poetry Prize as well as the PEN/Revson Fellowship. His fifth collection, *Imagine the Angels of Bread*, won the 1997 American Book Award for poetry. In a masterful fashion, Espada combines both the personal and the political in the poems of this collection. For all the injustices of the past, the poet expresses his hope that a better and more just future is possible. He takes pleasure in "the bread of the imagination, the bread of the table, and the bread of justice."

In Espada's 1998 collection of essays, *Zapata's Disciple*, he delineates "why poetry must matter," saying it is possible for suffering to be transformed into something positive, something beautiful. His sixth collection, *A Mayan Astronomer in Hell's Kitchen*, continues Espada's quest to speak up for those who do not have a voice. He is unashamedly an "advocate for the cause of freedom." The noted author Sandra Cisneros has stated that Espada must be considered "the Pablo Neruda of North American authors" and that she would "select him as the Poet Laureate of the United States." In 2003 his collection *Alabanza* was published. This collection brings together Espada's "earliest out-of-print work to seventeen new poems." The power of his poetry is clearly on display with *Alabanza*. As the acclaimed author Barbara Kingsolver has pointed out, a reader of Espada's poetry cannot but "come away changed" by the experience.

"Tony Went to the Bodega but He Didn't Buy Anything"

TYPE OF WORK: Poetry
FIRST PUBLISHED: 1987, in *Trumpets from the Islands of Their Eviction*

In an interview for the *Milwaukee Journal Sentinel*, Espada once recalled that being the only Puerto Rican in town while growing up in Long Island was difficult. His response was to compose poetry: "I needed a way to respond. I think poetry is a great way to assert your humanity." Thus Espada's poem about Tony reflects not only his own experience as a lawyer-poet but also the struggles of those who find themselves isolated or disenfranchised, seeking to reconcile different cultural, educational, or social realms.

Composed of forty-four lines of free verse, this poem is divided into stanzas of varying lengths that describe Tony's maturation from elementary to law school. Each verse encapsulates some feature of Tony's development as he seeks his place in the world: As a fatherless Puerto Rican boy, he tries to survive the "Long Island city projects." He takes a job at a local bodega and learns how to be polite to the *abuelas* (grandmothers) and how to grin at the customers. He receives a scholarship to law school away from New York but feels out of place. The academic environment of graduate school and the upwardly mobile condominium communities seem inhospitable, so he searches for a sense of belonging and finds it in a Hispanic neighborhood on Tremont Street. Tony finds refuge in a Boston bodega:

> he sat by the doorway satisfied
> to watch *la gente* (people
> island-brown as him)
> crowd in and out
> *hablando espanol.*

The inclusion of Spanish words and phrases shows the blend of English and Spanish that comprise Tony's world. The vocabulary of the poem is accessible, while the diction is suggestive and imagistic. The work possesses a contemporary sensibility with its references to New York, Boston, Long Island, and Tremont Street. The irony of the poem is that Tony has the ability and opportunity to escape the Long Island projects, but as an adult he returns to a similar neighborhood because that is where he feels at home. Espada suggests that true success for Tony means returning to his Hispanic roots, where the language and people are familiar—where he finds a sense of belonging that he does not find in academic or professional communities.

SUGGESTED READINGS
Browning, Sarah. "Give Politics a Human Face: An Interview with Lawyer-Poet-Professor Martín Espada." *Valley Advocate*, November 18, 1993.
Campo, Rafael. "Why Poetry Matters." *The Progressive* 63 (April, 1999): 43-44.

Espada, Martín. "Poetry and the Burden of History: An Interview with Martín Espada." Interview by Steven Ratiner. *The Christian Science Monitor*, March 6, 1991, p. 16.

_____. "A Poetry of Legacy: An Interview with Martín Espada." Interview by Ray Gonzalez. *The Bloomsbury Review*, July/August, 1997, 3.

_____. "The Politics of Advocacy: Three Poems." *Hopscotch: A Cultural Review* 2 (2001): 128-133.

Fink, Thomas. "Visibility and History in the Poetry of Martín Espada." *Americas Review* 25 (1999): 202-221.

Gonzalez, Ray. "A Poetry of Legacy: An Interview with Martín Espada." *The Bloomsbury Review*, July/August, 1997, pp. 3ff.

Keene, John R. Review of *City of Coughing and Dead Radiators*. *MELUS* 21 (Spring, 1996): 133-135.

Ratiner, Steven. "Poetry and the Burden of History: An Interview with Martín Espada." *The Christian Science Monitor*, March 6, 1991, pp. 16ff.

Ullman, Leslie. "To Speak on Behalf." *The Kenyon Review* 14 (Summer, 1992): 174-187.

Contributors: Jeffry Jensen and Paula M. Miller

Percival L. Everett

BORN: Fort Gordon, Georgia; December 22, 1956

AFRICAN AMERICAN

Refusing to bow to racial stereotypes, Everett transcends issues of racial identity by creating each principal character as a kind of Everyman.

PRINCIPAL WORKS

CHILDREN'S LITERATURE: *The One That Got Away*, 1992; *Damned If I Do*, 2004
LONG FICTION: *Suder*, 1983; *Walk Me to the Distance*, 1985; *Cutting Lisa*, 1986; *For Her Dark Skin*, 1990; *Zulus*, 1990; *God's Country*, 1994; *Watershed*, 1996; *Frenzy*, 1997; *Glyph*, 1999; *Erasure*, 2001; *Grand Canyon, Inc.*, 2001 (novella); *American Desert*, 2004; *Wounded*, 2005; *The Water Cure*, 2007
SHORT FICTION: *The Weather and Women Treat Me Fair*, 1987; *Big Picture*, 1996; *Damned If I Do*, 2004

Born on a military base outside Augusta, Georgia, and reared in Columbia, South Carolina, the child of Percival Leonard and Dorothy Stinson Everett, Percival Leonard Everett (EH-vreht) has since led the largely nomadic life of an academician. He received a bachelor's degree in philosophy from the University of Miami in 1977, pursued graduate study at the University of Oregon, and earned an A.M. in writing from Brown University in 1982. Since the publication of his first novel, *Suder*, Everett has balanced a life of writing with a life of teaching, holding consecutive faculty positions at the Universities of Kentucky, Notre Dame, Wyoming, California (Riverside), and Southern California (USC), where he also became chairperson of the English Department.

Despite his southern upbringing, Everett, from the age of twenty, was drawn to the American West, where the open spaces and the sparseness of the population appealed to his need for privacy and autonomy. The climax, for example, of his popular first novel, *Suder*, is set against the Cascade Mountain Range of Oregon, where the protagonist, black baseball player Craig Suder, seeks refuge from a career slump and a failed marriage. Following a series of improvised adventures that read like the riffs of bebop jazz, Suder resists the attempts of others to define him and seeks, instead, to soar above the problems of life by taking self-propelled flight.

In sharp contrast to the essentially comic spirit of *Suder* is the more somber tone of Everett's second novel, *Walk Me to the Distance*. Feeling displaced after his return from the Vietnam War, David Larson, the main character, drives west from his native South, eventually to find temporary work on a Wyoming sheep ranch. Passive participant in an impromptu lynching, and noninterventionist bystander to an imminent suicide, Larson accepts the often harsh demands of western self-sufficiency associated with the code of frontier justice.

As is true of the early careers of most writers, Everett draws on personal experience for much of the substance of his first two books. His part-time work as a jazz musician gave him the experiential background that informs the characterization, themes, and structure of *Suder*; his temporary stint as a hired hand on a sheep ranch provides the primary situation and setting for *Walk Me to the Distance*.

It can be argued, however, that Everett turned to his father's background as decision maker, first as an army sergeant and then as a dentist, when he created the character of Dr. Livesey, the protagonist of his third novel, *Cutting Lisa*. Critics have compared Livesey to an Old Testament prophet, since it is the retired medical man's radical patriarchal choice that provides the focus of the book. While visiting his son's family on the Oregon coast, Livesey discovers that his daughter-in-law is pregnant with a child not her husband's and independently decides to perform a kitchen-table abortion in order to preserve what he sees as the integrity of the family unit.

People taking unilateral responsibility for the world around them is also a prevailing theme in the fifteen very short stories in *The Weather and Women Treat Me Fair*. These tales are told in the same laconic style that marks all of Everett's work. His novelistic reworking of the ancient tale of Jason and Medea, *For Her Dark Skin*, for example, is plotted in ninety-nine short chapters, each told from the first-person perspective of one of the principal characters. Some chapters are only one sentence in length. While some critics feel that the leanness of Everett's prose undercuts the potential for emotional resonance in his narratives, others find that his terseness matches the often poetic blankness of his chosen landscapes.

Considering the concept of environment as an expression of identity, one is offered additional insight into Everett's work. Perhaps initially because of the influence of his wife, the artist Shere Coleman, Everett began to paint what he refers to as "abstract expressionist oils." Expressionism in painting as well as in literature involves an attempt to convey the outer manifestation of some inner state. In this regard, both Everett's narrative mode and his choice of setting can be said to serve as metaphors of his own fundamental belief about the nature of the world.

In addition, perhaps because of his undergraduate study of philosophy, Everett seems concerned with transcending the issue of racial identity by creating each principal character as a kind of Everyman. In fact, Everett, as an African American writer, has been criticized for choosing a white protagonist for *Walk Me to the Distance* and for devoting equal weight to black and white characters in his other narratives. *Zulus*, for example, is the story of a three-hundred-pound white woman who is the only fertile female in a post-thermonuclear war world; as such, she stumbles from one false sanctuary to another until she eventually falls into the arms of a black lover intent upon causing the final destruction of the planet. Everett's Old West tale *God's Country* features an interracial, two-person posse: the politically incorrect white rancher Curt Marder, who is seeking to find the men who burned his home, raped his wife, and shot his dog; and a black tracker named Bubba, who is reluctantly committed to helping the thick-headed Marder in his quest. Percival Everett has stretched the bounds of traditional African American literature to meet the demands of his own imagination.

In his highly acclaimed 2001 novel, *Erasure*, Everett speaks directly to some of his critics, to the publishing industry, and to racial stereotypes. The work is a novel within a novel about a classically trained, black academic writer who is criticized for not being "black" enough in his writing. He then writes an over-the-top, lingo-ridden "black" novel that becomes a best seller. *Erasure* was universally praised, and Everett received the inaugural Hurston/Wright Legacy Award from the Zora Neale Hurston/Richard Wright Foundation and Borders Books for the novel.

American Desert

TYPE OF WORK: Novel
FIRST PUBLISHED: 2004

American Desert, Percival Everett's fifteenth novel, opens with Theodore "Ted" Street on his way to drown himself. Ironically, Ted dies before he can kill himself. A UPS truck dodging a poodle with painted nails collides with Ted's car; Ted is decapitated. The plot progresses chronologically with startling, unexpected events. This irony produces a dark comedy.

Symbolically, on the third day after his death, Ted rises up from his casket at his funeral. Remarks from a preacher who does not know him and unflattering comments from his department chair precede Ted's revival.

Reactions to Ted's restoration vary. The chair and dean, never Ted's allies, suffer heart attacks and die. The congregation riots. Ted's family does not celebrate; they experience embarrassment and fear. Ted's wife selects her next husband. Society is more concerned with defining death than with Ted. A religious cult shows no compassion, calls Ted a demon, and captures him for execution.

Ironically, Ted remains decent in the decadence. He escapes the commune and returns to rescue the children.

Everett's figurative language and stylistic devices enhance the plot. For instance, Ted notes the approaching deadline for meeting requirements for permanent faculty status; Everett uses the metaphor of the "ticking of the giant tenure clock." At Ted's funeral, Everett humorously describes how Rachel Ruddy, Ted's replacement, pepper-sprays herself out of the church.

Everett's characterization includes realistic diction and omniscience. Ted's explicit messages state (1) silence is as important as words, (2) death is not frightening, and (3) even flawed people can contribute to society.

The denouement is abrupt and closed. Ted removes the stitches from his neck, places his head on his lap, closes his eyes, and stays dead.

Damned If I Do

TYPE OF WORK: Short fiction
FIRST PUBLISHED: 2004

Everett once said he does not want to talk about race; he just wants to make art—and, he might have added, make us laugh at ourselves in the process. In the collection *Damned If I Do*, even stories about racial prejudice are treated with a light satirical touch. In "The Appropriation of Cultures," a young black man buys a pickup truck with a confederate flag on the back and, by driving it around, gradually undermines a symbol of racial injustice more successfully than conventional protests. In another story that centers on a pickup truck, a romance novelist just trying to earn a living, enjoy his privacy, and protect the environment, finds a way to make Hollywood pay through the nose and, in the process, staves off real estate and commercial encroachment.

One is reminded in reading these stories that Everett can write about a man trying to escape an insane asylum without subjecting his audience to a tirade about better treatment of the mentally ill. He can write about a black government official trying to get a signature from a prejudiced old woman and get his point across without ranting about racial injustice. It is hard to resist a writer who makes us laugh and learn without preaching—a writer whose only agenda is to expose the vulnerability and absurdity of the human condition. Even Everett's messiah story, "The Fix," centers on a handyman who knows how to repair everything, from broken compressors to broken hearts.

SUGGESTED READINGS

Hoffman, Alice. "Slumps and Tailspins." *The New York Times Book Review*, October 2, 1983, 9, 26.

Matuz, Roger, ed. *Contemporary Literary Criticism.* Vol. 57. Detroit: Gale Research, 1990.

Pear, Nancy. "Percival L. Everett." In *Black Writers: A Selection of Sketches from Contemporary Authors*, edited by Sharon Malinowski. 2d ed. Detroit: Gale Research, 1994.

Smith, Wendy. "Walk Me to the Distance." *The New York Times Book Review*, March 24, 1985, 24.

Woods, Paula L. "Dint, Ax, Fo, Screet: *Erasure: A Novel.*" *Los Angeles Times*, October 28, 2001, p. 1.

Contributor: S. Thomas Mack

Jessie Redmon Fauset

BORN: Snow Hill, New Jersey; April 27, 1882
DIED: Philadelphia, Pennsylvania; April 30, 1961

AFRICAN AMERICAN

*In her novels, Fauset explores the problems of
identity through characters who triumph by
accepting their race, class, and gender.*

PRINCIPAL WORKS

LONG FICTION: *There Is Confusion*, 1924; *Plum Bun: A Novel Without a Moral*,
1928; *The Chinaberry Tree: A Novel of American Life*, 1931; *Comedy, American
Style*, 1933

Jessie Redmon Fauset (JEHS-see FAW-siht), the youngest of seven children born
to Redmon Fauset, an African Methodist Episcopal minister, and Annie Seamon
Fauset, was born in New Jersey on April 27, 1882. She attended the public schools
in Philadelphia and graduated as an honor student from the Philadelphia School for
Girls. When she sought admission to Bryn Mawr College, rather than admit an African American woman, they supported her application to Cornell University. Fauset
graduated Phi Beta Kappa from Cornell in 1904. Whether she was the first black
woman to attend Cornell or to be elected to Phi Beta Kappa, both of which are often
speculated, Fauset has been called "one of the best-educated Americans of her generation."

Denied employment in Philadelphia's integrated schools, Fauset began teaching high school in New York in 1905. After a year there and a year in Baltimore,
she moved to the M Street High School (later named Dunbar High School) in Washington, D.C., where she taught for fourteen years. In 1921, a few months after receiving her master's degree from the University of Pennsylvania, Fauset joined the
staff of *The Crisis* as literary editor. In 1924 she published her first novel. Fauset
left *The Crisis* and returned to teaching in 1926. In 1929, she married a businessman, Herbert Harris, and between 1929 and 1933, she completed three other novels. When her husband died in 1958, Fauset returned to Philadelphia, where she
died in 1961.

There Is Confusion

TYPE OF WORK: Novel
FIRST PUBLISHED: 1924

Fauset's first novel, *There Is Confusion*—a tale of two families—is structured by three separate but connected plotlines, the first of which focuses on the Marshalls, a well-to-do family. Joanna, the youngest of the four children, encouraged by her father's thwarted dreams of greatness, wants to become a dancer. The second plotline focuses on Peter Bye, the fourth-generation descendant of a family whose lives are intertwined with their wealthy white former owners. While Peter's grandfather, Isaiah, refuses to accept his relative's offer to serve as their coachman and goes on to found a school for black youths in Philadelphia, Peter's dreams of becoming a surgeon are thwarted because he longs to be recognized by the white Byes and is not. Meriwether, Peter's father, deciding instead that "the world owes [him] a living," does nothing. Influenced by his father's attitude, Peter becomes entangled in the legacy of racial hatred and aspires to nothing. It is only when he becomes attracted to Joanna and is influenced by her goals of greatness that he decides, in order to win her love, to become a doctor.

The third plotline, the story of Maggie Ellersley, the daughter of a washerwoman, involves a conventional marriage. Aspiring to the middle class, Maggie begins working for Joanna's father, where she meets and takes an interest in his son, Philip. The interest appears to be mutual; however, Joanna intervenes and tells Maggie that she should marry someone in her own class. A hurt Maggie does so, then becomes a successful businesswoman when the marriage fails. After a second failed marriage, Maggie goes to France to volunteer during the war and encounters the dying Philip. They marry, and she takes care of him until his death.

Within each plotline Fauset heavy-handedly reveals the obstacles to the achievement of each character's dreams: Joanna's dream of becoming a professional dancer is thwarted by race, Peter's dream (or lack thereof) is influenced by family legacy, Maggie's dream is hindered by class. Yet Fauset also reveals how each character achieves, despite the obstacles. Unable to dance in a white theater troupe, Joanna starts her own dance class but is asked to dance the role of the colored American in "The Dance of the Nations" when the white woman chosen for the part lacks the technique. Joanna attains instant success and is eventually asked to perform three roles.

Peter, because of his love for Joanna, becomes a surgeon; however, she has no interest in assuming the conventional roles of wife and mother. Therefore, caught in the web of circumstances characteristic of sentimental novels, and through a series of contrived coincidences, Peter ends up in Europe during the war and meets one of his white relatives. Young Meriwether dies in Peter's arms, but not before extracting the promise that Peter would visit the senior Meriwether. By moving beyond hate, Peter not only receives the long-awaited recognition from the white Byes but also wins Joanna as his wife.

As evidenced by the many hardships that Maggie undergoes, Fauset suggests that Maggie's aspiration—to transcend one's class through marriage—is the most problematic. Maggie achieves her desired middle-class status not through her marriages but rather through her business acumen. Moreover, by developing a political and racial consciousness and selflessness and traveling to Europe to aid black soldiers, she is reunited with her first love. *There Is Confusion* ends, as do all sentimental novels, on a happy note. While there are many ideas introduced in the novel, critic Carolyn Sylvander states that the theme that dominates is that "surviving the hardships engendered by discrimination places the black person and the race in a position of superiority."

Plum Bun

TYPE OF WORK: Novel
FIRST PUBLISHED: 1928

Fauset's second novel, *Plum Bun: A Novel Without a Moral*, is considered by most critics her best. As in *There Is Confusion*, a middle-class African American family is at the novel's center, but unlike *There Is Confusion*, the novel's plot centers on one protagonist, Angela. In addition, the novel is structured in five parts, using a nursery rhyme as its epigraph and unifying element:

> To market, to market
> To buy a plum bun;
> Home again, home again
> Market is done.

In the first section, titled "Home," Fauset's readers are introduced to the Murray family: Junius and Mattie and their two daughters, Angela and Virginia. This section also provides the background information important to the rest of the novel. Angela and Virginia are exposed early on to their mother's fairy-tale view of marriage. Just as important, they are exposed to her views on color. Although Junius and Virginia are both brown-skinned, Mattie and Angela are light enough to pass—which they often do "for fun." Junius is not opposed to this as long as no principle is being compromised. The result, however, is that Angela grows up seeing her mother on occasion publicly ignore her dark husband and daughter. When the parents die within two weeks of each other, Angela decides to move to New York in order to further her personal and professional goals. In "Market," Angela changes her name, becoming the art student Angèle Mory and is indoctrinated in the worldly ways of courtship. In section 3, entitled "Plum Bun," Angèle meets Roger Fielding, an affluent white man, whom she dates and eventually hopes to marry. Roger does not propose marriage but rather cohabitation. Angèle does not agree, and he eventually ends the relationship, but not before Angèle has publicly denied Virginia, who has also moved to New York.

In "Home Again," the novel's fourth section, Angèle, in search of companionship, admits her love for Anthony Cross, a fellow art student who is also passing. Having resolved never to marry a white woman, Anthony rejects Angèle and becomes engaged unknowingly to her sister.

In the final section, "Market Is Done," Angèle decides to focus on her art. She wins a scholarship to study in Paris but forfeits it by revealing that she, too, is black when fellow student Rachel Powell is denied money for her passage because of her race. Angèle decides to support her own study in Paris. Before she leaves the United States, she returns "home" to Philadelphia and is reunited with a former admirer, Matthew Henson. Knowing that Virginia is really in love with Matthew, and learning that Matthew loves Virginia, Angèle does not interfere. Instead she moves to Paris, seemingly destined to be alone; however, Anthony appears that Christmas Eve, sent with Matthew and Virginia's love. Like *There Is Confusion*, *Plum Bun* has a happy ending.

Jessie Redmon Fauset (Courtesy, Moorland-Spingarn Research Center, Howard University)

By including the nursery rhyme and fairy-tale motifs within the marriage plot, Fauset explores the choices and compromises women make regarding marriage. The novel "without a moral" indeed has one: Adhering to the traditional conceptions of marriage is problematic when race, class, and gender are factors.

The Chinaberry Tree

TYPE OF WORK: Novel
FIRST PUBLISHED: 1931

The Chinaberry Tree: A Novel of American Life, Fauset's third novel, is her attempt to illustrate that "to be a Negro in America posits a dramatic situation." Believing that fate plays an important role in the lives of blacks and whites, Fauset depicts the domestic lives of African Americans who are not struggling with the harsh realities of day-to-day existence.

The Chinaberry Tree relates the story of two cousins, Laurentine Strange and Melissa Paul. Because Laurentine is the product of an illicit romantic relationship between a former slave and her master, Laurentine accepts the community's opinion that she has "bad blood." Rejection from a male suitor reinforces her feelings of inadequacy and propels her to further isolation from the community. The young Melissa, although the daughter of an adulterous relationship between Judy Strange and Sylvester Forten, believes herself superior. Sent to Red Brook to live with her relatives, Melissa meets and falls in love with Malory Forten, who, unknown to her, is her half brother. The "drama" of the novel is the exploration of both women's responses to being innocent victims of fate. Laurentine overcomes her feelings of inadequacy, and Melissa learns that she, too, is a product of "bad blood."

The Chinaberry Tree is also Fauset's attempt to prove that African Americans are not so vastly different from any other American. To illustrate this, Fauset creates characters such as Dr. Stephen Denleigh (whom Laurentine eventually marries) and Mrs. Ismay and Mrs. Brown, wives of prominent physicians, who enjoy the leisurely pursuits of bridge and whist and travel to Newark or Atlantic City to view moving pictures or to shop. There are also their offspring, children who attend private schools, enjoy winter sports, and have servants. Fauset's characters are not very different in their daily lives from financially comfortable whites.

Fauset's characters experience the joys and sorrows of love. Sarah's and Colonel Halloway's was a forbidden love; they were denied marriage because of the times in which they lived. He could not marry Sarah, but Colonel Halloway provided a comfortable home for Sarah and Laurentine. Although Laurentine experiences rejection by her first suitor, she attains love and happiness after she learns to accept herself. Melissa, who cannot marry Malory, is loved by Asshur Lane, someone she initially rejects because he aspires to be a farmer. Fauset argues that the African American is "endowed with the stuff of which chronicles may be made." In this novel Fauset addresses issues of identity in terms of race and social standing amid the disorder of her characters' daily lives.

Comedy, American Style

TYPE OF WORK: Novel
FIRST PUBLISHED: 1933

Fauset structured her final novel, *Comedy, American Style*, around the elements of drama, with its chapters entitled "The Plot," "The Characters," "Teresa's Act," "Oliver's Act," "Phebe's Act," and "Curtain." In this, Fauset's darkest work, she returns to the format of the two-parent family. The novel chronicles the life of Olivia Blanchard Cary, a light-skinned African American, who, shaped by two incidents in her childhood, chooses a life of passing. She marries a black doctor, not for love but rather for status, and they have three children. Nonetheless, Olivia's obsession with color consciousness destroys the family. When the oldest child, Teresa, falls in love with the dark-skinned Henry Bates, Olivia intervenes and forces her to marry a French man.

The youngest child, Oliver, suffers the most because of his bronze skin color. Rejected by his mother from birth and often made to play the role of servant or denied in public, he commits suicide. Only Christopher survives intact through his marriage to Phebe Grant. When the novel ends, Olivia has finally achieved her objective: Living alone in France—her husband has divorced her, and her children have abandoned her—she passes as white. In this, her only novel that does not have a happy ending, Fauset's use of satire is quite evident. One critic, pointing to Fauset's subversion of the Cinderella motif, notes that neither mother nor daughter is happily married, and both are poor. Another critic illustrates the ironic use of the Snow White motif: Olivia pronounces the bitter truth in her pregnancy with Oliver that he would be "the handsomest and most attractive of us all," and by doing so she unwittingly proclaims that black is beautiful.

SUGGESTED READINGS

Feeney, Joseph J. "A Sardonic, Unconventional Jessie Fauset: The Double Structure and Double Vision of Her Novels." *CLA Journal* 22 (1979).

Johnson, Abby Arthur. "Literary Midwife: Jessie Redmon Fauset and the Harlem Renaissance." *Phylon* 39 (1978).

McDowell, Deborah. "Jessie Fauset." In *Modern American Women Writers*, edited by Lea Baechler and A. Walton Litz. New York: Charles Scribner's Sons, 1991.

McLendon, Jacquelyn Y. *The Politics of Color in the Fiction of Jessie Fauset and Nella Larsen*. Charlottesville: University of Virginia Press, 1995.

Sato, Hiroko. "Under the Harlem Shadow: A Study of Jessie Fauset and Nella Larsen." In *The Harlem Renaissance Remembered*, edited by Arna Bontemps. New York: Dodd, Mead, 1972.

Sylvander, Carolyn. *Jessie Redmon Fauset: Black American Writer*. Troy, N.Y.: Whitston, 1981.

Wall, Cheryl. *Women of the Harlem Renaissance*. Bloomington: Indiana University Press, 1995.

Contributor: Paula C. Barnes

Rosario Ferré

BORN: Ponce, Puerto Rico; 1938

PUERTO RICAN

*Considered Puerto Rico's leading woman of letters,
Ferré writes of the struggles of women of her
culture between duty and personal needs.*

PRINCIPAL WORKS

LONG FICTION: *Maldito amor*, 1986 (*Sweet Diamond Dust*, 1988); *La batalla de las virgenas*, 1993; *The House on the Lagoon*, 1995; *Eccentric Neighborhoods*, 1998; *Flight of the Swan*, 2001

POETRY: *Sonatinas*, 1989; *Language Duel/Duelo de lenguaje*, 2002

SHORT FICTION: *Papeles de Pandora*, 1976 (*The Youngest Doll*, 1991); *Las dos Venecias*, 1992

NONFICTION: *Sitio a Eros: Trece ensayos literarios*, 1980; *El árbol y sus sombras*, 1989; *El coloquio de las perras*, 1990; *Memorias de Ponce: Autobiografia de Luis A. Ferré*, 1992; *A la sombra de tu nombre*, 2001

Rosario Ferré (roh-ZAHR-ee-oh fah-RAY) is considered Puerto Rico's leading woman of letters. A prolific writer, she has published fiction, poetry, criticism, essays, and biography. Born in Ponce, Puerto Rico, to a family with position in both politics and business, Ferré was educated at Manhattanville College, the University of Puerto Rico, and the University of Maryland, College Park, where she earned a Ph.D. in Latin American literature in 1987. Her writing career began in the 1970's with her position as editor and publisher of *Zona de carga y descarga*, a student-generated journal concentrating on new Puerto Rican literature. She has also taught at Rutgers University, Harvard University, the University of California at Berkeley, The Johns Hopkins University, and the University of Puerto Rico, Rio Piedras. She has been awarded an honorary doctorate from Brown University. In addition, from 1977 to 1980, her column of literary criticism was published in *El Mundo*, a Puerto Rican newspaper.

Ferré also wrote a biography of her father, Luis Ferré, the pro-statehood governor of the Commonwealth of Puerto Rico from 1968 to 1972, but she is best known for her fiction. Her nonfiction essays in *Zona de carga y descarga* reflected her ideals of social reform and independent politics. This journal was the outcome of an idea generated in a master's degree class at the University of Puerto Rico. With other students, she founded a journal that offered an opportunity for publication to many young Puerto Rican writers who later became famous.

Ferré's feminist ideas also formed the basis for her short stories. Her children's literature, including fables and short stories, contains messages concerning the need for social and political reform. Ferré's fiction in the form of short stories and novels for adults tells the stories of women in her culture who struggle with issues of class, race, and economic status. In stories like "The Youngest Doll," she explores the conflicts between cultural expectations for women in a changing Puerto Rican society and the common human need for decency and respect. The use of symbolism and allegory in this story is reflected in many of her longer works. Influenced by her family (her mother was from the landed gentry, and her father was an industrialist before he became a politician), Ferré writes of the struggles of women of this culture between duty and personal needs. Early in her career, she was important primarily to feminist academics, until the publication of *The House on the Lagoon* in 1995. This is the first of her novels written initially in English. Upon its publication, she received international attention with her nomination for the National Book Award. Ferré's recent novels are written in English, but her poetry is published only in Spanish.

Many of her works, including *Sweet Diamond Dust* and *The House on the Lagoon*, illustrate the ties between Puerto Rico and Spain as well as the United States. Through multilevel plots dealing with generational conflict and gender constraints, Ferré explores what life is and has been like for people, both men and women, of Puerto Rican descent. Her use of layered time frames, wide plot scope, and vivid language has been compared to Isabel Allende and Gabriel García Márquez. Her stories of the people and the rich culture of her homeland provide an opportunity for readers to learn and appreciate her Caribbean heritage.

The House on the Lagoon
TYPE OF WORK: Novel
FIRST PUBLISHED: 1995

The House on the Lagoon tells the story of the Mendizabal family, beginning in the 1880's and focusing on the period from July 4, 1917, when Puerto Ricans were granted U.S. citizenship, to the day of a hotly contested plebiscite on statehood in 1993, when fictional *independentistas* staged a takeover. Ferré interweaves the family's passions and struggles with the history of Puerto Rico and its changing relations with Spain and the United States. The main characters, Quintín Mendizabal and his wife, Isabel Monfort, have conflicting political views. Isabel advocates Puerto Rican independence; Quintín supports close ties with the United States. Quintin believes in traditional women's roles; Isabel advocates feminism. They also disagree about the novel Isabel is writing, a history that includes stories about her family as well as her husband's family.

One day Quintín discovers his wife's manuscript hidden in a bookcase. Beginning with marginal notes and condescending comments, Quintín ultimately writes his own interpretation of events and becomes the novel's second narrator. He corrects glaring anachronisms, protests scandalous portrayals of his family's and his own behavior, and rewrites the stories from his own perspective. When Isabel's manuscript reveals his ruthless business practices, his complicity in the suicide of one of his brothers, and his harsh treatment of his rebellious sons, he feels threatened and decides to suppress her version of the truth. When all else fails, she decides to leave him and he resorts to violence. At the end of the novel, Isabel finds the courage to defend herself and her children; she hits Quintín with an iron bar, killing him.

Within this dual version of history, Ferré also maps out a geography of the haves and the have-nots on the island, centering the action on the Mendizabal family's San Juan mansion. Upstairs are the Mendizabals, with their materially successful fusion of Spanish conquistador and American capitalist methods, their hot tempers, and their self-destructive habits. Downstairs are the servants, the wise and patient Avilés family, brought as slaves from Angola in the eighteenth century. The Mendizabal patriarchs meet their match in elderly Petra Avilés, granddaughter of an African-born rebel slave. Threatened with censorship and control by her husband, Isabel finds natural allies in Petra and her family.

SUGGESTED READINGS

Castillo, Debra A. "Surfacing: Rosario Ferré and Julieta Campos, with Rosario Castellanos." In *Talking Back: Toward a Latin American Feminist Literary Criticism*, edited by Debra Castillo. Ithaca, N.Y.: Cornell University Press, 1992.

Erro-Peralta, Nora, and Caridad Silva, eds. *Beyond the Border: A New Age in Latin American Women's Fiction*. Gainesville: University of Florida Press, 2000.

Fernandez Olmos, Margarite. "From a Woman's Perspective: The Short Stories of Rosario Ferré and Ana Lydia Vega." In *Contemporary Women Authors of Latin America: Introducing Essays*, edited by Doris Meyers and Margarita Fernandez Olmos. Brooklyn, N.Y.: Brooklyn College, 1983.

Ferré, Rosario. "Interview with Rosario Ferré." Interview by Magdalena García Pinto. Translated by Trudy Balch and Magdalena García Pinto. In *Women Writers of Latin America*. Austin: University of Texas Press, 1991.

Hintz, Susanne H. *Rosario Ferré: A Search for Identity*. New York: Lang, 1995.

Contributors: Dolores A. D'Angelo and Genevieve Slomski

Harvey Fierstein

BORN: Brooklyn, New York; June 6, 1954

JEWISH

*Fierstein's work challenges assumptions regarding
the lives of gay and bisexual Americans.*

PRINCIPAL WORKS

CHILDREN'S LITERATURE: *The Sissy Duckling*, 2002
DRAMA: *In Search of the Cobra Jewels*, pr. 1972; *Freaky Pussy*, pr. 1973; *Cannibals
Just Don't Know Better*, pr. 1974; *Flatbush Tosca*, pr. 1975; *Torch Song Trilogy*,
pr. 1978-1979, pb. 1979 (includes *The International Stud, Fugue in a Nursery*,
and *Widows and Children First!*); *Spookhouse*, pr. 1982; *La Cage aux folles*, pr.
1983 (libretto; music and lyrics by Jerry Herman); *Safe Sex*, pr., pb. 1987 (trilogy; includes *Manny and Jake, Safe Sex*, and *On Tidy Endings*); *Legs Diamond*,
pr. 1988 (libretto; music and lyrics by Peter Allen)
SCREENPLAY: *Torch Song Trilogy*, 1988 (adaptation of his play)
TELEPLAYS: *Kaddish and Old Men*, 1987; *Tidy Endings*, 1988 (adaptation of his
play *On Tidy Endings*)

In the late 1970's, Harvey Fierstein (FIR-steen) premiered a trio of one-act plays
collecitively titled *Torch Song Trilogy* that introduced gay characters to the
American stage without apology. The central character, Arnold Becker, is a drag
queen with a desire to live a life consistent with the American Dream. He wants to
secure a loving family life and sees no reason why he should be denied the opportunity of creating one simply because of his sexual orientation. The uniqueness
of the play's statement lies in the fact that the work was premiered at the end of
the sexual revolution of the 1970's, when gay life was viewed by many as simply
a series of casual encounters. Americans seemed content with a view of gays
as emotional children who lived strange, uncommitted lives. Fierstein's characters challenge this view.

The son of a handkerchief manufacturer and a librarian, Fierstein grew up in a
tight family unit that accepted his gayness. His first encounters with the lifestyle
were through family friends who shared long-term, committed relationships. These
were his role models, who helped him develop his somewhat conservative view of
gay life.

Fierstein's reworking of the popular French film *La Cage aux folles* (1978)
is another example of the playwright's ability to present fully developed gay
characters for mixed audiences. Fierstein received a Tony Award for the best

book for a musical in 1984. The musical enjoyed a long run in the United States and abroad, including a much anticipated revival in 2004. Like *Torch Song Trilogy*, the play is an old-fashioned love story espousing the virtues of family and commitment.

Fierstein's writing style is a fusion of his several identities. His work is distinguished by a mixture of Jewish and gay humor interspersed with poignant self-revelation. It is this combination that has endeared him to straight and gay audiences. Through laughter and dramatic truth, his characters are able to tap the human thread that brings all people together.

Although best known as a playwright, Fierstein is also an actor who has played various roles on stage, on national television, and in film, notably as Frank, the gay brother in the film *Mrs. Doubtfire* (1993) and Tevye in the 2005 Broadway revival of *Fiddler on the Roof* (pr. 1964). In addition to his work as an artist, Fierstein is active in various gay rights organizations and devotes considerable time and energy as an activist for causes relating to the acquired immunodeficiency syndrome (AIDS).

Torch Song Trilogy

Type of work: Drama
First produced: pr. 1978-1979, pb. 1979

Torch Song Trilogy is Fierstein's groundbreaking portrait of a gay man's struggle for respect and love in a homophobic world. The play, comprising three one acts titled *The International Stud*, *Fugue in a Nursery*, and *Widows and Children First*, chronicles the journey of the central character, Arnold Becker, from a life of transitory sexual encounters with strangers in the back rooms of New York's gay bars to his insistence on relationships based on commitment, respect, and love.

Harvey Fierstein (AP/Wide World Photos)

In the first play, "International Stud," Arnold meets Ed Reiss in a gay bar. For Arnold, the encounter offers the possibility of an honest relationship that will put an end to his loneliness. Ed, however, sees his meeting with Arnold as simply a one-night stand and returns to his developing relationship with Laurel. He describes himself as bisexual but chooses to hide his homosexuality for fear of public opinion. Ed attempts to terminate the relationship but finds himself returning to Arnold and is even able to acknowledge his love for Arnold. Arnold, however, cannot accept an undercover and uncommitted relationship and finally walks away.

The International Stud presents the reader with two characters who are at different places regarding their understanding of themselves. Arnold is comfortable with himself as a gay man and is in search of a lover who is also a friend. Ed, however, is in denial as to his sexuality and, therefore, incapable of giving himself to anyone as either friend or lover.

Fugue in a Nursery takes place one year after *The International Stud*. By this time Ed and Arnold have what each wanted; Arnold has Alan, an eighteen-year-old model, and Ed is involved in a relationship with Laurel. The action of the play takes place on an oversized bed. Arnold and Alan have been invited to spend a weekend with Ed and Laurel. In a brilliantly written series of overlapping lines and interwoven actions, the playwright demonstrates the confusion of each character as he or she attempts to resolve the conflict between what one has and what one wants. It becomes clear that none of the characters has found all that he or she was seeking. In Alan, however, Arnold has found someone who loves and respects him.

Fugue in a Nursery continues the argument of *The International Stud*. It clearly demonstrates that one cannot give love until one has learned to love oneself. Alan and Arnold have a better chance of building a solid relationship because each is aware of who he is and can, therefore, be honest with the other. Ed, however, can talk to Laurel about his confusions but cannot confront the truth of his attraction to and preference for Arnold.

The final play in the trilogy, *Widows and Children First*, takes place five years after the preceding play. Arnold has lost Alan to a mob of gay-bashers and is currently in the process of adopting David, a gay teenager. Ed's marriage to Laurel has failed, and he is temporarily staying with Arnold. The action of the play centers around a visit from Arnold's recently widowed mother and her inability to accept her son's need for love and the security of a family. Although she is aware of Arnold's lifestyle, she does not accept it. She is insulted when he compares his suffering at the death of Alan to her loss of her husband, and she questions the morality of a gay man rearing a child. A series of arguments ensues, and Arnold states that his mother is unwelcome in his life unless she can respect him and the validity of his feelings and desires. She leaves. David affirms his love for his soon-to-be father, and Ed finally confronts the truth of his desire to be with Arnold.

Torch Song Trilogy addresses the issue of gay identity and asks its audience to deal with the broader questions of honesty and respect regardless of sexual preference or lifestyle.

SUGGESTED READINGS

Connema, Richard. "San Francisco's Torch Song." *Talkin' Broadway's Regional News: San Francisco Reviews*, June 27, 2000.

Ebert, Roger. "*Torch Song Trilogy*." *Chicago Sun-Times*, December 23, 1988.

Fierstein, Harvey. "His Heart Is Young and Gay." Interview by Jack Kroll. *Newsweek*, June 20, 1983.

_____. Interview by Harry Stein. *Playboy* 35 (August, 1988).

Hungerford, Jason. "My Reaction to *Torch Song Trilogy*." *Pflag-Talk*, January 19, 1997.

Contributor: Don Evans

Rudolph Fisher

BORN: Washington, D.C.; May 9, 1897
DIED: New York, New York; December 26, 1934

AFRICAN AMERICAN

*Fisher depicts the layers of Harlem life during the
1920's with humor, wit, and satirical grace.*

PRINCIPAL WORKS

DRAMA: *Conjur' Man Dies*, pr. 1936
LONG FICTION: *The Walls of Jericho*, 1928; *The Conjure-Man Dies: A Mystery Tale
of Dark Harlem*, 1932
SHORT FICTION: *The City of Refuge: The Collected Stories*, 1987 (John McCluskey,
editor); *Joy and Pain*, 1996

Rudolph Fisher was educated in the arts and sciences. His first short story, "The
City of Refuge," was published while Fisher was in medical school, and throughout
his life he maintained careers as a doctor and as a writer of fiction and medical research.

For all his medical degrees, Fisher wanted to be known as a writer who could interpret Harlem life. Little seemed to have escaped his vision and analysis. He saw
Harlem as a vast canvas upon which he painted characters from several different
levels of life. There were the "rats," a Harlem term for the working class; the
"dickties," which was Harlemese for upper-class aspirants to white values; Pull-
man porters; gangsters; barbers; pool hall owners; doctors; lawyers; misguided
white liberals; and white celebrants and aspirants to Harlem culture. In the novel
The Walls of Jericho, Fisher brings all of the economic, racial, and political strata of
Harlem together at the annual costume ball. The dickties and the rats mingle with
whites who are in search of what they think is black bohemia. The dance hall setting
that Fisher enlivens in *The Walls of Jericho* was modeled after the Harlem cabarets
and nightclubs he frequented.

Fisher achieved remarkable balance between the medical and artistic worlds.
His short stories were published in national magazines in which other Harlem Renaissance writers could not publish. *The Walls of Jericho* was well received. The
detective novel *The Conjure-Man Dies* was hailed as a first. From 1929 to 1934,
Fisher was a hospital superintendent, a roentgenologist, a first lieutenant in the
medical division of the 369th Infantry, and a lecturer at the 135th Street Branch of
the New York Public Library.

Fisher seemed to know that working-class blacks in Harlem led lives that were far removed from the artistic renaissance popularized by intellectuals. In such short stories as "The City of Refuge" and "Vestiges, Harlem Sketches," he sympathetically depicts the struggles of many who have come from the South and who are disappointed or tricked by the fast, indifferent ways of the city. Characters such as Jinx Jenkins, Bubber Brown, and Joshua "Shine" Jones in *The Walls of Jericho* are subject to the competition and physical dangers of furniture moving. A maid in *The Walls of Jericho* is viewed by her white employer as slightly better than most blacks because of her light skin.

In 1934, Fisher died of cancer caused by X-ray exposure. A retinue of Harlem artists, including Countée Cullen and Noble Sissle, joined Fisher's wife and son to mourn the loss of one of Harlem's visionaries.

The Conjure-Man Dies

Type of work: Novel
First published: 1932

In *The Conjure-Man Dies: A Mystery Tale of Dark Harlem*, Fisher combines his talent and comedic wit with his knowledge of medicine to produce the first-known detective novel by an African American. Fisher introduces a variety of Harlem characters, including Jinx Jenkins and Bubber Brown, unemployed furniture movers who also appear in *The Walls of Jericho* (1928). Other characters include John Archer, the doctor who helps Harlem police solve the murder.

The complex plot highlights characters and settings popularized in Fisher's works. When Jinx and Bubber discover the murdered conjure man, they become suspects with several others: a numbers-runner, Spider Webb, who works in Harlem's illegal lottery system; a drug addict named Doty Hicks; a railroad worker; and a church worker. Mr. Crouch, mortician and owner of the building in which the conjure man is a tenant, and Crouch's wife Martha are quickly dismissed as suspects. When the corpse disappears and reappears as the live conjure man, Archer and Detective Dart know that there has been a murder but are unable to find the corpse. The conjure man is seen burning a body in the furnace. The body is of his servant, who was mistakenly killed instead of the conjure man. The conjure man adamantly insists he is innocent and helps to set a trap for the real murderer, but the conjure man is fatally shot by the railroad worker. Distraught that he has killed her lover, Martha assaults the railroad man, and all discover he is none other than the avenging Mr. Crouch, in disguise.

The detective story framework of *The Conjure-Man Dies* does not overshadow Fisher's depiction of several issues of Harlem life. Residents of Harlem resort to creative means to survive as the Depression makes their difficult economic situations worse. Bubber becomes a self-appointed detective for spouses who suspect their partners are being unfaithful. The numbers racket provides a living for many, including the conjure man. African Americans who are "firsts" to achieve a specific rank are under pressure to prove themselves worthy. Such is the case for detective

Dart, who privately thanks Dr. Archer for promising that the city administration will be informed that Dart solved the murder.

Although Fisher's development of the hard-boiled character may have been influenced by the detective fiction of Dashiell Hammett, his most remarkable character is the conjure man, N'Gana Frimbo, a Harvard-educated West African king who imparts the traditions of his culture to Dr. Archer. Frimbo reflects Fisher's interest in the connections among blacks in Harlem, the Caribbean, and Africa. In the spirit of the Harlem Renaissance, Fisher creates a new path with *The Conjure-Man Dies*, one that would influence later writers such as Chester Himes and Walter Mosley.

SUGGESTED READINGS

Bell, Bernard W. *The Afro-American Novel and Its Tradition*. Amherst: University of Massachusetts Press, 1987.

Brown, Sterling A. *The Negro in American Fiction*. 1937. Reprint. New York: Arno Press, 1969.

Davis, Arthur P. *From the Dark Tower: Afro-American Writers, 1900 to 1960*. Washington, D.C.: Howard University Press, 1974.

De Jongh, James. *Vicious Modernism: Black Harlem and the Literary Imagination*. New York: Cambridge University Press, 1990.

Gayle, Addison, Jr. *The Way of the New World: The Black Novel in America*. Garden City, N.Y.: Anchor Press, 1975.

Gloster, Hugh M. *Negro Voices in American Fiction*. 1948. Reprint. New York: Russell & Russell, 1976.

Kramer, Victor, ed. *The Harlem Renaissance Re-examined*. New York: AMS Press, 1987.

Lewis, David Levering. *When Harlem Was in Vogue*. New York: Oxford University Press, 1989.

McCluskey, John, Jr., ed. *The City of Refuge: The Collected Stories of Rudolph Fisher*. Columbia: University of Missouri Press, 1987.

McGruder, Kevin. "Jane Ryder Fisher." *Black Scholar* 23 (Summer, 1993).

Perry, Margaret. *Silence to the Drums: A Survey of the Literature of the Harlem Renaissance*. Westport, Conn.: Greenwood Press, 1976.

Tignor, Eleanor Q. "Rudolph Fisher: Harlem Novelist." *Langston Hughes Review* 1 (Fall, 1982).

Contributor: Australia Tarver

Maria Irene Fornes

BORN: Havana, Cuba; May 14, 1930

CUBAN AMERICAN

A force in Off- and Off-Off-Broadway theater, Fornes has
written scores of plays, has directed many of her own and
other productions, and has been actively involved in
supporting other women and Latino playwrights.

PRINCIPAL WORKS

DRAMA: *The Widow*, pr., pb. 1961; *There, You Died!*, pr. 1963 (revised pr. 1964, pb.
1971; as *Tango Palace*); *Promenade*, pr. 1965, pb. 1971 (music by Al
Carmines); *The Successful Life of Three*, pr. 1965, pb. 1971; *The Office*, pr.
1966; *The Annunciation*, pr. 1967; *A Vietnamese Wedding*, pr. 1967, pb. 1971;
Dr. Kheal, pr. 1968, pb. 1971; *Molly's Dream*, pr. 1968, pb. 1971; *The Red
Burning Light: Or, Mission XQ3*, pr. 1968, pb. 1971; *The Curse of Langston
House*, pr. 1972; *Aurora*, pr. 1974; *Cap-a-Pie*, pr. 1975; *Fefu and Her Friends*,
pr. 1977, pb. 1980; *Lolita in the Garden*, pr. 1977; *In Service*, pr. 1978; *Eyes on
the Harem*, pr. 1979; *Blood Wedding*, pr. 1980 (adaptation of Federico García
Lorca's play); *Evelyn Brown: A Diary*, pr. 1980; *A Visit*, pr. 1981; *Life Is a
Dream*, pr. 1981 (adaptation of Pedro Calderón de la Barca's play); *The Danube*,
pr. 1982; *Mud*, pr. 1983, pb. 1986; *Abingdon Square*, pr. 1984, pb. 1988; *No
Time*, pr. 1984; *Sarita*, pr. 1984, pb. 1986; *The Conduct of Life*, pr. 1985, pb.
1986; *Drowning*, pr. 1986, pb. 1987 (adaptation of Anton Chekhov's story);
Lovers and Keepers, pr. 1986, pb. 1987 (music by Tito Puente); *And What of the
Night?*, pr. 1989; *Oscar and Bertha*, pr. 1991; *Enter the Night*, pr. 1993, pb.
1996; *Balseros*, pr. 1996; *Summer in Gossensass*, pr. 1998; *Letters from Cuba*,
pr. 2000

Maria Irene Fornes (mah-REE-ah i-REEN fohr-NAYS) was born in Havana,
Cuba, in 1930. Her father did not believe in formal schooling, so she attended only
the third through sixth grades. After her father's death, she went to New York in
1945 with her widowed mother and became a naturalized American citizen in
1951. She worked at a variety of menial jobs. Her first artistic interest was painting, and in 1954 she began studying with Hans Hofmann. She spent three years in
Europe in the mid-1950's. During this time, she has said, she knew nothing about
theater, but she did see the first production of Samuel Beckett's *En attendant
Godot* (1952; *Waiting for Godot*, 1954) in Paris, an experience that she has
described as profound. She credits this performance and her reading of Henrik

Ibsen's *Hedda Gabler* (1890; English translation, 1891) with inspiring her to become a playwright several years later.

Fornes returned to New York in 1957 and worked as a textile designer. She developed a relationship with Susan Sontag, who at that time wanted to become a writer. According to Fornes, she started writing as a kind of game to encourage Sontag; both women found success fairly rapidly. Fornes's play *There, You Died!* was produced by the Actors' Workshop in San Francisco in 1963. That same year, Fornes joined the playwriting unit of the Actors Studio in New York, which produced the same play under the title *Tango Palace* in 1964. In 1965 she won her first Obie (Off-Broadway award) for Distinguished Plays, for *Promenade* and *The Successful Life of Three*.

Although she is not as acclaimed in mainstream theater as her fans would like her to be, Fornes has been a force in Off- and Off-Off-Broadway theater. She has written more than forty plays, has directed many of her own and other productions, and has been actively involved in supporting other women and Latino playwrights. She cofounded the Women's Theater Council in 1972, with the purpose of supporting the writing and production of new plays by American women. In 1978 she began teaching Playwrights Workshop at INTAR (International Arts Relations), and in 1981 she became director of INTAR's Hispanic Playwrights-in-Residence Laboratory, a national program to support Hispanic playwrights.

She won additional Obies in 1977 (Playwriting, for *Fefu and Her Friends*), 1979 (Direction, for *Eyes on the Harem*), 1982 (Sustained Achievement), 1984 (Playwriting and Direction, for *The Danube*, *Sarita*, and *Mud*), 1985 (Playwriting, for *The Conduct of Life*), and 1988 (Best New American Play, for *Abingdon Square*). She has also been awarded numerous grants and fellowships (Guggenheim, Rockefeller, and the National Endowment for the Arts among them) and is sought after as a teacher and lecturer, both in the United States and abroad. In 1999 the Signature Theater Company in New York did a season-long retrospective of Fornes's work.

Critics and scholars find it impossible to compartmentalize the works of Fornes. Many regard her as a realistic playwright, but her plays also experiment with avant-garde techniques, expressionist and Cuban and American influences, and the influences of Ibsen, Beckett, and Bertolt Brecht. She eschews political and formal labels and emphasizes writing as a process of inventing, of always remaining on new ground. If the constant is her experimentation, the measure of her success is the number of contemporary playwrights who acknowledge her influence. Fellow dramatist Paula Vogel has noted that for these playwrights, there are only two stages— before and after reading Maria Irene Fornes.

The Conduct of Life

TYPE OF WORK: Drama
FIRST PRODUCED: 1985, pb. 1986

Perhaps Fornes's best-known play, *The Conduct of Life* partners violence against women with political violence. The play centers on the figure of Orlando, who is the head of his household and also an army officer involved in state-sponsored torture. Orlando mocks his wife, Leticia, and dominates his household, including Olympia, his housekeeper. He also beats and rapes Nena, a twelve-year-old girl whom he keeps in the basement for his sexual pleasures. As the action progresses, Fornes shows how violence breeds more violence: Leticia finally rebels and kills Orlando. She then gives the gun to Nena, and the play ends with her asking Nena to shoot her as well.

The Conduct of Life shows Fornes's continuing concern with the intersection of gender, power, and violence. Olympia survives because she is able to dismiss Orlando despite his threats, and Nena survives her brutal ordeal through a Christ-like acceptance of others' pain. Orlando is only able to perform sexually if violence is involved. He rapes Nena and forces himself on his wife at the end of the play. Leticia, who tries to endure this world, finally resorts to violence. With these characters, Fornes explores many different ways in which power and gender interact and shows how oppression breeds violence and hatred.

SUGGESTED READINGS

Delgado, Maria M., and Caridad Svetch, eds. *Conducting a Life: Reflections on the Theatre of Maria Irene Fornes*. Lyme, N.H.: Smith and Kraus, 1999.
Kent, Assunta Bartolomucci. *Maria Irene Fornes and Her Critics*. Westport, Conn.: Greenwood Press, 1996.
Moroff, Diane Lynn. *Fornes: Theater in the Present Tense*. Ann Arbor: University of Michigan Press, 1996.
Porterfield, Sally. "Black Cats and Green Trees: The Art of Maria Irene Fornes." *Modern Drama* 43 (Summer, 2000): 204-212.
Robinson, Marc. *The Other American Drama*. Baltimore, Md.: The Johns Hopkins University Press, 1994.
_____, ed. *The Theater of Maria Irene Fornes*. Baltimore: The Johns Hopkins University Press, 1999.

Contributors: Elsie Galbreath Haley and David Jortner

Charles Fuller

BORN: Philadelphia, Pennsylvania; March 5, 1939

AFRICAN AMERICAN

Fuller has helped break a long tradition of stereotyping blacks, especially black men, in literature.

PRINCIPAL WORKS

DRAMA: *Sun Flowers, The Rise*, pr. 1968 (one acts); *The Village: A Party*, pr. 1968, pr. 1969 (as *The Perfect Party*); *In My Many Names and Days*, pr. 1972; *First Love*, pr. 1974; *In the Deepest Part of Sleep*, pr. 1974; *The Candidate*, pr. 1974; *The Lay Out Letter*, pr. 1975; *The Brownsville Raid*, pr. 1976; *Sparrow in Flight*, pr. 1978; *Zooman and the Sign*, pr. 1980, pb. 1982; *A Soldier's Play*, pr., pb. 1981; *Eliot's Coming*, pr. 1988 (pr. as part of the musical revue *Urban Blight*); *Prince*, pr. 1988; *Sally*, pr. 1988; *We*, pr. 1989 (combined performance of *Sally* and *Prince*; parts 1 and 2 of five-part play series); *Burner's Frolic*, pr. 1990 (part 4 of *We* play series); *Jonquil*, pr. 1990 (part 3 of *We* play series)

SCREENPLAYS: *A Soldier's Story*, 1984 (adaptation of his play); *Zooman*, 1995 (adaptation of his play)

TELEPLAYS: *Roots, Resistance, and Renaissance*, 1967 (series); *Mitchell*, 1968; *Black America*, 1970-1971 (series); *The Sky Is Gray*, 1980 (from the story by Ernest J. Gaines); *A Gathering of Old Men*, 1987 (adaptation of the novel by Ernest J. Gaines); *Love Songs*, 1999

Charles Fuller was reared in comfortable circumstances in an extended family of many foster children in North Philadelphia. He attended a Roman Catholic high school with his lifelong friend, Larry Neal, and attended Villanova University from 1956 to 1958. After a four-year hiatus in the U.S. Army in Japan and Korea, he returned to complete his undergraduate studies at LaSalle College from 1965 to 1968. Fuller began writing short stories, poetry, and essays in the 1960's in Philadelphia mostly at night after working various daytime jobs. His interest in literature, largely a result of assuming the responsibility of proofreading his father's print jobs, began early and served as the fertile source for a formal writing career, which developed from his short stories long after he began writing.

Fuller wrote and produced his first play, *The Village: A Party*, in 1968. His place as a significant and talented playwright in contemporary African American theater is marked by an impressive number of dramas, among them *Zooman and the Sign*, for which he received two Obie Awards for best play and best playwright in 1980, and *A Soldier's Play*, which received the New York Drama Critics

Circle Award for best American play, the 1982 Pulitzer Prize in drama, and a film contract in 1984.

In addition to his Pulitzer Prize-winning *A Soldier's Play*, a number of his best-known plays have been produced by the Negro Ensemble Company, notably *The Brownsville Raid*, *Zooman and the Sign*, and the *We* plays.

As a social reformer, Fuller is concerned with brushing away deeply rooted stereotypes and uprooting preconceptions in order to explore the complexities of human relationships—particularly black-white relationships in America—and rectify the portrayals that distort African Americans, especially the black male. Critical of black hatred for and treatment of other blacks, Fuller is just as critical of the negative portrayal of the black male by the white media. Convinced that the stage is a powerful medium that can effectively rectify the stereotyped image of blacks shaped by white media, Fuller combined the mystery genre with his knowledge of the military structure of the U.S. Army to expose some of the real conflicts of white and black, and of black and black, in America.

The Brownsville Raid

TYPE OF WORK: Drama
FIRST PRODUCED: 1976

Engrossed by the history of the Civil War (he dates the African American relation to the United States from the Emancipation Proclamation), Fuller blended politics with history in *The Brownsville Raid*. While working in New York with the Negro Ensemble Company, which had previously staged his first play for the group (*In the Deepest Part of Sleep*), Fuller showed the direction that his future plays would take. Using a historical event as its basis, *The Brownsville Raid* dramatized the story of a company of black soldiers who, in 1906, were wrongfully accused of causing a riot in Texas and shooting a man. In the play, Fuller also explores the relationship between President Theodore Roosevelt and Booker T. Washington, who asks his black editors to play down the "incident" to preserve the peace. The soldiers are dishonorably discharged, and only sixty years later are they vindicated when the truth is discovered. For all of them, however, it is too late.

Zooman and the Sign

TYPE OF WORK: Drama
FIRST PRODUCED: 1980, pb. 1982

In *Zooman and the Sign*, Fuller uses the device of a murder investigation (which he had first tried in *The Brownsville Raid*) to propel the story. In addition, he began experimenting with the title character's soliloquies, which alternated with the general action, giving the play an abrupt, stop-start rhythm. The situation in

Charles Fuller (AP/Wide World Photos)

Zooman and the Sign is one all too recognizable today: A twelve-year-old girl is accidentally killed in a fight between two street gangs, and the play charts the efforts of her anguished parents to discover the killer. Equally harrowing is the underlying theme: The father, in despair that none of his neighbors will come forward to identify the killer (because they are afraid that as witnesses they will have to deal with the police, though they themselves are innocent), puts up a sign outside his house proclaiming that his daughter's killers are free because of the community's indifference. The neighbors, in turn, are so incensed by the accusation that they threaten his life and attempt to tear down the sign. Their rage, in short, is turned against one of their own people; they have lost their sense of responsibility to one another because it has been destroyed by the very institution that should be protecting them: the law.

Here, Fuller has touched on a universal theme, for in just such a way were Nazi concentration camp monitors, though prisoners themselves, wont to ally themselves against their fellow captives because of their own brutalization. Meanwhile, the killer, Zooman, has proclaimed himself to the audience and in his soliloquies explains his way of life, noting that if a black man kills a black man and is not caught immediately, the authorities forget about it. In an ironic twist, the dead girl's uncle, unaware of the murderer's identity, accidentally shoots him, just as the niece was accidentally killed. When the parents look at the dead face of the "perpetrator," it is that of a teenage boy who, in his mind, has made virility synonymous with violence.

A Soldier's Play

TYPE OF WORK: Drama
FIRST PRODUCED: 1981

A Soldier's Play, which won the Pulitzer Prize in drama in 1982, is a murder mystery in which Fuller examines many social issues and poses provocative questions. The play also won the New York Drama Critics Circle Award, with a citation for Best American Play. The screenplay adaptation, *A Soldier's Story* (1984), which Fuller wrote, garnered an Academy Award nomination for adapted screenplay.

A play in two acts, *A Soldier's Play* examines and evaluates the causes of oppression of African Americans and the obstacles to their advancement. Unlike Fuller's two other award-winning plays, *The Brownsville Raid* (1976) and *Zooman and the Sign* (1980), *A Soldier's Play* has no particular, actual historical source. The play very realistically describes, however, the complex social issues that pervade his work: institutional, systemic racism in the U.S. Army during World War II; race relations; black genocide and the search for the meaning and definition of blackness in America; the meaning of democracy and the place of African Americans in it; and what it means to be black in a racially biased society.

Outside a segregated U.S. Army camp in Tynin, Louisiana, during World War II, a tyrannical technical sergeant, Vernon Waters, is murdered. The local brass has succeeded in playing down the murder until a Howard-trained attorney, Captain Davenport, is sent by Washington, D.C., to investigate the case. Initially assumed to be racially motivated, the murder's prime suspects are the white townspeople. The Ku Klux Klan is the first suspect, then two white officers. Davenport's thorough investigation, conducted in an atmosphere of racial hostility, mistrust on all sides, and condescension, leads to a surprising discovery of the murderer and the motives for the murder. The murderer is Private Peterson, the least likely suspect.

Strong, outspoken, and opinionated, Peterson faces off with Waters, whose militant agenda for black destiny causes the innocent, naïve C. J. to commit suicide. Waters's heinous, sinister, and obsessive master plan to cleanse the black race of "geeches" such as C. J. meets its match in Peterson's own calculated perspective of how to refashion the black image. Mutual hatred eventually leads to murder, not before, however, Waters realizes the flaw in his inhumane master plan, grieves his obsession with blackness, and challenges the source of his misdirected self-justifying posture.

In focusing on the character of Waters rather than on the murder or the murderer, Fuller is able to engage and address the major causes and effects of the race problem, particularly the psychological. The play indicts all of the characters—white and black, except C. J.—for racially motivated violence informed by pervasive prejudice and dangerous stereotypical assumptions.

We

TYPE OF WORK: Drama
FIRST PRODUCED: 1989-1990

Once more, Fuller looks to American history for his subject. After watching the classic film *One Third of a Nation* (1939), with its infamous depiction of black-white relationships, Fuller decided to counter with his own perspective and planned his multi-play opus *We*.

Directed by Douglas Turner Ward of the Negro Ensemble Company in 1989, *Sally* and *Prince*, the first two plays in Fuller's projected cycle, provide a panoramic view of the American Civil War and its aftermath from an African American perspective. The mood of both plays is that of trust betrayed. *Sally*, set in South Carolina in the middle of the war, has a title character who is a recently freed slave and widow with a teenage son; she wishes for her son's safety, some land, and a man of her own. In one of several episodes dealing with freed slaves at loose ends or serving as Union soldiers, the black soldiers, resentful at being paid less than their white counterparts, bring about a strike and a betrayal. A black sergeant named Prince, who gains Sally's attention but has no wish to settle down, has the same kinds of ambitions and dreams common to white men. Forced to be an intermediary between the strikers and the sympathetic but firm-minded white general in charge, he is persuaded by the latter—who sees the strike as a rebellion against his authority—to identify the ringleaders, who are then shot. Prince faces a moral dilemma; he must choose whether to betray his fellow black soldiers or the army system of which he approves and in which he flourishes.

Recalling some of the same characters and more focused than the first play, *Prince* deals with the protagonist, a Union prison guard in Virginia, who fatally shoots a ruthlessly taunting Southern captive and runs off. Other characters include former slaves on a farm, who have long waited to be paid for picking cotton for the North. One worker named Burner (the title character of *Burner's Frolic*, the fourth play in the cycle) objects to the delay and is imprisoned by the well-meaning but benighted Northerner running the plantation. Burner's lover is a tough black businesswoman who makes a living selling sweetcakes and wants to have her own store. When Prince, ready to pursue his dream of heading west, refuses her request to free Burner, she stabs him, but he survives and continues on his way.

The third play in the cycle, *Jonquil*, reveals Sally with other freed women slaves being abused and raped by Klu Klux Klan members. Sally's rapist, she discovers from the blind Jonquil who recognizes him from his voice, is a judge known for his benevolence toward slaves and malignance toward those freed. Sally persuades her reluctant husband to form a black militia to fight against thuggish whites, but the results have sad consequences.

The plays received mixed but not largely positive reviews, owing to problems of focus and structure. In Fuller's plays, the focus is on the injury that blacks do to blacks, which always results ultimately from the racist infrastructure in which they find themselves. Fuller does not focus on problems between blacks and whites but rather the experiences of blacks among themselves. "I wanted," he said, "to put blacks and whites on stage as people. I didn't want to do the usual black and white confrontation piece."

Suggested Readings

Anadolu-Okur, Nilgun. *Contemporary African American Theater: Afrocentricity in the Works of Larry Neal, Amiri Baraka, and Charles Fuller.* New York: Garland, 1997.

Carter, Steven R. "The Detective as Solution: Charles Fuller's *A Soldier's Play*." *Clues* 12, no. 1 (Spring/Summer, 1991): 33-42.

Fuller, Charles. "Pushing Beyond the Pulitzer." Interview by Frank White. *Ebony* 38 (March, 1983): 116.

_____. "When Southern Blacks Went North." Interview by Helen Dudar. *The New York Times*, December 18, 1988, p. C5.

Harriot, Esther. "Charles Fuller: The Quest for Justice." In *American Voices: Five Contemporary Playwrights in Essays and Interviews.* Jefferson, N.C.: McFarland, 1988.

Richardson, Riché. "Charles Fuller's Southern Specter and the Geography of Black Masculinity." *American Literature* 77, no. 1 (March, 2005): 7-32.

Savran, David. *In Their Own Words: Contemporary American Playwrights.* New York: Theater Communications Group, 1988.

Contributors: Pamela J. Olubunmi Smith, Mildred C. Kuner, Christian H. Moe, and Elsie Galbreath Haley

Ernest J. Gaines

BORN: Oscar, Louisiana; January 15, 1933

AFRICAN AMERICAN

Gaines's regionalist short stories and novels are distinguished contributions to modern African American fiction.

PRINCIPAL WORKS

LONG FICTION: *Catherine Carmier*, 1964; *Of Love and Dust*, 1967; *The Autobiography of Miss Jane Pittman*, 1971; *In My Father's House*, 1978; *A Gathering of Old Men*, 1983; *A Lesson Before Dying*, 1993

SHORT FICTION: *Bloodline*, 1968; *A Long Day in November*, 1971

MISCELLANEOUS: *Porch Talk with Ernest Gaines*, 1990; *Mozart and Leadbelly: Stories and Essays*, 2005

Born on a southern Louisiana plantation, Ernest J. Gaines (gaynz) was raised by a disabled aunt who became the model for the strong women in his works, including Miss Jane Pittman. There was no high school for Gaines to attend, so he left Louisiana in 1948 to live with relatives in California, where he suffered from the effects of his displacement. Displacement—caused by racism, by Cajuns' acquisition of land, or by loss of community ties—is a major theme for Gaines.

Young Gaines discovered works by John Steinbeck, William Faulkner, and Anton Chekhov, who wrote about the land. Not finding acceptable literary depictions of African Americans, Gaines resolved to write stories illuminating the lives and identities of his people. After completing military service, he earned a degree in English, published his first short stories, and received a creative writing fellowship at Stanford University.

Gaines rejected California as a subject for fiction, chose southern Louisiana as his major setting, and, like the Southern literary giant Faulkner, invented his own county. *Catherine Carmier*, an uneven apprentice novel, is the first of Gaines's works revealing Louisiana's physical beauty and folk speech.

Receiving a grant from the National Endowment for the Arts, Gaines published *Of Love and Dust*, inspired by a blues song about an African American who escapes prison by doing hard labor on a Louisiana plantation. This and other works by Gaines are not protest fiction, but they are concerned with human rights, justice, and equality.

Years of listening to the conversations of plantation folk led Gaines to employ multiple narrators in "Just like a Tree" in *Bloodline*, a short-story collection. He also employs the technique in *A Gathering of Old Men*, which gives new form to another favorite theme, the achievement of manhood. Twelve elderly African American men, after a lifetime of passivity, stand up against ruthless Cajuns and rednecks who have mistreated them, taken over their farmland, and threatened to destroy their past, represented by family homes and graveyards. In Gaines's somber moral drama, *A Lesson Before Dying*, an African American teacher who has difficulty being a man in his segregated society learns to love. He helps to humanize an illiterate teenager wrongly condemned for murder and to convince the boy to die courageously. With a firmer personal and racial identity, the teacher becomes dedicated to educating young African Americans.

Gaines has served as a teacher in his position as writer-in-residence at a Louisiana university. His honors include a Guggenheim Fellowship and awards from the American Academy and Institute of Arts and Letters and the MacArthur Foundation.

Catherine Carmier

TYPE OF WORK: Novel
FIRST PUBLISHED: 1964

Gaines's first novel, *Catherine Carmier*, based on a work he wrote while an adolescent in Vallejo, has many of the characteristic weaknesses of a first novel and is more interesting for what it anticipates in Gaines's later career than for its intrinsic merits. Though it caused barely a ripple of interest when it was first published, the novel introduces many of the themes that Gaines treats more effectively in his mature fiction. The book is set in the country, near Bayonne, Louisiana, an area depicted as virtually a wasteland. Ownership of much of this region has devolved to the Cajuns, who appear throughout Gaines's novels as Snopes-like vermin, interested in owning the land only to exploit it. Like Faulkner, Gaines sees this kind of person as particularly modern, and the growing power of the Cajuns indicates a weakening of values and a loss of determination to live in right relationship to the land.

Onto the scene comes Jackson Bradley, a young black man born and reared in the area but (like Gaines himself) educated in California. Bradley is a hollow, rootless man, a man who does not know where he belongs. He has found the North and the West empty, with people living hurried, pointless lives, but he sees the South as equally empty. Feeling no link to a meaningful past and no hope for a productive future, Bradley is a deracinated modern man. He has returned to Louisiana to bid final farewell to his Aunt Charlotte, a representative of the older generation, and to her way of life.

While there and while trying to find a meaningful path for himself, Bradley meets and falls in love with Catherine Carmier. She, too, is living a blocked life, and he feels that if they can leave the area, they will be able to make a fulfilling life together. Catherine is the daughter of Raoul Carmier, in many ways the most interesting character in the novel. A Creole, he is caught between the races. Because of his black blood, he is not treated as the equal of whites, but because of his white blood, he considers blacks to be beneath him. He has a near incestuous relationship with Catherine, since after her birth his wife was unfaithful to him and he considers none of their subsequent children his. Feeling close only to Catherine, he forbids her to associate with any men, but especially with black men. A man of great pride and love of the land, Raoul is virtually the only man in the region to resist the encroachment of the Cajuns. His attitude isolates him all the more, which in turn makes him fanatically determined to hold on to Catherine.

Ernest J. Gaines (© Jerry Bauer)

Despite her love for and loyalty to her father, Catherine senses the dead end her life has become and returns Bradley's love. Though she wants to leave with him, she is paralyzed by her love of her father and by her knowledge of what her leaving would do to him. This conflict climaxes with a brutal fight between Raoul and Bradley over Catherine, a fight that Bradley wins. Catherine, however, returns home to nurse her father. The novel ends ambiguously, with at least a hint that Catherine will return to Bradley, although the thrust of the book militates against that eventuality. Gaines implies that history and caste are a prison, a tomb. No change is possible for the characters because they cannot break out of the cages their lives have become. Love is the final victim. Catherine will continue living her narrow, unhealthy life, and Jackson Bradley will continue wandering the earth, searching for something to fill his inner void.

Of Love and Dust

TYPE OF WORK: Novel
FIRST PUBLISHED: 1967

Gaines's second novel, *Of Love and Dust*, was received much more enthusiastically than was *Catherine Carmier*; with it, he began to win the largely positive, respectful reviews that have continued to the present time. Like *Catherine Carmier*, *Of Love and Dust* is a story of frustrated love. The setting is the same: rural Louisiana, where the Cajuns are gradually assuming ownership and control of the land. *Of Love and*

Dust is a substantial improvement over *Catherine Carmier*, however, in part because it is told in the first person by Jim Kelly, an observer of the central story. In this novel, one can see Gaines working toward the folk voice that became such an integral part of the achievement of *The Autobiography of Miss Jane Pittman*.

The plot of the novel concerns Marcus Payne, a young black man sentenced to prison for murder and then bonded out by a white plantation owner who wants him to work in his fields. Recognizing Marcus's rebelliousness and pride, the owner and his Cajun overseer, Sidney Bonbon, brutally attempt to break his spirit. This only makes Marcus more determined, and in revenge he decides to seduce Louise, Bonbon's neglected wife. What begins, however, as simply a selfish and egocentric act of revenge on Marcus's part grows into a genuine though grotesque love. When he and Louise decide to run away together, Bonbon discovers them and kills Marcus. Even though he dies, Marcus, by resisting brutalizing circumstances, retains his pride and attempts to prove his manhood and dignity. His attempts begin in a self-centered way, but as his love for Louise increases, he grows in stature in the reader's eyes until he becomes a figure of heroic dimensions.

Through his use of a first-person narrator, Gaines creates a double perspective in the novel, including on one hand the exploits of Marcus and on the other the black community's reactions to them. The narrator, Jim Kelly, is the straw boss at the plantation, a member of the black community but also accepted and trusted by the whites because of his dependability and his unwillingness to cause any problems. His initial reaction to Marcus—resentment and dislike of him as a troublemaker—represents that of the community at large. The older members of the community never move beyond that attitude because they are committed to the old ways, to submission and accommodation. To his credit, however, Jim's attitude undergoes a transformation. As he observes Marcus, his resentment changes to sympathy and respect, for he comes to see Marcus as an example of black manhood that others would do well to emulate.

Marcus's death gives evidence of the strain of fate and determinism in this novel as well, yet because he dies with his pride and dignity intact, *Of Love and Dust* is more hopeful than *Catherine Carmier*. Gaines indicates that resistance is possible and, through the character of Jim Kelly, that change can occur. Kelly leaves the plantation at the end of the novel, no longer passively accepting what fate brings him but believing that he can act and shape his own life. Though Marcus is an apolitical character, like Jackson Bradley, it is suggested that others will later build on his actions to force social change on the South. *Of Love and Dust* is a major step forward beyond *Catherine Carmier* both artistically and thematically. Through his use of the folk voice, Gaines vivifies his story, and the novel suggests the real possibility of free action by his characters.

Bloodline

TYPE OF WORK: Short fiction
FIRST PUBLISHED: 1968

Gaines, although popular, is a very serious and methodical writer. He works very hard to fashion a distinct voice richly imbued with its unique traditions. He also spins compelling stories, which are collected in the single volume *Bloodline*, first published in 1968. *Bloodline* comprises five long stories, all of which deal with a place and a people Gaines expresses so fully and so vividly that they are recognized as his own exclusive fictional property: the southern black communities living on a stretch of low-lying cotton and sugarcane country between the Atchafalaya and Mississippi Rivers, west and northwest of Baton Rouge. Setting is a central force in Gaines's work, and his fiction often focuses on this distinctive Louisiana region.

All the stories in *Bloodline* take place in and around the fictional town of Bayonne, a small country town not too far from the actual city of Baton Rouge. The lives of Gaines's men and women are shaped by fields, dirt roads, plantation quarters, and the natural elements of dust, heat, and rain. Whatever the differences among his characters—he has a rich diversity of race and culture to work with—the Cajun sharecroppers, the black tenants, and the white plantation owners all consider the soil and the crops part of their daily weather. Bayonne and the surrounding countryside provide local and cultural unity for the stories in *Bloodline*.

Equally important to the unity of *Bloodline* is the way the stories are presented. All of them are written in the form of oral narratives told by the characters in their own words. The first four stories are told by individual African Americans who participate in or are deeply affected by the stories they tell. The tellers range in age from the six-year-old boy of "A Long Day in November" to a seventy-year-old man in the title story. The final story, "Just like a Tree," is told by a group of relatives and friends, each in turn, as they attend the leave-taking ceremonies surrounding Aunt Fe, an old black woman who has been invited North to escape white reprisals against the Civil Rights movement. In all these stories the sound of individual voices rings out clearly and convincingly. Gaines has a keen, sure ear for his native speech patterns and recognizes the power of language in a predominantly oral culture to assert, affirm, and keep hold of personal and collective values. His stories deliberately call attention to the special virtues of the spoken word as a rich storehouse capable of keeping alive an otherwise impoverished community.

There is, however, a deeper unifying force to the stories than a common setting, race, and dependence on the spoken word. It consists of the movement of the stories through individual lives toward a sort of communal consciousness. There is a hint of this movement in the successive voices of the five stories. The first two are accounts of two young boys, the third of a young man in jail, the fourth of an old man of seventy, and the fifth of a household of friends, relatives, and one stranger. *Bloodline* begins with the private experience of a little boy and ends with a public event that affects the entire community.

The impression of development is strengthened by the recurrence in each story of one of Gaines's major themes, the impact of personal and communal codes of honor colliding with various forms of hostility, especially, in the last four stories, the discrimination, injustice, and violence the African American faced in the segregated South. This is not to imply that polemics or ideologies ever prevail over character in Gaines's stories. What interests him first and foremost is black experience, and some of his best writing centers on the lives and relationships of southern blacks within their own community, with sometimes little direct reference at all to the world of the whites around them. Inasmuch as discrimination and the crimes of segregation were an inescapable fact of southern black experience, the world Gaines describes is always—overtly or not—conditioned by the tensions of racial claims. In *Bloodline*, the questions raised by such claims become progressively more insistent, and the stories themselves roughly follow the chronology of the changing mood among blacks in modern times. Specific dates are not mentioned, but the stories obviously stretch back to the 1940's rural South of "A Long Day in November" up to the 1960's Civil Rights movement in Louisiana alluded to in the last story, "Just like a Tree."

"A Long Day in November"
TYPE OF WORK: Short fiction
FIRST PUBLISHED: 1968, in *Bloodline*

In the first story, "A Long Day in November," there are no direct references to racial struggles. It is a long tale told in the voice of a six-year-old boy, Sonny, whose world is suddenly shattered by the separation of his parents. His mother, Amy, leaves her husband, Eddie, because she feels he has become overenthusiastic about his car to the point of neglecting his family. She takes Sonny to her mother's house, and the remainder of the story charts Eddie's unsuccessful attempts to bring his wife home. Finally, on the advice of the local Voodoo woman, Madame Toussaint, Eddie burns his car publicly, and Sonny and Amy return home. For the entire story, Sonny does not act; he observes and suffers. He sees the world in terms of basic feelings—warmth, cold, hope, fear—and desires simply that his disrupted world be restored. The story ends where it began, with Sonny in bed, snug and safe under the blankets, only this time the night is not disturbed by his mother's calls or crying. Instead, Sonny is rocked to sleep by the sound of the springs in his parents' bed.

Gaines is a master at re-creating the words and sensations of children, and one of his main concerns in "A Long Day in November" is to contrast Sonny's simple, innocent needs of love and security with the complex world of adult conflicts. Neither his parents nor his grandmother seems to offer him what he needs most. His mother has become hard and bitter, and his father, more gentle, shows a weak streak and tends to use Sonny to win back his wife. The grandmother's irritability may be comic for the reader, but for Sonny she is the most hateful person in his life, rough spoken, harsh, and complaining. She is the one person Sonny would most like to be free of: "Lord knows I get tired of Gran'mon fussing all the time." The main character in the story, however, is Sonny's mother. She may be harsh and bitter, but she has forged for herself a code of personal behavior that finally brings her family into a new relationship. She forces the change at a great cost, especially in regards to her son.

One important feature of "A Long Day in November" is the presence of a well-defined community—the schoolteacher, the preacher, the schoolchildren, the Voodoo woman, Eddie's friends, and Amy's relatives—where conflict and separation may occur, but whose shared assumptions are not questioned. Increasingly, as the stories progress, not only individual codes but also communal values are brought under pressure.

"The Sky Is Gray"

TYPE OF WORK: Short fiction
FIRST PUBLISHED: 1968, in *Bloodline*

The second story in *Bloodline*, "The Sky Is Gray," is also narrated by a small boy. One of the most successful stories in the volume, it consists of thirteen episodes spanning the day. James, eight years old, goes with his mother to a dentist in Bayonne. Like Sonny in "A Long Day in November," James suffers more than he acts, but already, even at eight years old, he is beginning to adopt the code of stoic pride his mother is constantly encouraging. His world is even bleaker than Sonny's. His father has been called into the army, and his mother is left with three children and great poverty. Throughout the story, her hard words and harsh judgments must be measured against the fact that she has been placed in a situation in which mere survival is not always certain. She feels compelled to teach her oldest son how to take care of his family and to survive with dignity as a man.

While waiting in the dentist's office, James watches a young, educated African American argue with an older man who looks to James like a preacher. The young black has no faith in religion but reacts in such an extreme, self-confident way that he challenges their religious beliefs. Still, when he is hit by the "preacher," a man who maintains that no questions at all should be asked about God or traditional beliefs, it is the young man who wins the admiration of James: "When I grow up I want to be just like him. I want clothes like that and I want to keep a book with me, too."

The point seems to be that, given the extent of black suffering, most reactions tend to assume extreme, absolute forms that destroy man's full nature. The preacher is at once too submissive and too aggressive; the young man asserts his right to disbelieve but is unable to make sense out of his contradictory certitudes; and James's mother so overemphasizes stoic resistance that, in a later episode, she is incapable of compromising her rigid pride even when it means a meal for her son. Fortunately, the white lady who offers the meal knows exactly how to circumvent such pride so that natural help is not construed as demeaning charity. Such generosity has been too rare in the past, however, even among her fellow blacks, and the mother's attitude remains unchanged. At first, the story as a whole seems to reveal a world where gentleness and love and flexibility have no place: "The sleet's coming down heavy, heavy now, and I turn up my coat collar to keep my neck warm. My mama tells me to turn it right back down. 'You not a bum,' she says. 'You a man.'" James nevertheless knows that his mother loves her children and that they love her.

"Three Men"

TYPE OF WORK: Short fiction
FIRST PUBLISHED: 1968, in *Bloodline*

The third story, "Three Men," may have been placed at the center of the collection as a sort of hub toward which the first two stories approach and around which the whole book swings to return to the traditional rural society of the final stories, still rural and traditional, but now in the new context of the Civil Rights movement. Certainly it is the only story in which the central character undergoes anything resembling a change of heart or self-discovery.

Again, like the other stories, "Three Men" centers on a personal code of honor, this time specifically related to racial domination. A nineteen-year-old youth, Proctor Lewis, turns himself in to the law in Bayonne after stabbing another man in a fight over a girl. The story takes place in jail where his cellmates—an old convict, Munford, and a homosexual, Hattie—argue with each other and talk to Proctor. Munford, full of hate for a society based on racial stereotypes, hates himself for allowing his life to gratify the expectations of those same stereotypes. Recalling the way his own past has swung back and forth between fights and jail, he poses the dilemma of the story: whether Proctor should choose to get out of jail by accepting the bond he initially hopes the white plantation owner will pay or whether he should stay in jail, suffer the certain beating of the guards, and eventually go to the state penitentiary. Munford claims that the latter choice is the only way for Proctor to keep his manhood, something both Munford and Hattie have surrendered.

As the story ends, Proctor has almost made up his mind to refuse the bond and to abide by the code Munford has described. Although he is finally not sure if he can stand by his decision, a shift of attitude has been made, and the right questions have been clearly articulated. "Three Men" looks back to the seemingly fatalistic rounds of poverty, frustration, and rigid codes of the first two stories and anticipates the last two stories, in which individual acts of self-affirmation seem to offer something more than mere stoic resistance.

"Bloodline"

TYPE OF WORK: Short fiction
FIRST PUBLISHED: 1968, in *Bloodline*

"Bloodline," the title story of the collection, raises the old southern problem of mixed blood but in a new context, the "postsegregation" South. The story is told by a seventy-year-old African American, Felix, who works for the plantation's present owner Walter Laurent. Copper, the half-white illegitimate son of Laurent's dead brother, has returned to the plantation seeking what he considers his birthright, the land on which his "father" raped his mother. He calls himself the General and refuses to go through the back door of the plantation house to meet his uncle. Finally, after Copper has thwarted all attempts by Laurent to force him through the back door, Laurent relents and goes to meet him. Their meeting symbolizes the old order making way for the new. Laurent does not change his mind about the old rules; he simply stops applying them for a time. Copper represents the transformation that will eventually change the caste system of white over black and rewrite the rules Laurent is constantly talking about: "I didn't write the rules, and I won't try to change them."

The old men, Walter and Felix, are clearly part of the old order, but Gaines is careful to show how they both, especially Felix, manage to retain their individual dignity even though bound to the established tradition. There is a give-and-take between "master" and "servant" common to men who speak the same language, know the same people, and who have lived near each other all their lives. From this perspective, Copper comes back to his birthplace as an outsider, isolated from the rest of the blacks, whom he considers childlike lackeys. He embodies the same sort of absoluteness and aloofness represented earlier by the young man in the dentist's office in "The Sky Is Gray," but he also embodies the necessary wave of change that will eventually sweep through the plantation, a change whose consequences are already being felt in the final story, "Just Like a Tree."

"Just like a Tree"

TYPE OF WORK: Short fiction
FIRST PUBLISHED: 1968, in *Bloodline*

"Just like a Tree" revolves around Aunt Fe, an old black woman who is being taken North to escape the violence that has begun on the plantation. A young man, Emmanuel, has begun working for change, and in retaliation a tenant house has been bombed and a woman and her two children killed. More than any other story in the collection, "Just like a Tree" affirms the force of the community. The only outsider, an African American from the North, is clearly alien to the shared assumptions and beliefs of the others. He speaks a different "language"; he sets himself apart by his loud manners, his condescension, and his lack of feeling. The other people gathered in the house, even the white lady who has walked to the house to say good-bye, form a whole, united by shared speech and shared feelings. The ceremony itself of farewell and the narrative mode of the story, told in turn by several of the visitors, affirm the strong communal bonds of rural black society. Unlike the young man in "The Sky Is Gray" or the General in "Bloodline," Emmanuel belongs to the community even as he acts to change the old ways. He is a type of activist represented best in Gaines's work by Jimmy in *The Autobiography of Miss Jane Pittman*.

Aunt Fe's longtime presence in the community, her having touched, in some loving way, every member of the community, and her impending removal to the North provide clues to the tree symbolism of the story's title: Like a great, old, shade tree, she has protected and sheltered other living creatures, and her departure will leave a spiritual hole in the life of the community, like the hole that the removal, roots and all, of a large tree will leave in a meadow. Aunt Clo predicts that Aunt Fe will die when she is "transplanted" to the North. The personal diaspora being forced upon Aunt Fe also represents the mass diasporas suffered by African Americans through the centuries.

The story and the book end with Aunt Fe's death. She has refused to be moved, and once again the strong vital roots of individual pride show their strength. The difference is that Aunt Fe's pride affirms its strength within the community, not in aloof isolation from it. In terms of *Bloodline* as a whole, "Just like a Tree" offers the conclusion that change must involve sacrifice but that change must take place. The farewell ceremony and Aunt Fe's death also offer the reminder that the traditional community had values that the new order can deny only at its own peril and loss.

The Autobiography of Miss Jane Pittman

TYPE OF WORK: Novel
FIRST PUBLISHED: 1971

In *The Autobiography of Miss Jane Pittman* the heroine and many African Americans in south Louisiana move from passivity to heroic assertion and achieve a new identity. Gaines's best-known novel is not an autobiography but a first-person reminiscence of a fictional 110-year-old former slave whose memories extend from the Emancipation Proclamation to Martin Luther King, Jr. *The Autobiography of Miss Jane Pittman* tells her unschooled but adept version of state and national occurrences and personalities (Huey Long, the flood of 1927, the rise of black athletes such as Jackie Robinson and Joe Louis). Her version of history is given to a tape-recording young schoolteacher who wants historical facts; Jane helps him to understand the dynamics of living history, the way she remembers it. Her accounts are loving, sane, and responsible. Her language—speech patterns and pronunciations—is authentic, since Gaines read interviews with former slaves.

Renamed Jane Brown by a Union soldier because Ticey (her original name) is "a slave name," Jane wears her new designation proudly, as a badge of her identity as a free woman, when she and other former slaves attempt to escape from Louisiana. Many of them are brutally murdered by Klansmen. Jane, who is about ten at the time, escapes along with a small orphan, Ned. Jane becomes Ned's mother, and during Reconstruction she raises him when they settle on another plantation as field hands. Ned receives some schooling and as a teenager is involved in civil rights struggles. His life in danger, Ned escapes to Kansas. Jane chooses to remain in Louisiana.

Ned represents the first of three African American males in Jane's life who struggle to define their racial and personal identities. The second is Joe Pittman, with whom Jane lives after Ned leaves. Joe loves Jane and wants her with him even though she is barren as a result of childhood beatings. He finds personal fulfillment in breaking wild horses on a Texas ranch; he accepts danger and the risk of death unflinchingly. Like Ned, who is murdered after he returns to Louisiana and sets up a school for black children, Joe is also killed fulfilling his destiny. Ned describes his identity as that of a black American who cares, and will always struggle. With these men, Jane finds a personal identity as a woman and demonstrates her desire to work with her black men but not to control them.

When Jimmy, a young civil rights worker much loved by Jane and others, is murdered, Jane—age 110—goes into the nearby town to drink from the segregated water fountain at the courthouse. She moves from the safety of silence and obscurity to join the ranks of African Americans who assert themselves and who risk losing their homes and lives but gain courage, dignity, and a heroic identity.

In My Father's House

TYPE OF WORK: Novel
FIRST PUBLISHED: 1978

Gaines's fourth novel, *In My Father's House*, was the first he had written in the third person since *Catherine Carmier*; the effect of its point of view is to distance the reader from the action and characters, creating an ironic perspective. Set during a dreary winter in 1970, in the period of disillusionment following the assassination of Martin Luther King, Jr., the novel suggests that the progress which was implicit in the ending of *The Autobiography of Miss Jane Pittman* was temporary at best, if not downright illusory. The atmosphere of the novel is one of frustration and stagnation.

Both the setting and the protagonist of *In My Father's House* are uncharacteristic for Gaines. Instead of using the rural settings so familiar from his other works, he sets his story in a small town. Rather than focusing on the common people, Gaines chooses as his protagonist Philip Martin, one of the leaders of the black community, a public figure, a minister who is considering running for Congress. A success by practically any measure and pridefully considering himself a *man*, Martin is brought low in the course of the novel. His illegitimate son, Robert X, a ghostlike man, appears and wordlessly accuses him. Robert is evidence that, by abandoning him, his siblings, and their mother many years previously, Martin in effect destroyed their lives. Having been a drinker, a gambler, and irresponsible, he tries to explain to his son that his earlier weakness was a legacy of slavery. Even though he seems to have surmounted that crippling legacy, his past rises up to haunt him and forces him to face his weakness. Martin wants to effect a reconciliation with his son and thus with his past, but Robert's suicide precludes that. *In My Father's House* makes explicit a concern which was only implicit in Gaines's earlier novels, the relationship between fathers and sons. No communication is possible here, and the failure is illustrative of a more general barrier between the generations. While in the earlier novels the young people led in the struggle for change and the older characters held back, here the situation is reversed. Martin and members of his generation are the leaders, while the young are for the most part sunk in cynicism, apathy, and hopelessness, or devoted to anarchic violence. If the hope of a people is in the young, or in a reconciliation of old and young, hope does not exist in this novel.

A Gathering of Old Men

TYPE OF WORK: Novel
FIRST PUBLISHED: 1983

Hope does exist in Gaines's *A Gathering of Old Men*, for which Gaines returns to his more characteristic rural setting. Here he returns as well to the optimism with which *The Autobiography of Miss Jane Pittman* ended. This time, as at the end of that novel and in *In My Father's House*, it is up to the old among the black community to lead the struggle for change, this time primarily because there are no young men left to lead. All of them have escaped to towns and cities that promise more of a future than does rural Louisiana.

In this small corner of Louisiana, however, as elsewhere in Gaines's fiction, Cajuns are encroaching on the land, replacing men with machines and even threatening to plow up the old graveyard where generations of blacks have been buried. When Beau Boutan, son of the powerful Cajun Fix Boutan, is shot to death in the quarters of Marshall plantation, where Marshall blacks have worked the land since the days of slavery, the old black men who have lived there all of their lives are faced with one last chance to stand up and be men. They stand up for the sake of Matthu, the only one of them who ever stood up before and thus the most logical suspect in the murder. They also stand up because of all the times in their past when they should have stood up but did not. They prove one last time that free action is possible when eighteen or more of them, all in their seventies and eighties, arm themselves with rifles of the same gauge used in the shooting and face down the white sheriff, Mapes, each in his turn claiming to be the killer.

As shut off as the quarters are from the rest of the world, it is easy to forget that the events of the novel take place as recently as the late 1970's. Beau Boutan's brother Gil, however, represents the change that has been taking place in the world outside Marshall. He has achieved gridiron fame at Louisiana State University by working side by side with Cal, a young black man. Youth confronts age when Gil returns home and tries to persuade his father not to ride in revenge against Beau's murderer, as everyone expects him to do. Gil represents the possibility of change from the white perspective. He convinces his father to let the law find and punish Beau's murderer, but he pays a heavy price when his father disowns him. He cannot stop other young Cajuns, led by Luke Will, who are not willing to change but would rather cling to the vigilantism of the old South.

In spite of their dignity and pride, the old men at Marshall risk looking rather silly because after all these years they stand ready for a battle that seems destined never to take place once Fix Boutan decides not to ride on Marshall. Sheriff Mapes taunts them with the knowledge that they have waited too late to take a stand. Ironically, they are ultimately able to maintain their dignity and reveal their growth in freedom by standing up to the one person who has been most valiant in her efforts to help them: Candy Marshall, niece of the landowner. In her effort to protect Matthu, who was largely responsible for rearing her after her parents died, Candy has gone so far as to try to take credit for the murder herself. What she fails to realize is that the days are long past when black men need the protection of a white woman. She is stunned to realize that she too has been living in the past and has been guilty of treating grown black men like children.

The novel does eventually end with a gunfight, because Luke Will and his men refuse to let the murder of a white man by a black one go unavenged. It is fitting that the two men who fall in the battle are Luke Will, the one who was most resistant to change, and Charlie Biggs, the real murderer, who, at fifty, finally proves his manhood by refusing to be beaten by Beau Boutan and then by returning to take the blame for the murder that he has committed. Charlie's body is treated like a sacred relic as each member of the black community, from the oldest to the youngest, touches it, hoping that some of the courage that Charlie found late in life will rub off. Apparently it already has.

With *A Gathering of Old Men*, Gaines returns to first-person narration, but this time the history is told one chapter at a time by various characters involved in or witnessing the action. His original plan was to have the narrator be the white newspaperman Lou Dimes, Candy's boyfriend. He found, however, that there was still much that a black man in Louisiana would not confide to a white man, even a sympathetic one, so he let the people tell their own story, with Dimes narrating an occasional chapter.

A Lesson Before Dying

TYPE OF WORK: Novel
FIRST PUBLISHED: 1993

In *A Lesson Before Dying*, Gaines returns to the south Louisiana setting he has established in his earlier fiction as his own. The year is 1948. Jefferson, a barely literate young black man, sentenced to death for a shooting in which he was innocently involved, has heard his defense attorney say that executing Jefferson would be like putting a hog in the electric chair. Jefferson has suffered so many outrages to his manhood during his short lifetime that he is altogether too ready to accept his attorney's assessment.

But Jefferson's aged godmother resolves that, if Jefferson must die, he will first come to know that he is a man. She enlists as her reluctant instrument Grant Wiggins, a university graduate who teaches the children in the black quarter during the months when they are not working in the fields. At first, Grant and Jefferson seem a study in contrast, but as they slowly move toward mutual trust and respect, it is clear that Grant, as much as Jefferson, has a great deal to learn about what it is to be a man. Grant and Jefferson will finally share equally in the lesson all of us must learn before dying: what it means to be human.

What could degenerate into melodrama or didacticism becomes in Gaines's hands a probing and honestly felt study of human possibilities. Gaines creates a cast of sharply drawn minor characters, all of whom, including those of whose conduct he must disapprove, he treats with sympathy and insight. He is at his best in his nuanced observation of the ironies and intricacies of negotiation between races and between generations. Readers who have waited ten years for a new novel by Gaines will find in *A Lesson Before Dying* further confirmation of his assured, self-effacing, spiritually generous art.

SUGGESTED READINGS

Auger, Philip. *Native Sons in No Man's Land: Rewriting Afro-American Manhood in the Novels of Baldwin, Walker, Wideman, and Gaines*. New York: Garland, 2000.

Babb, Valerie Melissa. *Ernest Gaines*. Boston: Twayne, 1991.

Beavers, Herman. *Wrestling Angels into Song: The Fictions of Ernest J. Gaines and James Alan McPherson*. Philadelphia: University of Pennsylvania Press, 1995.

Carmean, Karen. *Ernest J. Gaines: A Critical Companion*. Westport, Conn.: Greenwood Press, 1998.

Clark, Keith. *Black Manhood in James Baldwin, Ernest J. Gaines, and August Wilson*. Urbana: University of Illinois Press, 2002.

Doyle, Mary Ellen. *Voices from the Quarters: The Fiction of Ernest J. Gaines*. Baton Rouge: Louisiana State University Press, 2001.

Estes, David E., ed. *Critical Reflections on the Fiction of Ernest J. Gaines*. Athens: University of Georgia Press, 1994.

Gaines, Ernest J., Marcia G. Gaudet, and Carl Wooton. *Porch Talk with Ernest Gaines: Conversations on the Writer's Craft*. Baton Rouge: Louisiana State University Press, 1990.

Lowe, John, ed. *Conversations with Ernest Gaines*. Jackson: University Press of Mississippi, 1995.

Simpson, Anne K. *A Gathering of Gaines: The Man and the Writer*. Lafayette: Center for Louisiana Studies at the University of Southwestern Louisiana, 1991.

Contributors: Philip A. Tapley, John W. Fiero, Ben Forkner, Frank W. Shelton, and Rebecca G. Smith

Ernesto Galarza

BORN: Jalcocotán, Mexico; August 15, 1905
DIED: San Jose, California; June 22, 1984

MEXICAN AMERICAN

*Out of his concern for the education of Mexican
American children, Galarza produced fiction and poetry
for children and young adults, as well as numerous studies
of Latin American immigrants and their history.*

PRINCIPAL WORKS

CHILDREN'S LITERATURE: *Zoo-Risa*, 1968 (*Zoo-Fun*, 1971); *Aquí y allá en California*, 1971; *Historia verdadera de una gota de miel*, 1971; *Poemas párvulos*,
1971; *Rimas tontas*, 1971; *La historia verdadera de una botella de leche*, 1972;
Más poemas párvulos, 1972; *Poemas pe-que pe-que peque-ñitos = Very Very
Short Nature Poems*, 1972; *Un poco de México*, 1972; *Chogorrom*, 1973; *Todo
mundo lee*, 1973

POETRY: *Kodachromes in Rhyme*, 1982

NONFICTION: *The Roman Catholic Church as a Factor in the Political and Social
History of Mexico*, 1928; *Argentina's Revolution and Its Aftermath*, 1931;
Debts, Dictatorship, and Revolution in Bolivia and Peru, 1931; *La industria
eléctrica en México*, 1941; *Labor in Latin America*, 1942; *Strangers in Our
Fields*, 1956; *Merchants of Labor: The Mexican Bracero Story*, 1964; *Spiders in
the House and Workers in the Field*, 1970; *Barrio Boy: The Story of a Boy's Acculturation*, 1971; *Farm Workers and Agri-Business in California, 1947-1960*,
1977; *Tragedy at Chular: El crucero de las treinta y dos cruces*, 1977

The writings of Ernesto Galarza (ehr-NAYS-toh gah-LAHR-sah) can be divided
into three phases: the Pan-Americanist, the farm-laborer advocate, and the educator. Galarza was born in a tiny mountain village in Mexico. When he was five, he,
his mother, and two uncles fled the Mexican Revolution. They traveled for three
years until they reached Sacramento, California.

At the age of twelve, Galarza lost his mother and one uncle to influenza. He continued his education with the assistance of his other uncle and worked after school
and during the summers as a farm laborer and in canneries. His flight northward, his
family's struggles for survival, and the process of acculturation are depicted in his
1971 autobiography, *Barrio Boy: The Story of a Boy's Acculturation*. This book is
perhaps Galarza's most outstanding contribution to Chicano literature for its pioneering spirit in the field of the essay and the fictionlike quality of its prose.

In 1923 Galarza received a scholarship from Occidental College in Los Angeles. In 1927 he received a fellowship from Stanford University, which awarded him a master's degree in Latin American history and political science in 1929. After marrying Mae Taylor, a teacher from Sacramento, Galarza entered Columbia University, where he obtained his Ph.D. in Latin American history in 1932.

Galarza's first publications belong to his Pan-American phase. In his book *The Roman Catholic Church as a Factor in the Political and Social History of Mexico*, Galarza defends the actions of the Mexican revolutionary governments, which aimed to limit the power of the Catholic Church. He wrote his other Pan-Americanist works, *Argentina's Revolution and Its Aftermath*; *Debts, Dictatorship, and Revolution in Bolivia and Peru*; and *Labor in Latin America*, while working for the Pan-American Union in Washington, D.C., which later became the Organization of American States.

Galarza worked in Washington, D.C., as a research associate in education and as the chief of the Division of Labor and Social Information at the Pan-American Union. He wrote and edited numerous Inter-American Reports and the Latin America for Young Readers series, published by the Pan-American Union. He became concerned about the living conditions of the *braceros*, the Mexican contract agricultural laborers who were brought to the United States in 1942 and remained until 1964. His book *Merchants of Labor: The Mexican Bracero Story* analyzes the *bracero* in California agriculture. This book initiates Galarza's farm labor advocate phase.

In 1947 Galarza resigned from the Pan-American Union to serve as the Director of Research and Education in California for the Southern Tenant Farmer's Union, which became the National Farm Labor Union. He became entangled in a union strike against the DiGiorgio Fruit Corporation. The strike gave rise to libel suits and countersuits, which Galarza analyzes in his book *Spiders in the House and Workers in the Field*.

In 1955 he conducted field surveys on the living conditions of Mexican nationals in the United States. This work culminated in his 1956 book *Strangers in Our Fields*, which produced an uproar among the members of the California State Board of Agriculture, the growers' associations, and all those who employed Mexican laborers. However, Galarza continued to make public sensitive issues involving agriculture. *Farm Workers and Agri-Business in California, 1947-1960* documents the rise of the corporations that precipitated the demise of the small farmer, and *Tragedy at Chular* examines the safety violations that caused the death of thirty-two laborers.

In the mid-1960's Galarza engaged in the study of learning theories and methodologies for an effective bilingual and bicultural education program. In 1971 he founded the Studio Laboratory for Bilingual Education in San Jose, California, to develop awareness of cultural values, nature, and the creative arts.

Out of his concern for the bilingual education of Mexican American children, he produced his Colección Mini-libros, which includes his children's books. Between 1971 and 1973 he wrote a total of thirteen prose and poetry "mini-libros" (mini-books), each equipped with a bilingual appendix. Galarza's creativity is also evident in his *Kodachromes in Rhyme*, which contains poetry for adults and young adults. Galarza is regarded as one of the most prominent Mexican American contributors to American culture.

Barrio Boy

TYPE OF WORK: Autobiographical novel
FIRST PUBLISHED: 1971

Barrio Boy is an autobiographical novel that divides the author's life story into five parts, each corresponding roughly to a place in which his family lived. The first part tells of the family's early history and Galarza's first five years of life in Jalcocotán, a village high in the Sierra Madre range. The second part details the family's movements over the next two years, from 1910 to 1912, and the third part describes the family's travels to the United States. Part 4 brings Galarza's family to the Mexican American barrio in Sacramento and later to a five-room house on the edge of Sacramento, in the town of Oak Park. With a new bicycle, he delivered newspapers and thought about becoming a doctor or a lawyer, but his middle-class life dissolved when his uncle and mother died from influenza. In the final part, Galarza describes how he and José moved back to the Sacramento barrio. The story ends with the author looking forward to entering high school in the barrio in 1921.

The details of each home, village, train car, and street are recorded in the smallest detail. Readers will be fascinated by scenes in which Galarza recounts his escape from Jalcocotán, the fighting around Tepic, the stagecoach and train rides through fighting armies, and life in the besieged city of Mazatlán, with cannon fire landing all around his house. Galarza also offers extensive details of life in Sacramento, his family's move to the suburbs, what it was like to be one of the few Mexican Americans in the new school, and his adolescent thoughts of becoming a doctor or lawyer.

Galarza's narrative is an outward-looking autobiography, sharing little of the author's inner feelings. Instead it reads like an encyclopedic description of the various places that he lived during these sixteen years. Galarza maintains the narrative stance of a newspaper report, and even the loss of his mother and uncle in the influenza epidemic—forcing his move back to the barrio and crushing his hopes for a profession—is related without emotion. In a way, however, such traumatic events need no emotional description. The story, told through rich experience and objective detail, records the facts of an immigrant boy's coming-of-age and overcoming of obstacles. The emotions are self-evident.

SUGGESTED READINGS
Bustamante, Jorge. *Ernesto Galarza's Legacy to the History of Labor Migration.* Stanford, Calif.: Stanford Center for Chicano Research, 1996.

Galarza, Ernesto. *The Burning Light: Action and Organizing in the Mexican Community in California*. Interviews by Gabrielle Norris and Timothy Beard. Berkeley: University of California Press, 1982.

Gomez, Laura E. *From Barrio Boys to College Boys: Ethnic Identity, Ethnic Organizations, and the Mexican American Elite. The Cases of Ernesto Galarza and Manuel Ruiz, Jr.* Stanford, Calif.: Stanford Center for Chicano Research, 1989.

Meister, Dick. "Ernesto Galarza: From Barrio Boy to Labor Leader/Philosopher." *Leabhrach: News from the University of Notre Dame Press*, Autumn, 1978.

Meister, Dick, and Amme Loftis. *A Long Time Coming: The Struggle to Unionize America's Farm Workers*. New York: Macmillan, 1977.

Revelle, Keith. "A Collection for La Raza." *Library Journal*, November 15, 1971.

Contributors: Cida S. Chase and Jamie Myers

Cristina García

BORN: Havana, Cuba; July 4, 1958

CUBAN AMERICAN

Immigrating to the United States in the wake of the
Cuban Revolution, García grew up to become a bicultural
Cuban American writer, drawing on the contradictions
of being simultaneously "both" and "neither."

PRINCIPAL WORKS

LONG FICTION: *Dreaming in Cuban*, 1992; *The Agüero Sisters*, 1997; *Monkey Hunting*, 2003; *A Handbook to Luck*, 2007
NONFICTION: *Cars of Cuba*, 1995
EDITED TEXTS: *Cubanisimo! The Vintage Book of Contemporary Cuban Literature*, 2003; *Bordering Fires: The Vintage Book of Contemporary Mexican and Chicana/o Literature*, 2006

Cristina García (krihs-TEE-nah gahr-SEE-ah) is a highly regarded Cuban American writer. Born in Havana, Cuba, she was brought to the United States at the age of two, when her family emigrated after Fidel Castro came to power. She grew up in New York City, studied in Catholic schools, and attended Barnard College, from where she went to the School of Advanced International Studies at The Johns Hopkins University. In 1993, after working for *Time* magazine as a journalist in Miami, San Francisco, and Los Angeles, García was a Hodder Fellow at Princeton University. She then moved to Los Angeles.

As a young adult García read American, Russian, and French novelists. Later she discovered her Latin American literary heritage. She cites Wallace Stevens, Gabriel García Márquez, and Toni Morrison as particular literary inspirations for her when writing her novels. Perhaps her greatest inspiration, however, was a trip back to Cuba in 1984, where she learned about her family and, as for so many bicultural writers, regained a sense of her own culture of origin and her part in it from the experience of "going home."

As a bicultural Cuban American writer, García is part of a vibrant group of individuals of various ethnicities who draw on the contradictions of being simultaneously both and neither. Other American writers sharing this multiethnic common ground are Julia Alvarez, Gloria Anzaldúa, Sandra Cisneros, Amy Tan, Maxine Hong Kingston, Diana Abu-Jaber, Oscar Hijuelos, Pablo Medina, and Omar Torres. They too write of the delicate balance, double consciousness, and multiple resonances of living "on the borderlands," as Anzaldúa phrased it. They share an

425

ability to "pass," as well as the knowledge, sometimes painful yet often a source of great pride, of their difference from mainstream American culture. They chronicle intergenerational immigrant experience and displacement, exile and double exile, for even the culture of origin feels like a strange place to the hybrid child who, unlike its parents, has become at least partially identified with the adopted American culture. The formation of identity, in all its complex manifestations, is the overarching theme in this kind of work.

The relativity of perception is another powerful theme in the works of these writers, and García is particularly skillful in the way her narrative structure and chronology reflect this relativity. Given the element of the autobiographical in novels that explore identity formation, it is no surprise that García has experienced this relativity personally, not only culturally but also politically. When interviewed by Allan Vorda in 1993 García mentioned that her parents were extremely anticommunist, but that her other relatives, whom she had met on her 1984 trip, were procommunist if not Party members.

Dreaming in Cuban is set alternately in Brooklyn and Havana, with multiple narrators tracing their memories, their family lines, and their complex interconnections. Granddaughter Pilar and grandmother Celia communicate wordlessly over the years, and only when the grandchild comes to visit do both feel complete again. In her novel García plays with Magical Realism, politics, the diary and epistolary forms, and the accretion of layers of culture. The locations shift, just as do the barriers of time and space, life and death, and García draws on the puzzle that is memory to show how identity is formed. The novel was nominated for the National Book Award in 1992, and in 1994 García received a Guggenheim Fellowship.

The Agüero Sisters draws upon the pro- and anticommunist allegiances found in García's own family. The novel contrasts two sisters, Constancia, who fled Cuba when Castro came to power, and Reina, who remained. Each has achieved a different kind of success in her chosen environment. Like *Dreaming in Cuban*, *The Agüero Sisters* is strongly marked by Magical Realism. *Monkey Hunting* is also about Cuban Americans, but this time Chinese Cuban Americans, tracing the Chen family from 1857 to the present as they emigrate from country to country.

Dreaming in Cuban

TYPE OF WORK: Novel
FIRST PUBLISHED: 1992

Dreaming in Cuban, García's first novel, chronicles the lives of three generations of women as they strive for self-fulfillment. This bittersweet novel also illustrates the Cuban American immigrant experience in the United States, focusing on the search for cultural identity in exile. In Cuba, for twenty-five years, the matriarch Celia del Pino writes letters to Gustavo, a long lost lover. She never sends the self-revealing correspondence and stops writing in 1959, at the time of the Cuban Revolution, when the family becomes divided by politics and her granddaughter Pilar is born.

Celia, who believes that "to survive is an act of hope," sublimates her unfulfilled romantic desires by imagining herself as a heroine of the revolution. In need of recognition, she supports Fidel Castro devotedly. As her husband Jorge del Pino leaves her to join their daughter Lourdes in the United States, she spends her days scanning the sea for American invaders and daydreaming about a more exciting life.

Felicia, Celia's youngest daughter, abused and abandoned by her first husband, Hugo Villaverde, suffers from fits of madness and violence. A stranger to herself and her children, she seeks refuge in music and the Afro-Cuban cult of Santeria; after becoming a priestess, she finds peace in death. Lourdes, Celia's eldest daughter, is raped and tortured by the revolutionaries and loses her unborn son. She escapes from Castro's Cuba with her husband Rufino del Puente and their daughter Pilar. Emotionally unfulfilled, she develops eating disorders; while her family dreams of returning to Cuba, she supports the anti-Castro movement, establishes a chain of Yankee Doodle bakeries, and focuses on achieving the American Dream.

Raised in Brooklyn, in conflict with her Americanized mother, Pilar identifies with her grandmother Celia in Cuba. She visits the homeland in search of her true identity and, as she receives Celia's legacy of letters and family stories, she becomes aware of the magic inner voice that inspires artistic creativity. Pilar returns to America with a positive self-image, accepting her double identity as a bilingual and bicultural Latina.

Dreaming in Cuban represents the coming-of-age memoir narrative. Through recollections and nostalgic remembrances, the novel illustrates issues of identity and separation, women's survival strategies, and cultural dualism.

SUGGESTED READINGS

Alvarez-Borland, Isabel. "Displacements and Autobiography in Cuban-American Fiction." *World Literature Today* 68 (Winter, 1994): 43.

Davis, Rocio G. "Back to the Future: Mothers, Languages, and Homes in Cristina García's *Dreaming in Cuban*." *World Literature Today* 74 (Winter, 2000): 60-68.

Firmat, Gustavo Pérez. *Life on the Hyphen: The Cuban-American Way*. Austin: University of Texas Press, 1994.

Payant, Katherine B. "From Alienation to Reconciliation in the Novels of Cristina García." *MELUS* 26 (Fall, 2001): 163-182.

Stefanko, Jacqueline. "New Ways of Telling: Latinas' Narratives of Exile and Return." *Frontiers* 17, no. 2 (1996): 50-69.

Contributors: Tanya Gardiner-Scott and Ludmila Kapschutschenko-Schmitt

Lionel G. García

BORN: San Diego, Texas; August 20, 1935

MEXICAN AMERICAN

García's works document the experience of Mexican immigrants coming to make lives in the southwestern United States.

PRINCIPAL WORKS

CHILDREN'S/YOUNG ADULT LITERATURE: *The Elephant and the Ant*, 2000
DRAMA: *An Acorn on the Moon*, pr. 1995
LONG FICTION: *Leaving Home*, 1985; *A Shroud in the Family*, 1987; *Hardscrub*, 1990; *To a Widow with Children*, 1994
SHORT FICTION: *I Can Hear the Cowbells Ring*, 1994; *The Day They Took My Uncle, and Other Stories*, 2001

Born in 1935 in the remote brush country of Texas near the Mexican border to Gonzalo Guzman and Maria Saenz García, Lionel G. García (LI-nehl gahr-SEE-ah) was later to write fiction for nearly three decades before seeing significant publication of and attention to his works. A regional writer, García has lived most of his life in this desolate, dirt-ridden part of the United States.

Interested in science and biology, García entered Texas A&M University. He earned a B.S. in 1956; he also took classes in and otherwise pursued creative writing as an undergraduate. García twice served two-year terms in the U.S. Army, the first of which was in 1957-1958. A year after leaving the military, he married Noemi Barrera. He returned to active duty in 1959.

Resolved not to pursue a military career, he returned to Texas A&M in the early 1960's, where he eventually earned the D.V.M. degree, which would provide most of his life's work outside the literary world. He became a practicing veterinarian in the late 1960's, after spending three years as an assistant professor of anatomy, again at Texas A&M. Perhaps surprisingly, though, he makes little use of his biology and primary profession in his fiction.

While serving in the military and teaching college classes, García's side interest—perhaps at heart it was always his main one—was writing short stories. He had published his first story in the undergraduate literary magazine during his senior year of college, continuing to write thereafter. It was not until 1983, however, that he would receive recognition for his work; he was awarded the PEN Southwest Discovery Prize for his first novel, *Leaving Home*, which at the time was unpublished.

Like the terrain in South Texas, García's characters—while colorful—are often bleak and desolate in their attitudes and behavior. Both *Leaving Home* and *A*

Shroud in the Family are about family life among first- and second-generation immigrants coming from Mexico to Texas. About this time, he also began to give public readings of his fiction, a mode of performance that well serves his storytelling abilities.

His next novel, *Hardscrub*, is set in the 1950's and also tells of a family confronting the problems of everyday life in South Texas. It won several honors, all regional in nature, including the Texas Literary Award. In the mid-1990's García changed his focus to other subgenres of fiction: He published the highly autobiographical collection of personal writings titled *I Can Hear the Cowbells Ring*, and he tried his luck with a play called *An Acorn on the Moon*, which was locally produced but never published. He also wrote a children's book, *The Elephant and the Ant*, and collected his stories, most of which had been previously published, in *The Day They Took My Uncle, and Other Stories*. García's works have generally been well received as popular writings of fiction, regional in scope but more than expansive in their appreciation of the experience of Mexican immigrants coming to make lives in the southwestern United States.

Leaving Home

TYPE OF WORK: Novel
FIRST PUBLISHED: 1985

García's *Leaving Home* offers an intimate view of one Latino family in the early 1940's. The novel traces the wanderings of the aging Adolfo, a former baseball pitcher who ruined his career with alcohol, as he moves from the home of his sister Maria to San Diego, hoping to live with his former lover, Isabel. Carmen, Maria's daughter, goes with Adolfo, hoping to move in with an aunt and find a better job.

Turned away by her aunt, Carmen is allowed to stay with Isabel. Adolfo, however, is forced to return to Maria's house. Maria promises to help him find a job, but his pride prevents him from working in the fields or holding down a gardener's job. He travels to Los Angeles, meeting a con artist, Antonia, who persuades him to move in with her so she can get his pension checks. She eventually tires of his alcoholism and throws him out, and he moves in with the Professor, another of Antonia's victims.

When the United States enters World War II, the Professor returns to Tijuana to avoid the draft, remembering that during World War I Hispanics were drafted before whites. Adolfo accompanies him and marries a prostitute. He soon leaves her, however, and returns to Maria's house.

In the meantime, Carmen has improved her life, discovering that she wants to be a nurse. She applies for a job at the Navy hospital in San Diego, is hired to wash pots, is promoted to orderly, and shortly thereafter is recommended for nurses' training in the U.S. Navy. She graduates at the top of her class and becomes an officer. Although Carmen is capable, her promotion is partly based on the fact that she is Latina: The Department of Defense uses her as a symbol. When Carmen becomes engaged to a white naval officer in the Philippines, Maria believes that she has lost Carmen.

Maria, too, experiences significant changes. She begins to question God's judgment when Carmen gets sick. When one of her sons is killed in battle, she loses her faith in God. She is alone and lonely. When Adolfo returns, Maria feels happy again. The two agree that Adolfo has wasted his life, but they are happy to have each other.

SUGGESTED READINGS

Anhalt, Diana. "South Texas Buckshot Stories." *The Texas Observer*, November 9, 2001.

Golden, Dorothy. Review of *To a Widow with Children*, by Lionel G. García. *Library Journal* 119, no. 6 (April 1, 1994): 131.

Mutter, John. Review of *A Shroud in the Family*, by Lionel G. García. *Publishers Weekly* 232, no. 4 (July 24, 1987): 181.

Ray, Karen. Review of *Hardscrub*, by Lionel G. García. *The New York Times Book Review* 125, no. 1705 (February 25, 1990): 7, 24.

Contributors: Carl Singleton and Wilma Shires